THE AGE OF
MOVIES
::
SELECTED
WRITINGS OF
PAULINE
KAEL

THE AGE OF MOVIES

SELECTED WRITINGS OF PAULINE KAEL

Edited by Sanford Schwartz

A SPECIAL PUBLICATION OF THE LIBRARY OF AMERICA

For sources and acknowledgments see page 787.
Material from *I Lost it at the Movies* and *Going Steady* is reprinted
by permission of Marion Boyars Publishers.
The letters of Pauline Kael are reprinted courtesy of
The Lilly Library, Indiana University, Bloomington.

Distributed to the trade in the United States
by Penguin Group (USA) Inc.
and in Canada by Penguin Books Canada Ltd.

Book designed by David Bullen.

Library of Congress Control Number: 2011923053
ISBN 978-1-59853-109-1

First Printing

Printed in the United States of America

:: CONTENTS

Introduction xi

Movies, the Desperate Art 1

from I Lost it at the Movies

The Glamour of Delinquency 25
The Golden Coach 40
Shoeshine 44
Breathless, and the Daisy Miller Doll 46
West Side Story 51
Lolita 58
Jules and Jim 64
Billy Budd 70
Yojimbo 75
Devi 80
Hud, Deep in the Divided Heart of Hollywood 90

from Kiss Kiss Bang Bang

Laurence Olivier as Othello 107
Marlon Brando: An American Hero 110
Movie Brutalists 118
Tourist in the City of Youth [*Blow-Up*] 127

Movies on Television 135

Orson Welles: There Ain't No Way [*Falstaff / Chimes at Midnight*] . . 146

Bonnie and Clyde 154

from **Going Steady**

Movies as Opera [*China Is Near*] 177

A Minority Movie [*La Chinoise*] 182

Faces 190

A Sign of Life [*Shame*] 194

Trash, Art, and the Movies 201

Saintliness [*Simon of the Desert*] 235

from **Deeper into Movies**

The Bottom of the Pit [*Butch Cassidy and the Sundance Kid*] 245

High School 251

Fellini's "Mondo Trasho" [*Fellini Satyricon*] 257

Notes on Heart and Mind 263

The Poetry of Images [*The Conformist*] 273

Pipe Dream [*McCabe & Mrs. Miller*] 279

Helen of Troy, Sexual Warrior [*The Trojan Women*] 284

Louis Malle's Portrait of the Artist as a Young Dog

    [*Murmur of the Heart*] 290

Urban Gothic [*The French Connection*] 296

The Fall and Rise of Vittorio De Sica

    [*The Garden of the Finzi-Continis*] 303

Stanley Strangelove [*A Clockwork Orange*] 310

Alchemy [*The Godfather*] 316

Collaboration and Resistance [*The Sorrow and the Pity*] 323

from **Reeling**

Tango [*Last Tango in Paris*] 331

Pop Versus Jazz [*Lady Sings the Blues*] 340

The Fred Astaire & Ginger Rogers Book 347

Days and Nights in the Forest 353

A Rip-off with Genius [*Marilyn*] 358

After Innocence [*The Last American Hero*] 367

Everyday Inferno [*Mean Streets*] 376

Movieland—The Bums' Paradise [*The Long Goodbye*] 384

Moments of Truth [*The Iceman Cometh*] 393

Politics and Thrills 400

Survivor [*Sleeper*] 409

Killing Time [*Magnum Force*] 414

Cicely Tyson Goes to the Fountain
   [*The Autobiography of Miss Jane Pittman*] 420

The Used Madonna [*The Mother and the Whore*] 426

When the Saints Come Marching In [*Lenny*] 432

Fathers and Sons [*The Godfather, Part II*] 440

Beverly Hills as a Big Bed [*Shampoo*] 448

Coming: *Nashville* 456

from **When the Lights Go Down**

The Man from Dream City [Cary Grant] 465

All for Love [*The Story of Adèle H.*] 500

Walking into Your Childhood [*The Magic Flute*] 506

Notes on the Nihilist Poetry of Sam Peckinpah
   [*The Killer Elite*] 511

The Artist as a Young Comedian [*Next Stop, Greenwich Village*] 520

Underground Man [*Taxi Driver*] 525

Sparkle 530

Notes on Evolving Heroes, Morals, Audiences 533

Hot Air [*Network*] 545

Marguerite Duras [*The Truck*] 552

A Woman for All Seasons? [*Julia*] 557

Shivers [*The Fury*] 564

Fear of Movies 569

Bertrand Blier 586

The God-Bless-America Symphony [*The Deer Hunter*] 596

Pods [*Invasion of the Body Snatchers*] 606

from Taking It All In

Why Are Movies So Bad? or, The Numbers 615

The Chant of Jimmie Blacksmith 630

The Man Who Made Howard Hughes Sing

    [*Melvin and Howard*] 638

Used Cars 647

Religious Pulp, or The Incredible Hulk [*Raging Bull*] 652

Atlantic City 659

Hey, Torquemada [*History of the World—Part I*] 666

Portrait of the Artist as a Young Gadgeteer [*Blow Out*] 671

Pennies from Heaven 677

Shoot the Moon 684

Richard Pryor Live on the Sunset Strip 691

E.T. The Extra-Terrestrial 695

Up the River [*Fitzcarraldo, Burden of Dreams*] 700

Tootsie 708

Memory [*The Night of the Shooting Stars*] 713

from State of the Art

A Masterpiece [*The Leopard*] 723

The Perfectionist [*Yentl*] 730

Golden Kimonos [*The Makioka Sisters*] 737

from Hooked

Out There and In Here [*Blue Velvet*] 745

Irish Voices [*The Dead*] 753

The Lady From the Sea [*High Tide*] 758

from **Movie Love**

Unreal [*Women on the Verge of a Nervous Breakdown*] 765
A Wounded Apparition [*Casualties of War*] 769
Satyr [*My Left Foot*] 779
The Grifters 783

Sources and Acknowledgments 787
Index 789

Describing the Italian film *The Night of the Shooting Stars*, in 1984, in *The New Yorker*, Pauline Kael wrote, in words that readers of hers over the years might have used to describe her own reviews, that the movie "is so good it's thrilling." Kael's movie criticism, with its racing, urgent, crystal clear way of making us see the depth, liveliness, or speciousness of whatever film she was handling, and the funny and uncannily intimate way she got into the skin of actors, or presented miniaturized biographies of directors, or drew out the larger social or ethical implications of a given film, affected readers in precisely that manner. We were given writing replete with so many separate, brilliant awarenesses as to take us, as we absorbed them, to another sphere. The very phrasing Kael used about the Tavianis' movie — "so good it's thrilling" — has her transformative power. The words are plain and conversational, yet they have been brought together with a blunt assurance that makes us pause and see them anew.

When she stepped down from writing movie reviews at *The New Yorker*, in 1991, at seventy-two, Kael's retirement was a national news story. For the little over two decades that she had been at the magazine she was undoubtedly the most fervently read American critic of any art. But her renown was based on far more than her coverage of the films of the 1970s and 1980s. In a 1977 review of Steven Spielberg's *Close Encounters of the Third Kind*, she wrote that Spielberg "is a magician in the age of movies," and perhaps more deeply than any other writer Kael gave shape to the idea of an "age of movies." In a career that began in the mid-1950s and was fully underway by the early 1960s, she explored movies as an art, an industry, and a sociological phenomenon. A romantic and a visionary, she believed that movies could feed our imaginations in intimate and immediate—and liberating, even subversive—ways that literature and plays and other arts could not. But she also understood the financial realities and artistic compromises behind moviemaking, and she described them with a specificity and a pertinacity that few other critics did. As concerned with audience reactions as with her own, she could be caught up in how movies stoke our fantasies regardless of their qualities as movies.

She was also, as she wrote, "lucky" in her timing. Her tenure as a regularly reviewing critic coincided with the modern flowering of movies, the period, primarily the 1960s (for foreign films) and the 1970s (for American films), when moviemakers were working more than ever with the autonomy associated with poets, novelists, and painters. While hardly always laudatory (and to some readers plain wrongheaded), she nonetheless, in the earlier decade, gave a breathing, textured life to the aims and sensibilities of Ingmar Bergman, Jean-Luc Godard, Federico Fellini, Satyajit Ray, Akira Kurosawa, François Truffaut, and Michelangelo Antonioni, among other European and Asian directors; and she endowed Robert Altman, Martin Scorsese, Paul Mazursky, Brian De Palma, and Francis Ford Coppola, among American directors of the following decade, with the same full-bodied presence.

Kael's grasp of film history was encyclopedic. She had seen silent films as a child, in the 1920s, sometimes taking them in on her parents' laps. Speaking for her generation, she could thus write of motion pictures that "We were in almost at the beginning, when something new was added to human experience"; and in her full-length reviews and essays (put together over the years in eleven volumes), and her short notices on films (collected in the mammoth *5001 Nights at the Movies*), she encompassed much of that "something new." (Her literal output can be gauged by noting that Kael described her 1994 *For Keeps*, an over 1,200-page selection of what she thought was her best writing, as representing about a fifth of her complete work.)

She had few occasions to write about silent films; but she kept them a living part of her universe by maintaining, for instance, that D. W. Griffith's *Intolerance* was "perhaps the greatest movie ever made" and that Maria Falconetti gave possibly the "finest performance ever recorded on film" in Carl Dreyer's *The Passion of Joan of Arc*. Her views on individual

American, European, and Asian movies of the 1930s, 1940s, and 1950s also exist somewhat in the background of her work as she wrote about them mainly in compressed reviews. But these highly factual and irresistibly readable reviews, which appear in *5001 Nights* alongside entries on movies made up through the 1980s, provide for countless films what feel like both perfect introductions and last words.

What gives Kael a distinctive place in American writing, however, has as much to do with what movies prompt in her as it does with her capturing so much of the breadth and lore of movies. Following through on her conviction that movies release us from our normal emotional and social guardedness, she built her criticism, whether her subject is an epochal masterpiece or a tinny Hollywood product, on her most spontaneous and sensory reactions. In a body of work that as a result sometimes has the impact of a single long, indirect, and utterly original kind of autobiography, she immerses us in a flow of dazzlingly stated, unpredictable, sometimes needling and exhortatory, and always humanly large and forthright perceptions. Speaking with the insights of simultaneously a drama coach, a club comedian, a social agitator, a connoisseur, and a psychotherapist, she illuminates the ways that artists of any kind succeed or fail. When she shows how movies can excite, demean, frighten, or stretch us, she makes it seem as if she were talking about the power and capacities of art no matter what its form. Her deepest subject, in the end, almost isn't movies at all—it is how to live more intensely.

Kael might have been describing herself when she called François Truffaut's *The Story of Adèle H*. "damnably intelligent—almost frighteningly so, like some passages in Russian literature which strip the characters bare." Kael had such an intelligence. Analyzing, say, political movies (whether *Z*, *The Battle of Algiers*, or *The First Circle*), or movies with or about stand-up and TV comedians (including Lenny Bruce, Sid Caesar, or Richard Pryor), or movies based on literary works of some stature (by D. H. Lawrence, Henry James, Melville, Joyce, or Henry Miller, among others), her observations were often so fresh, percipient, and commanding that a reader believed it was this particular subject that drove her to write about movies in the first place.

She often said of movie stars she particularly loved—Laurence Olivier, or Sean Connery, or Morgan Freeman—that everything they did was permeated by a sense of wit. Kael's own prose certainly was. But except in the case of terrible movies, when only sarcastic observations could do justice to the depressing products on hand, her own humor was more like a pervasive tone. There were zingers, of course, as when she wrote about a moment of comic confusion at a gravesite in *Indiana Jones and the Last Crusade* that "It's a good gag—I've always liked it," or noted of John Boorman that many of his movies might have been thought "classics if we hadn't known English"—or said of a scene in *Young Frankenstein* that "the laboratory machines give off enough sparks to let us know that's their only function."

As memorable as her jokes were Kael's little torpedoes of common sense, perceptions that could lodge in a reader's mind, such as her observation about "message" Westerns that their message was that the "myths we never believed in anyway were false," or when, analyzing the bogus hustle of the movie business, she wrote that "Hollywood is the only place where you can die of encouragement." About moviegoing habits, she could note that some people "go to the innocuous hoping for the charming."

Kael's consistently richest writing, though, may be her descriptions of actors. She brings actors to life and gives them at times the fullness of characters in fiction—as when she said that Ava Gardner "never looked really happy in her movies; she wasn't quite there, but she never suggested that she was anywhere else, either," or called the young Katharine Hepburn (whose work Kael often thought glorious) "someone who could be intensely wrong about everything." Paul Newman, she commented, "is good at small blowhards who reveal the needs behind their transparent lies."

Kael's reactions to performers could lead her far beyond the subject at hand. She wrote of Orson Welles in *Citizen Kane*, for instance, that he rouses in us "the kind of empathy we're likely to feel for smart kids who grin at us when they're showing off in the school play. It's a beautiful kind of emotional nakedness—ingenuously exposing the sheer love of playacting—that most actors lose long before they become 'professional.'" At times, by analyzing technique alone, Kael brings back the precise spirit of an actor and even of an era. John Candy in *Splash*, she said, "makes you aware of his bulk by the tricks in his verbal timing: when [Tom] Hanks has said something to him and you expect him to answer, his hesitation—it's like a few seconds of hippo torpor—is what makes his answer funny." Sometimes Kael needed less than a sentence to catch the essence of a performer, telling us, for instance, that in *Big Business* Bette Midler "breezes through, kicking one gong after another."

Pauline Kael herself seemed to breeze through the many aspects of her heroically large subject. Our chief source of information about her formative years—her unpublished letters to her college friends the poet and writer Robert Duncan and Violet (Rosenberg) Ginsburg—shows that her confidence was there from early on. In these letters dated from the late 1930s to the mid-1940s, when she was in her early twenties, her voice as a writer was little different from the voice she would have years later as a published critic. We hear it in her telling Duncan, in 1940, that *Civilization and Its Discontents* is perhaps Freud's "worst work," having a "logical structure that is more baffling and stupid than genuinely provocative"—or when, in 1944, first reading film history, she found that film writers "don't conceive that acting can be an extension of understanding and knowledge." But the setbacks she experienced in being a child of the Depression, and a woman, and the fact that movies as a subject took hold over her only over time, meant that it was a matter of decades before that voice was heard by a large audience.

Born on June 19, 1919, in Petaluma, California, she was the fifth and last child of Judith and Isaac Kael, who had moved west from New York City with their two sons and two daughters before Pauline's birth. In 1927, Isaac lost his money. The family had to give up its egg farm and move down to San Francisco; and from the time she entered the University of California, Berkeley, in 1936, at seventeen, until some thirty years later, when she landed work on national publications, Kael generally needed to take on one "crummy" (as she called them) job after another to make ends meet. When non-crummy work was available, positions such as writing advertising copy and editing manuscripts at a publishing house—at which she was clearly good and that would have led to promotions—she had to turn them down because they would have exhausted her energies for her own writing. So over the years she answered demands for a nanny or a cook, edited manuscripts for clients on a private basis, taught violin, and worked as a seamstress. In college, she graded papers for as many as three professors at a time and, as a teaching assistant, saw students in an office after school where, according to her detailed letters, she occasionally offered frank life-counseling advice — as when "I suggested to some prissy students from Piedmont that their grades mightn't be so low if they would get their minds dirtied up a bit and provided book titles for the process."

Kael's major at Berkeley was the philosophy of history, and she took part in left-wing causes on campus and was on the staff of the *Grizzly*, a student journal. She vaguely thought she might go on to law school. But although she was usually an A student, she was unhappy in college. Her teachers, courses, and fellow students often seemed simply insufficient to her, and as a sign of her boredom she didn't take a course required for her major and so did not receive a degree. Her mind was set, in any event, on getting to New York, where she went, in 1941, with the poet and dance critic Robert Horan. Especially at the beginning, she had to live quite frugally, sometimes even pawning her fountain pen for a needed sum, and she told about weeping on the subway while on one of her grueling job searches. But her letters also bubble up with shared gossip about friends and are full of lively accounts of attending political meetings chaired by Dwight Macdonald (about whose thinking and public speaking style she had grave doubts), and going to concerts and the theater, art shows, movies, jazz clubs, and dance performances — sometimes in the company of Samuel Barber, whom she met through Robert Horan (and about whose music she also had doubts).

She wrote plays and short fiction in her free time. But her letters suggest that she was most fired by reading authors in great depth and making notes for critical articles. In college, her chief concerns — Marx, John Dewey, Freud (on whose work she wrote an immensely long paper) — had not been essentially literary. Stimulated perhaps by Robert Duncan, himself equally involved in poetry, fiction, and political theory, Kael now plunged into the great modernist and nineteenth-century American and European writers, and they became over time her touchstones for all artistic achievement. Even as an undergrad, she kept up with small literary and political quarterlies, particularly *Partisan Review*; and before leaving for New York she wrote, with Horan, an article (which found no takers) on contemporary American fiction, and contemplated a piece on recent literary criticism. The writing style she would become known for, with its brusque assertiveness and belief that artworks must be seen as part of a larger social or moral terrain, was much the house style of *Partisan Review*.

Like other writers associated with the magazine, including Alfred

Kazin and Saul Bellow, Kael was the child of European Jewish immigrants. It is a detail which may help account for her affinity for American themes and artists (as was the case for Kazin), and her desire to sound "American" in her prose (as it was for Bellow)—even while she was concerned, like many *Partisan* writers, with the differences in substance and energy between American and European creators. Kael was especially drawn to the critic and poet R. P. Blackmur, whose work she was intimate with already in college. In New York, she read in depth the writers he tackled and, as she later acknowledged, he probably had an influence. Her portrait of Marlon Brando, for example, in her 1966 "Marlon Brando: An American Hero," as an artist who is too big and awkward for his time and culture, and becomes an eccentric and a clown to preserve himself, clearly echoes Blackmur's writing about the idea of failure and his conception of the isolated Henry Adams.

Kael returned to San Francisco in 1946, and became close to Weldon Kees, James Broughton, and other writers and experimental filmmakers in the area. With Broughton, she had a child—named Gina James—in 1948, but she and Broughton didn't marry and Gina was brought up entirely by Pauline, which gave her the very real stigma at the time of being an unwed mother. It wasn't until 1953, with a negative review of Chaplin's *Limelight*, that Kael finally got into print. But there was no money in writing about films, nor was she paid for a show on movies that she began on radio station KPFA.

She was able to live off movies at least to a slight extent when, in the latter half of the 1950s, she ran the Berkeley Cinema Guild and Studio. She had initially been approached by the owner of the repertory theaters, Edward Landberg, for advice. She and Landberg married, and Kael took over every aspect of theater management—and made it a thriving business. She programmed the various revivals, answered the phone, hired and fired people, and wrote notices about the films for the theaters' mailed-out programs. She even made the posters for the display cases by the entrance (and some were painted by a friend, the artist Jess Collins, who would become known as Jess).

By 1960, her marriage to Landberg and her involvement in running movie theaters was over, and she had more opportunity to write about new movies, publishing in *Sight and Sound, Film Quarterly*, and elsewhere. Yet it was only in 1965, when her first collection of essays and reviews,

I Lost it at the Movies, was met with national acclaim—and she and Gina moved to New York and Kael began reviewing for mass-circulation magazines—that she, at forty-six, could actually live off her writing. Even then there were hitches. Her writer's voice turned out not to suit the editors at *Life* or *McCall's* or a number of other magazines. In 1966 and 1967, she had more space to write at *The New Republic*, but differences with her editor led to her being let go there as well.

In 1967, she also had two significant essays taken by *The New Yorker*, "Movies on Television" and a long analysis of *Bonnie and Clyde*. So it was not altogether unexpected when William Shawn, editor of *The New Yorker*, offered her a job reviewing movies. It was doubly providential since Kael, fired by *The New Republic*, had no job and no idea where to turn, and at *The New Yorker* she was given the secure berth and the wide national audience she had sought for years.

Kael was always looking, in any endeavor, for a freedom from rules and expected structures. Growing up with a great love of jazz and dancing (she played in a girls' jazz band in her youth), she was after, it might be said, an unstructuredness that yet had a backbone to it. Her feeling for plot lines where the audience has little idea of what is coming next and yet the story as a whole has an organic unity is what drew her to write with such excitement and perception about Robert Altman, Jean-Luc Godard, John Guare, and the screwball comedy screenwriters of the 1930s. Kael's own writing has precisely this sense of apparently structureless tautness. Her reviews rarely begin with setting-the-stage introductions and they rarely end with grand wrap-ups. They manage to be entirely lucid even while seeming almost improvisatory in the way the material has been set out.

Her thinking conveys the same simultaneity of disparate elements. Her criticism has a Shakespearian variety of heroes, heroines, villains, conflicts, and expressions of social or artistic value; and her multifariousness is in good part what keeps her such an energizing writer. Kael had an unusually many-sided idea of what makes for beauty or power in art. Writing at age twenty-five to Robert Duncan about Joyce, she said it was "disgusting to have his morality aestheticized out of existence," and she remained impatient with purely formal approaches to art. Part of her desire to write about movies in the first place was because, as commercial products, they weren't only aesthetic objects; they were inherently about the battle film artists faced with the corporations that control which pictures get made and how they are made.

Kael knew in her bones how entangled art, personal freedom, and economic dependency are. Her experience surely fueled the scathing and moralistic way she treated the Hollywood moguls who created the studio system and the faceless executives who followed them. (Her anger can be heard in a letter she wrote even before film became her chosen subject.) In words that one is surprised to read were published in *The New Yorker* in the 1970s, she hit out repeatedly, to give a sense of her invective, against the industry's "thieving, high-salaried executives and their entourage of whores and underlings."

She was in love, however, with the idea of a sensual and amoral world. Like writers before her, she perceived, and wanted to celebrate, that there was something inherently sexual in the nature of movies. But her belief in the power of sheer carnal energy was hardly tied to movies alone. Kael saw the erotic force as inhibition-breaking. Her certainty in the matter is what made her so ready to champion Bernardo Bertolucci's 1972 *Last Tango in Paris*, where sexuality was presented with a new frankness and was practically the movie's subject. By the same token, she might state in a characteristic moment that "A pretty fair case could be made that a little corruption is good for the soul: it humanizes you."

As deep as her feeling for the sensuous was her need for a story or a character to ring true in emotional terms. The "revelation of human character," she wrote, is the highest dramatic function of movies (and of the stage). It was because the characters in genre movies, whether Westerns, science fiction, or film noir, were almost by definition impersonal, stock types that these kinds of films generally seemed stunted and vaguely wearisome to her.

Describing the particular power of movies, Kael set forth a kind of rationale for popular culture no matter what its form. In a major 1968 essay, "Trash, Art, and the Movies," she held that, watching movies, we can dispense with "the proper responses required of us in our official (school) culture." We are relieved of the "responsibility to pay attention and to appreciate," and in this zone of freedom and irresponsibility we can often get closer to the real spirit of art—we can "develop our own aesthetic response." Kael's prose, with its colloquial and slangy expressions, its contractions and "you feel" constructions, demonstrated in itself how "our official" culture could be shed.

Her social predilections were of a piece with this aim. She had an instinctive affinity for questioners and dislodgers of propriety. Her long-standing high regard for Marlon Brando, whom she saw as "our genius" among American actors, and for Norman Mailer, who, despite her not much caring for his movies and his biography of Marilyn Monroe, held the same standing among our writers for her, owed much to the way that she saw both seeking, in their respective arts, to bring unorthodox, disruptive, even perilous feelings up to the surface of life.

Kael's taste, though, was hardly that of a populist. She wrote that art has "got to be too much or it's not enough," and surely few critics pointed out so continually and exasperatedly how vacuous and cliché-ridden movies generally are. Her heightened degree of opinionatedness—her ability to have at the very moment crisply definitive feelings about everything in her path—was, actually, mesmerizing (and a little alienating). Critics are supposed to have strong opinions and to be able to change their minds about their subjects over time. But, regarding any kind of artist, Kael could go from admiration to antipathy overnight, and whichever way she was going she made her judgments feel moral, aesthetic, and personal all at once. If a reader didn't agree with her view it could come as a personal challenge; one felt the need to square one's view with hers.

And where most critics, when they have an opinion that isolates them from the general taste of their time—such as Edmund Wilson dissenting on Kafka or Clement Greenberg rejecting Picasso's later work—tend to leave the issue once it has been voiced, and so let it come to seem like an aberrant or private notion (thereby making people feel they don't have to take it seriously), Kael reiterated and forthrightly explored tastes and emotions of hers that were radically different from that of consensus thinking. She wasn't the only critic to believe, for example, that Alfred Hitchcock was wildly overrated or to find most of Stanley Kubrick's films cold and rigid; but her clear and essential rejection of the regular claims of importance for them, and her similar clarity about what she felt were the profound limitations of Fellini, Antonioni, and Ingmar Bergman (at different times in his career), remains salutary, even if one disagrees with her specific conclusions. Few writers, by their example, have said so forcefully and inspiringly that, in judging the arts, no artists are above criticism.

Much of the seductive power of Kael's first book, the best-selling *I Lost it at the Movies*, which brought together pieces she wrote when still in Berkeley, came from the way she seemed to offer alternatives to conventional thinking of every stripe. Often quoting the notices the movie under review had already been given by New York critics, and then talking back to those critics, she presented the voice of a Californian. Describing how unimpressed she was with such vaunted European films of the time as *Hiroshima, Mon Amour* or *8 ½*, she seemed to speak, in addition, for a completely valid other, and very American, way of responding. With her wisecracking and ballsy tone, she even gave some readers a new idea of what a woman writer could sound like.

I Lost it at the Movies remains perhaps Kael's best-known collection, but it isn't her richest book (she certainly didn't think it was). She had real sympathy with only elements of recent European filmmaking, and, in articles that became almost sociological attacks on the educated audience that was responding to the new movies, her voice could be hectoring and strident. But Kael's questioning of theories that said there were inherent values in certain kinds of movies, whether the "auteur theory" or any other, was tonic; and her overall thinking, which was that of a liberal writer admonishing what she saw as the myopia of her fellow liberals, had much the same drive that Jane Jacobs, in her 1961 classic *The Death and Life of Great American Cities*, brought to her encounter with what she saw as the theory-driven blind spots of architects and city planners. When we read Kael clearing the air of academic systems of grading movies, and getting us to put more trust in our visceral and instinctive reactions to movies, we are only a step away from Jacobs describing in everyday language how free-flowing and unregimented city life usually is when it is making the greatest numbers of its residents happiest.

In her later work, Kael's viewpoint was much less that of a gadfly. In the 1970s, at *The New Yorker*, she seized opportunities to delve into aspects of American filmmaking—or the "American consciousness," as Mailer put it—that she found elating, whether writing about the movie past or developments in current movies. For Kael the second half of the 1930s represented a high point in American films but one that had not been given its due. She redressed the issue in the juicily detailed 1971 "Raising Kane," about the making of *Citizen Kane* (her longest piece of writing, not included here for reasons of space), and in the 1975 "The Man from Dream City," a profile of Cary Grant. However different their subjects, the essays concern a time, as Kael presents it, when the deprivations of the early Depression years had subsided, Hollywood was buoyed up by wry, witty, and ornery screenwriters from the East Coast, and the best American movies had a formal glamour, an adult sexiness, a hardboiled disdain for sentimentality, and a sense of what she called a "happy effrontery" that the studio system hardly matched again.

Citizen Kane, for her—it is not everyone's idea of the film—was the "culmination" of that "sustained feat of careless magic we call 'thirties comedy'"; and the same verbal slapstick that animated what has also been referred to as the "newspaper comedy" (which Orson Welles's film certainly is in many ways) was a core ingredient in fashioning Cary Grant's glistening, romantic, and farcical screen presence. Both studies revolve, in a sense, around an original and poetic way of thinking about the word "shallow." Kael pointedly employed the word as early as 1956, in "Movies, The Desperate Art," to distinguish an American, as opposed to a European, response to experience, and she did not mean it pejoratively. Shallow for her could connote energy, joy, and sass combined, and she somehow makes it a meaningful accolade for *Citizen Kane*, Cary Grant, and the time they came out of.

In the American movies of the 1970s, though, Kael was tracking edgier and riskier responses to experience. Already in her probing 1967 analysis of *Bonnie and Clyde* she had spotted a new kind of American film. With its then novel mixture of bloody deaths and absurdist humor, coolly untouched by any accompanying moral lessons, Arthur Penn's movie, she saw, was a rarity in being a commercial Hollywood venture whose unsettling spirit owed a lot to the French New Wave and whose candor about death reflected a new mood of disillusionment in the country. (She didn't mention the Vietnam War, but its presence is felt in her piece.) The film was a harbinger of a period of more personal and experimental, and more emotionally and physically violent, American movies—a period that Kael was prepared to meet head on.

During the 1970s, Kael seemed to be putting in perspective, in the very weeks the movies opened, what the onrush of new directors, new actors, and new themes meant to the large audience responding to them. She was in her fifties and many of her most dynamic subjects, including Altman,

Spielberg, Scorsese, De Palma, and Coppola, were a good bit younger, if not half her age. Yet she moved without hesitation into their different imaginative worlds and intuitively grasped the relative significance of their efforts. It is hard to imagine that there will be better evocations of the rash and explosive spirit of Scorsese's early films, the muffled and disorienting beauty of Altman's *McCabe & Mrs. Miller*, the believable sweetness of Spielberg's early fables, the blend De Palma made of the scary, the pictorially sumptuous, and the ingenious, or of the way Coppola's *The Godfather* attained what she called a "new tragic realism."

It was Kael's close involvement with current filmmaking that prompted Warren Beatty to propose that she leave reviewing and work as an executive consultant at Paramount Pictures, doing for films before they were made what she did in print. This made sense to her, and for five months in 1979 she had an office in Hollywood, talking, she said in a later interview, "to anybody who stopped by and wanted to talk" (a position oddly echoing what she did with fellow students at Berkeley four decades earlier). But Kael "missed writing," she said, and returned to *The New Yorker* in 1980. She came back from Los Angeles confirmed in her belief that the movie industry, which a few years back had let itself be galvanized by a number of talented moviemakers with fresh approaches, was now in a state of retrenchment. It had found ways, she wrote in the 1980 "Why Are Movies So Bad? or, The Numbers," to insure itself against financial losses—and therefore could bottle up the artistically challenging as well.

In her last decade at *The New Yorker* Kael worked with the sense that film as an art and as a mirror of national life had lost its momentum and urgency. She continued, however, to find certain directors and, especially, actors exciting. She was eager to mark the arrival of emerging filmmakers from Australia, New Zealand, and Spain, the resurgence of John Huston and Kon Ichikawa at the end of their lives, and the coming into their own of, among others, Richard Pryor, Barbra Streisand, Burt Lancaster, Diane Keaton, and Daniel Day-Lewis.

Movie reviewing itself, though, had become arduous. Kael had bought a house in Great Barrington, Massachusetts, in 1971, and came to divide her time between New York, where she saw movies and turned in her articles, and the Berkshires, where she wrote. By the late 1980s, when she was in her late sixties, the commuting began to wear on her. In the ten years of life that remained to her after her retirement—she died on

September 3, 2001, at eighty-two—she suffered considerably from heart ailments and Parkinson's disease. But her concern for movies, for the screenplays she was sent to comment on, and for books and music, remained unabated.

Kael's openness throughout her life to so many unrelated artists and themes makes one understand why, of all directors, Jean Renoir, whom she covered in a number of short reviews and often mentioned, may have meant the most to her. With her hip, wary, street-smart language and insights and her desire for sheer contemporaneity, she didn't always seem temperamentally connected to the French director, whose films often expressed a sympathetic awareness of people no matter what their motivations or behavior. Yet there was a part of Kael that clearly did have a rapport with the elemental naturalism, and the kind of filmmaking that doesn't call attention to itself, that can be associated with Renoir. Her feeling for such a view of art, and people, was certainly evident over the years in her writing on Satyajit Ray and Jan Troell. And in some of her strongest pieces from the late 1970s and 1980s, whether on *The Deer Hunter*, *Melvin and Howard*, *The Chant of Jimmie Blacksmith*, *The Leopard*, or *Casualties of War*, she described the stories and textures of the films in ways that showed her to be this kind of artist herself. She increasingly could write with the same calm, wide empathy for events as they unfolded that marked some of Renoir's strongest films.

She came increasingly as well to label as a comedy movies she particularly loved, and her use of the word was as distinctive and personal as her use of "shallow" in that she often called a film a comedy even when it wasn't especially funny. Kael was, of course, in her language, a bit of a comedian herself, and she wrote that some of the best reasons to go to movies in the 1980s were to see Bill Murray, Bette Midler, or Steve Martin, among other comic performers, in action. But "comedy" for her meant more than jokes, or flashes of impudence, or a feeling for the absurdity of some experiences. The word suggested that a movie, or any artwork, had a self-awareness. It could take itself seriously and stand outside itself at the same time. It could bring together sorrow and violence and silliness and wild exaggeration and a lyrical beauty and make them all feel like part of one fabric. This is what Kael's own vast body of work does, and perhaps it also can best be called a comedy—a comedy of awareness and perception.

Books by Pauline Kael

I Lost it at the Movies, 1965
Kiss Kiss Bang Bang 1968
Going Steady, 1970
The Citizen Kane Book, 1971
Deeper into Movies, 1973
Reeling, 1976
When the Lights Go Down, 1980
5001 Nights at the Movies, 1982; expanded edition, 1991
Taking It All In, 1984
State of the Art, 1985
Hooked, 1989
Movie Love, 1991
For Keeps, 1994

Interviews:
Will Brantley, ed. *Conversations with Pauline Kael*, 1996
Francis Davis. *Afterglow: A Last Conversation with Pauline Kael*, 2002

:: Movies, the Desperate Art

The film critic in the United States is in a curious position: the greater his interest in the film medium, the more enraged and negative he is likely to sound. He can assert his disgust, and he can find ample material to document it, but then what? He can haunt film societies and re-experience and reassess the classics, but the result is an increased burden of disgust; the directions indicated in those classics are not the directions Hollywood took. A few writers, and not Americans only, have taken a rather fancy way out: they turn films into Rorschach tests and find the most elaborate meanings in them (bad acting becomes somnambulism, stereotyped situations become myths, and so forth). The deficiency of this technique is that the writers reveal a great deal about themselves but very little about films.

Size

Hollywood films have attempted to meet the "challenge" of television by the astonishingly simple expedient of expanding in size; in the course of this expansion the worst filmic tendencies of the past thirty years have reached what we may provisionally call their culmination. Like a public building designed to satisfy the widest public's concept of grandeur, the big production loses the flair, the spontaneity, the rhythm of an artist working to satisfy his own conception. The more expensive the picture, the bigger the audience it must draw, and the fewer risks it can take. The big film is the disenchanted film: from the outset, every element in a multi-million-dollar production is charged with risk and anxiety, the fear of calamitous failure—the loss of "big" money. The picture becomes less imaginative in inverse ratio to its cost. But the idiot solution has worked: size *has* been selling, and Hollywood has learned to inflate everything, even romance (*Three Coins in the Fountain*) or murder mystery (*Black Widow*)—the various genres become indistinguishable. A "small" picture would probably seem retrogressive to Hollywood—as if the industry were not utilizing its full resources, and, indeed, when the CinemaScope screen contracts for an "old-fashioned"-size picture, the psychological effect is of a going *back*. Films must be big to draw the mass audience, but the heroes and heroines, conceived to flatter the "ordinary," "little" persons who presumably make up the audience, must be inanities who will offend no one.

The magic that films advertise is the magic of bloated production methods—it is no longer the pyramid the company photographed at Gizeh which is the selling point (that has become too easy) but the pyramid they have *built*. It is the "magic" of American industry—the feats of production presumed to be possible nowhere else (musical extravaganzas like *Easy to Wed* or *Latin Lovers* are incarnations of American speed and efficiency, vigor and abundance, held together by the conviction that all this is the good life). Abroad, especially, the glamour of American movies emanates from the wastefulness of Hollywood methods as much as from the land of plenty revealed in film stories.

Those who see the era of the wide screen and the traveling camera crew as encouraging evidence that movies will once again become magical and exciting recall their childhood when the wonder of film lay in the extraordinary scope of the camera. But the panoramic views of a CinemaScope or VistaVision production are about as magical as a Fitzpatrick travelogue, and the actors are not unlike the girls that travelogue makers love to place at the entrance to each glorious temple—commonplace, anachronistic and reassuring. In a film like *Soldier of Fortune* the story material and the exotic backgrounds do not support each other (as they do in Carol Reed's *Outcast of the Islands*); the company goes to Hong Kong to tell a story that could just as easily be told in Southern California—the location shots are used to make the familiar seem unusual.

The split between background and foreground in pictures with foreign settings develops into schizophrenia in historical and Biblical spectacles. A reconstruction of Egypt (usually filtered through Maxfield Parrish) means authenticity; the audience is supposed to feel that the film is "real" and important because the background material has been thoroughly researched (the sets are real sets). But the heroes and heroines are not really intended to look of the period at all; the audience might lose its bearings if Susan Hayward or Alan Ladd did not hold them in the familiar present. Would *20,000 Leagues under the Sea* have been such a commercial success if Kirk Douglas had not been there to destroy the illusion of the nineteenth century? The emotions and actions recorded by novelists and historians might insult American tastes and mores; audiences rest easier when characters do only those things modern young men and women are supposed to do (Salome can dance, but she can't get the head). Accuracy (or what passes for accuracy) in background details becomes enormously important—it gives the shoddy, sexy films the sanction of educational and religious values. (The fantastic emphasis on accurate sets and costumes may indicate also a last desperate stand by the artists and technicians who have failed to grapple with the most restrictive censorship—the tastes of the national audience—but who still cling to some kind of pride in their work.) There is a crude appeal in Hollywood's "realism." Arliss made up to look like Disraeli was a living display of ingeniousness for the same public that appreciates a painted horse that looks real enough to ride. There is an instinct for what the public respects that works beneath film methods: the backgrounds of *Seven Brides for Seven Brothers* are painted to fool the audience into seeing real snow on real mountains. In proving that it can make things look real (reality rates higher with the mass audience than style and illusion) Hollywood comes full circle—back to before the beginnings of art.

Hollywood follows the mass audience and the mass audience follows Hollywood; there is no leader. The worst of the past is preserved with new dust. How many films that we once groaned at do we now hear referred to nostalgically? When the bad is followed by the worse, even the bad seems good. (Film addicts talk about *Grand Hotel* or Busby Berkeley's choreography, as if *those* were the days.) The hostility toward art and highbrowism that infects much of our culture helps to explain the popularity of so many untrained and untalented screen performers. Richard Burton and Daniel O'Herlihy do not stimulate the fans; Tony Curtis, Tab Hunter, Janet Leigh, Jane Powell do. Fans like untrained actors; perhaps they like even the embarrassment of untrained actors (why should they tolerate the implied criticism of speech or gesture that derives from a higher culture?).

The office girl says, "No, I don't want to go see Howard Keel—he was a professional singer, you know." The tastes of the mass audience belong to sociology, not aesthetics. Those who make big films do not consider primarily the nature of the medium and what they want to do with it, they try to keep ahead of the mass audience.

As the mass media developed, the fine points of democratic theory were discarded, and a parody of democracy became public dogma. The film critic no longer considers that his function is the formation and reformation of public taste (that would be an undemocratic presumption); the old independent critic who would trumpet the good, blast the bad, and tell his readers they were boobs if they wasted their money on garbage, gives way to the amiable fellow who feels responsible not to his subject matter but to the tastes of his stratum of the public. Newspaper critics are, in many cases, not free to attack big films (too much is at stake), but they are usually free to praise what they wish; yet they seem too unsure of themselves, too fearful of causing a breach with their readers, to praise what may be unpopular. It is astonishing how often they attack the finest European productions and the most imaginative American ones—safe targets. Attitudes become more important than judgments. The critic need not make any definite adverse comments; his descriptive tone is enough to warn his readers off. Praise which includes such terms as "subtle," "low-keyed" or "somber" is damnation; the critic saves his face but helps kill the movie.

There are people, lots of them, who take big pictures seriously. What is one to say to the neo-Aristotelianism of the salesgirl who reports, "I saw *The Student Prince* last night—it was so wonderful and so sad. I cried and cried, and when it was over, why, I just felt all cleaned out." Only snobs howl at *Duel in the Sun* ($11.3 million gross), and if you crawled out on *Quo Vadis* ($10.5 million gross) you not only showed your disrespect for heavy labor, you implied contempt for those who were awed by it. Hollywood productions are official parts of American life, proofs of technological progress; derision is subversive. You will be reproved with "What right have you to say *Samson and Delilah* is no good when millions of people liked it?" and you will be subjected to the final devastation of "It's all a matter of taste and one person's taste is as good as another's." One does not make friends by replying that although it *is* all a matter of taste (and education and intelligence and sensibility) one person's taste is *not* as good as another's.

Three or four years ago, films by Huston and Zinnemann and, at times, Mankiewicz, Kazan and a few others, stood out from the thick buttered-up products and showed the working of individual creative responsibility. The wide screen and the rediscovery of Christianity have restored films to their second childhood. In the thirties we thought Cecil B. DeMille passé; the American film of 1955 represents his full triumph. In the infancy of films there was promise and fervor; the absurdities were forgivable—we could find them amusing and primitive because we thought we saw the beginnings of a prodigy and we knew there were real obstacles ahead. But this synthetic infancy is monstrous—a retracing of the steps, not to discover the lost paths of development, but to simulate the charms of infancy—and, for all we know, there may be a return to each previous (and doomed) period of film. Something must be done to keep a huge film in motion—in desperation everything gets thrown in. *Grand Hotel* itself becomes a model: put in enough characters and stories and perhaps the huge screen will fuse what it encompasses (Mankiewicz' *The Barefoot Contessa*, Kazan's *East of Eden*, as well as *Violent Saturday*, *Soldier of Fortune*, *The Cobweb*). The biggest productions often look like a compendium of the worst filmic crimes of the past, achieving a really massive staleness. Some directors, feeling possibly that spectacles are a joke, attempt elaborate spoofs like *Athena* or *Jupiter's Darling*. But films have got so close to no conviction and no believability that there is very little difference when they cross the line into satire of themselves. If an audience can accept *Mambo* as a serious film, how is it to know, the next week, that *Many Rivers to Cross* is supposed to be funny? When the spectacular production scale is used for comedy, audiences may be too stunned by size and expense to see the humor.

One reason recent spectacles are so much worse than the earliest ones is the addition of sound; it was bad enough to look at the Saviour on the cross, now we must hear his gasps. And the wide screen, which theoretically expands filmic possibilities in certain areas of material, in general limits what can be done—while the areas in which it offers possibilities will probably never be explored. A master could use the vast medium; he could even find themes and dialogue adequate to it (*The Dynasts* or *Peer Gynt* perhaps—or *Road to Damascus*), but what master would be entrusted with the cost of such a venture? It was Michael Todd who enlisted the Yugoslav Army for *War and Peace* ("We're going to make this movie accurate down to the last bit of hairdress and harness") while David Selznick, the Civil War behind him, commands another *War and Peace* (even the legions and larders of Hollywood may be exhausted building the steppes of Russia). Selznick and his peers continue the worst heritage of Griffith, not the visual inventiveness which is his glory but the spread of his conceptions and the spliced sentiments and ideas which substituted for structure. Erich von Stroheim's synopses of *Walking down Broadway* and *Queen Kelly* (recently published in *Film Culture*) are extraordinary documents (as high-school themes they would be hilarious); is it possible that early film makers did not realize that they were heirs to *any* traditions, that because the film medium was new they thought it should be approached with an empty mind? The egotism of the self-taught, which is a practical, though often paranoid, defense against commercial pressure, has had considerable effect on film development. The megalomaniacs who make films can think of no bigger subject than *War and Peace* (Italians, Finns and Russians all race to complete their versions); what can they do next—recreate the creation of the world? All these companies but one will probably lose their shirts; if *all* lose their shirts, perhaps producers will heed the Tolstoyan lesson and learn to approach film making with the economy of a peasant.

Action

The best films of recent years have not been spectacles and they have not been geared to a large audience; they have made more and more demands on concentrated attention. The trained eye of an adult may find magic in the sustained epiphanies of *Day of Wrath*, the intricate cutting and accumulating frenzy of *La Règle du Jeu*, the visual chamber drama of *Les Parents Terribles*. American attempts in these directions have met with resistance not only from the public but from American film critics as well. The critics' admiration for "action" and "the chase" leads them to praise sleazy suspense films but to fret over whether *A Streetcar Named Desire* or *The Member of the Wedding* is really "cinematic."

For the gullible, advertising provides a rationale for spectacles (the duplication of big historical events is edifying, and the films themselves are triumphs comparable in status to the original events); a more sophisticated audience finds its own rationale for suspense films: crime and punishment suggest some connection with the anxieties and terrors of modern man. The police pursuing a mad killer in the most routine chase seems more "realistic" than a spectacle, and have not some film theorists decided that the chase is "pure cinema"? Suspense films may reflect modern anxieties but they don't deal with them; the genre offers the spring of tension, the audience recoils. For critics, the suspense film has been a safety valve: they could praise it and know themselves to be in accord both with high "technical" standards and a good-size audience.

But critics have been quick to object to a film with a difficult theme, a small camera range, or a markedly verbal content (they object even when the words are worth listening to). Because action *can* be extended over a wide area on the screen, they think it must be — or what they're seeing isn't really a movie at all. The camera is supposed to get outside, even when it has no place to go. According to *Time*, *The Member of the Wedding* "comes most vibrantly alive when it forsakes the one-set stage original and untrammeled by high-flown talk, roves through the neighborhood, e.g., Frankie's journey through blaring, glaring honky-tonk town." The drama, however, was in the "high-flown talk," and the excursion into town was the least dramatically interesting sequence in the film (and, as a matter of fact, the camera moved more fluidly within the room than it did outside). *Miss Julie* was a beautifully executed "cinematic" treatment of a play with the action extended over acres and generations. Yet when it was over one wanted to see the play itself — that confined, harrowing drama which had been dissipated in additional material and lyrical compositions from nature. The closed framework employed in *Les Parents Terribles* could have brought us *Miss Julie* as we could never see it on the stage, with the camera intensifying our consciousness of the human face and body, picking up details, and directing the eye toward the subtleties of performance. The film *Miss Julie* treats the play as if stage and screen were opposed media and the play had to be subjected to a chemical change. (What is chemically changed in the process is the material and meaning of the play.) But, of course, it was dramatists like Strindberg and Ibsen who reformed stage movement and acting technique and created the modern style — the style to which virtually all film directors are indebted. They are the dramatists who taught film how to behave.

Concerned to distinguish between the "proper" functions of stage and screen, critics tend to overlook that most important dramatic function which they share: the revelation of human character. Instead of asking,

"Does the film mean anything?" they ask, "Does the film move?" It is not surprising that there should be many in the mass audience who can see action only in a cavalry charge, but it is surprising how many film critics have the same basic notion of action. (The idea that filmic action must be red-blooded turns up in surprising places. Why did Olivier as Hamlet feel it necessary to throw Ophelia down as if to break every bone in her body?) Most of the elements they condemn as "stagy" were taken over from films anyway—the theatrical devices of Tennessee Williams, for example. Kazan's transition from stage director to film director was so smooth because he had already been adapting film techniques to the stage. The most widely applauded "advanced" staging derives from films: revolving stages (*Lady in the Dark*) simulate rapid cutting, scrim sets (*Death of a Salesman*) conjure variable perspectives, unit sets (*Tea and Sympathy*) attempt a controlled panorama, light-plot sets (*The Trial*) imitate the whole process of the dissolve and montage. And to confound the issue, Griffith and the other film pioneers who developed these techniques extracted them in large part from Max Reinhardt—who was bursting the bounds of the stage frame. Few, if any, of the devices of film originated exclusively with film.

The giveaway in the critics' demand for action is that fine films in which the camera is brilliantly active over considerable terrain often disturb and displease them; they found *Miracle in Milan* too fantastic and imaginative, *Los Olvidados* too grim, *The Beggar's Opera* too contrived, *The Earrings of Madame de . . .* too chic and decadent. When they asked for action they didn't mean action with intellectual content (they want the chase to be pure). One of the strongest critical terms of condemnation is that a film is *slow*. This is understood to mean dull, but what it may really indicate is complexity or subtlety. Renoir's lovely comedy *The Golden Coach* was described as "slow" (and died at the box office), though after sitting through it twice I still had not had time to catch up with everything in it. Those who are used to films which underscore and overscore every point for them are bewildered when they are required to use their own eyes and ears—nothing seems to be going on. Perhaps the effects of a few decades of radio have been underestimated: film audiences don't want images to carry the dramatic idea; they don't know what's happening unless there are words to tell them. And they want the same kind of words they are used to on the radio. When the simplest kind of visual image is added to the verbal plane of soap opera or radio humor, you have the style of

Hollywood films. One of the reasons for their extraordinary popularity all over the world is that once the audience gets used to this visual-verbal redundancy (which is remarkably easy to understand) it dislikes the effort of adjusting to more complex types of film. The patrons of "action" houses, steady customers for the heroics of Jeff Chandler or Rory Calhoun, are displeased only when there is some content that slows up the "action." The speed of Hollywood films is a necessity; there is nothing for the eye to linger on and nothing verbal that requires thought.

So many film pedants have insisted that one portion "belongs" to the camera and one portion "belongs" to the stage that it has become a mark of culture to discuss movies in terms of their cinematic properties and their theatrical deviations. In place of this tug of war (which would split both film and stage down the middle) may one propose simple basic terms for the evaluation of film: does the frame of meaning support the body of photographic, directorial, and acting styles; and conversely, do these styles define the frame of meaning? Examples of this integrity are Keaton's *The Navigator* or *The General*, Guitry's *Les Perles de la Couronne*, *On Approval*, *The Fallen Idol*, *Rashomon*. There are other examples, where the meaning may vitiate our interest in the film, but where the film is obviously of a piece — *The Maltese Falcon* or *Sunset Boulevard*. The integration of meaning and style is almost always the result of the director's imaginative grasp of the story material and control over the production. A great film is one in which the range of meaning is so imaginatively new, compelling, or exciting that we experience a new vision of human experience (*Grand Illusion*). One might also call a film great because it triumphantly achieves a style (René Clair's *Le Million*) or because it represents a new method and approach (*Potemkin*). Only rarely does an American film, as a whole, sustain an interesting range of meanings, but frequently there are meaningful sections and efforts in a film. For example, the theme of *On the Waterfront* is inflated and the directorial style is overscaled, but certain sections of the film are more dramatically meaningful than anything else in recent American movies. When the latent meanings in the material are disintegrated in the photography, direction and acting, we have fiascoes like *The Caine Mutiny* and *The Bridges at Toko-Ri*. When the meanings are too obvious and too absurd to support the body, we have the typical bloated film (*The Prodigal*, *Garden of Evil*, *Daddy Long Legs*, or that CinemaScope edition of *Reader's Digest*, *A Man Called Peter*).

Academic "Craftsmanship"

The serious, literate audiences share with the larger American audience the fear of being duped. Even the small audiences at cinema guilds and art houses are suspicious of new artists, who might be charlatans pulling tricks and willfully obscuring things. Americans are susceptible to the widespread democratic propaganda that the really great artists of history were simple and lucid; they don't want to be *had*. Music lovers who listen to nothing later than Mozart are saved from errors in taste; they are certain to consider themselves discriminating. The film audience dedicated to Pudovkin or von Stroheim or the early René Clair are playing it just as safe.

While it is not easy to recognize or understand new art, meticulous, ponderous craftsmanship—the emulation of already recognized art—can be appreciated at once. George Stevens used to direct some pictures with good moments (*Alice Adams, The More the Merrier*); now that he makes heavy, expensive pictures full of obese nuances (*I Remember Mama, A Place in the Sun, Shane*) he is highly regarded. Literate carefulness is the much advertised "quality" of Samuel Goldwyn productions (assemble "distinguished" writers, a costly story property, director and actors and technicians with artistic reputations, and you have a "prestige" picture—though the results may suggest the old Community Chest slogan "Suppose nobody cared . . ."). The production values of a Goldwyn picture (*The North Star, The Best Years of Our Lives, Hans Christian Andersen*) are not as banal and vulgar as those of *A Woman's World*, but crudity has often been the only sign of life in American movies; the prestige picture sacrifices even this feeble vitality for an impressive façade.

The look of solid, serious construction seems to be very important to the educated audience; they are fearful of approving the films of Cocteau—perhaps, like Gulley Jimson, he may be painting for pleasure on walls that are collapsing. Readers who put down *The Horse's Mouth* and ask anxiously if Gulley Jimson is really supposed to be a great painter are, no doubt, part of the same audience that feels reassured when George Stevens says, "I don't make films for pleasure." Work without joy is respectable; it doesn't raise doubts that it may not be serious. Cocteau, with his enigmas and ambiguities, is he not perhaps trying to put something over? His high style is suspicious; members of the serious audience don't want to go out on a limb for something that may turn out to be merely chic and fashionable. Though they are educated beyond the fat production values of routine pictures, they still want the fat of visible artistic effort. And there is something they want even more, something they value even higher than "artistic values"—the fat of "important ideas" and paraphrasable content (in the thirties, Warner Brothers was the chief purveyor; in the late forties, Stanley Kramer took over). While the less educated mass audience may be in awe of the man-hours and banker's dollars that go into a colossal production, the educated audience, uncertain and self-sacrificial, respects the good a movie will do for others.

Pressures

Our films are stuffed with good intentions. A *Life* editorial pointed out that "in 1951 Americans bought more tickets to symphony concerts than they did to baseball games. . . . The hunger of our citizenry for culture and self-improvement has always been grossly underestimated." Is it hunger or is it a nutritional deficiency? These educated people of conscience don't feel they should waste their time; they reserve their interest for films with praiseworthy aims. The themes favored by the serious audience in the thirties and forties—race relations and mob violence—are perfectly good themes, but treatment of them in conformity with the moral and social aims of conscientious people bleached the interest out. The morally awakened audience banished the early subhuman racial stereotypes from the screen; they developed their own stereotypes—which they must know to be lies and yet feel are *necessary* lies. Could Melville's *Benito Cereno* be filmed, a century after it was written, without a barrage of protests from the educated audience—an audience that cannot admit to the dread and terror of Melville's white man held captive by Negroes?

It is the enlightened message, e.g., *Gentleman's Agreement*, that people must be educated into tolerance; prejudice is wrong. Any motives indicated for the prejudice must be superficial or wrongheaded, so that the prejudiced character can be exposed, if not to himself, at least to the audience. At the lowest level in *It's a Big Country* (a bottom-grade big picture) the Jewish soldier was the usual Hollywood boy next door, and the woman's hostility toward him was the product of sheer ignorance; we left her enlightened by the recognition that he was exactly like the boy next door, only better, and she was about to correspond with his mother. At a more complex level in *Crossfire* the Jew-hater was a fanatic who never learned; but what the audience saw was once again the liberal stereotype: the murdered Jew was a decorated war hero. (Suppose the murdered man was a draft dodger, or a conscientious objector, would the audience then feel no sting, would the fanatic have been justified in killing him?) In John Sturges' *Bad Day at Black Rock* (one of the few reasonably good films to come out of Hollywood this year) the pattern is the same: the period is 1945 and the victim of the townspeople is a murdered Japanese farmer—this time it is the victim's son (killed in action) who is the decorated war hero. By a quota system, war films admitted carefully selected minority representatives, clean-cut Jewish and Negro soldiers whose participation in the national defense apparently gave them a special claim to equality over and above mere membership in the human species. Can it be that even in liberal thinking there is a stigma which can be rubbed off only if minority characters behave heroically?

The fantasy structure is familiar: We have had countless movie heroines who sin (i.e., express sexual passion) and repent by way of almost automatic illegitimate births and various forms of social condemnation. Eventually they "work off" the sin by self-sacrifice, commonly the sacrifice of mother for child. This pleasure-pain bookkeeping (for which the production code, and hence the pressure groups, are partly responsible) tells you that you pay for pleasure by the sacrifice of all future pleasures. Can it be that for the middle classes, Jews and Negroes also need to work off something? Pinky gave up the white doctor and dedicated her life to her people; in what sense they were her people at all it was hard to say, but as a partly Negro heroine she was expected to behave sacrificially—like the escaped convict she had to return to prison to pay her debt to society.

How effective, one wonders, are the "necessary" lies of well-meaning people when the mass audience lives in a world full of the very people that the movies tell us are figments of prejudiced thinking—the Negroes of Harlem or the Fillmore, the Jews of Broadway and Central Park West, and the Hollywood producers of the Hillcrest Country Club, with its own gentleman's agreement (no Gentiles accepted). Films may "expose" anti-Semitism or anti-Negroism but they dare not deal with Semitism or Negroism (the existence of which they deny). Behind the pressures that destroy the thematic possibilities in race relations (and similar pressures obtain in sex relations) is the fear that some portions of the public are not intelligent enough to understand that if one Jew is pictured as aggressive, this does not mean that all are aggressive; or if one Negro pulls a knife in a fight, all will; or, for that matter, if one dentist overcharges, all do. This fear has been played upon by the leaders of minorities and pressure groups: Negroes or Jews are made to feel that because others might associate them with the actions of Josephine Baker or Walter Winchell, they are somehow responsible for those actions. Any Italian or doctor or psychiatrist on the screen is considered as a *representative* of the group, who might, by his action, discredit the whole group. In order to protect themselves, minorities act upon the premise which they ascribe to the ignorant public.

The situation is not simple. Art derives from human experience, and the artist associates certain actions and motivations with certain cultural and vocational groups because that is how he has observed and experienced them. Would Jews be so fearful of the depiction of Jewish characters as ostentatious and vulgar, aggressive and secretive, if they did not recognize that these elements often converge in "Jewishness"? Would Negroes be so sensitive to the images of sullen bestiality and economic irresponsibility if they did not feel the impact? It is the germ of observed truth that pressure groups fear, a germ which infects only the individual but which the group treats as epidemic. The whole group becomes defensive under the guidance of pressuring leaders who inoculate them with false responsibilities. All these inoculations have produced a real democratic disease: a mass culture made up of stereotypes, models, whitewashes, smiles and lies. To allow the artist to treat his experience freely may be dangerous, but it is a step toward the restoration of individual responsibility. And how else can American indifference and cynicism be cured?

Truth is feared most of all in the visualization of sex relations. The presumption is that romantic models of happiness are less dangerous than truth, that if youngsters saw in films the same kind of problems they experience and see all about them, they would be "misled" into believing that human relations are often difficult, painful and unsatisfactory, that society is unwilling to consider the problems of adolescents, and that the impetus for divorce is not an absurd, unmotivated quarrel which will be patched up in the last reel (*Phffft!*) but a miserable impasse. These lies are certainly more dangerous than truth; the split between the romantic glorifications of love, marriage and family life and our actual mores adds to the perplexity and guilt of those whom the films seek to protect.

Films do not suffer from the pressure to do something; they turn into drivel because of the pressures not to do almost everything. One may suspect that there is something fundamentally corrupt in a concept of democracy which places safety, harmony and conformity above truth. The educated audience deplores the films offered to the less educated audience, but, in order to protect the ignorant, and in the cause of democracy, they effectively prevent an exploration of the living world. Art, perhaps unfortunately, is not the sphere of good intentions.

Is Anything Left?

If there are almost no films (except the suspense variety) set in contemporary America, the reason is clear: there are almost no modern themes acceptable to the mass audience. The treatment of historical subjects generally reduces them to nothing (*Desirée*), but it is easier to dress up nothing in a foreign or period setting. The hollowness of the big productions is a direct result of the effort to please the public while doing nothing that might displease countless sections within the public. (A competent movie like *Blackboard Jungle* has to fight its way against pressure groups and legal action.) To a marked degree, the effort is self-defeating: when nothing is left to hang the *décor* on, audiences get bored. They were amazed and delighted when *On the Waterfront* and, before that, *From Here to Eternity* made contact with some areas in their experience; it's as if they had forgotten that movies could mean anything at all. It may be that such box-office successes as *The Robe* and *Quo Vadis* are among the last belches of the giant. Spectacles will cease to be events, and audiences can be more comfortably bored at home. Tony Curtis and Janet Leigh can easily transfer to television, which has inherited not only the worst of radio and vaudeville but the content of B movies as well (the dreary humors of family life). Americans do have some sort of taste: they will accept mediocrity, but they don't like to *pay* for it. Vaudeville died because people refused to support it in its decrepitude, but they were perfectly willing to listen to its ghost on the radio. They will suffer, on television, chopped-up, incoherent prints of bad movies—the very worst specimens of what destroyed their enthusiasm for going out to a theater. (David Riesman's suggestion that people over thirty may be staying away from theaters because "films are too mature, move too fast, for older people to catch on to and catch up with" is altogether remarkable. No doubt, Americans as they age do tend to lose the youngsters' lively interest in the world, but American movies show the same middle-aged spread. To a sociologist, movies can be a constant source of material on up-to-date habits and manners. But one interested in film as an art form finds these surface shifts about as significant as a sculptor finds the cosmetic lore of Forest Lawn. Riesman offers us possibilities of "mature" comedy. Documentary camera in hand, one would like to follow the proposed team of "humanists and social scientists" as they "come together to see what each set of skills might contribute to heighten the awareness of Americans of all ages for the imaginative qualities of their best films." The man who described for us the outlines of the American mousetrap now calls for mice to walk in. Skilled teamwork, having already destroyed movies, will now take over movie criticism.)

Americans don't have to go to the movies at all. They spend as much money on equipment for fishing as they do at movie box offices; they spend as much on hunting and bowling. Sports not only invite participation, they provide suspense about the outcome (something which our movies have failed to do for a long time); sports are geared to leisure interests, travel, photography and a whole range of consumer goods—casual clothes, equipage. And sports comprise the proper interests for getting along and getting ahead in a sociable way.

Drama, on the other hand, posits intense interest in the character and destiny of the individual, and American culture is indifferent, and even hostile, to strong individuality. The American film is no longer concerned with characters of real dramatic stature; it gives the actor few chances for any interesting or full characterizations and often constricts acting possibilities to the barest minimum. Films do not center as much as they used to on one or two heroic individuals who were often engaged in a grand passion, or a drive toward money or power, or even in some struggle against society and conventions. The new heroes and heroines of film and television are dismaying—not because they're not attractive and presentable (often they're competently played), but because they represent the death of drama as we have known it. They are not protagonists in any meaningful sense; they represent the voice of adjustment, the caution against individuality, independence, emotionality, art, ambition, personal vision. They represent the antidrama of American life. Biblical spectacles convey magnitude of character by magnitude of close-up. Film versions of the lives of the "great" turn out to be success stories drawn from the mass media—Knute Rockne, Marty Mahrer, Glenn Miller, Eva Tanguay, Ruth Etting, Jackie Robinson, Houdini, Cole Porter, Rodgers and Hart, Sigmund Romberg, Jane Froman, "Crazy-Legs" Hirsch, Lou Gehrig, Joe Louis, etc. And with Valentino, Al Jolson, Eddie Cantor, and the projected Jean Harlow and Theda Bara, Hollywood feeds upon itself—a confection only for jaded palates. The heroism of Hollywood is the gift of itself to the world: *A Star Is Born* is the epic of Hollywood's self-sacrifice. The new path for success is to enact the success of someone else in the same field; when you have reached the summits, you re-enact your own success.

Other arts show an internal logic in their development, the constant solving of aesthetic challenges; films have changed simply by following the logic of the market. When one cycle was exhausted, a new personality (embodying some recognizable form of human experience and a new kind of sexual excitement) in a new type of picture usually set off another. Joan Crawford doing the Charleston on the table in *Our Dancing Daughters* incarnated a new youthful abandon for her period, just as Valentino had brought dark, exotic sensuality to his, and Fairbanks joy of life to his. Bette Davis introduced a more complicated sexual character—driving, neurotic. When the public interest in gangsters and the socially downtrodden was exhausted, and the war over, Hollywood lacked a social orientation. Kirk Douglas injected something new into melodrama: he represented a new type—the guy who's got the stuff, but who is really a wrong guy, the ambitious heel in a disoriented society. Now Marlon Brando breathes some life into films: he projects the tensions of displaced, alienated American youth—characters who reject the hypocritical society that denies their instincts. Refresher personalities don't, of course, stay fresh; their roles become stale; the public becomes satiated. Idolatry turns to mockery and boredom, and new idols appear. When his magic was gone, it didn't matter that Charles Boyer was an excellent actor. Sometimes the public gets the full spectacle of the fall: John Barrymore became a buffoon. And the public was more than willing to turn Garbo into a national butt of humor.

Though even the biggest stars have not remained at the zenith, we are now witnessing a desperately contrived effort to keep them there: waning stars provide the "big" names for the big productions. Clark Gable or Gary Cooper, Robert Taylor or James Stewart add size and importance, but do they have any vital star quality left? Advertising announces "the *new* Greer Garson" or "Lana as you've never seen her before"—obviously the public wasn't buying the old Greer or Lana. Can Hollywood manufacture the artificial asteroid? (Joan Crawford has come to represent the tenacity of a woman determined to remain a star: her survival power is the only drawing power she has left. She shows us her legs to prove that they are *still* good.) From time to time newspapers or the radio play upon the popular nostalgia about old favorites, but the public stopped buying a Norma Shearer or a Janet Gaynor long before they faded. The camera itself uses up an Esther Williams rapidly; her expressive resources are so limited that close-ups are like billboard ads—the image is constant, only the backgrounds vary. Can a new refresher find so much as a toe hold in the blubber of big films? The old big name or the actor who can impersonate a model American is safer than a challenging new personality; the studios are rather resentful of Brando's drawing power: what big pictures does he really fit into? He will, of course, be remade to fit.

When the remains of Christianity are returned to their caskets, Hollywood may delve into Buddhism or Mohammedanism (all gods are pretty much alike and resemblance to the Christian god will, no doubt, lend the others a certain respectability). This step is foreshadowed in *The Egyptian*. A clash of cymbals announces the name of Darryl F. Zanuck, but, with all modesty, the letters of fire are reserved for the postscript: "All these things happened thirteen centuries before the birth of Christ." (Obviously the producers would like to get precedence on *The Robe*—an estimated $19 million gross.) Why should Americans be offended by other religions when they can all be depicted as anticipations of the true faith? Hollywood will probably also "adjust" itself. *Rogue Cop* is a somewhat longer and bigger version of the typical glossy MGM melodrama of the thirties and forties. It is what might be called the "academic commercial" film—competently done, considering that it's not worth doing. Can films like this, over a period of time, draw people away from television and into theaters? It's more than doubtful—the material of television drama *is* old movie melodrama; when films recapitulate their past, they're in a deadlock with television. And the film becomes increasingly subject to pressure. That *Rogue Cop* has been banned in some states, at the insistence of police departments who argue that the crooked cop of the film might give some juvenile delinquents the wrong idea about policemen, suggests that there is almost no subject matter left for the mass-audience film. When everybody knows that there is widespread police corruption, the movies are not supposed to show even one cop who isn't a model (the police have good reason to be so sensitive). Obviously if one made a film about an incompetent teacher's effect upon a child, or dramatized the results of a doctor's mistaken diagnosis, one would be in trouble. (Artists, on the other hand, may be pictured as pathological cowards, cheats and murderers — they're not organized.) Every group wants glorification, but even glorification carries risks (audiences can be derisive about the discrepancies between film and fact), so perhaps it is safer to leave all subjects untouched. This feat is virtually accomplished in films like *White Christmas* and *The Long Gray Line*. Fear of offending someone — anyone — may help to account for the death of American film comedy. Films like *Roxie Hart*, *His Girl Friday*, *A Letter to Three Wives*, and the Preston Sturges comedies didn't seem so important when we had them; in retrospect, after a *Sabrina*, they acquire new luster. While serious drama is smothered by moral restrictions and the preordained ending (characters must get their "just deserts"), the verve and zest of comedy dribble away when you're half afraid to make a joke of anything.

Who Cares About Movies?

It may be that in a few years the film situation will be comparable to the present stage situation. The few dozen Broadway plays a year are supplemented by thousands of little theaters and college groups. It would not be unlikely that a few hundred big houses showing big Hollywood productions would be surrounded by a swarm of small "art" houses, catering to a fairly limited audience and showing foreign films, revivals and new American films — experimental or, at least, inexpensive ones. The art houses might even be forced to help finance small new films. Good American films like *The Treasure of the Sierra Madre* have often failed financially — possibly because they attempted to succeed in the wrong places; if Hollywood could make good pictures on a low-budget basis, book them into art houses, and give them months and even years to return the investment, they might show a modest profit.

Small houses cannot grow to a swarm on foreign films alone. After the initial enthusiasm for French, Italian and English films, Americans begin to lose interest. The acceptance of life in European films, the acceptance of joys and defeats, does not make vital contact with American experience. We do not live in those terms, and *our* terms are apparently somewhat incomprehensible to Europeans. Representations of Americans in foreign films always feel wrong to an American audience. It is true we are shallow, but we are not carefree and irresponsible, we are shallowly *serious*. Even the worst American films have often had more energy than the imports. English comedies, with their high level of craftsmanship, their quiet charm and their tiny scope, become almost as wearisome to us as the shoddy tasteless products of Hollywood. Success within such small limits is ultimately not very interesting, especially to Americans. *Genevieve* is delightful, but have you missed anything if you didn't see it? And just how many *Genevieve*s do you want to see? The economy of the enterprise is so straitened; you can't accuse the English of not fulfilling large intentions because they don't aim very high. Where is the insolence that gives bite to comedy? The English have their own way of playing it safe. Not every moving picture can be great or even good, and there can be no objection to honest failure or modest success. But every work of art has a core of risk and it is around this core that the work takes form.

Our commercialized culture never integrates all the individuals with energy and talent. They constitute a reserve of independence and dissidence, and idiosyncrasy. And in this reserve there is, perhaps, a more vital hope for the American film.

There are people who can sit around for hours discussing early films, giving detailed accounts of dialogue, action, gesture, even costume, exchanging remembered reactions to Colin Clive, or what Nils Asther was like in *The Bitter Tea of General Yen*, or Bette Davis in *Cabin in the Cotton*. Sentiment and romance may be attached to the memories, but, more important, these people remember movies because they were alert to them. They were fascinated by what went on in the films — the personalities, the talents, the inadvertences, the reactions of the audience, the mélange of techniques, the actress working against hopeless material, the director injecting a clever bit of business, the glaring close-ups as in a strip tease revealing the human material. The people who love movies are a knowing audience; the early period of going to movies has not deadened their taste, it has cultivated it. They are capable of judging in advance just about what a given production will be like, though they may want to taste for themselves the precise flavor even of horseradish. Films are at the mercy of this knowing audience: it goes to see everything it can in a film, and often comes out with much more than it was intended to see. In a sense, every movie is a documentary: the actor is as exposed as the tenant farmer, the sets as exposed as the Aran Islands. In one way or another, everyone who goes to the movies knows this; when the film fails to hold the attention of the audience and when the theater situation permits, the disgruntled patrons comment on what is exposed to them.

Just as there are people alive to poetry but blind to painting, there are literate people who don't care for movies. The quality of most Hollywood films has made it easy for them to say they are not interested, without even that nod at acknowledging a failing that usually accompanies the state-ment that one draws a blank on opera or poetry. They tend, in fact, to view lack of interest in films as evidence of superiority and to be contemptuous of the "low tastes" of those who go to films frequently (many of them *do* go to movies—in guilty secrecy). One is inclined to suspect that these people who dismiss movies as a lost cause and a circus for the masses never could tell a good picture from a poor one.

With all the waste and disappointment, growing up at the films was, for our generation, an extraordinary education of the senses. We were in almost at the beginning, when something new was added to human expe-rience. In high school and college we formed friendships as much on the basis of film tastes as of literature or politics. When the commercialized Hollywood films could no longer satisfy our developing tastes, *Le Jour se Lève* and *La Grande Illusion* restored us. After more than fifteen years one still recalls the rage one felt toward the college boy who was so busy point-ing out the biographical falsifications in *Beethoven* that he had no eyes for Harry Bauer. Arguments about films were formative, and, by the logic of developing taste, those who cared enough to argue found that film-going resulted in disgust. It took a couple of decades for Hollywood films to wear us out; we wearied more quickly of the imports. While in the mass audi-ence older people abandoned movies to the kids, we could not abandon film-going any more than we could give up other vital appetites.

Cocteau, after revivals of *Blood of a Poet*, emerged as the most important film maker, not necessarily because one especially liked the film, but because Cocteau suggested to us the shattering possibilities of an artist using the medium for his own ends, not just to make movies, but to say what he wanted to say in movies. Because of him, we began to look at films in a new way: we were no longer merely audience, we were potential film makers. And we discovered new ancestors. Searching through early film experiments, looking for the excitement that our senses told us the medium could produce, we found the early experimenters who had discovered the film medium for themselves. When we arrived at the infant beginnings of film art, we realized that we had grown up in a period of steady decline, scarcely aware of what films had started out to be.

From the beginning, American film makers have been crippled by business financing and the ideology it imposed: they were told that they had an obligation to entertain the general public, that this was a democratic function and a higher obligation than to give their best to a few hundred or a few million people. This "obligation" forced even the early innovators to lard their work with sentimentality. And this "obligation" has contributed to fear of the medium itself—they began to use titles and music to explain and add to what they were already doing with images; when sound became possible, they were fearful of imaginative or difficult speech and music. It is clear now that there is more than one audience, and that artists must judge their own obligations. The film artist knows what happened to the innovators; he knows he can't expect the banks and studios to finance him. Fortunately his experience at expensive movies should have surfeited him—his tastes need not be so extravagant. If he wants to make movies he must cadge and borrow and save and fill out fellowship forms and beg from foundations—like other American artists. And if he produces a squiggly little mess of abstract patterns or a symbolic drama full of knives, keys and figures receding in the night, at least the responsibility is where it should be.

The responsibility is on the artist, even when he tries to evade responsibility. If, so far, American experimental and "little" films haven't received much support, most of them haven't deserved it, either. All too frequently, after an evening of avant-garde cinema, one wants to go see a movie (at least a little fresh air comes in through the holes in Hollywood plots). Though avant-garde film makers don't always know what they're doing when they make a film, they demonstrate a marvelous talent for the post-factum scenario; often their greatest effort at composition is in explaining

away the lack of it in their films. They become so adept at escaping consideration of their failures and limitations that they rarely develop at
all; what they fail to put in they deride you for not seeing there. You're
supposed to find a whole world of meaning in that three-minute cinepoem.
The times are out of joint: the poisonous atmosphere of Hollywood premieres is distilled to pure pretension at avant-garde premieres. Object to
the Hollywood film and you're an intellectual snob, object to the avant-
garde films and you're a Philistine. But, while in Hollywood, one must
often be a snob; in avant-garde circles one must often be a Philistine.

{*The Berkley Book of Modern Writing No. 3*, 1956; rev. for *Film: An Anthology*, 1959}

from
I LOST IT AT THE MOVIES

:: The Glamour of Delinquency

A "regular" movie says yes to the whole world or it says not much of anything. What is there in *The Long Gray Line*, *A Man Called Peter*, *The Prodigal* or *Not as a Stranger* that can stir an audience out of its apathy—an exposed beating heart, a man fighting a vulture—and who cares? And who really cares about the bland prosperity that produces these entertainments? The United States has now achieved what critics of socialism have always posited as the end result of a socialist state: a prosperous, empty, uninspiring uniformity. (If we do not have exactly what Marx meant by a classless society, we do have something so close to it that the term is certainly no longer an alluring goal.) What promises does maturity hold for a teen-ager: a dull job, a dull life, television, freezers, babies and baby sitters, a guaranteed annual wage, taxes, social security, hospitalization insurance, and death. Patriotism becomes a series of platitudes; even statements that are true seem hypocritical when no longer informed with fire and idealism. It may be because this culture offers nothing that stirs youthful enthusiasm that it has spewed up a negative reaction: for the first time in American history we have a widespread nihilistic movement, so nihilistic it doesn't even have a program, and, ironically, its only leader is a movie star: Marlon Brando.

Our mass culture has always been responsive to the instincts and needs of the public. Though it exploits those needs without satisfying them, it does nonetheless throw up images that indicate social tensions and undercurrents. Without this responsiveness, mass culture would sink of its own weight. But it doesn't sink—there *is* a kind of vitality in it. Even the most routine adventure pictures, with Jeff Chandler or Rory Calhoun or Randolph Scott or John Wayne, empty and meaningless as they are, cater to unsatisfied appetites for action and color and daring—ingredients that are absent from the daily lives of patrons. But if films and other areas of mass culture did not produce anything that moved us more directly, they would become as rigid and formalized as ballet—a series of repeated gestures for a limited audience of connoisseurs (the western has reached this point). When more ambitious film makers want to make a film with dramatic conflict, they draw upon the hostility to conformity embodied in the crazy, mixed-up kid.

The phenomenon of films touching a social nerve is not new. The gangster films in the thirties expressed a fundamental hostility to society and authority; the gangsters made their own way, even if they paid for it by prison or death. But in the thirties the gangsters were not the only rebels, there was a large active body of political rebellion, given partial expression in films by the dispossessed heroes who asked for a job, a home, and a life. In the fifties there is no American political rebellion, there is not even enough political theory to give us a feasible explanation of delinquency itself—the new dissidents who say that a job, a home, and the life that goes with them aren't worth the trouble. One thing seems evident: when the delinquent becomes the hero in our films, it is because the image of instinctive rebellion expresses something in many people that they don't dare express. These kids seem to be the only ones who are angry about apathy: they seem to be the only ones with guts enough, or perhaps they are the only ones irresponsible enough, to act out a *no* to the whole system of authority, morality and prosperity.

The depth of Brando's contact with some sections of the public may be gauged by the extraordinary resentments expressed toward James Dean for what was considered an imitation of Brando in *East of Eden* (though Dean's acting suggests Montgomery Clift as much as it does Brando, while his facial qualities suggest Gregory Peck); and the jeers and walkouts on *Blackboard Jungle* because Vic Morrow employed a Brando style. The reaction is quite archaic—as if Brando fans feared that other actors were trying to take some power away from their god, that the public might worship graven images instead of the true god.

Alienation

Alienation, the central theme of modern literature, has, like everything else, entered mass culture. Films borrow the artist-hero of literature only to turn him into the boob of *A Song to Remember*, *Rhapsody in Blue*, *Moulin Rouge*, *Limelight*; the alienation of a Stephen Dedalus or a Marcel, the heroic expense of extending consciousness, becomes inexplicable, but glamorous, misery. (The artist suffers because he can't get the girl; she, lacking the audience's hindsight, doesn't know that he's so good a catch that one day a movie will solemnize his life. The irony of the artist's suffering is his inability to guess that Hollywood will make him immortal.) Those at work in films have, however, to one degree or another, projected alienated non-artist heroes and heroines in some of the best, though not always commercially successful, films of recent years: *The Stars Look Down*, *Odd Man Out*, *Outcast of the Islands*, *The Men*, *The Member of the Wedding*, *A Streetcar Named Desire*, *From Here to Eternity*. In these films, alienation is not merely the illusion of cynicism or cowardice which is dispelled in the rousing finish of a *Casablanca* or a *Stalag 17*.

The subject matter of *On the Waterfront* is alienation at the lowest social level. In *From Here to Eternity* Prewitt had formulated his position ("If a man don't go his own way, he's nothin'") and was willing to take the risks. Terry Malloy, the hero of *On the Waterfront*, is alienated at the instinctive level of the adolescent and the bum, and the drama, as those who made the film see it, is in his development of consciousness and responsibility, his taking his place as a man.

The attempt to create a hero for the mass audience is a challenge and a great big trap. *On the Waterfront* meets the challenge, falls into the trap. The creation of a simple hero is a problem that doesn't come up often in European films, where the effort is to create characters who move us by their humanity—their weaknesses, their wisdom, their complexity—rather than by their heroic dimensions. Our films, however, deny the human weaknesses and complexities that Europeans insist upon. It's as if we refused to accept the human condition: we don't want to see the image of ourselves in those cheats and cuckolds and cowards. We want heroes, and Hollywood produces them by simple fiat. Robert Taylor or John Wayne is cast as the hero and that's that; any effort to relate the hero's actions to his character is minimal or routine. Real heroism is too dangerous a subject for Hollywood—for there is no heroism without failure risked or faced, and failure, which is at the heart of drama, is an unpopular subject in America.

On the Waterfront succeeds brilliantly in creating a figure out of the American lower depths, a figure simple in reasoning power but complicated in motivation and meaning; it fails to win complete assent when it attempts to make this figure into a social and symbolic hero—by fiat. But how should we interpret the view of *Harper's* that, "if the makers of *On the Waterfront* had chosen to have it merely a decadently sophisticated underworld travelogue, a kind of American '*Quai des Brumes*,' they would have been truer to themselves, their subject and their art. Still better, they could have stood in bed." If I read this right, the implication is that if the film dealt with defeat, it would be more honest, but it would be decadent. This is a view which quite possibly *has* affected those who made the film, and *Harper's*, inadvertently and revealingly, justifies the artists' fear of "decadence" by its contempt for "decadence."

It's likely that those who made the film—Kazan, Schulberg, Spiegel, Brando, Bernstein—share in the American fantasy of success, a fantasy which they spectacularly act out in their own careers, and want to believe that their material fits into a drama of man's triumph. A drama of man's defeat would seem somehow antisocial, un-American, "arty," and even decadent. It's quite likely also that art to them is a call to action as much as a reach into consciousness, so that they feel bound to demonstrate a victory of good over evil; they want the film to "come out right" politically, though this demonstration probably moves the audience much less than if it had to take home an unresolved, disturbed recognition of social difficulties. (The motive power behind much of our commercial entertainment is: give the public a happy ending so they won't have to think about it afterwards.) Perhaps the artists of *On the Waterfront* fear the reality of failure not only for their hero but for themselves. If the film did not resolve its drama in triumph, it might not reach the mass audience, and if it reached a smaller audience, that—in America—would be failure.

From Here to Eternity did not convert its hero into a socially accepted leader, did not reduce issues to black and white, and it was a huge popular success. But a curious displacement occurred in the course of the film:

Prewitt's fate as hero got buried in the commotion of the attack on Pearl Harbor, and it was easy to get the impression that it didn't really matter what happened to him as he would probably have gotten killed anyway. And, as a related phenomenon, Montgomery Clift's fine performance as Prewitt was buried in the public praise for Frank Sinatra and Burt Lancaster. It was almost as if Prewitt wasn't there at all, as if the public wanted to forget his troublesome presence. Lancaster, an amazingly kinesthetic actor, has built-in heroism; his Sergeant Warden was closer to the conventional hero stereotype, and he had managed to stay alive. Or perhaps Prewitt wasn't troublesome enough: there was no mystery or confusion about why he behaved as he did. He had his own value system, and perhaps his clarity prevented him from stirring the audience. *Formulated* alienation seems already part of the past; Prewitt is the last Hollywood representative of depression-style alienation.

On the Waterfront is a more ambitious film, though its moral scheme is that battle of good versus evil which is a film commonplace. No doubt those who made the film, and many of those who see it, view the conflict in the film not as a commonplace, but as a rendering of the "supreme" theme. But this "supreme" theme has never been the theme of great drama because it tends to diminish man's humanity, rather than to illuminate it. Working with this theme, it is natural for the artists to take the next step and to employ the most easily accessible symbols that are ready-to-hand to the artists and perfectly familiar to the widest audience. The priest stands for conscience and humanity; the pure, selfless girl is the hero's reward; the union boss represents brutal avarice. And crucifixion is used in the broadest sense as an equivalent for suffering.

The center of the dramatic structure, the priest's speech over Dugan's body in the hold, is the poorest scene of the film. The priest speaks with such facility that the ideological mechanics become distressingly obvious, and the re-enactment of the stoning of saints is an embarrassing contrivance, an effort to achieve a supremely powerful effect by recall rather than creation. The scene appeals not only to Catholic interest but to what we have come to recognize as Catholic taste as well. And although the concept of crucifixion in the film is scarcely the Catholic Church's concept, in using the figure of the priest the artists acquire a certain amount of unearned increment by making the film more acceptable to Catholics.

When Terry tells the priest to go to hell, the patent intention is to shock the religious audience, and, of course, to cue us all: we know that such sacrilege is possible only for one who will shortly be redeemed.

On the theatrical level, most of the Christian symbolism functions well in the film. The artists have not further debased it; compared to what we are accustomed to in Hollywood pictures, they have given it considerable dignity. But theatricality can too easily be confused with dramatic strength and Christian mythology provides an all too convenient source of theatrical devices — the jacket, for example, that passes from one crucified figure to another. Such devices do not give meaning, they give only dramatic effect, the *look* of meaning.

The director, Elia Kazan, is undoubtedly a master of what is generally regarded as "good theater": all those movements, contrasts, and arrangements which have been developed to give inferior material the look of drama. "Good theater" is an elaborate set of techniques for throwing dust in the eyes of the audience, dust which, to many theater-trained minds, is pure gold. When Kazan has real dramatic material in *On the Waterfront*, his staging is simple and he lets the actors' faces and voices do the work; but when the material is poor or unrealized, he camouflages with "effective staging" — the theater term for what is really high pressure salesmanship. Your theater instinct tells you that these effects are supposed to do something for you, but you may be too aware of the manipulation to feel anything but admiration (or resentment) for the director's "know-how."

The advantages of Kazan's direction are in his fine eye for living detail (for example, in Terry's first interchange with the men from the crime commission); the disadvantages are that the best things are often overpowered by the emphasis given to the worst. Rod Steiger's fine performance as the brother stays within its own framework, while Malden's priest is so overburdened with reference and effect that it disintegrates. Though this priest is not cut from the same cloth as Paramount's priests, at times (and he has his coy moments) he adopts a similar protective coloration. The musical score is excellent; then at a crucial moment it stops, and the silence compels awareness of the music. There are a few places where Kazan's dexterity fails completely: moving the union men around as a herd is too "staged" to be convincing. And even "good theater" doesn't allow for elements that are tossed in without being thought out (the ship owner, an oddly ambiguous abstraction, possibly cartooned in obeisance

to the labor-union audience) or tossed in without being felt (the complacent, smiling faces of the priest and the girl at the end—converted, by a
deficiency of artistic sensibility, into pure plaster). Many weaknesses go
back to the script, of course (for example, the failure to show the reasons
for the union men's loyalty to the boss), but Kazan, by trying to make assets
out of liabilities, forces consideration of his responsibility.

If one feels bound to examine the flaws and facilities of *On the Waterfront* it is because, intermittently, and especially in Brando's scenes with
the girl in the saloon and with his brother in the cab, the film is great.
Brando's performance is the finest we have had in American films since
Vivien Leigh's Blanche DuBois. Marlon Brando has that ability shared by
most great actors: he can convey the multiple and paradoxical meanings
in a character.

Brando makes contact with previously untapped areas in American
social and psychological experience. If one had doubts about the authenticity of Terry's character, audience manifestations would confirm its
truth. Brando's inarticulate wise guy attracts a startling number of its kind;
there they are in the theater, gratified by their image, shouting at the
screen and guffawing at Brando. Their derision is just like Terry's derisive
compliments to the girl; they, too, are afraid to expose their vulnerability.
They are exhibitionistic in their excitement when Terry gestures and
voices disbelief in social values: it is not Terry as a candidate for redemption who excites them, but Terry the tough. They have a truer sense of
Terry and themselves than those who conceived the film.

The writer and director placed this imaginatively compelling figure in
a structure which, while theatrically fairly sound, is not the dramatic
complement the figure deserves. Terry has his own kind of consciousness;
he is *too* compelling to act out *their* consciousness and to fit the social role
they assign him. Terry is credible until he becomes a social hero. Does
moral awakening for a Terry mean that he acquires the ability to change
the external situation, or does it mean simply an intensification and a
broadening of his alienation? We know that movie heroes can always
conquer evil, but in the early sequences we didn't know that Terry was
going to be turned into this kind of "regular" hero. The other protagonists
have been oversimplified until they seem to be mere symbols rather than
human beings who might have some symbolic meaning. As dramatic characters they lack dimensions, as symbolic representations of the waterfront

struggle they are inadequate. Our social problems are much too complex to be dramatically rendered in a Christian parable. The artists who made the film have a remarkable negative similarity: they do not risk alienation from the mass audience. And they do not face up to the imaginative task— nor to the social risk—of creating fresh symbols. Have they earned the right to show their hero risking his life in order to save his soul?

The myth of the creation of a saint (or, indeed, a multiplicity of saints) which cripples the dramatic development of Terry's character, does an even more obvious disservice to the social questions the film raises. The myth structure forces a superficial answer to questions for which no one has a satisfactory answer. The honest union posited at the end is an abstraction, which could not even be dramatically posited if the film had not already abstracted the longshore local it treats from the total picture of waterfront unionism and American business. An item in *Time* for September 27, 1954, is to the point:

> John Dwyer, a brawny hiring boss on the brawling New York City docks (and a prototype of Marlon Brando's movie role in *On the Waterfront*), quit his $10,000-a-year job last year to fight the racket-ridden International Longshoremen's Association. As vice president of the A.F.L.'s new rival dock union, he won thousands of dock-wallopers away from the I.L.A. But last month the I.L.A. won a Labor Relations Board election (by a scant 263 votes out of 18,551), and thereby held on to control of waterfront jobs.
>
> The A.F.L. brasshats, retreating from their attempt to reform the docks, cut their organizing losses (about $1,000,000), ended their all-out campaign and fired John Dwyer. When Dwyer protested, they ignored his letters and hung up on phone calls. Last week Dwyer bitterly told his men to "forget about the A.F.L. and go back to the I.L.A." Brusquely, the I.L.A. snubbed Dwyer and said A.F.L. rank-and-filers could come back only if they paid up back dues. For a happy ending dockers could go to the movies.

This kind of data suggests why alienation is such a powerful theme in our art: if, for the individual, efforts to alter a situation end in defeat, and adjustment (with decency) is impossible, alienation may be all that's left. Would Terry seem so compelling if his behavior and attitudes did not express a profound mass cynicism and a social truth? More goes into his alienation than the activities of a John Friendly, and his character is powerful because it suggests much more—the desire of adolescents to find an acceptable ethic, quasi-homosexual elements in this ethic, adolescent hostility toward adult compromises, the identification with an antisocial code, the intensity of aspirations. Terry's scene with his brother in the cab is drama because these accumulated elements explode. These elements and many more derive, not merely from a corrupt union, but from the dislocation of youth in our society, and ultimately, if one takes a pessimistic view, they derive from the human condition. The betrayal experienced by the boy who kills the pigeons is not altogether mistaken. With *On the Waterfront* alienation reaches the widest audience at the level of the raw unconscious hero who suggests the unconscious alienation experienced at all social levels. The artists who wanted to affect everybody just about did.

Artists who aim at nobility may achieve something pretentious and overscaled, but their aim tells us something about the feeling and tone of American life that is not wholly to be deprecated. Abroad, it *is* deprecated, and the excesses of *On the Waterfront* gave European critics a gloating edge of triumph. Is it perhaps evidence of cultural condescension that the festival committees which had passed over *From Here to Eternity* and *On the Waterfront* honored *Marty*, a thin, mechanical piece of sentimental realism —as if to say, "Stick to little things, you Americans, when you try to do something bigger, you expose your dreadful vulgarity"?

On the Waterfront came as a public shock in 1954 because Hollywood films have stayed away from the real America, just as, while feeding Christians to the lions, they have stayed away from the real Rome. According to *Harper's*, "The things movies 'say' are so much better stated through indirect suggestion, and Hollywood has developed so many techniques of skillful evasion, that the burden of censorship and the pressure groups has always been more apparent than real. Art thrives on limitations." One wonders if *Harper's* goes to movies often enough to see Hollywood's "techniques of skillful evasion" in operation. If there is anything "skillful" in our films, it is merely in product differentiation—in making each new film just like the others that have sold, yet with some little difference in casting or locale or extra costliness that can give it special appeal. Within the temples of *The Egyptian* you can see the shape of the lowest theater, mouldy in motive and manner. When you hear the whore of Babylon ask the hero for "the greatest gift any man can give a woman—his innocence—that he can give only once" you know that those responsible for the film have long since surrendered their greatest gift. A bad film can be a good joke, as *Duel in the Sun* once so delightfully demonstrated; but *Valley of the Kings, Garden of Evil, The High and the Mighty* are not even very good jokes. Despite its defects, and they are major, *On the Waterfront* provides an imaginative experience. If one regrets that the artists, having created an authentic image of alienation, failed to take that image seriously enough, one remembers also that most films provide no experience at all.

Romance

The alienated hero acquires a new dimension in *East of Eden*: James Dean's Cal, even more inarticulate and animalistic than Terry, is a romantic figure, decorated with all sorts of charming gaucheries, and set, anachronistically, in a violent reverie of pre–World War I youth. At one level he's the All-American boy (and the reverse of the usual image of the artist as a youth): he's not too good at school, he's sexually active, he's not interested in politics but has a childlike responsiveness to parades, he doesn't care about words or ideas. Yet this lack of intellectual tendencies is projected as evidence of sensitivity and purity of feeling; the strangled speech, the confused efforts at gesture, as poetry. This is a new image in American films: the young boy as beautiful, disturbed animal, so full of love he's defenseless. Maybe his father doesn't love him, but the camera does, and we're supposed to; we're thrust into upsetting angles, caught in infatuated close-ups, and prodded, "Look at all that beautiful desperation."

The film is overpowering: it's like seeing a series of teasers—violent moments and highly charged scenes without structural coherence (one begins to wonder if the teaser is Kazan's special genre?). When Cain strikes Abel, the sound track amplifies the blow as if worlds were colliding; a short heavy dose of expressionism may be followed by a pastoral romp or an elaborate bit of Americana; an actor may suddenly assume a psychotic stance, another actor shatter a train window with his head. With so much going on, one might forget to ask why. The explanation provided (Cal wants his father to love him) is small reason for the grotesque melodramatic flux. But from a director's point of view, success can be seen as effectiveness, failure as dullness—and *East of Eden* isn't dull.

If, after the film, the air outside the theater seems especially clean and fresh, it is not only from relief at escaping the cracker-barrel humanism, it's the restorative power of normal, uncoerced perspective: it's a little like coming out of a loony bin. A boy's agonies should not be dwelt on so lovingly: being misunderstood may easily become the new and glamorous lyricism. With *East of Eden*, Hollywood has caught up with the main line of American avant-garde cinema—those embarrassingly autoerotic twelve-minute masterpieces in which rejected, inexplicable, and ambiguous figures are photographed in tortured chiaroscuro, films which exude symbolism as if modern man were going to find himself by chasing the shadow of an alter ego in a dark alley. When alienation is exploited for erotic gratification, film catches up with the cult realities of city parks and Turkish baths; clear meanings or definite values would be too grossly explicit—a vulgar intrusion on the Technicolor night of the soul.

The romance of human desperation is ravishing for those who wish to identify with the hero's amoral victory: everything he does is forgivable, his crimes are not crimes at all, because he was so terribly *misunderstood*. (And who in the audience, what creature that ever lived, felt he was loved enough?) This is the victory that we used to think of as a child's fantasy: now it is morality for nursery school and theater alike. The concept of Terry was a little behind the times: he was posited as heroic because he acted for the social good. Cal is the hero simply and completely because of his *need*, and his frenzied behavior, the "bad" things that he does, establish him as a hero by demonstrating his need. (When Peter Lorre as *M* said he couldn't help what he did, who would have thought him heroic? We have come a slippery distance.) This is a complete negation of previous conceptions of heroism: the hero is not responsible for his actions—the crazy, mixed-up kid becomes a romantic hero by being treated on an infantile level. And the climax of the film is not the boy's growing up beyond this need or transferring it to more suitable objects, but simply the satisfaction of an infantile fantasy: he displaces his brother and is at last accepted by his father.

In theater and film, the mixed-up kid has evolved from the depression hero, but the explanation from the thirties (poverty did this) no longer works, and the refinement of it in *On the Waterfront* (corruption did this) didn't work. It gives way in *East of Eden* to something even more facile and fashionable: the psychiatric explanation (lack of love did this). Although it's rather bizarre to place this hyped-up modern type in the setting of a historical novel, the reminiscent haze has some advantages: the basic incoherence of motive would probably be even more apparent in a modern setting. Cal's poetry of movement would be odd indeed if he were leaping and careening in the streets of 1955.

The type of heroism entrenched in most older and routine films is based on the obscenity: "right makes might and might makes right." (The hero can back up his moral and ethical edge on the villain with stronger fists.) And an absurd corollary is attached: the girl loves the man who fights for the right. *East of Eden* introduces a rather dismaying new formula: need for love makes right, and the girl loves the boy who most needs to be loved.

Films can, and most of them do, reduce all the deprivations and coercions, desires and hopes of social and individual experience, to the simple formula of needing love. In *Young at Heart*, the bitter depression hero once played by John Garfield is brought up to date: the young composer (Frank Sinatra) is simply an oddball, bitter because he is an orphan and the world has never made a place for him. But Doris Day accepts him and when he feels all warm and cozy in her middle-class family, his bitterness melts. (Most artists are, of course, bitter against precisely the middle-class coziness that Doris Day and her family represent.) In a more sophisticated version, we get Gloria Grahame in *The Cobweb*: she is all fixed-up and able to save her marriage (and square the Production Code) once she knows her husband really needs her. (Lauren Bacall gives her no real competition: she has been analyzed—she is mature and doesn't need anybody.) The convenient Hollywood explanation for alienation—for failure to integrate in the economy, for hostility to authority and society—is, then, lack of love and acceptance. You're bland and happy when you're loved, and if you're unhappy, it's not really your fault, you just haven't been loved. This is the language of the jukebox, and when Freud is reduced to this level, psychoanalysis becomes the language of idiocy. (In a few years, films will probably reflect the next national swing: so I got love, now what?)

Snow Jobs in Sunshine Land

Nobody is satisfied with Hollywood's approach to delinquency, but who has a better one? The psychiatrically-oriented social workers and teachers are advised that they will be included in the delinquent's hostility to authority and that they must get through to the boy. But is the boy mistaken in feeling that they are trying to give him a snow job and that they are part of the apparatus of deadly adjustment to what he is reacting against? *Blackboard Jungle* says that the boy *is* mistaken, and though in many ways a good film, like *The Wild One* it's a snow job. *The Wild One* had taken a news story as the basis for a nightmare image: the leather-jacketed pack of motorcyclists take over a town; their emblem is a death's head and crossed pistons and rods, and Brando is their leader, Lee Marvin his rival. But the movie seemed to be frightened of its subject matter and reduced it as quickly as possible to the trivial meaninglessness of misunderstood boy meets understanding girl; the audience could only savor the potentialities. *Blackboard Jungle* lifts a group of mixed-up kids from the headlines and tries to devise a dramatic structure for them out of the social problem drama. Delinquency is treated as a problem with a definite solution: the separation of the salvageable from the hopeless, and the drama is in the teacher's effort to reach the salvageable. (Like the newspapers, both films avoid discussion of why the boys form their own organizations, with rigid authority, strict codes, and leaders.) Although the script of *Blackboard Jungle* is sane and intelligible, the thematic resolution (like the end of *The Wild One*) is an uneasy dodge—not because it isn't well worked out, but because the film draws its impact from a situation that can't be so easily worked out. It's hard to believe in the good teacher's idealism; audiences audibly assent to the cynical cowardice of the other teachers—even though it's rather overdone. Somehow it's no surprise when we excavate the short story on which the rather shoddy novel was based to find that in the original version, "To Break the Wall," the teacher did *not* break through. This, like Dwyer's "forget about the A.F.L. and go back to the I.L.A.," has the ring of truth—what *Harper's* might call "decadence."

If a film deals with boys rejecting society and ignores *what* they reject, it's easy to pretend there are no grounds for rejection—they're just mixed-up. In denying that there are reasons for not wanting to adjust, the films are left to wrestle clinically, rather than dramatically, with the boys' anger, dealing with the boys at face value, just as the newspapers do. The strongest film element is always the truculent boy, whose mixture of shyness, fear and conceit has a peculiarly *physical* assertiveness: there's bravado in his display of energy. That energy—which adjusted, genteel types subdue or have had drained away or never had—is itself an assault upon the society that has no use for it. He can be invited to work it off only in games, or in leathercraft in some youth center.

The delinquent is disturbing because he is delinquent from values none of us really believe in; he acts out his indifference to what we are all somewhat indifferent to. And in acting it out, he shocks us by making us realize that *necessary* values are endangered. When he is moody and uncooperative and suspicious of the adult, official world we understand something of what he is reacting against and we think we perceive values that he must be struggling for. But when he attacks the weak, when he destroys promiscuously, when, as in *Mad at the World*, he wantonly throws a whisky bottle and kills a baby, we become possible targets and victims of a moral indifference that we both share and do not share.

In the gangster films we knew where we were: if we identified with the small businessmen trying to protect their livelihoods and their pride against extortion, the gangster was an enemy; and if the gangster rubbed out a rival or, when cornered, shot a policeman, these were occupational hazards for gangsters and police, and they were rational. But in the delinquent films we who feel ourselves to be innocent, and even sympathetic, become as vulnerable as a cop. Just as Negro hatred of whites includes even the whites who believe in equality, so the delinquent's violence may strike any one of us. The hold-up victim who offers no resistance is as likely to be beaten as the one who resists, and despised for his cowardice as well.

Confused feelings of identification and fear turn us into the mixed-up audience. There's been plenty of violence in Hollywood films for many years, but it did not stir up the violent audience reactions produced by *On the Waterfront* and *Blackboard Jungle* (many theaters have had, for the first time, to call in police to keep order). In these films the violence means something, it's not just there to relieve the boredom of the plot as in *The Prodigal*, and pressure groups are right in seeing it as a threat. This violence is discharged from boredom with American life, and we have no available patterns into which it fits, no solutions for the questions it raises, and, as yet, no social or political formulations that use indifference toward prosperity and success as a starting point for new commitments.

Though films take up social discontent only to dissolve it in unconvincing optimism, the discontent has grown out of that optimism. A Polynesian coming to an industrial country for the first time might see a technological civilization as a state of nature; Americans who have lost the passion for social involvement see the United States almost the same way (we have lost even the passion for technology). Our economic system, our social order, are accepted, not with respect, but as facts, accepted almost at the same level on which "regular" films are accepted—a convictionless acceptance which is only a hair's breadth away from violent negation. When language is debased to the level of the pitch man, why not use animal grunts? They're more honest, and they say more. Why respect authority which is weak, uncertain, and corrupt? Why care about social relations when they have reached such interpersonal virtuosity that no one shows off or presses an opinion too hard? Why care about acquiring the millionaire's equipment of the middle-class home; does anyone really enjoy a power-driven lawn mower? Everything in America makes life easier, and if Americans are not really happy, they're not really unhappy either. If they feel some pangs of dissatisfaction, what can they blame it on? Only themselves—guiltily—and so the IBM operator who begins to fantasize, the file clerk who can't fight off sleep, hie themselves to the analyst. What a relief to go to the movies and hear mixed-up kids say it out loud. They don't always say it in attractive ways, but it is a no and *somebody* has to say it. It's explosively present.

Though the expressions of the mixed-up kids are antisocial, in a society which insists that all is well, these expressions are interpreted as a psychological disorder. It's a social lie to pretend that these kids are only in conflict with themselves or that they merely need love or understanding. Instinctively, the audience knows better. Pressures can emasculate the theme and remove it from the screen: this exploitation and destruction of every theme is the history of American movies. Marlon Brando can be cleaned up and straightened out for the approval of the family magazines, just as he is in his movie roles; he can become a model of affirmation, impersonating baseball players or band leaders in "regular" pictures. But won't his fans want to kill his pigeons?

{1955}

:: *The Golden Coach**

At his greatest, Jean Renoir expresses the beauty in our common humanity—the desires and hopes, the absurdities and follies, that we all, to one degree or another, share. As a man of the theater (using this term in its widest sense to include movies) he has become involved in the ambiguities of illusion and "reality," theater and "life"—the confusions of identity in the role of man as a role-player. The methods and the whole range of ideas that were once associated with Pirandello and are now associated with Jean Genet are generally considered highly theatrical. But perhaps it is when theater becomes the most theatrical—when the theater of surprise and illusion jabs at our dim notions of reality—that we become conscious of the roles we play.

Jean Renoir's *The Golden Coach* (1953) is a comedy of love and appearances. In her greatest screen performance, Anna Magnani, as the actress who is no more of an actress than any of us, tries out a series of love roles in a play within a play within a movie. The artifice has the simplest of results: we become caught up in a chase through the levels of fantasy, finding ourselves at last with the actress, naked in loneliness as the curtain descends, but awed by the wonders of man's artistic creation of himself. Suddenly, the meaning is restored to a line we have heard and idly discounted a thousand times: "All the world's a stage."

The commedia dell'arte players were actors who created their own roles. They could trust in inspiration and the free use of imagination, they

*Based on Prosper Mérimée's one-act play, *Le Carrosse du Saint Sacrement*, which was derived from the same Peruvian story that served as source material for an episode in Thornton Wilder's *The Bridge of San Luis Rey.*

could improvise because they had an acting tradition that provided taken-for-granted situations and relationships, and they had the technique that comes out of experience. *The Golden Coach*, Renoir's tribute to the commedia dell'arte, is an improvisation on classic comedy, and it is also his tribute to the fabulous gifts, the inspiration, of Anna Magnani. At her greatest, she, too, expresses the beauty in our common humanity. It is probably not coincident with this that Renoir is the most sensual of great directors, Magnani the most sensual of great actresses. Though he has taken Prosper Mérimée's vehicle and shaped it for her, it will be forever debatable whether it contains her or is exploded by her. But as this puzzle is parallel with the theme, it adds another layer to the ironic comedy.

Perhaps only those of us who truly love this film will feel that Magnani, with her deep sense of the ridiculous in herself and others, Magnani with her roots in the earth so strong that she can pull them out, shake them in the face of pretension and convention, and sink them down again stronger than ever—the actress who has come to be the embodiment of human experience, the most "real" of actresses—is the miraculous choice that gives this film its gusto and its piercing beauty. If *this* woman can wonder who she is, then all of us must wonder. Renoir has shaped the material not only for her but out of her and out of other actresses' lives. Talking about the production, he remarked, "Anna Magnani is probably the greatest actress I have ever worked with. She is the complete animal—an animal created completely for the stage and screen . . . Magnani gives so much of herself while acting that between scenes . . . she collapses and the mask falls. Between scenes she goes into a deep state of depression . . ." Like the film itself, the set for the film is an unreal world where people suffer. In *The Golden Coach* we see Magnani in a new dimension: not simply the usual earthy "woman of the people," but the artist who exhausts her resources in creating this illusion of volcanic reality.

The work has been called a masque, a fairy tale, and a fable—each a good try, but none a direct hit: the target shimmers, our aim wavers. *The Golden Coach* is light and serious, cynical and exquisite, a blend of color, wit, and Vivaldi. What could be more unreal than the time and place—a dusty frontier in Renaissance Peru. (You can't even fix the time in the Renaissance—the architecture is already Baroque.) A band of Italian players attempts to bring art to the New World. Magnani is Camilla, the Columbine of the troupe; among her lovers is the Spanish viceroy, who, as the final token of his bondage—the proof of his commitment to love over position and appearances—presents her with the symbol of power in the colony, the golden coach. Through this formal "taken-for-granted" situation, life (that is to say, art) pours out—inventive, preposterous, outrageous, buoyant. And in the midst of all the pleasures of the senses, there is the charging force of Magnani with her rumbling, cosmic laughter, and her exultant cry—"Mama mia!"

The script has its awkward side, and those who don't get the feel of the movie are quick to point out the flaws. Some passages of dialogue are clumsily written, others embarrassingly over-explicit ("Where does the theatre end and life begin?"—which isn't even a respectable question). Much of the strained rhythm in the dialogue may be blamed on the fact that Renoir's writing in English doesn't do justice to Renoir the film artist. And, though Magnani herself, in her first English-speaking role, is vocally magnificent, some of the others speak in dreary tones and some of the minor characters appear to be dubbed. The "international" cast—in this case, largely Italian, English and French—never really seems to work; at the basic level they don't speak the same language. And Renoir allows some of the performers more latitude than their talent warrants; though Duncan Lamont and Riccardo Rioli are marvelous love foils, Paul Campbell is shockingly inept, and the scenes in which he figures go limp. Another defect is in the directorial rhythm. This was Renoir's second color film, and as in his first, *The River*, which was also a collaboration with his great cinematographer-nephew, Claude Renoir, static patches of dialogue deaden the movement; his sense of film rhythm seems to falter when he works in color. Instead of indulging in the fancy fool's game of Freudian speculation that he fails when he tries to compete with his father, it seems simpler to suggest that he gets so bemused by the beauty of color that he carelessly neglects the language of cinema which he himself helped to develop.

But in the glow and warmth of *The Golden Coach*, these defects are trifles. When the singing, tumbling mountebanks transform the courtyard of an inn into a playhouse, the screen is full of joy in creative make-believe. When, at a crucial point in the story, Magnani announces that it is the end of the second act, and the movie suddenly becomes a formalized stage set, we realize that we have been enchanted, that we had forgotten where we were. When the hand of the creator becomes visible, when the actor holds the mask up to view, the sudden revelation that this world we have been absorbed in is not life but theater brings us closer to the actor-characters. So many movies pretend to be life that we are brought up short, brought to consciousness, by this movie that proclaims its theatricality. And the presence of the artists — Renoir and Magnani — is like a great gift. When, in the last scene of *The Golden Coach*, one of the most exquisitely conceived moments on film, the final curtain is down, and Magnani as the actress stands alone on stage, bereft of her lovers, listening to the applause that both confirms and destroys the illusion, the depth of her loneliness seems to be the truth and the pity of all roles played.

{KPFA broadcast for revival showing, 1961}

:: *Shoeshine*

When *Shoeshine* opened in 1947, I went to see it alone after one of those terrible lovers' quarrels that leave one in a state of incomprehensible despair. I came out of the theater, tears streaming, and overheard the petulant voice of a college girl complaining to her boyfriend, "Well I don't see what was so special about that movie." I walked up the street, crying blindly, no longer certain whether my tears were for the tragedy on the screen, the hopelessness I felt for myself, or the alienation I felt from those who could not experience the radiance of *Shoeshine*. For if people cannot feel *Shoeshine*, what *can* they feel? My identification with those two lost boys had become so strong that I did not feel simply a mixture of pity and disgust toward this dissatisfied customer but an intensified hopelessness about everything . . . Later I learned that the man with whom I had quarreled had gone the same night and had also emerged in tears. Yet our tears for each other, and for *Shoeshine* did not bring us together. Life, as *Shoeshine* demonstrates, is too complex for facile endings.

Shoeshine was not conceived in the patterns of romance or melodrama; it is one of those rare works of art which seem to emerge from the welter of human experience without smoothing away the raw edges, or losing what most movies lose—the sense of confusion and accident in human affairs. James Agee's immediate response to the film was, "*Shoeshine* is about as beautiful, moving, and heartening a film as you are ever likely to see." A few months later he retracted his evaluation of it as a work of art and wrote that it was not a completed work of art but "the raw or at best the roughed-out materials of art." I think he should have trusted his initial response: the greatness of *Shoeshine* is in that feeling we get of human emotions that have not been worked-over and worked-into something (a pattern? a structure?) and cannot really be comprised in such a structure. We receive something more naked, something that pours out of the screen.

Orson Welles paid tribute to this quality of the film when he said in 1960, "In handling a camera I feel that I have no peer. But what De Sica can do, that I can't do. I ran his *Shoeshine* again recently and the camera disappeared, the screen disappeared; it was just life . . ."

When *Shoeshine* came to this country, *Life* Magazine wrote, "New Italian film will shock the world . . . will act on U.S. audiences like a punch in the stomach." But few Americans felt that punch in the stomach. Perhaps like the college girl they need to be hit by an actual fist before they can feel. Or, perhaps, to take a more charitable view of humanity, they feared the pain of the film. Just about everybody has heard of *Shoeshine*— it is one of the greatest and most famous films of all time—but how many people have actually seen it? They didn't even go to see it in Italy. As De Sica has said, "*Shoeshine* was a disaster for the producer. It cost less than a million lire but in Italy few people saw it as it was released at a time when the first American films were reappearing . . ." Perhaps in the U.S. people stayed away because it was advertised as a social protest picture— which is a little like advertising *Hamlet* as a political study about a struggle for power.

Shoeshine has a sweetness and a simplicity that suggest greatness of feeling, and this is so rare in film works that to cite a comparison one searches beyond the medium—if Mozart had written an opera set in poverty, it might have had this kind of painful beauty. *Shoeshine*, written by Cesare Zavattini, is a social protest film that rises above its purpose. It is a lyric study of how two boys* betrayed by society betray each other and themselves. The two young shoeshine boys who sustain their friendship and dreams amid the apathy of postwar Rome are destroyed by their own weaknesses and desires when sent to prison for black-marketeering. This tragic study of the corruption of innocence is intense, compassionate, and above all, humane.

{KPFA broadcast for revival showing, 1961}

---

*Rinaldo Smordoni (Guiseppe) became a baker; Franco Interlenghi (Pasquale) became a film star.

:: *Breathless*, and the Daisy Miller Doll

Breathless, the most important New Wave film which has reached the United States, is a frightening little chase comedy with no big speeches and no pretensions. Michel, the young Parisian hood (Jean-Paul Belmondo), steals a car, kills a highway patrolman, chases after some money owed him for past thefts, so he and his young American girl friend can get away to Italy. He finances this chase after the money by various other crimes along the way. Meanwhile, the police are chasing him. But both Michel's flight and the police chase are half-hearted. Michel isn't desperate to get away—his life doesn't mean that much to him; and the police (who are reminiscent of Keystone Cops) carry on a routine bumbling manhunt. Part of the stylistic peculiarity of the work—its art—is that while you're watching it, it's light and playful, off-the-cuff, even a little silly. It seems accidental that it embodies more of the modern world than other movies.

What sneaks up on you in *Breathless* is that the engagingly coy young hood with his loose, random grace and the impervious, passively butch American girl are as shallow and empty as the shiny young faces you see in sports cars and in suburban supermarkets, and in newspapers after unmotivated, pointless crimes. And you're left with the horrible suspicion that this is a new race, bred in chaos, accepting chaos as natural, and not caring one way or another about it or anything else. The heroine, who has literary interests, quotes *Wild Palms*, "Between grief and nothing, I will take grief." But that's just an attitude she likes at that moment; at the end she demonstrates that it's false. The hero states the truth for them both: "I'd choose nothing." The characters of *Breathless* are casual, carefree moral idiots. The European critic, Louis Marcorelles, describes their world as "total immorality, lived skin-deep." And possibly because we Americans live among just such people and have come to take them for granted, the film may not, at first, seem quite so startling as it is. And that's what's frightening about *Breathless*: not only are the characters familiar in an exciting, revealing way, they are terribly *attractive*.

If you foolishly depend on the local reviewers to guide you, you may have been put off *Breathless*. To begin with, where did they get the idea that the title refers to the film's fast editing? That's about like suggesting that the title *Two-Way Stretch* refers to the wide screen. The French title, *À Bout de Souffle*, means "Out of Breath," and it refers to the hero, who keeps going until he's winded. Their confusion is, however, a tribute to the film's fast, improvisatory style, the go go go rhythm. The jazz score, the comic technique are perfectly expressive of the lives of the characters; the jump-cuts convey the tempo and quality of the activities of characters who don't work up to anything but hop from one thing to the next. And as the film seems to explain the people *in their own terms*, the style has the freshness of "objectivity." It does seem breathlessly young, newly created.

If you hold the *Chronicle*'s review of *Breathless* up to the light, you may see H-E-L-P shining through it.

Certain scenes are presented with utter candor, lacking in form and impact in their frankness. A long encounter, for instance, in the small room of Jean Seberg, with whom Belmondo claims to be in love, is repetitious—but extremely lifelike. And then young Godard suddenly will present another scene in which a police inspector is tailing Miss Seberg and searching for Belmondo. This is staged so clumsily that one wonders whether parody is what the director intends. But Belmondo's peril is grave and his reaction to his predicament is sensitive. . . . Always energetic and arrogant, he still suggests both a lost quality and a tender humor. This is his facade to shield his small cynical world from all that he does not understand.

The hero of the film understands all that he wants to, but the critic isn't cynical enough to see the basic fact about these characters: they just don't give a damn. And that's what the movie is about. The *Examiner*'s critic lamented that *Breathless* was a "hodge-podge" and complained that he couldn't "warm up" to the characters—which is a bit like not being able to warm up to the four Mission District kids who went out looking for homosexuals to beat up, and managed to cause the death of a young schoolteacher. For sheer not-getting-the-point, it recalls the remark recently overheard from a well-groomed, blue-rinse-on-the-hair type elderly lady: "That poor Eichmann! I don't think he's got a Chinaman's chance."

How do we connect with people who don't give a damn? Well, is it really so difficult? Even if they weren't all around us, they'd still be (to quote *Double Indemnity*) closer than that.

They are as detached as a foreign colony, as uncommitted as visitors from another planet, yet the youth of several countries seem, to one degree or another, to share the same characteristics. They're not consciously against society: they have no ideologies at all, they're not even rebels without a cause. They're not rebelling against anything—they don't pay that much attention to what doesn't please or amuse them. There is nothing they really want to do, and there's nothing they won't do. Not that they're perverse or deliberately cruel: they have charm and intelligence—but they live on impulse.

The codes of civilized living presuppose that people have an inner life and outer aims, but this new race lives for the moment, because that is all that they care about. And the standards of judgment we might bring to bear on them don't touch them and don't interest them. They have the narcissism of youth, and we are out of it, we are bores. These are the youthful representatives of mass society. They seem giddy and gauche and amusingly individualistic, until you consider that this individualism is not only a reaction to mass conformity, but, more terrifyingly, is the new form that mass society takes: indifference to human values.

Godard has used this, as it were, documentary background for a gangster story. In the traditional American gangster films, we would have been cued for the gangster's fall: he would have shown the one vanity or sentimental weakness or misjudgment that would prove fatal. But *Breathless* has removed the movie gangster from his melodramatic trappings of gangs and power: this gangster is Bogart apotheosized and he is romantic in a modern sense just because he doesn't care about anything but the pleasures of love and fast cars. There is not even the American gangster's hatred of cops and squealers. Michel likes cops because they're cops. This gangster is post-*L'Etranger* and he isn't interested in motives: it's all simple to him, "Killers kill, squealers squeal." Nobody cares if Michel lives or dies, and he doesn't worry about it much either.

Yet Godard has too much affection for Michel to make *him* a squealer: a killer yes, a squealer no. Despite the unrest and anarchy in the moral atmosphere, Michel is as romantic as Pépé Le Moko and as true to love (and his death scene is just as operatic and satisfying). A murderer and a girl with artistic pretensions. She asks him what he thinks of a reproduction she is trying on the wall, and he answers, "Not bad." This doesn't show that he's sufficiently impressed and she reprimands him with, "Renoir was a very great painter." In disgust he replies, "I said 'Not bad.'" There's no doubt which of them responds more. He's honest and likable, though socially classifiable as a psychopath; she's a psychopath, too, but the non-classifiable sort—socially acceptable but a sad, sweet, affectless doll.

There are more ironies than can be sorted out in Patricia-Jean Seberg from Iowa, selected by Otto Preminger from among thousands of American girls to play the French national heroine, Joan of Arc, and now the national heroine of France—as the representative American girl abroad. Patricia, a naive, assured, bland and boyish creature, is like a new Daisy Miller—but not quite as envisioned by Henry James. She has the independence, but not the moral qualms or the Puritan conscience or the high aspirations that James saw as the special qualities of the American girl. She is, indeed, the heiress of the ages—but in a more sinister sense than James imagined: she is so free that she has no sense of responsibility or guilt. She seems to be playing at existence, at a career, at "love"; she's "trying them on." But that's all she's capable of in the way of experience. She doesn't want to be bothered; when her lover becomes an inconvenience, she turns him in to the police.

Shot down and dying, the young man gallantly tries to amuse her, and then looks up at her and remarks—without judgment or reproach, but rather, descriptively, as a grudging compliment: "You really are a bitch." (The actual word he uses is considerably stronger.) And in her flat, little-girl, cornbelt voice, she says, "I don't know what the word means." If she does know, she doesn't care to see how it applies to her. More likely, she really doesn't know, and it wouldn't bother her much anyway. The codes of love and loyalty, in which, if you betray a lover you're a bitch, depend on stronger emotions than her idle attachment to this lover—one among many. They depend on *emotions*, and she is innocent of them. As she had observed earlier, "When we look into each other's eyes, we get nowhere." An updated version of the betraying blonde bitches who destroyed so many movie gangsters, she is innocent even of guilt. As Jean Seberg plays her—and that's exquisitely—Patricia is the most terrifyingly *simple* muse-goddess-bitch of modern movies. Next to her, the scheming Stanwyck of *Double Indemnity* is as archaic as Theda Bara in *A Fool There Was.*

Jean-Paul Belmondo, who plays the hood, is probably the most exciting new presence on the screen since the appearance of Brando; nobody holds the screen this way without enormous reserves of talent. At twenty-six, he has already appeared in nine plays and nine movies; he may be, as Peter Brook says, the best young actor in Europe today. In minor parts, the Alfred Hitchcock personal-appearance bit is compounded, and Truffaut (*The 400 Blows*), Chabrol (*Le Beau Serge, The Cousins*), and Godard himself flit through. Truffaut supplied the news item on which Godard based the script; Chabrol lent his name as supervising producer. But it is Godard's picture, and he has pointed out how he works: "The cinema is not a trade. It isn't teamwork. One is always alone while shooting, as though facing a blank page." His movie is dedicated to Monogram Pictures—who were, of course, the producers of cheap American gangster-chase movies, generally shot in city locations. (*Breathless* was made for $90,000.) Another important director appears in the film—Jean-Pierre Melville—who a few years ago performed one of the most amazing feats on film: he entered into Jean Cocteau's universe and directed, with almost no funds, the brilliant film version of Cocteau's *Les Enfants Terribles*, sometimes known as *The Strange Ones.* He is regarded as a sort of spiritual father to the New Wave; he appears in the movie as a celebrity being interviewed. (The true celebrity and progenitor of the movement is, of course, Cocteau.) Asked by Patricia, "What is your ambition?" the celebrity teases her with a pseudo-profundity: "To become immortal, and then to die."

{KPFA broadcast, 1961}

:: *West Side Story*

Sex is the great leveler, taste the great divider. I have premonitions of the beginning of the end when a man who seems charming or at least remotely possible starts talking about movies. When he says, "I saw a great picture a couple years ago—I wonder what you thought of it?" I start looking for the nearest exit. His great picture generally turns out to be *He Who Must Die* or something else that I detested—frequently a socially conscious problem picture of the Stanley Kramer variety. Boobs on the make always try to impress with their high level of seriousness (wise guys, with their contempt for *all* seriousness).

It's experiences like this that drive women into the arms of truckdrivers —and, as this is America, the truckdrivers all too often come up with the same kind of status-seeking tastes: they want to know what you thought of *Black Orpheus* or *Never on Sunday* or something else you'd much rather forget.

When a really attractive Easterner said to me, "I don't generally like musicals, but have you seen *West Side Story*? It's really great," I felt a kind of gnawing discomfort. I *love* musicals and so I couldn't help being suspicious of the greatness of a musical that would be so overwhelming to somebody who *didn't* like musicals. The gentleman's remark correlated with other expressions of taste—the various encounters in offices and on trains and planes with men who would put on solemn faces as they said, "I don't ordinarily go for poetry but have you read *This Is My Beloved*?"

I had an uneasy feeling that maybe it would be better if I *didn't* go to see *West Side Story*—but, if you're driven to seek the truth, you're driven. I had to learn if this man and I were really as close as he suggested or as far apart as I feared. Well, it's a great musical for people who don't like musicals.

You will notice that nobody says *West Side Story* is a good movie; they say it's great—they accept the terms on which it is presented. It aims to be so much more than a "mere" musical like *Singin' in the Rain* (just about the best Hollywood musical of all time) that it is concerned with nothing so basic to the form as lightness, grace, proportion, diversion, comedy. It is not concerned with the musical form as a showcase for star performers in their best routines; it aspires to present the ballet of our times—our conflicts presented in music and dance. And, according to most of the critics, it succeeds. My anxiety as I entered the theater was not allayed by a huge blow-up of Bosley Crowther's review proclaiming the film a "cinematic masterpiece."

West Side Story begins with a blast of stereophonic music that had me clutching my head. Is the audience so impressed by science and technique, and by the highly advertised new developments that they accept this jolting series of distorted sounds gratefully—on the assumption, perhaps, that because it's so unlike ordinary sound, it must be *better*? Everything about *West Side Story* is supposed to stun you with its newness, its size, the wonders of its photography, editing, choreography, music. It's nothing so simple as a musical, it's a piece of cinematic technology.

Consider the feat: first you take Shakespeare's *Romeo and Juliet* and remove all that cumbersome poetry; then you make the Montagues and Capulets really important and modern by turning them into rival street gangs of native-born and Puerto Ricans. (You get rid of the parents, of course; America is a *young* country—and who wants to be bothered by the squabbles of older people?) There is Jerome Robbins to convert the street rumbles into modern ballet—though he turns out to be too slow and painstaking for high-powered moviemaking and the co-director Robert Wise takes over. (May I remind you of some of Robert Wise's previous credits—the names may be construed as symbolic. *So Big, Executive Suite, Somebody Up There Likes Me, I Want to Live!*) The writers include Arthur Laurents, Ernest Lehman, and, for the lyrics, Stephen Sondheim. The music is said to be by Leonard Bernstein. (Bernstein's father at a recent banquet honoring his seventieth birthday: "You don't expect your child to be a Moses, a Maimonides, a Leonard Bernstein." No, indeed, nor when you criticize

Bernstein's music do you expect people to jump in outrage as if you were demeaning Moses or Maimonides.) Surely, only Saul Bass could provide the titles for such a production, as the credits include more consultants and assistants, production designers, sound men, editors, special effects men, and so forth than you might believe possible—until you see the result. Is it his much-vaunted ingeniousness or a hidden streak of cynicism—a neat comment on all this technology—that he turns the credits into graffiti?

The irony of this hyped-up, slam-bang production is that those involved apparently don't really believe that beauty and romance *can* be expressed in modern rhythms—for whenever their Romeo and Juliet enter the scene, the dialogue becomes painfully old-fashioned and mawkish, the dancing turns to simpering, sickly romantic ballet, and sugary old stars hover in the sky. When true love enters the film, Bernstein abandons Gershwin and begins to echo Richard Rodgers, Rudolf Friml, and Victor Herbert. There's even a heavenly choir. When the fruity, toothsome Romeo-Tony meets his Juliet-Maria, everything becomes gauzy and dreamy and he murmurs, "Have we met before?" That's my favorite piece of synthetic mysticism since the great exchange in *Black Orpheus*: "My name is Orpheus." "My name is Eurydice." "Then we must be in love." When Tony, floating on the clouds of romance (Richard Beymer unfortunately doesn't look as if he *could* walk) is asked, "What have you been taking tonight?" he answers, "A trip to the moon." Match *that* for lyric eloquence! (You'd have to go back to *Golden Boy*.)

When Tony stabs Maria's brother and your mind fills in with "O, I am fortune's fool," the expensive scriptwriters come up with a brilliant exclamation for him. "Maria!" he cries. Do not let this exquisite simplicity mislead you—for they do not call the name "Maria" lightly. She is no mere girl like Juliet—she has the wisdom of all women, she is the mother of us all. And that is why, no doubt, they depart from Shakespeare's plot at the end: suffering Maria survives. And, of course, the appeal to the Catholic audience—which might otherwise become uneasy as both gangs are probably Catholic—is thereby assured. *West Side Story* plays the game in every conceivable way: it makes a strong appeal to youth by expressing the exuberant, frustrated desires of youth in the ugly, constricted city life, but it finally betrays this youth by representing the good characters as innocent and sweet, and making the others seem rather comic and foolish. They're like Dead End Kids dancing—and without much improvement in the humor of the Dead End Kids.

How can so many critics have fallen for all this frenzied hokum—about as original as, say, *South Pacific* at home—and with a score so derivative that, as we left the theater, and overheard some young man exclaiming "I could listen to that music forever," my little daughter answered "We *have* been listening to it forever." (At his father's banquet, Bernstein recalled that at his debut when he was thirteen he had played variations of a song "in the manner of Chopin, Liszt and Gershwin. Now I will play it in the manner of Bernstein." How, I wonder?) Perhaps the clue is in the bigness, and in the pretensions that are part of the bigness. Arthur Knight in the *Saturday Review* called it "A triumphant work of art"; Stanley Kauffmann in the *New Republic* says:

> The best film musical ever made. . . . When the film begins, and the Jets move down the streets of the West Side (studio settings faultlessly blended with location shots), as they mold swagger into ballet, we know that we are not seeing dance numbers, we are seeing street gangs for the first time *as they really are*—only we have not been able to perceive it for ourselves. . . . It is Robbins' vision—of city life expressed in stylized movement that sometimes flowers into dance and song—that lifts this picture high. If a time-capsule is about to be buried anywhere, this film ought to be included, so that possible future generations can know how an artist of ours made our most congenial theatrical form respond to some of the beauty in our time and to the humanity in some of its ugliness.

A candidate for a time-capsule is surely no ordinary multi-million-dollar spectacle. Hasn't Kauffmann, along with a lot of other people, fallen victim to the show of grandeur and importance? If there is anything great in the American musical tradition—and I think there is—it's in the light satire, the high spirits, the giddy romance, the low comedy, and the unpretentiously stylized dancing of men like Fred Astaire and the younger Gene Kelly. There's more beauty there—and a lot more humanity—than in all this jet-propelled ballet. Nothing in *West Side Story* gave me the pleasure of an honest routine like Donald O'Connor's "Make 'Em Laugh" number in *Singin' in the Rain* or almost any old Astaire and Rogers movie.

Despite Kauffmann's feeling that "we are seeing street gangs for the first time *as they really are*," I wonder how the actual street gangs feel about the racial composition of the movie's gangs. For, of course, the Puerto Ricans are *not* Puerto Ricans and the only real difference between these two gangs of what I am tempted to call ballerinas—is that one group has faces and hair darkened, and the other group has gone wild for glittering yellow hair dye; and their stale exuberance, though magnified by the camera to epic proportions, suggests no social tensions more world shaking than the desperation of young dancers to get ahead—even at the risk of physical injury. They're about as human as the Munchkins in *The Wizard of Oz*. Maria, the sweet virgin fresh from Puerto Rico, is the most machine-tooled of Hollywood ingenues—clever little Natalie Wood. Like the new Princess telephone, so ingeniously constructed that it transcends its function and makes communication superfluous (it seems to be designed so that teen-agers can read advertising slogans at each other), Natalie Wood is the newly-constructed love-goddess—so perfectly banal she destroys all thoughts of love. In his great silent film *Metropolis*, Fritz Lang had a robot woman named the false Maria: she had more spontaneity than Natalie Wood's Maria.

I had a sense of foreboding when I saw that Friar Lawrence had become a kindly old Jewish pharmacist called "Doc," but I was hardly prepared for his ultimate wisdom—"You kids make this world lousy! When will you stop?" These words Bosley Crowther tells us "should be heard by thoughtful people—sympathetic people—all over the land." Why, I wonder? What *is* there in this message that has anything to *do* with thought? These message movies dealing with Negro and white, or Puerto Rican and white, like to get a little extra increment of virtue—unearned—by tossing in a sweet, kindly, harmless old Jew full of prophetic cant. (Presumably, Jews should not be discriminated against because they are so philosophic and impotent.) The film makers wouldn't dream of having a young, pushing, aggressive Jew in the film—just as they don't dare to differentiate or characterize the racial backgrounds of the white gang. (Only sweet, reformed Tony can be identified as a Pole.) Yet this is a movie that pretends to deal with racial tensions. The lyrics keep telling us this is what it's about and the critics seem to accept the authors' word for it.

"But," counter the enthusiasts for the film, "surely you must admit the dancing is great." No, it isn't—it's trying so hard to be great it isn't even good. Those impressive, widely admired opening shots of New York from the air overload the story with values and importance—technological and sociological. The Romeo and Juliet story could, of course, be set anywhere, but *West Side Story* wrings the last drop of spurious importance out of the setting, which dominates the enfeebled love story. The dancing is also designed to be urgent and important: it is supposed to be the lyric poetry of the streets, with all the jagged rhythms of modern tensions. The bigger the leap the more, I suppose, the dancer is expressing—on the theory that America is a big, athletic country. Who would have thought that Busby Berkeley's amusing old geometric patterns and aerial views would come back *this* way? Add social ideas to geometry, and you have the new *West Side Story* concept of dance. And just as the American middle classes thought they were being daring and accepting jazz when they listened to the adaptations and arrangements of big orchestras that gave jazz themes the familiar thick, sweet sludge of bad symphonic music, and thought that jazz was being elevated and honored as an art when Louis Armstrong played with the lagging, dragging New York Philharmonic (under Leonard Bernstein), they now think that American dancing is elevated to the status of art by all this arranging and exaggerating—by being turned into the familiar "high" art of ballet. The movements are so huge and sudden, so portentously "alive" they're always near explosion point. The dancing is obviously trying to say something, to *glorify* certain kinds of move-ment. And looking at all those boys in blue jeans doing their calisthenic choreography, Americans say, "Why it's like ballet . . . it's art, it's really great!" What is lost is not merely the rhythm, the feel, the unpretentious movements of American dancing at its best—but its basic emotion, which, as in jazz music, is the contempt for respectability. The possibilities of dance as an expressive medium are not expanded in *West Side Story*; they're contracted. I would guess that in a few decades the dances in *West Side Story* will look as much like hilariously limited, dated period pieces as Busby Berkeley's "Remember the Forgotten Man" number in *Gold Diggers of 1933.*

After *West Side Story* was deluged with Academy Awards as the best movie of 1961, Murray Schumach reported in the *New York Times* that "there seemed to be general agreement that one reason" it won "was that its choreography, music, and direction were devoted to the serious theme of the brotherhood of man." A few weeks ago, in a talk with a Hollywood director, when I expressed surprise at the historical novel he had undertaken to film, he explained that the "idea" of the book appealed to him because it was really about "the brotherhood of man." I averted my eyes in embarrassment and hoped that my face wasn't breaking into a crooked grin. It's a great conversation closer—the "brotherhood of man." Some suggested new "serious" themes for big movies: the sisterhood of women, "no man is an island," the inevitability of death, the continuity of man and nature, "God Is All."

Sometimes, when I read film critics, I think I can do without brothers.

{KPFA broadcast, 1961; *Film Quarterly*, Summer 1962}

:: *Lolita*

The ads asked "How did they ever make a movie of *Lolita* for persons over 18 years of age?" A few days later the question mark was moved, and the ads asked "How did they ever make a movie of *Lolita*?" and after that, the caution: "for persons over 18 years of age." Either way, the suggestion was planted that the movie had "licked" the book, and that *Lolita* had been turned into the usual kind of sexy movie. The advertising has been slanted to the mass audience, so the art-house audience isn't going. A sizable part of the mass audience doesn't like the movie (their rejection is being interpreted as a vote for "wholesomeness," which according to *Variety* is about to stage a comeback) and the art-house audience is missing out on one of the few American films it might enjoy.

Recommend the film to friends and they reply, "Oh I've *had* it with *Lolita*." It turns out (now that *Lolita* can be purchased for fifty cents and so is in the category of ordinary popular books) that they never thought much of it; but even though they didn't really like the book, they don't want to see the movie because of all the changes that have been made in the book. (One person informed me that he wouldn't go to see the movie because he'd heard they'd turned it into a comedy.) Others had heard so much about the book, they thought reading it superfluous (they had as *good* as read it—they were *tired* of it); and if the book was too much talked about to necessitate a reading, surely going to the film was really *de trop*?

Besides, wasn't the girl who played Lolita practically a *matron*? The New York *Times* had said, "She looks to be a good seventeen," and the rest of the press seemed to concur in this peculiarly inexpert judgment. *Time* opened its review with "Wind up the Lolita doll and it goes to Hollywood and commits nymphanticide" and closed with "*Lolita* is the saddest and most important victim of the current reckless adaptation fad . . ." In the *Observer* the premiere of the film was described under the heading "Lolita fiasco" and the writer concluded that the novel had been "turned into a film about this poor English guy who is being given the runaround by this sly young broad." In the *New Republic* Stanley Kauffmann wrote, "It is clear that Nabokov respects the novel. It is equally clear that he does not respect the film—at least as it is used in America . . . He has given to films the *Lolita* that, presumably, he thinks the medium deserves . . ." After all this, who would expect anything from the film?

The surprise of *Lolita* is how enjoyable it is: it's the first *new* American comedy since those great days in the forties when Preston Sturges recreated comedy with verbal slapstick. *Lolita* is black slapstick and at times it's so far out that you gasp as you laugh. An inspired Peter Sellers creates a new comic pattern—a crazy quilt of psychological, sociological commentary so "hip" it's surrealist. It doesn't cover everything: there are structural weaknesses, the film falls apart, and there's even a forced and humiliating attempt to "explain" the plot. But when the wit is galloping who's going to look a gift horse in the mouth? Critics, who feel decay in their bones.

The reviews are a comedy of gray matter. Doubts may have remained after Arthur Schlesinger, Jr.'s, ex cathedra judgment that *Lolita* is "willful, cynical and repellent . . . It is not only inhuman; it is anti-human. I am reluctantly glad that it was made, but I trust it will have no imitators." Then, "for a learned and independent point of view, *Show* invited Dr. Reinhold Niebuhr, the renowned theologian, to a screening in New York and asked him for an appraisal." The higher primate discovered that "the theme of this triangular relationship exposes the unwholesome attitudes of mother, daughter, and lover to a mature observer." (Ripeness is all . . . but is it enough?) This mature observer does however find some "few saving moral insights"—though he thinks the film "obscures" them—such as "the lesson of Lolita's essential redemption in a happy marriage." (Had any *peripheral* redemptions lately?) If you're still hot on the trail of insights, don't overlook the *New Republic*'s steamy revelation that "the temper of the original might . . . have been tastefully preserved" if Humbert had narrated the film. "The general tone could have been: 'Yes, this is what I did then and thought lovely. Dreadful, wasn't it? Still . . . it has its funny side, no?'" It has its funny side, oui oui.

The movie adaptation tries something so far beyond the simple "narrator" that a number of the reviewers have complained: Bosley Crowther, who can always be counted on to miss the point, writes that "Mr. Kubrick inclines to dwell too long over scenes that have slight purpose, such as scenes in which Mr. Sellers does various comical impersonations as the sneaky villain who dogs Mr. Mason's trail." These scenes "that have slight purpose" are, of course, just what make *Lolita* new, these are the scenes that make it, for all its slackness of pace and clumsy editing, a more exciting comedy than the last American comedy, *Some Like It Hot*. Quilty, the success, the writer of scenarios and school plays, the policeman, the psychologist; Quilty the genius, the man whom Lolita loves, Humbert's brother and tormenter and parodist; Quilty the man of the world is a conception to talk about alongside Melville's *The Confidence Man*. "Are you with someone?" Humbert asks the policeman. And Quilty the policeman replies, "I'm not with someone. I'm with you."

The Quilty monologues are worked out almost like the routines of silent comedy—they not only carry the action forward, they comment on it, and this comment is the *new* action of the film. There has been much critical condescension toward Sellers, who's alleged to be an impersonator rather than an actor, a man with many masks but no character. Now Sellers does a turn with the critics' terms: his Quilty is a character employing masks, an actor with a merciless talent for impersonation. He is indeed "the sneaky villain who dogs Mr. Mason's trail"—and he digs up every bone that "Mr. Mason" ineptly tries to bury, and presents them to him. Humbert can conceal nothing. It is a little like the scene in Victor Sjöström's magnificent *The Wind*, in which Lillian Gish digs a grave for the man she has murdered and then, from her window, watches in horror as the windstorm uncovers the body. But in *Lolita* our horror is split by laughter: Humbert has it coming—*not* because he's having "relations" with a minor, but because, in order to conceal his sexual predilections, he has put on the most obsequious and mealy-minded of masks. Like the homosexual professors who are rising fast in American academia because they are so cautious about protecting their unconventional sex lives that they can be trusted not to be troublesome to the college administrations on any important issues (a convoluted form of blackmail), Humbert is a worm and Quilty knows it.

Peter Sellers works with miserable physical equipment, yet he has somehow managed to turn his lumbering, wide-hipped body into an advantage by *acting* to perfection the man without physical assets. The soft, slow-moving, paper-pushing middle-class man is his special self-effacing type; and though only in his mid-thirties he all too easily incarnates sly, smug middle-aged man. Even his facial muscles are kept flaccid, so that he always looks weary, too tired and cynical for much of a response. The rather frightening strength of his Quilty (who has enormous — almost sinister — reserves of energy) is peculiarly effective just because of his ordinary, "normal" look. He does something that seems impossible: he makes unattractiveness magnetic.

Quilty — rightly, in terms of the film as distinguished from the novel — dominates *Lolita* (which could use much more of him) and James Mason's Humbert, who makes attractiveness tired and exhausted and impotent, is a remarkable counterpart. Quilty who doesn't care, who wins Lolita and throws her out, Quilty the homewrecker is a winner; Humbert, slavishly, painfully in love, absurdly suffering, the lover of the ages who degrades himself, who cares about nothing but Lolita, is the classic loser. Mason is better than (and different from) what almost anyone could have expected. Mason's career has been so mottled: a beautiful *Odd Man Out*, a dull Brutus, an uneven, often brilliant Norman Maine in A *Star Is Born*, a good Captain Nemo, and then in 1960 the beginnings of comic style as the English naval commander who pretends to have gone over to the Russians in *A Touch of Larceny*. And now, in *Lolita* he's really in command of a comic style: the handsome face gloats in a rotting smile. Mason seems to need someone strong to play against. He's very good in the scenes with Charlotte and with her friends, and especially good in the bathtub scene (which Niebuhr thinks "may arouse both the laughter and the distaste of the audience" — imagine being so drained of reactions that you have to be *aroused* to distaste!) but his scenes with Lolita, when he must dominate the action, fall rather flat.

Perhaps the reviewers have been finding so many faults with *Lolita* because this is such an easy way to show off some fake kind of erudition: even newspaper reviewers can demonstrate that they've read a book by complaining about how different the movie is from the novel. The movie *is* different but not *that* different, and if you can get over the reviewers' preoccupation with the sacredness of the novel (they don't complain this much about Hollywood's changes in biblical stories) you'll probably find that even the characters that *are* different (Charlotte Haze, especially, who has become the culture-vulture rampant) are successful in terms of the film. Shelley Winters's Charlotte is a triumphant caricature, so overdone it recalls Blake's "You never know what is enough until you know what is more than enough."

Sue Lyon is perhaps a little less than enough—but not because she looks seventeen. (Have the reviewers looked at the schoolgirls of America lately? The classmates of my fourteen-year-old daughter are not merely nubile: some of them look badly used.) Rather it is because her role is insufficiently written. Sue Lyon herself is good (at times her face is amusingly suggestive of a miniature Elvis Presley) though physically too *young* to be convincing in her last scenes. (I don't mean that to sound paradoxical but merely descriptive.) Kubrick and company have been attacked most for the area in which they have been simply accurate: they could have done up Sue Lyon in childish schoolgirl clothes, but the facts of American life are that adolescents and even pre-adolescents wear nylons and make-up and two-piece strapless bathing suits and have *figures*.

Lolita isn't a consistently good movie but that's almost beside the point: excitement is sustained by a brilliant idea, a new variant on the classic chase theme—Quilty as Humbert's walking paranoia, the madness that chases Humbert and is chased by him, over what should be the delusionary landscape of the actual United States. This panoramic confusion of normal and mad that can be experienced traveling around the country is, unfortunately, lost: the film badly needs the towns and motels and highways of the U.S. It suffers not only from the genteel English landscapes, but possibly also from the photographic style of Oswald Morris—perhaps justly famous, but subtly wrong (and too tasteful) for *Lolita*. It may seem like a dreadfully "uncinematic" idea, but I rather wish that Kubrick, when he realized that he couldn't shoot in the U.S. (the reasons must have been economic), had experimented with stylized sets.

There *is* a paradox involved in the film *Lolita*. Stanley Kubrick shows talents in new areas (theme and dialogue and comedy), and is at his worst at what he's famous for. *The Killing* was a simple-minded suspense film about a racetrack robbery, but he structured it brilliantly with each facet shining in place; *Paths of Glory* was a simple-minded pacifist film, but he gave it nervous rhythm and a sense of urgency. *Lolita* is so clumsily structured that you begin to wonder what was shot and then cut out, why other pieces were left in, and whether the beginning was intended to be the end; and it is edited in so dilatory a fashion that after the first hour, almost every scene seems to go on too long. It's as if Kubrick lost his nerve. If he did, it's no wonder; the wonder is, that with all the pressures on American moviemakers — the pressures to evade, to conceal, to compromise, and to explain everything for the literal-minded — he had the nerve to transform this satire on the myths of love into the medium that has become conse-crated to the myths. *Lolita* is a wilder comedy for being, now, family enter-tainment. Movie theaters belong to the same world as the highways and motels: in first-run theaters, "for persons over 18 years of age" does not mean that children are prohibited but simply that there are no reduced prices for children. In second-run neighborhood theaters, "for persons over 18 years of age" is amended by "unless accompanied by a member of the family." That befits the story of Humbert Humbert.

{KPFA broadcast, 1962; *Partisan Review*, Fall 1962}

:: *Jules and Jim*

When the Legion of Decency condemned *Jules and Jim*, the statement read: the story has been developed "in a context alien to Christian and traditional natural morality." It certainly has. The Legion went on to say: "If the director has a definite moral viewpoint to express, it is so obscure that the visual amorality and immorality of the film are predominant and consequently pose a serious problem for a mass medium of entertainment." It would be possible to make a fraudulent case for the film's morality by pointing out that the adulterous individuals suffer and die, but this is so specious and so irrelevant to the meanings and qualities of the work that surely the Legion, expert in these matters, would recognize that it was casuistry. The Legion isn't wrong about the visual amorality either, and yet, *Jules and Jim* is not only one of the most beautiful films ever made, and the greatest motion picture of recent years, it is also, viewed as a work of art, exquisitely and impeccably *moral*. Truffaut does not have "a definite moral viewpoint to express" and he does not use the screen for messages or special pleading or to sell sex for money; he uses the film medium to express his love and knowledge of life as completely as he can.

The film is adapted from Henri-Pierre Roché's autobiographical novel, written when he was seventy-four, with some additional material from his even later work, *Deux Anglaises et le Continent*. If some of us have heard of Roché, it's probably just the scrap of information that he was the man who introduced Gertrude Stein to Picasso—but this scrap shouldn't be discarded, because both Stein and Picasso are relevant to the characters and period of *Jules and Jim*. Roché is now dead, but the model for Catherine, the Jeanne Moreau role, is a German literary woman who is still alive; it was she who translated *Lolita* into German. Truffaut has indicated, also, that some of the material which he improvised on location was suggested by Apollinaire's letters to Madeleine—a girl whom he had met for a half-hour on a train.

The film begins in Paris before the First World War. Jules the Austrian (Oskar Werner) and Jim the Frenchman (Henri Serre) are Mutt and Jeff, Sancho Panza and Don Quixote, devoted friends, contentedly arguing about life and letters. Catherine enters their lives, and Jules and Jim try to have both the calm of their friendship and the excitement of her imperious, magical presence. She marries Jules who can't hold her, and in despair he encourages Jim's interest in her—"That way she'll still be *ours*." But Catherine can't subjugate Jim: he is too independent to be dominated by her whims. Not completely captivated, Jim fails to believe in her love when she most desperately offers it. She kills herself and him.

The music, the camera and editing movement, the rhythm of the film carry us along without pauses for reflection. Truffaut doesn't linger; nothing is held too long, nothing is overstated or even *stated*. Perhaps that's why others besides the Legion of Decency have complained: Stanley Kauffmann in the *New Republic* says that *Jules and Jim* "loses sight of purposes . . . It is a confusion of the sheer happiness of being in the studio . . . with the reason for being there." Truffaut, the most youthfully alive and abundant of all the major film directors, needs a *reason* for making movies about as much as Picasso needs a reason for picking up a brush or a lump of clay. And of what film maker could a reference to a *studio* be less apt? He works everywhere and with anything at hand. Kauffmann says of *Jules and Jim*, "There is a lot less here than meets the eye," and Dwight Macdonald, who considers Kauffmann his only peer, is reassured: "one doesn't want to be the only square," he writes. If it gives him comfort to know there are two of them . . .

What is the film about? It's a celebration of life in a great historical period, a period of ferment and extraordinary achievement in painting and music and literature. Together Jules and Jim have a peaceful friendship (and Jim has a quiet love affair with Gilberte) but when Jules and Jim are with Catherine they feel alive. Anything may happen—she's the catalyst, the troublemaker, the source of despair as well as the source of joy. She is the enchantress who makes art out of life.

At the end, Jules, who has always given in to everything in order to keep

Catherine, experiences relief at her death, although he has always delighted in the splendor she conferred on his existence. (Don't we all experience this sort of relief when we say goodbye to a particularly brilliant house-guest?) The dullness in Jules, the bourgeois under the Bohemian, the passivity is made clear from the outset: it is why the girls don't fall in love with him. At the end, the excitements and the humiliations are over. He will have peace, and after a lifetime with Catherine he has earned it.

Catherine is, of course, a little crazy, but that's not too surprising. Pioneers can easily become fanatics, maniacs. And Catherine is part of a new breed—the independent, intellectual modern woman, so determined to live as freely as a man that while claiming equality she uses every feminine wile to gain extra advantages, to demonstrate her superiority, and to increase her power position. She is the emerging twentieth-century woman satirized by Strindberg, who also adored her; she is the woman with rights and responsibilities who entered Western literature after the turn of the century and has almost always been seen by the male authors as demanding the rights but refusing the responsibilities. This is the traditional male view of the feminist, and the film's view is not different. Don't we now hear complaints that Negroes are so sensitive about their rights that you can't treat them casually and equally as you would anybody else, you can't disagree on a job or question their judgment, you have to defer to their sensitivities and treat them as if they were super-whites—always in the right? So it is with Catherine.

Catherine, in her way, compensates for the homage she demands. She has, despite her need to intrude and to dominate, the gift for life. She holds nothing in reserve; she lives out her desires; when she can't control the situation, she destroys it. Catherine may be wrong-headed, as those who aspire to be free spirits often are (and they make this wrongness more visible than pliable, amiable people do), but she is devoid of hypocrisy and she doesn't lie. In one of the most upsetting and odd little scenes in the film she takes out a bottle which she says is "vitriol for lying eyes"—and Jim doesn't react any more than if it were aspirin. Catherine the free spirit has the insanity of many free spirits—she believes that she knows truth from lies, right from wrong. Her absolutism is fascinating, but it is also rather clearly *morally insane*. She punishes Jim because he has not broken with Gilberte, though she has not broken with Jules. Only the relationships *she* sets and dominates are *right*. Catherine suffers from the fatal ambivalence of the "free and equal" woman toward sex: she can leave men, but if they leave her, she is as abandoned and desolate, as destroyed and helpless as any clinging vine (perhaps *more* destroyed — she cannot even ask for sympathy). *Jules and Jim* is about the impossibility of freedom, as it is about the many losses of innocence.

All these elements are elliptical in the film — you catch them out of the corner of your eye and mind. So much happens in the span of an hour and three quarters that even if you don't take more than a fraction of the possible meanings from the material, you still get far more than if you examined almost any other current film, frame by frame, under a microscope. *Jules and Jim* is as full of character and wit and radiance as *Marienbad* is empty, and the performance by Jeanne Moreau is so vivid that the bored, alienated wife of *La Notte* is a faded monochrome. In *Jules and Jim* alienation is just one aspect of her character and we see how Catherine got there: she *becomes* alienated when she can't get her own way, when she is blocked. It is not a universal condition as in *La Notte* (neither Jules nor Jim shares in it): it is her developing insanity as she is cut off from what she wants and no longer takes pleasure in life.

Jules and Jim are portraits of artists as young men, but they are the kind of artists who grow up into something else — they become specialists in some field, or journalists; and the dedication to art of their youth becomes the *civilizing* influence in their lives. The war blasts the images of Bohemian life; both Jules and Jim are changed, but not Catherine. She is the unreconstructed Bohemian who does *not* settle down. She needed more strength, more will than they to live the artist's life — and this determination is the *un*civilizing factor. Bohemianism has made her, underneath all the graces, a moral barbarian: freedom has come to mean whatever she says it is. And when she loses what she believes to be freedom — when she can no longer dictate the terms on which Jim will live — she is lost, isolated. She no longer makes art out of life: she makes life hell.

She chooses death, and she calls on Jules to observe her choice, the last demonstration of her power over life and death, because Jules by a lifetime of yielding his own freedom to her has become, to her, a witness. He can only observe grand gestures; he cannot *make* them. In the last moment in the car, when self-destruction is completely determined, she smiles the smile of the statue: this was the mystery that drew them to her—the smile that looks so easy and natural but which is self-contained and impenetrable.

Jules and Jim ends after the burning of the books in Germany, the end of an epoch, as Truffaut has said, for intellectual Bohemians like Jules and Jim. The film is, in a way, a tribute to the books that were burned; I can't think of another movie so full of books, and of references to books and of writing and translating books. Books were the blood of these characters: they took their ideas of life from books, and writing books was their idea of living.

Jules and Jim is, among other things, the best movie ever made about what I guess most of us think of as the Scott Fitzgerald period (though it begins much earlier). Catherine jumping into the waters of the Seine to demonstrate her supremacy over Jules and Jim, who are discussing the weaknesses of women, is not unlike Zelda jumping over that balustrade. This film treatment of the period is a work of lyric poetry and a fable of the world as playground, a work of art as complex and suggestive in its way as the paintings and poetry and novels and music of the period that it is based on. It is a tribute to the school of Paris when art and Paris were synonymous; filmically it is a new school of Paris—and the new school of Paris is cinema. You go to movies, you talk movies, and you make movies. The young French painters don't compare with the Americans, and French literature is in a fancy trance, but oh, how the young French artists can make movies!

Several of the critics, among them Kauffmann, have complained that the song Jeanne Moreau sings is irrelevant to the action of the film. It's embarrassing to have to point out the obvious, that the song is the theme and spirit of the film: Jules and Jim and Catherine are the ones who "make their way in life's whirlpool of days—round and round together bound." And, in the film, the song is an epiphany: when Catherine sings, the story is crystallized, and the song, like Jim and the child rolling on the hill, seems to belong to memory almost before it is over. In the same way, the still shots catch for us, as for the characters, the distillation, the beauty of the moment. Throughout the film, Georges Delerue's exquisite music—simple and fragrant, popular without being banal—is part of the atmosphere; it is so evocative that if you put the music on the phonograph, like the little phrase from Vinteuil's sonata, it brings back the images, the emotions, the experience. Though emotionally in the tradition of Jean

Renoir, as a work of film craftsmanship *Jules and Jim* is an homage to D. W. Griffith. Truffaut explores the medium, plays with it, overlaps scenes, uses fast cutting in the manner of *Breathless* and leaping continuity in the manner of *Zero for Conduct*, changes the size and shape of the images as Griffith did, and in one glorious act of homage he recreates a frame out of *Intolerance*, the greatest movie ever made. *Jules and Jim* is the most exciting movie made in the West since *L'Avventura* and *Breathless* and Truffaut's earlier *Shoot the Piano Player*; because of the beauty and warmth of its images, it is a richer, a more satisfying film than any of them. I think it will rank among the great lyric achievements of the screen, right up there with the work of Griffith and Renoir.

{KPFA broadcast, 1962; *Partisan Review*, Fall 1962}

:: *Billy Budd*

Billy Budd is not a great motion picture, but it is a very good one—a clean, honest work of intelligence and craftsmanship. It ranks as one of the best films of 1962, and by contrast, it exposes what a slovenly, incoherent production *Mutiny on the Bounty* is. *Billy Budd* not only has a strong story line; it has a core of meaning that charges the story, gives it tension and intellectual excitement.

In the film version of *Billy Budd*, Melville's story has been stripped for action; and I think this was probably the right method—the ambiguities of the story probably come through more clearly than if the film were not so straightforward in its narrative line. The very cleanness of the narrative method, Peter Ustinov's efficient direction, Robert Krasker's stylized, controlled photography, help to release the meanings. The film could easily have been clogged by metaphysical speculation and homo-erotic overtones. Instead, it is a good, tense movie that doesn't try to tell us too much—and so gives us a very great deal.

Terence Stamp is a remarkably intelligent casting selection for Billy. If he were a more feminine type—as the role is often filled on the stage—all the overtones would be cheapened and limited. Stamp, fortunately, can wear white pants and suggest angelic splendor without falling into the narcissistic poses that juveniles so often mistake for grace. Robert Ryan gives a fine performance in the difficult role of Claggart. Ryan has had so few chances at anything like characterization in his movie career that each time he comes across, it seems amazing that he could have retained such power and technique. I don't know how many dozens of times I've seen him, but the roles that I remember are his prizefighter in *The Set-Up*, the anti-Semite in *Crossfire*, the vicious millionaire in Max Ophuls's *Caught*, the projectionist in *Clash by Night*, the central figure in *God's Little Acre*. Considering that he is a very specialized physical type—the tall, rangy American of Western mythology—his variety of characterizations is rather extraordinary. Perhaps just because he is the type who looks at home in cowboy movies, critics rarely single out his performances for commendation. The American reviewers of *Billy Budd* seem more concerned to complain that his Claggart doesn't have an English accent than to judge his performance. But it is not at all necessary that Claggart speak with an English accent: his antecedents are deliberately vague in Melville as in the film, and the men on board are drawn from all over. It may even be better that Claggart's accent does not define his background for us.

Ryan's Claggart has the requisite Satanic dignity: he makes evil comprehensible. The evil he defines is the way the world works, but it is also the self-hatred that makes it necessary for him to destroy the image of goodness. In the film Claggart is drawn to Billy but overcomes his momentary weakness. Melville, with all his circumlocutions, makes it overwhelmingly clear that Claggart's "depravity according to nature" is, among other things, homosexual, or as he coyly puts it, "a nut not to be cracked by the tap of a lady's fan." Billy's innocence and goodness are intolerable to Claggart because Billy is so beautiful.

Neither Stamp nor Ryan can be faulted. Unfortunately, the role of Captain Vere as played by Ustinov is a serious misconception that weakens the film, particularly in the last section. Ustinov gives a fine performance but it doesn't belong in the story of *Billy Budd*: it reduces the meanings to something clear-cut and banal. Ustinov's physical presence is all wrong; his warm, humane, sensual face turns Melville's Starry Vere into something like a cliché of the man who wants to do the right thing, the liberal. We *believe* him when he presents his arguments about justice and law.

Perhaps it is Ustinov's principles that have prevented him from seeing farther into Melville's equivocations. Ustinov has explained that he was concerned "with a most horrible situation where people are compelled by the letter of the law, which is archaic, to carry out sentences which they don't wish to do. That obviously produces a paradox which is tragic." This is, no doubt, an important subject for Ustinov, but it is not the kind of paradox that interested Melville. Melville, so plagued by *Billy Budd* that he couldn't get it in final form (he was still revising it when he died), had far more unsettling notions of its content. As Ustinov presents the film, the conflict is between the almost abstract forces of good (Billy) and evil (Claggart) with the Captain a human figure tragically torn by the rules and demands of authority. Obviously. But what gives the story its fascination, its greatness, is the ambivalent Captain; and there is nothing in Ustinov's performance, or in his conception of the story, to suggest the unseemly haste with which Vere tries to hang Billy. In Melville's account the other officers can't understand why Vere doesn't simply put Billy in confinement "in a way dictated by usage and postpone further action in so extraordinary a case to such time as they should again join the squadron, and then transfer it to the admiral." The surgeon thinks the Captain must be "suddenly affected in his mind." Melville's Vere, who looks at the dead Claggart and exclaims, "Struck dead by an angel of God. Yet the angel must hang!" is not so much a tragic victim of the law as he is Claggart's master and a distant relative perhaps of the Grand Inquisitor. Sweet Starry Vere is the evil we *can't* detect: the man whose motives and conflicts we can't fathom. Claggart we can spot, but he is merely the underling doing the Captain's work: it is the Captain, Billy's friend, who continues the logic by which saints must be destroyed.

Though it is short, *Billy Budd* is one of the most convoluted, one of the strangest works Melville wrote (in some ways even stranger than *Pierre*). Among its peculiarities is a chapter entitled "A Digression," which is given over to a discussion between the ship's purser and the ship's surgeon after Billy's death. Their subject is why Billy's body during the hanging did not go through the movements which are supposed to be invariable in such cases. The absence of spasm—which is a euphemism for ejaculation—is rather like a variation or a reversal of the famous death stink of Father Zossima in *The Brothers Karamazov*. I don't want to stretch the comparison too far, but it's interesting that Melville and Dostoyevsky, so closely contemporary—Melville born in 1819, Dostoyevsky in 1821—should both have been concerned in works written just before their own deaths with the physical phenomena of death. Billy Budd, by the absence of normal human reactions at the moment of death, turns into a saint, a holy innocent, both more and less than a man. Father Zossima, by the presence of all-too-mortal stench after death, is robbed of his saintliness. Melville's lingering on this singularity about Billy Budd's death didn't strike me so forcibly the first time I read the story, but reading it again recently, and, as it happened, reading it just after William Burroughs's *The Naked Lunch*, with all its elaborate fantasies of violent deaths and gaudy ejaculations, Melville's treatment seems odder than ever. Billy Budd's goodness is linked with presexuality or nonsexuality; his failure to comprehend evil in the universe is linked with his not being really quite a man. He is, in Melville's view, too pure and beautiful to be subject to the spasms of common musculature.

Before this rereading I had associated the story only with that other work of Dostoyevsky's to which it bears more obvious relationships—*The Idiot*. It is, of course, as a *concept* rather than as a character that Billy resembles Prince Myshkin. It may be worth pointing out that in creating a figure of abnormal goodness and simplicity, both authors found it important for their hero to have an infirmity—Myshkin is epileptic, Billy stammers. In both stories the figure is also both naturally noble and also of aristocratic birth: Myshkin a prince, Billy a bastard found in a silk-lined basket. And in the structure of both, the heroes have their opposite numbers—Myshkin and Rogozhin, Billy and Claggart. For both authors, a good man is not a whole man; there is the other side of the human coin, the dark side. Even with his last words, "God bless Captain Vere," Billy demonstrates that he is not a man: he is unable to comprehend the meaning of Vere's experience, unable to comprehend that he will die just because he is innocent.

What's surprising about the film is how much of all this *is* suggested and comes through. What is missing in the film—the reason it is a very good film but not a great one—is that passion which gives Melville's work its extraordinary beauty and power. I wonder if perhaps the key to this failure is in that warm, humane face of Peter Ustinov, who perhaps, not just as an actor, but also as adaptor and director, is too much the relaxed worldly European to share Melville's American rage—the emotionality that is blocked and held back and still pours through in his work. Melville is not a civilized, European writer; he is our greatest writer because he is the American primitive struggling to say more than he knows how to say, struggling to say more than he knows. He is perhaps the most confused of all great writers; he wrestles with words and feelings. It is probably no accident that Billy's speech is blocked. Dostoyevsky is believed to have shared Myshkin's epilepsy, and when Melville can't articulate, he flails in all directions. Even when we can't understand clearly what he is trying to say, we respond to his Promethean torment, to the unresolved complexities.

The movie does not struggle; it moves carefully and rhythmically through the action to the conclusion. Its precision—which is its greatest virtue—is, when compared with the oblique, disturbing novella, evidence of its limitations. Much of what makes the story great is in Melville's effort to achieve new meanings (and some of the meanings we can only guess at from his retreats and disguises) and it is asking rather too much of the moviemakers to say what he wasn't sure about himself. But as Ustinov interprets Vere, Billy is just a victim of unfortunate circumstances, and the film is no more than a tragedy of *justice*. There's a good deal in the film, but the grandeur of Melville is not there.

{KPFA broadcast, 1962; *Film Quarterly*, Spring 1963}

Kurosawa has made the first great shaggy-man movie. *Yojimbo* (The Bodyguard) is a glorious comedy-satire of force: the story of the bodyguard who kills the bodies he is hired to guard. Our Westerner, the freelance professional gunman, the fastest draw in the West, has become the unemployed samurai; the gun for hire has become the sword for hire. But when our Westerner came into town, although his own past was often shady, he picked the *right* side, the farmers against the gamblers and cattle thieves, the side of advancing law and order and decency and schools and churches. Toshiro Mifune, the samurai without a master, the professional killer looking for employment, walks into a town divided by two rival merchants quarreling over a gambling concession, each supporting a gang of killers. The hero is the Westerner all right, the stranger in town, the disinterested outsider with his special skills and the remnants of a code of behavior, but to whom can he give his allegiance? Nobody represents any principle, the scattered weak are simply weak.

The Westerner has walked into the gangster movie: both sides are treacherous and ruthless (trigger-happy, they would be called in American pictures). He hires out to each and systematically eliminates both. He is the agent of their destruction because they offend his sense of how things should be: he destroys them because they disgust him. This black Robin Hood with his bemused contempt is more treacherous than the gangsters; he can defend his code only by a masterly use of the doublecross, and he enjoys himself with an occasional spree of demolition ("Destruction's our delight"). The excruciating humor of his last line, as he surveys the carnage—"Now there'll be a little quiet in this town"—is that we've heard it so many times before, but not amidst total devastation. His clean-up has been so thorough and so outrageously bloody that it has achieved a hilarious kind of style.

We would expect violence carried to extremity to be sickening; Kurosawa, in a triumph of bravura technique, makes it explosively comic and exhilarating. By taking the soft romantic focus off the Westerner as played by Gary Cooper or Alan Ladd or John Wayne, Kurosawa has made him a comic hero—just because of what he does, which was always incredible. Without his nimbus, he is unbelievably, absurdly larger-than-life. In *Shane*, the rather ponderously "classic" version of the Western, good and evil were white and black. The settlers, morally strong but physically weak, naive and good but not very bright or glamorous, had to be represented in their fight against the rustling-gambling-murderous prince of darkness by a disinterested prince of light. Shane was Galahad. The Western dog, who howled at his master's grave in *Shane*, who crossed the road to frame the action at the beginning and end of *The Ox-Bow Incident*, has a new dimension in *Yojimbo*—he appears with a human hand for a bone. This dog signals us that in this movie the conventions of the form are going to be turned inside out, we'll have to shift expectations, abandon sentiments: in this terrain dog eats man. And if we think that man, having lost his best friend, can still count on his mother, Kurosawa has another shock for us. A boy from one gang, held prisoner by the other, is released; he rushes to his mother, crying "Oka" (ma or mother). She responds by slapping him. Mother isn't sentimental: first things first, and what she cares about is that gambling concession. This Eastern Western isn't merely a confusion in the points of the compass; Kurosawa's control and his sense of film rhythm are so sure that each new dislocation of values produces both surprise and delight, so that when the hero tries to free an old man who has been trussed-up and suspended in air, and the old man protests that he's safer where he is, we giggle in agreement.

Other directors attempt to recreate the pastness of a story, to provide distance, perspective. For Kurosawa, the setting may be feudal or, as in this case, mid-nineteenth century, but we react (as we are supposed to react) as modern men. His time is now, his action so immediate, sensuous, raging, that we are forced to disbelieve, to react with incredulity, to admire. (This is partly the result of using telephoto lenses that put us right into the fighting, into the confusion of bared teeth and gasps and howls.) He shakes spears in our faces. This is more alive than any living we know; this, all our senses tell us, is art, not life. Ironic detachment is our saving grace.

Of all art forms, movies are most in need of having their concepts of heroism undermined. The greatest action pictures have often been satirical: even before Douglas Fairbanks, Sr., mocked the American dreams, our two-reelers used the new techniques of the screen to parody the vacuous heroics of stage melodrama. George Stevens' *Gunga Din*, a model of the action genre, was so exuberant and high-spirited that it both exalted and mocked a schoolboy's version of heroism. But in recent years John Ford, particularly, has turned the Western into an almost static pictorial genre, a devitalized, dehydrated form which is "enriched" with pastoral beauty and evocative nostalgia for a simple, heroic way of life. The clichés we retained from childhood pirate, buccaneer, gangster, and Western movies have been awarded the status of myths, and writers and directors have been making infatuated tributes to the myths of our old movies. If, by now, we dread going to see a "great" Western, it's because "great" has come to mean slow and pictorially composed. We'll be lulled to sleep in the "affectionate," "pure," "authentic" scenery of the West (in "epics" like *My Darling Clementine*, *She Wore a Yellow Ribbon*, *Fort Apache*) or, for a change, we'll be clobbered by messages in "mature" Westerns like *The Gunfighter* and *High Noon* (the message is that the myths we never believed in anyway were false). Kurosawa slashes the screen with action, and liberates us from the pretensions of our "serious" Westerns. After all those long, lean-hipped walks across the screen with Cooper or Fonda (the man who knows how to use a gun is, by movie convention, the man without an ass), we are restored to sanity by Mifune's heroic personal characteristic—a titanic shoulder twitch.

The Western has always been a rather hypocritical form. The hero represents a way of life that is becoming antiquated. The solitary defender of justice is the last of the line; the era of lawlessness is over, courts are coming in. But the climax is the demonstration that the old way is the only way that works—though we are told that it is the last triumph of violence. The Westerner, the loner, must take the law into his hands for one last time in order to wipe out the enemies of the new system of justice. *Yojimbo* employs an extraordinary number of the conventions of the form, but takes the hypocrisy for a ride. The samurai is a killer with a code of honor and all that, but no system of justice is supplanting him. He's the last of the line not because law and order will prevail, but because his sword for hire is already anachronistic. Guns are coming in. One of his enemies is a gun-slinger, who looks and acts a parody of American Method actors. That ridiculous little gun means the end of the warrior caste: killing is going to become so easy that it will be democratically available to all. In *Yojimbo* goodness triumphs satirically: the foil at the point of the sword is a huge joke. The samurai is not a man with a poker face, and he's not an executioner who hates his job. He's a man of passion who takes savage satisfaction in his special talents. Violence triumphs whoever wins, and our ideas of courage, chivalry, strength, and honor bite the dust along with the "bad" men. The dogs will have their human fodder.

Yojimbo is not a film that needs much critical analysis; its boisterous power and good spirits are right there on the surface. Lechery, avarice, cowardice, coarseness, animality, are rendered by fire; they become joy in life, in even the lowest forms of human life. (Kurosawa's grotesque variants of the John Ford stock company include a giant—a bit mentally retarded, perhaps.) The whimpering, maimed and cringing are so vivid they seem joyful; what in life might be pathetic, loathsome, offensive is made comic and beautiful. Kurosawa makes us accept even the most brutish of his creatures as more alive than the man who doesn't yield to temptation. There is so much displacement that we don't have time or inclination to ask why we are enjoying the action; we respond kinesthetically. It's hard to believe that others don't share this response. Still, I should remember Bosley Crowther with his "the dramatic penetration is not deep, and the plot complications are many and hard to follow in Japanese." And Dwight Macdonald, who writes, "It is a dark, neurotic, claustrophobic film . . ." and, "The Japanese have long been noted for their clever mimicry of the West. *Yojimbo* is the cinematic equivalent of their ten-cent ball-point pens and their ninety-eight-cent mini-cameras. But one expects more of Kurosawa."

More? Kurosawa, one of the few great new masters of the medium, has had one weakness: he has often failed to find themes that were commensurate with the surge and energy of his images. At times he has seemed to be merely a virtuoso stylist, a painter turned director whose visual imagination had outstripped his content. But in at least three films, eye and mind have worked together at the highest levels. His first major international success, *Rashomon* (1950)—despite the longueurs of the opening and closing sequences—is still the classic film statement of the relativism, the unknowability of truth. *The Seven Samurai* (1954) is incomparable as a modern poem of force. It is the Western form carried to apotheosis—a vast celebration of the joys and torments of fighting, seen in new depth and scale, a brutal imaginative ballet on the nature of strength and weakness. Now, in *Yojimbo*, Kurosawa has made a farce of force. And now that he has done it, we can remember how good his comic scenes always were and that he frequently tended toward parody.

Ikiru is often called Kurosawa's masterpiece. (It *does* have one great moment—the old man's song in the swing. *Throne of Blood*, which I much prefer, has at least two great moments—Isuzu Yamada's handwashing scene, and that dazzling filmic achievement of Shakespeare's vision when Birnam Wood does come to Dunsinane.) Movies are, happily, a popular medium (which makes it difficult to understand why Dwight Macdonald with his dedication to high art sacrifices his time to them), but does that mean that people must look to them for confirmation of their soggiest humanitarian sentiments? The prissy liberals who wouldn't give a man with the D.T.'s a quarter for a shot ("He'll waste it on drink") are just the ones who love the message they take out of *Ikiru*, not that one man did manage to triumph over bureaucracy but that the meaning of life is in doing a bit of goody good good for others. I have talked to a number of these people about why they hated *The Manchurian Candidate* and I swear not one of them can remember that when the liberal senator is killed, milk pours out. *Yojimbo* seems so simple, so marvelously obvious, but those who are sentimental don't get it: they think it's a mistake, that it couldn't have been intended as a killing comedy. It's true that even Shakespeare didn't dare give his clowns hot blood to drink. But Kurosawa dares.

{KPFA broadcast, 1962; *Partisan Review*, Summer 1963}

<h1 style="text-align: right">:: *Devi*</h1>

The Apu Trilogy has been widely acclaimed as a master-piece, which indeed it is, though I would guess that in the years since its release fewer Americans have seen it than have seen *David and Lisa* in any *week* since its release. Fewer have seen Satyajit Ray's new film, *Devi*, than have seen *David and Lisa* in any *night* since its release. Ingmar Bergman, who was also a slow starter with American audiences, has definitely caught on; why not Ray?

Bergman is sensual and erotic; he provides "stark" beauty and exposed nerves and conventional dramatic conflicts and a theme that passes for contemporary—the coldness of intellectuals. Husbands fail their wives and drive them crazy because they don't understand them and all that. (Really, it's not people who don't understand us who drive us nuts—it's when those who shouldn't, *do*.) But I would guess that what gives his movies their immense appeal is their semi-intellectual, or, to be more rude, "metaphysical" content. His characters are like schoolboys who have just heard the startling new idea that "God is dead"; this sets them off on torments of deep thought. Bergman's greatest "dark" film, *The Seventh Seal*, reminds one of the nightmares of life and death and religion that one had as a child; the sense of mystery and the questions that no one will answer suggest the way religious symbols function in childhood and in fear. Bergman's power over audiences is that he has not developed philosophically beyond the awesome questions: audiences trained in more rational philosophy still respond emotionally to Bergman's kind of mysticism, his searching for "the meaning of life," his fatalism, and the archaic ogres of childhood and religion. Bergman is not a deep thinker, but he is an artist who moves audiences deeply by calling up their buried fears and feelings.

People come out of his movies with "something to think about" or, at least, to talk about.

Those who find Bergman profound and sophisticated are very likely to find Satyajit Ray rather too simple. I think that Ray, like Kurosawa, is one of the great new film masters, and that his simplicity is a simplicity arrived at, achieved, a master's distillation from his experience; but it is—and this may be another reason why audiences prefer Bergman—the simplicity to which we must respond with *feeling*. It is not the simplicity of a film like *David and Lisa*—which is simplicity at a pre-art level, the simplicity of those who don't perceive complexities and have not yet begun to explore their medium.

People say that *David and Lisa* is a "heartfelt" experience, but they gobble it up so easily because it appeals to feelings they already had. It's a movie about mental disturbances that couldn't disturb anybody. Similarly, *Sundays and Cybèle*, also a phenomenal box-office success, is gobbled up as "artistic" (it's "artistic" the same way that *Harper's Bazaar* fiction is "beautifully literate"). Bosley Crowther says that *Sundays and Cybèle* is "what *Lolita* might conceivably have been had it been made by a poet and angled to be a rhapsodic song of innocence and not a smirking joke." Surely only a satirist like Nabokov could have invented this eminent critic whose praise gives the show away—"angled to be a rhapsodic song of innocence."

(One of the delights of life in San Francisco is observing the cultural chauvinism of New York from a safe distance. *Variety* informs us that improvement is expected in West Coast movie tastes now that the Western edition of the New York *Times* brings us Bosley Crowther. And Dwight Macdonald, who calls any place outside New York "the provinces," has a solution for the problems of American movies: they should be made closer to the intellectual life of the nation—in New York. But it's the Eastern banks, not the Western minds, that are destroying our movies.)

The concept of humanity is so strong in Ray's films that a man who functioned as a villain could only be a limitation of vision, a defect, an intrusion of melodrama into a work of art which seeks to illuminate experience and help us feel. There is, for example, a defect of this kind in De Sica's *Umberto D*: the landlady is unsympathetically caricatured so that we do not understand and respond to her as we do to the others in the film. I don't think Ray ever makes a mistake of this kind: his films are so far from the world of melodrama that such a mistake is almost unthinkable.

We see his characters not in terms of good or bad, but as we see ourselves, in terms of failures and weaknesses and strength and, above all, as part of a human continuum—fulfilling, altering, and finally accepting ourselves as part of this humanity, recognizing that no matter how much we want to burst the bounds of experience, there is only so much we can do. This larger view of human experience—the simplicity of De Sica at his best, of Renoir at his greatest, is almost miraculously present in every detail of Satyajit Ray's films. Ray's method is perhaps the most direct and least impaired by commercial stratagems in the whole history of film. He does not even invent dramatic devices, shortcuts to feelings. He made no passes at the commercial market; he didn't even reach out toward Western conceptions of drama and construction, although as one of the founders of the Calcutta film society, he must have been familiar with these conceptions. He seems to have had, from the beginning, the intuitive knowledge that this was not what he wanted.

In the background of almost every major new figure in film today we see the same great man—Jean Renoir. In France, the critic André Bazin taught a film-loving juvenile delinquent named François Truffaut "first" as Truffaut says, "to love Renoir and then to know him." The lives of Ray and Renoir intersected in 1950, when Ray, a young painter working as a layout artist for a British advertising firm, was struggling to work out a film treatment for *Pather Panchali*, and Renoir was in Calcutta filming *The River*, a movie that despite its weaknesses is perhaps a genre in itself— the only fictional film shot in a remote culture in which the director had the taste and sensitivity to present an outsider's view without condescension or a perfunctory "documentary" style. Ray has said that "the only kind of professional encouragement I got came from one single man"—Jean Renoir, who "insisted that I shouldn't give up."

There is a common misconception that Ray is a "primitive" artist and although, initially, this probably worked to his advantage in this country (*Pather Panchali* was taken to be autobiographical, and "true" and important because it dealt with rural poverty), it now works to his disadvantage, because his later films are taken to be corrupted by exposure to "art," and thus less "true." *The Apu Trilogy* expresses India in transition, showing the development of the boy Apu's consciousness from the primitive, medieval village life of *Pather Panchali* through the modern city streets and schools of Benares to the University of Calcutta in *Aparajito*, and then, in *The*

World of Apu, beyond self-consciousness to the destruction of his egotism, and the rebirth of feeling, the renewal of strength. But Ray himself is not a primitive artist any more than, say, Robert Flaherty was when he chronicled the life of the Eskimos in *Nanook of the North*. Ray was a highly educated man at the beginning of his film career, and he was influenced by a wide variety of films, those of Renoir and De Sica in particular. (Sent by his employers to England for three months in 1950, he went to more than ninety films, and he has reported that the one that helped most to clarify his ideas was *The Bicycle Thief*.) Among his other influences are certainly Dovzhenko's *Earth* and Eisenstein, and probably Von Sternberg. Just as *Nanook*, although a great work, seems primitive compared with a later, more complex Flaherty film like *Man of Aran*, *Pather Panchali* has a different kind of beauty, a more primitive kind, than later Ray films. But Ray's background is not Apu's: "My grandfather was a painter, a poet, and also a scientist who, in addition to editing the first children's magazine in Bengal, had introduced the half-tone block to India. My father was equally well known. He . . . wrote, among other works, Bengal's classic Book of Nonsense — an Englishman might call him India's Edward Lear." After graduating from the University of Calcutta with honors in physics and economics, the nineteen-year-old Ray, at the urging of Rabindranath Tagore, went to study at Tagore's school, Santiniketan. There, he "developed some skill in drawing" and "read widely in the history of art . . . studying in particular Chinese calligraphy." After Tagore's death, he left the school ("There were no films there and somehow, I don't know how it happened, but films appealed to me"). In Calcutta he worked as art director for a British advertising firm: "I stayed with them a long while and went through every department. When I was in a position to do so I introduced into their advertisements a fusion of modern western and Bengal tradition, to give it a new look."

In addition, he illustrated books, and it was after he had illustrated an edition of the popular novel *Pather Panchali* that he began to think about visualizing it on the screen.

What I lacked was first-hand acquaintance with the *milieu* of the story. I could, of course, draw upon the book itself, which was a kind of encyclopaedia of Bengali rural life, but I knew that this was not enough. In any case, one had only to drive six miles out of the city to get to the heart of the authentic village. While far from being an adventure in the physical sense, these explorations . . . nevertheless opened up a new and fascinating world. To one born and bred in the city, it had a new flavor, a new texture; and its values were different. It made you want to observe and probe, to catch the revealing details, the telling gestures, the particular turns of speech. You wanted to fathom the mysteries of "atmosphere."

Ray's statements and articles have been widely published, and his English is perfectly clear, but the critics can't resist the chance to play sahib. *Pather Panchali* provided Crowther with an opportunity for a classic example of his style and perception: "Chief among the delicate revelations that emerge from its loosely formed account of the pathetic little joys and sorrows of a poor Indian family in Bengal is the touching indication that poverty does not nullify love and that even the most afflicted people can find some modest pleasures in their worlds . . . Any picture as loose in structure or as listless in tempo as this one is would barely pass as a 'rough cut' in Hollywood." In a review of *Aparajito*, Kingsley Amis, then *Esquire*'s movie critic, thought that "Satyajit Ray, the director, seems to have set out with the idea of photographing without rearrangement the life of a poor Indian family, of reporting reality in as unshaped a form as possible." *The World of Apu*, which died at the box-office, got short shrift from Macdonald: "*Pather* was about a family in a village, *Apu* is about a young writer in a city, a more complex theme, and I'm not sure Ray is up to it." (Somehow he makes us feel that he's more sure than he ought to be; he condescends promiscuously.)

Each of the films of *The Apu Trilogy* represents a change, I think a development, of style. Unfortunately, those who responded to the slow rhythm of *Pather Panchali* felt that this pace was somehow more true to India than the faster pace of the third film, *The World of Apu*. But Ray's rhythm is derived from his subject matter, and for the college students and artists of *The World of Apu*, the leisurely flow of the seasons on which *Pather Panchali* was based would be ludicrous. Even those who prefer *Pather Panchali* to his later work should recognize that an artist cannot retain his first beautiful awkward expressiveness and innocence, and that to attempt to do so would mean redoing consciously what had been beautiful because it was not completely conscious. An artist must either give up art or develop. There are, of course, two ways of giving up: stopping altogether or taking the familiar Hollywood course—making tricks out of what was once done for love.

Ray began his film career with a masterpiece, and a trilogy at that; this makes it easy to shrug off his other films as very fine but not really up to the trilogy (even critics who disparaged each film of the trilogy as it appeared, now use the trilogy as the measure to disparage his other works). It is true that the other films are smaller in scope. But, if there had been no trilogy, I would say of *Devi*, "This is the greatest Indian film ever made." And if there had been no trilogy and no *Devi*, I would say the same of his still later *Two Daughters*, based on Tagore stories, of which the first, *The Postmaster*, is a pure and simple masterpiece of the filmed short story form. (The second has memorable scenes, beauty, and wit, but is rather wearying.) Ray's least successful film that has been imported, *The Music Room* (made early, for respite, between the second and third parts of the trilogy), has such grandeur in its best scenes that we must revise customary dramatic standards. By our usual standards it isn't a good movie: it's often crude and it's poorly constructed; but it's a great experience. It's a study of *noblesse oblige* carried to extremity, to a kind of aesthetic madness. It recalls the film of *The Magnificent Ambersons* and, of course, *The Cherry Orchard* but, more painfully, it calls up hideous memories of our own expansive gestures, our own big-role playing. We are forced to see the recklessness and egomania of our greatest moments—and at the same time we are forced to see the sordid banality of being practical. The hero is great *because* he destroys himself; he is also mad. I was exasperated by the defects of *The Music Room* when I saw it; now, a month later, I realize that I will never forget it. Worrying over its faults as a film is like worrying over whether *King Lear* is well constructed: it doesn't really matter.

Ray is sometimes (for us Westerners, and perhaps for Easterners also?) a little boring, but what major artist outside film and drama isn't? What he has to give is so rich, so contemplative in approach (and this we are completely unused to in the film medium—except perhaps in documentary) that we begin to accept our lapses of attention during the tedious moments with the same kind of relaxation and confidence and affection that we feel for the boring stretches in the great novels, the epic poems.

Although India is second only to Japan in the number of movies it produces, Ray is the *only* Indian director; he is, as yet, in a class by himself.

Despite the financial conditions under which he works, despite official disapproval of his themes, despite popular indifference to his work, he is in a position that almost any film maker anywhere in the world might envy. The Indian film industry is so thoroughly corrupt that Ray could start fresh, as if it did not exist. Consider the Americans, looking under stones for some tiny piece of subject matter they can call their own, and then judge the wealth, the prodigious, fabulous heritage that an imaginative Indian can draw upon. Just because there has been almost nothing of value done in films in India, the whole country and its culture is his to explore and express to the limits of his ability; he is the first major artist to draw upon these vast and ancient reserves. The Hollywood director who re-makes biblical spectacles or Fannie Hurst stories for the third or sixth or ninth time is a poor man—no matter how big his budget—compared to the first film artist of India. American directors of talent can still try to beat the system, can still feel that maybe they can do something worth doing, and every once in a while someone almost does. In India, the poverty of the masses, and their desperate *need* for escapist films, cancels out illusions. Ray knows he can't reach a mass audience in India (he can't spend more than $40,000 on a production). Outside of West Bengal, his films are not understood (Bengali is spoken by less than fifteen percent of India's population—of those, only twenty percent can read). In other provinces his films, subtitled, appeal only to the Indian equivalent of the American art-house audience—the urban intellectuals—not only because the masses and the rural audiences want their traditional extravaganzas but because they can't read. Probably India produces so many films just because of the general illiteracy; if Indians could read subtitles, American and European films might be more popular. (India has so many languages, it's impractical to dub for the illiterates—the only justification for dubbing, by the way.)

It's doubtful if Ray could finance his films at all without the international audience that he reaches, even though it's shockingly small and he doesn't reach it easily. Indian bureaucrats, as "image" conscious as our own, and much more powerful in the control of films, prefer to send abroad the vacuous studio productions which they assure us are "technically" superior to Ray's films (everyone and everything in them is so clean and shiny and false that they suggest interminable TV commercials).

Devi, based on a theme from Tagore, is here thanks to the personal intercession of Nehru, who removed the censors' export ban. According to official Indian policy, *Devi* is misleading in its view of Indian life. We can interpret this to mean that, even though the film is set in the nine-teenth century, the government is not happy about the world getting the idea that there are or ever were superstitions in India. In the film, the young heroine is believed by her rich father-in-law to be an incarnation of the goddess Kali. I don't know why the Indian government was so con-cerned about this—anyone who has ever tried to tell children how, for example, saints function in Catholic doctrine may recognize that we have a few things to explain, too. Those who grow up surrounded by Christian symbols and dogmas are hardly in a position to point a finger of shame at Kali worship—particularly as it seems so closely related to prayers to the Virgin Mary, Mother of God. As the film makes clear, Kali is generally called "Ma."

The film has so many Freudian undertones that I was not surprised when the film maker sitting next to me in the empty theater muttered, "Think what Buñuel would do with this." I'm grateful that it's Ray, not Buñuel, and that the undertones stay where they belong—down under. Buñuel would have made it explicit. Ray never tells us that this is the old man's way of taking his son's bride away from him; he doesn't tell us that this is the old man's way of punishing his Westernized, Christianized son; he never says that religion is the last outpost of the old man's sensuality, his return to childhood and "Ma" love. But we experience all this, just as we experience the easy drift of the lovely silly young girl into the auto-intoxication, the narcissism of believing that she *is* a goddess. She is cer-tainly beautiful enough. In one sense the film is about what Christians might call the sin of pride: the girl who finds it not too difficult to believe that she is a goddess, fails to cure the nephew she adores; when the child dies, she goes mad. But that is a Christian oversimplification: what we see is the girl's readiness to believe, her liquid acquiescence; not so much *pride* as a desire to please—the culmination, we suspect, of what the culture expects of a high-born girl. And, surrounded by so much luxury, what is there for the girl to do but try to please? The whole indolent life is centered on pleasure.

Ray creates an atmosphere that intoxicates us as well; the household is so rich and the rich people so overripe. The handsome, soft-eyed men in their silks and brocades are unspeakably fleshly; the half-naked beggars on the steps outside are clothed in their skins, but the rich are eroticized by their garments. And perhaps because of the camera work, which seems to derive from some of the best traditions of the silent screen and the thirties, perhaps because of the Indian faces themselves, the eyes have depths—and a disturbing look of helplessness—that we are unused to. It's almost as if these people were isolated from us and from each other by their eyes. It is not just that they seem exotic to us, but that each is a stranger to the others. Their eyes link them to the painted eyes of the Hindu idols, and, in the film, it is this religion which separates them. They are lost behind their eyes.

Sharmila Tagore (Tagore's great-granddaughter), fourteen when she played Apu's bride, is the seventeen-year-old goddess; she is exquisite, perfect (a word I don't use casually) in both these roles. And the men are wonderfully selected—so that they manage to suggest both the hand-someness of almost mythological figures and the rotting weakness of their way of life. Ray has been developing his own stock company, and anyone who mistook the principal players in the trilogy for people just acting out their own lives for the camera may be startled now to see them in a nine-teenth-century mansion. In the early parts of the trilogy, Ray was able to convince many people that he had simply turned his cameras on life; he performs the same miracle of art on this decadent, vanished period. The setting of *Devi* seems to have been caught by the camera just before it decays. The past is preserved for us, disturbingly, ironically, in its jeweled frame. Are we not perhaps in the position of the "advanced," ineffective young husband who knows that his childish wife can't be Kali because he has "progressed" from Kali worship to the idols of Christianity? (Can we distinguish belief in progress from the sin of pride?)

It is a commentary on the values of *our* society that those who saw truth and greatness in *The Apu Trilogy*, particularly in the opening film with its emphasis on the mother's struggle to feed the family, are not drawn to a film in which Ray shows the landowning class and its collapse of beliefs. It is part of *our* heritage from the thirties that the poor still seem "real" and the rich "trivial." *Devi* should, however, please even Marxists if they would go to see it; it is the most convincing study of upper-class decadence I have ever seen. But it is Ray's feeling for the beauty within this disinte-grating way of life that makes it convincing. Eisenstein cartooned the upper classes and made them hateful; they became puppets in the show he was staging. Ray, by giving them the respect and love that he gives the poor and struggling, helps us to understand their demoralization. The rich, deluded father-in-law of *Devi* is as human in his dreamy sensuality as Apu's own poet father. Neither can sustain his way of life or his beliefs against the new pressures; and neither can adapt.

Like Renoir and De Sica, Ray sees that life itself is good no matter how bad it is. It is difficult to discuss art which is an affirmation of life, without fear of becoming maudlin. But is there any other kind of art, on screen or elsewhere? "In cinema," Ray says, "we must select everything for the camera according to the richness of its power to reveal."

{KPFA broadcast, 1962; *Partisan Review*, Summer 1963}

:: *Hud*, Deep in the Divided Heart of Hollywood

As a schoolgirl, my suspiciousness about those who attack American "materialism" was first aroused by the refugees from Hitler who so often contrasted their "culture" with our "vulgar materialism" when I discovered that their "culture" consisted of their having had servants in Europe, and a swooning acquaintance with the poems of Rilke, the novels of Stefan Zweig and Lion Feuchtwanger, the music of Mahler and Bruckner. And as the cultural treasures they brought over with them were likely to be Meissen porcelain, Biedermeier furniture, oriental carpets, wax fruit, and bookcases with glass doors, it wasn't too difficult to reconstruct their "culture" and discover that it was a stuffier, more middle-class materialism and sentimentality than they could afford in the new world.

These suspicions were intensified by later experience: the most grasping Europeans were, almost inevitably, the ones who leveled the charge of American materialism. Just recently, at a film festival, a behind-the-iron-curtain movie director, who interrupted my interview with him to fawn over every Hollywood dignitary (or supposed dignitary) who came in sight, concluded the interview with, "You Americans won't understand this, but I don't make movies just for money."

Americans are so vulnerable, so confused and defensive about prosperity —and nowhere more so than in Hollywood, where they seem to feel they can cleanse it, justify their right to it, by gilding it with "culture," as if to say, see, we're not materialistic, we appreciate the finer things. ("The hunting scene on the wall of the cabana isn't wallpaper: it's handpainted.")

Those who live by making movies showing a luxurious way of life worry over the American "image" abroad. But, the economics of moviemaking being what they are, usually all the producers do about it is worry—which is probably just as well because films made out of social conscience have generally given an even more distorted view of America than those made out of business sense, and are much less amusing.

The most conspicuous recent exception is *Hud*—one of the few entertaining American movies released in 1963 and just possibly the most completely schizoid movie produced anywhere anytime. *Hud* is a commercial Hollywood movie that is ostensibly an indictment of materialism, and it has been accepted as that by most of the critics. But those who made it protected their material interest in the film so well that they turned it into the opposite: a celebration and glorification of materialism—of the man who looks out for himself—which probably appeals to movie audiences just because it confirms their own feelings. This response to *Hud* may be the only time the general audience has understood film makers better than they understood themselves. Audiences ignored the cant of the makers' liberal, serious intentions, and enjoyed the film for its vital element: the nihilistic "heel" who wants the good things of life and doesn't give a damn for the general welfare. The writers' and director's "anti-materialism" turns out to be a lot like the refugees' anti-materialism: they had their Stefan Zweig side—young, tender Lon (Brandon de Wilde) and Melvyn Douglas's Homer, a representative of the "good" as prating and tedious as Polonius; and they had their protection, their solid salable property of Meissen and Biedermeier, in Paul Newman.

Somehow it all reminds one of the old apochryphal story conference— "It's a modern western, see, with this hell-raising, pleasure-loving man who doesn't respect any of the virtues, and, at the end, we'll fool them, he doesn't get the girl and he doesn't change!"

"But who'll want to see *that?*"

"Oh, that's all fixed—we've got Paul Newman for the part."

They could cast him as a mean man and know that the audience would never believe in his meanness. For there are certain actors who have such extraordinary audience rapport that the audience does not believe in their villainy except to relish it, as with Brando; and there are others, like Newman, who in addition to this rapport, project such a traditional heroic frankness and sweetness that the audience dotes on them, seeks to protect them from harm or pain. Casting Newman as a mean materialist is like writing a manifesto against the banking system while juggling your investments so you can break the bank. Hud's shouted last remark, his poor credo, "The world's so full of crap a man's going to get into it sooner or later, whether he's careful or not," has, at least, the ring of *his* truth. The generalized pious principles of the good old codger belong to nobody.

The day *Hud* opened in San Francisco the theater was packed with an audience that laughed and reacted with pleasure to the verve and speed and economy, and (although I can't be sure of this) enjoyed the surprise of the slightly perverse ending as much as I did. It was like the split movies of the war years—with those cynical heel-heroes whom we liked because they expressed contempt for the sanctimonious goody guys and over-stuffed family values, and whom we still liked (because they were played by actors who *seemed* contemptuous) even when they reformed.

It's not likely that those earlier commercial writers and directors were self-deceived about what they were doing: they were trying to put something over, and knew they could only go so far. They made the hero a "heel" so that we would identify with his rejection of official values, and then slyly squared everything by having him turn into a conventional hero. And it seems to me that we (my college friends) and perhaps the audience at large didn't take all this very seriously, that we enjoyed it for its obvious hokum and glamour and excitement and romance, and for the wisecracking American idiom, and the tempo and rhythm of slick style. We enjoyed the *pretense* that the world was like this—fast and funny; this pretense which was necessary for its enjoyment separated the good American commercial movie—the good "hack" job like *Casablanca* or *To Have and Have Not*—from film art and other art. This was the best kind of Hollywood *product*: the result of the teamwork of talented, highly paid professional hacks who were making a living; and we enjoyed it as a product, and assumed that those involved in it enjoyed the money they made.

What gave the Hollywood movie its vitality and its distinctive flavor was that despite the melodramatic situations, the absurd triumphs of virtue and the inordinate punishments for trivial vice—perhaps even because of the stale conventions and the necessity to infuse some life that would make the picture seem new within them—the "feel" of the time and place (Hollywood, whatever the locale of the story) came through, and often the attitudes, the problems, the tensions. Sometimes more of American life came through in routine thrillers and prison-break films and even in the yachting-set comedies than in important, "serious" films like *The Best Years of Our Lives* or *A Place in the Sun*, paralyzed, self-conscious imitations of European art, or films like *Gentleman's Agreement*, with the indigenous paralysis of the Hollywood "problem" picture, which is morally solved in advance. And when the commercial film makers had some freedom and leeway, as well as talent, an extraordinary amount came through—the rhythm of American life that gives films like *She Done Him Wrong*, *I'm No Angel*, the Rogers-Astaire musicals, *Bringing Up Baby*, *The Thin Man*, *The Lady Eve*, *Double Indemnity*, *Strangers on a Train*, *Pat and Mike*, *The Crimson Pirate*, *Singin' in the Rain*, *The Big Sleep*, or the more recent *The Manchurian Candidate* and *Charade* a freshness and spirit that makes them unlike the films of any other country. Our movies are the best proof that Americans are liveliest and freest when we don't take ourselves too seriously.

Taking *Hud* as a commercial movie, I was interested to see that the audience reacted to Hud as a Stanley Kowalski on the range, laughing with his coarseness and sexual assertiveness, and sharing his contempt for social values. Years before, when I saw the movie version of *A Streetcar Named Desire*, I was shocked and outraged at those in the audience who expressed their delight when Brando as Stanley jeered at Blanche. At the time, I didn't understand it when they laughed their agreement as Stanley exploded in rage and smashed things. It was only later, away from the spell of Vivien Leigh's performance, that I could reflect that Stanley was clinging to his brute's bit of truth, his sense that her gentility and coquetry were intolerably fake. And it seemed to me that this was one of the reasons why *Streetcar* was a great play—that Blanche and Stanley upset us, and complicated our responses. This was no Lillian Hellman melodrama with good and evil clay pigeons. The conflict was genuine and dramatic. But Hud didn't have a dramatic adversary; his adversaries *were* out of Lillian Hellmanland.

The setting, however, wasn't melodramatic, it was comic—not the legendary west of myth-making movies like the sluggish *Shane* but the modern West I grew up in, the ludicrous real West. The comedy was in the realism: the incongruities of Cadillacs and cattle, crickets and transistor radios, jukeboxes, Dr. Pepper signs, paperback books—all emphasizing the standardization of culture in the loneliness of vast spaces. My West wasn't Texas; it was northern California, but our Sonoma County ranch was very much like this one — with the frame house, and "the couple's" cabin like the housekeeper's cabin, and the hired hands' bunkhouse, and my father and older brothers charging over dirt roads, not in Cadillacs but in Studebakers, and the Saturday nights in the dead little town with its movie house and ice cream parlor. This was the small-town West I and so many of my friends came out of — escaping from the swaggering small-town hotshots like Hud. But I didn't remember any boys like Brandon de Wilde's Lon: he wasn't born in the West or in anybody's imagination; that seventeen-year-old blank sheet of paper has been handed down from generations of lazy hack writers. His only "reality" is from de Wilde's having played the part before: from *Shane* to *Hud*, he has been our observer, our boy in the West, testing heroes. But in *Hud*, he can't fill even this cardboard role of representing the spectator because Newman's Hud has himself come to represent the audience. And I didn't remember any clean old man like Melvyn Douglas's Homer: his principles and rectitude weren't created either, they were handed down from the authors' mouthpieces of the socially conscious plays and movies of the thirties and forties. Occupied towns in the war movies frequently spawned these righteous, prophetic elder citizens.

Somewhere in the back of my mind, Hud began to stand for the people who would vote for Goldwater, while Homer was clearly an upstanding Stevensonian. And it seemed rather typical of the weakness of the whole message picture idea that the good liberals who made the film made their own spokesman a fuddy-duddy, worse, made him inhuman — except for the brief sequence when he isn't a spokesman for anything, when he follows the bouncing ball and sings "Clementine" at the movies. Hud, the "villain" of the piece, is less phony than Homer.

In the next few days I recommended *Hud* to friends (and now "friends" no longer mean college students but academic and professional people) and was bewildered when they came back indignant that I'd wasted their time. I was even more bewildered when the reviews started coming out; what were the critics talking about? Unlike the laughing audience, they were taking *Hud* at serious message value as a work of integrity, and, even in some cases, as a tragedy. In the New York *Herald Tribune*, Judith Crist found that "Both the portraits and the people are completely without compromise—and therein is not only the foundation but also the rare achievement of this film." In the *Saturday Review*, Arthur Knight said that "it is the kind of creative collaboration too long absent from our screen . . . by the end of the film, there can be no two thoughts about Hud: he's purely and simply a bastard. And by the end of the film, for all his charm, he has succeeded in alienating everyone, including the audience." According to Bosley Crowther in the New York *Times*:

> Hud is a rancher who is fully and foully diseased with all the germs of materialism that are infecting and sickening modern man . . . And the place where he lives is not just Texas. It is the whole country today. It is the soil in which grows a gimcrack culture that nurtures indulgence and greed. Here is the essence of this picture. While it looks like a modern Western, and is an outdoor drama, indeed, *Hud* is as wide and profound a contemplation of the human condition as one of the New England plays of Eugene O'Neill. . . . The striking, important thing about it is the clarity with which it unreels. The sureness and integrity of it are as crystal-clear as the plot is spare . . . The great key scene of the film, a scene in which [the] entire herd of cattle is deliberately and dutifully destroyed . . . helps fill the screen with an emotion that I've seldom felt from any film. It brings the theme of infection and destruction into focus with dazzling clarity.

As usual, with that reverse acumen that makes him invaluable, Crowther has put his finger on a sore spot. The director carefully builds up the emotion that Crowther and probably audiences in general feel when the cattle, confused and trying to escape, are forced into the mass grave that has been dug by a bulldozer, and are there systematically shot down, covered with lime, and buried. This is the movie's big scene, and it can be no accident that the scene derives some of its emotional power from the Nazis' final solution of the Jewish problem; it's inconceivable that these overtones would not have occurred to the group—predominantly Jewish—who made the film. Within the terms of the story, this emotion that is worked up is wrong, because it is not Hud the bad man who wants to destroy the herd; it is Homer the good man who accedes to what is necessary to stop the spread of infection. And is all this emotion appropriate to the slaughter of animals who were, after all, raised to be slaughtered and would, in the normal course of events, be even more *brutally* slaughtered in a few weeks? What's involved is simply the difference in money between what the government pays for the killing of the animals and their market value. It would not have been difficult for the writers and director to arrange the action so that the audience would feel quick relief at the destruction of the herd. But I would guess that they couldn't resist the opportunity for a big emotional scene, a scene with *impact*, even though the emotions don't support the meaning of the story. They got their big scene: it didn't matter what it meant.

So it's pretty hard to figure out the critical congratulations for clarity and integrity, or such statements as Penelope Gilliatt's in the *Observer*, "*Hud* is the most sober and powerful film from America for a long time. The line of it is very skillfully controlled: the scene when Melvyn Douglas's diseased cattle have to be shot arrives like the descent of a Greek plague." Whose error are the gods punishing? Was Homer, in buying Mexican cattle, merely taking a risk, or committing hubris? One of the things you learn on a ranch, or any other place, is that nobody is responsible for natural catastrophes; one of the things you learn in movies and other dramatic forms is the symbolic use of catastrophe. The locusts descended on Paul Muni in *The Good Earth* because he had gotten rich and *bad*: a farmer in the movies who neglects his humble wife and goes in for high living is sure to lose his crops. *Hud* plays it both ways: the texture of the film is wisecracking naturalism, but when a powerful sequence is needed to jack up the action values, a disaster is used for all the symbolic overtones that can be hit—and without any significant story meaning. I don't think the line of *Hud* is so much "controlled" as adjusted, set by conflicting aims at seriousness and success.

It hardly seems possible but perhaps Crowther thought the *cattle* were symbolically "fully and foully diseased with all the germs of materialism that are infecting and sickening modern man." Those sick cattle must have *something* to do with the language he uses in describing the film. "It is a drama of moral corruption—of the debilitating disease of avaricious self-seeking—that is creeping across the land and infecting the minds of young people in this complex, materialistic age. It is forged in the smoldering confrontation of an aging cattleman and his corrupted son." Scriptwriters have only to toss in a few bitter asides about our expense-account civilization and strew a few platitudes like, "Little by little the country changes because of the men people admire," and the movie becomes "a drama of moral corruption."

The English critics got even more out of it: Derek Prouse experienced a "catharsis" in *The Sunday Times*, as did Peter John Dyer in *Sight and Sound*. Dyer seems to react to cues from his experience at *other* movies; his review, suggesting as it does a super-fan's identification with the film makers' highest aspirations, is worth a little examination. "From the ominous discovery of the first dead heifer, to the massacre of the diseased herd, to Homer's own end and Hud's empty inheritance of a land he passively stood by and watched die, the story methodically unwinds like a python lying sated in the sun." People will be going to *Hud*, as Charles Addams was reported to have gone to *Cleopatra*, "to see the snake." Dyer squeezes out more meaning and lots more symbolism than the film makers could squeeze in. (A) Homer just suddenly up and died, of a broken heart, one supposes. It wasn't prepared for, it was merely convenient. (B) Hud's inheritance isn't empty: he has a large ranch, and the land has oil. Dyer projects the notion of Hud's emptiness as a human being onto his inheritance. (C) Hud didn't passively stand by and watch the land die. The *land* hasn't changed. Nor was Hud passive: he worked the ranch, and he certainly couldn't be held responsible for the cattle becoming infected—unless Dyer wants to go so far as to view that infection as a symbol of or a punishment for Hud's sickness. Even Homer, who blamed Hud for just about everything else, didn't accuse him of infecting the cattle. Dyer would perhaps go that far, because somehow "the aridity of the cattle-less landscape mirrors his own barren future." Why couldn't it equally mirror Homer's barren past? In this scheme of symbolic interpretation, if there was a dog on the ranch, and it had worms, Hud the worm would be the reason. Writing of the "terse and elemental polarity of the film," Dyer says, "The earth is livelihood, freedom and death to Homer; an implacably hostile prison to Hud"—though it would be just as easy, and perhaps more true to the audience's experience of the film, to interpret Hud's opportunism as love of life and Homer's righteousness as rigid and life-destroying—and *unfair*. The scriptwriters give Homer principles (which are hardly likely to move the audience); but they're careful to show that Hud is misunderstood and rejected when he makes affectionate overtures to his father.

Dyer loads meaning onto Hud's actions and behavior: for example,

"Instead of bronco-busting he goes in for a (doubtless) metaphorical bout of pig-wrestling." Why "instead of"—as if there were bronco-busting to do and he dodged it—when there is nothing of the kind in the film? And what would the pig-wrestling be a metaphor for? Does Dyer take pigs to represent women, or does he mean that the pig-wrestling shows Hud's swinishness? Having watched my older brothers trying to catch greased pigs in this traditional western small-town sport, I took the sequence as an indication of how boring and empty small-town life is, and how coarse the games in which the boys work off a little steam. I had seen the same boys who wrestled greased pigs and who had fairly crude ideas of sex and sport enter a blazing building to save the lives of panic-stricken horses, and emerge charred but at peace with the world and themselves.

Are the reviewers trying to justify having enjoyed the movie, or just looking for an angle, when they interpret the illustrative details *morally?* Any number of them got their tip on Hud's character by his taking advantage of a husband's absence to go to bed with the wife. But he couldn't very well make love to her when her husband was home—although that would be par for the course of "art" movies these days. The summer nights are very long on a western ranch. As a child, I could stretch out on a hammock on the porch and read an Oz book from cover to cover while my grandparents and uncles and aunts and parents didn't stir from their card game. The young men get tired of playing cards. They either think about sex or try to do something about it. There isn't much else to do—the life doesn't exactly stimulate the imagination, though it does stimulate the senses. Dyer takes as proof of Hud's bad character that "his appetites are reserved for married women." What alternatives are there for a young man in a small town? Would it be proof of a *good* character to seduce young girls and wreck their reputations? There are always a few widows, of course, and, sometimes, a divorcee like Alma, the housekeeper. (Perhaps the first female equivalent of the "white Negro" in our films: Patricia Neal plays Alma as the original author Larry McMurtry described the Negro housekeeper, the "chuckling" Halmea with "her rich teasing laugh.") But they can hardly supply the demand from the married men, who are in a better position to give them favors, jobs, presents, houses, and even farms. I remember my father taking me along when he visited our local widow: I played in the new barn which was being constructed by workmen who seemed to take their orders from my father. At six or seven, I was very proud of my father for being the protector of widows.

I assumed the audience enjoyed and responded to Hud's chasing women because this represented a break with western movie conventions and myths, and as the film was flouting these conventions and teasing the audience to enjoy the change, it didn't occur to me that in *this* movie his activity would be construed as "bad." But Crowther finds that the way Hud "indulges himself with his neighbor's wife" is "one of the sure, unmistakable tokens of a dangerous social predator." Is this knowledge derived from the film (where I didn't discover it) or from Crowther's knowledge of life? If the latter, I can only supply evidence against him from my own life. My father who was adulterous, and a Republican who, like Hud, was opposed to any government interference, was in no sense and in no one's eyes a social predator. He was generous and kind, and democratic in the western way that Easterners still don't understand: it was not out of guilty condescension that mealtimes were communal affairs with the Mexican and Indian ranchhands joining the family, it was the way Westerners lived.

If Homer, like my father, had frequented married women or widows, would Dyer interpret that as a symbol of Homer's evil? Or, as Homer voiced sentiments dear to the scriptwriters and critics, would his "transgressions" be interpreted as a touching indication of human frailty? What Dyer and others took for symbols were the clichés of melodrama—where character traits are sorted out and separated, one set of attitudes and behavior for the good characters, another for the bad characters. In melodrama, human desires and drives make a person weak or corrupt: the heroic must be the unblemished good like Homer, whose goodness is not tainted with understanding. Reading the cues this way, these critics missed what audiences were reacting to, just as Richard Whitehall in *Films and Filming* describes Newman's Hud as "the-hair-on-the-chest-male"—although the most exposed movie chest since Valentino's is just as hairless.

I suppose we're all supposed to react on cue to movie rape (or as is usually the case, attempted rape); rape, like a cattle massacre, is a box-office value. No doubt in *Hud* we're really supposed to believe that Alma is, as Stanley Kauffmann says, "driven off by his [Hud's] vicious physical assault." But in terms of the modernity of the settings and the characters, as well as the age of the protagonists (they're at least in their middle thirties), it was more probable that Alma left the ranch because a frustrated rape is just too sordid and embarrassing for all concerned—for the drunken Hud who forced himself upon her, for her for defending herself so titanically, for young Lon the innocent who "saved" her. Alma obviously wants to go to bed with Hud, but she has been rejecting his propositions because she doesn't want to be just another casual dame to him; she wants to be treated differently from the others. If Lon hadn't rushed to protect his idealized view of her, chances are that the next morning Hud would have felt guilty and repentant, and Alma would have been grateful to him for having used the violence necessary to break down her resistance, thus proving that she *was* different. They might have been celebrating ritual rapes annually on their anniversaries.

Rape is a strong word when a man knows that a woman wants him but won't accept him unless he commits himself emotionally. Alma's mixture of provocative camaraderie plus reservations invites "rape." (Just as, in a different way, Blanche DuBois did—though Williams erred in having her go mad: it was enough, it was really *more*, that she was broken, finished.) The scriptwriters for *Hud*, who, I daresay, are as familiar as critics with theories of melodrama, know that heroes and villains both want the same things and that it is their way of trying to get them that separates one from the other. They impart this knowledge to Alma, who tells Hud that she wanted him and he could have had her if he'd gone about it differently. But this kind of knowingness, employed to make the script more clever, more frank, more modern, puts a strain on the credibility of the melodramatic actions it explicates—and embellishes. Similarly, the writers invite a laugh by having Alma, seeing the nudes Lon has on his wall, say, "I'm a girl, they don't do a thing for me." Before the Kinsey report on women, a woman might say, "They don't do a thing for me," but she wouldn't have prefaced it with "I'm a girl" because she wouldn't have known that erotic reactions to pictures are not characteristic of women.

The Ravetches have been highly praised for the screenplay: Penelope Gilliatt considers it "American writing at its abrasive best"; Brendan Gill says it is "honestly written"; *Time* calls it "a no-compromise script." Dyer expresses a fairly general view when he says it's "on a level of sophistication totally unexpected from their scripts for two of Ritt's least successful, Faulkner-inspired films." This has some special irony because not only is their technique in *Hud* a continuation of the episodic method they used in combining disparate Faulkner stories into *The Long Hot Summer*, but the dialogue quoted most appreciatively by the reviewers to illustrate their new skill (Alma's rebuff of Hud, "No thanks, I've had one cold-hearted bastard in my life, I don't want another") is lifted almost verbatim from that earlier script (when it was Joanne Woodward telling off Paul Newman). They didn't get acclaim for their integrity and honesty that time because, although the movie was entertaining and a box-office hit, the material was resolved as a jolly comedy, the actors and actresses were paired off, and Newman as Ben Quick the barn burner turned out not really to be a barn burner after all. They hadn't yet found the "courage" that keeps Hud what *Time* called him, "an unregenerate heel" and "a cad to the end." It may have taken them several years to learn that with enough close-ups of his blue, blue eyes and his hurt, sensitive mouth, Newman's Ben Quick could have burned barns all right, and audiences would have loved him more for it.

In neither film do the episodes and characters hold together, but Ritt, in the interim having made Hemingway's *Adventures of a Young Man* and failed to find a style appropriate to it, has now, with the aid of James Wong Howe's black and white cinematography, found something like a reasonably clean visual equivalent for Hemingway's prose. Visually *Hud* is so apparently simple and precise and unadorned, so skeletonic, that we may admire the bones without being quite sure of the name of the beast. This Westerner is part gangster, part *Champion*, part rebel-without-a-cause, part the traditional cynic-hero who pretends not to care because he cares so much. (And it is also part *Edge of the City*, at least the part about Hud's having accidentally killed his brother and Homer's blaming him for it. Ritt has plagiarized his first film in true hack style: the episode was integral in *Edge of the City* and the friendship of Cassavetes and Poitier—probably the most beautiful scenes Ritt has directed—drew meaning from it; in *Hud* it's a fancy "traumatic" substitute for explaining why Hud and Homer don't get along.)

When *Time* says *Hud* is "the most brazenly honest picture to be made in the U.S. this season" the key word is brazenly. The film brazens it out. In the *New Yorker* Brendan Gill writes, "It's an attractive irony of the situation that, despite the integrity of its makers, *Hud* is bound to prove a box-office smash. I find this coincidence gratifying. Virtue is said to be its own reward, but money is nice, too, and I'm always pleased to see it flowing toward people who have had other things on their minds." Believing in this coincidence is like believing in Santa Claus. Gill's last sentence lacks another final "too." In Hollywood, a "picture with integrity" is a moneymaking message picture. And that's what Crowther means when he says, "*Hud* is a film that does its makers, the medium and Hollywood proud." He means something similar when he calls his own praise of the film a "daring endorsement"—as if it placed him in some kind of jeopardy to be so forthright.

If most of the critics who acclaimed the film appeared as innocent as Lon and as moralistic as Homer, Dwight Macdonald, who perceived that "it is poor Hud who is forced by the script to openly practice the actual as against the mythical American Way of Life," regarded this perception as proof of the stupidity of the film.

But the movie wouldn't necessarily be a good movie if its moral message was dramatically sustained in the story and action, and perhaps it isn't necessarily a bad movie if its moral message is not sustained in the story and action. By all formal theories, a work that is split cannot be a work of art, but leaving the validity of these principles aside, do they hold for lesser works—not works of art but works of commerce and craftsmanship, sometimes fused by artistry? Is a commercial piece of entertainment (which may or may not aspire to be, or pretend to be, a work of art) necessarily a poor one if its material is confused or duplicit, or reveals elements at variance with its stated theme, or shows the divided intentions of the craftsmen who made it? My answer is no, that in some films the more ambivalence that comes through, the more the film may mean to us or the more fun it may be. The process by which an idea for a movie is turned into the product that reaches us is so involved, and so many compromises, cuts, and changes may have taken place, so much hope and disgust and spoilage and waste may be embodied in it or mummified in it, that the tension in the product, or some sense of urgency still left in it, may be our only contact with the life in which the product was processed. Commercial products in which we do not sense or experience divided hopes and aims and ideas may be the dullest—ones in which everything alive was processed out, or perhaps ones that were never alive even at the beginning. *Hud* is so astutely made and yet such a mess that it tells us much more than its message. It is redeemed by its fundamental dishonesty. It is perhaps an archetypal Hollywood movie: split in so many revealing ways that, like *On the Waterfront* or *From Here to Eternity*, it is the movie of its year (even though it's shallow and not nearly so good a film as either of them).

My friends were angry that I'd sent them to *Hud* because, like Macdonald, they "saw through it," they saw that Hud was not the villain, and they knew that though he expressed vulgar notions that offended *them*, these notions might not be unpopular. The film itself flirts with this realization: when Homer is berating Hud, Lon asks, "Why pick on Hud, Grandpa? Nearly everybody around town is like him."

My friends, more or less socialist, detest a crude Hud who doesn't believe in government interference because they believe in more, and more drastic, government action to integrate the schools and end discrimination in housing and employment. However, they are so anti-CIA that at Thanksgiving dinner a respected professor could drunkenly insist that he had positive proof that the CIA had engineered the murder of Kennedy with no voice but mine raised in doubt. They want centralized power when it works for their civil-libertarian aims, but they dread and fear its international policies. They hate cops but call them at the first hint of a prowler: they are split, and it shows in a million ways. I imagine they're very like the people who made *Hud*, and like them they do rather well for themselves. They're so careful to play the game at their jobs that if they hadn't told you that they're *really* screwing the system, you'd never guess it.

[*Film Quarterly*, Summer 1964]

from
KISS KISS
BANG BANG

:: Laurence Olivier as Othello

Othello with Laurence Olivier is a filmed record of the theatrical production; it would be our loss if we waited for posterity to discover it. Olivier's Negro Othello—deep voice with a trace of foreign music in it; happy, thick, self-satisfied laugh; rolling buttocks; grand and barbaric and, yes, a little lewd—almost makes this great, impossible play work. It has always made more than sense; now it almost makes sense, too—not only dramatic poetry, but a comprehensible play. Frank Finlay's pale, parched little Iago is not a plotting maniac who's lucky for theatrical convenience, but a man consumed with sexual jealousy and irrational hatred. And because Iago is consumed by sexual jealousy, he infects Othello with the same disease. Maggie Smith's Desdemona is strong and quiet and willful enough to have wanted Othello and gone after him. And Othello, who thought himself almost accepted by these civilized whites, is destroyed by primitive, irrational forces in them that he has no knowledge of. His "civilization" is based on theirs and goes because he believed in theirs.

Olivier is the most physical Othello imaginable. As a lord, this Othello is a little vulgar—too ingratiating, a boaster, an arrogant man. Reduced to barbarism, he shows us a maimed African prince inside the warrior-hero. Iago's irrationality has stripped him bare to a different kind of beauty. We are sorry to see it, and we are not sorry, either. To our eyes, the African prince is more beautiful in his isolation than the fancy courtier in his reflected white glory.

Part of the pleasure of the performance is, of course, the sheer feat of Olivier's transforming himself into a Negro; yet it is not wasted effort, not mere exhibitionism or actor's vanity, for what Negro actor at this stage in the world's history could dare bring to the role the effrontery that Olivier does, and which Negro actor could give it this reading? I saw Paul Robeson and he was not black as Olivier is; Finlay can hate Olivier in a way José Ferrer did not dare—indeed did not have the provocation—to hate Robeson. Possibly Negro actors need to sharpen themselves on white roles before they can *play* a Negro. It is not enough to *be*: for great drama, it is the awareness that is everything.

Every time we single out the feature that makes Olivier a marvel—his lion eyes or the voice and the way it seizes on a phrase—he alters it or casts it off in some new role, and is greater than ever. It is no special asset, it is the devilish audacity and courage of this man. Olivier, who, for Othello, changed his walk, changed his talk, is a man close to sixty who, in an ordinary suit in an ordinary role, looks an ordinary man, and can look even smaller in a role like Archie Rice in *The Entertainer*. What is extraordinary is inside, and what is even more extraordinary is his determination to give it outer form. He has never leveled off; he goes on soaring.

Olivier once said of his interpretation of Henry V: "When you are young, you are too bashful to play a hero; you debunk it. It isn't until you're older that you can understand the pictorial beauty of heroism." And perhaps there is a tendency for people to debunk the kind of heroism necessary to develop your art in a society that offers so many rewards and honors to those who give up and sell out early at the highest market price. One might suspect that in a democratic society the public is on better terms with the mighty after they have fallen. Our mass media are full of the once mighty: they are called "celebrities." Olivier's presence on the screen is the pictorial beauty of heroism. Perhaps that is why we may leave the photographed version of *Othello* with a sense of exaltation and the wonder of sheer admiration.

This *Othello* is history already; it's something to remember. And *Othello* isn't even much of a "movie." Just a reasonably faithful (one assumes) record of a stage interpretation. After thirty-five years in movies and masterpiece upon masterpiece acclaimed in the theatre—every new season seems to bring the tidings that Olivier has exceeded himself as Oedipus, as Lear, in Chekhov—he still could not raise the money to do a real movie version of his Othello. And of his Macbeth, acclaimed as the greatest since—Macbeth, we have not even a record.

Olivier's greatness is in his acting; as a movie director, he is merely excellent and intelligent. Yet his Shakespearean performances deserve—at the minimum—the kind of movie he or other talented directors might do, what he brought to *Henry V*, *Hamlet*, *Richard III*. It is a scandal, an indictment of Anglo-American civilization and values, that eight million dollars can go into a spy spoof, twelve into a comic chase, twenty-seven into a spectacle, and for Olivier in *Othello*, we and history must content ourselves with a quickie recording process. And yet the joke is on the spoofs, chases and spectacles. *Othello* lives.

Yes, it's lovely that foundations give all that money to regional theatres, to training ballet students, to raising the pay of symphony orchestras, to encouraging the young and promising and possibly gifted, and that our government is talking about encouraging "standards of excellence"—that eerie schoolteacher's terminology that suggests magical measuring sticks. But do artists have to *aspire* to "excellence" to get help? Where is the help when they have overachieved their promise? Where is the help when Orson Welles botched his great movie version of *Othello* for want of cash, when Olivier can only record a stage production on film? What, then, is the purpose of all the encouragement of "creativity"?

The movies, the one art that people don't have to be encouraged, prodded, or "stimulated" to enjoy, which they go to without the path being greased by education and foundations, are still at the mercy of the economics of the mass market, which have broken the heart of almost every artist who has tried to work in the movies.

{*McCall's*, March 1966}

:: Marlon Brando:
An American Hero

      The history of the motion-picture industry might be summed up as the development from the serials with the blade in the sawmill moving closer and closer to the heroine's neck, to modern movies with the laser beam zeroing in on James Bond's crotch. At this level, the history of movies is a triumph of technology. I'm not putting down this kind of movie: I don't know anybody who doesn't enjoy it more or less at some time or other. But I wouldn't be much interested if that were the only kind of movie, any more than I'd be interested if all movies were like *Last Year at Marienbad* or *The Red Desert* or *Juliet of the Spirits*. What of the other kinds?

      While American enthusiasm for movies has never been so high, and even while teachers prepare to recognize film-making as an art, American movies have never been so contemptible. In other parts of the world there has been a new golden age: great talents have fought their way through in Japan, India, Sweden, Italy, France; even in England there has been something that passes for a renaissance. But not here: American enthusiasm is fed largely by foreign films, memories, and innocence. The tragic or, depending on your point of view, pitiful history of American movies in the last fifteen years may be suggested by a look at the career of Marlon Brando.

      It used to be said that great clowns, like Chaplin, always wanted to play Hamlet, but what happens in this country is that our Hamlets, like John Barrymore, turn into buffoons, shamelessly, pathetically mocking their public reputations. Bette Davis has made herself lovable by turning herself into a caricature of a harpy—just what, in one of her last good roles, as Margo Channing in *All About Eve*, she feared she was becoming. The women who were the biggest stars of the forties are either retired, semi-retired, or, like Davis, Crawford, and de Havilland, have become the mad queens of Grand Guignol in the sixties, grotesques and comics, sometimes inadvertently.

Marlon Brando's career indicates the new speed of these processes. Brando, our most powerful young screen actor, the only one who suggested tragic force, the major protagonist of contemporary American themes in the fifties, is already a self-parodying comedian.

I mean by protagonist the hero who really strikes a nerve—not a Cary Grant who delights with his finesse, nor mushy heartwarmers like Gary Cooper and James Stewart with their blubbering sincerity (sometimes it seemed that the taller the man, the smaller he pretended to be; that was his notion of being "ordinary" and "universal" and "real"), but men whose intensity on the screen stirs an intense reaction in the audience. Not Gregory Peck or Tyrone Power or Robert Taylor with their conventional routine heroics, but James Cagney or Edward G. Robinson in the gangster films, John Garfield in the Depression movies, Kirk Douglas as a postwar heel. These men are not necessarily better actors, but through the accidents of casting and circumstances or because of what they themselves embodied or projected, they *meant* something important to us. A brilliant actor like Jason Robards, Jr., may never become a protagonist of this kind unless he gets a role in which he embodies something new and relevant to the audience.

Protagonists are always loners, almost by definition. The big one to survive the war was the Bogart figure—the man with a code (moral, aesthetic, chivalrous) in a corrupt society. He had, so to speak, inside knowledge of the nature of the enemy. He was a sophisticated, urban version of the Westerner who, classically, knew both sides of the law and was tough enough to go his own way and yet, romantically, still do right.

Brando represented a reaction against the postwar mania for security. As a protagonist, the Brando of the early fifties had no code, only his instincts. He was a development from the gangster leader and the outlaw. He was antisocial because he knew society was crap; he was a hero to youth because he was strong enough not to take the crap. (In England it was thought that *The Wild One* would incite adolescents to violence.)

There was a sense of excitement, of danger in his presence, but perhaps his special appeal was in a kind of simple conceit, the conceit of tough kids. There was humor in it—swagger and arrogance that were vain and childish, and somehow seemed very American. He was explosively dangerous without being "serious" in the sense of having ideas. There was no theory, no cant in his leadership. He didn't care about social position or a job or respectability, and because he didn't care he was a big man; for what is less attractive, what makes a man smaller, than his worrying about his status? Brando represented a contemporary version of the free American.

Because he had no code, except an aesthetic one—a commitment to a *style* of life—he was easily betrayed by those he trusted. There he was, the new primitive, a Byronic Dead End Kid, with his quality of vulnerability. His acting was so physical—so exploratory, tentative, wary—that we could sense with him, feel him pull back at the slightest hint of rebuff. We in the audience felt protective: we knew how lonely he must be in his assertiveness. Who even in hell wants to be an outsider? And he was no intellectual who could rationalize it, learn somehow to accept it, to live with it. He could only feel it, act it out, be "The Wild One"—and God knows how many kids felt, "That's the story of my life."

Brando played variations on rebel themes: from the lowbrow, disturbingly inarticulate brute, Stanley Kowalski, with his suggestions of violence waiting behind the slurred speech, the sullen face, to his Orpheus standing before the judge in the opening scene of *The Fugitive Kind*, unearthly, mythic, the rebel as artist, showing classic possibilities he was never to realize (or has not yet realized).

He was our angry young man—the delinquent, the tough, the rebel— who stood at the center of our common experience. When, as Terry Malloy in *On the Waterfront*, he said to his brother, "Oh Charlie, oh Charlie . . . you don't understand. I could have had class. I could have been a contender. I could have been somebody, instead of a bum—which is what I am," he spoke for all our failed hopes. It was the great American lament, of Broadway, of Hollywood, as well as of the docks.

I am describing the Brando who became a star, not the man necessarily, but the boy-man he projected, and also the publicity and the come-on. The publicity had a built-in ambivalence. Though the fan magazines might describe him alluringly as dreamy, moody, thin-skinned, easily hurt, gentle, intense, unpredictable, hating discipline, a defender of the underdog, other journalists and influential columnists were not so sympathetic toward what this suggested.

It is one of the uglier traditions of movie business that frequently when a star gets big enough to want big money and artistic selection or control of his productions, the studios launch large-scale campaigns designed to cut him down to an easier-to-deal-with size or to supplant him with younger, cheaper talent. Thus, early in movie history the great Lillian Gish was derided as unpopular in the buildup of the young Garbo (by the *same* studio), and in newspapers all over the country Marilyn Monroe, just a few weeks before her death, was discovered to have no box-office draw. The gossip columnists serve as the shock troops with all those little items about how so-and-so is getting a big head, how he isn't taking the advice of the studio executives who know best, and so forth.

In the case of Brando, the most powerful ladies were especially virulent because they were obviously part of what he was rebelling against; in flouting their importance, he might undermine their position with other new stars who might try to get by without kowtowing to the blackmailing old vultures waiting to pounce in the name of God, Motherhood, and Americanism. What was unusual in Brando's case were the others who joined in the attack.

In 1957, Truman Capote, having spent an evening with Brando and then a year writing up that evening (omitting his own side of the conversation and interjecting interpretations), published "The Duke in His Own Domain" in the *New Yorker*. The unwary Brando was made to look public ass number one. And yet the odd thing about this interview was that Capote, in his supersophistication, kept using the most commonplace, middlebrow evidence and arguments against him—for example, that Brando in his egotism was not impressed by Joshua Logan as a movie director. (The matter for astonishment was that Capote *was*—or was willing to use anything to make his literary exercise more effective.) Despite Capote's style and venomous skill, it is he in this interview, not Brando, who equates money and success with real importance and accomplishment. His arrows fit snugly into the holes they have made only if you accept the usual middlebrow standards of marksmanship.

It was now open season on Brando: Hollis Alpert lumbered onto the pages of *Cosmopolitan* to attack him for not returning to the stage to become a great actor—as if the theatre were the citadel of art. *What* theatre? Was Brando really wrong in feeling that movies are more relevant to our lives than the dead theatre which so many journalists seem to regard as the custodian of integrity and creativity? David Susskind was shocked that a mere actor like Brando should seek to make money, might even dare to consider his own judgment and management preferable to that of millionaire producers. Dwight Macdonald chided Brando for not being content to be a craftsman: "Mr. Brando has always aspired to something Deeper and More Significant, he has always fancied himself as like an intellectual"—surely a crime he shares with Mr. Macdonald.

If he had not been so presumptuous as to try to think for himself in Hollywood and if he hadn't had a sense of *irony*, he could have pretended—and convinced a lot of people—that he was still a contender. But what crown could he aspire to? Should he be a "king" like Gable, going from one meaningless picture to another, performing the rituals of manly toughness, embracing the studio stable, to be revered, finally, because he was the company actor who never gave anybody any trouble? Columnists don't attack that kind of king on his papier-mâché throne; critics don't prod him to return to the stage; the public doesn't turn against him.

Almost without exception, American actors who don't accept trashy assignments make nothing, not even superior trash. Brando accepts the trash, but unlike the monochromatic, "always dependable" Gable, he has too much energy or inventiveness or contempt just to go through the motions. And when he appears on the screen, there is a special quality of recognition in the audience: we know he's too big for the role.

Perhaps, as some in picture business say, Brando "screws up" his pictures by rewriting the scripts; certainly he hasn't been very astute in the directors and writers he has worked with. What he needed was not more docility, but more strength, the confidence to work with young talent, to try difficult roles. But he's no longer a contender, no longer a protagonist who challenges anything serious. Brando has become a comic.

The change was overwhelmingly apparent in the 1963 *Mutiny on the Bounty*, which, rather surprisingly, began with a miniature class conflict between Brando, as the aristocratic Fletcher Christian, and Trevor Howard, as the lowborn Captain Bligh, who cannot endure Christian's contempt for him. Brando played the fop with such relish that audiences shared in the joke; it was like a Dead End Kid playing Congreve. The inarticulate grunting Method actor is showing off, and it's a classic and favorite American joke: the worm turns, Destry gets his guns, American honor is redeemed. He can talk as fancy as any of them, even fancier. (In the action sequences he's uninteresting, not handsome or athletic enough to be a stock romantic adventure hero. He seems more eccentric than heroic, with his bizarre stance, his head held up pugnaciously, his face unlined in a peculiar bloated, waxen way. He's like a short, flabby tenor wandering around the stage and not singing: you wonder what he's doing there.)

In *The Ugly American* (1963) once again he is very funny as he sets the character—a pipe-smoking businessman-ambassador who parries a Senate subcommittee with high-toned clipped speech and epigrammatic sophistication. When he plays an articulate role, it is already rather a stunt, and in this one he is talking about personal dignity and standards of proper behavior. His restraint becomes a source of amusement because he is the chief exponent of the uncouth, the *charged*. Even his bull neck, so out of character, adds to the joke. His comedy is volatile. It has the unpredictable element that has always been part of his excitement: at any moment we may be surprised, amazed. When he submerges himself in the role, the movie dies on the screen.

Brando is never so American as when his English or foreign accent is thickest. It's a joke like a child's impersonation of a foreigner, overplaying the difference, and he offers us complicity in his accomplishments at pretending to be gentlemen or foreigners. What is funny about these roles is that they seem foreign to the Brando the audience feels it knows. When he does rough, coarse American serviceman comedy, as in *Bedtime Story*, he is horribly nothing (except for one farcical sequence when he impersonates a mad Hapsburg). Worse than nothing, because when his vulnerability is gone, his animal grace goes too, and he is left without even the routine handsomeness of his inferiors.

He had already implicated us in his amusement at his roles earlier in his career, in 1954 with his Napoleon in *Desirée*, in 1957 with his hilarious Southern gentleman-officer in *Sayonara*, but these could still be thought of as commercial interludes, the bad luck of the draw. Now he doesn't draw anything else. Is it just bad luck, or is it that he and so many of our greatest talents must play out their "creative" lives with a stacked deck?

It is easy these days to "explain" the absence of roles worth playing by referring to the inroads of television and the end of the studio system. Of course, there's some truth in all this. But Brando's career illustrates something much more basic: the destruction of meaning in movies; and this is not a new phenomenon, nor is it specially linked to television or other new factors. The organic truth of American movie history is that the new theme or the new star that gives vitality to the medium is widely imitated and quickly exhausted before the theme or talent can develop. Everything good can be turned into a trick.

What's left of the rebel incarnate is what we see of Brando in the 1965 *Morituri*: his principal charm is his apparent delight in his own cleverness. Like many another great actor who has become fortune's fool, he plays the great ham. He seems as pleased with the lines as if he'd just thought them up. He gives the best ones a carefully timed double-take so that we, too, can savor his cleverness and the delight of his German accent. And what else is there to do with the role? If his presence did not give it the extra dimension of comedy, it would be merely commonplace.

In *Morituri* all we need is one look at the cynical aesthete Brando in his escapist paradise, telling us that he's "out of it," that war never solves anything, and we know that he's going to become the greatest warrior of them all. It can be argued that this hurdle of apathy or principle or convictions to be overcome gives a character conflict and makes his ultimate action more significant. Theoretically, this would seem to explain the plot mechanism, but as it works, no matter how absurd the terms in which the initial idealism or cynicism or social rejection is presented (as in such classic movie examples of character reformation as *Casablanca*, *To Have and Have Not*, *Stalag 17*), it is the final, socially acceptable "good" behavior which seems fantasy, fairy tale, unbelievable melodrama—in brief, fake. And the initial attitudes to be overcome often seem to have a lot of strength; indeed, they are likely to be what drew us to the character in the first place, what made him pass for a protagonist.

In *Morituri*, as in movies in general, there is rarely a *difference* shown, except to bring it back to the "norm." The high-minded, like the Quakers in *High Noon* or *Friendly Persuasion*, are there only to violate their convictions. They must be brought down low to common impulses, just as the low cynical materialists must be raised high to what are supposed to be our shared ideals. This democratic leveling of movies is like a massive tranquilizer. The more irregular the hero, the more offbeat, the more necessary it is for him to turn square in the finale.

Brando's *career* is a larger demonstration of the same principle at work in mass culture; but instead of becoming normal, he (like Norman Mailer) became an eccentric, which in this country means a clown, possibly the only way left to preserve some kind of difference.

When you're larger than life you can't just be brought down to normalcy. It's easier to get acceptance by caricaturing your previous attitudes and aspirations, by doing what the hostile audience already has been doing to you. Why should Bette Davis let impersonators on television make a fool of her when she can do it herself and reap the rewards of renewed audience acceptance?

Perhaps Brando has been driven to this self-parody so soon because of his imaginative strength and because of that magnetism that makes him so compelling an expression of American conflicts. His greatness is in a range that is too disturbing to be encompassed by regular movies. As with Bette Davis, as with John Barrymore, even when he mocks himself, the self he mocks is more prodigious than anybody else around. It's as if the hidden reserves of power have been turned to irony. Earlier, when his roles were absurd, there was a dash of irony; now it's taken over: the nonconformist with no roles to play plays *with* his roles. Brando is still the most exciting American actor on the screen. The roles may not be classic, but the actor's dilemma is.

Emerson outlined the American artist's way of life a century ago—"Thou must pass for a fool and a churl for a long season." We used to think that the season meant only youth, before the artist could prove his talent, make his place, achieve something. Now it is clear that for screen artists, and perhaps not only for screen artists, youth is, relatively speaking, the short season; the long one is the degradation *after* success.

{*Atlantic Monthly*, March 1966}

:: Movie Brutalists

The basic ideas among young American film-makers are simple: the big movies we grew up on are corrupt, obsolete or dead, or are beyond our reach (we can't get a chance to make Hollywood films) — so we'll make films of our own, cheap films that we can make in our own way. For some this is an attempt to break into the "industry"; for others it is a different approach to movies, a view of movies not as a popular art or a mass medium but as an art form to be explored.

Much of the movie style of young American film-makers may be explained as a reaction against the banality and luxuriant wastefulness which are so often called the superior "craftsmanship" of Hollywood. In reaction, the young become movie brutalists.

They, and many in their audiences, may prefer the rough messiness — the uneven lighting, awkward editing, flat camera work, the undramatic succession of scenes, unexplained actions, and confusion about what, if anything, is going on — because it makes their movies seem so different from Hollywood movies. This inexpensive, inexperienced, untrained look serves as a kind of testimonial to sincerity, poverty, even purity of intentions. It is like the sackcloth of true believers which they wear in moral revulsion against the rich in their fancy garments. The look of poverty is not necessarily a necessity. I once had the experience, as chairman of the jury at an experimental film festival, of getting on the stage, in the black silk dress I had carefully mended and ironed for the occasion, to present the check to the prizewinner, who came forward in patched, faded dungarees. He got an ovation, of course. I had seen him the night before in a good dark suit, but now he had dressed for his role (deserving artist) as I had dressed for mine (distinguished critic).

Although many of the American experimentalists have developed extraordinary kinds of technique, it is no accident that the virtuoso technicians who can apparently do almost anything with drawing board or camera are not taken up as the heroes of youth in the way that brutalists are. Little is heard about Bruce Baillie or Carroll Ballard whose camera skills expose how inept, inefficient, and unimaginative much of Hollywood's self-praised work is, or about the elegance and grandeur of Jordan Belson's short abstract films, like *Allures*, that demonstrate that one man working in a basement can make Hollywood's vaunted special effects departments look archaic. Craftsmanship and skill don't, in themselves, have much appeal to youth. Rough work looks rebellious and sometimes it is: there's anger and frustration and passion, too, in those scratches and stains and multiple superimpositions that make our eyes swim. The movie brutalists, it's all too apparent, are hurting our eyes to save our souls.

They are basically right, of course, in what they're *against*. Aesthetically and morally, disgust with Hollywood's fabled craftsmanship is long overdue. I say fabled because the "craft" claims of Hollywood, and the notion that the expensiveness of studio-produced movies is necessary for some sort of technical perfection or "finish," are just hucksterism. The reverse is closer to the truth: it's becoming almost impossible to produce a decent-looking movie in a Hollywood studio. In addition to the touched-up corpses of old dramatic ideas, big movies carry the dead weight of immobile cameras, all-purpose light, whorehouse décor. The production values are often ludicrously inappropriate to the subject matter, but studio executives, who charge off roughly 30 percent of a film's budget to studio overhead, are very keen on these production values which they frequently remind us are the hallmark of American movies.

In many foreign countries it is this very luxuriousness that is most envied and admired in American movies: the big cars, the fancy food, the opulent bachelor lairs, the gadget-packed family homes, even the loaded freeways and the noisy big cities. What is not so generally understood is the studio executives' implicit assumption that this is also what American audiences like. The story may not involve more than a few spies and counterspies, but the wide screen will be filled. The set decorator will pack the sides of the image with fruit and flowers and furniture.

When Hollywood cameramen and editors want to show their expertise, they imitate the effects of Japanese or European craftsmen, and then the result is pointed to with cries of "See, we can do anything in Holly-wood." The principal demonstration of art and ingenuity among these "craftsmen" is likely to be in getting their sons and nephews into the unions and in resisting any attempt to make Hollywood movie-making flexible enough for artists to work there. If there are no cinematographers in modern Hollywood who can be discussed in the same terms as Henri Decaë or Raoul Coutard or the late Gianni di Venanzo, it's because the studio methods and the union restrictions and regulations don't make it possible for talent to function. The talent is strangled in the business bureaucracy, and the best of our cinematographers perform safe, sane academic exercises. If the most that a gifted colorist like Lucien Ballard can hope for is to beautify a John Michael Hayes screenplay—giving an old tart a fresh complexion—why not scratch up the image?

The younger generation doesn't seem much interested in the obstacles to art in Hollywood, however. They don't much care about why the older directors do what they do or whether some of the most talented young directors in Hollywood, like Sam Peckinpah (*Ride the High Country*, *Major Dundee*) or Irvin Kershner (*The Hoodlum Priest*, *The Luck of Ginger Coffey*, *A Fine Madness*), will break through and do the work they should be doing. There is little interest in the work of gifted, intelligent men outside the industry, like James Blue (*The Olive Trees of Justice*) or John Korty (*The Crazy Quilt*), who are attempting to make inexpensive feature films as honestly and independently as they can. These men (and their films) are not flamboyant; they don't issue manifestos, and they don't catch the imagination of youth. Probably, like the students in film courses who often do fresh and lively work, they're not surprising enough, not different enough. The new film enthusiasts are, when it comes down to it, not any more interested in simple, small, inexpensive pictures than Hollywood is. The workmen's clothes and crude movie techniques may cry out, "We're poor and honest. They're rich and rotten." But, of course, you can be poor and not so very honest and, although it's harder to believe, you can even be rich and not so very rotten. What the young seem to be interested in is brutalism. In certain groups, automatic writing with a camera has come to be considered the most creative kind of film-making.

Their hero, Jean-Luc Godard—one of the most original talents ever to work in film and one of the most uneven—is not a brutalist at so simple a level, yet he comprises the attitudes of a new generation. Godard is what is meant by a "film-maker." The concept of a "film-maker"—as distinguished from a director (or even writer-directors like Bergman or Fellini)—is a response and reaction to traditional methods of financing as well as shooting, and to traditional concepts of what a movie is. Godard works with a small crew and shifts ideas and attitudes from movie to movie and even within movies. While Hollywood producers straddle huge fences trying to figure out where the action is supposed to be—and never find out—Godard in himself is where the action is.

There is a disturbing quality in Godard's work that perhaps helps to explain why the young are drawn to his films and identify with them, and why so many older people call him a "coterie" artist and don't think his films are important. *His characters don't seem to have any future.* They are most alive (and most appealing) just because they don't conceive of the day after tomorrow; they have no careers, no plans, only fantasies of roles they could play—of careers, thefts, romance, politics, adventure, pleasure, a life like in the movies. Even his world of the future, *Alphaville*, is, photographically, a documentary of Paris in the present. (All of his films are in that sense documentaries—as were also, and also by necessity, the grade B American gangster films that influenced him.) And even before *Alphaville*, the people in *The Married Woman* were already science fiction—so blank and affectless no mad scientist was required to destroy their souls.

His characters are young, unrelated to families and background. Whether deliberately or unconsciously, he makes his characters orphans who, like the students in the theatres, feel only attachments to friends, to lovers—attachments that will end with a chance word or the close of the semester. They're orphans, by extension, in a larger sense, too, unconnected with the world, feeling out of relationship to it. They're a generation of familiar strangers.

An elderly gentleman recently wrote me, "Oh, they're such a bore, bore, bore, modern youth! All attitudes and nothing behind the attitudes. When I was in my twenties, I didn't just loaf around, being a rebel, I went places and did things. The reason they all hate the squares is because the squares remind them of the one thing they are trying to forget: there *is* a Future and you must build for it."

He's wrong, I think. The young are not "trying to forget": they just don't think in those terms. Godard's power—and possibly his limitation—as an artist is that he so intensely expresses how they do feel and think. His characters don't plan or worry about careers or responsibilities; they just live. Youth makes them natural aristocrats in their indifference to sustenance, security, hard work; and prosperity has turned a whole generation—or at least the middle-class part of it—into aristocrats. And it's astonishing how many places they do go to and how many things they can do. The difference is in how easily they do it all. Even their notion of creativity—as what comes naturally—is surprisingly similar to the aristocratic artist's condescension toward those middle-class plodders who have to labor for a living, for an education, for "culture."

Here, too, Godard is the symbol, exemplar, and proof. He makes it all seem so effortless, so personal—just one movie after another. Because he is so skillful and so incredibly disciplined that he can make his pictures for under a hundred thousand dollars, and because there is enough of a youthful audience in France to support these pictures, he can do almost anything he wants within those budgetary limits. In this achievement of independence, he is almost alone among movie directors: it is a truly heroic achievement. For a younger generation he is the proof that it is possible to make and go on making films your own way. And yet they don't seem aware of how rare he is or how hard it is to get in that position. Even if colleges and foundations make it easier than it has ever been, they will need not only talent but toughness to be independent.

As Godard has been able to solve the problems of economic freedom, his work now poses the problems of artistic freedom—problems that few artists in the history of movies have been fortunate enough to face. The history of great film directors is a history of economic and political obstacles—of compromises, defeats, despair, even disgrace. Griffith, Eisenstein, von Stroheim, von Sternberg, Cocteau, Renoir, Max Ophuls, Orson Welles—they were defeated because they weren't in a position to do what they wanted to do. If Godard fails, it will be because what he wants to do—which is what he *does*—isn't good enough.

Maybe he is attempting to escape from freedom when he makes a beautiful work and then, to all appearances, just throws it away. There is a self-destructive urgency in his treatment of themes, a drive toward a quick finish. Even if it's suicidal for the hero or the work, Godard is impatient for the ending: the mood of his films is that there's no way for things to work out anyway, something must be done even if it's disastrous, no action is intolerable.

It seems likely that many of the young who don't wait for others to call them artists, but simply announce that they are, don't have the patience to make art. A student's idea of a film-maker isn't someone who has to sit home and study and think and work—as in most of the arts—but someone who goes out with friends and shoots—a social activity. It is an extroverted and egotistic image of the genius-creator. It is the Fellini-Guido figure of *8½*, the movie director as star. Few seem to have noticed that by the time of *Juliet of the Spirits* he had turned into a professional party-giver. Film-making, carried out the way a lot of kids do it, is like having a party. And their movie "ideas" are frequently no more than staging and shooting a wild, weird party.

"Creativity" is a quick route to power and celebrity. The pop singer or composer, the mod designer, says of his work, "It's a creative way to make a living"—meaning it didn't take a dull lot of study and planning, that he was able to use his own inventiveness or ingenuity or talent to get to the top without much sweat. I heard a young film-maker put it this way to a teen-age art student: "What do you go to life class for? Either you can draw or you can't. What you should do is have a show. It's important to get exposure." One can imagine their faces if they had to listen to those teachers who used to tell us that you had to be able to do things the traditional ways before you earned the right to break loose and do things *your* way. They simply take shortcuts into other art forms or into pop arts where they can "express themselves" now. Like cool Peter Pans, they just take off and fly.

Godard's conception of technique can be taken as a highly intellectual-ized rationale for these attitudes. "The ideal for me," he says, "is to obtain right away what will work—and without retakes. If they are necessary, it falls short of the mark. The immediate is chance. At the same time it is definitive. What I want is the definitive by chance." Sometimes, almost magically, he seems to get it—as in many scenes of *Breathless* and *Band of Outsiders*—but often, as in *The Married Woman*, he seems to settle for arbi-trary effects.

A caricature of this way of talking is common among young American film-makers. Some of them believe that everything they catch on film is definitive, so they do not edit at all. As proof that they do not mar their instinct with pedantry or judgment, they may retain the blank leader to the roll of film. As proof of their creative sincerity they may leave in the blurred shots.

Preposterous as much of this seems, it is theoretically not so far from Godard's way of working. Although his technical control is superb, so complete that one cannot tell improvisation from planning, the ideas and bits of business are often so arbitrary that they appear to be (and probably are) just things that he chanced to think of that day, or that he came across in a book he happened to be reading. At times there is a disarming, an almost ecstatic innocence about the way he uses quotes as if he had just heard of these beautiful ideas and wanted to share his enthusiasm with the world. After smiling with pleasure as we do when a child's discovery of the beauty of a leaf or a poem enables us to re-experience the wonder of responsiveness, we may sink in spirit right down to incredulity. For this is the rapture with "thoughts" of those whose minds aren't much sullied by thought. These are "thoughts" without thought: they don't come out of a line of thought or a process of thinking, they don't arise from the situation. They're "inspirations"—bright illuminations from nowhere—and this is what kids who think of themselves as poetic or artistic or creative think ideas are: noble sentiments. They decorate a movie and it is easy for viewers to feel that they give it depth, that if followed, these clues lead to understanding of the work. But if those who follow the clues come out with odd and disjunctive interpretations, this is because the "clues" are *not* integral to the movie but are clues to what else the artist was involved in while he was making the movie.

Putting into the work whatever just occurred to the artist is its own rationale and needs no justification for young Americans encouraged from childhood to express themselves creatively and to say whatever came into their heads. Good liberal parents didn't want to push their kids in academic subjects but oohed and aahed with false delight when their children presented them with a baked ashtray or a woven doily. Did anyone guess or foresee what narcissistic confidence this generation would develop in its banal "creativity"? Now we're surrounded, inundated by artists. And a staggering number of them wish to be or already call themselves "filmmakers."

A few years ago a young man informed me that he was going to "give

up" poetry and avant-garde film (which couldn't have been much of a sacrifice as he hadn't done anything more than talk about them) and devote
himself to writing "art songs." I remember asking, "Do you read music?"
and not being especially surprised to hear that he didn't. I knew from other
young men that the term "art" used as an adjective meant that they were
bypassing even the most rudimentary knowledge in the field. Those who
said they were going to make art movies not only didn't consider it worth
their while to go to see ordinary commercial movies, but usually didn't
even know anything much about avant-garde film. I did not pursue the
subject of "art songs" with this young man because it was perfectly clear
that he wasn't going to do anything. But some of the young who say they're
going to make "art movies" are actually beginning to make movies. Kids
who can't write, who have never developed any competence in photography, who have never acted in nor directed a play, see no deterrent to making movies. And although most of the results are bad beyond our wildest
fears, as if to destroy all our powers of prediction a few, even of the most
ignorant, pretentious young men and women, are doing some interesting
things.

Yet why are the Hollywood movies, even the worst overstuffed ones,
often easier to sit through than the short experimental ones? Because they
have actors and a story. Through what is almost a technological fluke,
16 mm movie cameras give the experimental film-maker greater flexibility
than the "professional" 35 mm camera user, but he cannot get adequate
synchronous sound. And so the experimentalists, as if to convert this
liability into an advantage, have asserted that their partial use of the capa-
bilities of the medium is the true art of the cinema, which is said to be
purely visual. But their visual explorations of their states of consciousness
(with the usual implicit social protest) get boring, the mind begins to wander, and though this lapse in attention can be explained to us as a new kind
of experience, as even the purpose of cinema, our desire to see a movie
hasn't been satisfied. (There are, of course, some young film-makers who
are not interested in movies as we ordinarily think of them, but in film as
an art medium like painting or music, and this kind of work must be looked
at a different way—without the expectation of story content or meaning.)
They probably won't be able to make satisfying *movies* until the problems
of sound are solved not only technically but in terms of drama, structure,
meaning, relevance.

It is not an answer to toss on a spoofing semi-synchronous sound track as a number of young film-makers do. It can be funny in a cheap sort of way—as in Robert Downey's *Chafed Elbows* where the images and sound are, at least, in the same style; but this isn't fundamentally different from the way George Axelrod works in *Lord Love a Duck* or Blake Edwards in *What Did You Do in the War, Daddy?*, and there's no special reason to congratulate people for doing underground what is driving us down there. Total satire is opportunistic and easy; what's difficult is to make a movie in which something is taken seriously without making a fool of yourself.

Is Hollywood interested in the young movement? If it attracts customers, Hollywood will eat it up, the way *The Wild Angels* has already fed upon *Scorpio Rising*. At a party combining the commercial and noncommercial worlds of film, a Hollywood screen writer watched as an underground film-maker and his wife entered. The wife was wearing one of those classic film-makers' wives' outfits: a simple sack of burlap in natural brown, with scarecrow sleeves. The screen writer greeted her enthusiastically, "I really dig your dress, honey," he said, "I used to have a dress like that once."

{*The New Republic*, September 24, 1966}

:: Tourist in the City of Youth

Some years ago I attended an evening of mime by Marcel Marceau, an elaborate exercise in aesthetic purification during which the audience kept applauding its own appreciation of culture and beauty, i.e., every time they thought they recognized what was supposed to be going on. It had been bad enough when Chaplin or Harpo Marx pulled this beauty-of-pathos stuff, and a whole evening of it was truly intolerable. But afterwards, when friends were acclaiming Marceau's artistry, it just wouldn't do to say something like "I prefer the Ritz Brothers" (though I do, I passionately do). They would think I was being deliberately lowbrow, and if I tried to talk in terms of Marceau's artistry versus Harry Ritz's artistry, it would be stupid, because "artist" is already too pretentious a term for Harry Ritz and so I would be falsifying what I love him for. I don't want to push this quite so far as to say that Marceau is to comedians I like as Antonioni's *Blow-Up* is to movies I like, but the comparison may be suggestive. And it may also be relevant that Antonioni pulls a Marceau-like expressionist finale in this picture, one of those fancy finishes that seems to say so much (but what?) and reminds one of so many naïvely bad experimental films.

Will *Blow-Up* be taken seriously in 1968 only by the same sort of cultural diehards who are still sending out five-page single-spaced letters on their interpretation of *Marienbad*? (No two are alike, no one interesting.) It has some of the *Marienbad* appeal: a friend phones for your opinion and when you tell him you didn't much care for it, he says, "You'd better see it again. I was at a swinging party the other night and it's all anybody talked about!" (Was there ever a good movie that everybody was talking about?) It probably won't blow over because it also has the *Morgan!–Georgy Girl* appeal; people identify with it so strongly, they get *upset* if you don't like it—as if you were rejecting not just the movie but *them*. And in a way they're right, because if you don't accept the peculiarly slugged consciousness of *Blow-Up*, you *are* rejecting something in them. Antonioni's new mixture of suspense with vagueness and confusion seems to have a kind of numbing fascination for them that they associate with art and intellectuality, and they are responding to it as *their* film—and hence as a masterpiece.

Antonioni's off-screen conversation, as reported to us, is full of impeccable literary references, but the white-faced clowns who open and close *Blow-Up* suggest that inside his beautifully fitted dinner jacket he carries—next to his heart—a gilt-edged gift edition of Khalil Gibran. From the way people talk about the profundity of *Blow-Up*, that's probably what they're responding to. What would we think of a man who stopped at a newsstand to cluck at the cover girls of *Vogue* and *Harper's Bazaar* as tragic symbols of emptiness and sterility, as evidence that modern life isn't "real," and then went ahead and bought the magazines? Or, to be more exact, what would we think of a man who conducted a leisurely tour of "swinging" London, lingering along the flashiest routes and dawdling over a pot party and mini-orgy, while ponderously explaining that although the mod scene appears to be hip and sexy, it represents a condition of spiritual malaise in which people live only for the sensations of the moment? Is he a foolish old hypocrite or is he, despite his tiresome moralizing, a man who knows he's hooked?

It's obvious that there's a new kind of noninvolvement among youth, but we can't get at what that's all about by Antonioni's terms. He is apparently unable to respond to or to convey the new sense of community among youth, or the humor and fervor and astonishing speed in their rejections of older values; he sees only the emptiness of pop culture.

Those who enjoy seeing this turned-on city of youth, those who say of *Blow-Up* that it's the trip, it's where we are now in consciousness and that Antonioni is in it, part of it, ahead of it like Warhol, may have a better sense of what Antonioni is about than the laudatory critics. Despite Antonioni's negativism, the world he presents looks harmless, and for many in the audience, and not just the youthful ones, sex without "connecting" doesn't really seem so bad—naughty, maybe, but nice. Even the smoke at the pot party is enough to turn on some of the audience. And there's all that pretty color which delights the critics, though it undercuts their reasons for praising the movie because it's that bright, cleaned-up big-city color of I-have-seen-the-future-and-it's-fun. Antonioni, like his fashion-photographer hero, is more interested in getting pretty pictures than in what they mean. But for reasons I can't quite fathom, what is taken to be shallow in his hero is taken to be profound in him. Maybe it's because of the symbols: do pretty pictures plus symbols equal art?

There are the revelers who won't make room on the sidewalk for the nuns (spirit? soul? God? love?) and jostle them aside; an old airplane propeller is found in an antique shop; the hero considers buying the antique shop; two homosexuals walk their poodle, etc. Antonioni could point out that the poodle is castrated, and he'd probably be acclaimed for that, too—one more bitter detail of modern existential agony. There is a mock copulation with camera and subject that made me laugh (as the planes fornicating at the beginning of *Strangelove* did). But from the reviews of *Blow-Up* I learn that this was "tragic" and "a superbly realized comment on the values of our time" and all that. People seem awfully eager to abandon sense and perspective and humor and put on the newest fashion in hair shirts; New York critics who are just settling into their Upper East Side apartments write as if they're leaving for a monastery in the morning.

Hecht and MacArthur used to write light satirical comedies about shallow people living venal lives that said most of what Antonioni does and more, and were entertaining besides; they even managed to convey that they were in love with the corrupt milieu and were part of it without getting bogged down. And Odets, even in late work like his dialogue for *Sweet Smell of Success*, also managed to convey both hate and infatuation. Love-hate is what makes drama not only exciting but possible, and it certainly isn't necessary for Antonioni to resolve his conflicting feelings. But in *Blow-Up* he smothers this conflict in the kind of platitudes the press loves to designate as proper to "mature," "adult," "sober" art. Who the hell goes to movies for mature, adult, sober art, anyway? Yes, we want more from movies than we get from the usual commercial entertainments, but would anybody use terms like mature, adult, and sober for *The Rules of the Game* or *Breathless* or *Citizen Kane* or *Jules and Jim*?

The best part of *Blow-Up* is a well-conceived and ingeniously edited sequence in which the hero blows up a series of photographs and discovers that he has inadvertently photographed a murder. It's a good murder mystery sequence. But does it symbolize (as one reviewer says) "the futility of seeking the hidden meanings of life through purely technological means"? I thought the hero did rather well in uncovering the murder. But this kind of symbolic interpretation is not irrelevant to the appeal of the picture: Antonioni loads his atmosphere with so much confused symbolism and such a heavy sense of importance that the viewers use the movie as a Disposall for intellectual refuse. We get the stock phrases about "the cold death of the heart," "the eroticism is chilling in its bleakness," a "world so cluttered with synthetic stimulations that natural feelings are overwhelmed," etc., because Antonioni *inspires* this jargon.

When the photographer loses the photographic record of the murder, he loses interest in it. According to *Time*, "Antonioni's anti-hero"—who is said to be a "little snake" and "a grincingly accurate portrait of the sort of squiggly little fungus that is apt to grow in a decaying society"—"holds in his possession, if only for an instant, the alexin of his cure: the saving grace of the spirit." (My Webster doesn't yield a clue to "grincingly"; an "alexin" is "a defensive substance, found normally in the body, capable of destroying bacteria.") In other words, if he did something about the murder, like going to the police, he would be accepting an involvement with the life or death of others, and he would find his humanity and become an OK guy to *Time*. (Would he then not be a representative of a decaying society, or would the society not then decay? Only *Time* can tell.)

This review, and many others, turn the murder into something like what the press and TV did with the Kitty Genovese case: use it as an excuse for another of those what-are-we-coming-to editorials about alienation and indifference to human suffering. What was upsetting about the Genovese case was not those among the "witnesses" who didn't want to get involved even to the degree of calling the police (cowardice is not a new phenomenon), but our recognition that in a big city we don't know when our help is needed, and others may not know when we need help. This isn't a new phenomenon, either; what is new is that it goes against the grain of modern social consciousness, i.e., we feel responsible even though we don't know how to act responsibly. The press turned it into one more chance to cluck, and people went around feeling very superior to those thirty-eight witnesses because they were sure *they* would have called the police.

The moral satisfaction of feeling indignant that people take away from these cases (though I'm not sure that *Time*'s moral is what Antonioni intended; probably not) is simple and offensive. Do all the times that the police are called when they are or aren't needed prove how humanly involved with each other we are? The editorial writers don't tell us. And they couldn't do much with the West Coast case of the young academic beaten, tied to his bed, moaning and crying for help for days before he died. His friends and neighbors heard him all right, but as that's how he customarily took his pleasure, they smiled sympathetically and went about their own affairs, not knowing that this time the rough trade he had picked up to beat him had been insanely earnest.

The quick rise to celebrity status of young fashion photographers, like the quick success of pop singers, makes them ideal "cool" heroes, because they don't come up the slow, backbreaking Horatio Alger route. And the glamour of the rich and famous and beautiful rubs off on the photographer who shoots them, making him one of them. Antonioni uses David Hemmings in the role very prettily—with his Billy Budd hair-do, he's like a Pre-Raphaelite Paul McCartney. But if we're supposed to get upset because this young man got rich quick—the way some people get morally outraged at the salaries movie stars make—that's the moral outrage television personalities specialize in and it's hardly worth the consideration of art-house audiences. Yet a surprising lot of people seem willing to accept assumptions such as: the fashion photographer is symbolic of life in our society and time; he turns to easy sex because his life and ours are empty, etc. Mightn't people like easy sex even if their lives were reasonably full? And is sex necessarily empty just because the people are strangers to each other, or is it just different? And what's so terrible about fast, easy success? Don't most of the people who cluck their condemnation wish they'd had it?

Vanessa Redgrave, despite an odd mod outfit, has a tense and lovely presence, and because she has been allowed to act in this film (in which almost no one else is allowed to project) she stands out. However, someone has arranged her in a wholly gratuitous mood—laughing with her head back and teeth showing in a blatant imitation of Garbo. It's almost a subliminal trailer for *Camelot* in which, according to advance publicity, she will be "the Garbo of the sixties." This little deformation does not stick out as it might in another movie because this movie is so ill-formed anyway. The exigencies of the plot force Antonioni to alter his typical "open" construction (famous partly because it was the most painstakingly planned openness in movie history). In *Blow-Up* he prepares for events and plants characters for reappearances when they will be needed, but limply, clumsily; and he finds poor excuses for getting into places like the discotheque and the pot party, which "use" London to tell us about dehumanization. In some terrible way that I suppose could be called Antonioni's genius, he complains of dehumanization in a dehumanized way, and it becomes part of noninvolvement to accept a movie like this as "a chronicle of our time."

Just as *Marienbad* was said to be about "time" and/or "memory," *Blow-Up* is said (by Antonioni and the critics following his lead) to be about "illusion and reality." They seem to think they are really saying something, and something impressive at that, though the same thing can be said about almost any movie. In what sense is a movie "about" an abstract concept? Probably what Antonioni and the approving critics mean is that high fashion, mod celebrity, rock and roll, and drugs are part of a sterile or frenetic existence, and they take this to mean that the life represented in the film is not "real" but illusory. What seems to be implicit in the prattle about illusion and reality is the notion that the photographer's life is based on "illusion" and that when he discovers the murder, he is somehow face to face with "reality." Of course this notion that murder is more real than, say, driving in a Rolls-Royce convertible, is nonsensical (it's more shocking, though, and when combined with a Rolls-Royce it gives a movie a bit of box office—it's practical). They're not talking about a concept of reality but what used to be called "the real things in life," the solid values they approve of versus the "false values" of "the young people today."

Antonioni is the kind of thinker who can say that there are "no social or moral judgments in the picture": he is merely showing us the people who have discarded "all discipline," for whom freedom means "marijuana, sexual perversion, anything," and who live in "decadence without any visible future." I'd hate to be around when he's making judgments. Yet in some sense Antonioni is right: because he doesn't *connect* what he's showing to judgment. And that dislocation of sensibility is probably why kids don't notice the moralizing, why they say *Blow-Up* is hip.

The cultural ambience of a film like this becomes mixed with the experience of the film: one critic says Antonioni's "vision" is that "the further we draw away from reality, the closer we get to the truth," another that Antonioni means "we must learn to live with the invisible." All this can sound great to those who don't mind not knowing what it's about, for whom the ineffable seems most important. "It's about the limits of visual experience. The photographer can't go beyond make-believe," a lady lawyer who loved the movie explained to me. "But," I protested, "visual experience is hardly make-believe any more than your practice is—perhaps less." Without pausing for breath she shifted to, "Why does it have to mean anything?" That's the game that's being played at parties this year at Marienbad. They feel they understand *Blow-Up*, but when they can't explain it, or why they feel as they do, they use that as the grounds for saying the movie is a work of art. *Blow-Up* is the perfect movie for the kind of people who say, "now that films have become an art form . . ." and don't expect to understand art.

Because the hero is a *photographer* and the blow-up sequence tells a story in pictures, the movie is also said to be about Antonioni's view of himself as an artist (though even his worst enemies could hardly accuse him of "telling stories" in pictures). Possibly it is, but those who see *Blow-Up* as Antonioni's version of *8 ½*—as making a movie about making a movie— seem to value that much more than just making a movie, probably because it puts the film in a class with the self-conscious autobiographical material so many young novelists struggle with (the story that ends with their becoming writers . . .) and is thus easy to mistake for the highest point of the artistic process.

There is the usual post-*Marienbad* arguing about whether the murder is "real" or "hallucinatory." There seems to be an assumption that if a movie can be interpreted as wholly or partially a dream or fantasy, it is more artistic, and I have been hearing that there is no murder, it's all in the photographer's head. But then the movie makes even less sense because there are no indications of anything in his character that relate to such fantasies. Bosley Crowther has come up with the marvelously involuted suggestion that as the little teeny-bopper orgy wasn't "real" but just the hero's "juvenile fantasy," the Production Code people shouldn't have thought they were seeing real titbits on the screen.

What is it about the symbolic use of characters and details that impresses so many educated people? It's not very hard to do: almost any detail or person or event in our lives can be pressed into symbolic service, but to what end? I take my dogs for a walk in New York City in January and see examples of "alienation." An old Negro woman is crooning, "The world out here is lonely and cold." A shuffling old man mutters, "Never did and never will, never again and never will." And there's a crazy lady who glowers at my dogs and shouts, "They're not fit to shine my canary's shoes!" Do they tell us anything about a "decaying society"? No, but if you had some banal polemical, social, or moral point to make, you could turn them into cardboard figures marked with arrows. In so doing I think you would diminish their individuality and their range of meaning, but you would probably increase your chances of being acclaimed as a deep thinker.

When journalistic details are used symbolically—and that is how Antonioni uses "swinging" London—the artist does not create a frame of reference that gives meaning to the details; he simply exploits the ready-made symbolic meanings people attach to certain details and leaves us in a profound mess. (The middlebrow moralists think it's profound and the hippies enjoy the mess.) And when he tosses in a theatrical convention like a mimed tennis game without a ball—which connects with the journalistic data only in that it, too, is symbolic—he throws the movie game away. It becomes ah-sweet-mystery-of-life we-are-all-fools, which, pitched too high for human ears, might seem like great music beyond our grasp.

{*The New Republic*, February 11, 1967}

:: Movies on Television

A few years ago, a jet on which I was returning to California after a trip to New York was instructed to delay landing for a half hour. The plane circled above the San Francisco area, and spread out under me were the farm where I was born, the little town where my grandparents were buried, the city where I had gone to school, the cemetery where my parents were, the homes of my brothers and sisters, Berkeley, where I had gone to college, and the house where at that moment, while I hovered high above, my little daughter and my dogs were awaiting my return. It was as though my whole life were suspended in time—as though no matter where you'd gone, what you'd done, the past were all still there, present, if you just got up high enough to attain the proper perspective.

Sometimes I get a comparable sensation when I turn from the news programs or the discussion shows on television to the old movies. So much of what formed our tastes and shaped our experiences, and so much of the garbage of our youth that we never thought we'd see again—preserved and exposed to eyes and minds that might well want not to believe that this was an important part of our past. Now these movies are there for new generations, to whom they cannot possibly have the same impact or meaning, because they are all jumbled together, out of historical sequence. Even what may deserve an honorable position in movie history is somehow dishonored by being so available, so meaninglessly present. Everything is in hopeless disorder, and that is the way new generations experience our movie past. In the other arts, something like natural selection takes place: only the best or the most significant or influential or successful works compete for our attention. Moreover, those from the past are likely to be touched up to accord with the taste of the present. In popular music, old tunes are newly orchestrated. A small repertory of plays is continually reinterpreted for contemporary meanings—the great ones for new relevance, the not so great rewritten, tackily "brought up to date," or deliberately treated as period pieces. By contrast, movies, through the accidents of commerce, are sold in blocks or packages to television, the worst with the mediocre and the best, the successes with the failures, the forgotten with the half forgotten, the ones so dreary you don't know whether you ever saw them or just others like them with some so famous you can't be sure whether you actually saw them or only imagined what they were like. A lot of this stuff never really made it with any audience; it played in small towns or it was used to soak up the time just the way TV in bars does.

There are so many things that we, having lived through them, or passed over them, never want to think about again. But in movies nothing is cleaned away, sorted out, purposefully discarded. (The destruction of negatives in studio fires or deliberately, to save space, was as indiscriminate as the preservation and resale.) There's a kind of hopelessness about it: what does not deserve to last lasts, and so it all begins to seem one big pile of junk, and some people say, "Movies never really were any good—except maybe the Bogarts." If the same thing had happened in literature or music or painting—if we were constantly surrounded by the piled-up inventory of the past—it's conceivable that modern man's notions of culture and civilization would be very different. Movies, most of them produced as fodder to satisfy the appetite for pleasure and relaxation, turned out to have magical properties—indeed, to *be* magical properties. This fodder can be fed to people over and over again. Yet, not altogether strangely, as the years wear on it doesn't please their palates, though many will go on swallowing it, just because nothing tastier is easily accessible. Watching old movies is like spending an evening with those people next door. They bore us, and we wouldn't go out of our way to see them; we drop in on them because they're so close. If it took some effort to see old movies, we might try to find out which were the good ones, and if people saw only the good ones maybe they would still respect old movies. As it is, people sit and watch movies that audiences walked out on thirty years ago. Like Lot's wife, we are tempted to take another look, attracted not by evil but by something that seems much more shameful—our own innocence. We don't try to reread the girls' and boys' "series" books of our adolescence— the very look of them is dismaying. The textbooks we studied in grammar school are probably more "dated" than the movies we saw then, but we never look at the old schoolbooks, whereas we keep seeing on TV the movies that represent the same stage in our lives and played much the same part in them—as things we learned from and, in spite of, went beyond.

Not all old movies look bad now, of course; the good ones are still good—surprisingly good, often, if you consider how much of the detail is lost on television. Not only the size but the shape of the image is changed, and, indeed, almost all the specifically visual elements are so distorted as to be all but completely destroyed. On television, a cattle drive or a cavalry charge or a chase—the climax of so many a big movie—loses the dimensions of space and distance that made it exciting, that sometimes made it great. And since the structural elements—the rhythm, the buildup, the suspense—are also partly destroyed by deletions and commercial breaks and the interruptions incidental to home viewing, it's amazing that the bare bones of performance, dialogue, story, good directing, and (especially important for close-range viewing) good editing can still make an old movie more entertaining than almost anything new on television. (That's why old movies are taking over television—or, more accurately, vice versa.) The verbal slapstick of the newspaper-life comedies—*Blessed Event*, *Roxie Hart*, *His Girl Friday*—may no longer be fresh (partly because it has been so widely imitated), but it's still funny. Movies with good, fast, energetic talk seem better than ever on television—still not great but, on television, better than what *is* great. (And as we listen to the tabloid journalists insulting the corrupt politicians, we respond once again to the happy effrontery of that period when the targets of popular satire were still small enough for us to laugh at without choking.) The wit of dialogue comedies like Preston Sturges's *Unfaithfully Yours* isn't much diminished, nor does a tight melodrama like *Double Indemnity* lose a great deal. Movies like Joseph L. Mankiewicz's *A Letter to Three Wives* and *All About Eve* look practically the same on television as in theatres, because they have almost no visual dimensions to lose. In them the camera serves primarily to show us the person who is going to speak the next presumably bright line—a scheme that on television, as in theatres, is acceptable only when the line *is* bright. Horror and fantasy films like Karl Freund's *The Mummy* or Robert Florey's *The Murders in the Rue Morgue*—even with the loss, through miniaturization, of imaginative special effects—are surprisingly effective, perhaps because they are so primitive in their appeal that the qualities of the imagery matter less than the basic suggestions. Fear counts for more than finesse, and viewing horror films is far more frightening at home than in the shared comfort of an audience that breaks the tension with derision.

Other kinds of movies lose much of what made them worth looking at—the films of von Sternberg, for example, designed in light and shadow, or the subleties of Max Ophuls, or the lyricism of Satyajit Ray. In the box the work of these men is not as lively or as satisfying as the plain good movies of lesser directors. Reduced to the dead grays of a cheap television print, Orson Welles's *The Magnificent Ambersons*—an uneven work that is nevertheless a triumphant conquest of the movie medium—is as lifelessly dull as a newspaper Wirephoto of a great painting. But when people say of a "big" movie like *High Noon* that it has dated or that it doesn't hold up, what they are really saying is that their judgment was faulty or has changed. They may have overresponded to its publicity and reputation or to its attempt to deal with a social problem or an idea, and may have ignored the banalities surrounding that attempt; now that the idea doesn't seem so daring, they notice the rest. Perhaps it was a traditional drama that was new to them and that they thought was new to the world; everyone's "golden age of movies" is the period of his first moviegoing and just before—what he just missed or wasn't allowed to see. (The Bogart films came out just before today's college kids started going.)

Sometimes we suspect, and sometimes rightly, that our memory has improved a picture—that imaginatively we made it what we knew it could have been or should have been—and, fearing this, we may prefer memory to new contact. We'll remember it better if we don't see it again—we'll remember what it meant to us. The nostalgia we may have poured over a performer or over our recollections of a movie has a way of congealing when we try to renew the contact. But sometimes the experience of reseeing is wonderful—a confirmation of the general feeling that was all that remained with us from childhood. And we enjoy the fresh proof of the rightness of our responses that reseeing the film gives us. We re-experience what we once felt, and memories flood back. Then movies seem magical—all those *madeleines* waiting to be dipped in tea. What looks bad in old movies is the culture of which they were part and which they expressed—a tone of American life that we have forgotten. When we see First World War posters, we are far enough away from their patriotic primitivism to be amused at the emotions and sentiments to which they appealed. We can feel charmed but superior. It's not so easy to cut ourselves off from old movies and the old selves who responded to them, because they're not an isolated part of the past held up for derision and amusement and wonder. Although they belong to the same world as stories in *Liberty*, old radio shows, old phonograph records, an America still divided between hayseeds and city slickers, and although they may seem archaic, their pastness isn't so very past. It includes the last decade, last year, yesterday.

Though in advertising movies for TV the recentness is the lure, for many of us what constitutes the attraction is the datedness, and the earlier movies are more compelling than the ones of the fifties or the early sixties. Also, of course, the movies of the thirties and forties look better technically, because, ironically, the competition with television that made movies of the fifties and sixties enlarge their scope and their subject matter has resulted in their looking like a mess in the box—the sides of the image lopped off, the crowds and vistas a boring blur, the color altered, the epic themes incongruous and absurd on the little home screen. In a movie like *The Robe*, the large-scale production values that were depended on to attract TV viewers away from their sets become a negative factor. But even if the quality of the image were improved, these movies are too much like the ones we can see in theatres to be interesting at home. At home, we like to look at those stiff, carefully groomed actors of the thirties, with their clipped, Anglophile stage speech and their regular, clean-cut features—walking profiles, like the figures on Etruscan vases and almost as remote. And there is the faithless wife—how will she decide between her lover and her husband, when they seem as alike as two wax grooms on a wedding cake? For us, all three are doomed not by sin and disgrace but by history. Audiences of the period may have enjoyed these movies for their action, their story, their thrills, their wit, and all this high living. But through our window on the past we see the actors acting out other dramas as well. The Middle European immigrants had children who didn't speak the king's English and, after the Second World War, didn't even respect it so much. A flick of the dial and we are in the fifties amid the slouchers, with their thick lips, shapeless noses, and shaggy haircuts, waiting to say their lines until they think them out, then mumbling something that is barely speech. How long, O Warren Beatty, must we wait before we turn back to beautiful stick figures like Phillips Holmes?

We can take a shortcut through the hell of many lives, turning the dial from the social protest of the thirties to the films of the same writers and directors in the fifties—full of justifications for blabbing, which they shifted onto characters in oddly unrelated situations. We can see in the films of the forties the displaced artists of Europe—the anti-Nazi exiles like Conrad Veidt, the refugees like Peter Lorre, Fritz Kortner, and Alexander Granach. And what are they playing? Nazis, of course, because they have accents, and so for Americans—for the whole world—they become images of Nazi brutes. Or we can look at the patriotic sentiments of the Second World War years and those actresses, in their orgies of ersatz nobility, giving their lives—or, at the very least, their bodies—to save their country. It was sickening at the time; it's perversely amusing now—part of the spectacle of our common culture.

Probably in a few years some kid watching *The Sandpiper* on television will say what I recently heard a kid say about *Mrs. Miniver*: "And to think they really believed it in those days." Of course, we didn't. We didn't accept nearly as much in old movies as we may now fear we did. Many of us went to see big-name pictures just as we went to *The Night of the Iguana*, without believing a minute of it. The James Bond pictures are not to be "believed," but they tell us a lot about the conventions that audiences now accept, just as the confessional films of the thirties dealing with sin and illegitimacy and motherhood tell us about the sickly-sentimental tone of American entertainment in the midst of the Depression. Movies indicate what the producers thought people would pay to see—which was not always the same as what they *would* pay to see. Even what they enjoyed seeing does not tell us directly what they believed but only indirectly hints at the tone and style of a culture. There is no reason to assume that people twenty or thirty years ago were stupider than they are now. (Consider how *we* may be judged by people twenty years from now looking at today's movies.) Though it may not seem obvious to us now, part of the original appeal of old movies—which we certainly understood and responded to as children—was that, despite their sentimental tone, they helped to form the liberalized modern consciousness. This trash—and most of it was, and is, trash—probably taught us more about the world, and even about values, than our "education" did. Movies broke down barriers of all kinds, opened up the world, helped to make us aware. And they were almost always on the side of the mistreated, the socially despised. Almost all drama is. And, because movies were a mass medium, they had to be on the side of the poor.

Nor does it necessarily go without saying that the glimpses of something really good even in mediocre movies—the quickening of excitement at a great performance, the discovery of beauty in a gesture or a phrase or an image—made us understand the meaning of art as our teachers in appreciation courses never could. And—what is more difficult for those who are not movie lovers to grasp—even after this sense of the greater and the higher is developed, we still do not want to live only on the heights. We still want that pleasure of discovering things for ourselves; we need the sustenance of the ordinary, the commonplace, the almost-good as part of the anticipatory atmosphere. And though it all helps us to respond to the moments of greatness, it is not only for this that we want it. The educated person who became interested in cinema as an art form through Bergman or Fellini or Resnais is an alien to me (and my mind goes blank with hostility and indifference when he begins to talk). There isn't much for the art-cinema person on television; to look at a great movie, or even a poor movie carefully designed in terms of textures and contrasts, on television is, in general, maddening, because those movies lose too much. (Educational television, though, persists in this misguided effort to bring the television viewer movie classics.) There are few such movies anyway. But there are all the not-great movies, which we probably wouldn't bother going to see in museums or in theatre revivals—they're just not that important. Seeing them on television is a different kind of experience, with different values—partly because the movie past hasn't been filtered to conform to anyone's convenient favorite notions of film art. We make our own, admittedly small, discoveries or rediscoveries. There's Dan Dailey doing his advertising-wise number in *It's Always Fair Weather*, or Gene Kelly and Fred Astaire singing and dancing "The Babbitt and the Bromide" in *Ziegfeld Follies*. And it's like putting on a record of Ray Charles singing "Georgia on My Mind" or Frank Sinatra singing "Bim Bam Baby" or Elisabeth Schwarzkopf singing operetta, and feeling again the elation we felt the first time. Why should we deny these pleasures because there are other, more complex kinds of pleasure possible? It's true that these pleasures don't deepen, and that they don't change *us*, but maybe that is part of what makes them seem our own—we realize that we have some emotions and responses that *don't* change as we get older.

People who see a movie for the first time on television don't remember it the same way that people do who saw it in a theatre. Even without the specific visual loss that results from the transfer to another medium, it's doubtful whether a movie could have as intense an impact as it had in its own time. Probably by definition, works that are not truly great cannot be as compelling out of their time. Sinclair Lewis's and Hemingway's novels were becoming archaic while their authors lived. Can *On the Waterfront* have the impact now that it had in 1954? Not quite. And revivals in movie theatres don't have the same kind of charge, either. There's something a little stale in the air, there's a different kind of audience. At a revival, we must allow for the period, or care because of the period. Television viewers seeing old movies for the first time can have very little sense of how and why new stars moved us when they appeared, of the excitement of new themes, of what these movies meant to us. They don't even know which were important in their time, which were "hits."

But they can discover *something* in old movies, and there are few discoveries to be made on dramatic shows produced for television. In comedies, the nervous tic of canned laughter neutralizes everything; the laughter is as false for the funny as for the unfunny and prevents us from responding to either. In general, performances in old movies don't suffer horribly on television except from cuts, and what kindles something like the early flash fire is the power of personality that comes through in those roles that made a star. Today's high school and college students seeing *East of Eden* and *Rebel Without a Cause* for the first time are almost as caught up in James Dean as the first generation of adolescent viewers was, experiencing that tender, romantic, marvelously masochistic identification with the boy who does everything wrong because he cares so much. And because Dean died young and hard, he is not just another actor who outlived his myth and became ordinary in stale roles—he is the symbol of misunderstood youth. He is inside the skin of moviegoing and television-watching youth—even educated youth—in a way that Keats and Shelley or John Cornford and Julian Bell are not. Youth can respond—though not so strongly—to many of our old heroes and heroines: to Gary Cooper, say, as the elegant, lean, amusingly silent romantic loner of his early Western and aviation films. (And they can more easily ignore the actor who sacrificed that character for blubbering righteous bathos.) Bogart found his myth late, and Dean fulfilled the romantic myth of self-destructiveness, so they look good on television. More often, television, by showing us actors before and after their key starring roles, is a myth-killer. But it keeps acting ability alive.

There is a kind of young television watcher seeing old movies for the first time who is surprisingly sensitive to their values and responds almost with the intensity of a moviegoer. But he's different from the moviegoer. For one thing, he's housebound, inactive, solitary. Unlike a moviegoer, he seems to have no need to discuss what he sees. The kind of television watcher I mean (and the ones I've met are all boys) seems to have extreme empathy with the material in the box (new TV shows as well as old movies, though rarely news), but he may not know how to enter into a conversation, or even how to come into a room or go out of it. He fell in love with his baby-sitter, so he remains a baby. He's unusually polite and intelligent, but in a mechanical way—just going through the motions, without interest. He gives the impression that he wants to withdraw from this human interference and get back to his real life—the box. He is like a prisoner who has everything he wants in prison and is content to stay there. Yet, oddly, he and his fellows seem to be tuned in to each other; just as it sometimes seems that even a teen-ager locked in a closet would pick up the new dance steps at the same moment as other teen-agers, these television watchers react to the same things at the same time. If they can find more intensity in this box than in their own living, then this box can provide *constantly* what we got at the movies only a few times a week. Why should they move away from it, or talk, or go out of the house, when they will only experience that as a loss? Of course, we can see why they should, and their inability to make connections outside is frighteningly suggestive of ways in which we, too, are cut off. It's a matter of degree. If we stay up half the night to watch old movies and can't face the next day, it's partly, at least, because of the fascination of our own movie past; *they* live in a past they never had, like people who become obsessed by places they have only imaginative connections with—Brazil, Venezuela, Arabia Deserta. Either way, there is always something a little shameful about living in the past; we feel guilty, stupid—as if the pleasure we get needed some justification that we can't provide.

For some moviegoers, movies probably contribute to that self-defeating romanticizing of expectations which makes life a series of disappointments. They watch the same movies over and over on television, as if they were constantly returning to the scene of the crime — the life they were so busy dreaming about that they never lived it. They are paralyzed by longing, while those less romantic can leap the hurdle. I heard a story the other day about a man who ever since his school days had been worship-fully "in love with" a famous movie star, talking about her, fantasizing about her, following her career, with its ups and downs and its stormy romances and marriages to producers and agents and wealthy sportsmen and rich businessmen. Though he became successful himself, it never occurred to him that he could enter her terrain — she was so glamorously above him. Last week, he got a letter from an old classmate, to whom, years before, he had confided his adoration of the star; the classmate — an unattractive guy who had never done anything with his life and had a crummy job in a crummy business — had just married her.

Movies are a combination of art and mass medium, but television is so single in its purpose — selling — that it operates without that painful, poignant mixture of aspiration and effort and compromise. We almost never think of calling a television show "beautiful," or even of complaining about the absence of beauty, because we take it for granted that television operates without beauty. When we see on television photographic records of the past, like the pictures of Scott's Antarctic expedition or those series on the First World War, they seem almost too strong for the box, too pure for it. The past has a terror and a fascination and a beauty beyond almost anything else. We are looking at the dead, and they move and grin and wave at us; it's an almost unbearable experience. When our wonder and our grief are interrupted or followed by a commercial, we want to destroy the ugly box. Old movies don't tear us apart like that. They do something else, which we can take more of and take more easily: they give us a sense of the passage of life. Here is Elizabeth Taylor as a plump matron and here, an hour later, as an exquisite child. That charmingly petulant little gigolo with the skinny face and the mustache that seems the most substantial part of him — can he have developed into the great Laurence Olivier? Here is Orson Welles as a young man, playing a handsome old man, and here is Orson Welles as he has really aged. Here are Bette Davis and Charles Boyer traversing the course of their lives from ingenue and juvenile, through major roles, into character parts — back and forth, endlessly, embodying the good and bad characters of many styles, many periods. We see the old character actors put out to pasture in television serials, playing gossipy neighbors or grumpy grandpas, and then we see them in their youth or middle age, in the roles that made them famous—and it's startling to find how good they were, how vital, after we've encountered them caricaturing themselves, feeding off their old roles. They have almost nothing left of that young actor we responded to—and still find ourselves responding to—except the distinctive voice and a few crotchets. There are those of us who, when we watch old movies, sit there murmuring the names as the actors appear (Florence Bates, Henry Daniell, Ernest Thesiger, Constance Collier, Edna May Oliver, Douglas Fowley), or we recognize them but can't remember their names, yet know how well we once knew them, experiencing the failure of memory as a loss of our own past until we can supply it (Maude Eburne or Porter Hall)—with great relief. After a few seconds, I can always remember them, though I cannot remember the names of my childhood companions or of the prizefighter I once dated, or even of the boy who took me to the senior prom. We are eager to hear again that line we know is coming. We hate to miss anything. Our memories are jarred by cuts. We want to see the movie to the end.

The graveyard of *Our Town* affords such a tiny perspective compared to this. Old movies on television are a gigantic, panoramic novel that we can tune in to and out of. People watch avidly for a few weeks or months or years and then give up; others tune in when they're away from home in lonely hotel rooms, or regularly, at home, a few nights a week or every night. The rest of the family may ignore the passing show, may often interrupt, because individual lines of dialogue or details of plot hardly seem to matter as they did originally. A movie on television is no longer just a drama in itself; it is part of a huge ongoing parade. To a new generation, what does it matter if a few gestures and a nuance are lost, when they know they can't watch the parade on all the channels at all hours anyway? It's like traffic on the street. The television generation knows there is no end; it all just goes on. When television watchers are surveyed and asked what kind of programming they want or how they feel television can be improved, some of them not only have no answers but can't understand the questions. What they get on their sets is television—that's it.

{*The New Yorker*, June 3, 1967}

:: Orson Welles:
There Ain't No Way

What makes movies a great popular art form is that certain artists can, at moments in their lives, reach out and unify the audience — educated and uneducated — in a shared response. The tragedy in the history of movies is that those who have this capacity are usually prevented from doing so. The mass audience gets its big empty movies full of meaningless action; the art-house audience gets its studies of small action and large inaction loaded with meaning.

Almost everyone who cares about movies knows that Orson Welles is such an artist. Even audiences who don't know that Welles is a great *director* sense his largeness of talent from his presence as an actor. Audiences are alert to him, as they often were to John Barrymore, and later to Charles Laughton, as they sometimes are to Bette Davis, as they almost always are to Brando — actors too big for their roles, who play the clown, and not always in comedy but in roles that for an artist of intelligence can only be comedy. Like Brando, Welles is always being attacked for not having fulfilled his prodigious promise; but who has ever beaten the mass culture fly-by-night system of economics for long? What else could Welles do with his roles in *Black Magic* or *Prince of Foxes* or *The Black Rose* or *Trent's Last Case* but play them as comedy? Could one take such work seriously? The mediocre directors and the cynical hacks got money when he couldn't. His ironic playing is all that one remembers from those movies anyway; like Brando, he has the greatness to make effrontery a communicated, shared experience — which lesser artists had better not attempt. It takes large *latent* talent to tell the audience that you know that what you're doing isn't worth doing and still do it better than anyone else in the movie.

Waiting for a train in Grand Central station recently, I was standing next to a group of Negroes. To everything that they talked about, one of them—a young girl—said, "There ain't no way"; and it fit perfectly each time.

Orson Welles's *Falstaff* came and went so fast there was hardly time to tell people about it, but it should be back (it should be around forever) and it should be seen. It's blighted by economics and it will never reach the audience Welles might have and should have reached, because there just ain't no way. So many people—and with such complacent satisfaction, almost, one would say, delight—talk of how Welles has disappointed them, as if he had willfully thrown away his talent through that "lack of discipline" which is always brought in to explain failure. There is a widespread notion that a man who accomplishes a great deal is thus a "genius" who should be able to cut through all obstacles; and if he can't (and who can?), what he does is too far beneath what he should have done to be worth consideration. On the contrary, I think that the more gifted and imaginative a director, the greater the obstacles. It is the less imaginative director who has always flourished in the business world of movies—the "adaptable," reliable fellow who is more concerned to get the movie done than to do it his way, who, indeed, after a while has no way of his own, who is as anonymous as the director of *Prince of Foxes*. And the more determined a man is to do it his way or a new way, the more likelihood that this man (quickly labeled a "troublemaker" or "a difficult person" or "self-destructive" or "a man who makes problems for himself"—standard Hollywoodese for an artist and, of course, always true at some level, and the greater the artist, the more true it's likely to become) won't get the support he needs to complete the work his way. In the atmosphere of anxiety surrounding him, the producers may decide to "save" the project by removing him or adding to or subtracting from his work, or finally dumping the film without publicity or press screenings, consigning it to the lower half of double bills.

All these things have happened to Welles (*Citizen Kane* was not big enough at the box office and it caused trouble; he was not allowed to finish his next picture, *The Magnificent Ambersons*). Treatment of this sort, which usually marks the end of great movie careers, was for Welles the beginning. Most of these things have happened to men as pacific as Jean Renoir, whom few could accuse of being "undisciplined." (Renoir turned to writing a novel, his first, in 1966, when he could not raise money to make a movie, though the budget he required was less than half that allotted to movies made to be premiered on television.) And they are still happening to men in Hollywood like Sam Peckinpah. Such men are always blamed for the eventual failure of whatever remains of their work, while men who try for less have the successes (and are forgiven their routine failures because they didn't attempt anything the producers didn't understand). Joseph L. Mankiewicz's *Julius Caesar* was considered a success and Orson Welles's *Othello* a failure. The daring of doing Shakespeare at all was enough for Mankiewicz and his producer, John Houseman, who was to be ritualistically referred to as "the distinguished producer John Houseman" because of this film—not from his early theatre work with Orson Welles—much as George Schaefer is referred to as "the distinguished director" because of his specialty of embalming old war horses for television. Mankiewicz's luck held good on *Julius Caesar*: it's perfectly suited to the small screen, where it recently appeared, while Welles's *Othello*—with its disastrous, imperfectly synchronized soundtrack—isn't even intelligible. How could it be? A movie shot over a period of four years with Welles dashing off periodically to act in movies like *The Black Rose* to earn the money to continue; and then, his cast scattered, trying to make a soundtrack, reading half the roles himself (not only Roderigo, but if my ear is to be trusted, parts of Iago, too), selecting long shots and shots with the actors' backs to the camera to conceal the sound problem. This, of course, looked like "affectation." And his splendid, flawed production—visually and emotionally a near-masterpiece—was a "failure." Earlier, working on a Republic Pictures budget (for Republic Pictures), Welles had shot his barbaric *Macbeth*—marred most by his own performance—in twenty-three days because "no one would give me any money for a further day's shooting."

In the early fifties, Welles as an actor was in top flamboyant form. Nobody seemed to enjoy the sheer physical delight of acting as much as he in roles like his Lord Mountdrago in *Three Cases of Murder*. Still very young, he played like a great ham of the old school—which was marvelous to watch in his Father Mapple in *Moby Dick* and in *The Roots of Heaven*. This lesser talent that he could live on was a corollary to his great talent.

It was a demonstration of his love of (and prowess in) traditional theatre—like the way Vittorio De Sica (also an actor from adolescence) could go from being the romantic singing star of Italian musical comedy to make *Shoeshine* and then back again (he, too, to raise money for his own films) to playing in an ornate style, Gina's lawyer or Sophia's papa, a whole Barzini gallery of glory-ridden, mustachioed Italians. But Welles was beginning to turn into America's favorite grotesque. Like Barrymore and Laughton and Brando, he seemed to be developing an obsession with false noses, false faces. He had once, at least, played a role in his own face, Harry Lime in *The Third Man*, a role he had written for himself; by the sixties he was encased in makeup and his own fat—like a huge operatic version of W. C. Fields. Audiences laughed when he appeared on the screen. He didn't need to choose the role of Falstaff: it chose him.

When Welles went to Europe, he lost his single greatest asset as a movie director: his sound. (He had already lost the company that *talked* together, the Mercury players he had brought to Hollywood—Joseph Cotten, Agnes Moorehead, Everett Sloane, et al.—who were now working separately.) Welles had first skyrocketed to public attention on radio, and what he had brought to movies that was distinctively new was the radio sound—with an innovative use of overlapping dialogue—which was used for trick shock purposes, almost playfully, in *Citizen Kane*. But by the time of *The Magnificent Ambersons* he was using this technique for something deeper (the family bickering was startling in its almost surreal accuracy; the sound was of arguments overheard from childhood, with so many overtones they were almost mythic). Welles himself had a voice that seemed to carry its own echo chamber; somehow, in becoming the whiz kid of vocal effects, in simulating so many deep, impersonal voices, he had emptied his own voice of emotion, and when he spoke his credit at the end of *The Ambersons*, audiences laughed at the hollow voice (and perhaps at the comic justice of the *spoken* credit). Ironically, sound—the area of his greatest mastery—became his worst problem as he began to work with actors who didn't speak English and actors who did but weren't around when he needed them (for the post-synchronization which is standard practice in Europe, because the actors don't speak the same language, and is becoming standard here, too, because it saves shooting time). Welles compensated by developing greater visual virtuosity.

Yeats said "Rhetoric is heard, poetry overheard," and though I don't agree, I think I see what he means, and I think this assumption is involved in much of the rejection of a talent like Welles's. His work is often referred to as flashy and spectacular as if this also meant cheap and counterfeit. Welles is unabashedly theatrical in a period when much of the educated audience thinks theatrical flair vulgar, artistry intellectually respectable only when subtle, hidden. Welles has the approach of a *popular* artist: he glories in both verbal and visual rhetoric. He uses film *theatrically* — not stagily, but with theatrical bravado. He makes a show of the mechanics of film. He doesn't, if I may be forgiven the pun, hide his tracks. Movies gave him the world for a stage, and his is not the art that conceals art, but the showman's delight in the flourishes with which he pulls the rabbit from the hat. (This is why he was the wrong director for *The Trial*, where the poetry needed to be overheard.) I think that many people who enjoy those flourishes, who really love them — as I do — are so fearfully educated that they feel they must put them down. It's as if people said he's a mountebank, an actor showing off. But there's life in that kind of display: it's part of an earlier theatrical tradition that Welles carries over into film, it's what the theatre has lost, and it's what brought people to the movies.

Welles might have done for American talkies what D. W. Griffith did for the silent film. But when he lost his sound and his original, verbal wit, he seemed to lose his brashness, his youth, and some of his vitality. And he lost his American-ness; in Europe he had to learn a different, more exclusively visual language of film. An *enfant terrible* defeated ages fast. At fifty-one, Welles seems already the grand old master of film, because, of course, everybody knows that he'll never get in the position to do what he might have done. Governments and foundations will prattle on about excellence and American film companies will rush to sign up Englishmen and Europeans who have had a hit, hoping to snare that magic moneymaking gift. And tired transplanted Europeans will go on making big, lousy American movies, getting financed because they once had a hit and maybe the magic will come back. And Welles — the one great creative force in American films in our time, the man who might have redeemed our movies from the general contempt in which they are (and for the most part, rightly) held — is, ironically, an expatriate director whose work thus reaches only the art-house audience. And he has been so crippled by the problems of working as he does, he's lucky to reach that. The distributors of *Falstaff* tested it out of town before risking Bosley Crowther's displeasure in New York.

You may want to walk out during the first twenty minutes of *Falstaff*. Although the words on the soundtrack are intelligible, the sound doesn't match the images. We hear the voices as if the speakers were close, but on the screen the figures may be a half mile away or turned from us at some angle that doesn't jibe with the voice. In the middle of a sentence an actor may walk away from us while the voice goes on. Often, for a second, we can't be sure who is supposed to be talking. And the cutting is maddening, designed as it is for camouflage—to keep us from seeing faces closely or from registering that mouths which should be open and moving are closed. Long shots and Shakespearean dialogue are a crazy mix. It's especially jarring because the casting is superb and the performance beautiful. It's not hard to take Shakespeare adapted and transformed by other cultures—like Kurosawa's *Throne of Blood*, a *Macbeth* almost as much related to Welles's as to Shakespeare's—but the words of Shakespeare slightly out of synch! This is as intolerable as those old prints of *Henry V* that the miserly distributors circulate—chewed up by generations of projection machines, crucial syllables lost in the splices. The editing rhythm of *Falstaff* is at war with the rhythm and comprehension of the language. Welles, avoiding the naturalistic use of the outdoors in which Shakespeare's dialogue sounds more stagey than on stage, has photographically stylized the Spanish locations, creating a theatrically darkened, slightly unrealistic world of angles and low beams and silhouettes. When this photographic style is shattered by the cuts necessary to conceal the dialogue problems, the camera angles seem unnecessarily exaggerated and pretentious. But then despite everything—the angles, the doubles in long shots, the editing that distracts us when we need to concentrate on the dialogue—the movie begins to be great. The readings in *Falstaff* are great even if they don't always go with the images, which are often great, too.

Welles has brought together the pieces of Falstaff that Shakespeare had strewn over the two parts of *Henry IV* and *The Merry Wives of Windsor*, with cuttings from *Henry V* and *Richard II*, and fastened them into place with narration from Holinshed's Chronicles (read by Ralph Richardson). Those of us who resisted our schoolteachers' best efforts to make us appreciate the comic genius of Shakespeare's fools and buffoons will not be surprised that Welles wasn't able to make Falstaff very funny: he's a great conception of a character, but the charades and practical jokes seem meant to be funnier than they are. This movie does, however, provide the best Shakespearean comic moment I can recall: garrulous Falstaff sitting with Shallow (Alan Webb) and Silence (Walter Chiari), rolling his eyes in irritation and impatience at Silence's stammer. But Welles's Falstaff isn't essentially comic; W. C. Fields's Micawber wasn't either: these actors, so funny when they're playing with their own personae in roles too small for them, are not so funny when they're trying to measure up. The carousing and roistering in the tavern doesn't seem like such great fun either, though Welles and the cast work very hard to convince us it is. Oddly, we never really see the friendship of Prince Hal—played extraordinarily well by Keith Baxter —and Falstaff; the lighter side in *Henry IV, Part I* is lost—probably well lost, though we must take it for granted in the film. What we see are the premonitions of the end: Hal taking part in games that have gone stale for him, preparing himself for his final rejection of his adopted father Falstaff in order to turn into a worthy successor of his father the king. And we see what this does to Falstaff, the braggart with the heart of a child who expects to be forgiven everything, even what he knows to be unforgivable—his taking the credit away from Hal for the combat with Hotspur (Norman Rodway). Falstaff lacks judgment, which kings must have.

John Gielgud's Henry IV is the perfect contrast to Welles; Gielgud has never been so monkishly perfect in a movie. Welles could only get him for two weeks of the shooting and the makeshift of some of his scenes is obvious, but his performance gives the film the austerity it needs for the conflict in Hal to be dramatized. Gielgud's king is so refined—a skeleton too dignified for any flesh to cling to it, inhabited by a voice so modulated it is an exquisite spiritual whine. Merrie England? Falstaff at least provides a carcass to mourn over.

Welles as an actor had always been betrayed by his voice. It was too much and it was inexpressive; there was no warmth in it, no sense of a life lived. It was just an instrument that he played, and it seemed to be the key to something shallow and unfelt even in his best performances, and most fraudulent when he tried to make it tender. I remember that once, in *King Lear* on television, he hit a phrase and I thought his voice was emotionally right; it had beauty—and what a change it made in his acting! In *Falstaff*

Welles seems to have grown into his voice; he's not too young for it anymore, and he's certainly big enough. And his emotions don't seem fake anymore; he's grown into them, too. He has the eyes for the role. Though his Falstaff is short on comedy, it's very rich, very full.

He has directed a sequence, the battle of Shrewsbury, which is unlike anything he has ever done, indeed unlike any battle ever done on the screen before. It ranks with the best of Griffith, John Ford, Eisenstein, Kurosawa—that is, with the best ever done. How can one sequence in this movie be so good? It has no dialogue and so he isn't handicapped: for the only time in the movie he can edit, not to cover gaps and defects but as an artist. The compositions suggest Uccello and the chilling ironic music is a death knell for all men in battle. The soldiers, plastered by the mud they fall in, are already monuments. It's the most brutally somber battle ever filmed. It does justice to Hotspur's great "O, Harry, thou hast robbed me of my youth."

Welles has filled the cast with box-office stars. Margaret Rutherford, Jeanne Moreau, Marina Vlady are all in it (though the girl I like best is little Beatrice Welles as the pageboy). And Falstaff is the most popular crowd-pleasing character in the work of the most enduringly popular writer who ever lived. Yet, because of technical defects due to poverty, Welles's finest Shakespearean production to date—another near-masterpiece, and this time so very close—cannot reach a large public. There ain't no way.

{*The New Republic*, June 24, 1967}

:: *Bonnie and Clyde*

How do you make a good movie in this country without being jumped on? *Bonnie and Clyde* is the most excitingly American American movie since *The Manchurian Candidate*. The audience is alive to it. Our experience as we watch it has some connection with the way we reacted to movies in childhood: with how we came to love them and to feel they were ours—not an art that we learned over the years to appreciate but simply and immediately ours. When an American movie is contemporary in feeling, like this one, it makes a different kind of contact with an American audience from the kind that is made by European films, however contemporary. Yet any movie that is contemporary in feeling is likely to go further than other movies—go too far for some tastes—and *Bonnie and Clyde* divides audiences, as *The Manchurian Candidate* did, and it is being jumped on almost as hard. Though we may dismiss the attacks with "What good movie doesn't give some offense?," the fact that it is generally *only* good movies that provoke attacks by many people suggests that the innocuousness of most of our movies is accepted with such complacence that when an American movie reaches people, when it makes them react, some of them think there must be something the matter with it—perhaps a law should be passed against it. *Bonnie and Clyde* brings into the almost frighteningly public world of movies things that people have been feeling and saying and writing about. And once something is said or done on the screens of the world, once it has entered mass art, it can never again belong to a minority, never again be the private possession of an educated, or "knowing," group. But even for that group there is an excitement in hearing its own private thoughts expressed out loud and in seeing something of its own sensibility become part of our common culture.

Our best movies have always made entertainment out of the anti-heroism of American life; they bring to the surface what, in its newest forms and fashions, is always just below the surface. The romanticism in American movies lies in the cynical tough guy's independence; the sentimentality lies, traditionally, in the falsified finish when the anti-hero turns hero. In 1967, this kind of sentimentality wouldn't work with the audience, and *Bonnie and Clyde* substitutes sexual fulfillment for a change of heart. (This doesn't quite work, either; audiences sophisticated enough to enjoy a movie like this one are too sophisticated for the dramatic uplift of the triumph over impotence.)

Structurally, *Bonnie and Clyde* is a story of love on the run, like the old Clark Gable–Claudette Colbert *It Happened One Night* but turned inside out; the walls of Jericho are psychological this time, but they fall anyway. If the story of Bonnie Parker and Clyde Barrow seemed almost from the start, and even to them while they were living it, to be the material of legend, it's because robbers who are loyal to each other—like the James brothers—are a grade up from garden-variety robbers, and if they're male and female partners in crime and young and attractive they're a rare breed. The Barrow gang had both family loyalty and sex appeal working for their legend. David Newman and Robert Benton, who wrote the script for *Bonnie and Clyde*, were able to use the knowledge that, like many of our other famous outlaws and gangsters, the real Bonnie and Clyde seemed to others to be acting out forbidden roles and to relish their roles. In contrast with secret criminals—the furtive embezzlers and other crooks who lead seemingly honest lives—the known outlaws capture the public imagination, because they take chances, and because, often, they enjoy dramatizing their lives. They know that newspaper readers want all the details they can get about the criminals who do the terrible things they themselves don't dare to do, and also want the satisfaction of reading about the punishment after feasting on the crimes. Outlaws play to this public; they show off their big guns and fancy clothes and their defiance of the law. Bonnie and Clyde established the images for their own legend in the photographs they posed for: the gunman and the gun moll. The naïve, touching doggerel ballad that Bonnie Parker wrote and had published in newspapers is about the roles they play for other people contrasted with the coming end for them. It concludes:

Someday they'll go down together;
They'll bury them side by side;
To few it'll be grief—
To the law a relief—
But it's death for Bonnie and Clyde.

That they did capture the public imagination is evidenced by the many movies based on their lives. In the late forties, there were *They Live by Night*, with Farley Granger and Cathy O'Donnell, and *Gun Crazy*, with John Dall and Peggy Cummins. (Alfred Hitchcock, in the same period, cast these two Clyde Barrows, Dall and Granger, as Loeb and Leopold, in *Rope*.) And there was a cheap—in every sense—1958 exploitation film, *The Bonnie Parker Story*, starring Dorothy Provine. But the most important earlier version was Fritz Lang's *You Only Live Once*, starring Sylvia Sidney as "Joan" and Henry Fonda as "Eddie," which was made in 1937; this version, which was one of the best American films of the thirties, as *Bonnie and Clyde* is of the sixties, expressed certain feelings of its time, as this film expresses certain feelings of ours. (*They Live by Night*, produced by John Houseman under the aegis of Dore Schary, and directed by Nicholas Ray, was a very serious and socially significant tragic melodrama, but its attitudes were already dated thirties attitudes: the lovers were very young and pure and frightened and underprivileged; the hardened criminals were sordid; the settings were committedly grim. It made no impact on the postwar audience, though it was a great success in England, where our moldy socially significant movies could pass for courageous.)

Just how contemporary in feeling *Bonnie and Clyde* is may be indicated by contrasting it with *You Only Live Once*, which, though almost totally false to the historical facts, was *told* straight. It is a peculiarity of our times—perhaps it's one of the few specifically modern characteristics—that we don't take our stories straight any more. This isn't necessarily bad. *Bonnie and Clyde* is the first film demonstration that the put-on can be used for the purposes of art. *The Manchurian Candidate almost* succeeded in that, but what was implicitly wild and far-out in the material was nevertheless presented on screen as a straight thriller. *Bonnie and Clyde* keeps the audience in a kind of eager, nervous imbalance—holds our attention by throwing our disbelief back in our faces. To be put on is to be put on the spot, put on the stage, made the stooge in a comedy act. People in the audience at *Bonnie and Clyde* are laughing, demonstrating that they're not stooges—that they appreciate the joke—when they catch the first bullet right in the face. The movie keeps them off balance to the end. During the first part of the picture, a woman in my row was gleefully assuring her companions, "It's a comedy. It's a comedy." After a while, she didn't say anything. Instead of the movie spoof, which tells the audience that it doesn't need to feel or care, that it's all just in fun, that "we were only kidding," *Bonnie and Clyde* disrupts us with "And you thought we were only kidding."

This is the way the story was told in 1937. Eddie (Clyde) is a three-time loser who wants to work for a living, but nobody will give him a chance. Once you get on the wrong side of the law, "they" won't let you get back. Eddie knows it's hopeless—once a loser, always a loser. But his girl, Joan (Bonnie)—the only person who believes in him—thinks that an innocent man has nothing to fear. She marries him, and learns better. Arrested again and sentenced to death for a crime he didn't commit, Eddie asks her to smuggle a gun to him in prison, and she protests, "If I get you a gun, you'll kill somebody." He stares at her sullenly and asks, "What do you think they're going to do to me?" He becomes a murderer while escaping from prison; "society" has made him what it thought he was all along. *You Only Live Once* was an indictment of "society," of the forces of order that will not give Eddie the outcast a chance. "We have a right to live," Joan says as they set out across the country. During the time they are on the run, they become notorious outlaws; they are blamed for a series of crimes they didn't commit. (They do commit holdups, but only to get gas or groceries or medicine.) While the press pictures them as desperadoes robbing and killing and living high on the proceeds of crime, she is having a baby in a shack in a hobo jungle, and Eddie brings her a bouquet of wild flowers. Caught in a police trap, they die in each other's arms; they have been denied the right to live.

Because *You Only Live Once* was so well done, and because the audience in the thirties shared this view of the indifference and cruelty of "society," there were no protests against the sympathetic way the outlaws were pictured—and, indeed, there was no reason for any. In 1958, in *I Want to Live!* (a very popular, though not very good, movie), Barbara Graham, a drug-addict prostitute who had been executed for her share in the bludgeoning to death of an elderly woman, was presented as gallant, wronged,

morally superior to everybody else in the movie, in order to strengthen
the argument against capital punishment, and the director, Robert Wise,
and his associates weren't accused of glorifying criminals, because the
"criminals," as in *You Only Live Once*, weren't criminals but innocent victims. Why the protests, why are so many people upset (and not just the
people who enjoy indignation), about *Bonnie and Clyde*, in which the criminals *are* criminals—Clyde an ignorant, sly near psychopath who thinks
his crimes are accomplishments, and Bonnie a bored, restless waitress-slut
who robs for excitement? And why so many accusations of historical inac-
curacy, particularly against a work that is far more accurate historically
than most and in which historical accuracy hardly matters anyway? There
is always an issue of historical accuracy involved in any dramatic or literary
work set in the past; indeed, it's fun to read about Richard III vs. Shakespeare's Richard III. The issue is always with us, and will always be with
us as long as artists find stimulus in historical figures and want to present
their versions of them. But why didn't movie critics attack, for example,
A Man for All Seasons—which involves material of much more historical
importance—for being historically inaccurate? Why attack *Bonnie and
Clyde* more than the other movies based on the same pair, or more than
the movie treatments of Jesse James or Billy the Kid or Dillinger or Capone
or any of our other fictionalized outlaws? I would suggest that when a
movie so clearly conceived as a new version of a legend is attacked as historically inaccurate, it's because it shakes people a little. I know this is
based on some pretty sneaky psychological suppositions, but I don't see
how else to account for the use only against a *good* movie of arguments
that could be used against almost all movies. When I asked a nineteen-
year-old boy who was raging against the movie as "a cliché-ridden fraud"
if he got so worked up about other movies, he informed me that that was
an argument *ad hominem*. And it is indeed. To ask why people react so
angrily to the best movies and have so little negative reaction to poor ones
is to imply that they are so unused to the experience of art in movies that
they fight it.

Audiences at *Bonnie and Clyde* are not given a simple, secure basis for
identification; they are made to feel but are not told *how* to feel. *Bonnie
and Clyde* is not a serious melodrama involving us in the plight of the innocent but a movie that assumes—as William Wellman did in 1931 when he
made *The Public Enemy*, with James Cagney as a smart, cocky, mean little

crook—that we don't need to pretend we're interested only in the falsely accused, as if real criminals had no connection with us. There wouldn't be the popular excitement there is about outlaws if we didn't all suspect that—in some cases, at least—gangsters must take pleasure in the profits and glory of a life of crime. Outlaws wouldn't become legendary figures if we didn't suspect that there's more to crime than the social workers' case studies may show. And though what we've always been told will happen to them—that they'll come to a bad end—does seem to happen, some part of us wants to believe in the tiny possibility that they can get away with it. Is that really so terrible? Yet when it comes to movies people get nervous about acknowledging that there must be some fun in crime (though the gleam in Cagney's eye told its own story). *Bonnie and Clyde* shows the fun but uses it, too, making comedy out of the banality and conventionality of that fun. What looks ludicrous in this movie isn't *merely* ludicrous, and after we have laughed at ignorance and helplessness and emptiness and stupidity and idiotic deviltry, the laughs keep sticking in our throats, because what's funny isn't only funny.

In 1937, the movie-makers knew that the audience wanted to believe in the innocence of Joan and Eddie, because these two were lovers, and inno-cent lovers hunted down like animals made a tragic love story. In 1967, the movie-makers know that the audience wants to believe—maybe even pre-fers to believe—that Bonnie and Clyde were guilty of crimes, all right, but that they were innocent in general; that is, naïve and ignorant *compared with us.* The distancing of the sixties version shows the gangsters in an already legendary period, and part of what makes a legend for Americans is viewing anything that happened in the past as much simpler than what we are involved in now. We tend to find the past funny and the recent past campy-funny. The getaway cars of the early thirties are made to seem hilarious. (Imagine anyone getting away from a bank holdup in a tin lizzie like that!) In *You Only Live Once*, the outlaws existed in the same present as the audience, and there was (and still is, I'm sure) nothing funny about them; in *Bonnie and Clyde* that audience is in the movie, transformed into the poor people, the Depression people, of legend—with faces and poses out of Dorothea Lange and Walker Evans and *Let Us Now Praise Famous Men*. In 1937, the audience felt sympathy for the fugitives because they weren't allowed to lead normal lives; in 1967, the "normality" of the Barrow gang and their individual aspirations toward respectability are the craziest things about them—not just because they're killers but because thirties "normality" is in itself funny to us. The writers and the director of *Bonnie and Clyde* play upon our attitudes toward the American past by making the hats and guns and holdups look as dated as two-reel comedy; emphasizing the absurdity with banjo music, they make the period seem even farther away than it is. The Depression reminiscences are not used for purposes of social consciousness; hard times are not the reason for the Barrows' crimes, just the excuse. "We" didn't make Clyde a killer; the movie deliberately avoids easy sympathy by picking up Clyde when he is already a cheap crook. But Clyde is not the urban sharpster of *The Public Enemy*; he is the hick as bank robber—a countrified gangster, a hillbilly killer who doesn't mean any harm. People so simple that they are alienated from the results of their actions—like the primitives who don't connect babies with copulation—provide a kind of archetypal comedy for us. It may seem like a minor point that Bonnie and Clyde are presented as not mean and sadistic, as having killed only when cornered; but in terms of legend, and particularly movie legend, it's a major one. The "classic" gangster films showed gang members betraying each other and viciously murdering the renegade who left to join another gang; the gang-leader hero no sooner got to the top than he was betrayed by someone he had trusted or someone he had double-crossed. In contrast, the Barrow gang represent family-style crime. And Newman and Benton have been acute in emphasizing this—not making them victims of society (they are never that, despite Penn's cloudy efforts along these lines) but making them absurdly "just-folks" ordinary. When Bonnie tells Clyde to pull off the road—"I want to talk to you"—they are in a getaway car, leaving the scene of a robbery, with the police right behind them, but they are absorbed in family bickering: the traditional all-American use of the family automobile. In a sense, it is the absence of sadism—it is the violence without sadism—that throws the audience off balance at *Bonnie and Clyde*. The brutality that comes out of this innocence is far more shocking than the calculated brutalities of mean killers.

Playfully posing with their guns, the real Bonnie and Clyde mocked the "Bloody Barrows" of the Hearst press. One photograph shows slim, pretty Bonnie, smiling and impeccably dressed, pointing a huge gun at Clyde's chest as he, a dimpled dude with a cigar, smiles back. The famous picture of Bonnie in the same clothes but looking ugly squinting into the sun, with a foot on the car, a gun on her hip, and a cigar in her mouth, is obviously a joke—her caricature of herself as a gun moll. Probably, since they never meant to kill, they thought the "Bloody Barrows" were a joke—a creation of the lying newspapers.

There's something new working for the Bonnie-and-Clyde legend now: our nostalgia for the thirties—the unpredictable, contrary affection of the prosperous for poverty, or at least for the artifacts, the tokens, of poverty, for Pop culture seen in the dreariest rural settings, where it truly seems to belong. Did people in the cities listen to the Eddie Cantor show? No doubt they did, but the sound of his voice, like the sound of Ed Sullivan now, evokes a primordial, pre-urban existence—the childhood of the race. Our comic-melancholic affection for thirties Pop has become sixties Pop, and those who made *Bonnie and Clyde* are smart enough to use it that way. Being knowing is not an artist's highest gift, but it can make a hell of a lot of difference in a movie. In the American experience, the miseries of the Depression are funny in the way that the Army is funny to draftees—a shared catastrophe, a leveling, forming part of our common background. Those too young to remember the Depression have heard about it from their parents. (When I was at college, we used to top each other's stories about how our families had survived: the fathers who had committed suicide so that their wives and children could live off the insurance; the mothers trying to make a game out of the meals of potatoes cooked on an open fire.) Though the American derision of the past has many offensive aspects, it has some good ones, too, because it's a way of making fun not only of our forebears but of ourselves and our pretensions. The toughness about what we've come out of and what we've been through—the honesty to see ourselves as the Yahoo children of yokels—is a good part of American popular art. There is a kind of American poetry in a stickup gang seen chasing across the bedraggled backdrop of the Depression (as true in its way as Nabokov's vision of Humbert Humbert and Lolita in the cross-country world of motels)—as if crime were the only activity in a country stupefied by poverty. But Arthur Penn doesn't quite have the toughness of mind to know it; it's not what he means by poetry. His squatters'-jungle scene is too "eloquent," like a poster making an appeal, and the Parker-family-reunion sequence is poetic in the gauzy mode. He makes the sequence a fancy lyric interlude, like a number in a musical (*Funny Face*, to be exact); it's too "imaginative"—a literal dust bowl, as thoroughly becalmed as Sleeping Beauty's garden. The movie becomes dreamy-soft where it should be hard (and hard-edged).

If there is such a thing as an American tragedy, it must be funny. O'Neill undoubtedly felt this when he had James Tyrone get up to turn off the lights in *Long Day's Journey Into Night*. We are bumpkins, haunted by the bottle of ketchup on the dining table at San Simeon. We garble our foreign words and phrases and hope that at least we've used them right. Our heroes pick up the wrong fork, and the basic figure of fun in the American theatre and American movies is the man who puts on airs. Children of peddlers and hod carriers don't feel at home in tragedy; we are used to failure. But, because of the quality of American life at the present time, perhaps there can be no real comedy—nothing more than stupidity and "spoof"—without true horror in it. Bonnie and Clyde and their partners in crime are comically bad bank robbers, and the backdrop of poverty makes their holdups seem pathetically tacky, yet they rob banks and kill people; Clyde and his good-natured brother are so shallow they never think much about anything, yet they suffer and die.

If this way of holding more than one attitude toward life is already familiar to us—if we recognize the make-believe robbers whose toy guns produce real blood, and the Keystone cops who shoot them dead, from Truffaut's *Shoot the Piano Player* and Godard's gangster pictures, *Breathless* and *Band of Outsiders*—it's because the young French directors discovered the poetry of crime in American life (from our movies) and showed the Americans how to put it on the screen in a new, "existential" way. Melo-dramas and gangster movies and comedies were always more our speed than "prestigious," "distinguished" pictures; the French directors who grew up on American pictures found poetry in our fast action, laconic speech, plain gestures. And because they understood that you don't express your love of life by denying the comedy or the horror of it, they brought out the poetry in our tawdry subjects. Now Arthur Penn, working with a script heavily influenced—one might almost say inspired—by Truffaut's *Shoot the Piano Player*, unfortunately imitates Truffaut's artistry instead of going back to its tough American sources. The French may tenderize their American material, but we shouldn't. That turns into another way of mak-ing "prestigious," "distinguished" pictures.

Probably part of the discomfort that people feel about *Bonnie and Clyde* grows out of its compromises and its failures. I wish the script hadn't provided the upbeat of the hero's sexual success as a kind of sop to the audience. I think what makes us not believe in it is that it isn't consistent with the intelligence of the rest of the writing—that it isn't on the same level, because it's too manipulatively clever, too much of a gimmick. (The scene that shows the gnomish gang member called C.W. sleeping in the same room with Bonnie and Clyde suggests other possibilities, perhaps discarded, as does C.W.'s reference to Bonnie's liking his tattoo.) Compromises are not new to the Bonnie-and-Clyde story; *You Only Live Once* had a tacked-on coda featuring a Heavenly choir and William Gargan as a dead priest, patronizing Eddie even in the afterlife, welcoming him to Heaven with "You're free, Eddie!" The kind of people who make a movie like *You Only Live Once* are not the kind who write endings like that, and, by the same sort of internal evidence, I'd guess that Newman and Benton, whose Bonnie seems to owe so much to Catherine in *Jules and Jim*, had more interesting ideas originally about Bonnie's and Clyde's (and maybe C.W.'s) sex lives.

But people also feel uncomfortable about the violence, and here I think they're wrong. That is to say, they *should* feel uncomfortable, but this isn't an argument *against* the movie. Only a few years ago, a good director would have suggested the violence obliquely, with reaction shots (like the famous one in *The Golden Coach*, when we see a whole bullfight reflected in Anna Magnani's face), and death might have been symbolized by a light going out, or stylized, with blood and wounds kept to a minimum. In many ways, this method is more effective; we feel the violence more because so much is left to our imaginations. But the whole point of *Bonnie and Clyde* is to rub our noses in it, to make us pay our dues for laughing. The dirty reality of death—not suggestions but blood and holes—is necessary. Though I generally respect a director's skill and intelligence in inverse ratio to the violence he shows on the screen, and though I questioned even the Annie Sullivan–Helen Keller fight scenes in Arthur Penn's *The Miracle Worker*, I think that this time Penn is right. (I think he was also right when he showed violence in his first film, *The Left Handed Gun*, in 1958.) Suddenly, in the last few years, our view of the world has gone beyond "good taste." Tasteful suggestions of violence would at this point be a more grotesque form of comedy than *Bonnie and Clyde* attempts. *Bonnie and Clyde* needs violence; violence is its meaning. When, during a comically botched-up getaway, a man is shot in the face, the image is obviously based on one of the most famous sequences in Eisenstein's *Potemkin*, and the startled face is used the same way it was in *Potemkin*—to convey in an instant how someone who just happens to be in the wrong place at the wrong time, the irrelevant "innocent" bystander, can get it full in the face. And at that instant the meaning of Clyde Barrow's character changes; he's still a clown, but *we've* become the butt of the joke.

It is a kind of violence that says something to us; it is something that movies must be free to use. And it is just because artists must be free to use violence—a legal right that is beginning to come under attack—that we must also defend the legal rights of those film-makers who use violence to sell tickets, for it is not the province of the law to decide that one man is an artist and another man a no-talent. The no-talent has as much right to produce works as the artist has, and not only because he has a surprising way of shifting from one category to the other but also because men have an inalienable right to be untalented, and the law should not discriminate against lousy "artists." I am not saying that the violence in *Bonnie and Clyde* is legally acceptable because the film is a work of art; I think that *Bonnie and Clyde*, though flawed, is a work of art, but I think that the violence in *The Dirty Dozen*, which isn't a work of art, and whose violence offends me *personally*, should also be legally defensible, however morally questionable. Too many people—including some movie reviewers—want the law to take over the job of movie criticism; perhaps what they really want is for their own criticisms to have the force of law. Such people see *Bonnie and Clyde* as a danger to public morality; they think an audience goes to a play or a movie and takes the actions in it as examples for imitation. They look at the world and blame the movies. But if women who are angry with their husbands take it out on the kids, I don't think we can blame *Medea* for it; if, as has been said, we are a nation of mother-lovers, I don't think we can place the blame on *Oedipus Rex*. Part of the power of art lies in showing us what we are *not* capable of. We see that killers are not a different breed but are us without the insight or understanding or self-control that works of art strengthen. The tragedy of *Macbeth* is in the fall from nobility to horror; the comic tragedy of *Bonnie and Clyde* is that although you can't fall from the bottom you can reach the same horror. The movies may set styles in dress- or love-making, they may advertise cars or beverages, but art is not examples for imitation—that is not what a work of art does for us—though that is what guardians of morality *think* art is and what they want it to be and why they think a good movie is one that sets "healthy," "cheerful" examples of behavior, like a giant all-purpose commercial for the American way of life. But people don't "buy" what they see in a movie quite so simply; Louis B. Mayer did not turn us into a nation of Andy Hardys, and if, in a film, we see a frightened man wantonly take the life of another, it does not encourage us to do the same, any more than seeing an ivory hunter shoot an elephant makes us want to shoot one. It may, on the contrary, so sensitize us that we get a pang in the gut if we accidentally step on a moth.

Will we, as some people have suggested, be lured into imitating the violent crimes of Clyde and Bonnie because Warren Beatty and Faye Dunaway are "glamorous"? Do they, as some people have charged, confer glamour on violence? It's difficult to see how, since the characters they play are horrified by it and ultimately destroyed by it. Nobody in the movie gets pleasure from violence. Is the charge based on the notion that simply by their presence in the movie Warren Beatty and Faye Dunaway make crime attractive? If movie stars can't play criminals without our all wanting to be criminals, then maybe the only safe roles for them to play are movie stars—which, in this assumption, everybody wants to be anyway. After all, if they played factory workers, the economy might be dislocated by everybody's trying to become a factory worker. (Would having criminals played by dwarfs or fatties discourage crime? It seems rather doubtful.) The accusation that the beauty of movie stars makes the anti-social acts of their characters dangerously attractive is the kind of contrived argument we get from people who are bothered by something and are clutching at straws. Actors and actresses are *usually* more beautiful than ordinary people. And why not? Garbo's beauty notwithstanding, her Anna Christie did not turn us into whores, her Mata Hari did not turn us into spies, her Anna Karenina did not make us suicides. We did not want her to be ordinary looking. Why should we be deprived of the pleasure of beauty? Garbo could be all women in love because, being more beautiful than life, she could more beautifully express emotions. It is a supreme asset for actors and actresses to be beautiful; it gives them greater range and greater possibilities for expressiveness. The handsomer they are, the more roles they can play; Olivier can be anything, but who would want to see Ralph Richardson, great as he is, play Antony? Actors and actresses who are beautiful start with an enormous advantage, because we love to look at them. The joke in the glamour charge is that Faye Dunaway has the magazine-illustration look of countless uninterestingly pretty girls, and Warren Beatty has the kind of high-school good looks that are generally lost fast.

It's the roles that make *them* seem glamorous. Good roles do that for actors.

There is a story told against Beatty in a recent *Esquire*—how during the shooting of *Lilith* he "delayed a scene for three days demanding the line 'I've read *Crime and Punishment* and *The Brothers Karamazov*' be changed to 'I've read *Crime and Punishment* and *half* of *The Brothers Karamazov*.'" Considerations of professional conduct aside, what is odd is why his adversaries waited three days to give in, because, of course, he was right. That's what the character he played *should* say; the other way, the line has no point at all. But this kind of intuition isn't enough to make an actor, and in a number of roles Beatty, probably because he doesn't have the technique to make the most of his lines in the least possible time, has depended too much on intuitive non-acting—holding the screen far too long as he acted out self-preoccupied characters in a lifelike, boringly self-conscious way. He has a gift for slyness, though, as he showed in *The Roman Spring of Mrs. Stone*, and in most of his films he could hold the screen—maybe because there seemed to be something going on in his mind, some kind of calculation. There was something smart about him—something shrewdly private in those squeezed-up little non-actor's eyes—that didn't fit the clean-cut juvenile roles. Beatty was the producer of *Bonnie and Clyde*, responsible for keeping the company on schedule, and he has been quoted as saying, "There's not a scene that we have done that we couldn't do better by taking another day." This is the hell of the expensive way of making movies, but it probably helps to explain why Beatty is more intense than he has been before and why he has picked up his pace. His business sense may have improved his timing. The role of Clyde Barrow seems to have released something in him. As Clyde, Beatty is good with his eyes and mouth and his hat, but his body is still inexpressive; he doesn't have a trained actor's use of his body, and, watching him move, one is never for a minute convinced he's impotent. It is, however, a tribute to his performance that one singles this failure out. His slow timing works perfectly in the sequence in which he offers the dispossessed farmer his gun; there may not be another actor who would have dared to prolong the scene that way, and the prolongation until the final "We rob banks" gives the sequence its comic force. I have suggested elsewhere that one of the reasons that rules are impossible in the arts is that in movies (and in the other arts, too) the new "genius"—the genuine as well as the fraudulent or the dubious—is often the man who has enough audacity, or is simpleminded enough, to do what others had the good taste not to do. Actors before Brando did not mumble and scratch and show their sweat; dramatists before Tennessee Williams did not make explicit a particular substratum of American erotic fantasy; movie directors before Orson Welles did not dramatize the techniques of film-making; directors before Richard Lester did not lay out the whole movie as cleverly as the opening credits; actresses before Marilyn Monroe did not make an asset of their ineptitude by turning faltering misreadings into an appealing style. Each, in a large way, did something that people had always enjoyed and were often embarrassed or ashamed about enjoying. Their "bad taste" shaped a new accepted taste. Beatty's non-actor's "bad" timing may be this kind of "genius"; we seem to be watching him *think out* his next move.

It's difficult to know how Bonnie should have been played, because the character isn't worked out. Here the script seems weak. She is made too warmly sympathetic—and sympathetic in a style that antedates the style of the movie. Being frustrated and moody, she's not funny enough—neither ordinary, which, in the circumstances, would be comic, nor perverse, which might be rather funny, too. Her attitude toward her mother is too loving. There could be something funny about her wanting to run home to her mama, but, as it has been done, her heading home, running off through the fields, is unconvincing—incompletely motivated. And because the element of the ridiculous that makes the others so individual has been left out of her character she doesn't seem to belong to the period as the others do. Faye Dunaway has a sixties look anyway—not just because her eyes are made up in a sixties way and her hair is wrong but because her personal style and her acting are sixties. (This may help to make her popular; she can seem prettier to those who don't recognize prettiness except in the latest styles.) Furthermore, in some difficult-to-define way, Faye Dunaway as Bonnie doesn't keep her distance—that is to say, an *actor's* distance—either from the role or from the audience. She doesn't hold a characterization; she's in and out of emotions all the time, and though she often hits effective ones, the emotions seem *hers*, not the character's. She has some talent, but she comes on too strong; she makes one conscious that she's a willing worker, but she doesn't seem to know what she's doing—rather like Bonnie in her attempts to overcome Clyde's sexual difficulties.

...

Although many daily movie reviewers judge a movie in isolation, as if the people who made it had no previous history, more serious critics now commonly attempt to judge a movie as an expressive vehicle of the director, and a working out of his personal themes. Auden has written, "Our judgment of an established author is never simply an aesthetic judgment. In addition to any literary merit it may have, a new book by him has a historic interest for us as the act of a person in whom we have long been interested. He is not only a poet . . . he is also a character in our biography." For a while, people went to the newest Bergman and the newest Fellini that way; these movies were greeted like the latest novels of a favorite author. But Arthur Penn is not a writer-director like Bergman or Fellini, both of whom began as writers, and who (even though Fellini employs several collaborators) compose their spiritual autobiographies step by step on film. Penn is far more dependent on the talents of others, and his primary material—what he starts with—does not come out of his own experience. If the popular audience is generally uninterested in the director (unless he is heavily publicized, like DeMille or Hitchcock), the audience that is interested in the art of movies has begun, with many of the critics, to think of movies as a directors' medium to the point where they tend to ignore the contribution of the writers—and the directors may be almost obscenely content to omit mention of the writers. The history of the movies is being rewritten to disregard facts in favor of celebrating the director as the sole "creative" force. One can read Josef von Sternberg's autobiography and the text of the latest books on his movies without ever finding the name of Jules Furthman, the writer who worked on nine of his most famous movies (including *Morocco* and *Shanghai Express*). Yet the appearance of Furthman's name in the credits of such Howard Hawks films as *Only Angels Have Wings*, *To Have and Have Not*, *The Big Sleep*, and *Rio Bravo* suggests the reason for the similar qualities of good-bad-girl glamour in the roles played by Dietrich and Bacall and in other von Sternberg and Hawks heroines, and also in the Jean Harlow and Constance Bennett roles in the movies he wrote for *them*. Furthman, who has written about half of the most entertaining movies to come out of Hollywood (Ben Hecht wrote most of the other half), isn't even listed in new encyclopedias of the film. David Newman and Robert Benton may be good enough to join this category of unmentionable men who do what the directors are glorified for. The Hollywood writer is becoming a ghostwriter. The writers who succeed in the struggle to protect their identity and their material by becoming writer-directors or writer-producers soon become too rich and powerful to bother doing their own writing. And they rarely have the visual sense or the training to make good movie directors.

Anyone who goes to big American movies like *Grand Prix* and *The Sand Pebbles* recognizes that movies with scripts like those don't have a chance to be anything more than exercises in technology, and that this is what is meant by the decadence of American movies. In the past, directors used to say that they were no better than their material. (Sometimes they said it when they weren't even up to their material.) A good director can attempt to camouflage poor writing with craftsmanship and style, but ultimately no amount of director's skill can conceal a writer's failure; a poor script, even well directed, results in a stupid movie—as, unfortunately, does a good script poorly directed. Despite the new notion that the direction is everything, Penn can't redeem bad material, nor, as one may surmise from his *Mickey One*, does he necessarily know when it's bad. It is not fair to judge Penn by a film like *The Chase*, because he evidently did not have artistic control over the production, but what happens when he does have control and is working with a poor, pretentious mess of a script is painfully apparent in *Mickey One*—an art film in the worst sense of that term. Though one cannot say of *Bonnie and Clyde* to what degree it shows the work of Newman and Benton and to what degree they merely enabled Penn to "express himself," there are ways of making guesses. As we hear the lines, we can detect the intentions even when the intentions are not quite carried out. Penn is a little clumsy and rather too fancy; he's too much interested in being cinematically creative and artistic to know when to trust the script. *Bonnie and Clyde* could be better if it were simpler. Nevertheless, Penn is a remarkable director when he has something to work with. His most interesting previous work was in his first film, *The Left Handed Gun* (and a few bits of *The Miracle Worker*, a good movie version of the William Gibson play, which he had also directed on the stage and on television). *The Left Handed Gun*, with Paul Newman as an ignorant Billy the Kid in the sex-starved, male-dominated Old West, has the same kind of violent, legendary, nostalgic material as *Bonnie and Clyde*; its script, a rather startling one, was adapted by Leslie Stevens from a Gore Vidal television play. In interviews, Penn makes high, dull sounds—more like a politician than a movie director. But he has a gift for violence, and, despite all the violence in movies, a gift for it is rare. (Eisenstein had it, and Dovzhenko, and Buñuel, but not many others.) There are few memorable violent moments in American movies, but there is one in Penn's first film: Billy's shotgun blasts a man right out of one of his boots; the man falls in the street, but his boot remains upright; a little girl's giggle at the boot is interrupted by her mother's slapping her. The mother's slap—the seal of the awareness of horror—says that even children must learn that some things that look funny are not only funny. That slap, saying that only idiots would laugh at pain and death, that a child must develop sensibility, is the same slap that *Bonnie and Clyde* delivers to the woman saying "It's a comedy." In *The Left Handed Gun*, the slap is itself funny, and yet we suck in our breath; we do not dare to laugh.

Some of the best American movies show the seams of cuts and the confusions of compromises and still hold together, because there is enough energy and spirit to carry the audience over each of the weak episodes to the next good one. The solid intelligence of the writing and Penn's aura of sensitivity help *Bonnie and Clyde* triumph over many poorly directed scenes: Bonnie posing for the photograph with the Texas Ranger, or—the worst sequence—the Ranger getting information out of Blanche Barrow in the hospital. The attempt to make the Texas Ranger an old-time villain doesn't work. He's in the tradition of the mustachioed heavy who foreclosed mortgages and pursued heroines in turn-of-the-century plays, and this one-dimensional villainy belongs, glaringly, to spoof. In some cases, I think, the writing and the conception of the scenes are better (potentially, that is) than the way the scenes have been directed and acted. If Gene Hackman's Buck Barrow is a beautifully controlled performance, the best in the film, several of the other players—though they are very good— needed a tighter rein. They act too much. But it is in other ways that Penn's limitations show—in his excessive reliance on meaning-laden closeups, for one. And it's no wonder he wasn't able to bring out the character of Bonnie in scenes like the one showing her appreciation of the fingernails on the figurine, for in other scenes his own sense of beauty appears to be only a few rungs farther up that same cultural ladder.

The showpiece sequence, Bonnie's visit to her mother (which is a bit reminiscent of Humphrey Bogart's confrontation with his mother, Marjorie

Main, in the movie version of *Dead End*), aims for an effect of alienation, but that effect is confused by all the other things attempted in the sequence: the poetic echoes of childhood (which also echo the child sliding down the hill in *Jules and Jim*) and a general attempt to create a frieze from our national past—a poetry of poverty. Penn isn't quite up to it, though he is at least good enough to communicate what he is trying to do, and it is an attempt that one can respect. In 1939, John Ford attempted a similar poetic evocation of the legendary American past in *Young Mr. Lincoln*; this kind of evocation, by getting at how we *feel* about the past, moves us far more than attempts at historical re-creation. When Ford's Western evocations fail, they become languorous; when they succeed, they are the West of our dreams, and his Lincoln, the man so humane and so smart that he can outwit the unjust and save the innocent, is the Lincoln of our dreams, as the Depression of *Bonnie and Clyde* is the Depression of our dreams—the nation in a kind of trance, as in a dim memory. In this sense, the effect of blur is justified, is "right." Our memories *have* become hazy; this is what the Depression has faded into. But we are too conscious of the technical means used to achieve this blur, of the *attempt* at poetry. We are aware that the filtered effects already include our responses, and it's too easy; the lines are good enough so that the stylization wouldn't have been necessary if the scene had been played right. A simple frozen frame might have been more appropriate.

The editing of this movie is, however, the best editing in an American movie in a long time, and one may assume that Penn deserves credit for it along with the editor, Dede Allen. It's particularly inventive in the robberies and in the comedy sequence of Blanche running through the police barricades with her kitchen spatula in her hand. (There is, however, one bad bit of editing: the end of the hospital scene, when Blanche's voice makes an emotional shift without a corresponding change in her facial position.) The quick panic of Bonnie and Clyde looking at each other's face for the last time is a stunning example of the art of editing.

The end of the picture, the rag-doll dance of death as the gun blasts keep the bodies of Bonnie and Clyde in motion, is brilliant. It is a horror that seems to go on for eternity, and yet it doesn't last a second beyond what it should. The audience leaving the theatre is the quietest audience imaginable.

...

Still, that woman near me was saying "It's a comedy" for a little too long, and although this could have been, and probably was, a demonstration of plain old-fashioned insensitivity, it suggests that those who have attuned themselves to the "total" comedy of the last few years may not know when to stop laughing. Movie audiences have been getting a steady diet of "black" comedy since 1964 and *Dr. Strangelove, Or: How I Learned to Stop Worrying and Love the Bomb*. Spoof and satire have been entertaining audiences since the two-reelers; because it is so easy to do on film things that are difficult or impossible in nature, movies are ideally suited to exaggerations of heroic prowess and to the kind of lighthearted nonsense we used to get when even the newsreels couldn't resist the kidding finish of the speeded-up athletic competition or the diver flying up from the water. The targets have usually been social and political fads and abuses, together with the heroes and the clichés of the just preceding period of film-making. *Dr. Strangelove* opened a new movie era. It ridiculed *everything* and *everybody* it showed, but concealed its own liberal pieties, thus protecting itself from ridicule. A professor who had told me that *The Manchurian Candidate* was "irresponsible," adding, "I didn't like it—I can suspend disbelief only so far," was overwhelmed by *Dr. Strangelove*: "I've never been so involved. I had to keep reminding myself it was only a movie." *Dr. Strangelove* was clearly intended as a cautionary movie; it meant to jolt us awake to the dangers of the bomb by showing us the insanity of the course we were pursuing. But artists' warnings about war and the dangers of total annihilation never tell us how we are supposed to regain control, and *Dr. Strangelove*, chortling over madness, did not indicate any possibilities for sanity. It was experienced not as satire but as a confirmation of fears. Total laughter carried the day. A new generation enjoyed seeing the world as insane; they *literally* learned to stop worrying and love the bomb. Conceptually, we had already been living with the bomb; now the mass audience of the movies—which is the youth of America—grasped the idea that the threat of extinction can be used to devaluate everything, to turn it all into a joke. And the members of this audience do love the bomb; they love feeling that the worst has happened and the irrational are the sane, because there is the bomb as the proof that the rational are insane. They love the bomb because it intensifies their feelings of hopelessness and powerlessness and innocence. It's only three years since Lewis Mumford was widely acclaimed for saying about *Dr. Strangelove* that "unless the spectator was purged by laughter he would be paralyzed by the unendurable anxiety this policy, once it were honestly appraised, would produce." Far from being purged, the spectators are paralyzed, but they're still laughing. And how odd it is now to read, "*Dr. Strangelove* would be a silly, ineffective picture if its purpose were to ridicule the characters of our military and political leaders by showing them as clownish monsters—stupid, psychotic, obsessed." From *Dr. Strangelove* it's a quick leap to *MacBird* and to a belief in exactly what it was said we weren't meant to find in *Dr. Strangelove*. It is not war that has been laughed to scorn but the possibility of sane action.

Once something enters mass culture, it travels fast. In the spoofs of the last few years, everything is gross, ridiculous, insane; to make sense would be to risk being square. A brutal new melodrama is called *Point Blank* and it is. So are most of the new movies. This is the context in which *Bonnie and Clyde*, an entertaining movie that has some feeling in it, upsets people —people who didn't get upset even by *Mondo Cane*. Maybe it's because *Bonnie and Clyde*, by making us care about the robber lovers, has put the sting back into death.

{*The New Yorker*, October 21, 1967}

from
GOING
STEADY

:: Movies as Opera

Movies have been doing so much of the same thing—in slightly different ways—for so long that few of the possibilities of this great hybrid art have yet been explored. At the beginning, movies served many of the functions of primitive theatre; they were Punch-and-Judy shows. But by bringing simple forms of theatre and great actors and dancers and singers to the small towns of the world, they helped to create a taste for more complex theatre, and by bringing the world to people who couldn't travel they helped to develop more advanced audiences. When Méliès photographed his magic shows, when D. W. Griffith recreated the Civil War or imagined the fall of Babylon, when Pabst made a movie with Chaliapin, when Flaherty went to photograph life in the Aran Islands or the South Seas, they were just beginning to tap the infinite possibilities of movies to explore, to record, to dramatize. Shipped in tins, movies could go anywhere in the world, taking a synthesis of almost all the known art forms to rich and poor. In terms of the number of people they could reach, movies were so inexpensive that they could be hailed as the great democratic art form. Then, as businessmen gained control of the medium, it became almost impossibly difficult for the artists to try anything new. Movies became in one way or another remakes of earlier movies, and until inexpensive pictures from abroad began to attract large audiences the general public probably believed what the big studios advertised—that great movies meant big stars, best-seller stories, expensive production. The infinite variety of what was possible on film was almost forgotten, along with the pioneers, and many of those who loved movies lost some of their own vision. They began to ask what cinema "really" was, as if ideal cinema were some preëxistent entity that had to be discovered; like

Platonists turned archeologists, they tried to unearth the true essence of cinema. Instead of celebrating the multiplicity of things that movies can do better or more easily than the other arts, and in new ways and combinations, they looked for the true nature of cinema in what cinema can do that the other arts can't—in artistic apartheid. Some decided on "montage," others on "purely visual imagery." (There was even a period when true cinema was said to be "the chase," and for a while audiences were being chased right out of the theatres.) They wanted to prove that cinema was a real art, like the other arts, when the whole world instinctively preferred it because it was a bastard, cross-fertilized super-art.

"Cinema" in a pure state is not to be found, but movies in the sixties began to expand again, and so quickly it's hard to keep up with them. In France men like Jean Rouch and Chris Marker are extending movies into what were previously thought to be the domains of anthropologists, sociologists, and journalists, while in *Masculine Feminine* Jean-Luc Godard made a modern love lyric out of journalism and essays and interviews, demonstrating that there are no boundaries in the arts that talent can't cross. Not even the grave. In *China Is Near* the young Italian director Marco Bellocchio now brings back to startling life a form that had been laid to rest with modern ceremony—that is, with a few regrets, kicks, and jeers. The new, great talent—perhaps the genius—of Godard brought chance into the art of movies. Bellocchio's talent—so distinctive that already it resembles genius—flourishes within the confines of intricate plot. *China Is Near* has the boudoir complications of a classic comic opera.

Among the five principals in *China Is Near*, who use each other in every way they can, are a pair of working-class lovers—a secretary and an accountant who scheme to marry into the rich landed gentry. Their targets are a professor, Vittorio (Glauco Mauri), who is running for municipal office on the Socialist ticket, and his sister, Elena, a great lady who lets every man in town climb on top of her but won't marry because socially they're all beneath her. Vittorio, the rich Socialist candidate, is that role so essential to comic opera—the ridiculous lover, the man whose mission in life is to be deceived—and Bellocchio, who wrote the film (with Elda Tattoli, who plays Elena) as well as directed it, has produced a classic modern specimen of the species: a man who's out of it, who doesn't get anything while it's going on. The fifth principal is their little brother, Camillo, who is a prissy, sneering despot—a seventeen-year-old seminary student turned Maoist who looks the way Edward Albee might look in a drawing by David Levine. Camillo provides the title when he scrawls "China Is Near" on the walls of the Socialist Party building—his brother's campaign headquarters.

Bellocchio uses the underside of family life—the inbred family atmosphere—for borderline horror and humor. His people are so awful they're funny. One might say that Bellocchio, though he is only twenty-eight, sees sex and family and politics as a dirty old man would, except that his movie is so peculiarly exuberant; perhaps only a very young (or a very old) director can focus on such graceless, mean-spirited people with so much enjoyment. As the pairs of lovers combine and recombine and the five become one big, ghastly family (with a yapping little house pet as an emblem of domesticity), Bellocchio makes it all rhyme. He provides the grace of formal design. The grand manner of the movie is hilarious. I found myself smiling at the wit of his technique; it was pleasurable just to see the quick way doors open and close, or how, when the scene shifts to a larger, more public area, there's always something unexpected going on— surprises that explode what has seemed serious. Bellocchio's visual style is almost incredibly smooth; the camera glides in and out and around the action. He uses it as if there were no obstructions, as if he could do anything he wanted with it; it moves as simply and with as much apparent ease as if it were attached to the director's forehead. In *China Is Near*, as in his first film (*I Pugni in Tasca*, or *Fists in the Pocket*, which was made in 1965 and is soon to open in this country), he probably exhibits the most fluid directorial technique since Max Ophuls, and I don't know where it came from—that is, how he developed it so fast.

Fists in the Pocket must surely be one of the most astonishing directorial débuts in the history of movies, yet it is hard to know how to react to the movie itself. The material is wild, the direction cool and assured. *Fists in the Pocket*, which Bellocchio made fresh from film schools in Italy and England, is also about a prosperous family, but a family of diseased monsters. And as epileptic fits multiply between bouts of matricide, fratricide, and incest, one is too busy gasping at the director's technique and the performances of a cast of unknown actors (Lou Castel, with his pug-dog manner, and Paola Pitagora, looking like a debauched gazelle, are the best strange brother-and-sister act since Édouard Dermithe and Nicole Stéphane in *Les Enfants Terribles*) to doubt his directorial genius. But the movie is a portrait of the genius as a very young man. It is so savage it often seems intended to be funny, but *why* it was so intended isn't clear. Though *Fists in the Pocket* is exhilarating because it reveals a new talent, not everybody cares about movies enough to want to see a movie—no matter how brilliant—about a family cage of beasts, and to a casual moviegoer *Fists in the Pocket* may seem as heavily charged with misguided energy as one of those epileptic seizures. But in a few years people will probably be going to see it as, after seeing Ingmar Bergman's later films, they went to see his early ones. After only two films, Bellocchio's characters already seem his, in the way that the characters of certain novelists seem theirs—a way uncommon in movies except in the movies of writer-directors of especially individual temperaments. Bellocchio's characters are as much a private zoo as Buñuel's.

It was not just coincidence when, a few years ago, first one young French director broke through, then another and another; it was obvious not only that they took encouragement from each other but that they literally inspired each other. Bellocchio was preceded in this way by another young Italian, Bernardo Bertolucci, who at twenty-one directed *La Commare Secca* and at twenty-two wrote and directed the sweepingly romantic *Before the Revolution*, which also dealt with a provincial family and sex and politics, and which suggested a new, operatic approach to movie-making. Both these young directors refer to opera the way the French refer to American movies; they not only use operatic structure and themes but actually introduce performances and recordings of operas—especially Verdi operas— into their work. (The bit of opera performed in *China Is Near* is the damnedest thing since *Salammbô* in *Citizen Kane*.) In the analogy they draw with opera, they seem to glory in the hybrid nature of movies, and to Italians movies may seem almost an outgrowth of the hybrid art of opera. If Verdi wrote a larger number of enduring operas than any other composer (perhaps a fifth of the total standard repertory), it's not only because he wrote great music but also because he filled the stage with action and passion and a variety of good roles for different kinds of voice—which is how these two directors make their movies. Maybe, too, these directors are saying that sex and family and politics in modern Italy are still out of Verdi. Both these young Italians are different from the older Italian directors— even those just a little older, like Pasolini—in the way that their movies move. Men like Fellini and Antonioni developed their techniques over the years, laboriously, and their early movies attest to how long it took them to become Fellini and Antonioni. This is not to put them down—most of us take a long time and never become anything—but to contrast them with Bertolucci and Bellocchio, who started their movie careers with masterly techniques, proving that it doesn't take decades of apprenticeship or millions of dollars to tell planned and acted stories, and that there is still joy in this kind of movie-making. I think Godard is the most exciting director working in movies today, and it's easy to see how and why he is influencing movie-makers all over the world. But chance and spontaneity and improvisation and the documentary look are only one way to go—not, as some have begun to think, the only way. The clear triumph of *China Is Near* is that it demonstrates how good other ways can be.

{*The New Yorker*, January 13, 1968}

:: A Minority Movie

A few weeks ago, I was startled to see a big Pop poster of Che Guevara—startled not because students of earlier generations didn't have comparable martyrs and heroes but because they didn't consider their heroes part of popular culture, though their little brothers and sisters might have been expected to conceive of them in comic-strip terms. Jean-Luc Godard, who said on the sound track of a recent film, "One might almost say that to live in society today is something like living inside an enormous comic strip," has already made a movie about the incorporation of revolutionary heroes and ideas into Pop—*La Chinoise*. In the narration of an earlier movie, Godard defined his field as "the present, where the future is more present than the present." In *Masculine Feminine*, which was about "the children of Marx and Coca-Cola," a man about to burn himself up needed to borrow a match, and many people were irritated by the levity and absurdity of it—but the *Times* reported just such an incident this month. In the further adventures of those children, in *La Chinoise*, the heroine wants to blow up the Louvre; someone threw a stink bomb into a party at the Museum of Modern Art last week. We don't have time to catch up with the future that is here, and Godard is already making movie critiques of it—documentaries of the future in the present. His movies have become a volatile mixture of fictional narrative, reporting, essay, and absurdist interludes. His tempo is so fast that it is often difficult to keep up with the dialogue, let alone the punctuation of advertising art and allusions to history, literature, movies, and current events. There is little doubt that many of us react to movies in terms of how the tempo suits our own tempo (as a child, I could never sit still through a Laurel-and-Hardy feature, and

I have something of the same problem with most of Antonioni's recent work). Since Godard's tempo is too fast for many people—perhaps most people—they have some ground for anger and confusion. But I think he is driven to ignore the difficulties that audiences may experience—not because he wants to assault them or to be deliberately "uncommercial," not out of pretentiousness or arrogance, but out of the nature of his material and his talent.

Though Godard is a social critic, using largely documentary material, he does not work in the expository manner of television documentaries but intuitively seizes new, rapidly changing elements and dramatizes them as directly as possible, projecting his feelings and interpretations into the material. He assumes in his audience an Americanized sensibility—that is, a quick comprehension of devices and conventions derived from American film style—and his temperamental affinity with American popular art probably seems particularly disreputable and trivial to those educated Americans who go to art-film houses for the European cultural ambiance. Antonioni's ponderously serious manner serves as a guarantee of quality; Godard is so restless and inquiring that he hardly develops his ideas at all. In a new picture he may leap back to rework a theme when he sees how to develop what was only partly clear before. His style is a form of shorthand, and this irritates even some people who one might assume are perfectly able to read it. We all know that an artist can't discover anything for himself—can't function as an *artist*—if he must make everything explicit in terms accessible to the widest possible audience. This is one of the big hurdles that defeat artists in Hollywood: they aren't allowed to assume that anybody knows anything, and they become discouraged and corrupt when they discover that studio thinking is not necessarily wrong in its estimate of the mass audience. Godard, like many American novelists, works in terms of an audience that is assumed to have the same background he has. And, of course, many people do—perhaps a majority of the people in the art-house audiences, though they're not used to making connections among fast references at the movies. No one complains about the quotation from Kafka's *Metamorphosis* in *The Producers*, or about Gene Wilder's being named Leo Bloom in the same film, or even about another character's being called Carmen Giya; this is considered cute "inside humor" when it's obviously done just for a laugh. But if, as in *La Chinoise*, some of the names are used as a shortcut to the characters' roles — Kirilov, for example, for the most desperately confused of the revolutionaries — people are sure to object, though this is done in novels all the time. There are many references that may be incomprehensible to some in the audience, but should Godard stop to explain who Rosa Luxembourg was or what Malraux stands for or why he brings in Sartre and Aragon or Artaud or Theatre Year Zero or Daniel and Sinyavsky? Can't he assume that those who care about the kind of film he is making — those who are involved with the issues of his art — already share most of his frame of reference and are prepared to respond to someone's using it in movies, that they are no longer much involved with movies in the same old frame of reference, which doesn't permit dealing with the attitudes of, as in this case, radical youth? This is minority art not by desire but by necessity. Most innovative artists working in movies have tried to reach the mass audience and failed — failed to reach it as artists. Godard, who is perhaps a symptom of the abandonment of hope for a great popular art, works as artists do in less popular media — at his own highest level.

Inventive and visually gifted, Godard is also, and perhaps even primarily, literary in his approach, and his verbal humor presupposes an educated audience. In *La Chinoise* he uses words in more ways than any other filmmaker: they're in the dialogue and on the walls, on book jackets and in headlines; they're recited, chanted, shouted, written, broken down; they're in commentaries, quotations, interviews, narration; they're in slogans and emblems and signs. Those who dislike verbal allusions will be irritated constantly, and those who want only straightforward action on the screen may be driven wild by his neo-Brechtian displacement devices (his voice on the sound track, a cut to Raoul Coutard at the camera) and by his almost novelistic love of digression — his inclusion of anecdotes and of speculations about movie art and of direct-to-the-camera interviews. And his doubts can be irritating in a medium that is customarily used for banal certainties. Not many movie directors regard their movies as a place to raise the questions that are troubling them. Sometimes Godard's questioning essays come apart like hasty puddings, and then his whole method falls open to question. He is also prone to the use of the *acte gratuit*, so common in philosophical French fiction of this century but rather maddening in films because such acts violate the basic premise of dramatic construction — that the author will show us what led to the crimes or deaths. Godard gives us quick finishes that are not resolutions of what has gone before.

Some of these factors are genuine deterrents to moviegoing, but Godard is, at the moment, the most important single force keeping the art of the film alive—that is to say, responsive to the modern world, moving, reaching out for new themes. The last year has been a relatively good year for American movies—there have been more pictures fit to look at than there were in the preceding few years, when Hollywood seemed to have become a desert, but, with the exception of *Bonnie and Clyde*, if you missed any or all of them you would hardly have missed a thing, because they are merely genre pieces brought up to date: thrillers, Westerns, or "strikingly new" films, which is to say films about adolescent rebellion that take over material, attitudes, and sensibility already commonplace to anybody who reads books or goes to plays. We can go to foreign films, and a romantic tragedy set in another period and culture, like *Elvira Madigan*, may be highly satisfying when we want to dream away and weep a little and look at lovely pictures—as we did at *Mayerling* in the thirties. And a slick thriller or a Western may still be entertaining enough and basically, crudely satisfying when we are tired and just want to go sit and see some action. But what these late-sixties versions of standard movies don't have is the excitement of contemporaneity, of using movies in new ways. Going to the movies, we sometimes forget—because it so rarely happens—that when movies are used in new ways there's an excitement about them much sharper than there is about the limited-entertainment genres. Godard's films—the good ones, that is—are funny, and they're funny in a new way: *La Chinoise* is a comic elegy on a group of modern revolutionary youth— naïve, forlorn little ideologues who live out a Pop version of *The Possessed*.

Godard once wrote, "I want to be able sometimes to make you feel far from the person when I do a closeup." We feel far from Véronique, the teen-age philosophy student of *La Chinoise*, all the time, and it's a scary sensation, because she is so much like every other girl on campus these days. As embodied by Anne Wiazemsky, the granddaughter of Mauriac who made her début in Bresson's *Balthazar* and is now married to Godard, Véronique may be more of a representative of the new radical youth than any other movie has come up with. She is an engaged nihilist, an activist who wants to close the universities by acts of terrorism; she thinks that this will open the way for a new educational system, and that a few deaths don't matter. She is politically engaged, and yet this condition seems to go hand in hand with a peculiar, and possibly new, kind of detachment. She and the four other members of her Maoist group who share the apartment where most of the movie takes place seem detached from the life around them, from how they live, from feelings of any kind. In her soft, small voice, and with the unself-conscious, frightened, yet assured face of so many American college girls, Véronique makes rigid formulations about morals and philosophy; she has no resonance. The group live in a political wonderland of slogans lifted out of historical continuity; they prattle about correct programs and objective conditions and just, progressive wars and the Treaty of Brest Litovsk. They have none of the strength or the doubts that come from experience. They are disparately together in their communal life; they could just as easily recombine in another grouping. Véronique is a new version of Godard's unreachable, perfidious girl, but this unreachable ideologue, though as blankly affectless as the heroines of *Breathless* and *Masculine Feminine*, is not treacherous, nor is there any deep enough emotional involvement between the boys and the girls for deceit to be necessary or for betrayal or victimization to be possible. Sex is taken for granted, is so divorced from emotion that the members of the group seem almost post-sexual, which may be just about the same as pre-sexual. They study Marxism-Leninism, and chant Chairman Mao's sayings from the little red book like nursery rhymes; they play with lethal toys, and—in that bizarre parroting of the Red Guard which is so common here, too—they attack not the economic system and the advertising culture that has produced them but the culture of the past and its institutions, and bourgeois "compromisers," and Russian-style Communists. Véronique wants to bomb the Sorbonne, the Louvre, the Comédie-Française; she murders a Soviet cultural emissary visiting Paris, a representative of the culture stifling the universities, who is selected almost at random to be the first in a series. The group's political life in the flat is a contained universe that almost seems to dematerialize the more familiar world, because it is such a separate, paper-thin universe. Their conspiratorial plots seem like games; they are too open and naïve to hide anything. They expel a member for "revisionism," and the little bespectacled boy goes to the foot of the table and consoles himself with bread and jam. Yet from the flat where they play-act revolution they go out and commit terrorist acts with the same affectless determination. Véronique kills the wrong man and is not fazed by it; she goes back and gets "the right one" as unemotionally as she might correct a mistake in an examination. Godard shows the horror, the beauty, and the absurdity of their thinking and their living, all at the same time.

La Chinoise is a satire of new political youth, but a satire from within, based on observation, and a satire that loves its targets more than it loves anything else—that, perhaps, can see beauty and hope only in its targets. But not much hope. In a section toward the end, the movie goes outside comedy. Godard introduces Francis Jeanson, an older man with political experience, a humane radical who *connects*. Jeanson tries to explain to Véronique that her terrorist actions will not have the consequences she envisions. She describes her tactics for closing the universities, and, gently but persistently, he raises the question "What next?" There is no question whose side Godard is on—that of the revolutionary children—but in showing their styles of action and of thought he has used his doubts, and his fears for them. Though his purpose is didactic, the movie is so playful and quick-witted and affectionate that it's possible—indeed, likely—that audiences will be confused about Godard's "attitude."

How can the modern "possessed" be *funny*? The fusion of attitudes— seeing characters as charming and poetic and, at the same time, preposterous and absurd—is one of Godard's contributions to modern film. (Truffaut worked in almost the same mode in *Shoot the Piano Player*—the mode that in America led to *Bonnie and Clyde*.) Godard's attitude toward his characters is similar to Scott Fitzgerald's in that he loves beautiful, doomed youth, but his style is late-sixties. If one examines books on modern movies, the stills generally look terrible—shlocky, dated, cluttered, and artificially lighted. Stills from Godard's films provide such a contrast that they can be spotted at once. In natural light, his figures are isolated and clearly defined in space against impersonal modern buildings with advertising posters or in rooms against white walls with unframed pictures from magazines. The look is of modern graphics, and that, of course, is why the stills reproduce so well. The ironic elegance of his hard-edge photographic compositions on screen is derived from graphics, comic strips, modern décor, and the two-dimensional television image. The frames in a Godard film are perfectly suited to fast comprehension—one can see everything in them at a glance—and to quick cutting. They can move with the speed of a comic strip, in which we also read the whole picture and the words at once. This visual style, which enables him to make a comedy out of politics and despair, has, however, often been misinterpreted as an attempt to achieve "pure form" on screen. Godard is not trying to create a separate world of abstract film that might be analogous to the arts of music and abstract painting, and it is a way not of explaining his movies but of explaining them away to say that they are works of art because they are going in the same direction as painting—as if every art reached its culmination when it was emptied of verbal meaning and of references to this world. Godard uses abstract design because he responds to the future in the present and because he is trying to show how human relationships are changing in this new world of advertising art, dehumanized housing, multiple forms of prostitution. He does not work in a studio; he selects locations that reveal how abstract modern urban living already is. He fills the screen with a picture of Brecht and the definition "Theatre is a commentary on reality." He uses words as words—for what they mean (and he satirizes the characters in *La Chinoise* for using words abstractly). He is no more an abstractionist than the comic-strip artist, who also uses simplified compositions and bright primary colors as a visual-verbal shorthand technique. If the meaning is conveyed by a balloon containing the word "Splat!" you don't need to paint in the leaves on the branches of the trees or the herringbone design on the pants. And if modern life is seen in terms of the future, the leaves and the weave are already gone. It's folly to view Godard's stripped-down-for-speed-and-wit visual style as if he were moving away from the impurities of meaning; that's a way of cancelling out everything that goes on in a movie like *La Chinoise*—of "appreciating" everything the "artist" does and not reacting to or understanding anything the person says.

For a movie-maker, Godard is almost incredibly intransigent. At this point, it would be easy for him to court popularity with the young audience (which is the only audience he has ever had, and he has had little of that one) by making his revolutionaries romantic, like the gangster in *Breathless*. Romantic revolutionaries could act out political plots instead of robberies. But he does not invest the political activists of *La Chinoise* with glamour or mystery, or even passion. His romantic heroes and heroines were old-fashioned enough to believe in people, and hence to be victimized;

the members of Véronique's group believe love is impossible, and for them it is. Godard does just what will be hardest to take: he makes them infantile and funny—victims of Pop culture. And though he likes them because they are ready to convert their slogans into action, because they want to do something, the movie asks, "And after you've closed the universities, what next?"

{*The New Yorker*, April 6, 1968}

::   *Faces*

Although I am far from being an enthusiast of John Cassavetes' kind of movie-making, after seeing something like *Joanna* one may think back on the glum, naïve realism of *Faces* with respect, if not quite affection. When his *Shadows* came out, almost a decade ago, it was generally thought of as a group improvisation rather than as a first film by John Cassavetes. But from bits of his two intervening, commercially produced films (*Too Late Blues* and *A Child Is Waiting*), and now from *Faces*, in which he apparently had full control, it is clear that either he made *Shadows* or working on *Shadows* made his style. Cassavetes' method is peculiar in that its triumphs and its failures are not merely inseparable from the method but often truly hard to separate from each other. The acting that is so bad it's embarrassing sometimes seems also to have revealed something, so we're forced to reconsider our notions of good and bad acting. In 1961, I commented on *Shadows*, "As the creative effort of a group, it has the rawness and insistence of a form of psychodrama, but it has a special fascination—it reveals a good deal about what actors think is the content of drama (and what they think life is)." In *Faces*, the people are older and richer, and the milieu is southern California rather than New York, yet not only is the method the same (though the technique is infinitely smoother and the *cinéma-vérité*-style photography is generally handsome and effective) but the attitudes are the same. The heroine, after a night of extramarital sex, experiences the very same pathos and guilt and disgust that the virgin in *Shadows* experienced when she was seduced. In fact, nobody seems to have got very far, except downhill. *Faces* is going to be a big success and it doesn't need critical generosity, so, still awarding Cassavetes high marks for doing something "interesting,"

I would like to point out some of the limitations and implications of the method.

Cassavetes' approach to making a film is not unlike Andy Warhol's in *The Chelsea Girls* and Norman Mailer's in *Wild 90* and *Beyond the Law*; by depending on the inspiration of the amateurs and professionals in their casts, they attempt to get at something more truthful than ordinary movies do. And the actors act away. The movie equivalent of primitive painters may be movie-makers like these, who expect the movie to happen when the camera is on. Their movies become the games actors play (and this can be true even when there is a conventional script, as in *Rachel, Rachel*). They are likely to go for material that they feel is being left out of commercial films, but they make their movies in terms of what impressed them in their childhood — the stars — and ignore the other elements of movies. In Warhol and in Mailer, the best moments may be when the actors have a good time performing for the camera. Cassavetes has a good, clear sense of structure; he uses a script and allows improvisation only within strict limits, and, as a result, *Faces* — which is like an upper-middle-class, straight version of *The Chelsea Girls* — has the unified style of an agonizing honesty. Many professional and non-professional actors have something they're particularly good at, and in this kind of movie they may get a chance to show it: in *Shadows*, the heroine's flirtatiousness, the quarrelling of the two men in the train station; in *Faces*, Lynn Carlin's comic rapport with John Marley in her first scene. And there are nuances and inventions we get from such scenes which in context seem remarkable — seem to be unlike what we get in ordinary movies. But these actors may be inadequate or awful in the rest of the film, because, working out of themselves this way, they can't create a character. Their performances don't have enough range, so one tends to tire of them before the movie is finished. It's my feeling that nothing makes one so aware of acting as this self-conscious kind of willed realism, and I think we may overreact to the occasional small victories because we sit there waiting for the actors to think up something to say and do. The actors dominate, as they do on a stage, and they can bring something like the tedium of dull people on the stage to the screen. But what actors think is true to life, and what, given the impetus to be sincere and the opportunity to improvise, they come up with, is very much like what the public thinks is true to life.

Glowering with integrity, determined not to pander to commercial tastes, Cassavetes has stumbled on a very commercial idea. His great commercial asset is that he thinks not like a director but like an actor. His deliberately raw material about affluence and apathy, loneliness and middle age, the importance of sex and the miseries of marriage may not say any more about the subject than glossy movies on the same themes, and the faces with blemishes may not be much more revealing than faces with a little makeup, but the unrelieved effort at honesty is, for some people, intensely convincing. When it's done as psychodrama rather than as entertainment, they seem to accept all this bruising-searing stuff, the sad whore and the tender hustler, and the false-laughter bit, and the-lies-people-live-by, etc. Watching the kind of drunken salesmen one would have sense enough to avoid in life can, I suppose, seem an illumination. Watching a fat, drunken old woman fall on top of a man she has just begged for a kiss can seem an epiphany. There are scenes in *Faces* so dumb, so crudely conceived, and so badly performed that the audience practically burns incense. I think embarrassment is not a quality of art but our reaction to failed art, yet many members of the audience apparently feel that embarrassment is a sign of flinching before the painful truth, and hence they accept what is going on as deeper and truer because they have been embarrassed by it. Cassavetes' people are empty, lecherous middle-aged failures, like Benjamin's parents and their friends in *The Graduate*, seen not in terms of comedy but in terms of bitterness and despair—a confirmation of the audience's anxieties. The theme of *Faces* is exactly the same theme as that of many now fashionable films—sex as the last quest for meaning in this meaningless, godless, etc., life, or "We who are about to die want to try everything." But the aging people and the Los Angeles setting (which, of course, makes it all seem suburban) have the ghastliness and monotonousness of the commonplace. The heroine is the most banal of all statistical entities—"housewife." And no matter how much is written on aesthetics people think something is good because "I've known people just like that. It's so true to life."

Artists use their technique in order to express themselves more fully; the actors in *Faces* strip away technique as if it were a falsehood that stood between them and "reality." This idea has great popular appeal; it's like the theory of character in *The Boys in the Band*—that when you peel away the protective layers of personality you get to the real person inside. *Faces* has the kind of seriousness that a serious artist couldn't take seriously—the kind of seriousness that rejects art as lies and superficiality. And this lumpen-artists' anti-intellectualism, this actors' unformulated attack on art may be what much of the public also believes—that there is a real thing that "art" hides. The audience comes out shaken and in no mood for levity—as I discovered when I attempted to cheer someone up by remarking that if people's lives were so empty, wasn't it lucky that they had a little money to ease the pain? I was reprimanded with "The pain is due to America and money." (A) I don't believe it, and (B) just about every "serious" movie lately has been saying it. But audiences really seem to want to hear it. I have tried to describe the audience reaction rather than just my own because that reaction may be important to the future of movies. A movie like *Joanna* makes one want to throw up, but *Faces* makes a sacrament of throwing up modern life and American society. Like a number of new forms of theatre, *Faces* is being taken as a religious experience. It's almost a form of self-flagellation to go to a movie like this—"to see yourself," which, of course, means to see how awful you are. And the hushed seriousness with which people respond (to what is really not much more than the routine sorrows of middle age or a bad office party) seems almost hysterical. They come out chanting the liberal forms of "Mea culpa."

{*The New Yorker*, December 7, 1968}

:: A Sign of Life

"Ingmar Bergman's *Shame*," the screening invitation said, "is that director's ultimate personal vision of war and its effects on two people," and if there was anything I didn't want to see, it was another Ingmar Bergman picture, and Bergman on *war*! Years had passed, but I hadn't yet fully recovered from that tank creaking along on the plywood streets in the nameless country of *The Silence*, and recent Bergman pictures had been organized so subconsciously that they were only partly on the screen—the rest still in his head. I have always thought it rather funny that Bergman's most famous statement is that his purpose is to be like one of the anonymous artisans involved in the collective building of the Cathedral of Chartres. Every time I hear that reverentially quoted, I marvel at the power of fancy sentiments to seduce people—because no moviemaker is less of an anonymous artisan on a collective project than Ingmar Bergman. There is teamwork—of a kind—in Hollywood, but Bergman's team is *his* team, working to express *his* vision. I have seen more than twenty of his twenty-nine feature films, and if ever there was a "personal" and "individual" movie director, it's Ingmar Bergman. Before *Shame*, he had, indeed, become so personal that he was beginning to treat his own mind as a cathedral—sanctifying his ideas and obsessions. Movies like *Persona* and *Hour of the Wolf*, despite brilliant passages, were so disordered and so full of associations with his earlier work that though one could respond to parts of them emotionally, trying to understand what he was getting at required exegesis and, finally, guesswork. He seemed to be dealing with material that was only semiconscious—material so close to him and so confused that he was unable to make it accessible.

In recent years, the movie audience has split into the audience for popular films—the mass audience—and the art-house audience, and movies, once heralded as the great new democratic art, have followed the route of the other arts. The advances are now made by "difficult" artists who reach a minority audience, and soon afterward, the difficult artists, or their bowdlerizers, are consumed by the mass audience. Yesterday's interesting, difficult new directors become commercial, and their work becomes part of the film industry's anonymous product, which will never be compared to Chartres. Infrequent moviegoers are likely to be irritated when they go to a highly recommended art-house picture and find it bewildering and obscure. What they may not be aware of is that in this new, divided world of film the commercial movies have become so omnivorous and so grossly corrupt that frequent moviegoers may, for the first time in movie history, be looking for traces of talent and for evidence of thought, and may care more for an "interesting" failure than for a superficially entertaining "hit." During the last New York film festival, I, for example, was impressed by a film called *Signs of Life*, written and directed by a young German, Werner Herzog, even though the film was maddeningly dull and lacked flair and facility, because Herzog was clearly highly intelligent and was struggling toward a distinctive new approach. As a casual moviegoer, I might have thought: What a bore! As a constant one, I thought: This young man, I hope, will invent the techniques he needs, and the movie itself is a sign of life. For constant moviegoers, facility is no longer very important. Television commercials and the tricks of thousands of clever technicians have devalued facility; it's like the graceful literary style of all those college writers who will never have anything to say.

Bergman was one of the few directors who had managed to stay clear of international financing and the big industry; he had worked out his own techniques and gone his own way. But his own way had become a bleak and thorny path in a landscape by Edvard Munch and he took it so often, with the same actors representing "the artist's"—i.e., *his*—conflicts and anguish, that it was becoming a well-travelled psychotic freeway. By *Hour of the Wolf*, released earlier this year, I no longer found him "interesting"; if a movie director isn't going to provide a joke or two and some dancing girls, if he's going to be serious, then he'd better have something serious to say. I knew a Catholic girl in college who was losing her faith and who spent a semester extracting the last dregs of drama from her spiritual crisis by going around asking everybody, "If you don't believe in God, what basis do you have for going on living?" Bergman pulled that same dumb stunt for a much longer period, and when he graduated to the agony-of-the-creator theme, it really seemed about time for him to give us more creation and less agony. I wanted a sign of life from him—not just masterly passages like the great erotic monologue in *Persona* but the kind of sign I thought I had seen back in the mid-fifties when *Summer Interlude* first turned up (as an exploitation picture), followed by *Smiles of a Summer Night* and *The Seventh Seal* and his early *Törst*. But then came ten years that were a regular death knell of movies, from *Wild Strawberries* to *Hour of the Wolf*, though he developed an extraordinary expressive technique and an extraordinary control over actors, and though, intermittently, he produced sequences of great intensity. But what a tiresome deep thinker of second-rate thoughts he had become—the Billy Graham of the post-analytic set. And how absurdly gloomy and self-absorbed—a man living alone in the world and stewing in his own intellectual juice. When the heroine of *Persona* turned on the television and saw Vietnam atrocities, we in the audience experienced culture shock—a medievalist had crossed the time barrier. If, despite his erratic brilliance, I was fed up with Bergman, it was because of the pall of profundity that hung over his work and because so many people had come to think that that pall was art.

Shame is a masterpiece, and it is so thoroughly accessible that I'm afraid some members of the audience may consider it too obvious. They have had so many years now of grappling with puzzles that they may consider all that figuring out *responding* to a work of art; when they devised a theory about what was going on in a film, they took their own ingenuity as proof that the film was art. And now here is Bergman, of all people, making a direct and lucid movie; they may, in self-defense, decide it's banal. But if *Shame* is banal, it's the most powerful banal movie ever made—the obvious redeemed. Bergman has pulled himself together and objectified his material. There are no demons, no delusions. Everybody is exactly who he appears to be, so we can observe the depth and complexity of what he is. There is no character who may or may not represent Bergman; he is not lost in the work but is in control of it, and is thus more fully present than before. *Shame* is indeed a vision of the effect of war on two people, but there are a great many people in the movie—it is full of characters and incidents—and as the movie started to develop and *people* began to appear, I began to breathe easier about what Bergman was doing this time.

Although he had earlier made several films I didn't like, I think I really first despaired of him in *Through a Glass Darkly*, because that was when he began to empty the screen and make chamber dramas. Though limiting the cast to a girl, her brother, her husband, and her father and setting them on an island marked the beginning of a new concentration on screen technique for him, and though he began to make severe *formal* demands on himself, he also made incredible demands on the audience. One of the blessings of movies was to liberate us from the lighthouses and remote cottages of the theatre; he was taking us back to them, and not for convenience. Using few people is as difficult for a movie director as using a great many people is for a stage director. One always knows that a young moviemaker is impossibly ignorant when he says he's going to do something simple, like a monologue; that's probably even more difficult to do successfully on the screen than an epic battle of angels is to do on the stage. Bergman, of course, knew the difficulties—knew that the fewer people on the screen and the simpler the settings, the more surely the director must be in control and the more crucial every nuance becomes—but the very fact that he was determined to do something so difficult, when it is so much easier to keep a movie audience interested with a variety of faces and backgrounds, suggested that he was wrestling with material that he felt had to be worked out in isolated settings, that was "private" material. When people go off somewhere "to think," they're generally just hung up, and his austerity made one suspect the worst. In film, concentrating on a few elements gives those elements such importance that the material can easily become inflated, and the method is generally attempted by people who overvalue their few ideas and have little sense of the abundance of ideas that must go into a good movie. Bergman was not in such straitened intellectual circumstances, but he was given to inflation of "dark" and messy ideas. The order he imposed on his chamber dramas was a false order. The films looked formal and disciplined, but (as often happens in movies) that "abstract" look concealed conceptual chaos. If a movie director cannot control both his thematic material and the flux of visual material, it is far better to have inner order and outer chaos, because then there is at least a lot to look at—different people and things and places to distract one—even if it is disorganized, while if the movie looks formally strict but the ideas and emotions are disturbed, the viewer may feel that the fault is in himself for not understanding the work, or, worse, feel that this kind of artistic-looking, disturbing ambiguity is what art *is*. As Bergman went from one isolated-island or unknown-country situation to the next, with characters who spoke little and loomed large in closeup, his movies became so private that one began to wonder what he was doing by exposing this unresolved mass of anxieties and guilts and fears. In *Shame*, on the contrary, he has full control of the material, and though the film, set in the chaotic last stages of war—the mopping-up operations—is a narrative of complex incidents, the outer chaos, too, is controlled. It is the chaos of life in wartime seen through an ordering intelligence.

Shame has an almost magical lack of surprise; it has the inevitability of a common dream. Although, in order to project us just a little beyond our current situation, it is set a tiny step into the future—1971—we feel we have already known this time. This world of 1971 has been at war long enough for events to have become confused, and (like the characters) we are the civilians in the middle of it even though we feel out of it. It is all so exactly detailed that it seems to be war as we have always known it—a war that is so familiar from our fears that it is normal, everyday total war. Liv Ullmann and Max von Sydow become survivors—as in our dreams of war we are the survivors. Bergman's war is the imaginary war we remember at night. It's the semi-documentary war we know from *The Moon Is Down* and *Edge of Darkness* and Rossellini and *Les Carabiniers* and television coverage of Vietnam. There's nothing startling about it; even the weapons are conventional. It doesn't, after all, take a hydrogen bomb to finish us—a rifle can do the job. This is just degrading, ordinary old war, and it takes a while before we realize that Bergman has put us in the position of the Vietnamese and all those occupied peoples we have seen being interrogated and punished and frightened until they can no longer tell friend from enemy, extermination from liberation. *Shame* is too exact and too strongly simplified to be merely realistic; the details register upon us with an intensity and a consistency beyond realism. Sven Nykvist's photography is so straightforward it's like an unblinking eye on the universe—realistic photography that achieves an aesthetic effect beyond realism.

Shame, it is true, "says" nothing new, but then neither did our great national elegy *The Birth of a Nation*. *Shame* is an elegy written in advance for a civilization that seems already lost. Bergman finally took the death knell itself for his theme, and no one could say he hadn't prepared. He had already played around with so many macabre fantasies that he may have worked the fantastic out of his system. When he got to this vision of man's last days on earth, he looked at his subject with astonishing purity. The terror in *Shame* is in how prosaically awful the end can be. *Shame* is, in many ways, Bergman's equivalent of Godard's *Weekend*—also an account of what people do to survive—but artists of different temperaments see the destruction of their world very differently. There is not a trace of the surreal or the comic in *Shame*; Bergman does not have Godard's daring wit or his gift for making the contemporary fantastic. But it's a much more nearly perfect work than *Weekend*. In the past, it was a weakness of Bergman as an artist that although he can do comedy and he can do tragic material, he cannot (as yet) combine them in one film. (When he tried, it was disastrous.) In *Shame*, his unvarying, unchanging mood is effective in a new way; I have never been fond of "brooding" minds at work in film, but the vision here creates its own suspense. Can the picture possibly sustain this level of tension? It does. And without even the time-honored crutch of music. Bergman uses the sounds of war percussively—war becomes a monster beating and waiting. Maybe all those years of developing the technical mastery that made sketches of madness look controlled gave him the equipment to do precisely what he wanted to do. This is part of the excitement of watching a movie artist develop—seeing his new films the way one reads the new books of a contemporary writer, and finding, just when one is ready to give him up, that he has renewed himself, transformed his materials, demonstrated that what he has learned can be used in a new direction. Bergman's austerity of style—when it is applied to objectified material—is splendid. He is now a master at creating effects of dislocation without any need for the superficial apparatus of movie surrealism. And he is a master of what is perhaps most difficult of all on film—the simple domestic scene. The way a husband and wife sit together, the way a lover's body leans as he observes his mistress, white wine in a crystal glass—the pleasures and the amenities are plainly stated, without emphasis or atmospheric touches. *Shame* is a *just* elegy, without false emotion.

Liv Ullmann is superb in the demanding central role—one that calls for emotional involvements with both von Sydow and Gunnar Björnstrand. The screen uses up actors in certain roles the way television uses up political figures—and particularly in roles in which they exhibit their least attractive qualities. Von Sydow is perhaps too familiar—and therefore slightly tiresome—in this slack-faced incarnation (he isn't when he's playing magnetic roles); we already know how good he is at it, just as we know how good Dirk Bogarde is at weaklings. Björnstrand, however, is beautifully restrained as an aging man clinging to the wreckage of his life.

There is a search through a house I thought was shot too dramatically and was excessively edited, and I could have done without the explicit formulation of the theme (which diminishes it with "poetry"), and a few confusing details, but these faults are so minor one might as well go ahead and call *Shame* a flawless work and a masterly vision. Treating the most dreaded of all subjects, the film makes one feel elated. The subject is our responses to death, but a work of art is a true sign of life.

{*The New Yorker*, December 28, 1968}

:: Trash, Art, and the Movies

I

Like those cynical heroes who were idealists before they discovered that the world was more rotten than they had been led to expect, we're just about all of us displaced persons, "a long way from home." When we feel defeated, when we imagine we could now perhaps settle for home and what it represents, that home no longer exists. But there are movie houses. In whatever city we find ourselves we can duck into a theatre and see on the screen our familiars—our old "ideals" aging as we are and no longer looking so ideal. Where could we better stoke the fires of our masochism than at rotten movies in gaudy seedy picture palaces in cities that run together, movies and anonymity a common denominator. Movies—a tawdry corrupt art for a tawdry corrupt world—fit the way we feel. The world doesn't work the way the schoolbooks said it did and we are different from what our parents and teachers expected us to be. Movies are our cheap and easy expression, the sullen art of displaced persons. Because we feel low we sink in the boredom, relax in the irresponsibility, and maybe grin for a minute when the gunman lines up three men and kills them with a single bullet, which is no more "real" to us than the nursery-school story of the brave little tailor.

We don't have to be told those are photographs of actors impersonating characters. We know, and we often know much more about both the actors and the characters they're impersonating and about how and why the movie has been made than is consistent with theatrical illusion. Hitchcock teased us by killing off the one marquee-name star early in *Psycho*, a gambit which startled us not just because of the suddenness of the murder or how it was committed but because it broke a box-office convention and so it was a joke played on what audiences have learned to expect. He broke the rules of the movie game and our response demonstrated how aware we are of commercial considerations. When movies are bad (and in the bad parts of good movies) our awareness of the mechanics and our cynicism about the aims and values is peculiarly alienating. The audience talks right back to the phony "outspoken" condescending *The Detective*; there are groans of dejection at *The Legend of Lylah Clare*, with, now and then, a desperate little titter. How well we all know that cheap depression that settles on us when our hopes and expectations are disappointed *again*. Alienation is the most common state of the knowledgeable movie audience, and though it has the peculiar rewards of low connoisseurship, a miser's delight in small favors, we long to be surprised out of it—not to suspension of disbelief nor to a Brechtian kind of alienation, but to pleasure, something a man can call good without self-disgust.

A good movie can take you out of your dull funk and the hopelessness that so often goes with slipping into a theatre; a good movie can make you feel alive again, in contact, not just lost in another city. Good movies make you care, make you believe in possibilities again. If somewhere in the Hollywood-entertainment world someone has managed to break through with something that speaks to you, then it isn't *all* corruption. The movie doesn't have to be great; it can be stupid and empty and you can still have the joy of a good performance, or the joy in just a good line. An actor's scowl, a small subversive gesture, a dirty remark that someone tosses off with a mock-innocent face, and the world makes a little bit of sense. Sitting there alone or painfully alone because those with you do not react as you do, you know there must be others perhaps in this very theatre or in this city, surely in other theatres in other cities, now, in the past or future, who react as you do. And because movies are the most total and encompassing art form we have, these reactions can seem the most personal and, maybe the most important, imaginable. The romance of movies is not just in those stories and those people on the screen but in the adolescent dream of meeting others who feel as you do about what you've seen. You do meet them, of course, and you know each other at once because you talk less about good movies than about what you love in bad movies.

II

There is so much talk now about the art of the film that we may be in danger of forgetting that most of the movies we enjoy are not works of art. *The Scalphunters*, for example, was one of the few entertaining American movies this past year, but skillful though it was, one could hardly call it a work of art—if such terms are to have any useful meaning. Or, to take a really gross example, a movie that is as crudely made as *Wild in the Streets*—slammed together with spit and hysteria and opportunism—can nevertheless be enjoyable, though it is almost a classic example of an unartistic movie. What makes these movies—that are not works of art—enjoyable? *The Scalphunters* was more entertaining than most Westerns largely because Burt Lancaster and Ossie Davis were peculiarly funny together; part of the pleasure of the movie was trying to figure out what made them so funny. Burt Lancaster is an odd kind of comedian: what's distinctive about him is that his comedy seems to come out of his physicality. In serious roles an undistinguished and too obviously hardworking actor, he has an apparently effortless flair for comedy and nothing is more infectious than an actor who can relax in front of the camera as if he were having a good time. (George Segal sometimes seems to have this gift of a wonderful amiability, and Brigitte Bardot was radiant with it in *Viva Maria!*) Somehow the alchemy of personality in the pairing of Lancaster and Ossie Davis—another powerfully funny actor of tremendous physical presence—worked, and the director Sydney Pollack kept tight control so that it wasn't overdone.

And *Wild in the Streets*? It's a blatantly crummy-looking picture, but that somehow works for it instead of against it because it's smart in a lot of ways that better-made pictures aren't. It looks like other recent products from American International Pictures but it's as if one were reading a comic strip that looked just like the strip of the day before, and yet on this new one there are surprising expressions on the faces and some of the balloons are really witty. There's not a trace of sensitivity in the drawing or in the ideas, and there's something rather specially funny about wit without *any* grace at all; it can be enjoyed in a particularly crude way—as Pop wit. The basic idea is corny—*It Can't Happen Here* with the freaked-out young as a new breed of fascists—but it's treated in the paranoid style of editorials about youth (it even begins by blaming everything on the parents). And a cheap idea that is this current and widespread has an almost lunatic charm, a nightmare gaiety. There's a relish that people have for the idea of drug-taking kids as monsters threatening them—the daily papers merging into *Village of the Damned*. Tapping and exploiting this kind of hysteria for a satirical fantasy, the writer Robert Thom has used what is available and obvious but he's done it with just enough mockery and style to make it funny. He throws in touches of characterization and occasional lines that are not there just to further the plot, and these throwaways make odd connections so that the movie becomes almost frolicsome in its paranoia (and in its delight in its own cleverness).

If you went to *Wild in the Streets* expecting a good movie, you'd probably be appalled because the directing is unskilled and the music is banal and many of the ideas in the script are scarcely even carried out, and almost every detail is messed up (the casting director has used bit players and extras who are decades too old for their roles). It's a paste-up job of cheap movie-making, but it has genuinely funny performers who seize their opportunities and throw their good lines like boomerangs—Diane Varsi (like an even more zonked-out Geraldine Page) doing a perfectly quietly convincing freak-out as if it were truly a put-on of the whole straight world; Hal Holbrook with his inexpressive actorish face that is opaque and uninteresting in long shot but in closeup reveals tiny little shifts of expression, slight tightenings of the features that are like the movement of thought; and Shelley Winters, of course, and Christopher Jones. It's not so terrible—it may even be a relief—for a movie to be without the look of art; there are much worse things aesthetically than the crude good-natured crumminess, the undisguised reach for a fast buck, of movies without art. From *I Was a Teen-Age Werewolf* through the beach parties to *Wild in the Streets* and *The Savage Seven*, American International Pictures has sold a cheap commodity, which in its lack of artistry and in its blatant and sometimes funny way of delivering action serves to remind us that one of the great appeals of movies is that we don't have to take them too seriously.

Wild in the Streets is a fluke—a borderline, special case of a movie that is entertaining because some talented people got a chance to do something at American International that the more respectable companies were too nervous to try. But though I don't enjoy a movie so obvious and badly done as the big American International hit, *The Wild Angels*, it's easy to see why kids do and why many people in other countries do. Their reasons are basically why we all started going to the movies. After a time, we may want more, but audiences who have been forced to wade through the thick middle-class padding of more expensively made movies to get to the action enjoy the nose-thumbing at "good taste" of cheap movies that stick to the raw materials. At some basic level they *like* the pictures to be cheaply done, they enjoy the crudeness; it's a breather, a vacation from proper behavior and good taste and required responses. Patrons of burlesque applaud politely for the graceful erotic dancer but go wild for the lewd lummox who bangs her big hips around. That's what they go to burlesque for. Personally, I hope for a reasonable minimum of finesse, and movies like *Planet of the Apes* or *The Scalphunters* or *The Thomas Crown Affair* seem to me minimal entertainment for a relaxed evening's pleasure. These are, to use traditional common-sense language, "good movies" or "good bad movies" —slick, reasonably inventive, well-crafted. They are not art. But they are almost the maximum of what we're now getting from American movies, and not only these but much worse movies are talked about as "art"—and are beginning to be taken seriously in our schools.

It's preposterously egocentric to call anything we enjoy art—as if we could not be entertained by it if it were not; it's just as preposterous to let prestigious, expensive advertising snow us into thinking we're getting art for our money when we haven't even had a good time. I did have a good time at *Wild in the Streets*, which is more than I can say for *Petulia* or *2001* or a lot of other highly praised pictures. *Wild in the Streets* is not a work of art, but then I don't think *Petulia* or *2001* is either, though *Petulia* has that kaleidoscopic hip look and *2001* that new-techniques look which combined with "swinging" or "serious" ideas often pass for motion picture art.

III

Let's clear away a few misconceptions. Movies make hash of the schoolmarm's approach of how well the artist fulfilled his intentions. Whatever the original intention of the writers and director, it is usually supplanted, as the production gets under way, by the intention to make money—and the industry judges the film by how well it fulfills that intention. But if you could see the "artist's intentions" you'd probably

wish you couldn't anyway. Nothing is so deathly to enjoyment as the relentless march of a movie to fulfill its obvious purpose. This is, indeed, almost
a defining characteristic of the hack director, as distinguished from an
artist.

The intention to make money is generally all too obvious. One of the
excruciating comedies of our time is attending the new classes in cinema
at the high schools where the students may quite shrewdly and accurately
interpret the plot developments in a mediocre movie in terms of manipulation for a desired response while the teacher tries to explain everything
in terms of the creative artist working out his theme—as if the conditions
under which a movie is made and the market for which it is designed were
irrelevant, as if the latest product from Warners or Universal should be
analyzed like a lyric poem.

People who are just getting "seriously interested" in film always ask a
critic, "Why don't you talk about technique and 'the visuals' more?" The
answer is that American movie technique is generally more like technology and it usually isn't very interesting. Hollywood movies often have the
look of the studio that produced them—they have a studio style. Many
current Warner films are noisy and have a bright look of cheerful ugliness,
Universal films the cheap blur of money-saving processes, and so forth.
Sometimes there is even a *spirit* that seems to belong to the studio. We
can speak of the Paramount comedies of the Thirties or the Twentieth-
Century Fox family entertainment of the Forties and CinemaScope comedies of the Fifties or the old MGM gloss, pretty much as we speak of
Chevvies or Studebakers. These movies look alike, they move the same
way, they have just about the same engines because of the studio policies
and the *kind* of material the studio heads bought, the ideas they imposed,
the way they had the films written, directed, photographed, and the labs
where the prints were processed, and, of course, because of the presence
of the studio stable of stars for whom the material was often purchased
and shaped and who dominated the output of the studio. In some cases,
as at Paramount in the Thirties, studio style was plain and rather tacky
and the output—those comedies with Mary Boland and Mae West and
Alison Skipworth and W. C. Fields—looks the better for it now. Those
economical comedies weren't slowed down by a lot of fancy lighting or the
adornments of "production values." Simply to be enjoyable, movies don't

need a very high level of craftsmanship: wit, imagination, fresh subject matter, skillful performers, a good idea—either alone or in any combination—can more than compensate for lack of technical knowledge or a big budget.

The craftsmanship that Hollywood has always used as a selling point not only doesn't have much to do with art—the expressive use of techniques— it probably doesn't have very much to do with actual box-office appeal, either. A dull movie like Sidney Furie's *The Naked Runner* is technically competent. The appalling *Half a Sixpence* is technically astonishing. Though the large popular audience has generally been respectful of expenditure (so much so that a critic who wasn't impressed by the money and effort that went into a *Dr. Zhivago* might be sharply reprimanded by readers), people who like *The President's Analyst* or *The Producers* or *The Odd Couple* don't seem to be bothered by their technical ineptitude and visual ugliness. And on the other hand, the expensive slick techniques of ornately empty movies like *A Dandy in Aspic* can actually work against one's enjoyment, because such extravagance and waste are morally ugly. If one compares movies one likes to movies one doesn't like, craftsmanship of the big-studio variety is hardly a decisive factor. And if one compares a movie one likes by a competent director such as John Sturges or Franklin Schaffner or John Frankenheimer to a movie one doesn't much like by the same director, his technique is probably not the decisive factor. After directing *The Manchurian Candidate* Frankenheimer directed another political thriller, *Seven Days in May*, which, considered just as a piece of direction, was considerably more confident. While seeing it, one could take pleasure in Frankenheimer's smooth showmanship. But the material (Rod Serling out of Fletcher Knebel and Charles W. Bailey II) was like a straight (i.e., square) version of *The Manchurian Candidate*. I have to chase around the corridors of memory to summon up images from *Seven Days in May*; despite the brilliant technique, all that is clear to mind is the touchingly, desperately anxious face of Ava Gardner—how when she smiled you couldn't be sure if you were seeing dimples or tics. But *The Manchurian Candidate*, despite Frankenheimer's uneven, often barely adequate, staging, is still vivid because of the script. It took off from a political double entendre that everybody had been thinking of ("Why, if Joe McCarthy were working for the Communists, he couldn't be doing them more good!")

and carried it to startling absurdity, and the extravagances and conceits and conversational non sequiturs (by George Axelrod out of Richard Condon) were ambivalent and funny in a way that was trashy yet liberating.

Technique is hardly worth talking about unless it's used for something worth doing: that's why most of the theorizing about the new art of television commercials is such nonsense. The effects are impersonal—dexterous, sometimes clever, but empty of art. It's because of their emptiness that commercials call so much attention to their camera angles and quick cutting—which is why people get impressed by "the art" of it. Movies are now often made in terms of what television viewers have learned to settle for. Despite a great deal that is spoken and written about young people responding visually, the influence of TV is to make movies visually less imaginative and complex. Television is a very noisy medium and viewers listen, while getting used to a poor quality of visual reproduction, to the absence of visual detail, to visual obviousness and overemphasis on simple compositions, and to atrociously simplified and distorted color systems. The shifting camera styles, the movement, and the fast cutting of a film like *Finian's Rainbow*—one of the better big productions—are like the "visuals" of TV commercials, a disguise for static material, expressive of nothing so much as the need to keep you from getting bored and leaving. Men are now beginning their careers as directors by working on commercials—which, if one cares to speculate on it, may be almost a one-sentence résumé of the future of American motion pictures.

I don't mean to suggest that there is not such a thing as movie technique or that craftsmanship doesn't contribute to the pleasures of movies, but simply that most audiences, if they enjoy the acting and the "story" or the theme or the funny lines, don't notice or care about how well or how badly the movie is made, and because they don't care, a hit makes a director a "genius" and everybody talks about his brilliant technique (i.e., the technique of grabbing an audience). In the brief history of movies there has probably never been so astonishingly gifted a large group of directors as the current Italians, and not just the famous ones or Pontecorvo (*The Battle of Algiers*) or Francesco Rosi (*The Moment of Truth*) or the young prodigies, Bertolucci and Bellocchio, but dozens of others, men like Elio Petri (*We Still Kill the Old Way*) and Carlo Lizzani (*The Violent Four*). *The Violent Four* shows more understanding of visual movement and more talent for movie-making than anything that's been made in America this year.

But could one tell people who are not crazy, dedicated moviegoers to go see it? I'm not sure, although I enjoyed the film enormously, because *The Violent Four* is a gangster genre picture. And it may be a form of aestheticism—losing sight of what people go to movies for, and particularly what they go to foreign movies for—for a critic to say, "His handling of crowds and street scenes is superb," or, "It has a great semi-documentary chase sequence." It does, but the movie is basically derived from our old gangster movies, and beautifully made as it is, one would have a hard time convincing educated people to go see a movie that features a stunning performance by Gian Maria Volonté which is based on Paul Muni and James Cagney. Presumably they want something different from movies than a genre picture that offers images of modern urban decay and is smashingly directed. If a movie is interesting primarily in terms of technique then it isn't worth talking about except to students who can learn from seeing how a good director works. And to talk about a movie like *The Graduate* in terms of movie technique is really a bad joke. Technique at this level is not of any aesthetic importance; it's not the ability to achieve what you're after but the skill to find something acceptable. One must talk about a film like this in terms of what audiences enjoy it for or one is talking gibberish—and might as well be analyzing the "art" of commercials. And for the greatest movie artists where there is a unity of technique and subject, one doesn't need to talk about technique much because it has been subsumed in the art. One doesn't want to talk about how Tolstoi got his effects but about the work itself. One doesn't want to talk about how Jean Renoir does it; one wants to talk about what he has done. One can try to separate it all out, of course, distinguish form and content for purposes of analysis. But that is a secondary, analytic function, a scholarly function, and hardly needs to be done explicitly in criticism. Taking it apart is far less important than trying to see it whole. The critic shouldn't need to tear a work apart to demonstrate that he knows how it was put together. The important thing is to convey what is new and beautiful in the work, not how it was made—which is more or less implicit.

Just as there are good actors—possibly potentially great actors—who have never become big stars because they've just never been lucky enough to get the roles they needed (Brian Keith is a striking example) there are good directors who never got the scripts and the casts that could make their reputations. The question people ask when they consider going to a movie is not "How's it made?" but "What's it about?" and that's a perfectly legitimate question. (The next question—sometimes the first—is generally, "Who's in it?" and that's a good, honest question, too.) When you're at a movie, you don't have to believe in it to enjoy it but you do have to be interested. (Just as you have to be interested in the human material, too. Why should you go see *another* picture with James Stewart?) I don't want to see another samurai epic in exactly the same way I never want to read *Kristin Lavransdatter*. Though it's conceivable that a truly great movie director could make any subject interesting, there are few such artists working in movies and if they did work on unpromising subjects I'm not sure we'd really enjoy the results even if we did *admire* their artistry. (I recognize the greatness of sequences in several films by Eisenstein but it's a rather cold admiration.) The many brilliant Italian directors who are working within a commercial framework on crime and action movies are obviously not going to be of any great interest unless they get a chance to work on a subject we care about. Ironically the Czech successes here (*The Shop on Main Street*, *Loves of a Blonde*, *Closely Watched Trains*) are acclaimed for their techniques, which are fairly simple and rather limited, when it's obviously their human concern and the basic modesty and decency of their attitudes plus a little barnyard humor which audiences respond to. They may even respond partly because of the *simplicity* of the techniques.

IV

When we are children, though there are categories of films we don't like—documentaries generally (they're too much like education) and, of course, movies especially designed for children—by the time we can go on our own we have learned to avoid them. Children are often put down by adults when the children say they enjoyed a particular movie; adults who are short on empathy are quick to point out aspects of the plot or theme that the child didn't understand, and it's easy to humiliate a child in this way. But it is one of the glories of eclectic arts like opera and movies that they include so many possible kinds and combinations of pleasure. One may be enthralled by Leontyne Price in *La Forza del Destino* even if one hasn't boned up on the libretto, or entranced by *The Magic Flute* even if one has boned up on the libretto, and a movie may be enjoyed for many reasons that have little to do with the story or the subtleties (if any) of theme or character. Unlike "pure" arts which are often defined in terms of what only they can do, movies are open and unlimited. Probably everything that can be done in movies can be done some other way, but — and this is what's so miraculous and so expedient about them — they can do almost anything any other art can do (alone or in combination) and they can take on some of the functions of exploration, of journalism, of anthropology, of almost any branch of knowledge as well. We go to the movies for the variety of what they can provide, and for their marvellous ability to give us easily and inexpensively (and usually painlessly) what we can get from other arts also. They are a wonderfully *convenient* art.

Movies are used by cultures where they are foreign films in a much more primitive way than in their own; they may be enjoyed as travelogues or as initiations into how others live or in ways we might not even guess. The sophisticated and knowledgeable moviegoer is likely to forget how new and how amazing the different worlds up there once seemed to him, and to forget how much a child reacts to, how many elements he is taking in, often for the first time. And even adults who have seen many movies may think a movie is "great" if it introduces them to unfamiliar subject matter; thus many moviegoers react as naïvely as children to *Portrait of Jason* or *The Queen*. They think they're wonderful. The oldest plots and corniest comedy bits can be full of wonder for a child, just as the freeway traffic in a grade Z melodrama can be magical to a villager who has never seen a car. A child may enjoy even a movie like *Jules and Jim* for its sense of fun, without comprehending it as his parents do, just as we may enjoy an Italian movie as a sex comedy although in Italy it is considered social criticism or political satire. Jean-Luc Godard liked the movie of *Pal Joey*, and I suppose that a miserable American movie musical like *Pal Joey* might look good in France because I can't think of a single good dance number performed by French dancers in a French movie. The French enjoy what they're unable to do and we enjoy the French studies of the pangs of adolescent love that would be corny if made in Hollywood. A movie like *The Young Girls of Rochefort* demonstrates how even a gifted Frenchman who adores American musicals misunderstands their conventions. Yet it would be as stupid to say that the director Jacques Demy couldn't love American musicals because he doesn't understand their conventions as to tell a child he couldn't have liked *Planet of the Apes* because he didn't get the jokey references to the Scopes trial.

Every once in a while I see an anthropologist's report on how some preliterate tribe reacts to movies; they may, for example, be disturbed about where the actor has gone when he leaves the movie frame, or they may respond with enthusiasm to the noise and congestion of big-city life which in the film story are meant to show the depths of depersonalization to which we are sinking, but which they find funny or very jolly indeed. Different cultures have their own ways of enjoying movies. A few years ago the new "tribalists" here responded to the gaudy fantasies of *Juliet of the Spirits* by using the movie to turn on. A few had already made a trip of *8 ½*, but *Juliet*, which was, conveniently and perhaps not entirely accidentally, in electric, psychedelic color, caught on because of it. (The color was awful, like in bad MGM musicals — so one may wonder about the quality of the trips.)

The new tribalism in the age of the media is not necessarily the enemy of commercialism; it is a direct outgrowth of commercialism and its ally, perhaps even its instrument. If a movie has enough clout, reviewers and columnists who were bored are likely to give it another chance, until on the second or third viewing, they discover that it affects them "viscerally" — and a big expensive movie is likely to do just that. *2001* is said to have caught on with youth (which can make it happen); and it's said that the movie will stone you — which is meant to be a recommendation. Despite a few dissident voices — I've heard it said, for example, that *2001* "gives you a bad trip because the visuals don't go with the music" — the promotion has been remarkably effective with students. "The tribes" tune in so fast that college students thousands of miles apart "have heard" what a great trip *2001* is before it has even reached their city.

Using movies to go on a trip has about as much connection with the art of the film as using one of those Doris Day–Rock Hudson jobs for ideas on how to redecorate your home — an earlier way of stoning yourself. But it is relevant to an understanding of movies to try to separate out, for purposes of discussion at least, how we may personally *use* a film — to learn how to dress or how to speak more elegantly or how to make a grand entrance or even what kind of coffee maker we wish to purchase, or to take off from the movie into a romantic fantasy or a trip — from what makes it a good movie or a poor one, because, of course, we can *use* poor films as easily as good ones, perhaps *more* easily for such non-aesthetic purposes as shopping guides or aids to tripping.

V

We generally become interested in movies because we *enjoy* them and what we enjoy them for has little to do with what we think of as art. The movies we respond to, even in childhood, don't have the same values as the official culture supported at school and in the middle-class home. At the movies we get low life and high life, while David Susskind and the moralistic reviewers chastise us for not patronizing what they think we should, "realistic" movies that would be good for us—like *A Raisin in the Sun*, where we could learn the lesson that a Negro family can be as dreary as a white family. Movie audiences will take a lot of garbage, but it's pretty hard to make us queue up for pedagogy. At the movies we want a different kind of truth, something that surprises us and registers with us as funny or accurate or maybe amazing, maybe even amazingly beautiful. We get little things even in mediocre and terrible movies—José Ferrer sipping his booze through a straw in *Enter Laughing*, Scott Wilson's hard scary all-American-boy-you-can't-reach face cutting through the pretensions of *In Cold Blood* with all its fancy bleak cinematography. We got, and still have embedded in memory, Tony Randall's surprising depth of feeling in *The Seven Faces of Dr. Lao*, Keenan Wynn and Moyna Macgill in the lunch-counter sequence of *The Clock*, John W. Bubbles on the dance floor in *Cabin in the Sky*, the inflection Gene Kelly gave to the line, "I'm a rising young man" in *Du Barry Was a Lady*, Tony Curtis saying "avidly" in *Sweet Smell of Success*. Though the director may have been responsible for releasing it, it's the human material we react to most and remember longest. The art of the performers stays fresh for us, their beauty as beautiful as ever. There are so many kinds of things we get—the hangover sequence wittily designed for the CinemaScope screen in *The Tender Trap*, the atmosphere of the newspaper offices in *The Luck of Ginger Coffey*, the automat gone mad in *Easy Living*. Do we need to lie and shift things to false terms—like those who have to say Sophia Loren is a great actress as if her *acting* had made her a star? Wouldn't we rather watch her than better actresses because she's so incredibly charming and because she's probably the greatest model the world has ever known? There are great moments—Angela Lansbury singing "Little Yellow Bird" in *Dorian Gray*. (I don't think I've ever had a friend who didn't also treasure that girl and that song.) And there are absurdly right little moments—in *Saratoga Trunk* when Curt Bois says to Ingrid Bergman, "You're very beautiful," and she says, "Yes, isn't it lucky?" And those things have closer relationships to art than what the schoolteachers told us was true and beautiful. Not that the works we studied in school weren't often great (as we discovered *later*) but that what the teachers told us to admire them for (and if current texts are any indication, are still telling students to admire them for) was generally so false and prettified and moralistic that what might have been moments of pleasure in them, and what might have been cleansing in them, and subversive, too, had been coated over.

Because of the photographic nature of the medium and the cheap admission prices, movies took their impetus not from the desiccated imitation European high culture, but from the peep show, the Wild West show, the music hall, the comic strip—from what was coarse and common. The early Chaplin two-reelers still look surprisingly lewd, with bathroom jokes and drunkenness and hatred of work and proprieties. And the Western shoot-'em-ups certainly weren't the schoolteachers' notions of art—which in my school days, ran more to didactic poetry and "perfectly proportioned" statues and which over the years have progressed through nice stories to "good taste" and "excellence"—which may be more poisonous than homilies and dainty figurines because then you had a clearer idea of what you were up against and it was easier to fight. And this, of course, is what we were running away from when we went to the movies. All week we longed for Saturday afternoon and sanctuary—the anonymity and impersonality of sitting in a theatre, just enjoying ourselves, not having to be responsible, not having to be "good." Maybe you just want to look at people on the screen and know they're not looking back at you, that they're not going to turn on you and criticize you.

Perhaps the single most intense pleasure of moviegoing is this non-aesthetic one of escaping from the responsibilities of having the proper responses required of us in our official (school) culture. And yet this is probably the best and most common basis for developing an aesthetic sense because responsibility to pay attention and to appreciate is anti-art, it makes us too anxious for pleasure, too bored for response. Far from supervision and official culture, in the darkness at the movies where nothing is asked of us and we are left alone, the liberation from duty and constraint allows us to develop our own aesthetic responses. Unsupervised enjoyment is probably not the only kind there is but it may feel like the only kind. Irresponsibility is part of the pleasure of all art; it is the part the schools cannot recognize. I don't like to buy "hard tickets" for a "road show" movie because I hate treating a movie as an occasion. I don't want to be pinned down days in advance; I enjoy the casualness of moviegoing—of going in when I feel like it, when I'm in the mood for a movie. It's the feeling of freedom from respectability we have always enjoyed at the movies that is carried to an extreme by American International Pictures and the Clint Eastwood Italian Westerns; they are stripped of cultural values. We may want more from movies than this negative virtue but we know the feeling from childhood moviegoing when we loved the gamblers and pimps and the cons' suggestions of muttered obscenities as the guards walked by. The appeal of movies was in the details of crime and high living and wicked cities and in the language of toughs and urchins; it was in the dirty smile of the city girl who lured the hero away from Janet Gaynor. What draws us to movies in the first place, the opening into other, forbidden or surprising, kinds of experience, and the vitality and corruption and irreverence of that experience are so direct and immediate and have so little connection with what we have been taught is art that many people feel more secure, feel that their tastes are becoming more cultivated when they begin to *appreciate* foreign films. One foundation executive told me that he was quite upset that his teen-agers had chosen to go to *Bonnie and Clyde* rather than with him to *Closely Watched Trains*. He took it as a sign of lack of maturity. I think his kids made an honest choice, and not only because *Bonnie and Clyde* is the better movie, but because it is closer to us, it has some of the qualities of direct involvement that make us care about movies. But it's understandable that it's easier for us, as Americans, to see *art* in foreign films than in our own, because of how we, as Americans, think of art. Art is still what teachers and ladies and foundations believe in, it's civilized and refined, cultivated and serious, cultural, beautiful, European, Oriental: it's what America isn't, and it's especially what American movies are not. Still, if those kids had chosen *Wild in the Streets* over *Closely Watched Trains* I would think that was a sound and honest choice, too, even though *Wild in the Streets* is in most ways a terrible picture. It connects with their lives in an immediate even if a grossly frivolous way, and if we don't go to movies for excitement, if, even as children, we accept the cultural standards of refined adults, if we have so little drive that we accept "good taste," then we will probably never really begin to care about movies at all. We will become like those people who "may go to American movies sometimes to relax" but when they want "a little more" from a movie, are delighted by how colorful and artistic Franco Zeffirelli's *The Taming of the Shrew* is, just as a couple of decades ago they were impressed by *The Red Shoes*, made by Powell and Pressburger, the Zeffirellis of their day. Or, if they like the cozy feeling of uplift to be had from mildly whimsical movies about timid people, there's generally a *Hot Millions* or something musty and faintly boring from Eastern Europe—one of those movies set in World War II but so remote from our ways of thinking that it seems to be set in World War I. Afterward, the moviegoer can feel as decent and virtuous as if he'd spent an evening visiting a deaf old friend of the family. It's a way of taking movies back into the approved culture of the schoolroom—into gentility—and the voices of schoolteachers and reviewers rise up to ask why America can't make such movies.

VI

Movie art is not the opposite of what we have always enjoyed in movies, it is not to be found in a return to that official high culture, it is what we have always found good in movies only more so. It's the subversive gesture carried further, the moments of excitement sustained longer and extended into new meanings. At best, the movie is totally informed by the kind of pleasure we have been taking from bits and pieces of movies. But we are so used to reaching out to the few good bits in a movie that we don't need formal perfection to be dazzled. There are so many arts and crafts that go into movies and there are so many things that can go wrong that they're not an art for purists. We want to experience that elation we feel when a movie (or even a performer in a movie) goes farther than we had expected and makes the leap successfully. Even a film like Godard's *Les Carabiniers*, hell to watch for the first hour, is exciting to think about after because its one good sequence, the long picture-postcard sequence near the end, is so incredible and so brilliantly prolonged. The picture has been crawling and stumbling along and then it climbs a high wire and walks it and keeps walking it until we're almost dizzy from admiration. The tight-rope is rarely stretched so high in movies, but there must be a sense of tension somewhere in the movie, if only in a bit player's face, not just mechanical suspense, or the movie is just more hours down the drain. It's the rare movie we really *go* with, the movie that keeps us tense and attentive. We learn to dread Hollywood "realism" and all that it implies. When, in the dark, we concentrate our attention, we are driven frantic by events on the level of ordinary life that pass at the rhythm of ordinary life. That's the self-conscious striving for integrity of humorless, untalented people. When we go to a play we expect a heightened, stylized language; the dull realism of the streets is unendurably boring, though we may escape from the play to the nearest bar to listen to the same language with relief. Better life than art imitating life.

If we go back and think over the movies we've enjoyed—even the ones we knew were terrible movies while we enjoyed them—what we enjoyed in them, the little part that was good, had, in some rudimentary way, some freshness, some hint of style, some trace of beauty, some audacity, some craziness. It's there in the interplay between Burt Lancaster and Ossie Davis, or, in *Wild in the Streets*, in Diane Varsi rattling her tambourine, in Hal Holbrook's faint twitch when he smells trouble, in a few of Robert Thom's lines; and they have some relation to art though they don't look like what we've been taught is "quality." They have the joy of playfulness. In a mediocre or rotten movie, the good things may give the impression that they come out of nowhere; the better the movie, the more they seem to belong to the world of the movie. Without this kind of playfulness and the pleasure we take from it, art isn't art at all, it's something punishing, as it so often is in school where even artists' little *jokes* become leaden from explanation.

Keeping in mind that simple, good distinction that all art is entertainment but not all entertainment is art, it might be a good idea to keep in mind also that if a movie is said to be a work of art and you don't enjoy it, the fault may be in you, but it's probably in the movie. Because of the money and advertising pressures involved, many reviewers discover a fresh masterpiece every week, and there's that cultural snobbery, that hunger for respectability that determines the selection of the even bigger annual masterpieces. In foreign movies what is most often mistaken for "quality" is an imitation of earlier movie art or a derivation from respectable, approved work in the other arts—like the demented, suffering painter-hero of *Hour of the Wolf* smearing his lipstick in a facsimile of expressionist anguish. Kicked in the ribs, the press says "art" when "ouch" would be more appropriate. When a director is said to be an artist (generally on the basis of earlier work which the press failed to recognize) and especially when he picks artistic subjects like the pain of creation, there is a tendency to acclaim his new bad work. This way the press, in trying to make up for its past mistakes, manages to be wrong all the time. And so a revenge-of-a-sour-virgin movie like Truffaut's *The Bride Wore Black* is treated respectfully as if it somehow revealed an artist's sensibility in every frame. Reviewers who would laugh at Lana Turner going through her *femme fatale* act in another Ross Hunter movie swoon when Jeanne Moreau casts significant blank looks for Truffaut.

In American movies what is most often mistaken for artistic quality is box-office success, especially if it's combined with a genuflection to importance; then you have "a movie the industry can be proud of" like *To Kill a Mockingbird* or such Academy Award winners as *West Side Story*, *My Fair Lady*, or *A Man for All Seasons*. Fred Zinnemann made a fine modern variant of a Western, *The Sundowners*, and hardly anybody saw it until it got on television; but *A Man for All Seasons* had the look of prestige and the press felt honored to praise it. I'm not sure most movie reviewers consider what they honestly enjoy as being central to criticism. Some at least appear to think that that would be relying too much on their own tastes, being too personal instead of being "objective"—relying on the ready-made terms of cultural respectability and on consensus judgment (which, to a rather shocking degree, can be arranged by publicists creating a climate of importance around a movie). Just as movie directors, as they age, hunger for what was meant by respectability in their youth, and aspire to prestigious cultural properties, so, too, the movie press longs to be elevated in terms of the cultural values of their old high schools. And so they, along with the industry, applaud ghastly "tour-de-force" performances, movies based on "distinguished" stage successes or prize-winning novels, or movies that are "worthwhile," that make a "contribution"—"serious" messagy movies. This often involves praise of bad movies, of dull movies, or even the praise in good movies of what was worst in them.

This last mechanism can be seen in the honors bestowed on *In the Heat of the Night*. The best thing in the movie is that high comic moment when Poitier says, "I'm a police officer," because it's a reversal of audience expectations and we laugh in delighted relief that the movie is not going to be another self-righteous, self-congratulatory exercise in the gloomy old Stanley Kramer tradition. At that point the audience sparks to life. The movie is fun largely because of the amusing central idea of a black Sherlock Holmes in a Tom and Jerry cartoon of reversals. Poitier's color is used for comedy instead of for that extra dimension of irony and pathos that made movies like *To Sir, with Love* unbearably sentimental. He doesn't really play the super sleuth very well: he's much too straight even when spouting the kind of higher scientific nonsense about right-handedness and left-handedness that would have kept Basil Rathbone in an ecstasy of clipped diction, blinking eyes and raised eyebrows. Like Bogart in *Beat the Devil* Poitier doesn't seem to be in on the joke. But Rod Steiger compensated with a comic performance that was even funnier for being so unexpected— not only from Steiger's career which had been going in other directions, but after the apparently serious opening of the film. The movie was, however, praised by the press as if it had been exactly the kind of picture that the audience was so relieved to discover it wasn't going to be (except in its routine melodramatic sequences full of fake courage and the climaxes such as Poitier slapping a rich white Southerner or being attacked by white thugs; except that is, in its worst parts). When I saw it, the audience, both black and white, enjoyed the joke of the fast-witted, hyper-educated black detective explaining matters to the backward, blundering Southern-chief-of-police slob. This racial joke is far more open and inoffensive than the usual "irony" of Poitier being so good and so black. For once it's *funny* (instead of embarrassing) that he's so superior to everybody.

In the Heat of the Night isn't in itself a particularly important movie; amazingly alive photographically, it's an entertaining, somewhat messed-up comedy-thriller. The director Norman Jewison destroys the final joke when Steiger plays redcap to Poitier by infusing it with tender feeling, so it comes out sickly sweet, and it's too bad that a whodunit in which the whole point is the demonstration of the Negro detective's ability to unravel what the white man can't, is never clearly unraveled. Maybe it needed a Negro super director. (The picture might have been more than just a lively whodunit if the detective had proceeded to solve the crime not by "scientific" means but by an understanding of relationships in the South that the white chief of police didn't have.) What makes it interesting for my purposes here is that the audience enjoyed the movie for the vitality of its surprising playfulness, while the industry congratulated itself because the film was "hard-hitting"—that is to say, it flirted with seriousness and spouted warm, worthwhile ideas.

Those who can accept *In the Heat of the Night* as the socially conscious movie that the industry pointed to with pride can probably also go along with the way the press attacked Jewison's subsequent film, *The Thomas Crown Affair*, as trash and a failure. One could even play the same game that was played on *In the Heat of the Night* and convert the *Crown* trifle into a sub-fascist exercise because, of course, Crown, the superman, who turns to crime out of boredom, is the crooked son of *The Fountainhead*, out of Raffles. But that's taking glossy summer-evening fantasies much too seriously: we haven't had a junior executive's fantasy-life movie for a long time and to attack this return of the worldly gentlemen-thieves genre of Ronald Colman and William Powell *politically* is to fail to have a sense of humor about the little romantic-adolescent fascist lurking in most of us. Part of the fun of movies is that they allow us to see how silly many of our fantasies are and how widely they're shared. A light romantic entertainment like *The Thomas Crown Affair*, trash undisguised, is the kind of chic crappy movie which (one would have thought) nobody could be fooled into thinking was art. Seeing it is like lying in the sun flicking through fashion magazines and, as we used to say, feeling rich and beautiful beyond your wildest dreams.

But it isn't easy to come to terms with what one enjoys in films, and if an older generation was persuaded to *dismiss* trash, now a younger generation, with the press and the schools in hot pursuit, has begun to talk about trash as if it were really very serious art. College newspapers and the new press all across the country are full of a hilarious new form of scholasticism, with students using their education to cook up impressive reasons for enjoying very simple, traditional dishes. Here is a communication from Cambridge to a Boston paper:

> To the Editor:
> *The Thomas Crown Affair* is fundamentally a film about faith between people. In many ways, it reminds me of a kind of updated old fable, or tale, about an ultimate test of faith. It is a film about a love affair (note the title), with a subplot of a bank robbery, rather than the reverse. The subtlety of the film is in the way the external plot is used as a matrix to develop serious motifs, much in the same way that the *Heat of the Night* functioned.
> Although Thomas Crown is an attractive and fascinating

character, Vicki is the protagonist. Crown is consistent, predictable: he courts personal danger to feel superior to the system of which he is a part, and to make his otherwise overly comfortable life more interesting. Vicki is caught between two opposing elements within her, which, for convenience, I would call masculine and feminine. In spite of her glamour, at the outset she is basically masculine, in a man's type of job, ruthless, after prestige and wealth. But Crown looses the female in her. His test is a test of her femininity. The masculine responds to the challenge. Therein lies the pathos of her final revelation. Her egocentrism had not yielded to his.

In this psychic context, the possibility of establishing faith is explored. The movement of the film is towards Vicki's final enigma. Her ambivalence is commensurate with the increasing danger to Crown. The suspense lies in how she will respond to her dilemma, rather than whether Crown will escape.

I find *The Thomas Crown Affair* to be a unique and haunting film, superb in its visual and technical design, and fascinating for the allegorical problem of human faith.

The Thomas Crown Affair is pretty good trash, but we shouldn't convert what we enjoy it for into false terms derived from our study of the other arts. That's being false to what we enjoy. If it was priggish for an older generation of reviewers to be ashamed of what they enjoyed and to feel they had to be contemptuous of popular entertainment, it's even more priggish for a new movie generation to be so proud of what they enjoy that they use their education to try to place trash within the acceptable academic tradition. What the Cambridge boy is doing is a more devious form of that elevating and falsifying of people who talk about Loren as a great actress instead of as a gorgeous, funny woman. Trash doesn't belong to the academic tradition, and that's part of the *fun* of trash—that you know (or *should* know) that you don't have to take it seriously, that it was never meant to be any more than frivolous and trifling and entertaining.

It's appalling to read solemn academic studies of Hitchcock or von Sternberg by people who seem to have lost sight of the primary reason for seeing films like *Notorious* or *Morocco*—which is that they were not intended solemnly, that they were playful and inventive and faintly (often deliberately) absurd. And what's good in them, what relates them to art, is that playfulness and absence of solemnity. There is talk now about von Sternberg's technique—his use of light and décor and detail—and he is, of course, a kitsch master in these areas, a master of studied artfulness and pretty excess. Unfortunately, some students take this technique as proof that his films are works of art, once again, I think, falsifying what they really respond to—the satisfying romantic glamour of his very pretty trash. *Morocco* is great trash, and movies are so rarely great art, that if we cannot appreciate great *trash*, we have very little reason to be interested in them. The kitsch of an earlier era—even the best kitsch—does not become art, though it may become camp. Von Sternberg's movies became camp even while he was still making them, because as the romantic feeling went out of his trash—when he became so enamored of his own pretty effects that he turned his human material into blank, affectless pieces of décor—his absurd trashy style was all there was. We are now told in respectable museum publications that in 1932 a movie like *Shanghai Express* "was completely misunderstood as a mindless adventure" when indeed it was completely *understood* as a mindless adventure. And enjoyed as a mindless adventure. It's a peculiar form of movie madness crossed with academicism, this lowbrowism masquerading as highbrowism, eating a candy bar and cleaning an "allegorical problem of human faith" out of your teeth. If we always wanted works of complexity and depth we wouldn't be going to movies about glamorous thieves and seductive women who sing in cheap cafés, and if we loved *Shanghai Express* it wasn't for its mind but for the glorious sinfulness of Dietrich informing Clive Brook that, "It took more than one man to change my name to Shanghai Lily" and for the villainous Oriental chieftain (Warner Oland!) delivering the classic howler, "The white woman stays with me."

If we don't deny the pleasures to be had from certain kinds of trash and accept *The Thomas Crown Affair* as a pretty fair example of entertaining trash, then we may ask if a piece of trash like this has any relationship to art. And I think it does. Steve McQueen gives probably his most glamorous, fashionable performance yet, but even enjoying him as much as I do, I wouldn't call his performance art. It's artful, though, which is exactly what is required in this kind of vehicle. If he had been luckier, if the script had provided what it so embarrassingly lacks, the kind of sophisticated dialogue—the sexy shoptalk—that such writers as Jules Furthman and William Faulkner provided for Bogart, and if the director Norman Jewison had Lubitsch's lightness of touch, McQueen might be acclaimed as a suave, "polished" artist. Even in this flawed setting, there's a self-awareness in his performance that makes his elegance funny. And Haskell Wexler, the cinematographer, lets go with a whole bag of tricks, flooding the screen with his delight in beauty, shooting all over the place, and sending up the material. And Pablo Ferro's games with the split screen at the beginning are such conscious, clever games designed to draw us in to watch intently what is of no great interest. What gives this trash a lift, what makes it entertaining is clearly that some of those involved, knowing of course that they were working on a silly shallow script and a movie that wasn't about anything of consequence, used the chance to have a good time with it. If the director, Norman Jewison, could have built a movie instead of putting together a patchwork of sequences, *Crown* might have had a chance to be considered a movie in the class and genre of Lubitsch's *Trouble in Paradise*. It doesn't come near that because to transform this kind of kitsch, to make art of it, one needs that unifying grace, that formality and charm that a Lubitsch could sometimes provide. Still, even in this movie we get a few grace notes in McQueen's playfulness, and from Wexler and Ferro. Working on trash, feeling free to play, can loosen up the actors and craftsmen just as seeing trash can liberate the spectator. And as we don't get this playful quality of art much in movies except in trash, we might as well relax and enjoy it freely for what it is. I don't trust anyone who doesn't admit having at some time in his life enjoyed trashy American movies; I don't trust *any* of the tastes of people who were born with such good taste that they didn't need to find their way through trash.

There is a moment in *Children of Paradise* when the rich nobleman (Louis Salou) turns on his mistress, the pearly plebeian Garance (Arletty). He complains that in all their years together he has never had her love, and she replies, "You've got to leave something for the poor." We don't ask much from movies, just a little something that we can call our own. Who at some point hasn't set out dutifully for that fine foreign film and then ducked into the nearest piece of American trash? We're not only educated people of taste, we're also common people with common feelings. And our common feelings are not all *bad*. You hoped for some aliveness in that trash that you were pretty sure you wouldn't get from the respected "art film." You had long since discovered that you wouldn't get it from certain kinds of American movies, either. The industry now is taking a neo-Victorian tone, priding itself on its (few) "good, clean" movies—which are always its worst movies because almost nothing can break through the smug surfaces, and even performers' talents become cute and cloying. The lowest action trash is preferable to wholesome family entertainment. When you clean them up, when you make movies respectable, you kill them. The wellspring of their *art*, their greatness, is in not being respectable.

VII

Does trash corrupt? A nutty Puritanism still flourishes in the arts, not just in the schoolteachers' approach of wanting art to be "worthwhile," but in the higher reaches of the academic life with those ideologues who denounce us for enjoying trash as if this enjoyment took us away from the really disturbing, angry new art of our time and somehow destroyed us. If we had to *justify* our trivial silly pleasures, we'd have a hard time. How could we possibly *justify* the fun of getting to know some people in movie after movie, like Joan Blondell, the brassy blonde with the heart of gold, or waiting for the virtuous, tiny, tiny-featured heroine to say her line so we could hear the riposte of her tough, wisecracking girlfriend (Iris Adrian was my favorite). Or, when the picture got too monotonous, there would be the song interlude, introduced "atmospherically" when the cops and crooks were both in the same never-neverland nightclub and everything stopped while a girl sang. Sometimes it would be the most charming thing in the movie, like Dolores Del Rio singing "You Make Me That Way" in *International Settlement*; sometimes it would drip with maudlin meaning, like "Oh Give Me Time for Tenderness" in *Dark Victory* with the dying Bette Davis singing along with the chanteuse. The pleasures of this kind of trash are not intellectually defensible. But why should pleasure need justification? Can one demonstrate that trash desensitizes us, that it prevents people from enjoying something better, that it limits our range of aesthetic response? Nobody I know of has provided such a demonstration. Do even Disney movies or Doris Day movies do us lasting harm? I've never known a person I thought had been harmed by them, though it does seem to me that they affect the tone of a culture, that perhaps—and I don't mean to be facetious—they may poison us collectively though they don't injure us individually. There are women who want to see a world in which everything is pretty and cheerful and in which romance triumphs

(*Barefoot in the Park, Any Wednesday*); families who want movies to be an innocuous inspiration, a good example for the children (*The Sound of Music, The Singing Nun*); couples who want the kind of folksy blue humor (*A Guide for the Married Man*) that they still go to Broadway shows for. These people are the reason slick, stale, rotting pictures make money; they're the reason so few pictures are any good. And in that way, this terrible conformist culture does affect us all. It certainly cramps and limits opportunities for artists. But that isn't what generally gets attacked as trash, anyway. I've avoided using the term "harmless trash" for movies like *The Thomas Crown Affair*, because that would put me on the side of the angels—against "harmful trash," and I don't honestly know what that is. It's common for the press to call cheaply made, violent action movies "brutalizing" but that tells us less about any actual demonstrable effects than about the finicky tastes of the reviewers—who are often highly appreciative of violence in more expensive and "artistic" settings such as *Petulia*. It's almost a class prejudice, this assumption that crudely made movies, movies without the look of art, are bad for people.

If there's a little art in good trash and sometimes even in poor trash, there may be more trash than is generally recognized in some of the most acclaimed "art" movies. Such movies as *Petulia* and *2001* may be no more than trash in the latest, up-to-the-minute guises, using "artistic techniques" to give trash the look of art. The serious art look may be the latest fashion in *expensive* trash. All that "art" may be what prevents pictures like these from being *enjoyable* trash; they're not honestly crummy, they're very fancy and they take their crummy ideas seriously.

I have rarely seen a more disagreeable, a more dislikable (or a bloodier) movie than *Petulia* and I would guess that its commercial success represents a triumph of publicity—and not the simple kind of just taking ads. It's a very strange movie and people may, of course, like it for all sorts of reasons, but I think many may dislike it as I do and still feel they should be impressed by it; the educated and privileged may now be more susceptible to the mass media than the larger public—they're certainly easier to reach. The publicity about Richard Lester as an artist has been gaining extraordinary momentum ever since *A Hard Day's Night*. A critical success that is also a hit makes the director a genius; he's a magician who made money out of art. The media are in ravenous competition for ever bigger stories, for "trend" pieces and editorial essays, because once the process starts it's considered news. If Lester is "making the scene" a magazine that hasn't helped to build him up feels it's been scooped. *Petulia* is the come-dressed-as-the-sick-soul-of-America-party and in the opening sequence the guests arrive—rich victims of highway accidents in their casts and wheel chairs, like the spirit of '76 coming to opening night at the opera. It's science-horror fiction—a garish new world with charity balls at which you're invited to "Shake for Highway Safety."

Lester picked San Francisco for his attack on America just as in *How I Won the War* he picked World War II to attack war. That is, it looks like a real frontal attack on war itself if you attack the war that many people consider a just war. But then he concentrated not on the issues of that war but on the class hatreds of British officers and men—who were not engaged in defending London or bombing Germany but in building a cricket pitch in Africa. In *Petulia*, his hate letter to America, he relocates the novel, shifting the locale from Los Angeles to San Francisco, presumably, again, to face the big challenge by showing that even the best the country has to offer is rotten. But then he ducks the challenge he sets for himself by making San Francisco look like Los Angeles. And if he must put carnival barkers in Golden Gate Park and invent Sunday excursions for children to Alcatraz, if he must invent such caricatures of epicene expenditure and commercialism as bizarrely automated motels and dummy television sets, if he must provide his own ugliness and hysteria and lunacy and use filters to destroy the city's beautiful light, if, in short, he must falsify America in order to make it appear hateful, what is it he really hates? He's like a crooked cop framing a suspect with trumped-up evidence. We never find out *why*: he's too interested in making a flashy case to examine what he's doing. And reviewers seem unwilling to ask questions which might expose them to the charge that they're *still* looking for meaning instead of, in the new cant, just reacting to images—such questions as why does the movie keep juxtaposing shots of bloody surgery with shots of rock groups like the Grateful Dead or Big Brother and the Holding Company and shots of the war in Vietnam. What are these little montages supposed to do to us—make us feel that even the hero (a hardworking life-saving surgeon) is implicated in the war and that somehow contemporary popular music is also allied to destruction and death? (I thought only the moralists of the Soviet Union believed that.) The images of *Petulia* don't make valid connections, they're joined together for shock and excitement, and I don't believe in the brilliance of a method which equates hippies, war, surgery, wealth, Southern decadents, bullfights, etc. Lester's mix is almost as fraudulent as *Mondo Cane*; *Petulia* exploits any shocking material it can throw together to give false importance to a story about Holly Golightly and The Man in the Gray Flannel Suit. The jagged glittering mosaic style of *Petulia* is an armor protecting Lester from an artist's task; this kind of "style" no longer fools people so much in writing but it knocks them silly in films.

Movie directors in trouble fall back on what they love to call "personal style"—though how impersonal it often is can be illustrated by *Petulia*—which is not edited in the rhythmic, modulations-of-graphics style associated with Lester (and seen most distinctively in his best-edited, though not necessarily best film, *Help!*) but in the style of the movie surgeon, Anthony Gibbs, who acted as chopper on it, and who gave it the same kind of scissoring which he had used on *The Loneliness of the Long Distance Runner* and in his rescue operation on *Tom Jones*. This is, in much of *Petulia*, the most insanely obvious method of cutting film ever devised; keep the audience jumping with cuts, juxtapose startling images, anything for effectiveness, just make it *brilliant*—with the director taking, apparently, no responsibility for the *implied* connections. (The editing style is derived from Alain Resnais, and though it's a debatable style in his films, he uses it responsibly not just opportunistically.)

Richard Lester, the director of *Petulia*, is a shrill scold in Mod clothes. Consider a sequence like the one in which the beaten-to-a-gruesome-pulp heroine is taken out to an ambulance, to the accompaniment of hippies making stupid, unfeeling remarks. It is embarrassingly reminiscent of the older people's comments about the youthful sub-pre-hippies of *The Knack*. Lester has simply shifted villains. Is he saying that America is so rotten that even our hippies are malignant? I rather suspect he is, but why? Lester has taken a fashionably easy way to attack America, and because of the war in Vietnam some people are willing to accept the bloody montages that make them feel we're all guilty, we're rich, we're violent, we're spoiled, we can't relate to each other, etc. Probably the director who made three celebrations of youth and freedom (*A Hard Day's Night*, *The Knack*, and *Help!*) is now desperate to expand his range and become a "serious" director, and this is the new look in seriousness.

It's easy to make fun of the familiar ingredients of trash—the kook heroine who steals a tuba (that's not like the best of Carole Lombard but like the worst of Irene Dunne), the vaguely impotent, meaninglessly hand-some rotter husband, Richard Chamberlain (back to the rich, spineless weaklings of David Manners), and Joseph Cotten as one more insanely vicious decadent Southerner spewing out villainous lines. (Even Victor Jory in *The Fugitive Kind* wasn't much meaner.) What's terrible is not so much this feeble conventional trash as the director's attempts to turn it all into scintillating art and burning comment; what is really awful is the trash of his ideas and artistic effects.

Is there any art in this obscenely self-important movie? Yes, but in a format like this the few good ideas don't really shine as they do in simpler trash; we have to go through so much unpleasantness and showing-off to get to them. Lester should trust himself more as a director and stop the cinemagician stuff because there's good, tense direction in a few sequences. He got a good performance from George C. Scott and a sequence of post-marital discord between Scott and Shirley Knight that, although over-wrought, is not so glaringly overwrought as the rest of the picture. It begins to suggest something interesting that the picture might have been about. (Shirley Knight should, however, stop fondling her hair like a miser with a golden hoard; it's time for her to get another prop.) And Julie Chris-tie is extraordinary just to look at—lewd and anxious, expressive and empty, brilliantly faceted but with something central missing, almost as if there's no woman inside.

VIII

2001 is a movie that might have been made by the hero of *Blow-Up*, and it's fun to think about Kubrick really doing every dumb thing he wanted to do, building enormous science-fiction sets and equip-ment, never even bothering to figure out what he was going to do with them. Fellini, too, had gotten carried away with the Erector Set approach to movie-making, but his big science-fiction construction, exposed to view at the end of *8½*, was abandoned. Kubrick never really made his movie either but he doesn't seem to know it. Some people like the Amer-ican International Pictures stuff because it's rather idiotic and maybe some people love *2001* just because Kubrick did all that stupid stuff, acted out a kind of super sci-fi nut's fantasy. In some ways it's the biggest amateur movie of them all, complete even to the amateur-movie obligatory scene—the director's little daughter (in curls) telling daddy what kind of present she wants.

There was a little pre-title sequence in *You Only Live Twice* with an astronaut out in space that was in a looser, more free style than *2001*—a daring little moment that I think was more fun than all of *2001*. It had an element of the unexpected, of the shock of finding death in space lyrical. Kubrick is carried away by the idea. The secondary title of *Dr. Strangelove*, which we took to be satiric, *How I learned to stop worrying and love the bomb*, was not, it now appears, altogether satiric for Kubrick. *2001* celebrates the invention of tools of death, as an evolutionary route to a higher order of *non-human* life. Kubrick literally learned to stop worrying and love the bomb; he's become his own butt—the Herman Kahn of extraterrestrial games theory. The ponderous blurry appeal of the picture may be that it takes its stoned audience out of this world to a consoling vision of a graceful world of space, controlled by superior godlike minds, where the hero is reborn as an angelic baby. It has the dreamy somewhere-over-the-rainbow appeal of a new vision of heaven. *2001* is a celebration of cop-out. It says man is just a tiny nothing on the stairway to paradise, something better is coming, and it's all out of your hands anyway. There's an intelligence out there in space controlling your destiny from ape to angel, so just follow the slab. Drop up.

It's a bad, bad sign when a movie director begins to think of himself as a myth-maker, and this limp myth of a grand plan that justifies slaughter and ends with resurrection has been around before. Kubrick's story line—accounting for evolution by an extraterrestrial intelligence—is probably the most gloriously redundant plot of all time. And although his intentions may have been different, *2001* celebrates the *end of man*; those beautiful mushroom clouds at the end of "Strangelove" were no accident. In *2001, A Space Odyssey*, death and life are all the same: no point is made in the movie of Gary Lockwood's death—the moment isn't even defined—and the hero doesn't discover that the hibernating scientists have become corpses. That's unimportant in a movie about the beauties of resurrection. Trip off to join the cosmic intelligence and come back a better mind. And as the trip in the movie is the usual psychedelic light show, the audience doesn't even have to worry about getting to Jupiter. They can go to heaven in Cinerama.

It isn't accidental that we don't care if the characters live or die; if Kubrick has made his people so uninteresting, it is partly because characters and individual fates just aren't big enough for certain kinds of big movie directors. Big movie directors become generals in the arts; and they want subjects to match their new importance. Kubrick has announced that his next project is *Napoleon*—which, for a movie director, is the equivalent of Joan of Arc for an actress. Lester's "savage" comments about affluence and malaise, Kubrick's inspirational banality about how we will become as gods through machinery, are big-shot show-business deep thinking. This isn't a new show-business phenomenon; it belongs to the genius tradition of the theatre. Big entrepreneurs, producers, and directors who stage big spectacular shows, even designers of large sets have traditionally begun to play the role of visionaries and thinkers and men with answers. They get too big for art. Is a work of art possible if pseudo-science and the technology of movie-making become more important to the "artist" than man? This is central to the failure of *2001*. It's a monumentally unimaginative movie: Kubrick, with his $750,000 centrifuge, and in love with gigantic hardware and control panels, is the Belasco of science fiction. The special effects—though straight from the drawing board—are good and big and awesomely, expensively detailed. There's a little more that's good in the movie, when Kubrick doesn't take himself too seriously—like the comic moment when the gliding space vehicles begin their Johann Strauss waltz; that is to say, when the director shows a bit of a sense of proportion about what he's doing, and sees things momentarily as comic—when the movie doesn't take itself with such idiot solemnity. The light-show trip is of no great distinction; compared to the work of experimental filmmakers like Jordan Belson, it's third-rate. If big film directors are to get credit for doing badly what others have been doing brilliantly for years with no money, just because they've put it on a big screen, then businessmen are greater than poets and theft is art.

IX

Part of the fun of movies is in seeing "what everybody's talking about," and if people are flocking to a movie, or if the press can con us into thinking that they are, then ironically, there is a sense in which we want to see it, even if we suspect we won't enjoy it, because we want to know what's going on. Even if it's the worst inflated pompous trash that is the most talked about (and it usually is) and even if that talk is manufactured, we want to see the movies because so many people fall for whatever is talked about that they make the advertisers' lies true. Movies absorb material from the culture and the other arts so fast that some films that have been widely *sold* become culturally and sociologically important whether they are good movies or not. Movies like *Morgan!* or *Georgy Girl* or *The Graduate* —aesthetically trivial movies which, however, because of the ways some people react to them, enter into the national bloodstream—become cultural and psychological equivalents of watching a political convention—to observe what's going on. And though this has little to do with the art of movies, it has a great deal to do with the appeal of movies.

An analyst tells me that when his patients are not talking about their personal hangups and their immediate problems they talk about the situations and characters in movies like *The Graduate* or *Belle de Jour* and they talk about them with as much personal involvement as about their immediate problems. I have elsewhere suggested that this way of reacting to movies as psychodrama used to be considered a pre-literate way of reacting but that now those considered "post-literate" are reacting like pre-literates. The high school and college students identifying with Georgy Girl or Dustin Hoffman's Benjamin are not that different from the stenographer who used to live and breathe with the Joan Crawford-working girl and worry about whether that rich boy would really make her happy—and considered her pictures "great." They don't see the movie as a movie but as part of the soap opera of their lives. The fan magazines used to encourage this kind of identification; now the *advanced* mass media encourage it, and those who want to sell to youth use the language of "just let it flow over you." The person who responds this way does not respond more freely but less freely and less fully than the person who is aware of what is well done and what badly done in a movie, who can accept some things in it and reject others, who uses all his senses in reacting, not just his emotional vulnerabilities.

Still, we care about what other people care about—sometimes because we want to know how far we've gotten from common responses—and if a movie is important to other people we're interested in it because of what it means to them, even if it doesn't mean much to us. The small triumph of *The Graduate* was to have domesticated alienation and the difficulty of communication, by making what Benjamin is alienated from a middle-class comic strip and making it absurdly evident that he has nothing to communicate—which is just what makes him an acceptable hero for the large movie audience. If he said anything or had any ideas, the audience would probably hate him. *The Graduate* isn't a *bad* movie, it's entertaining, though in a fairly slick way (the audience is just about programmed for laughs). What's surprising is that so many people take it so seriously. What's funny about the movie are the laughs on that dumb sincere boy who wants to talk about art in bed when the woman just wants to fornicate. But then the movie begins to pander to youthful narcissism, glorifying his innocence, and making the predatory (and now crazy) woman the villain-ess. Commercially this works: the inarticulate dull boy becomes a roman-tic hero for the audience to project into with all those squishy and now conventional feelings of look, his parents don't communicate with him; look, he wants truth not sham, and so on. But the movie betrays itself and its own expertise, sells out its comic moments that click along with the rhythm of a hit Broadway show, to make the oldest movie pitch of them all—asking the audience to identify with the simpleton who is the latest version of the misunderstood teen-ager and the pure-in-heart boy next door. It's almost painful to tell kids who have gone to see *The Graduate* eight times that once was enough for you because you've already seen it eighty times with Charles Ray and Robert Harron and Richard Barthel-mess and Richard Cromwell and Charles Farrell. How could you convince them that a movie that sells innocence is a very commercial piece of work when they're so clearly in the market to buy innocence? When *The Grad-uate* shifts to the tender awakenings of love, it's just the latest version of *David and Lisa*. *The Graduate* only wants to succeed and that's fundamen-tally what's the matter with it. There is a pause for a laugh after the men-tion of "Berkeley" that is an unmistakable sign of hunger for success; this kind of movie-making shifts values, shifts focus, shifts emphasis, shifts everything for a sure-fire response. Mike Nichols' "gift" is that he lets the audience direct him; this is demagoguery in the arts.

Even the cross-generation fornication is standard for the genre. It goes back to Pauline Frederick in *Smouldering Fires*, and Clara Bow was at it with mama Alice Joyce's boyfriend in *Our Dancing Mothers*, and in the Forties it was *Mildred Pierce*. Even the terms are not different: in these movies the seducing adults are customarily sophisticated, worldly, and corrupt, the kids basically innocent, though not so humorless and blank as Benjamin. In its basic attitudes *The Graduate* is corny American, it takes us back to before *The Game of Love* with Edwige Feuillère as the sympathetic older woman and *A Cold Wind in August* with the sympathetic Lola Albright performance.

What's interesting about the success of *The Graduate* is sociological: the revelation of how emotionally accessible modern youth is to the same old manipulation. The recurrence of certain themes in movies suggests that each generation wants romance restated in slightly new terms, and of course it's one of the pleasures of movies as a popular art that they can answer this need. And yet, and yet—one doesn't expect an *educated* generation to be so soft on itself, much softer than the factory workers of the past who didn't go back over and over to the same movies, mooning away in fixation on themselves and thinking this fixation meant movies had suddenly become an art, and *their* art.

X

When you're young the odds are very good that you'll find something to enjoy in almost any movie. But as you grow more experienced, the odds change. I saw a picture a few years ago that was the sixth version of material that wasn't much to start with. Unless you're feeble-minded, the odds get worse and worse. We don't go on reading the same kind of manufactured novels—pulp Westerns or detective thrillers, say—all of our lives, and we don't want to go on and on looking at movies about cute heists by comically assorted gangs. The problem with a popular art form is that those who want something more are in a hopeless minority compared with the millions who are always seeing it for the first time, or for the reassurance and gratification of seeing the conventions fulfilled again. Probably a large part of the older audience gives up movies for this reason—simply that they've seen it before. And probably this is why so many of the best movie critics quit. They're wrong when they blame it on the movies going bad; it's the odds becoming so bad, and they can no longer bear the many tedious movies for the few good moments and the tiny shocks of recognition. Some become too tired, too frozen in fatigue, to respond to what *is* new. Others who *do* stay awake may become too demanding for the young who are seeing it all for the first hundred times.

The critical task is necessarily comparative, and younger people do not truly know what is new. And despite all the chatter about the media and how smart the young are, they're incredibly naïve about mass culture — perhaps *more* naïve than earlier generations (though I don't know why). Maybe watching all that television hasn't done so much for them as they seem to think; and when I read a young intellectual's appreciation of *Rachel, Rachel* and come to "the mother's passion for chocolate bars is a superb symbol for the second coming of childhood" I know the writer is still in his first childhood, and I wonder if he's going to come out of it.

One's moviegoing tastes and habits change — I still like in movies what I always liked but now, for example, I really want documentaries. After all the years of stale stupid acted-out stories, with less and less for me in them, I am desperate to know something, desperate for facts, for information, for faces of non-actors and for knowledge of how people live — for revelations, not for the little bits of show-business detail worked up for us by show-business minds who got them from the same movies we're tired of.

But the big change is in our *habits*. If we make any kind of decent, useful life for ourselves we have less need to run from it to those diminishing pleasures of the movies. When we go to the movies we want something good, something sustained, we don't want to settle for just a bit of something, because we have other things to do. If life at home is more interesting, why go to the movies? And the theatres frequented by true moviegoers — those perennial displaced persons in each city, the loners and the losers — depress us. Listening to them — and they are often more audible than the sound track — as they cheer the cons and jeer the cops, we may still share their disaffection, but it's not enough to keep us interested in cops and robbers. A little nose-thumbing isn't enough. If we've grown up at the movies we know that good work is continuous not with the academic, respectable tradition but with the glimpses of something good in trash, but we want the subversive gesture carried to the domain of discovery. Trash has given us an appetite for art.

{*Harper's*, February 1969}

:: Saintliness

We are so often bathed in emotion at the movies by all those directors whose highest ambition is to make us feel feelings that aren't worth feeling that the cool detachment of Luis Buñuel has a surprising edge. Buñuel doesn't make full contact with us, and the distance can be fun; it can result in the pleasure of irony, though it can also result in the dissatisfaction of feeling excluded. His indifference to whether we understand him or not can seem insolent, and yet this is part of what makes him fascinating. Indifference can be tantalizing in art, as in romance, and by keeping us at a distance in a medium with which most directors try to involve us he deliberately undermines certain concepts that are almost axiomatic in drama and movies—especially drama and movies in their mass-culture form. Buñuel, who regards all that tender involvement as "bourgeois morality," deliberately assaults us for being so emotional. His most distinctive quality as a movie-maker is the lack of certainty he inflicts on us about how we should feel toward his characters. Buñuel shoots a story simply and directly, to make just the points he wants to make, though if he fails to make them or doesn't make them clearly he doesn't seem to give a damn. He leaves in miscalculations, and fragments that don't work—like the wheelchair on the sidewalk in *Belle de Jour*. He's a remarkably fast, economical, and careless movie-maker, and the carelessness no doubt accounts for some of the ambiguity in the films, such as the unresolved trick endings that leave us dangling. From the casting and the listless acting in many of his movies, one can conclude only that he's unconcerned about such matters; often he doesn't seem to bother even to cast for type, and one can't easily tell if the characters are meant to be what they appear to be. He uses actors in such an indifferent way that they scarcely even stand for the characters. Rather than allow the bad Mexican actors that he generally works with to act, he seems to dispense with acting by just rushing them through their roles without giving them time to understand what they're doing. Clearly, he prefers no acting to bad acting. The mixture of calculation and carelessness in his ambiguity can be maddening, as in some of *Viridiana* (1961) and in most of the slackly directed *The Exterminating Angel* (1962). But sometimes what makes an artist great and original is that in his lack of interest in (or lack of talent for) what other artists have been concerned with he helps us see things differently and develops the medium in new ways. Like Borges, who won't even bother to write a book, Buñuel probably doesn't think casting or acting is important enough to bother about. And casting without worrying about whether the actors suit the role — casting almost *against* type — and not allowing the actors to work up characterizations can give movies a new kind of tone. Without the conventional emotional resonances that actors acting provide, his movies have a thinner texture that begins to become a new kind of integrity, and they affect us as fables. Most movies are full of actors trying to appeal to us, and the movies themselves try so hard to win us over that the screen is practically kissing us. When Buñuel is at his most indifferent, he is sometimes at his best and most original, as in parts of *Nazarin* (1958), which opened here last summer, and in almost all of his newly released — and peculiarly exhilarating — *Simon of the Desert*.

Other movie directors tell us how we should feel; they want our approval for being such good guys, and most of them are proudest when they can demonstrate their commitment to humanitarian principles. Buñuel makes the charitable the butt of humor and shows the lechery and mendacity of the poor and misbegotten. As a movie-making comedian, he is a critic of mankind. One can generally define even a critic's position, but there is no way to get a hold on what Buñuel believes in. There is no characteristic Buñuel hero or heroine, and there is no kind of behavior that escapes his ridicule. His movies are full of little sadistic jokes that we can't quite tell how to take. The movie director most influenced by de Sade, and the only one still at work who had close ties to the Surrealist movement, Buñuel has gone on using the techniques of the Surrealists in the medium that once seemed their natural habitat. We may not really like his jokes, yet they make us laugh. A perturbing example that comes all too readily to mind: When Jorge, in *Viridiana*, frees a mistreated dog that has been tied to a cart and then we see another cart coming from the opposite direction with another dog tied to it, is Buñuel saying that Jorge is a realist who does what he can, or does Buñuel really mean what the audience, by its laughter, clearly takes the scene to mean—that Jorge's action was useless, since there are so many mistreated dogs? This "joke" could be extended to the "comedy" of saving one Jew from the ovens or one Biafran baby from starvation, and I think we are aware of the obscenity in the humor even as we laugh—we laugh at the recognition that we are capable of participating in the obscenity. His jokes are perverse and irrational and blasphemous, and it may feel liberating to laugh at them just because they are a return to a kind of primitive folk comedy—the earliest form of black comedy, enjoyed by those who laugh at deformity and guffaw when a man kicks a goat or squeezes an udder too hard. Buñuel reminds us of the cruelty that he feels sentimental art tries to hide, and we respond by laughing at horrors. This is partly, I think, because we are conscious of the anti-sentimentality of his technique—of his toughness and his willingness to look things in the eye.

Some of his recurrent jokes are really rather private jokes—the udders and little torture kits and objects turned into fetishes—and Buñuel throwing his whammies can seem no more than a gigantic, Spanish Terry Southern. Bad Buñuel is like good Terry Southern—a putdown and a cackle. Sometimes when we laugh at a Buñuel film we probably want to sound more knowledgeable than we are; we just know it's "dirty." Yet this is the vindication of the Surrealist idea of the power of subjective images: we *do* feel certain things to be "dirty" and some kinds of violence to be funny, and we laugh at them without being able to explain why. Buñuel gets at material we've buried, and it's a release to laugh this impolite laughter, which is like laughter from out of nowhere, at jokes we didn't know we knew.

Once, in Berkeley, after a lecture by LeRoi Jones, as the audience got up to leave, I asked an elderly white couple next to me how they could applaud when Jones said that all whites should be killed. And the little gray-haired woman replied, "But that was just a metaphor. He's a wonderful speaker." I think we're inclined to react similarly to Buñuel—who once referred to some of those who praised *Un Chien Andalou* as "that crowd of imbeciles who find the film beautiful or poetic when it is fundamentally a desperate and passionate call to murder." To be blind to Buñuel's meanings as a way of being open to "art" is a variant of the very sentimentality that he satirizes. The movie-goers apply the same piousness to "art" that his mock saints do to humanity: both groups would rather swallow insults than be tough-minded. Buñuel is the opposite of a flower child.

Simon of the Desert, a short (forty-five-minute) feature made in Mexico in 1965, just before he made *Belle de Jour*, is a playful little travesty on the temptations of St. Simeon Stylites, the fifth-century desert anchorite who spent thirty-seven years preaching to pilgrims from his perch on top of a column. It is, in both a literal and a figurative sense, a shaggy-saint story, and (unlike much of Buñuel's work) it is charming. The narrative style of *Simon* is so straightforward and ascetically simple that it may be easier to see what he is saying in this film than in his more elaborate divertissements about saintliness turning into foolishness—*Nazarin* and the complicated, allusive *Viridiana*, which was cluttered with Freudian symbols. Buñuel seems to have a grudging respect for Nazarin and Simon that he didn't show for Viridiana, whom he made sickly, chaste, and priggish. *Viridiana* seemed dramatically out of focus because Buñuel didn't even dignify her desire to do good, and so the film had to depend on the pleasures and shocks of blasphemy—probably not inconsiderable for insiders, but insufficient for others. The tone of *Simon* is almost jovial, though the style is direct—just one incident after another—and as bare and objective as if he were documenting a scientific demonstration; even the Surreal details (like a coffin skittering over the ground) are presented in a matter-of-fact way. Buñuel has himself in the past given in to temptation: with more money than he was accustomed to, he fell for the fanciness of all that French *mise-en-scène* that made his *Diary of a Chambermaid* so revoltingly "beautiful." But there's very little money in "Simon," and there was, apparently, none to finish it; the bummer of an ending was just a way to wind it up.

Simon (Claudio Brook) performs his miracles, and the crowds evaluate them like a bunch of New York cabdrivers discussing a parade: whatever it was, it wasn't much. He restores hands to a thief whose hands have been chopped off; the crowds rate the miracle "not bad," and the thief's first act with his new hands is to slap his own child. The Devil, in the female form of Silvia Pinal (much more amusing as the Devil than she was in her guises in other Buñuel films), tempts him, and, at one point, frames him in front of the local priests, who are more than willing to believe the worst of him. Simon is a saint, and yet not only are his miracles worthless—they can't change men's natures—but even he is dragged down by his instincts. Buñuel is saying that saintliness is sentimentality, that, as the platitude has it, human nature doesn't change. This is not, God knows, a very interesting point, nor do I think it has the slightest validity; the theme is an odd mixture—a Spanish schoolboy's view of life joined to an adult atheist's disbelief in redemption. This outlook creates some problems when it comes to responding to Buñuel's work.

There are probably many lapsed Catholics who still believe in sin though they no longer believe in redemption, who have the disease though they have lost faith in the cure. In this they are not much different from the Socialists who still accept the general Socialist analysis of capitalism without having much confidence in the Socialist solutions. But psychologically there is an enormous difference between those who regard man as the victim of violent instinctual drives and those who live by a belief in justice and decency, even without any real conviction that society will ever be better. The pessimistic view can be so offensive to our ameliorative, reforming disposition that it's almost inconceivable to us that an artist whose work we respond to on many levels can disagree with us at such a fundamental level. And so with Luis Buñuel in films, as, in literature, with D. H. Lawrence and T. S. Eliot and Pound, we often contrive to overlook what the artist is saying that is alien to us. Because Buñuel is anti-Church and is a Spaniard at odds with Franco, because he satirizes bourgeois hypocrisy, there is, I think, a tendency to applaud his work as if this were all it encompassed. At the movies, when we see horrors we expect the reformer's zeal; that is the convention in democratic art, and perhaps we project some of our outraged virtue onto Buñuel's films. We feel free to enjoy his anarchic humor—which is often funniest when it is cruelest— because we can feel we're laughing at Fascism and at the human stupidity that reinforces Fascism. But though his work is a series of arguments against the Grand Inquisitor's policies, his basic view of man is the Grand Inquisitor's. Buñuel attacks the Church as the perverter and frustrater of man—the power trying to hold down sexuality, animality, irrationality, man's "instinctual nature." He sees bourgeois hypocrisy as the deceptions that men practice to deny the truth of their urges. His movies satirize the blindness of the spiritual; his would-be saints are fools—denying the instinctive demands not only in others but in themselves. Surrealism is both a belief in the irrationality of man and a technique for demonstrating it. In his *Land Without Bread*, Spain itself—that country that seems to be left over from something we don't understand—was a Surreal joke, a country where the only smiling faces were those of cretins. Like other passionate artists who fling horrors at us, Buñuel is an outraged lover of man, a disenchanted idealist; being a Spaniard, he makes comedy of his own disgust. He can't let go of the Church; he's an anti-Catholic the way Bogart was an anti-hero. He wants man to be purged of inhibitions, yet the people in his movies become grotesque when they're uninhibited. And when his saintly characters wise up and lose their faith, he can't show us that they're useful or better off, or even happier. He is overtly anti-romantic and anti-religious, yet he is obsessed with romantic, religious fools. He has never made a movie of *Don Quixote*, but he keeps pecking away at the theme of *Don Quixote*, and gets himself so enraged by the unfulfillment of ideals that he despises dreamers who can't make their dreams come true. In *Viridiana*, he twisted the theme into knots—turning in on himself so far that he came out the other end.

How can Buñuel in *Simon of the Desert* make a comedy out of a demonstration of what liberals have always denied and yet make liberals (rather than conservatives) laugh at it? It's as if someone made a comedy demonstrating that if you divided the world's wealth equally, it would all be back in the hands of the same people in a year, and this comedy became a big hit in Communist countries—which, however, it might very well do if the style of the comedy and the characters and details were the kind that the Communists responded to. And it might become an underground hit if it had jokes that brought something hidden out into the open: Buñuel's Freudian symbols and blasphemous gags alienate the conservatives and, of course, please the liberals. And then there is the matter of style. Buñuel doesn't pour on the prettiness, he doesn't turn a movie into a catered affair. There is such a thing as mass bourgeois movie sentimentality; we are surrounded by it, inundated by it, sinking in it, and Buñuel pulls us out of this muck. *Simon* is so palpably clean that it's an aesthetic assault on conservative taste. It's hard to love man; Hollywood movies pretend it's easy, but every detail gives the show away. Buñuel's style tells the truth of his feelings; the Spanish stance is too strong for soft emotions like pity. Though, as in *Diary of a Chambermaid*, he can be so coldly unpleasant that we are repelled (and happy to be excluded), he never makes people pitiable lumps. And though he may turn Quixote into a cold green girl or a dithering man, in his films the quixotic gestures of the simple peasants are the only truly human gestures. A dwarf gives his inamorata an apple and his total love; a woman offers Nazarin a pineapple and her blessing. Nazarin is so stubbornly proud that it's a struggle for him to accept, and Buñuel himself is so proud that he will hardly give in to the gesture. Humility is so difficult for him that he just tosses in the pineapple ambiguously—he's so determined not to give in to the folly of tenderness that he cops out.

At the end of *Simon of the Desert* Simon is transported to the modern world, and we see him, a lost soul, in a Greenwich Village discothèque full of dancing teen-agers. This is a disastrous finish for the movie—a finish of the careless kind that Buñuel is prone to. The primitive Mexican desert setting situates the story plausibly, but New York is outside the movie's frame of reference, nor does this discothèque conceivably represent what Simon's temptation might be. What Buñuel intended as another little joke is instead a joke on his gloomy view. "It's the last dance," the Devil says, though what is presented to us as a vision of a mad, decaying world in its final orgy looks like a nice little platter party.

{*The New Yorker*, February 15, 1969}

from
DEEPER
INTO
MOVIES

:: The Bottom of the Pit

A college-professor friend of mine in San Francisco who has always tried to stay in tune with his students looked at his class recently and realized it was time to take off his beads. There he was, a superannuated flower child wearing last year's talismans, and the young had become austere, even puritanical. Movies and, even more, movie audiences have been changing. The art houses are now (for the first time) dominated by American movies, and the young audiences waiting outside, sitting on the sidewalk or standing in line, are no longer waiting just for entertainment. The waiting together may itself be part of the feeling of community, and they go inside almost for sacramental purposes. For all the talk (and fear) of ritual participation in the "new" theatre, it is really taking place on a national scale in the movie houses, at certain American films that might be called cult films, though they have probably become cult films because they are the most interesting films around. What is new about *Easy Rider* is not necessarily that one finds its attitudes appealing but that the movie conveys the mood of the drug culture with such skill and in such full belief that these simplicities are the truth that one can understand why these attitudes are appealing to others. *Easy Rider* is an expression and a confirmation of how this audience feels; the movie attracts a new kind of "inside" audience, whose members enjoy tuning in together to a whole complex of shared signals and attitudes. And although one may be uneasy over the satisfaction the audience seems to receive from responding to the general masochism and to the murder of Captain America, the movie obviously rings true to the audience's vision. It's cool to feel that you can't win, that it's all rigged and hopeless. It's even cool to believe in purity and sacrifice. Those of us who reject the heroic central character and the statements of

Easy Rider may still be caught by something edgy and ominous in it—the acceptance of the constant danger of sudden violence. We're not sure how much of this paranoia isn't paranoia.

Some of the other cult films *try* to frighten us but are too clumsy to, though they succeed in doing something else. One has only to talk with some of the people who have seen *Midnight Cowboy*, for example, to be aware that what they care about is not the camera and editing pyrotechnics; they are indifferent to all that by now routine filler. John Schlesinger in *Midnight Cowboy* and, at a less skillful level, Larry Peerce in *Goodbye, Columbus* hedge their bets by using cutting and camera techniques to provide a satirical background as a kind of enrichment of the narrative and theme. But it really cheapens and impoverishes their themes. Peerce's satire is just cheesy, like his lyricism, and Schlesinger's (like Tony Richardson's in *The Loved One* and Richard Lester's in *Petulia*) is offensively inhuman and inaccurate. If Schlesinger could extend the same sympathy to the other Americans that he extends to Joe Buck and Ratso, the picture might make better sense; the point of the picture must surely be to give us some insight into these derelicts—two of the many kinds of dreamers and failures in the city. Schlesinger keeps pounding away at America, determined to expose how horrible the people are, to dehumanize the people these two are part of. The spray of venom in these pictures is so obviously the directors' way of showing off that we begin to discount it. To varying degrees, these films share the paranoid view of America of *Easy Rider*—and they certainly reinforce it for the audience—but what the audience really reacts to in *Midnight Cowboy* is the two lost, lonely men finding friendship. The actors save the picture, as the actors almost saved parts of *Petulia*; the leading actors become more important because the flamboyantly "visual" exhibitionism doesn't hold one's interest. Despite the recurrent assertions that the star system is dead, the audience is probably more interested than ever in the human material on the screen (though the new stars don't always resemble the old ones). At *Midnight Cowboy*, in the midst of all the grotesque shock effects and the brutality of the hysterical, superficial satire of America, the audiences, wiser, perhaps, than the director, are looking for the human feelings—the simple, *Of Mice and Men* kind of relationship at the heart of it. Maybe they wouldn't accept the simple theme so readily in a simpler setting, because it might look square, but it's what they're taking from the movie. They're looking for "truth"—for some signs of emotion, some evidence of what keeps people together. The difference between the old audiences and the new ones is that the old audiences wanted immediate gratification and used to get restless and bored when a picture didn't click along; these new pictures don't all click along, yet the young audiences stay attentive. They're eager to respond, to love it—eager to *feel*.

Although young movie audiences are far more sentimental now than they were a few years ago (Frank Capra, whose softheaded populism was hooted at in college film societies in the fifties, has become a new favorite at U.C.L.A.), there is this new and good side to the sentimentality. They are going to movies looking for feelings that will help synthesize their experience, and they appear to be willing to feel their way along with a movie like Arthur Penn's *Alice's Restaurant*, which is also trying to feel its way. I think we (from this point I include myself, because I share these attitudes) are desperate for some sensibility in movies, and that's why we're so moved by the struggle toward discovery in *Alice's Restaurant*, despite how badly done the film is. I think one would have to lie to say *Alice's Restaurant* is formally superior to the big new Western *Butch Cassidy and the Sundance Kid*. In formal terms, neither is very good. But *Alice's Restaurant* is a groping attempt to express something, and *Butch Cassidy* is a glorified vacuum. Movies can be enjoyed for the *quality* of their confusions and failures, and that's the only way you can enjoy some of them now. Emotionally, I stayed with Penn during the movie, even though I thought that many of the scenes in it were inept or awful, and that several of the big set pieces were expendable (to put it delicately). But we're *for* him, and that's what carries the movie. Conceptually, it's unformed, with the director trying to discover his subject as well as its meaning and his own attitudes. And, maybe for the first time, there's an audience for American pictures which is willing to accept this.

Not every movie has to matter; generally we go hoping just to be relaxed and refreshed. But because most of the time we come out slugged and depressed, I think we care far more now about the reach for something. We've simply spent too much time at movies made by people who didn't enjoy themselves and who didn't respect themselves or us, and we rarely enjoy ourselves at their movies anymore. They're big catered affairs, and we're humiliated to be there among the guests. I look at the list of movies playing, and most of them I genuinely just can't face, because the odds are so strong that they're going to be the same old insulting failed entertainment, and, even though I may have had more of a bellyful than most people, I'm sure this isn't just my own reaction. Practically everybody I know feels the same way. This may seem an awfully moral approach, but it comes out of surfeit and aesthetic disgust. There's something vital to enjoyment which we haven't been getting much of. Playfulness? Joy? Perhaps even honest cynicism? What's missing isn't anything as simple as talent; there's lots of talent, even on TV. But the business conditions of moviemaking have soured the spirit of most big movies. That's why we may be willing to go along with something as strained and self-conscious as *Alice's Restaurant*. And it's an immensely hopeful sign that the audience isn't derisive, that it wishes the movie well.

All this is, in a way, part of the background of why, after a few minutes of *Butch Cassidy and the Sundance Kid*, I began to get that depressed feeling, and, after a half hour, felt rather offended. We all know how the industry men think: they're going to try to make "now" movies when now is already then, they're going to give us orgy movies and plush skinflicks, and they'll be trying to feed youth's paranoia when youth will, one hopes, have cast it off like last year's beads. This Western is a spinoff from *Bonnie and Clyde*; it's about two badmen (Paul Newman and Robert Redford) at the turn of the century, and the script, by William Goldman, which has been published, has the prefatory note "Not that it matters, but most of what follows is true." Yet everything that follows rings false, as that note does.

It's a facetious Western, and everybody in it talks comical. The director, George Roy Hill, doesn't have the style for it. (He doesn't really seem to have the style for anything, yet there is a basic decency and intelligence in his work.) The tone becomes embarrassing. Maybe we're supposed to be charmed when this affable, loquacious outlaw Butch and his silent, "dangerous" buddy Sundance blow up trains, but how are we supposed to feel when they go off to Bolivia, sneer at the country, and start shooting up poor Bolivians? George Roy Hill is a "sincere" director, but Goldman's script is jocose; though it reads as if it might play, it doesn't, and probably this isn't just Hill's fault. What can one do with dialogue like Paul Newman's Butch saying, "Boy, I got vision. The rest of the world wears bifocals"? It must be meant to be sportive, because it isn't witty and it isn't dramatic. The dialogue is all banter, all throwaways, and that's how it's delivered; each line comes out of nowhere, coyly, in a murmur, in the dead sound of the studio. (There is scarcely even an effort to supply plausible outdoor resonances or to use sound to evoke a sense of place.) It's impossible to tell whose consciousness the characters are supposed to have. Here's a key passage from the script—the big scene when Sundance's girl, the schoolteacher Etta (Katharine Ross), decides to go to Bolivia with the outlaws:

> ETTA *(For a moment, she says nothing. Then, starting soft, building as she goes)*: I'm twenty-six, and I'm single, and I teach school, and that's the bottom of the pit. And the only excitement I've ever known is sitting in the room with me now. So I'll go with you, and I won't whine, and I'll sew your socks and stitch you when you're wounded, and anything you ask of me I'll do, except one thing: I won't watch you die. I'll miss that scene if you don't mind . . . *(Hold on Etta's lovely face a moment—)*

It's clear who is at the bottom of the pit, and it isn't those frontier schoolteachers, whose work was honest.

Being interested in good movies doesn't preclude enjoying many kinds of crummy movies, but maybe it does preclude acceptance of this enervated, sophisticated business venture—a movie made by those whose talents are a little high for mere commercial movies but who don't break out of the mold. They're trying for something more clever than is attempted in most commercial jobs, and it's all so archly empty—Conrad Hall's virtuoso cinematography providing constant in-and-out-of-focus distraction, Goldman's decorative little conceits passing for dialogue. It's all posh and josh, without any redeeming energy or crudeness. Much as I dislike the smugness of puritanism in the arts, after watching a put-on rape and Conrad Hall's *Elvira Madigan* lyric interlude (and to our own Mozart—Burt Bacharach) I began to long for something simple and halfway *felt*. If you can't manage genuine sophistication, you may be better off simple. And when you're as talented as these fellows, perhaps it's necessary to descend into yourself sometime and try to find out what you're doing—maybe, even, to risk banality, which is less objectionable than this damned waggishness.

Butch Cassidy will probably be a hit; it has a great title, and it has star appeal for a wide audience. Redford, who is personable and can act, is overdue for stardom, though it will be rather a joke if he gets it out of this non-acting role. Newman throws the ball to him often—that's really exactly what one feels he's doing—and is content to be his infectiously good-humored (one assumes) self. He plays the public image of himself (as an aging good guy), just as Arlo Guthrie plays himself as a moonchild. Yet, hit or no, I think what this picture represents is finished. Butch and Sundance will probably be fine for a TV series, which is what I mean by finished.

One can't just take the new cult movies head on and relax, because they're too confused. Intentions stick out, as in the thirties message movies, and you may be so aware of what's wrong with the movies while you're seeing them that you're pulled in different directions, but if you reject them because of the confusions, you're rejecting the most hopeful symptoms of change. Just when there are audiences who may be ready for something, the studios seem to be backing away, because they don't understand what these audiences want. The audiences themselves don't know, but they're looking for *something* at the movies. This transition into the seventies is maybe the most interesting as well as the most confusing period in American movie history, yet there's a real possibility that, because the tastes of the young audience are changing so fast, the already tottering studios will decide to minimize risks and gear production straight to the square audience and the networks. That square audience is far more alienated than the young one—so alienated that it isn't looking for *anything* at the movies.

{*The New Yorker*, September 27, 1969}

:: *High School*

Movies sometimes connect with our memories in surprising ways. My vocabulary loosened up during my freshman year at
Berkeley, and I was quite pleased when my mother remarked that the more
educated I got the more I sounded like a truck driver. When I was a sophomore, a group of us went on a trip to Los Angeles, and our car broke down
in Oxnard; we were huddled there in the garage at night when two garage
mechanics got into an argument and started swearing at each other. As
the rhythm of their fury and venom built up, those words that I had been
so free with sounded hideous. I hadn't understood their function as swear-
words — hadn't understood that they were meant to insult the person
receiving them, that they were a way of degrading another person. That
night at Oxnard came back when I saw Frederick Wiseman's *Law and
Order* on N.E.T.: the police were cursed constantly by thieves and drunks.
I had assumed that the police, coming from stricter and more religious
backgrounds, didn't understand that college kids use the words in that
liberated way that empties them of degradation or any real power; I hadn't
considered that they hear that kind of talk so much they probably just
can't stand it anymore. They're drowning in obscenity. College students
are sometimes contemptuous of the cops for fearing *words*, but in the film
those words really *are* weapons — often the *only* weapons of angry, frustrated people — and they're directed against the police all the time. *Law
and Order* was the most powerful hour and a half of television that I've seen
all year, and, since it won an Emmy, one might suppose that it would stir
up interest in Wiseman's other films, but the New York Film Festival,
which featured so many mindless forms of "artistic" moviemaking in the
main auditorium, tossed some of the best new American pictures into the

two-hundred-seat hall, and among them was Wiseman's *High School*, in its first New York showing.

There's a good deal to be said for finding your way to moviemaking—as most of the early directors did—after living for some years in the world and gaining some knowledge of life outside show business. We are beginning to spawn teen-age filmmakers who at twenty-five may have a brilliant technique but are as empty-headed as a Hollywood hack, and they will become the next generation of hacks, because they don't know anything except moviemaking. Wiseman is a law professor and urban planner turned filmmaker, a muckraking investigative journalist who looks into American institutions with a camera and a tape recorder, and because he doesn't go in with naïve and limiting concepts, what he finds ties in with one's own experience.

Many of us grow to hate documentaries in school, because the use of movies to teach us something seems a cheat—a pill disguised as candy—and documentaries always seem to be about something we're not interested in. But Wiseman's documentaries show what is left out of both fictional movies and standard documentaries that simplify for a purpose, and his films deal with the primary institutions of our lives: *Titicut Follies* (Bridgewater, an institution in which we lock away the criminally insane), *High School* (a high school in a large Eastern city), and *Law and Order* (the Kansas City police force). Television has been accustoming us to a horrible false kind of "involvement"; sometimes it seems that the only thing the news shows can think of is to get close to emotion. They shove a camera and a microphone in front of people in moments of stress and disaster and grief, and ram their equipment into any pores and cavities they can reach. Wiseman made comparable mistakes in *Titicut Follies*, but he learned better fast.

High School is so familiar and so extraordinarily evocative that a feeling of empathy with the students floods over us. How did we live through it? How did we keep any spirit? When you see a kid trying to make a phone call and being interrupted with "Do you have a pass to use the phone?" it all floods back—the low ceilings and pale-green walls of the basement where the lockers were, the constant defensiveness, that sense of always being in danger of breaking some pointless, petty rule. When since that time has one ever needed a pass to make a phone call? This movie takes one back to where, one discovers, time has stood still. Here is the girl humiliated for having worn a short dress to the Senior Prom, being told it was "offensive" to the whole class. Here it is all over again—the insistence that you be "respectful," and the teachers' incredible instinct for "disrespect," their antennae always extended for that little bit of reservation or irony in your tone, the tiny spark that you desperately need to preserve your *self*-respect. One can barely hear it in the way a boy says "Yes, sir" to the dean, but the dean, ever on the alert, snaps, "Don't give me that 'Yes, sir' business! . . . There's no sincereness behind it." Here, all over again, is the dullness of high-school education:

> TEACHER: What on the horizon or what existed that forced labor to turn to collective bargaining? What was there a lack of?

> GIRL: Communications?

> TEACHER: Security, yes, communications, lack of security, concern for the job. The important thing is this, let's get to the beginning. First of all, there was the lack of security; second of all, there was a lack of communication. . . .

The same old pseudo-knowledge is used to support what the schools think is moral. The visiting gynecologist in a sex-education class lectures the boys:

> The more a fellow gets into bed with more different girls, the more insecure he is, and this shows up actually later in all the divorce statistics in America. . . . You can graph right on a graph, the more girls fellows got into bed with or vice-versa the higher the divorce rate, the greater the sexual inadequacy. . . .

And there's the beautiful military doubletalk when it's a question of a teacher's incompetence or unfairness. A boy protests a disciplinary action against him by a teacher, and after he has explained his innocence, the dean talks him into accepting the punishment "to establish that you can be a man and that you can take orders." The teachers are masters here;

they're in a superior position for the only time in their lives, probably, and most of the petty tyrannies—like laying on the homework—aren't fully conscious. They justify each other's actions as a matter of course, and put the students in the wrong in the same indifferent way. They put a student down with "It's nice to be individualistic, but there are certain places to be individualistic," yet they never tell you where. How can one stand up against such bland authoritarianism? The teachers, crushing and processing, are the most insidious kind of enemy, the enemy with corrupt values who means well. The counsellor advising on college plans who says "You can have all your dream schools, but at the bottom you ought to have some college of last resort where you could be sure that you would go, if none of your dreams came through" certainly means to be realistic and helpful. But one can imagine what it must feel like to be a kid trudging off to that bottom college of last resort. There's a jolly good Joe of a teacher staging a fashion show who tells the girls, "Your legs are all too heavy. . . . Don't wear it too short; it looks miserable." And she's not wrong. But, given the beauty norms set up in this society, what are they to do? Cut off their legs? Emigrate? They're defeated from the legs up. Mediocrity and defeat sit in the offices and classrooms, and in those oppressive monitored halls.

We went through it all in order to graduate and be rid of passes forever, and once it was over we put it out of our minds, and here are the students still serving time until graduation, still sitting in class staring out the windows or watching the crawling hands of those ugly school clocks. So much of this education is part of an obsolete system of authority that broke down long ago, yet the teachers and administrators are still out there, persevering, "building character." *High School* seems an obvious kind of film to make, but as far as I know no one before has gone into an ordinary, middle-class, "good" (most of the students go to college) high school with a camera and looked around to see what it's like. The students are even more apathetic than we were. Probably the conflicts over the restrictions come earlier now—in junior high—and by high school the kids either are trying to cool it and get through to college or are just beaten down and sitting it out. We may have had a few teachers who really got us interested in something—it was one of the disappointments of the movie *Up the Down Staircase* that, treating this theme, it failed to be convincing—and, remembering our good luck, we could always say that even if a school was rotten, there were bound to be a few great teachers in it. This movie shows competent teachers and teachers who are trying their best but not one teacher who really makes contact in the way that means a difference in your life. The students are as apathetic toward the young English teacher playing and analyzing a Simon & Garfunkel record as toward the English teacher reciting "Casey at the Bat," and, even granted that as poetry there might not be much to choose between them—and perhaps Casey has the edge—still, one might think the students would, just as a *courtesy*, respond to the young teacher's attempt, the way one always gave the ingénue in the stock company a special round of applause. But it's very likely that high schools no longer *are* saved by live teachers, if hostility and cynicism and apathy set in right after children learn their basic skills. The students here sit on their hands even when a teacher tries. That's the only visible difference between this school and mine. I think we would have responded appreciatively to obvious effort, even if we thought the teacher was a jerk; these kids are beyond that. So the teachers are trapped, too. The teachers come off much worse than the police do in *Law and Order*. *High School* is a revelation because now that we see school from the outside, the teachers seem to give themselves away every time they open their mouths—and to be unaware of it.

At the end, the principal—a fine-looking woman—holds up a letter from a former student, on stationery marked "U.S.S. Okinawa," and reads it to the faculty:

> I have only a few hours before I go. Today I will take a plane trip from this ship. I pray that I'll make it back but it's all in God's hands now. You see, I am going with three other men. We are going to be dropped behind the D.M.Z. (the Demilitarized Zone). The reason for telling you this is that all my insurance money will be given for that scholarship I once started but never finished, if I don't make it back. I am only insured for $10,000. Maybe it could help someone. I have been trying to become a Big Brother in Vietnam, but it is very hard to do. I have to write back and forth to San Diego, California, and that takes time. I only hope that I am good enough to become one. God only knows. My personal family usually doesn't understand me. . . . They say: "Don't you value life? Are you crazy?" My answer is: "Yes. But I value all the lives of South Vietnam and the free world so that they and all of us can live in peace." Am I wrong? If I do my

best and believe in what I do, believe that what I do is right—that
is all I can do. . . . Please don't say anything to Mrs. C. She would
only worry over me. I am not worth it. I am only a body doing a job.
In closing I thank everyone for what they all have done for me.

And the principal comments, "Now, when you get a letter like this, to me
it means that we are very successful at [this] high school. I think you will
agree with me."

It's a great scene—a consummation of the educational process we've
been watching: They are successful at turning out bodies to do a job. Yet
it's also painfully clear that the school must have given this soldier more
kindness and affection than he'd ever had before. There must be other
students who respond to the genuine benevolence behind the cant and
who are grateful to those who labor to turn them into men. For those
students, this schooling in conformity is successful.

Wiseman extends our understanding of our common life the way novelists used to—a way largely abandoned by the modern novel and left to
the journalists but not often picked up by them. What he's doing is so
simple and so basic that it's like a rediscovery of what we knew, or should
know. We often want more information about the people and their pre-
dicaments than he gives, but this is perhaps less a criticism of Wiseman's
method than it is a testimonial to his success in making us care about his
subjects. With fictional movies using so little of our shared experience,
and with the big TV news "specials" increasingly using that idiot "Mc-
Luhanite" fragmentation technique that scrambles all experience—as if
the deliberate purpose were to make us indifferent to the life around us—
it's a good sign when a movie sends us out wanting to know more and
feeling that there is more to know. Wiseman is probably the most sophisticated intelligence to enter the documentary field in recent years.

{*The New Yorker*, October 18, 1969}

:: Fellini's "Mondo Trasho"

Fellini Satyricon uses the pre-Christian Roman world of debauchery during the time of Nero as an analogue of the modern post-Christian period. Like Cecil B. De Mille, who was also fond of pagan infernos, Fellini equates sexual "vice" with apocalypse; in *La Dolce Vita* he used the orgies of modern Rome as a parallel to ancient Rome, and now he reverses the analogy to make the same point. The idea that sticks out in every direction from *Fellini Satyricon* is that man without a belief in God is a lecherous beast. I think it's a really bad movie—a terrible movie—but Fellini has such intuitive rapport with the superstitious child in the adult viewer that I imagine it will be a considerable success. If it were put to members of the foreign-film audience rationally, probably few of them would identify the problems in the world today with fornication and licentiousness, or with the loss of faith in a divine authority. But when people at the movies are shown an orgiastic world of human beasts and monsters it's easy for them to fall back upon the persistent cliché that godlessness is lawlessness. De Mille, whose specialty was also the photogenic demonstration that modern immorality resembles the hedonism of declining Rome, used to satisfy the voyeuristic needs of the God-abiding by showing them what they were missing by being good and then soothe them by showing them the terrible punishments they escaped by being good. Fellini is not a sanctimonious manipulator of that kind; he makes fantasy extravaganzas out of tabloid sensationalism, but he appears to do it from emotional conviction, or, perhaps more exactly, from a master entertainer's feeling for the daydreams of the audience. He seems to draw upon something in himself that many people respond to as being profound, possibly because it has been long buried in them. When he brings it out, they think he is a great artist.

Fellini's pagans are freaks—bloated or deformed, or just simulated freaks with painted faces and protruding tongues. This is not the first time Fellini has used freaks in a movie; he has been using them, though in smaller numbers, to represent mystery and depravity all along, and especially since *La Dolce Vita*. Often they were people made up freakishly, as if in his oddly sophisticated-naïve eyes decadence were a wig and a heavy makeup job. His homosexual boys with gold dust in their hair were the "painted women" of naughty novels. It's the most simple-minded and widespread of all attitudes toward sin—identical with De Mille's. And so it wasn't surprising that some enthusiasts of *La Dolce Vita* took it as "a lesson to us"—a lesson that Rome fell because of high living and promiscuity, and we would, too. The labors of Gibbon and other historians never really permeated people's minds the way banalities about retribution for sin did. The freak show of *Fellini Satyricon* is a grotesque interpretation of paganism, yet I think many people in the audience will accept it without question. When we were children, we may have feared people wth physical defects, assuming that they were frightening to look at because they were *bad*. In our fairy tales, it was the ugly witches who did wicked deeds, and didn't we pick up the idea that if we were good we would be beautiful but if we did forbidden things it would show in our faces? Some of us probably thought that depravity caused deformity; at the most superstitious level, ugliness was God's punishment for disobedience. Many of us have painfully learned to overcome these superstitions, and yet the buried feelings can be easily touched. Fellini's popular strength probably comes from primitive elements such as these in a modern style that enables audiences to respond as if the content were highly sophisticated. Perhaps the style enables some viewers to think that the primitive fantasies are Jungian, or whatever, and so are somehow raised to the status of art. But there is no evidence that Fellini is using them consciously, or using them *against* their original impact; they're not even fully brought to light. In Fellini's films, buried material isn't jabbed at and released in obscene jokes, as in Buñuel's films. Our primitive fears are tapped and used just as they are by a punishing parent or an opportunistic schoolteacher who's unaware of what he's doing—except that Fellini does it more playfully.

Like a naughty Christian child, Fellini thinks it's a ball to be a pagan, but a naughty ball, a *bad* one, which can't really be enjoyed. In *La Dolce Vita*, Fellini's hero was a society reporter who got caught up in the life of the jaded rich international party set; in *8½*, the hero was a movie director who lived out the public fantasy of what a big movie director's life is like— a big, swirling party; in *Juliet of the Spirits*, the hero was some sort of official greeter and partygiver whose wife dreamed of fruity, balletistic parties. In *Fellini Satyricon* the party scenes are no longer orgiastic climaxes. Fellini uses Petronius and other classic sources as the basis for a movie that is one long orgy of eating, drinking, cruelty, and copulation, and he goes all the way with his infatuation with transvestism, nymphomania, homosexuality, monsters.

Fellini Satyricon is *all* phantasmagoria, and though from time to time one may register a face or a set or an episode, for most of the film one has the feeling of a camera following people walking along walls. The fresco effect becomes monotonous and rather oppressive. It's almost as if the movie were a theatrically staged panorama, set on a treadmill. At first, while we're waiting for Fellini to get into the material and involve us, there's a sequence on an ancient stage which seems to promise that the movie will be a theatrical spectacle in the modern theatre-of-cruelty sense. But Fellini never does involve us: we seem to be at a stoned circus, where the performers go on and on whether we care or not. And though there's a story, we anticipate the end a dozen times—a clear sign that his episodic structuring has failed. Afterward, one recalls astonishingly little; there are many episodes and anecdotes, but, for a work that is visual if it is anything, it leaves disappointingly few visual impressions. Giton, the adolescent boy whom the two heroes battle over, *is* memorable, because Max Born makes him a soft, smiling coquette full of sly promise; he's the complete whore, who takes pleasure in being used. The one charming episode is a sweetly amoral Garden of Eden sexual romp of the two heroes with a beautiful slave girl in a deserted house. Except for Giton's scenes and the slave girl's, and perhaps a shipboard-rape-and-marriage sequence, the picture isn't particularly sensual—though one assumes that carnality is part of its subject matter, and though Fellini has previously shown a special gift for carnal fantasies, as in the harem sequence of *8½*. Some of the set designs (by Danilo Donati) have a hypnotic quality—a ship like a sea serpent, a building with many stories and no front wall, so that we look into it as if it were a many-layered stage set—but the photography isn't very distinguished.

It's a tired movie; during much of it, we seem to be moving past clumsily arranged groups and looking at people exhibiting their grossness or their abnormalities and sticking their tongues out at us. If you have ever been at a high-school play in which the children trying to look evil stuck their tongues out, you'll know exactly why there's so little magic in Fellini's apocalyptic extravaganza. It's full of people making faces, the way people do in home movies, and full of people staring at the camera and laughing and prancing around, the way they often do in 16-millimetre parodies of sex epics, like *Mondo Trasho*. Fellini's early films had a forlorn atmosphere, and there were bits of melancholy still drifting through *La Dolce Vita* and *8½*; if the people were lost, at least their sorrow gave them poetic suggestions of depth. There was little depth in *Juliet of the Spirits*, and there is none in this *Satyricon*. Perhaps Fellini thinks Christ had to come before people could have souls, but, lacking emotional depth, the movie is so transient that elaborate episodes like Trimalchio's banquet barely leave a trace in the memory.

Somewhere along the line—I think it happened in *La Dolce Vita*—Fellini gave in to the luxurious basking in sin that has always had such extraordinary public appeal. He became the new De Mille—a purveyor of the glamour of wickedness. And, though he doesn't appear in them, he became the star of his movies, which are presented as emanations of his imagination, his genius; he functioned as if the creative process had no relation to experience, to thought, or to other art. As this process has developed, the actors, and the characters, in his movies have become less and less important, so at *Fellini Satyricon* one hardly notices the familiar people in it—it's all a masquerade anyway, and they are made up to be hideous, and they come and go so fast—and one hardly knows or cares who the leads are, or which actor is Encolpius, which Ascyltus. (Encolpius, the blond Botticelli-angel face, is an English stage and TV actor named Martin Potter; Ascyltus, the goatish brunet, is Hiram Keller, an American who was in *Hair*. Encolpius and Ascyltus look as if they might be found among the boys cruising the Spanish Steps, and that is certainly right for the ancient-modern parallel Fellini makes, but Potter appears uncomfortable in his role.) I feel that what has come over Fellini is a movie director's megalomania, which has not gone so far with anyone else, and that part of the basis for his reputation is that his narcissistic conception of his role is exactly what celebrity worshippers have always thought a movie director to be. His idea of a movie seems to be to gather and exhibit all the weird people he can find, and one gets the feeling that more excitement and energy go into casting than into what he does with his cast, because, after the first sight of them, the faces don't yield up anything further to the camera. People coming out of *La Dolce Vita* and *8½* could be heard asking, "Where do you suppose he found them?"—as if he were a magician of a zookeeper who had turned up fabulous specimens. This increasingly strange human zoo into which he thrusts us is what people refer to when they say that there is a Fellini world. The partygoers of *La Dolce Vita*, with their masklike faces of dissatisfaction and perversity, have given way to this parade of leering, grinning cripples. And these primitive caricatures of what depravity supposedly does to us are used as cautionary images. In interviews, Fellini frequently talks of the need to believe in miracles, and of how "we have not the strength" to do without religion or myth. My guess would be that Fellini, as a Catholic, and a notably emotional one, has small knowledge of or interest in any forms of control outside the Church. As an artist, he draws upon the imagination of a Catholic schoolboy and presents us with a juvenile version of the Grand Inquisitor's argument.

Fellini's work has an eerie, spellbinding quality for some people which must be not unlike the powerful effect the first movies were said to have. Perhaps the opulence and the dreamlike movement of his films and the grotesques who populate them are what some people want from the movies—a return to frightening fairy tales. Following the Kubrick line in selling pictures, Fellini, in an interview, says, "Even the young ones not smoking, not with drugs—they grasp the picture, they feel the picture, eat the picture, breathe it, without asking, 'What does it mean?' This film—I don't want to sound presumptuous, but it is a very good test just to choose friends with, a test if people are free or not. The young kids, they pass the test." I should say that emotionally his *Satyricon* is just about the opposite of "free"; emotionally, it's a hip version of *The Sign of the Cross*. There's a certain amount of confusion in it about what's going on and where, so some people may take it "psychedelically" and swallow it whole, though the audience at *Fellini Satyricon* is already on to part of the con: there was a big laugh when Encolpius identifies himself as a student. But this new selling technique of congratulating youth for not thinking—which is also a scare selling technique to reviewers who are afraid of being

left behind "free" youth—puts the audience at the mercy of shrewd promotion. "The young, they just love and feel," says Fellini, "and if there is a
new cinema, pictures such as *2001*—and, yes, *Satyricon*—it is for them."
Sure it's for them, because they constitute about fifty per cent of the paid
admissions, and so poor old *Fantasia* has now been reissued as a trip movie,
and the ads for *Zabriskie Point* say "It blows your mind," and so on. When
Susan Kohner, sobbing, clutched the flowers on her black mother's casket
in *Imitation of Life*, you might have felt the anguish in your chest even as
you laughed at yourself for reacting. Maybe if Fellini personally didn't
impress people so much as a virtuoso they'd become as conscious of the
emotional and intellectual shoddiness they're responding to in *his* films.
The usual refrain is "With Fellini, I'm so captivated by the images I don't
ask what it means." But suppose it's not the "beauty" of the images they're
reacting to so much as that step-by-step intuitive linkage between Fellini's
emotions and their own almost forgotten ones? I'm sure there are people
who will say that it doesn't matter if Fellini's movies are based on shallow
thinking, or even ignorance, because he uses popular superstitions for a
poetic vision, and makes art out of them. The large question in all this is:
Can movie art be made out of shallow thinking and superstitions? The
answer may, I think, be no. But even if it's yes, I don't think Fellini transformed anything in *Fellini Satyricon*.

{*The New Yorker*, March 14, 1970}

:: Notes on Heart and Mind

Is anyone surprised that the critics and journalists who only a few weeks ago were acclaiming the new creative freedom of young American moviemakers are now climbing aboard the new sentimentality? The press may use the term "romance" for this deliberately fabricated regression in recent movies, but in Hollywood the businessmen talk more crassly. They say, "We're going back to heart." The back-to-heart movement is accompanied by strong pressures on reviewers, who are informed that they have lost touch with the public. Reviewers are supposed to show *their* heart by puckering up for every big movie.

As part of the Pop impulse of the sixties, movies have been elevated to a central position among the arts—a dominant, almost overwhelming position. Those who grew up during this period have been so sold on Pop and so saturated with it that they appear to have lost their bearings in the arts. And so when they discover that, of course, Pop isn't enough, and they want some depth and meaning from movies, they head right for the slick synthetic. Those who have abandoned interest in literature except for the à-la-mode mixture of Pop and sticky, such as Vonnegut, Hesse, Tolkien, Brautigan, and a little I Ching, are likely to have comparably fashionable tastes in movies. To the children of *Blow-Up* movies that are literary in the worst way—movies that superficially resemble head books and art films—can seem profound and suggestive. Every few months, there is a new spate of secondhand lyrical tricks. Robert Redford is impaled, like a poor butterfly, in frozen frames at the end of picture after picture. Directors have become so fond of telescopic lenses that any actor crossing a street in a movie may linger in transit for a hazy eternity—the movie equivalent of a series of dots. The audience accepts this sort of thing in movies that not only are without the vitality of Pop but are enervated and tenuous—like the worst of what earlier generations of college students fled from when they went to the movies. If you don't have that sense of the range of possibilities and pleasures which is developed from reading, from an interest in drama and the other arts, or even from a longer span of moviegoing, it's easy to overrate the fancy, novelettish alienation of a *Five Easy Pieces*. But while it's perfectly understandable that those without much to compare such a movie to may think it's great—just as a child's judgment of a movie may be ingenuous and droll because he has so few previous experiences to relate it to—this inexperience provides the opening for the media-hype. There is probably more insensate praise in movie reviews now than in any other field, including writing on rock. The new tendency is to write appreciatively at the highest possible pitch, as if the reviewer had no scale of values but only a hearsay knowledge of the peaks. And everything he likes becomes a new peak.

If one opens a newspaper to the movie pages and reads the quotes, one is confronted with a choice of masterpieces, but I didn't write a column last week because the new movies defeated me—I couldn't think of anything worth saying about them. You come out of a movie like *There's a Girl in My Soup* or *I Love My Wife* feeling that your pocket has been picked and your mind has been stunted.

Movie critics have always had to become acrobats, jumping from level to level, trying not to attack the timid amateurs the way we attack the successful hacks. The danger in this act is that one may fall into the trap of condescension. This used to take the form of that horrible debonair style which was once the gentleman-critics' specialty. They were so superior to the subject that they never dealt with it. Now it more frequently takes the form of a wisecracking put-down. And that's the bottom of the trap, because, as all critics know, the worst danger of the profession is that one may sink to the level of what one is reviewing. What sustains a critic from falling to the level of an *I Love My Wife* and making shrivelling bad jokes about its shrivelling bad jokes? Last week, I couldn't find anything sustaining; rage isn't condescending, but one wears oneself down, and these films weren't worth it.

Though sinking to the level of the work is a danger to the critic, to movies the more serious danger, of course, is that critics may not *rise* to the level of what they're reviewing. And, even with movies as bad as they are now, I think this is often the case, because those who stoop to review become insensitive.

I don't trust critics who say they care only for the highest and the best; it's an inhuman position, and I don't believe them. I think it's simply their method of exalting themselves. It's not always easy to analyze what is going wrong in movies, what is going right—even if only in small ways—and why. One might think this an exercise in futility, but, ideally, the regular reviewer provides a touchstone for movie lovers—so that they have a basis for checking themselves out—and for all those actively involved in movies. The regular reviewer knows he will not effect a radical transformation of movies, but he may be able to help us keep our bearings. Movies, far more than the traditional arts, are tied to big money. Without a few independent critics, there's nothing between the public and the advertisers.

Movie executives often say critics should be the same age as the average moviegoer; sometimes they say reviewers shouldn't go on for more than three years or they won't have the same enthusiasm as the audience. The executives don't understand what criticism is; they want it to be an extension of their advertising departments. They want moviegoers to be uninformed and without memory, so they can be happy consumers.

In most cases, the conglomerates that make the movies partly own the magazines and radio stations and TV channels, or, if they don't own them, advertise in them or have some interlocking connection with them. That accounts for a lot of the praise that is showered on movies. Then, too, many critics, knowing that the young dig movies, are afraid of being left behind. Besides, the critics don't get quoted in the ads unless they rhapsodize over a picture (or are willing to accept being misquoted and distorted), and each time they get quoted, their bosses are happy and their names become better known. There are critics whose reviews hardly anybody ever sees but who are widely known for their ecstatic quotes. The radio and TV boys get the point: their reviews *are* quotes.

...

A reviewer delivering quickie reviews at the end of a radio or television news program typically reacts to a picture "strictly on its own merits"; that is, he tells the theme, he praises or pans the structure, he says a few words about the acting, the photography, etc. He reviews a movie in a cheerful vacuum, and he is generally perfectly sincere when he tells you that he says exactly what he thinks.

To be the movie critic for a network, no training or background is necessary; "too much" interest in movies may be a disqualification. Novices are thought to speak to the public on the public's own terms. They age, but, like the critic on your home-town paper, they remain novices in criticism, because there is no need for them to learn; they understand that their job is dependent on keeping everybody happy, and they are generally not the kind of people who learn anyway. They can say "what they think" with more sincerity if they're the kind of people who don't realize they can say what they think because they don't think.

It is often said that it doesn't matter how bad a reviewer is as long as he stays in the job, because people learn how to read him. It's true they may learn how to interpret his enthusiasms, but what about the young practitioners of an art form? Bad notices—or being ignored—are death to them. In this mass medium, in which big-budget productions are hugely advertised—they're like epidemics spreading over the media—a new artist or a young artist working on a small budget doesn't stand a chance unless he gets the help of the press. A writer or a painter can generally keep going even if he fails to reach an audience; even a dramatist may be able to keep going, though he is creatively crippled if his plays aren't staged. But if a movie director fails to reach an audience, he simply can't get the money to go on making pictures.

The industry and many established actors on talk shows love the idea that the public doesn't need the critics; the young filmmaker knows different. Most of the new pictures that try to break the molds risk confusing audiences, and just about all the pictures that express new social impulses or that are critical or rebellious are small-budget pictures. If a few critics don't go all the way for them, the public doesn't hear about them in time to keep the directors working and to keep the art of film alive. It cannot be kept alive by pictures like *The Odd Couple*, *Cactus Flower*, or *Airport*;

those are the ones that don't require the help of the press (though they often get it). The audience finds its way to them with the help of the advertising.

The casual moviegoer is often drawn to new versions of what he used to enjoy—the TV watcher to *Airport*, the aging art-house patron to the latest Chabrol. One can't quarrel with his enjoyment of them, only with his evaluation of them. A critic's point of view is likely to be somewhat different from the casual moviegoer's. The successful second-rate will probably anger him more than the fifth-rate, because it represents the triumph of aesthetic senility.

Since a critic may cost his publication advertising revenue—and no longer just from the loss of movie advertising but from records and whatever else the conglomerate is into—independent, disinterested criticism becomes rarer than ever just at the time when, because of the central importance of movies, it is needed most. The pressure is so strong on reviewers to do what is wanted of them that many of them give in and reserve their fire for pathetic little sex pictures—cheap porny pix—which they can safely attack because there's no big advertising money behind them. That way, the reviewer can keep his paper happy and at the same time get credit for high-mindedness in his community. Most of the people who give him credit never go to the movies anyway. Middle-aged people, particularly women, often use pornography as a self-congratulatory excuse for not reading and for not going to the movies. It becomes a righteous form of abstention for those who prefer *Hee Haw* or *The Beverly Hillbillies*.

In some ways, last week's movies probably aren't worse than movies of a decade or two or three ago, but there is something dead and nerveless about them; they don't know how to connect with the audience, and they have lost the simplicity and the narrative strength that used to pull one through bad movies. TV has destroyed the narrative qualities of older movies, but the restlessness one feels while watching a chopped-up movie on TV is mitigated by the fact that one isn't necessarily paying much attention. In a movie theatre, with nothing else to do, one is likely to become depressed. We've been told for some years now that visual excitement is what matters, but even the rare movie that is extraordinary to look at may be demoralizing. When it's obvious that the picture is going nowhere, there's an awful letdown of expectations, and for most people there seems to be nothing left but dumb submission; walking out may be too positive an act for the depressed state one falls into.

Yet even those who go enough to know how awful movies have been this year say, "But what else is there? Bad as they are, movies are better than the theatre." However, the thing that has happened to the theatre in the past decade is happening now to movies. On the average, Americans go to only seven movies a year. And as there were scarcely seven halfway good American movies for them to go to last year (and few from abroad), chances are they'll go to even fewer in 1971. *There's a Girl in My Soup* reminds you of why you stopped going to Broadway comedies. One never even knows what the principal characters are meant to be; it's not merely that this movie has no connection with any people who ever lived but that it doesn't sustain its own artifices. It's like going to see *Swan Lake* and finding that no one knew the dancers should be trained to get on their points.

When movies were bad a decade ago, it wasn't such a serious matter; despite the greatness of some films, movies in general weren't expected to be more than casual, light entertainment. You weren't expected to get your ideas of artistic possibilities from movies. I remember seeing *To Have and Have Not* the night it opened, in 1944, and I remember how everyone loved it, but if anyone I knew had said that it was a masterpiece comparable to the greatest works of literature or drama, he would have been laughed at as a fool who obviously didn't know literature or drama. Now, by and large, even the college-educated moviegoer isn't expected to, and the media constantly apply superlatives to works that lack even the spirit and energy of a *To Have and Have Not*.

What must it be like for those who know and love only movies, and not literature as well? Even if they don't consciously miss it, surely the loss of the imaginative ranging over experience is irreparable.

There's been almost no fight for it. Fiction has been abandoned casually and quickly. There haven't even been journalists to defend it. On TV talk shows, the hosts have generally given up even the pretense of having read the books that are being plugged. There are several cooking celebrities on TV but no TV personality who discusses books. If you ask college students to name half a dozen movie critics, they have no trouble supplying names.

If you ask them to name three book critics, they flounder, and finally one of them may triumphantly recall the name of a critic who abandoned regular reviewing before they were born.

If a movie is a bowdlerization of a book and the movie's director is acclaimed for his artistry, surely something has gone askew. In some cases, directors add virtually nothing, and diminish and cheapen what was in the original, and yet the fraction of the original they manage to reproduce is sufficient to make their reputations.

Film theorists often say that film art is, "by its nature," closest to painting and music, but all these years movie companies haven't been buying paintings and symphonies to adapt, they've been buying plays and novels. And although the movies based on those plays and novels have visual and rhythmic qualities, their basic material has nevertheless come from the theatre and from books.

When a movie based on a book goes wrong but one isn't sure exactly how or why, one of the best ways to find out is to go to the book. The changes that have been made in the course of the adaptation frequently upset the structure, the characterizations, and the theme itself.

Generally speaking, when people become angry if you refer to the original novel or play while you're discussing a movie, it means they haven't read it. Twenty years ago, they hadn't always, either, but they didn't feel they didn't need to. McLuhanism and the media have broken the back of the book business; they've freed people from the shame of not reading. They've rationalized becoming stupid and watching television.

And television has become the principal advertising medium for movies. Even the few talk shows that held out against the show-biz personalities for a while are now loaded with movie people plugging away and often inflicting pain and embarrassment by trying to sing. Talk shows are becoming amateur hours for professionals.

Although good movies have often been made from inferior books, in the last few years I've been embarrassed to discover that even when movies have been made from books that aren't especially worth reading, the books are still often superior. That is to say, even our second- and third-string writers have more complex sensibilities than the movies that cannibalize them. A very minor novel like Ken Kolb's *Getting Straight* is a case in point. And I think reading Thomas Berger's *Little Big Man*—which is almost a major novel—is probably stronger than the movie even as a visual experience. American fiction seems to have reached a fairly high plateau at the very time when college students were deciding movies were more interesting. They didn't make that decision without encouragement from the media. *Would* they have made it without encouragement? I don't know. But the new dominance of Pop is the culmination of processes that have been at work in the mass media for many years. Gradually, as the things people used to fear would happen happened, ways were found to refer to the changes positively instead of negatively, and so "the herd instinct" that mass culture was expected to lead to became "the new tribalism."

If some people would rather see the movie than read the book, this may be a fact of life that we must allow for, but let's not pretend that people get the same things out of both, or that nothing is lost. The media-hype encourages the sacrifice of literature.

Movies are good at action; they're not good at reflective thought or conceptual thinking. They're good for immediate stimulus, but they're not a good means of involving people in the other arts or in learning about a subject. The film techniques themselves seem to stand in the way of the development of curiosity.

Movies don't help you to develop independence of mind. They don't give you much to mull over, and they don't give you the data you need in order to consider the issues they raise.

A young film critic recently told me that he needed to read more books than he did before he got the job—that he felt empty after seeing films daily. I don't have any doubts about movies' being a great art form, and what makes film criticism so peculiarly absorbing is observing—and becoming involved in—the ongoing battle of art and commerce. But movies alone are not enough: a steady diet of mass culture is a form of deprivation. Most movies are shaped by calculations about what will sell; the question they're asking about new projects in Hollywood is "In what way is it like *Love Story?*"

A teacher writes that "literate students are getting into the terms of film and the history of film in the same way that they have always got into the terms of literature, for example, and the history and evolution of that art form." If movies had become what they might be, this would make sense, but to study mass culture in the same terms as traditional art forms is to accept the shallowness of mass culture. It could mean that the schools are beginning to accept the advertisers' evaluations; the teachers don't want to be left behind, either.

The Faulkner who collaborated on the screenplay for *To Have and Have Not* is not commensurate with the Faulkner of the novels. Faulkner's work for hire is fun, but it's not his major work (though, as things are going, he and many other writers may remain known only for the hackwork they did to support the work they cared about). Yet until writers as well as directors can bring their full powers to American movies, American movies are not going to be the works of imagination and daring that the media claim they are already.

Writers who go to Hollywood still follow the classic pattern: either you get disgusted by "them" and you leave or you want the money and you become them.

Allowing for exceptions, there is still one basic difference between the traditional arts and the mass-media arts: in the traditional arts, the artist grows; in a mass medium, the artist decays profitably.

From indications in the press, the new line will be that the moviemakers have had too much freedom; the unstated corollary is that the businessmen know what's best. Moviemakers need more freedom, not less, or they'll never work through the transitional stage that American movies are in. If Hollywood tries to return to its childhood via romantic slop, movies will just get worse and worse. But if the advertisers and the media can blur the distinction between movies that are made in freedom as collaborative forms of expression and movies that are packaged, how many moviemakers will be strong enough to fight against success?

The film medium is too expensive for the kind of soft, sweet college students who want to work in it. Some of the most talented are lovely innocents; they will be the first to fall.

The great men of the screen have had to be tough; perhaps because of this, the great men of the screen have been crazy men. Jean Renoir is the only proof that it is possible to be great and sane in movies, and he hasn't worked often in recent years.

{*The New Yorker*, January 23, 1971}

:: The Poetry of Images

What makes Bernardo Bertolucci's films different from the work of older directors is an extraordinary combination of visual richness and visual freedom. In a Hollywood movie, the big scenes usually look prearranged; in a film by David Lean, one is practically wired to react to the hard work that went into gathering a crowd or dressing a set. Bertolucci has been working on a big scale since his first films — *La Commare Secca*, made when he was twenty, and *Before the Revolution*, a modern story derived from *The Charterhouse of Parma*, made when he was twenty-two — and his films just seem to flow, as if the life he photographs had not been set up for the camera but were all there and he were moving in and out of it at will. Most young filmmakers now don't attempt period stories — the past is not in good repute, and period pictures cost more and tend to congeal — but Bertolucci, because of the phenomenal ease of his sweeping romanticism, is ideally suited to them; he moves into the past, as he works in the present, with a lyrical freedom almost unknown in the history of movies. He was a prize-winning poet at twenty-one, and he has a poet's gift for using objects, landscapes, and people expressively, so that they all become part of his vision. It is this gift, I think, that makes *The Conformist* a sumptuous, emotionally charged experience.

Bertolucci's adaptation of the Alberto Moravia novel about the psychology of an upper-class follower of Mussolini is set principally in 1938 (Bertolucci was born in 1941), and I think it's not unfair to say that except for Jean-Louis Trintignant's grasp of the central character — it's an extraordinarily prehensile performance — the major interest is in the way everything is imbued with a sense of the past. It's not the past we get from films that survive from the thirties but Bertolucci's evocation of the past—the thirties made expressive through the poetry of images.

Trintignant, who has quietly come to be the key French actor that so many others (such as Belmondo) were expected to be, digs into the character of the intelligent coward who sacrifices everything he cares about because he wants the safety of normality. Trintignant has an almost incredible intuitive understanding of screen presence; his face is never too full of emotion, never completely empty. In this role, as an indecisive intellectual, he conveys the mechanisms of thought through tension, the way Bogart did, and he has the grinning, teeth-baring reflexes of Bogart—cynicism and humor erupt in savagery. And, playing an Italian, he has an odd, ferrety resemblance to Sinatra. Everything around him seems an emanation of the director's velvet style—especially the two beautiful women: Stefania Sandrelli, an irresistible comedienne, as Trintignant's deliciously corrupt middle-class wife, and Dominique Sanda, with her swollen lips and tiger eyes, as the lesbian wife of an anti-Fascist professor he is ordered to kill. (She's rather like a prowling, predatory stage lesbian, but she's such an ecstatic erotic image that she becomes a surreal figure, and Bertolucci uses her as an embodiment of repressed desires. She also appears, only slightly disguised, in two other roles—conceived to be almost subliminal.) The film succeeds least with its ideas, which are centered on Trintignant's Fascist. I think we may all be a little weary—and properly suspicious—of psychosexual explanations of political behavior; we can make up for ourselves these textbook cases of how it is that frightened, repressed individuals become Fascists. In an imaginative work, one might hope for greater illumination—for a Fascist seen from inside, not just a left view of his insides. Yet though the ideas aren't convincing, the director makes the story itself seem organic in the baroque environment he has created, and the color is so soft and deep and toned down, and the texture so lived in, that the work is, by its nature, ambiguous—not in the tedious sense of confusing us but in the good sense of touching the imagination. The character Trintignant plays is by no means simple; when he says "I want to build a normal life," it's clear that he needs to *build* it because it's not normal for him. He shows a streak of bravura enjoyment as he watches himself acting normal.

Bertolucci's view isn't so much a reconstruction of the past as an infusion from it; *The Conformist* cost only seven hundred and fifty thousand dollars—he brought together the décor and architecture surviving from that modernistic period and gave it all a unity of style (even with the opening titles). Visconti used the thirties-*in-extremis* in *The Damned*—as a form of estrangement. Bertolucci brings the period close, and we enter into it. His nostalgia is open; it's a generalized sort of empathy, which the viewer begins to share. You don't think in terms of watching a story being acted out, because he provides a consciousness of what's going on under the scenes; they're fully orchestrated. Bertolucci is perhaps the most operatic of movie directors. I don't mean simply that he stages movies operatically, in the way that other Italians—notably Zeffirelli—do, but that he conceives a movie operatically; the distinction is something like that between an opera director and an opera composer. Visconti in *The Damned* was somewhere in the middle—composing, all right, but in a single, high-pitched scale, as if the music were to be howled by wolves. *The Damned* was hysterical; *The Conformist* is lyrical. You come away with sequences in your head like arias: a party of the blind that opens with the cry of "*Musica!*"; an insane asylum situated in a stadium—a theatre-of-the-absurd spectacle of madness; a confession-box satirical duet between priest and non-believer; a wedding-night scherzo, the bride describing her sins, to the groom's amusement; the two women on a late-afternoon shopping expedition in Paris; a French working-class dance hall (a *Bal Populaire*) where the women dance a parody of passion that is one of the most romantic screen dances since Rogers and Astaire, and where the crowd join hands in a farandole. The political assassination in the forest—an operatic love-death—is the emotional climax of the film; Trintignant sits in his car, impotent—paralyzed by conflicting impulses—while the woman he loves is murdered.

Two years ago, Bertolucci made *Partner*, an inventive but bewildering modernization of Dostoyevsky's *The Double*, in which the hero, a young drama teacher (Pierre Clémenti), had fantasies of extending the theatre of cruelty into political revolution. This basic idea is shared by many young filmmakers, including, probably, Bertolucci, but Clémenti never conveyed enough intellectuality for us to understand the character, who seemed to be a comic-strip Artaud. Despite the fascination of *Partner* (I recall one image in particular, in which books were piled up in heaps on the floor of a room like the Roman ruins outside), the film was shown here only at the 1968 New York Film Festival. It was a political vaudeville for the movie generation bred on Godard's *La Chinoise*; the meanings were lost in the profusion of images and tricks of his original, daring high style. Bertolucci seemed to have forgotten the story of his own *Before the Revolution*, in which his Fabrizio discovered that he was not single-minded enough to be a Communist—that he was too deeply involved in the beauty of life as it was *before* the revolution. Bertolucci, like Fabrizio, has "a nostalgia for the present." This may seem a bourgeois weakness to him (and to some others), but to be deeply involved in the beauty of life as it is is perhaps the first requisite for a great movie director. (And, far from precluding activity for social change, it is, in a sense, the only sane basis for such activity.) It's a bit ironic that the young director who has the greatest natural gifts of his generation for making movies as sensual celebrations should have sought refuge for this talent in the Fascist period.

After *Partner*, Bertolucci made a television film about a plot to murder Mussolini during a performance of *Rigoletto—The Spider's Stratagem*. Based on a Borges story, it was attenuated—it didn't have enough content to justify the atmosphere of mystification. *The Conformist* is his most accessible, least difficult film from an audience point of view. I don't put that accessibility down; despite the intermittent brilliance of *Partner*, it *is* a failure, and trying to figure out what a director has in mind is maddening when it's apparent he hasn't worked it out himself. *The Conformist*, though in some ways less audacious, is infinitely more satisfying. One may wish that Bertolucci had been able to integrate some of the Godard influence, but no one has been able to do that; Bertolucci has simply thrown the discordant notes out of his system and gone back to his own natural flowing film rhythm. (Is it perhaps an in-joke that the saintly bespectacled professor who is murdered faintly resembles Godard?) In this film, one knows that Bertolucci knows who he is and what he's doing; young as he is, he's a master director. Except for the unconvincing and poorly staged concluding sequence, the flaws in *The Conformist* are niggling. It's very tempting for young filmmakers, through cutting, to make their films difficult; the filmmakers look at their own footage so many times that they assume an audience can apprehend connections that are barely visible. Bertolucci uses an organizing idea that puts an unnecessary strain on the viewer: the film begins with the dawn of the assassination day, and the events that led up to it unfold while Trintignant and a Fascist agent are driving to the forest. The editing at the outset is so fast anyway that cutting to and from that car is slightly confusing, but as one gets caught up in the imagery that slight confusion no longer matters. In a Bertolucci film, in any case, there are occasional images that have no logical explanation but that work on an instinctive level—as surreal poetry, like the piles of books in *Partner* or the desk here, in a Fascist's office, that is covered with neatly arranged walnuts. However, I don't think *The Conformist* is a great movie. It's the best movie this year by far, and it's a film by a prodigy who—if we're all lucky—is going to make great films. But it's a triumph of style; the substance is not sufficiently liberated, and one may begin to feel a little queasy about the way the movie left luxuriates in Fascist decadence.

One of the peculiarities of movies as a mass medium is that what the directors luxuriate in—and what we love to look at—has so often been held up as an example of vice. Except for the sophisticated comedies of the past and occasional thrillers about classy crooks, we get most of our views of elegance under the guise of condemnation. Our desire for grace and seductive opulence is innocent, I think, except to prigs, so when it's satisfied by movies about Fascism or decadence we get uncomfortable, because our own enjoyment is turned against us. One wants modern directors to be able to use the extravagant emotional possibilities of the screen without falling into the De Mille–Fellini moralistic bag. There are some sequences in *The Conformist* that suggest the moralistic extremism of *The Damned*—that party of the blind, for example, and the blue light on Trintignant's and Sanda's faces in the cloakroom of a ballet school.

The old puritanism imposed on moviemakers is now compounded by the puritanism of the left which coerces filmmakers into a basically hypocritical position: they begin to deny the very feelings that brought them to movies in the first place. The democratic impulse that informed the earliest screen masterpieces was to use the new medium to make available to all what had been available, through previous art forms, only to the rich and aristocratic. It was the dream of a universalization of the best work that could be done. As this dream became corrupted by mass culture produced for the lowest common denominator, the young filmmakers had to fight to free themselves from mass culture, and the fervor of the earlier democratic spirit was lost. Most young American filmmakers, in college and after, now think of themselves as artists in the same way American poets or painters do—and the poets have long since abandoned

Whitman's dream of the great American audience. Filmmakers often talk as if it were proof of their virtue that they think in terms of a minority art. American movies have now reached just about the place the American theatre did a decade or so back, when, except for the rare big hits, it had dwindled into a medium for the few.

The radicalized young are often the most antidemocratic culturally, and they push radical filmmakers to the point where no one can enjoy their work. Any work that is enjoyable is said to be counter-revolutionary. The effect may be to destroy the most gifted filmmakers (who are also—not altogether coincidentally—mostly left) unless the young left develops some tolerance for what the pleasures of art can mean to people. These issues become central when one considers a Bertolucci film, because his feeling for the sensuous surfaces of life suggests the revelatory abandon of the Russian film poet Dovzhenko. If anyone can be called a born moviemaker, it's Bertolucci. Thus far, he is the only young moviemaker who suggests that he may have the ability of a Griffith to transport us imaginatively into other periods of history—and without this talent movies would be even more impoverished than they are. The words that come to mind in connection with his work—sweeping, operatic, and so on—describe the talents of the kind of moviemaker who has the potential for widening out the appeal of movies once again. But movies—the great sensual medium—are still stuck with the idea that sensuality is decadent. If Bertolucci can break all the way through this barrier—and he has already broken through part way—the coast is clear. But if he uses his talent—as "commercial" directors so often do—at half-mast, and somewhat furtively, to celebrate life under the guise of exposing decadence, he'll make luscious, fruity movies. When "period" becomes more important than subject, the result is often decorator-style—as in the worst of Minnelli. Bertolucci has such a feeling for detail that one fears he could go this route into empty, gorgeous filmmaking. That would be one more devastating blow to the art of motion pictures; sensuality is what they have lost. Except for *The Conformist* (and *Claire's Knee*), the new movies in New York have—for what I think must be the first time in decades—sunk below the level of the theatre season (which happens to be an unusually good one). People say you have to psych yourself up to go to a movie these days, and that's not far from the truth.

{*The New Yorker*, January 23, 1971}

:: Pipe Dream

McCabe & Mrs. Miller is a beautiful pipe dream of a movie—a fleeting, almost diaphanous vision of what frontier life might have been. The film, directed by Robert Altman, and starring Warren Beatty as a small-time gambler and Julie Christie as an ambitious madam in the turn-of-the-century Northwest, is so indirect in method that it throws one off base. It's not much like other Westerns; it's not really much like other movies. We are used to movie romances, but this movie is a figment of the romantic imagination. Altman builds a Western town as one might build a castle in the air—and it's inhabited. His stock company of actors turn up quietly in the new location, as if they were part of a floating crap game. Altman's most distinctive quality as a director here, as in *M*A*S*H*, is his gift for creating an atmosphere of living interrelationships and doing it so obliquely that the viewer can't quite believe it—it seems almost a form of effrontery. He has abandoned the theatrical convention that movies have generally clung to of introducing the characters and putting tags on them. Though Altman's method is a step toward a new kind of movie naturalism, the technique may seem mannered to those who are put off by the violation of custom—as if he simply didn't want to be straightforward about his storytelling. There are slight losses in his method—holes that don't get filled and loose ends that we're used to having tied up—but these losses (more like temporary inconveniences, really) are, I think, inseparable from Altman's best qualities and from his innovative style.

There's a classical-enough story, and it's almost (though not quite) all there, yet without the usual emphasis. The fact is that Altman is dumping square conventions that don't work anymore: the spelled-out explanations of motive and character, the rhymed plots, and so on—all those threadbare remnants of the "well-made" play which American movies have clung to. He can't be straightforward in the old way, because he's improvising meanings and connections, trying to find his movie in the course of making it—an incredibly risky procedure under modern union conditions. But when a director has a collaborative team he can count on, and when his instinct and his luck both hold good, the result can be a *McCabe & Mrs. Miller*. The classical story is only a thread in the story that Altman is telling. Like the wartime medical base in *M*A*S*H*, the West here is the life that the characters are part of. The people who drop in and out and the place—a primitive mining town—are not just background for McCabe and Mrs. Miller; McCabe and Mrs. Miller are simply the two most interesting people in the town, and we catch their stories, in glimpses, as they interact with the other characters and each other. But it isn't a slice-of-life method, it's a peculiarly personal one—delicate, elliptical. The picture seems to move in its own quiet time, and the faded beauty of the imagery works a spell. Lives are picked up and let go, and the sense of how little we know about them becomes part of the texture; we generally know little about the characters in movies, but since we're assured that that little is all we need to know and thus all there is to know, we're not bothered by it. Here we seem to be witnesses to a vision of the past—overhearing bits of anecdotes, seeing the irrational start of a fight, recognizing the saloon and the whorehouse as the centers of social life. The movie is so affecting it leaves one rather dazed. At one point, cursing himself for his inability to make Mrs. Miller understand the fullness of his love for her, McCabe mutters, "I got poetry in me. I do. I got poetry in me. Ain't gonna try to put it down on paper . . . got sense enough not to try." What this movie reveals is that there's poetry in Robert Altman and he *is* able to put it on the screen. Emotionally far more complex than *M*A*S*H*, *McCabe & Mrs. Miller* is the work of a more subtle, more deeply gifted—more mysterious—intelligence than might have been guessed at from *M*A*S*H*.

The picture is testimony to the power of stars. Warren Beatty and Julie Christie have never been better, and they *are* the two most interesting people in the town. They seem to take over the screen by natural right—because we want to look at them longer and more closely. Altman brings them into focus so unobtrusively that it's almost as if we had sorted them out from the others by ourselves. Without rigid guidelines, we observe them differently, and as the story unfolds, Beatty and Christie reveal more facets of their personalities than are apparent in those star vehicles that sell selected aspects of the stars to us. Julie Christie is no longer the androgynous starlet of *Darling*, the girl one wanted to see on the screen not for her performances but because she was so great-looking that she was compelling on her own, as an original. She had the profile of a Cocteau drawing—tawdry-classical—and that seemed enough: who could expect her to act? I think this is the first time (except, perhaps, for some of the early scenes in *Doctor Zhivago*) that I've believed in her as an *actress*—a warm and intense one—and become involved in the role she was playing, instead of merely admiring her extraordinary opaque mask. In this movie, the Cocteau girl has her opium. She's a weird, hounded beauty as the junky madam Mrs. Miller—that great, fat underlip the only flesh on her, and her gaunt, emaciated face surrounded by frizzy ringlets. She's like an animal hiding in its own fur. Julie Christie has that gift that beautiful actresses sometimes have of suddenly turning ugly and of being even more fascinating because of the crossover. When her nose practically meets her strong chin and she gets the look of a harpy, the demonstration of the thin line between harpy and beauty makes the beauty more dazzling—it's always threatened. The latent qualities of the one in the other take the character of Mrs. Miller out of the realm of ordinary movie madams. It is the depth in her that makes her too much for the cocky, gullible McCabe; his inexpressible poetry is charming but too simple. An actor probably has to be very smart to play a showoff so sensitively; Beatty never overdoes McCabe's foolishness, the way a foolish actor would. It's hard to know what makes Beatty such a magnetic presence; he was that even early in his screen career, when he used to frown and loiter over a line of dialogue as if he hoped to find his character during the pauses. Now that he has developed pace and control, he has become just about as attractive a screen star as any of the romantic heroes of the past. He has an unusually comic romantic presence; there's a gleefulness in Beatty, a light that comes on when he's onscreen that says "Watch this—it's fun." McCabe pantomimes and talks to himself through much of this movie, complaining of himself to himself; his best lines are between him and us. Beatty carries off this tricky yokel form of soliloquy casually, with good-humored self-mockery. It's a fresh, ingenious performance; we believe McCabe when he says that Mrs. Miller is freezing his soul.

A slightly dazed reaction to the film is, I think, an appropriate one. Right from the start, events don't wait for the viewers' comprehension, as they do in most movies, and it takes a while to realize that if you didn't quite hear someone's words it's all right—that the exact words are often expendable, it's the feeling tone that matters. The movie is inviting, it draws you in, but at the opening it may seem unnecessarily obscure, perhaps too "dark" (at times it suggests a dark version of Sam Peckinpah's genial miss *The Ballad of Cable Hogue*), and later on it may seem insubstantial (the way Max Ophuls' *The Earrings of Madame de* . . . seemed—to some—insubstantial, or Godard's *Band of Outsiders*). One doesn't quite know what to think of an American movie that doesn't pretend to give more than a partial view of events. The gaslight, the subdued, restful color, and Mrs. Miller's golden opium glow, Leonard Cohen's lovely, fragile, ambiguous songs, and the drifting snow all make the movie hazy and evanescent. Everything is in motion, and yet there is a stillness about the film, as if every element in it were conspiring to tell the same incredibly sad story: that the characters are lost in their separate dreams.

The pipe dreamer is, of course, Robert Altman. *McCabe & Mrs. Miller* seems so strange because, despite a great deal of noise about the art of film, we are unaccustomed to an intuitive, quixotic, essentially impractical approach to moviemaking, and to an exploratory approach to a subject, particularly when the subject is the American past. Improvising as the most gifted Europeans do has been the dream of many American directors, but few have been able to beat the economics of it. In the past few years, there have been breakthroughs, but only on sensational current subjects. Can an American director get by with a movie as personal as this—personal not as in "personal statement" but in the sense of giving form to his own feelings, some not quite defined, just barely suggested? A movie like this isn't made by winging it; to improvise in a period setting takes phenomenal discipline, but *McCabe & Mrs. Miller* doesn't look "disciplined," as movies that lay everything out for the audience do. Will a large enough American public accept American movies that are delicate and understated and searching—movies that don't resolve all the feelings they touch, that don't aim at leaving us *satisfied*, the way a three-ring circus satisfies? Or do we accept such movies only from abroad, and then only a small group of us—enough to make a foreign film a hit but not enough to make an American film, which costs more, a hit? A modest picture like

Claire's Knee would probably have been a financial disaster if it had been made in this country, because it might have cost more than five times as much and the audience for it is relatively small. Nobody knows whether this is changing—whether we're ready to let American moviemakers grow up to become artists or whether we're doomed to more of those "hard-hitting, ruthlessly honest" American movies that are themselves illustrations of the crudeness they attack. The question is always asked, "Why aren't there American Bergmans and Fellinis?" Here is an American artist who has made a beautiful film. The question now is "Will enough people buy tickets?"

{*The New Yorker*, July 3, 1971}

:: Helen of Troy, Sexual Warrior

The flaws in the Michael Cacoyannis film of Euripides' *The Trojan Women* seem unimportant compared to the simple fact that here is a movie of one of the supreme works of the theatre, and not a disgraceful movie, either. The play is not just the first but the one great anti-war play. What Euripides did was to look at war's other side, and the view from the losing side was not pomp and glory but cruelty and pain. The Trojan women are powerless, defenseless. As Andromache, Hector's widow, says, "I cannot save my child from death. Oh, hide my head for shame . . ." The shame of these captive women is that they can do nothing but yield to the victors. When the play opens, their children have been taken from them and sent to unknown destinations, and the women are waiting to be shipped into slavery; it closes when they have all been consigned and the city is burned. *The Trojan Women* is the greatest lament for the loss of freedom ever written, the greatest lament for the suffering of the victims of war. An Athenian, Euripides staged this profoundly radical play in Athens in 416 B.C., during a long war, only a few months after Athens had conquered a small island in the Aegean that was trying to stay neutral, killing the men and enslaving the women and children. The play might be called *Woman's Fate*. The dramatist's vision of the women whose husbands and sons have been slaughtered is austere and controlled and complete, so that, in a way, he said it all, and for all time. And because he said it all, and yet said it simply, the play is inexorable; we go from step to step until it is all there and the full effect has us by the throat. We knew about the miseries of war before. The play does more than confirm what we knew: it lays it out so clearly that we feel a deeper and higher understanding. Euripides has put it into words for us; he distills the worst that can happen. ("The gods—I prayed, they never listened." "Count no one happy, however fortunate, before he dies.") Despite the makeshift style of the film, one may come out grateful for this clarity, grateful to be caught by the throat, because it has been achieved by the most legitimate of all means—by a drama that states its case, and achieves nobility, through simplicity.

Katharine Hepburn, always forthright, starts as a fine, tough Hecuba, plainspoken and direct, but she comes to seem pitiful and mummified. Too many "O sorrow"s and references to her old gray head, and your mind begins to wander, asking vagrant questions such as "Why are all the women listening to the Queen—don't they have troubles enough of their own?" That is to say, you stop accepting the classical stage convention of the chorus and ask the questions you normally ask at movies. Actually, Euripides was so acutely sensible that within the convention of the chorus he provided the answers to one's natural questions. But in the movie the chorus, instead of going through their own hells, appear to be passive witnesses to Hecuba's, and she, instead of expressing the emotions of all of them, seems to be speaking of her own grief only, and her voice begins to seem thin and querulous. Hepburn is splendid when she's angry—when she has an antagonist. Perhaps our awareness of her as Hepburn makes us a little impatient with the weak, resigned side of the character.

A false nose (a trifle pale but very becoming) gives Genevieve Bujold's mad seeress Cassandra a classical look, and Bujold is becoming a daring and fascinating actress. She stretches the traditional sensitive-young-actress effects with a bursting conviction that they are good effects, and by strength of will, makes some of them work. That her performance doesn't come off is probably not entirely her fault. The role is the least modern, and the hokiest, in the play—Cassandra's virginal oaths and her prophecies don't mean much to us—and Cacoyannis has staged it with Ophelia-like flutters and with so much camera and chorus commotion that the narrative line goes out of whack. Bujold makes a stunning try, however, especially in her final fit. This performance is a leap in her career; her ambitiousness in tackling a role like this suggests prodigies ahead.

As Andromache, Vanessa Redgrave—that great goosey swan of the screen—fares better. Andromache is not as showy a role as Cassandra; it is written in a no-frills, clear-purpose style that pushes the narrative forward, and Redgrave's Andromache is magnificently uncomplicated. There are those who think that Vanessa Redgrave is a bad screen actress—that she jumps out of the screen at you, that she's always acting and does not allow you to *discover* anything in her performances. I think she *is* always acting, always "on." Though many moviegoers would probably be happy just to bask in her goddess image, she insists on doing something for them, on giving them the most imaginative performance she can. It's true one could look into Garbo, whereas Redgrave often seems to be staring one down, but there's a marvellous romantic excitement about this woman, because one never knows what audacity she will attempt, what heights she'll scale. This may prevent unconscious involvement, because we are always conscious of a *performance*, but our conscious involvement in the tension she creates has its own kind of excitement. She seems to act with her whole soul: you don't see her as a woman trying to play a role—the woman has been consumed by the determination to give the role all she has. Vanessa Redgrave never does the expected, and is never sloppy or overexpressive. Her Andromache is being freshly thought out while we watch—a dazed, pale-golden matron, unflirtatious, enough like Hepburn to suggest that Hector chose her because she was as free from guile and as naturally regal as his mother. Redgrave holds us by the quiet power of her concentration; she does odd little things—a tiny half sob gurgles from her throat. As an actress, she is such an embodiment of the idealistic, romantic spirit that I find myself rooting for her when she reaches for something new and difficult. There is a long meant-to-sound-wild cry when she is told that her child is to be slaughtered. She brings the cry to a sensational screaming finish; I realized I was hoping that others hadn't noticed how carefully it had begun. (Only once have I stopped rooting for her: I thought her dancing in *The Loves of Isadora* unforgivable, because she lacked the fluidity and lyricism to transform calisthenics into dance.)

Vanessa Redgrave gives the finest performance in the movie, but Cacoyannis demonstrates his love of the material, and his right to film it, in casting her as Andromache, and not in the obvious role for her—Helen. Because it is Irene Papas as Helen of Troy who cancels out the clichés of the legend and lifts the movie right out of the women's-college virtuous cultural ambience that plagues stage productions. *The Trojan Women* is not just a plainsong elegy disguised as a play. Euripides gave it one great melodramatic stroke. Helen, the adulterous wife of King Menelaus of Sparta, she whose flight with Paris, Prince of Troy, precipitated the war, is among the Trojan women survivors. The women would kill her if she were not protected from them by guards. Papas's Helen is a force of nature—a greedy woman who wants what she wants and who means to live. She has the vitality of a natural aggressor. She is first introduced prowling behind the slats of the stockade that protects her, and all we see are her brown-black eyes, as fiercely alive as a wolf's. While the other women mourn their dead, Helen uses all her animal cunning to survive. Cacoyannis makes the point that she is not defenseless—that the ruthless have weapons that the righteous don't have. Irene Papas is on her own turf in this play, and her Helen is a great winner—right there in the flesh. This Helen breathes sexuality; she is not merely a beauty but the strongest woman one has ever seen, and the more seductive because of her strength. You can *believe* that men would kill for her. She is not merely the cause of war, she is the spirit of war. When Hecuba says, "Fire comes from her to burn homes," it is perfectly plausible. The words of Andromache that seem like rhetoric on the page are given body:

> O Helen,
> many the fathers you were born of,
> Madness, Hatred, Red Death,
>   whatever poison
> the earth brings forth—God curse
>   you,
> with those beautiful eyes that
>   brought to shame and ruin
> Troy's far-famed plains.

The phrasing of the speeches is not always satisfying, however, and ends of phrases get swallowed when the characters are especially upset or are in motion. These variations in audibility may make the play superficially lifelike on the screen, but we regret not hearing all the words. And why oh why was the movie shot in the kind of muted dark color that dummies think is right for tragedy? The drained, gloomy spectrum looks like stage lighting. An even more fundamental problem is Cacoyannis's sense of movement and place. In a movie, before characters enter a room we are customarily shown their arrival on the street and at the house and some-times in the foyer or a passageway. This isn't mere filler. In the live theatre, we know exactly where the characters are — they're on that stage right in front of us. But at movies we seem to need to get our bearings — to know where people are coming from and where they're going and where things are happening. Most of the time, movies provide this information and we take it in unconsciously. When we don't get it, the movie appears to be impoverished and *stagy*. When people enter and leave an area that we cannot locate in terms of surrounding areas, the area is, inescapably, stage space, and we become even more aware of this when the area is outdoors — and therefore unconfined — than when it's indoors. Everything in *The Trojan Women* is outdoors, and yet the movie is claustrophobic, because the locations — the harbor, Cassandra's cave, a field of corpses, and so on — have no more connection with each other than if they were stage sets replacing each other. I would guess that Cacoyannis was working on a relatively small budget and had to piece his Troy together from bits of Spain. But, with all consideration made for the problem, the fact is that he didn't solve it. And he doesn't seem to know how to use the ground he's got. You're not sure where the people are in relation to each other even when they're in the same shot.

It obviously took extraordinary dedication and talent to make this movie — to inspire the actresses to test themselves, and to coach them and blend their voices so that an American, a French-Canadian, and an Englishwoman become acceptable as a family. Yet I question whether a director with so little feeling for the most basic elements of moviemaking can ever be a good movie director. A director with a "film sense" knows where to put the camera so that you don't question the shot; for others every setup looks arbitrary. This play demands a plain, consistent cinematic style, with no flourishes — a style as supremely matter-of-fact as Euripides' language. Cacoyannis tries to make the movie impressive — there's embalming fluid in the images — and the tragic line breaks down into sequences. Some are derivative, such as the whirling camera when Cassandra spins about, the cacophonous music and fast cuts when the chorus is distraught; some are effective in an overly prestigious way, such as the freeze frames in the opening sequence while the narrator speaks — like the breaks for words in Stravinsky's *Oedipus Rex*. These are the attempts of a man without a film sense to make a drama cinematic; it winds up an anthology of second-rate film styles.

One may long for the ideal — for a great play transformed by a great movie artist into a great movie. But great movie artists are not often tempted to tackle great plays, and when they do, it sometimes turns out that they don't have the right skills. Short of the ideal, what it comes down to is whether in seeing a movie version one can still respond to what makes the play great. By that standard, I count the Cacoyannis film a success. Even if one is aware of everything the matter with it, the emotion of the play gets to you, and the emotion of Greek tragedy has a purity that you *can't get from anything else*. That's a very good reason to make a movie—to bring people the emotions that only a few in our time have experienced in the theatre. (And the productions they see are flawed and stilted, too—though, of course, in different ways.) Beautiful as the Edith Hamilton translation is, the movie has something you can't get from a reading: Irene Papas's Helen is a demonic illumination of the text. I think one would have to be maybe a little foolish to let aesthetic scruples about the movie's mediocrity as cinema deprive one of seeing *The Trojan Women* with a cast that one could never hope to see on the stage. The actresses come from different cultures, but they bring intensity of life to the screen; that's what makes them stars. If a movie releases that intensity, it hasn't bungled what matters most.

{*The New Yorker*, October 16, 1971}

:: Louis Malle's Portrait of
the Artist as a Young Dog

Murmur of the Heart is mellow and smooth, like a fine old jazz record, but when it's over it has the kick of a mule—a *funny* kick, which sends you out doubled over grinning. Assured and unflamboyant in technique, it is yet an exhilarating film—an irresistible film, one might say if one had not heard word of some resistance, especially by the jury at Cannes, which chose to ignore it, managing even to pass over Lea Massari's full-scale portrait of the carelessly sensual mother of a bourgeois brood of sons in favor of Kitty Winn's drab, meagre-spirited performance in *The Panic in Needle Park*. Massari's Clara is a woman without discretion or calculation; she's shamelessly loose and free, and she's loved by her sons because of her indifference to the bourgeois forms, which they nevertheless accept—on the surface, that is. What makes this movie so different from other movies about bourgeois life is that the director, Louis Malle, sees not only the prudent, punctilious surface but the volatile and slovenly life underneath. He looks at this bourgeois bestiary and sees it as funny and appalling and also—surprisingly—hardy and happy. It is perhaps the first time on film that anyone has shown us the bourgeoisie *enjoying* its privileges.

From the way Malle observes the sex education of the youngest, brightest son of the family, fourteen-year-old Laurent (Benoît Ferreux), one knows that the movie is a portrait of the artist as a young dog. It comes after a succession of Malle films, but in its subject, and in the originality and the special sure-footedness that the director (who also wrote the script) brings to the material, it is, clearly, the obligatory first film. The picture is set in Dijon—also the setting for Malle's *The Lovers*—in 1954, at the time of Dien Bien Phu (which must have been only a few years after the director's schoolboy days), and before the children of the bourgeoisie became radicalized. Though the film itself reveals the sources of Malle's humor, this story probably wouldn't have been nearly so funny or, perhaps, so affectionate if Malle had told it fifteen years ago. It is a film by someone who doesn't have to simplify in order to take a stand, who no longer needs to rebel; he has come a distance, and the story is additionally distanced by the changes in French student life that Godard recorded in *Masculine Feminine* and *La Chinoise*. In 1954, the sons of the successful gynecologist (Daniel Gélin) and the Italian-born Clara could still enjoy their wealth as their due. Seen with the vivacity of fresh intelligence, they're a family of monsters, all right, but normal monsters—no more monstrous than other close-knit families—and they're happy hypocrites.

I'm not sure how the picture was sustained and brought off so that we see the stuffiness and snobbery of the privileged class on the outside and the energetic amorality underneath, but the story moves toward its supremely logical yet witty and imaginative conclusion so stealthily that the kicker joke is perfect. Advance word had suggested that the picture was a serious, shocking view of incest, but the only shock is the joke that, for all the repressions these bourgeois practice and the conventions they pretend to believe in, they are such amoral, instinct-satisfying creatures that incest doesn't mean any more to them than to healthy animals. The shock is that in this context incest *isn't* serious—and that, I guess, may really upset some people, so they won't be able to laugh.

I can't remember another movie in which family life and adolescence have been used for such high comedy. The details are as singular, as deeply rooted in the period and the place, as the details in Truffaut's *The 400 Blows*, and the picture has that kind of candor. But no one in the film requires sympathy. Malle's approach has some of Buñuel's supple objectivity and aberrant humor. Malle satirizes the family from inside as Buñuel satirizes Catholicism from inside. The boys casually loot their own home, turn the dining room into a tennis court with a ball of spinach. Members of the family tease and squabble, but they enjoy the squabbling, because it is part of their intimacy and their security. Home is chaos; the three boys are not subdued even when there are guests. The vinegar-face father, severe and disgusted, though in a sort of ineffectual, ritualistic way, is tolerant—perhaps even, like the old family servant, proud that his boys are such irresponsible, uncontrollable *boys*. They're expensive pets, expected to commit outrages, and also expected to shape up eventually. In a poor environment, the boys would be brats, or even punks and delinquents; here they're the young masters. Papa's distaste is amusing, and the boys goad him; the grumblings of a put-upon father are a reassuring sound. And when you're furious with a brother, he's still a brother, and you have the pride and safety in that that you can never feel when you quarrel with those outside the family. This movie catches the way people care about each other in a family, and the feeling of a household in which there's no discipline. Which I think is probably generally the case but is something that movies like to lie about. The mixture of contempt and affection that the boys feel toward the old servant is so accurate—even if one has never been near a fuddy-duddy family retainer—that it sweeps away all those false, properly respected movie servants.

The only quality common to the films of Louis Malle is the restless intelligence one senses in them, and it must be this very quality that has led Malle to try such different subjects and styles. A new Chabrol or a Losey is as easily recognizable as a Magritte, but even film enthusiasts have only a vague idea of Malle's work. Had Malle gone on making variations of almost any one of his films, it is practically certain he would have been acclaimed long ago, but a director who is impatient and dissatisfied and never tackles the same problem twice gives reviewers trouble and is likely to be dismissed as a dilettante. Malle, though he is still under forty, predates the New Wave, and has made amazingly good films in several styles. Born in 1932, he was co-director with Cousteau of *The Silent World*, then assistant to Bresson on *A Man Escaped*, and then, in 1957, at twenty-five, he made his first film, the ingenious, slippery thriller *Lift to the Scaffold* (also called *Frantic*), with Maurice Ronet and Jeanne Moreau, and a Miles Davis score. The following year, he had his biggest American success—*The Lovers*, with its flowing rhythms and its Brahms, the message of woman's desire for sexual fulfillment and the wind rippling through Moreau's white chiffon. It was facile movie-poetry but erotic and beautifully made. In 1960, he did a flipover to *Zazie dans le Métro*, from the Queneau novel—a fiendishly inventive slapstick comedy about a foulmouthed little girl, which was too fast and too freakish for American tastes, so that Americans did not credit Malle with the innovative editing, and later gave the credit instead to Tony Richardson's *Tom Jones* and to Richard Lester and others. *Zazie*, a comedy that owed a debt to Tati but carried Tati's dry, quick style to nightmarish anxiety, included satirical allusions to *La Dolce Vita* and *The Lovers*. After the wild *Zazie* came *Vie Privée*, with Brigitte Bardot and about her life as a sex-symbol star. *Le Feu Follet*, in 1963, the film that first convinced me that Malle was a superb director, shows the influence of Bresson but is without the inhuman pride that I think poisons so much of Bresson's later work. *Le Feu Follet* (sometimes called *The Fire Within*) has been seen by few people in this country. It received some generous reviews (especially in *The New Yorker*), and no one appears to be very clear about the reasons for its commercial failure—whether it got snarled in distribution problems or whether the film was simply "not commercial" in American terms. An elegy for a wasted life, adapted by Malle from a thirties novel, it dealt with the forty-eight hours before the suicide of a dissolute playboy (Maurice Ronet again) who, at thirty, has outlived his boyish charm and his social credit. It is a study of despair with no possibility of relief; the man has used up his slim resources and knows it. He does not want to live as what he has become; his taste is too good. It was directed in a clean, deliberate style, with a lone piano playing Satie in the background. Genêt wrote of the director, "He has effected something phenomenal this time, having turned literature into film, photographed the meaning of an unsubstantial, touching, and rather famous book, and given its tragic intention a clarity it never achieved in print." And Brendan Gill said, "Between them, Malle and Ronet have composed a work as small and vast, as affecting, and, I think, as permanent as Fitzgerald's *Babylon Revisited*." It was a masterly film, and it seemed almost inconceivable that a director still so young could produce a work about such anguish with such control. *Le Feu Follet* should have made Malle's reputation here—in the way that *L'Avventura* made Antonioni's. After that painful, claustrophobic film, Malle did another flip, to the outdoors and the New World—to the frivolous, picaresque *Viva Maria!*, set in the Latin America of La Belle Epoque, with Moreau and Bardot. At the opening, the child who will become Bardot helps her imperialist-hating father dynamite a British fortress in Ireland, and the contrast between the father's act and the child's blooming, innocent happiness as she plays in the fields planting explosives is rapturously comic. *Viva Maria!* was lavish and visually beautiful, but the subsequent bombings and shootings weren't so funny; the central conceit involved in the pairing of Bardot and Moreau didn't work out, so the slap-stick facetiousness was just left there, with nothing under it. But Bardot—not because of any *acting*—has never been more enchanting than in parts of this movie. When Malle put her into boys' clothes, with a cap and a smudge on her cheek, she was a tomboy looking for fun: Zazie grown up but still polymorphously amoral. After *The Thief of Paris*, with Jean-Paul Belmondo, Malle went to India, where he shot documentaries, the most famous of which, *Calcutta*, has never opened in New York.*

The director travelled a long road before looking into his own back yard; now, when he goes back to it in *Murmur of the Heart*, we can see in that gleeful, chaotic household the origins of the radiant prankishness of *Zazie* and *Viva Maria!* and of those riffs that don't stop for breath, and we can see the sources of the studied, overblown romanticism of *The Lovers*, and also of the caustic view of romanticism in the great *Le Feu Follet*. I don't think *Murmur of the Heart* is a greater film than *Le Feu Follet*, but in exclud-ing all joy that film was a very special sort of film: getting so far inside a suicide's attitude toward himself can really wipe viewers out. This is a joyous and accessible work, and so the anguish of *Le Feu Follet* begins to seem youthful—like an early spiritual crisis that has been resolved. Although *Murmur of the Heart* is obviously semi-autobiographical, it's a movie not about how one has been scarred but about how one was formed. You can see that Malle is off the hook by the justice he does to the other characters. (The only character that seems to me a failure and no more than a stereotype is the lecherous priest, played by Michel Lonsdale.)

Lea Massari (she was the girl who disappeared in *L'Avventura*) has, as Clara, the background of a libertarian father—reminiscent of Bardot's background in *Viva Maria!* Clara says she grew up "like a savage," and when she smiles her irregular teeth show her to be a spiritual relative of the impudent Zazie. Malle's films have swung back and forth between the eroticism of the Moreau characters and the anarchic, childish humor of the Zazies; Massari's ravishing Clara combines them. Her relaxed sensuality is the essence of impropriety. There is a moment when Clara, who has blithely remarked to her sons as they watch her changing clothes, "I

Calcutta was shown on Channel 13 in New York early in December, followed by *The Impos-sible Camera*—the first in a series of seven films that make up *Phantom India*. All eight later opened in a theatre.

simply have no modesty," catches Laurent peeping at her in her bath. She instinctively slaps him; he is deeply offended, and she apologizes and says he should have slapped her back. This many-layered confusion of principle and hypocrisy and instinct and injustice is one of the rare occasions when a movie has shown how knotted the ties of family life really are for most of us. Clara comes alive because of that freak bit of Zazie in her; she will never grow up and become the mature mother of simplified fiction. She is not one of those Fay Bainter mothers, born at forty full of wisdom and christened "Mother."

As for Laurent—or Renzino, as Clara calls him—Benoît Ferreux probably is only about fourteen, but, without being fey, he looks enough like the Lauren Bacall of an earlier era to hold the camera in a vise, and he appears to have an impeccable sense of what's wanted. You're never quite sure how you feel about Laurent. His musical tastes—Charlie Parker and the other jazz greats we hear on the track—are irreproachable, and, in their irreproachability, marks of fashion and caste. He's extraordinarily clever, but he's also an arrogant, precocious little snot who thinks that people were put in the world to serve him; he despises a snob Fascist boy because the boob hasn't mastered the right tone—the acceptable amount of snobbery. The movie is about the childhood and growing into manhood of those who are pampered from birth, and at every step it shows what they take for granted. It defines the ways in which the rich are not like you and me, and the ways in which they are. Malle resembles Fitzgerald, but a Fitzgerald with a vision formed from the inside, and with the intelligence for perspective. His is a deeply realistic comic view—free of Fitzgerald's romantic ruined dreams. In pulling his different styles together in *Murmur of the Heart*, Malle finds a new ripe vein of comedy: believable comedy; that is to say, life seen in its comic aspects. There's a sequence in which smart Laurent outsmarts himself: he attempts to disrupt a meeting that his mother is having with her lover, and his intrusion results in her going off with the lover for a few days. When it comes to family ties and basic affections and how to lose one's virginity, even the smart and the dumb aren't so very far apart.

{*The New Yorker*, October 23, 1971}

:: Urban Gothic

When Mayor Lindsay began his efforts to attract the movie-production business, it probably didn't occur to him or his associates that they were ushering in a new movie age of nightmare realism. The Los Angeles area was selected originally for the sunshine and so that the movie-business hustlers — patent-violators who were pirating inventions as well as anything else they could get hold of — could slip over the border fast. As it turned out, however, California had such varied vegetation that it could be used to stand in for most of the world, and there was space to build whatever couldn't be found. But New York City is always New York City; it can't be anything else, and, with practically no studios for fakery, the movie companies use what's really here, so the New York–made movies have been set in Horror City. Although recent conflicts between the producers and the New York unions seem to have ended this Urban Gothic period,* the New York–made movies have provided a permanent record of the city in breakdown. I doubt if at any other time in American movie history there has been such a close relationship between the life on the screen and the life of a portion of the audience. Los Angeles–made movies were not *about* Los Angeles; often they were not about any recognizable world. But these recent movies are about New York, and the old sentimentalities are almost impossible here — physically impossible, because the city gives them the lie. (I'm thinking of such movies as *Klute*, *Little Murders*, *The Anderson Tapes*, *Greetings*, *The Landlord*, *Where's Poppa?*, *Mid-*

---

*After two and a half months, the five major companies signed an agreement with the unions and production in New York was resumed.

night Cowboy, Harry Kellerman, Diary of a Mad Housewife, No Way to Treat a Lady, Shaft, Cotton Comes to Harlem, The Steagle, Cry Uncle, The Owl and the Pussycat, The Panic in Needle Park, Bananas, and the forthcoming *Born to Win*.) The city of New York has helped American movies grow up; it has also given movies a new spirit of nervous, anxious hopelessness, which is the true spirit of New York. It is literally true that when you live in New York you no longer believe that the garbage will ever be gone from the streets or that life will ever be sane and orderly.

The movies have captured the soul of this city in a way that goes beyond simple notions of realism. The panhandler in the movie who jostles the hero looks just like the one who jostles you as you leave the movie theatre; the police sirens in the movie are screaming outside; the hookers and junkies in the freak show on the screen are indistinguishable from the ones in the freak show on the streets. Famous New York put-on artists and well-known street people are incorporated in the movies; sometimes they are in the movie theatre, dressed as they are in the movie, and sometimes you leave the theatre and see them a few blocks away, just where they were photographed. There's a sense of carnival about this urban-crisis city; everyone seems to be dressed for a mad ball. Screams in the theatre at Halloween movies used to be a joke, signals for laughter and applause, because nobody believed in the terror on the screen. The midnight show-ings of horror films now go on all year round, and the screams are no longer pranks. Horror stories and brutal melodramas concocted for profit are apparently felt on a deeper level than might have been supposed. People don't laugh or applaud when there's a scream; they try to ignore the sound. It is assumed that the person yelling is stoned and out of con-trol, or crazy and not to be trifled with—he may want an excuse to blow off steam, he may have a knife or a gun. It is not uncommon now for fights and semi-psychotic episodes to take place in the theatres, especially when the movies being played are shockers. Audiences for these movies in the Times Square area and in the Village are highly volatile. Probably the unstable, often dazed members of the audiences are particularly suscep-tible to the violence and tension on the screen; maybe crowds now include a certain number of people who simply can't stay calm for two hours. But whether the movies bring it out in the audience or whether the particular audiences that are attracted bring it into the theatre, it's *there* in the theatre, particularly at late shows, and you feel that the violence on the screen may at any moment touch off violence in the theatre. The audience is explosively *live*. It's like being at a prizefight or a miniature Altamont.

Horror is very popular in Horror City—old horror films and new ones. The critics were turned off by the madness of *The Devils*; the audiences were turned on by it. They wanted the benefits of the sexual pathology of religious hysteria: bloody tortures, burning flesh, nuns violated on altars, lewd nuns stripping and orgying, and so on. Almost all the major movie companies are now, like the smaller ones, marginal businesses. The losses of the American film industry since 1968 are calculated at about five hundred and twenty-five million dollars. Besides Disney, the only company that shows profits is A.I.P.—the producers of ghouls-on-wheels schlock pictures, who are now also turning out movies based on Gothic "classics." I don't believe that people are going to shock and horror films because of a need to exorcise their fears; that's probably a fable. I think they're going for entertainment, and I don't see how one can ignore the fact that the kind of entertainment that attracts them now is often irrational and horrifyingly brutal. A few years ago, *The Dirty Dozen* turned the audience on so high that there was yelling in the theatre and kicking at the seats. And now an extraordinarily well-made new thriller gets the audience sky-high and keeps it up there—*The French Connection*, directed by William Friedkin, which is one of the most "New York" of all the recent New York movies. It's also probably the best-made example of what trade reporters sometimes refer to as "the cinema du zap."

How's this for openers? A peaceful day in Marseille. A *flic* strolls into a boulangerie, comes out carrying a long French bread, and strolls home. As he walks into his own entranceway, a waiting figure in a leather coat sticks out an arm with a .45 and shoots him in the face and then in the torso. The assassin picks up the bread, breaks off a piece to munch, and tosses the remainder back onto the corpse. That's the first minute of *The French Connection*. The film then jumps to New York and proceeds through chases, pistol-whippings, slashings, beatings, murders, snipings, and more chases for close to two hours. The script, by Ernest Tidyman (who wrote *Shaft*), is based on the factual account by Robin Moore (of *The Green Berets*) of the largest narcotics haul in New York police history until the recent Jaguar case. The producer, Philip D'Antoni, also produced *Bullitt*, and the executive producer was G. David Schine, of Cohn and Schine. That's not a creative team, it's a consortium. The movie itself is pretty businesslike. There are no good guys in this harsh new variant of cops-and-robbers; *The French Connection* features the latest-model sadistic cop, Popeye (Gene Hackman). It's undeniably gripping, slam-bang, fast, charged with suspense, and so on—a mixture of *Razzia* and *Z*, and hyped up additionally with a television-thriller-style score that practically lays you out all by itself. At one point, just in case we might lose interest if we didn't have our minute-to-minute injections of excitement, the camera cuts from the street conversation of a few cops to show us the automobile smashup that brought them to the scene, and we are treated to two views of the bloody faces of fresh corpses. At first, we're confused as to who the victims are, and we stare at them thinking they must be characters in the movie. It takes a few seconds to realize that they bear no relation whatsoever to the plot.

It's no wonder that *The French Connection* is a hit, but what in hell is it? It uses eighty-six separate locations in New York City—so many that it has no time for carnival atmosphere: it crashes right through. I suppose the answer we're meant to give is that it's an image of the modern big city as Inferno, and that Popeye is an Existential hero, but the movie keeps zapping us. Though *The French Connection* achieves one effect through timing and humor (when the French Mr. Big, played by Fernando Rey, outwits Popeye in a subway station by using his silver-handled umbrella to open the train doors) most of its effects are of the *Psycho*-derived blast-in-the-face variety. Even the expert pacing is achieved by somewhat questionable means; the ominous music keeps tightening the screws and heating things up. The noise of New York already has us tense. The movie is like an aggravated case of New York: it raises this noise level to produce the kind of painful tension that is usually described as almost unbearable suspense. But it's the same kind of suspense you feel when someone outside your window keeps pushing down on the car horn and you think the blaring sound is going to drive you out of your skull. This horn routine is, in fact, what the cop does throughout the longest chase sequence. The movie's suspense is magnified by the sheer pounding abrasiveness of its means; you don't have to be an artist or be original or ingenious to work on the raw nerves of an audience this way—you just have to be smart and brutal. The high-pressure methods that one could possibly accept in *Z* because they were tools used to try to show the audience how a Fascist conspiracy works are used as ends in themselves. Despite the dubious methods, the purpose of the brutality in *Z* was moral—it was to make you hate brutality. Here you love it, you wait for it—that's all there is. I know that there are many people—and very intelligent people, too—who love this kind of fast-action movie, who say that this is what movies do best and that this is what they really want when they go to a movie. Probably many of them would agree with everything I've said but will still love the movie. Well, it's not what I want, and the fact that Friedkin has done a sensational job of direction just makes that clearer. It's not what I want not because it fails (it doesn't fail) but because of what it is. It is, I think, what we once feared mass entertainment might become: jolts for jocks. There's nothing in the movie that you enjoy thinking over afterward —nothing especially clever except the timing of the subway-door-and-umbrella sequence. Every other effect in the movie—even the climactic car-versus-runaway-elevated-train chase—is achieved by noise, speed, and brutality.

On its own terms, the picture makes few mistakes, though there is one small but conspicuous one. A good comic contrast of drug dealers dining at their ease in a splendid restaurant while the freezing, hungry cops who are tailing them curse in a cold doorway and finally eat a hunk of pizza is spoiled because, for the sake of a composition with the two groups in the same shot, the police have been put where the diners could obviously see them. It is also a mistake, I think, that at the end the picture just stops instead of coming to a full period. The sloppy plotting, on the other hand, doesn't seem to matter; it's amazing how much implausibility speed and brutality can conceal. Hitchcock's thrillers were full of holes, but you were having too good a time to worry about them; *The French Connection* is full of holes, but mostly you're too stunned to notice them. There's no logic in having the Lincoln Continental that has been shipped from France with the heroin inside abandoned on a back street at night rather than parked snugly in the garage of its owner's hotel; it appears to be on the street just so the narcotics agents can spot it and grab it. There's an elaborate sequence of an auction at an automobile graveyard which serves no clear purpose. And if you ever think about it you'll realize that you have no idea who that poor devil was who got shot in the overture, or why. For all the movie tells you, it may have been for his French bread. But you really know what it's all in there for. It's the same reason you get those juicy pictures of the corpses: zaps.

Listen to Popeye's lines and you can learn the secrets of zap realism. A crude writer can give his crummy, cheap jokes to a crude character, and the jokes really pay off. The rotten jokes get laughs and also show how ugly the character's idea of humor is. Popeye risks his life repeatedly and performs fabulously dangerous actions, yet the movie debases him in every possible way. Hackman has turned himself into a modern Ted Healy type—porkpie hat, sneaky-piggy eyes, and a gut-first walk, like Robert Morley preceded by his belly coming toward us in those BOAC "Visit Britain" commercials. Popeye (the name is out of Faulkner, I assume) has a filthy mouth and a complete catalogue of race prejudices, plus some "cute" fetishes; e.g., he cases girls who wear boots. He is the anti-hero carried to a new lumpenprole low—the mean cop who used to figure on the fringes of melodrama (as in *Sweet Smell of Success*) moved to the center. Sam Spade might play dirty, but he had a code and he had personal style; even Bullitt, a character contrived to hold the chases and bloodshed together, was a super-cop with style and feelings. This movie turns old clichés into new clichés by depriving the central figure of *any* attractive qualities. Popeye is insanely callous, a shrewd bully who enjoys terrorizing black junkies, and the film includes raids on bars that are gratuitous to the story line just to show what a subhuman son of a bitch he is. The information is planted early that his methods have already cost the life of a police officer, and at the end this plant has its pat payoff when he accidentally shoots an F.B.I. agent, and the movie makes the point that he doesn't show the slightest remorse. The movie presents him as the most ruthlessly lawless of characters and yet—here is where the basic amorality comes through—shows that this is the kind of man it takes to get the job done. It's the vicious bastard who gets the results. Popeye, the lowlifer who makes Joe or Archie sound like Daniel Ellsberg, is a cop the way the movie Patton was a general. When Popeye walks into a bar and harasses blacks, part of the audience can say, "That's a real pig," and another part of the audience can say, "That's the only way to deal with those people. Waltz around with them and you get nowhere."

I imagine that the people who put this movie together just naturally think in this commercially convenient double way. This right-wing, left-wing, take-your-choice cynicism is total commercial opportunism passing itself off as an Existential view. And maybe that's why Popeye's determination to find the heroin is not treated unequivocally as socially useful but is made obsessive. Popeye's low character is used to make the cops-and-robbers melodrama superficially modern by making it *meaning-less*; his brutality serves to demonstrate that the cops are no better than the crooks. In personal style and behavior, he is, in fact, deliberately shown as worse than the crooks, yet since he's the cop with the hunches that pay off, the only cop who gets results, the movie can be seen as a way of justifying police brutality. At the end, a Z-style series of titles comes on to inform us that the dealers who were caught got light sentences or none at all. The purpose of giving us this information is also probably double: to tell us to get tougher judges and to make tougher laws, and to provide an ironic coda showing that Popeye's efforts were really futile. A huge haul of heroin was destroyed, but the movie doesn't bother to show us that—to give a man points for anything is unfashionable. The series of titles is window-dressing anyway. The only thing that this movie believes in is giving the audience jolts, and you can feel the raw, primitive response in the theatre. This picture says Popeye is a brutal son of a bitch who gets the dirty job done. So is the picture.

{*The New Yorker*, October 30, 1971}

:: The Fall and Rise of
Vittorio De Sica

Twenty years ago, André Bazin wrote that "the Neapolitan charm of De Sica becomes, thanks to the cinema, the most sweeping message of love that our times have heard since Chaplin." De Sica's characters are "lit from within by the tenderness he feels for them," Bazin wrote. "Rossellini's style is a way of seeing, while De Sica's is primarily a way of feeling." Vittorio De Sica is one of those directors "whose entire talent derives from the love they have for their subject, from their ultimate understanding of it." But in the years since Bazin wrote those words De Sica's films have diminished in interest, and the routine jobs have obscured the work of his great neo-realist period. After a career in the late twenties and the thirties as a movie matinée idol—the handsome singing star of dozens of romantic musicals—De Sica had become a director, at first of highly successful light comedies and then, with the collaboration of the writer Cesare Zavattini, of a series of movies that were aesthetically revolutionary. The style that they initiated in 1942 with *The Children Are Watching Us* reached international critical recognition, after the war, with *Shoeshine*, in 1947, and then, in 1948, achieved its only financial success with the classic *The Bicycle Thief*. They followed that with the comic fantasy *Miracle in Milan*, in 1951, and, finally, later that year, the luminous, slightly flawed masterwork *Umberto D.* Commercially, *Umberto D.* was an abject failure; it didn't even get an opening in the United States until 1955. And the film was attacked by Italian government officials—which was financially crippling, because De Sica and Zavattini needed government subsidies in order to finance their projects. They gave up; they went on working together, but in the commercial cinema. Later, they made one last attempt—*The Roof*, in 1957—but the impulse that had motivated their greatest work seemed spent, and *The Roof* was tired. It had less life than their commercial jobs, which, though star vehicles and conventional crowd-pleasers, were often crowd-pleasers in the best sense—high-spirited satirical entertainments, with that non-professional actress Sophia Loren, who in De Sica's hands blossomed into the most luscious comedienne the screen has ever known. In full bloom, she is a glory, yet without De Sica she is not quite so funny and her humor and beauty lack roots.

There were few so holy that they could cry "Sellout!" to Vittorio De Sica and Cesare Zavattini, who openly abandoned their hopes. Maybe they could have fought their way through if they had been younger, but De Sica was born in 1901 and Zavattini in 1902. Movies have been a young man's medium (largely, one assumes, because of the business pressures that drain an artist's energy), and De Sica had made his greatest films at an age when most good directors have their best work behind them. It may have been the mellowed emotions of this late beginner that gave that series of neo-realist films their special purity. Though those films (which used actual locations and, as actors, people who actually were what they were supposed to be) were made on aesthetic principles that appear to have been formulated by Zavattini, it was De Sica's way of feeling that provided the soul for Zavattini's theory of a direct seizure of "reality." (The films that Zavattini wrote on the same principles for other directors turned out to be rather unpleasant.) But De Sica's famous "limpidity"—the technique that one was not aware of, because all one saw was the subject made radiant—was lost when he moved into the commercial cinema. It was by means of his limpid style that he and Zavattini had extended our sense of the beauty in common experience and of the elegance of simple gestures. It was a selfless director's art, an art so transparent that we think of those De Sica films purely in terms of emotion. When we recall moments from *Shoeshine*, or Umberto D.'s voice calling "Flick," or Emma Gramatica hopping over the spilled milk in *Miracle in Milan*, we are likely, I think, to experience a poignancy so strong that it amounts to an ache, like the ache we feel when we recall moments in a D. W. Griffith film or a Chaplin comedy. Like Griffith and Chaplin, De Sica achieved images that one feels to be essences of human experience—suffering or joy turned into poetry.

Bazin tried to explain this phenomenon when he said, "Poetry is but the active and creative form of love, its projection into the world." Because of De Sica's selflessness and the way he has disappeared into the subject, those great films stay almost incredibly distinct in the memory, the characters separately imprinted.

The later entertainments run together; they were often agreeable enough, but they leave few memories. *The Gold of Naples, Marriage—Italian Style, Yesterday, Today, and Tomorrow*, and a host of short-story films in big-director packages are not entirely bad, but they don't mean much to us, and, far from being limpid, they are careless, crowded, on occasion downright ugly. If De Sica became somewhat indifferent to how the commercial entertainments were made, who is to say that it mattered much? These were "lusty" films, not intended to be lingered over. Both as actor and as director, De Sica is a man of different sides. In his fifties, he became a superb ham actor in a florid tradition, but as the arm-waving lawyer defending Gina Lollobrigida in the trial for murder in *Times Gone By*, and in such movies as *Bread, Love, and Dreams, The Miller's Beautiful Wife*, and *The Anatomy of Love*, he is a different man from the restrained, civilized diplomat in *The Earrings of Madame De* . . . The hammy, extravagantly good-natured actor seems to be the director of the entertainments, which, though coarse, are not coarsely *felt*. In his crowd-pleasers, as in his refined work, De Sica is the true democrat of directors: his love of people has nothing to do with rank—he can be generous even toward the rich. His courtly tact extends to everyone, and he never swarms all over a character. The distance he keeps is an implicit homage to the dignity of the characters; he reveals more by not invading their privacy—and that takes art.

This doesn't mean, however, that one looked forward to the *next* De Sica film. He had, after all, first appeared on the screen as the boy Clemenceau in *The Clemenceau Case*, in 1915, and men of seventy don't often make good movies. (Buñuel is about the only exception who comes to mind.) De Sica's work had seemed in fairly obvious decline, as if he no longer had the energy—or perhaps the interest—to hold the complex elements of filmmaking together. And so *The Garden of the Finzi-Continis* is a beautiful surprise—a return not to neo-realism but to the limpid style of his neo-realist days.

Graceful and leisurely, *The Garden of the Finzi-Continis*, which is set in Ferrara in the Fascist period of the late thirties and early forties, is unmistakably novelistic in style, and different from anything else De Sica has ever done. The movie, from a semi-autobiographical novel by Giorgio Bassani published in Italy in 1962, is about a now vanished group of people and a vanished mood, and you can feel a novelist's sensibility in the tenuous relationships and the romantically charged decadence of the aristocratic setting. But though the relationships are tenuous, you feel that the movie is complete—that the tenuousness is an expression of the writer's obsession with this incompletely understood part of his past.

The movie not only is faithful to this obsession but validates the obsession—and without making a great to-do about it. De Sica's early films call up waves of emotion in us because the great moments are not overstated; he seems incapable of the cultural inflation that goes on in a film like *The Go-Between*, in which all that "style" is looking over our shoulders and telling us that there are deep things lurking in the empty spaces. That movie, I feel, did not validate the boy outsider's obsession. In the De Sica film—to borrow from Flip Wilson—what you see is what you get. The protagonist, Giorgio, from whose point of view we perceive the characters and events, is a middle-class Jewish-Italian student (Lino Capolicchio) who falls in love with Micòl (Dominique Sanda), the young daughter of the Finzi-Continis—rich, cultivated Sephardic Jews, descendants of the Venetian merchants who fled the Spanish Inquisition and intermarried with the leading Jewish families of Europe. Landowners with vast holdings, the Finzi-Continis live in a huge old house surrounded by a private park, with tennis courts and stables. Micòl, intelligent but imperious and contrary, and her languid, sickly brother, Alberto (Helmut Berger), live behind their garden walls in a decaying world that they haven't the strength or the will to change or to escape. It's an enchanted world for Giorgio, the middle-class outsider who is drawn into it—to play tennis when the Jews are expelled from the local tennis club, to use the Finzi-Continis' library when he can no longer use the city library. He is drawn in only part way, and obsessively, because Micòl does not return his love. Giorgio is not unlike the hero of *Goodbye, Columbus*, and the characters here, too, are predominantly Jewish, but the Finzi-Continis are the very opposite of vulgar nouveaux riches: the parents, with their distant, benevolent smiles for the young, seem detached and bloodless, the father an antiquarian preoccupied with seventeenth-century studies, the mother vague and formal. And if Giorgio, like Roth's hero, has difficulty comprehending the family's way of life, it's for the opposite reason: the Patimkins are survivors, the Finzi-Continis—assimilated to a nineteenth-century liberalism—are not. They have lost connection with the realities of Mussolini's Italy, which will soon de-assimilate them.

At the beginning of the movie, I thought that Dominique Sanda was shot like a young Garbo, and that I hadn't seen a brother and sister who were such glamorous look-alikes since Greta Garbo and Douglas Fairbanks, Jr., in *A Woman of Affairs*, the movie version of *The Green Hat*. Not that Dominique Sanda and Helmut Berger are quite in that league, but they're close enough to it to suggest the earlier pair and to be fairly dazzling. Then my reaction shifted as I realized that their relationship was reminiscent of Elisabeth (Nicole Stéphane) and Paul (Édouard Dermithe), the brother and sister in *Les Enfants Terribles*. A moment later, Micòl was reading the Cocteau novel and remarking on how chic it was. And then I understood that the connections I had been making were implicit in the scheme. If Dominique Sanda's Micòl seems to suggest both Garbo and Elisabeth, it should be recalled that Cocteau (as Francis Steegmuller explained in his biography) had Garbo in mind when he wrote Elisabeth—Garbo at eighteen, Cocteau said. And the novel *Les Enfants Terribles*, which was published in 1929, did have an unusual influence on the life style of adolescents in the thirties, who, Cocteau said, "found themselves mirrored in Paul and Elisabeth." Paul and Elisabeth were natural aristocrats by virtue of a narcissistic mixture of youth, pride, beauty—and contempt for all other values, especially self-preservation. It's apparent that Bassani (who also worked on the movie) intended Micòl and her brother to be among the mirror images. The sense of youth as an élite in *The Garden of the Finzi-Continis* is linked to Cocteau's reckless adolescents, just as the atmosphere of the youth-filled summer garden is, inevitably, Proustian.

Though Dominique Sanda's face is that of a perverse goddess, it isn't very expressive, but she has a great slouch, and if she stalks around her castle looking maybe a little more opaque than is absolutely necessary, she is nevertheless wonderfully *remote*—which is what Micòl is meant to be, since Giorgio and we never get to understand her. This novelistic approach is not, however, totally satisfying on the screen. De Sica's neo-realist films were dramatically structured so that we grasped everything there was to understand in the situation; here our point of view is Giorgio's—which is tentative, slightly bewildered. We want to perceive more than Giorgio does; we want to understand Micòl even if he doesn't. And at this level I think De Sica's fidelity to the novel becomes a limitation. Obviously, the author, looking back on the time, is fascinated by the Jewish landed gentry and their paralysis of will; the movie records Mussolini's small oppressive edicts—the gradual loss of rights—and we know where it will end. But we Americans have an aversion to watching people drift to destruction; many young Americans were furious at the suicide of the lovers in *Elvira Madigan*, and I believe they may also get angry at Micòl, lazing around putting on the same record year after year and dressing up. We want to know: Why don't they do something? But this is the elusive part of the story, which I'm afraid we must take as the given in this movie, just as the suicide was the given in *Elvira Madigan*. The fact is that these people didn't save themselves. What's unsatisfying is in the nature of the material—that it's auto-biographical and historical and rather precious, and that it's a minor novel when we want the insights and explanations that a major novelist could give us. A major novelist solves the mysteries for us; Bassani dwells on what he doesn't understand. You feel that the author is more involved in his own responses—in his own style—than in the subject. And that might be a definition of decadence. It is what links Giorgio Bassani to Micòl and pale Alberto and to Cocteau's gorgeously corrupt children and to the ancestral super-elegant tribe of *The Green Hat*. This is not the highest form of art, but, as it happens, the movies of *The Garden of the Finzi-Continis* and *Les Enfants Terribles* are, in different ways, quite marvellous, and Garbo has never been more extraordinary than in *A Woman of Affairs*. In their own terms, these movies are honest. *The Go-Between* pretends to be an attack on decadence, and the style of the movie gives it the lie; these movies openly love their spoiled beautiful people.

André Bazin was right when he said that De Sica drew his art from his understanding of his subjects, and it's a happy coincidence that Bazin's supremely perceptive essays on him should be available in English for the first time—in Volume II of *What Is Cinema?*—just when *The Garden of the Finzi-Continis*, which might be an illustration of his thesis, is opening. I think the only disappointment in the film is that Vittorio De Sica is a major film artist translating to the screen a minor novel. It has provided him with his finest subject in many years, but, except in a few moments of faultless intuition, he can't transcend it. The novel is not one of those sprawling second-rate novels that a movie director can use as a skeleton; it is a true minor novel, unmistakably slender. There was no way, I think, for De Sica to give it more body—to provide a fuller psychology and a richer social context—without destroying the mysteriously lyric quality of Bassani's memories.

There is an instant toward the end that is, however, purest De Sica. When the Finzi-Continis have been arrested, Micòl and her grandmother are herded into a room with other Jews from the town, and the bewildered old lady tries to smile sociably and keep her composure. The anxious face of the dignified old lady, who a moment later crumples in tears on her granddaughter's shoulder, is one of those faces lit from within by the director's love. And at the end there is a daring stroke that raises the movie above itself: we are not shown the gas chambers, but we hear a great, full-throated cantor singing a lament for the dead, and the lament brings to earth the melancholy glamour of the Finzi-Continis.

{*The New Yorker*, December 18, 1971}

:: Stanley Strangelove

Literal-minded in its sex and brutality, Teutonic in its humor, Stanley Kubrick's *A Clockwork Orange* might be the work of a strict and exacting German professor who set out to make a porno-violent sci-fi comedy. Is there anything sadder—and ultimately more repellent—than a clean-minded pornographer? The numerous rapes and beatings have no ferocity and no sensuality; they're frigidly, pedantically calculated, and because there is no motivating emotion, the viewer may experience them as an indignity and wish to leave. The movie follows the Anthony Burgess novel so closely that the book might have served as the script, yet that thick-skulled German professor may be Dr. Strangelove himself, because the meanings are turned around.

Burgess's 1962 novel is set in a vaguely Socialist future (roughly, the late seventies or early eighties)—a dreary, routinized England that roving gangs of teen-age thugs terrorize at night. In perceiving the amoral destructive potential of youth gangs, Burgess's ironic fable differs from Orwell's *1984* in a way that already seems prophetically accurate. The novel is narrated by the leader of one of these gangs—Alex, a conscienceless schoolboy sadist—and, in a witty, extraordinarily sustained literary conceit, narrated in his own slang (Nadsat, the teen-agers' special dialect). The book is a fast read; Burgess, a composer turned novelist, has an ebullient, musical sense of language, and you pick up the meanings of the strange words as the prose rhythms speed you along. Alex enjoys stealing, stomping, raping, and destroying until he kills a woman and is sent to prison for fourteen years. After serving two, he arranges to get out by submitting to an experiment in conditioning, and he is turned into a moral robot who becomes nauseated at thoughts of sex and violence. Released when he is harmless, he falls prey to his former victims, who beat him and torment him until he attempts suicide. This leads to criticism of the government that robotized him—turned him into a clockwork orange—and he is deconditioned, becoming once again a thug, and now at loose and triumphant. The ironies are protean, but Burgess is clearly a humanist; his point of view is that of a Christian horrified by the possibilities of a society turned clockwork orange, in which life is so mechanized that men lose their capacity for moral choice. There seems to be no way in this boring, dehumanizing society for the boys to release their energies except in vandalism and crime; they do what they do as a matter of course. Alex the sadist is as mechanized a creature as Alex the good.

Stanley Kubrick's Alex (Malcolm McDowell) is not so much an expression of how this society has lost its soul as he is a force pitted against the society, and by making the victims of the thugs more repulsive and contemptible than the thugs Kubrick has learned to love the punk sadist. The end is no longer the ironic triumph of a mechanized punk but a real triumph. Alex is the only likable person we see—his cynical bravado suggests a broad-nosed, working-class Olivier—and the movie puts us on his side. Alex, who gets kicks out of violence, is more alive than anybody else in the movie, and younger and more attractive, and McDowell plays him exuberantly, with the power and slyness of a young Cagney. Despite what Alex does at the beginning, McDowell makes you root for his foxiness, for his crookedness. For most of the movie, we see him tortured and beaten and humiliated, so when his bold, aggressive punk's nature is restored to him it seems not a joke on all of us but, rather, a victory in which we share, and Kubrick takes an exultant tone. The look in Alex's eyes at the end tells us that he isn't just a mechanized, choiceless sadist but prefers sadism and knows he can get by with it. Far from being a little parable about the dangers of soullessness and the horrors of force, whether employed by individuals against each other or by society in "conditioning," the movie becomes a vindication of Alex, saying that the punk was a free human being and only the good Alex was a robot.

The trick of making the attacked less human than their attackers, so you feel no sympathy for them, is, I think, symptomatic of a new attitude in movies. This attitude says there's no moral difference. Stanley Kubrick has assumed the deformed, self-righteous perspective of a vicious young punk who says, "Everything's rotten. Why shouldn't I do what I want?

They're worse than I am." In the new mood (perhaps movies in their cumulative effect are partly responsible for it), people want to believe the hyperbolic worst, want to believe in the degradation of the victims—that they are dupes and phonies and weaklings. I can't accept that Kubrick is merely reflecting this post-assassinations, post-Manson mood; I think he's catering to it. I think he wants to dig it.

This picture plays with violence in an intellectually seductive way. And though it has no depth, it's done in such a slow, heavy style that those prepared to like it can treat its puzzling aspects as oracular. It can easily be construed as an ambiguous mystery play, a visionary warning against "the Establishment." There are a million ways to justify identifying with Alex: Alex is fighting repression; he's alone against the system. What he does isn't nearly as bad as what the government does (both in the movie and in the United States now). Why shouldn't he be violent? That's all the Establishment has ever taught him (and us) to be. The point of the book was that we must be as men, that we must be able to take responsibility for what we are. The point of the movie is much more *au courant*. Kubrick has removed many of the obstacles to our identifying with Alex; the Alex of the book has had his personal habits cleaned up a bit—his fondness for squishing small animals under his tires, his taste for ten-year-old girls, his beating up of other prisoners, and so on. And Kubrick aids the identification with Alex by small directorial choices throughout. The writer whom Alex cripples (Patrick Magee) and the woman he kills are cartoon nasties with upper-class accents a mile wide. (Magee has been encouraged to act like a bathetic madman; he seems to be preparing for a career in horror movies.) Burgess gave us society through Alex's eyes, and so the vision was deformed, and Kubrick, carrying over from *Dr. Strangelove* his joky adolescent view of hypocritical, sexually dirty authority figures and extending it to all adults, has added an extra layer of deformity. The "straight" people are far more twisted than Alex; they seem inhuman and incapable of suffering. He alone suffers. And how he suffers! He's a male Little Nell—screaming in a straitjacket during the brainwashing; sweet and helpless when rejected by his parents; alone, weeping, on a bridge; beaten, bleeding, lost in a rainstorm; pounding his head on a floor and crying for death. Kubrick pours on the hearts and flowers; what is done to Alex is far worse than what Alex has done, so society itself can be felt to justify Alex's hoodlumism.

The movie's confusing—and, finally, corrupt—morality is not, however, what makes it such an abhorrent viewing experience. It is offensive long before one perceives where it is heading, because it has no shadings. Kubrick, a director with an arctic spirit, is determined to be pornographic, and he has no talent for it. In *Los Olvidados*, Buñuel showed teen-agers committing horrible brutalities, and even though you had no illusions about their victims—one, in particular, was a foul old lecher—you were appalled. Buñuel makes you understand the pornography of brutality: the pornography is in what human beings are capable of doing to other human beings. Kubrick has always been one of the least sensual and least erotic of directors, and his attempts here at phallic humor are like a professor's lead balloons. He tries to work up kicky violent scenes, carefully estranging you from the victims so that you can *enjoy* the rapes and beatings. But I think one is more likely to feel cold antipathy toward the movie than horror at the violence—or enjoyment of it, either.

Kubrick's martinet control is obvious in the terrible performances he gets from everybody but McDowell, and in the inexorable pacing. The film has a distinctive style of estrangement: gloating closeups, bright, hard-edge, third-degree lighting, and abnormally loud voices. It's a style, all right—the movie doesn't look like other movies, or sound like them—but it's a leering, portentous style. After the balletic brawling of the teen-age gangs, with bodies flying as in a Western saloon fight, and after the gang-bang of the writer's wife and an orgy in speeded-up motion, you're primed for more action, but you're left stranded in the prison sections, trying to find some humor in tired schoolboy jokes about a Hitlerian guard. The movie retains a little of the slangy Nadsat but none of the fast rhythms of Burgess's prose, and so the dialect seems much more arch than it does in the book. Many of the dialogue sequences go on and on, into a stupor of inactivity. Kubrick seems infatuated with the hypnotic possibilities of static setups; at times you feel as if you were trapped in front of the frames of a comic strip for a numbing ten minutes per frame. When Alex's correctional officer visits his home and he and Alex sit on a bed, the camera sits on the two of them. When Alex comes home from prison, his parents and the lodger who has displaced him are in the living room; Alex appeals to his seated, unloving parents for an inert eternity. Long after we've got the point, the composition is still telling us to appreciate its cleverness. This ponderous technique is hardly leavened by the structural use of classical music to characterize the sequences; each sequence is scored to Purcell (synthesized on a Moog), Rossini, or Beethoven, while Elgar and others are used for brief satiric effects. In the book, the doctor who has devised the conditioning treatment explains why the horror images used in it are set to music: "It's a useful emotional heightener." But the whole damned movie is heightened this way; yes, the music is effective, but the effect is self-important.

When I pass a newsstand and see the saintly, bearded, intellectual Kubrick on the cover of *Saturday Review*, I wonder: Do people notice things like the way Kubrick cuts to the rival teen-age gang before Alex and his hoods arrive to fight them, just so we can have the pleasure of watching that gang strip the struggling girl they mean to rape? Alex's voice is on the track announcing his arrival, but Kubrick can't wait for Alex to arrive, because then he couldn't show us as much. That girl is stripped for our benefit; it's the purest exploitation. Yet this film lusts for greatness, and I'm not sure that Kubrick knows how to make simple movies anymore, or that he cares to, either. I don't know how consciously he has thrown this film to youth; maybe he's more of a showman than he lets on — a lucky showman with opportunism built into the cells of his body. The film can work at a pop-fantasy level for a young audience already prepared to accept Alex's view of the society, ready to believe that that's how it is.

At the movies, we are gradually being conditioned to accept violence as a sensual pleasure. The directors used to say they were showing us its real face and how ugly it was in order to sensitize us to its horrors. You don't have to be very keen to see that they are now in fact desensitizing us. They are saying that everyone is brutal, and the heroes must be as brutal as the villains or they turn into fools. There seems to be an assumption that if you're offended by movie brutality, you are somehow playing into the hands of the people who want censorship. But this would deny those of us who don't believe in censorship the use of the only counterbalance: the freedom of the press to say that there's anything conceivably damaging in these films — the freedom to analyze their implications. If we don't use this critical freedom, we are implicitly saying that no brutality is too much for us — that only squares and people who believe in censorship are concerned with brutality. Actually, those who believe in censorship are primarily concerned with sex, and they generally worry about violence only when it's eroticized. This means that practically no one raises the issue of the possible cumulative effects of movie brutality. Yet surely, when night after night atrocities are served up to us as entertainment, it's worth some anxiety. We become clockwork oranges if we accept all this pop culture without asking what's in it. How can people go on talking about the dazzling brilliance of movies and not notice that the directors are sucking up to the thugs in the audience?

{*The New Yorker*, January 1, 1972}

:: Alchemy

If ever there was a great example of how the best popular movies come out of a merger of commerce and art, *The Godfather* is it. The movie starts from a trash novel that is generally considered gripping and compulsively readable, though (maybe because movies more than satisfy my appetite for trash) I found it unreadable. You're told who and what the characters are in a few pungent, punchy sentences, and that's all they are. You're briefed on their backgrounds and sex lives in a flashy anecdote or two, and the author moves on, from nugget to nugget. Mario Puzo has a reputation as a good writer, so his potboiler was treated as if it were special, and not in the Irving Wallace–Harold Robbins class, to which, by its itch and hype and juicy *roman-à-clef* treatment, it plainly belongs. What would this school of fiction do without Porfirio Rubirosa, Judy Garland, James Aubrey, Howard Hughes, and Frank Sinatra? The novel *The Godfather*, financed by Paramount during its writing, features a Sinatra stereotype, and sex and slaughter, and little gobbets of trouble and heartbreak. It's gripping, maybe, in the same sense that Spiro Agnew's speeches were a few years back. Francis Ford Coppola, who directed the film, and wrote the script with Puzo, has stayed very close to the book's greased-lightning sensationalism and yet has made a movie with the spaciousness and strength that popular novels such as Dickens' used to have. With the slop and sex reduced and the whoremongering guess-who material minimized ("Nino," who sings with a highball in his hand, has been weeded out), the movie bears little relationship to other adaptations of books of this kind, such as *The Carpetbaggers* and *The Adventurers*. Puzo provided what Coppola needed: a storyteller's outpouring of incidents and details to choose from, the folklore behind the headlines, heat and immediacy, the richly familiar. And Puzo's shameless turn-on probably left Coppola looser than if he had been dealing with a better book; he could not have been cramped by worries about how best to convey its style. Puzo, who admits he was out to make money, wrote "below my gifts," as he puts it, and one must agree. Coppola uses his gifts to reverse the process — to give the public the best a moviemaker can do with this very raw material. Coppola, a young director who has never had a big hit, may have done the movie for money, as *he* claims — in order to make the pictures he really wants to make, he says — but this picture was made at peak capacity. He has salvaged Puzo's energy and lent the narrative dignity. Given the circumstances and the rush to complete the film and bring it to market, Coppola has not only done his best but pushed himself farther than he may realize. The movie is on the heroic scale of earlier pictures on broad themes, such as *On the Waterfront*, *From Here to Eternity*, and *The Nun's Story*. It offers a wide, startlingly vivid view of a Mafia dynasty. The abundance is from the book; the quality of feeling is Coppola's.

The beginning is set late in the summer of 1945; the film's roots, however, are in the gangster films of the early thirties. The plot is still about rival gangs murdering each other, but now we see the system of patronage and terror, in which killing is a way of dealing with the competition. We see how the racketeering tribes encroach on each other and why this form of illegal business inevitably erupts in violence. We see the ethnic subculture, based on a split between the men's conception of their responsibilities — all that they keep dark — and the sunny false Eden in which they try to shelter the women and children. The thirties films indicated some of this, but *The Godfather* gets into it at the primary level; the willingness to be basic and the attempt to understand the basic, to look at it without the usual preconceptions, are what give this picture its epic strength.

The visual scheme is based on the most obvious life-and-death contrasts; the men meet and conduct their business in deep-toned, shuttered rooms, lighted by lamps even in the daytime, and the story moves back and forth between this hidden, nocturnal world and the sunshine that they share with the women and children. The tension is in the meetings in the underworld darkness; one gets the sense that this secret life has its own poetry of fear, more real to the men (and perhaps to the excluded women also) than the sunlight world outside. The dark-and-light contrast is so operatic and so openly symbolic that it perfectly expresses the basic nature of the material. The contrast is integral to the Catholic background of the characters: innocence versus knowledge—knowledge in this sense being the same as guilt. It works as a visual style, because the Goyaesque shadings of dark brown into black in the interiors suggest (no matter how irrationally) an earlier period of history, while the sunny, soft-edge garden scenes have their own calendar-pretty pastness. Nino Rota's score uses old popular songs to cue the varying moods, and at one climactic point swells in a crescendo that is both Italian opera and pure-forties movie music. There are rash, foolish acts in the movie but no acts of individual bravery. The killing, connived at in the darkness, is the secret horror, and it surfaces in one bloody outburst after another. It surfaces so often that after a while it doesn't surprise us, and the recognition that the killing is an integral part of business policy takes us a long way from the fantasy outlaws of old movies. These gangsters don't satisfy our adventurous fantasies of disobeying the law; they're not defiant, they're furtive and submissive. They are required to be more obedient than we are; they live by taking orders. There is no one on the screen we can identify with—unless we take a fancy to the pearly teeth of one shark in a pool of sharks.

Even when the plot strands go slack about two-thirds of the way through, and the passage of a few years leaves us in doubt whether certain actions have been concluded or postponed, the picture doesn't become softheaded. The direction is tenaciously intelligent. Coppola holds on and pulls it all together. The trash novel is there underneath, but he attempts to draw the patterns out of the particulars. It's amazing how encompassing the view seems to be—what a sense you get of a broad historical perspective, considering that the span is only from 1945 to the mid-fifties, at which time the Corleone family, already forced by competitive pressures into dealing in narcotics, is moving its base of operations to Las Vegas.

The enormous cast is headed by Marlon Brando as Don Vito Corleone, the "godfather" of a powerful Sicilian-American clan, with James Caan as his hothead son, Sonny, and Al Pacino as the thoughtful, educated son, Michael. Is Brando marvellous? Yes, he is, but then he often is; he was marvellous a few years ago in *Reflections in a Golden Eye*, and he's shockingly effective as a working-class sadist in a current film, *The Nightcomers*, though the film itself isn't worth seeing. The role of Don Vito—a patriarch in his early sixties—allows him to release more of the gentleness that was so seductive and unsettling in his braggart roles. Don Vito could be played as a magnificent old warrior, a noble killer, a handsome bull-patriarch, but Brando manages to debanalize him. It's typical of Brando's daring that he doesn't capitalize on his broken-prow profile and the massive, sculptural head that has become the head of Rodin's Balzac—he doesn't play for statuesque nobility. The light, cracked voice comes out of a twisted mouth and clenched teeth; he has the battered face of a devious, combative old man, and a pugnacious thrust to his jaw. The rasp in his voice is particularly effective after Don Vito has been wounded; one almost feels that the bullets cracked it, and wishes it hadn't been cracked before. Brando interiorizes Don Vito's power, makes him less physically threatening and *deeper*, hidden within himself.

Brando's acting has mellowed in recent years; it is less immediately exciting than it used to be, because there's not the sudden, violent discharge of emotion. His effects are subtler, less showy, and he gives himself over to the material. He appears to have worked his way beyond the self-parody that was turning him into a comic, and that sometimes left the other performers dangling and laid bare the script. He has not acquired the polish of most famous actors; just the opposite—less mannered as he grows older, he seems to draw directly from life, and from himself. His Don is a primitive sacred monster, and the more powerful because he suggests not the strapping sacred monsters of movies (like Anthony Quinn) but actual ones—those old men who carry never-ending grudges and ancient hatreds inside a frail frame, those monsters who remember minute details of old business deals when they can no longer tie their shoelaces. No one has aged better on camera than Brando; he gradually takes Don Vito to the close of his life, when he moves into the sunshine world, a sleepy monster, near to innocence again. The character is all echoes and shadings, and no noise; his strength is in that armor of quiet. Brando has lent Don Vito some of his own mysterious, courtly reserve: the character is not explained; we simply assent to him and believe that, yes, he could become a king of the underworld. Brando doesn't dominate the movie, yet he gives the story the legendary presence needed to raise it above gang warfare to archetypal tribal warfare.

Brando isn't the whole show; James Caan is very fine, and so are Robert Duvall and many others in lesser roles. Don Vito's sons suggest different aspects of Brando—Caan's Sonny looks like the muscular young Brando but without the redeeming intuitiveness, while as the heir, Michael,

Al Pacino comes to resemble him in manner and voice. Pacino creates a quiet, ominous space around himself; his performance—which is marvellous, too, big yet without ostentation—complements Brando's. Like Brando in this film, Pacino is simple; you don't catch him acting, yet he manages to change from a small, fresh-faced, darkly handsome college boy into an underworld lord, becoming more intense, smaller, and more isolated at every step. Coppola doesn't stress the father-and-son links; they are simply there for us to notice when we will. Michael becomes like his father mostly from the inside, but we also get to see how his father's face was formed (Michael's mouth gets crooked and his cheeks jowly, like his father's, after his jaw has been smashed). Pacino has an unusual gift for conveying the divided spirit of a man whose calculations often go against his inclinations. When Michael, warned that at a certain point he must come out shooting, delays, we are left to sense his mixed feelings. As his calculations will always win out, we can see that he will never be at peace. The director levels with almost everybody in the movie. The women's complicity in their husbands' activities is kept ambiguous, but it's naggingly there—you can't quite ignore it. And Coppola doesn't make the subsidiary characters lovable; we look at Clemenza (Richard Castellano) as objectively when he is cooking spaghetti as we do when he is garrotting a former associate. Many of the actors (and the incidents) carry the resonances of earlier gangster pictures, so that we almost unconsciously place them in the prehistory of this movie. Castellano, with his resemblance to Al Capone and Edward G. Robinson (plus a vagrant streak of Oscar Levant), belongs in this atmosphere; so does Richard Conte (as Barzini), who appeared in many of the predecessors of this movie, including *House of Strangers*, though perhaps Al Lettieri (as Sollozzo) acts too much like a B-picture hood. And perhaps the director goes off key when Sonny is blasted and blood-splattered at a toll booth; the effect is too garish.

The people dress in character and live in character—with just the gewgaws that seem right for them. The period details are there—a satin pillow, a modernistic apartment-house lobby, a child's pasted-together greeting to Grandpa—but Coppola doesn't turn the viewer into a guided tourist, told what to see. Nor does he go in for a lot of closeups, which are the simplest tool for fixing a director's attitude. Diane Keaton (who plays Michael's girl friend) is seen casually; her attractiveness isn't labored. The only character who is held in frame for us to see exactly as the character looking at her sees her is Apollonia (played by Simonetta Stefanelli), whom Michael falls in love with in Sicily. She is fixed by the camera as a ripe erotic image, because that is what she means to him, and Coppola, not having wasted his resources, can do it in a few frames. In general, he tries not to fix the images. In *Sunday Bloody Sunday*, John Schlesinger showed a messy knocked-over ashtray being picked up in closeup, so that there was nothing to perceive in the shot but the significance of the messiness. Coppola, I think, would have kept the camera on the room in which the woman bent over to retrieve the ashtray, and the messiness would have been just one element among many to be observed—perhaps the curve of her body could have told us much more than the actual picking-up motion. *The Godfather* keeps so much in front of us all the time that we're never bored (though the picture runs just two minutes short of three hours)—we keep taking things in. This is a heritage from Jean Renoir—this uncoercive, "open" approach to the movie frame. Like Renoir, Coppola lets the spectator roam around in the images, lets a movie breathe, and this is extremely difficult in a period film, in which every detail must be carefully planted. But the details never look planted: you're a few minutes into the movie before you're fully conscious that it's set in the past.

When one considers the different rates at which people read, it's miraculous that films can ever solve the problem of a pace at which audiences can "read" a film together. A hack director solves the problem of pacing by making only a few points and making those so emphatically that the audience can hardly help getting them (this is why many of the movies from the studio-system days are unspeakably insulting); the tendency of a clever, careless director is to go too fast, assuming that he's made everything clear when he hasn't, and leaving the audience behind. When a film has as much novelistic detail as this one, the problem might seem to be almost insuperable. Yet, full as it is, *The Godfather* goes by evenly, so we don't feel rushed, or restless, either; there's classic grandeur to the narrative flow. But Coppola's attitudes are specifically modern—more so than in many films with a more jagged surface. Renoir's openness is an expression of an almost pagan love of people and landscape; his style is an embrace. Coppola's openness is a reflection of an exploratory sense of complexity; he doesn't feel the need to comment on what he shows us, and he doesn't want to reduce the meanings in a shot by pushing us this way or that. The assumption behind this film is that complexity will engage the audience.

These gangsters *like* their life style, while we—seeing it from the outside—are appalled. If the movie gangster once did represent, as Robert Warshow suggested in the late forties, "what we want to be and what we are afraid we may become," if he expressed "that part of the American psyche which rejects the qualities and the demands of modern life, which rejects 'Americanism' itself," that was the attitude of another era. In *The Godfather* we see organized crime as an obscene symbolic extension of free enterprise and government policy, an extension of the worst in America— its feudal ruthlessness. Organized crime is not a rejection of Americanism, it's what we fear Americanism to be. It's our nightmare of the American system. When "Americanism" was a form of cheerful, bland official optimism, the gangster used to be destroyed at the end of the movie and our feelings resolved. Now the mood of the whole country has darkened, guiltily; nothing is resolved at the end of *The Godfather*, because the family business goes on. Terry Malloy didn't clean up the docks at the end of *On the Waterfront*; that was a lie. *The Godfather* is popular melodrama, but it expresses a new tragic realism.

{*The New Yorker*, March 18, 1972}

:: Collaboration and Resistance

Inexplicably, despite everything—the suicidal practices of the film industry, the defeat of many people of talent, the financial squeeze here and abroad—this has been a legendary period in movies. Just since last March: *The Conformist, McCabe & Mrs. Miller, Sunday Bloody Sunday, The Last Picture Show, Fiddler on the Roof, Murmur of the Heart, The Garden of the Finzi-Continis, Cabaret, The Godfather,* and, of course, the films one may have major reservations about—the smash-bang cops-and-robbers *The French Connection* and the controversial *A Clockwork Orange* and *Straw Dogs.* In addition: Jane Fonda's portrait of a call girl in *Klute,* George Segal's wild, comic hustling junkie in *Born to Win,* George C. Scott's bravura hamminess in *The Hospital,* the documentary-style *Derby,* the childishly primitive, touching, messed-up *Billy Jack,* the casually diverting *Skin Game,* and the comedies *Bananas* and *Made for Each Other.* A reviewer could hardly ask for more from any art, high or popular, and that list shows how far movies have gone in blurring the distinction. And now *The Sorrow and the Pity,* a documentary epic on the themes of collaboration and resistance.

The Hollywood war movies were propaganda for our side, and put us in the comfortable position of identifying with the heroic anti-Nazis. *The Sorrow and the Pity* makes us ask what we and our friends and families would actually have done if our country had been invaded, like France. Wartime France presents one of the most intricately balanced moral dilemmas imaginable, since, of all the countries occupied by the Nazis, the French were the only people to cave in and support a regime (the Pétain government, with its capital in Vichy) that actively collaborated with Hitler. That fact has been buried from sight in France, and a legend of national heroism has been officially encouraged; the government decided that the public was "not yet mature enough" to see this film on television. "Myths," according to the Gaullist official who made the decision, "are important in the life of a people. Certain myths must not be destroyed."

The Sorrow and the Pity is both oral history and essay: people who lived through the German occupation tell us what they did during that catastrophic period, and we see and hear evidence that corroborates or corrects or sometimes flatly contradicts them. A good portion of the material is no more than informed, intelligent television interviewing; what makes the film innovative is the immediate annotation of what has just been said, and the steady accumulation of perspectives and information. As the perspectives ramify—when we see the people as they are now and, in old snapshots and newsreel footage, as they were then—we begin to get a sense of living in history: a fuller sense of what it was like to participate in the moral drama of an occupied nation than we have ever before had. When history literally becomes the story of people's lives, we can't help but feel the continuity of those lives and our own. There's nothing comparable to *The Sorrow and the Pity*. Yet the director, Marcel Ophuls, didn't need to invent a new kind of mirror to hold up to us; all he needed to do was to hold up the old mirrors at different angles.

The Second World War was heavily recorded on film, and Ophuls draws upon newsreels from several countries and also upon propaganda shorts designed to educate and inspire the citizenry. The bits are fresh—selected, it might almost seem at first, to make marginal points; even those of us who know that period on film haven't seen much of this material. A piece of Nazi newsreel shows captured black troops from the French Army as evidence of France's racial decadence; another bit, on how to recognize a Jew, shows a collection of photos, including a glimpse of an infamous poster of Ernst Lubitsch—which, it is said, broke his heart when he realized he was being used as the model of Jewish bestiality. Pétain, visiting a schoolroom, talking high-mindedly, is the model of rectitude. There are fragments that in context gain a new meaning: the viciousness of shaving the heads of the women who had slept with Germans is horrible enough without the added recognition that probably those who did the shaving had spiritually slept with the Germans themselves. Ophuls sustains a constant ironic interplay between the old film clips and the interviews with those who gave orders, those who took orders, those who suffered and survived, and those who went on as before. The period (1940–44) is so recently past that it's still possible to delve into the psychology of history: *The Sorrow and the Pity* is about the effects of character upon political action.

It's one of the most demanding movies ever made—four hours and twenty minutes of concentrated attention. Narration, titles, voice-over translations that finish quickly so you can hear the actual voices in their own languages—Ophuls employs a variety of devices to get the data to the audience, and he tries to be aboveboard, as in the matter of the voices. (You can decide for yourself whether the dubber misrepresents the person's character.) You really process information, and doing so makes you aware of how falsely the phrase is applied to the unconscious soaking up of TV commercials and banalities. You experience the elation of using your mind—of evaluating the material, and perceiving how it's all developing, while you're storing it up. There's a point of view, but judgments are left to you, and you know that Ophuls is reasonable and fairminded, and trying to do justice to a great subject: how and why the French accepted Nazism, and then rejected what they had done, so that it was lost even from public memory. The Occupation has long been demythologized in print, and this film does not attempt to replace the printed studies; it does something different. On film it's possible to incorporate the historian's process of research—to show us the witnesses and the participants, so that we are put in the position of the investigators, seeing what they see and trying to frame some conclusions. Inevitably, the picture gets better as it goes along: the more we have to work with, the more complex our own reactions become. There's grace in Ophuls' method; he helps us to see that the issues go way beyond conventional ideas of assessing guilt—that the mysteries of human behavior in the film are true mysteries.

The cast is made up of the known, such as Pierre Mendès-France, Georges Bidault, Anthony Eden, and Albert Speer, and the unknown, who are principally from the small industrial city of Clermont-Ferrand, which the movie focusses on. Clermont-Ferrand is near Vichy and was the home base of Pierre Laval, and it is in the Auvergne, which was one of the centers of the Resistance. Those interviewed are, in their own terms, articulate and clearheaded, and are at their ease; *no one* appears to feel any guilt about past conduct. Whatever they did, they have, from what we can see, made their peace with themselves, though an upper-class Frenchman who fought alongside the Nazis in Russia appears to be almost in mourning for his duped and wasted youth. Some are less reflective and more open than we could have expected: Pétain's Minister of Youth discusses his morale-building among French children; a former Wehrmacht captain who was stationed in Clermont-Ferrand defends his right to wear his war decorations. From England, Anthony Eden, who used to look weak and foolish, suggests that anyone who did not live under the Occupation cannot judge the French. He comments on those days with great dignity and humanity: who would have expected him to age so intelligently? The heroes of the Resistance are the most unlikely people—stubborn, rebellious "misfits": a genial, though formidable, farmer, a bohemian aristocrat who at one time smoked opium, a diffident homosexual who became a British agent in France in order, he says, to prove that he was as brave as other men. They're not like the fake heroes in Hollywood's anti-Nazi movies, and they're impossible for us to project onto: we would be diminishing them if we tried. People who suffered tell stories of iniquities that we can scarcely bear to hear; others remember nothing, selectively. One man saw no Nazis and doesn't believe Clermont-Ferrand was occupied.

Were the French perhaps so passive in the Second World War because they were still depleted by their courage and sacrifices in the First World War? All sorts of speculative questions come to mind, and there are aspects of what happened in France in the early forties that I wish the film had clarified; for example, that the Germans had taken two million French prisoners of war, and that the promise of liberating these prisoners was a factor in encouraging France to fill its industrial quotas. Still . . . the French coöperation was peerless. The picture neglects to point out that the French Communists, serving the interests of Russian foreign policy (it was during the period of the Hitler-Soviet pact), were collaborationists until Hitler invaded Russia. But then the movie doesn't go into the close ties between the Catholic Church and the Vichy government, either. There are probably countless areas in which specialists would ask for more emphasis or greater detail, but that is true of almost any written work of history, and such works do not provide the psychological understanding that this film does.

We see that those who were inactive were not necessarily indifferent to the suffering of others: a sane, prosperous pharmacist sits, surrounded by his handsome children, and, without attempting to deny knowledge of what was going on, tells his reasons for remaining apolitical. They're not bad reasons—and who could call a man a coward for not having the crazy, aberrant nobility it takes to risk his life (and maybe his family)? (It's especially difficult for a woman to pass judgment, since women are traditionally exempted from accusations of cowardice. For most women, the risk of being separated from their children is a sufficient deterrent from any dangerous political acts, and who considers them immoral for that, even though they constitute a huge body of the docile and fearful?) It's only when you think of a country full of decent, reasonable people with such good reasons that you experience revulsion. The inactive, like the pharmacist, and the actual collaborators are easily accessible to the camera—perhaps more so than the resisters, because there is something special about the nature of intransigence, and maybe for that we need a literary or dramatic artist rather than a documentarian. But this film goes very far in bringing those approaches together. There may be a streak of romanticism in the way Ophuls leads us to the theory that only loners and black sheep—and workers and youth—are free enough to resist authority; I wasn't convinced, but I was charmed. I would like to know more of Louis Grave, the Maquis farmer who was betrayed by a neighbor and sent to Buchenwald: what formed this man that makes him so solid and contained, so beautifully rooted? When he tells about an old German's slipping him an apple when he was starving, you know that "documentary" has no boundaries. Louis Grave and his apple might be out of *Grand Illusion*, while Maurice Chevalier singing away becomes a little like the m.c. in *Cabaret*. We enjoy him, yet his entertainer's soul is perplexing; there's an element of the macabre in his good cheer. A German comedian entertaining troops and straining for laughs has that same macabre gaiety—the emblem of show business—but he's coarser (and German), and so less troubling. Chevalier's recurrent presence gives the film a lilt of satirical ambiguity.

It was in France during the Occupation that Simone Weil wrote, "Nothing is so rare as to see misfortune fairly portrayed. The tendency is either to treat the unfortunate person as though catastrophe were his natural vocation or to ignore the effects of misfortune on the soul; to assume, that is, that the soul can suffer and remain unmarked by it—can fail, in fact, to be recast in misfortune's image." She was writing about the *Iliad*, but she was writing about it because the Nazis, like the Greek and Trojan warriors, were modifying the human spirit by the use of force. It is the highest praise I can offer *The Sorrow and the Pity* to say that in it misfortune *is* fairly portrayed. One is left with the question of whether (and how much) the French really have been marked—in the long run—by the Nazi experience.

:: Tango

Bernardo Bertolucci's *Last Tango in Paris* was presented for the first time on the closing night of the New York Film Festival, October 14, 1972; that date should become a landmark in movie history comparable to May 29, 1913—the night *Le Sacre du Printemps* was first performed—in music history. There was no riot, and no one threw anything at the screen, but I think it's fair to say that the audience was in a state of shock, because *Last Tango in Paris* has the same kind of hypnotic excitement as the *Sacre*, the same primitive force, and the same thrusting, jabbing eroticism. The movie breakthrough has finally come. Exploitation films have been supplying mechanized sex—sex as physical stimulant but without any passion or emotional violence. The sex in *Last Tango in Paris* expresses the characters' drives. Marlon Brando, as Paul, is working out his aggression on Jeanne (Maria Schneider), and the physical menace of sexuality that is emotionally charged is such a departure from everything we've come to expect at the movies that there was something almost like fear in the atmosphere of the party in the lobby that followed the screening. Carried along by the sustained excitement of the movie, the audience had given Bertolucci an ovation, but afterward, as individuals, they were quiet. This must be the most powerfully erotic movie ever made, and it may turn out to be the most liberating movie ever made, and so it's probably only natural that an audience, anticipating a voluptuous feast from the man who made *The Conformist*, and confronted with this unexpected sexuality and the new realism it requires of the actors, should go into shock. Bertolucci and Brando have altered the face of an art form. Who was prepared for that?

Many of us had expected eroticism to come to the movies, and some of us had even guessed that it might come from Bertolucci, because he seemed to have the elegance and the richness and the sensuality to make lushly erotic movies. But I think those of us who had speculated about erotic movies had tended to think of them in terms of Terry Southern's deliriously comic novel on the subject, *Blue Movie*; we had expected *artistic* blue movies, talented directors taking over from the *Shlockmeisters* and making sophisticated voyeuristic fantasies that would be gorgeous fun—a real turn-on. What nobody had talked about was a sex film that would churn up everybody's emotions. Bertolucci shows his masterly elegance in *Last Tango in Paris*, but he also reveals a master's substance.

The script (which Bertolucci wrote with Franco Arcalli) is in French and English; it centers on a man's attempt to separate sex from everything else. When his wife commits suicide, Paul, an American living in Paris, tries to get away from his life. He goes to look at an empty flat and meets Jeanne, who is also looking at it. They have sex in an empty room, without knowing anything about each other—not even first names. He rents the flat, and for three days they meet there. She wants to know who he is, but he insists that sex is all that matters. We see both of them (as they don't see each other) in their normal lives—Paul back at the flophouse-hotel his wife owned, Jeanne with her mother, the widow of a colonel, and with her adoring fiancé (Jean-Pierre Léaud), a TV director, who is relentlessly shooting a sixteen-millimeter film about her, a film that is to end in a week with their wedding. Mostly, we see Paul and Jeanne together in the flat as they act out his fantasy of ignorant armies clashing by night, and it *is* warfare—sexual aggression and retreat and battles joined.

The necessity for isolation from the world is, of course, his, not hers. But his life floods in. He brings into this isolation chamber his sexual anger, his glorying in his prowess, and his need to debase her and himself. He demands total subservience to his sexual wishes; this enslavement is for him the sexual truth, the real thing, sex without phoniness. And she is so erotically sensitized by the rounds of lovemaking that she believes him. He goads her and tests her until when he asks if she's ready to eat vomit as a proof of love, she is, and gratefully. He plays out the American male tough-guy sex role—insisting on his power in bed, because that is all the "truth" he knows.

What they go through together in their pressure cooker is an intensified, speeded-up history of the sex relationships of the dominating men and the adoring women who have provided the key sex model of the past few decades—the model that is collapsing. They don't know each other, but their sex isn't "primitive" or "pure"; Paul is the same old Paul, and Jeanne, we gradually see, is also Jeanne, the colonel's daughter. They bring their cultural hangups into sex, so it's the same poisoned sex Strindberg wrote about: a battle of unequally matched partners, asserting whatever dominance they can, seizing any advantage. Inside the flat, his male physical strength and the mythology he has built on it are the primary facts. He pushes his morose, romantic insanity to its limits; he burns through the sickness that his wife's suicide has brought on—the self-doubts, the need to prove himself and torment himself. After three days, his wife is laid out for burial, and he is ready to resume his identity. He gives up the flat: he wants to live normally again, and he wants to love Jeanne as a *person*. But Paul is forty-five, Jeanne is twenty. She lends herself to an orgiastic madness, shares it, and then tries to shake it off—as many another woman has, after a night or a twenty years' night. When they meet in the outside world, Jeanne sees Paul as a washed-up middle-aged man—a man who runs a flophouse.

Much of the movie is American in spirit. Brando's Paul (a former actor and journalist who has been living off his French wife) is like a drunk with a literary turn of mind. He bellows his contempt for hypocrisies and orthodoxies; he keeps trying to shove them all back down other people's throats. His profane humor and self-loathing self-centeredness and street "wisdom" are in the style of the American hardboiled fiction aimed at the masculine-fantasy market, sometimes by writers (often good ones, too) who believe in more than a little of it. Bertolucci has a remarkably unbiased intelligence. Part of the convulsive effect of *Last Tango in Paris* is that we are drawn to Paul's view of society and yet we can't help seeing him as a self-dramatizing, self-pitying clown. Paul believes that his animal noises are more honest than words, and that his obscene vision of things is the way things really are; he's often convincing. After Paul and Jeanne have left the flat, he chases her and persuades her to have a drink at a ballroom holding a tango contest. When we see him drunkenly sprawling on the floor among the bitch-chic mannequin-dancers and then baring his bottom to the woman official who asks him to leave, our mixed emotions may be like those some of us experienced when we watched Norman Mailer put himself in an indefensible position against Gore Vidal on the Dick

Cavett show, justifying all the people who were fed up with him. Brando's Paul carries a yoke of masculine pride and aggression across his broad back; he's weighed down by it and hung on it. When Paul is on all fours barking like a crazy man-dog to scare off a Bible salesman who has come to the flat,* he may—to the few who saw Mailer's *Wild 90*—be highly reminiscent of Mailer on his hands and knees barking at a German shepherd to provoke it. But Brando's barking extends the terms of his character and the movie, while we are disgusted with Mailer for needing to prove himself by teasing an unwilling accomplice, and his barking throws us outside the terms of his movie.

Realism with the terror of actual experience still alive on the screen—that's what Bertolucci and Brando achieve. It's what Mailer has been trying to get at in his disastrous, ruinously expensive films. He was right about what was needed but hopelessly wrong in how he went about getting it. He tried to pull a new realism out of himself onto film, without a script, depending wholly on improvisation, and he sought to bypass the self-consciousness and fakery of a man acting himself by improvising within a fictional construct—as a gangster in *Wild 90*, as an Irish cop in *Beyond the Law* (the best of them), and as a famous director who is also a possible Presidential candidate in *Maidstone*. In movies, Mailer tried to will a work of art into existence without going through the steps of making it, and his theory of film, a rationale for this willing, sounds plausible until you see the movies, which are like Mailer's shambling bouts of public misbehavior, such as that Cavett show. His movies trusted to inspiration and were stranded when it didn't come. Bertolucci builds a structure that supports improvisation. Everything is prepared, but everything is subject to change, and the whole film is alive with a sense of discovery. Bertolucci builds the characters "on what the actors are in themselves. I never ask them to interpret something preëxistent, except for dialogue—and even that changes a lot." For Bertolucci, the actors "make the characters." And Brando knows how to improvise: it isn't just Brando improvising, it's Brando improvising as Paul. This is certainly similar to what Mailer was trying to do as the gangster and the cop and the movie director, but when Mailer improvises, he expresses only a bit of himself. When Brando improvises within Bertolucci's structure, his full art is realized. His performance

---

*This scene was deleted by the director after the New York Film Festival showing.

is not like Mailer's acting but like Mailer's best writing: intuitive, rapt, princely. On the screen, Brando is our genius as Mailer is our genius in literature. Paul is Rojack's expatriate-failure brother, and Brando goes all the way with him.

We all know that movie actors often merge with their roles in a way that stage actors don't, quite, but Brando did it even on the stage. I was in New York when he played his famous small role in *Truckline Café* in 1946; arriving late at a performance, and seated in the center of the second row, I looked up and saw what I thought was an actor having a seizure onstage. Embarrassed for him, I lowered my eyes, and it wasn't until the young man who'd brought me grabbed my arm and said "Watch this guy!" that I realized he was *acting*. I think a lot of people will make my old mistake when they see Brando's performance as Paul; I think some may prefer to make this mistake, so they won't have to recognize how deep down he goes and what he dredges up. Expressing a character's sexuality makes new demands on an actor, and Brando has no trick accent to play with this time, and no putty on his face. It's perfectly apparent that the role was conceived for Brando, using elements of his past as integral parts of the character. Bertolucci wasn't surprised by what Brando did; he was ready to use what Brando brought to the role. And when Brando is a full creative presence on the screen, the realism transcends the simulated actuality of any known style of *cinéma vérité*, because his surface accuracy expresses what's going on underneath. He's an actor: when he shows you something, he lets you know what it means. The torture of seeing Brando—at his worst—in *A Countess from Hong Kong* was that it was a *reductio ad absurdum* of the wastefulness and emasculation (for both sexes) of Hollywood acting; Chaplin, the director, obviously allowed no participation, and Brando was like a miserably obedient soldier going through drill. When you're nothing but an inductee, you have no choice. The excitement of Brando's performance here is in the revelation of how creative screen acting can be. At the simplest level, Brando, by his inflections and rhythms, the right American obscenities, and perhaps an improvised monologue, makes the dialogue his own and makes Paul an authentic American abroad, in a way that an Italian writer-director simply couldn't do without the actor's help. At a more complex level, he helps Bertolucci discover the movie in the process of shooting it, and that's what makes moviemaking an art. What Mailer never understood was that his *macho* thing prevented flexibility and that in terms of his own personality he *couldn't* improvise—he was consciously acting. And he couldn't allow others to improvise, because he was always challenging them to come up with something. Using the tactics he himself compared to "a commando raid on the nature of reality," he was putting a gun to their heads. Lacking the background of a director, he reduced the art of film to the one element of acting, and in his confusion of "existential" acting with improvisation he expected "danger" to be a spur. But acting involves the joy of self-discovery, and to improvise, as actors mean it, is the most instinctive, creative part of acting—to bring out and give form to what you didn't know you had in you; it's the surprise, the "magic" in acting. A director has to be supportive for an actor to feel both secure enough and free enough to reach into himself. Brando here, always listening to an inner voice, must have a direct pipeline to the mystery of character.

Bertolucci has an extravagant gift for sequences that are like arias, and he has given Brando some scenes that really sing. In one, Paul visits his dead wife's lover (Massimo Girotti), who also lives in the run-down hotel, and the two men, in identical bathrobes (gifts from the dead woman), sit side by side and talk. The scene is miraculously basic—a primal scene that has just been discovered. In another, Brando rages at his dead wife, laid out in a bed of flowers, and then, in an excess of tenderness, tries to wipe away the cosmetic mask that defaces her. He has become the least fussy actor. There is nothing extra, no flourishes in these scenes. He purifies the characterization beyond all that: he brings the character a unity of soul. Paul feels so "real" and the character is brought so close that a new dimension in screen acting has been reached. I think that if the actor were anyone but Brando many of us would lower our eyes in confusion.

His first sex act has a boldness that had the audience gasping, and the gasp was caused—in part—by our awareness that this was Marlon Brando doing it, not an unknown actor. In the flat, he wears the white T-shirt of Stanley Kowalski, and he still has the big shoulders and thick-muscled arms. Photographed looking down, he is still tender and poetic; photographed looking up, he is ravaged, like the man in the Francis Bacon painting under the film's opening titles. We are watching *Brando* throughout this movie, with all the feedback that that implies, and his willingness to run the full course with a study of the aggression in masculine sexuality and how the physical strength of men lends credence to the insanity that grows out of it gives the film a larger, tragic dignity. If Brando knows this hell, why should we pretend we don't?

The colors in this movie are late-afternoon orange-beige-browns and pink—the pink of flesh drained of blood, corpse pink. They are so delicately modulated (Vittorio Storaro was the cinematographer, as he was on *The Conformist*) that romance and rot are one; the lyric extravagance of the music (by Gato Barbieri) heightens this effect. Outside the flat, the gray buildings and the noise are certainly modern Paris, and yet the city seems muted. Bertolucci uses a feedback of his own—the feedback of old movies to enrich the imagery and associations. In substance, this is his most American film, yet the shadow of Michel Simon seems to hover over Brando, and the ambience is a tribute to the early crime-of-passion films of Jean Renoir, especially *La Chienne* and *La Bête Humaine*. Léaud, as Tom, the young director, is used as an affectionate takeoff on Godard, and the movie that Tom is shooting about Jeanne, his runaway bride, echoes Jean Vigo's *L'Atalante*. Bertolucci's soft focus recalls the thirties films, with their lyrically kind eye for every variety of passion; Marcel Carné comes to mind, as well as the masters who influenced Bertolucci's technique—von Sternberg (the controlled lighting) and Max Ophuls (the tracking camera). The film is utterly beautiful to look at. The virtuosity of Bertolucci's gliding camera style is such that he can show you the hype of the tango-contest scene (with its own echo of *The Conformist*) by stylizing it (the automaton-dancers do wildly fake head turns) and still make it work. He uses the other actors for their associations, too—Girotti, of course, the star of so many Italian films, including *Senso* and *Ossessione*, Visconti's version of *The Postman Always Rings Twice*, and, as Paul's mother-in-law, Maria Michi, the young girl who betrays her lover in *Open City*. As a maid in the hotel (part of a weak, diversionary subplot that is soon dispensed with), Catherine Allégret, with her heart-shaped mouth in a full, childishly beautiful face, is an aching, sweet reminder of her mother, Simone Signoret, in her *Casque d'Or* days. Bertolucci draws upon the movie background of this movie because movies are as active in him as direct experience—perhaps more active, since they may color everything else. Movies are a past we share, and, whether we recognize them or not, the copious associations are at work in the film and we feel them. As Jeanne, Maria Schneider, who has never had a major role before, is like a bouquet of Renoir's screen heroines and his father's models. She carries the whole history of movie passion in her long legs and baby face.

Maria Schneider's freshness—Jeanne's ingenuous corrupt innocence—gives the film a special radiance. When she lifts her wedding dress to her waist, smiling coquettishly as she exposes her pubic hair, she's in a great film tradition of irresistibly naughty girls. She has a movie face—open to the camera, and yet no more concerned about it than a plant or a kitten. When she speaks in English, she sounds like Leslie Caron in *An American in Paris*, and she often looks like a plump-cheeked Jane Fonda in her *Barbarella* days. The role is said to have been conceived for Dominique Sanda, who couldn't play it, because she was pregnant, but surely it has been reconceived. With Sanda, a tigress, this sexual battle might have ended in a draw. But the pliable, softly unprincipled Jeanne of Maria Schneider must be the winner: it is the soft ones who defeat men and walk away, consciencelessly. A Strindberg heroine would still be in that flat, battling, or in another flat, battling. But Jeanne is like the adorably sensual bitch-heroines of French films of the twenties and thirties—both shallow and wise. These girls know how to take care of themselves; they know who No. 1 is. Brando's Paul, the essentially naïve outsider, the romantic, is no match for a French bourgeois girl.

Because of legal technicalities, the film must open in Italy before it opens in this country, and so *Last Tango in Paris* is not scheduled to play here until January. There are certain to be detractors, for this movie represents too much of a change for people to accept it easily or gracefully. They'll grab at aesthetic flaws—a florid speech or an oddball scene—in order to dismiss it. Though Americans seem to have lost the capacity for being scandalized, and the Festival audience has probably lost the cultural confidence to admit to being scandalized, it might have been easier on some if they could have thrown things. I've tried to describe the impact of a film that has made the strongest impression on me in almost twenty years of reviewing. This is a movie people will be arguing about, I think, for as long as there are movies. They'll argue about how it is intended, as they argue again now about *The Dance of Death*. It is a movie you can't get out of your system, and I think it will make some people very angry and disgust others. I don't believe that there's *anyone* whose feelings can be totally resolved about the sex scenes and the social attitudes in this film.

For the very young, it could be as antipathetic as *L'Avventura* was at first—more so, because it's closer, more realistic, and more emotionally violent. It could embarrass them, and even frighten them. For adults, it's like seeing pieces of your life, and so, of course, you can't resolve your feelings about it—our feelings about life are never resolved. Besides, the biology that is the basis of the "tango" remains.

{*The New Yorker*, October 28, 1972}

:: Pop Versus Jazz

Lady Sings the Blues fails to do justice to the musical life of which Billie Holiday was a part, and it never shows what made her a star, much less what made her an artist. The sad truth is that there is no indication that those who made the picture understand that jazz is any different from pop corruptions of jazz. And yet when the movie was over I wrote "I love it" on my pad of paper and closed it and stuffed it back in my pocket. In certain kinds of movies, the chemistry of pop vulgarization is all-powerful. You don't want to resist the pull of it, because it has a celebrity-star temperament you don't get from anything else; this kitsch has its own kind of authenticity. It's a compliment to the brand of tarnished-lady realism Motown has produced that one thinks of Warners and such Bette Davis vehicles as *Dark Victory* and *Dangerous* rather than of M-G-M. This movie isn't heavy and glazed. Factually it's a fraud, but emotionally it delivers. It has what makes movies work for a mass audience: easy pleasure, tawdry electricity, personality—great quantities of personality. Pop music provides immediate emotional gratifications that the subtler and deeper and more lasting pleasures of jazz can't prevail against. Pop drives jazz back underground. And that's what this pop movie does to the career of a great jazz singer.

How can you trash an artist's life and come up with a movie as effective as *Lady Sings the Blues?* Well, at one level Billie Holiday trashed her own life, and so her morbid legend works for the picture. Movie-trade reporters say that movies with "lose" or "loser" in the title always make money; a movie about Billie Holiday hardly needs the word in the title. Who could be a more natural subject for a flamboyant downer than Billie Holiday, whose singing can send the cheeriest extroverts into a funk? Good Morning,

Heartache. Billie Holiday expressed herself in her bantering with lachrymose lyrics, making them ironic and biting, or else exploiting them for their full measure of misery, giving in so deeply to cheap emotions that she wrung a truth of her own out of them. Maybe not quite a truth but an essence. How many masochists have sated themselves on her "Gloomy Sunday"? And the defiance of her "Ain't Nobody's Business If I Do" was always borderline self-pity: the subtext was "I don't need any of you, I'm so miserable." We've all got a lot of slop in us, and she glorified it, so she was irresistible. She lived so close to those self-destructive suffering-star myths epitomized by the term "a Susan Hayward picture" that only by suggesting the Billie Holiday who was an intuitive innovator and played her oboe voice like a jazz instrument, the artist who was fully happy only when she was singing, could the movie have transcended the old gallant-victim-paying-the-price-of-fame routine. Instead, it stays snugly within commercial confines, relying on the variation of the black sufferer to make it new. This bio-melodrama wasn't made with love for Billie Holiday, exactly (except perhaps from Diana Ross, who plays the role), but *I'll Cry Tomorrow* and *Love Me or Leave Me* (which we think of as "forties" but which were actually mid-fifties—not very far in the past) didn't show much love, either, and they were made with much less energy and spirit.

Still, it's shocking to see a great black artist's experience poured into the same Hollywood mold, and to see that it works—and works far better than it did on the white singers' lives. There's an obvious, external cause for the torments Billie Holiday goes through, and black experience is still new and exotic on the screen—a fresh setting with a new cast of characters, a new vernacular, and a different kind of interplay. And since you can show almost anything in movies now, you don't have to find euphemisms and substitutions. A whore is no longer a "hostess." But this freedom in language and atmosphere isn't to be confused with freedom from commercialism. The movie prefers invented horrors to the known (and much worse) horrors of Billie Holiday's actual life. Her promiscuity has been jettisoned; the lovers and domestic messes and quick affairs all disappear, and her third husband, Louis McKay (Billy Dee Williams), becomes the only man she loves and wants. It's when they're separated (because of her career) that she's so lonely and unhappy she tries drugs; and she falls back on them again later on when he must be away for a few months. Billie Holiday's music certainly doesn't send us messages about a good man

who's always there when she needs him; her torch blues express the disorder and dissatisfaction of her human relations. How could anybody
listen to her high-wire singing and write this monogamous script? Well,
that's not what the troop of writers were listening to.

When this Billie Holiday announces that she is giving up singing to
marry Louis and spend her time in the kitchen, audiences cheer. The way
they have been conditioned by movies and TV, how else can they react?
In terms of the movie, they're reacting *appropriately*; the movie itself can't
deal with why Billie wants to go on singing after she has married her fairy-
tale prince. The picture is solidly aimed at a mass audience that knows a
junkie is damned lucky to get a fine, substantial husband to take care of
her, and Louis McKay has been made such a deep-voiced, sexy Mr. Right
that the audience's sympathies tend to go to him rather than to her. At
times, the movie seems deliberately shaped to make Billy Dee Williams a
star. One can almost feel the calculation that swooning teenagers will say
to themselves, "*I* wouldn't take dope if I had a man like that waiting for
me." McKay is black, but he's an early-model Clark Gable dreamboat. This
ridiculously suave, couth man (who is involved in some unspecified business that permits him to be a hot-shot big spender) belongs in another
sort of movie altogether. Since he doesn't save her, what's he here for? For
black popular romance, of course, and maybe it's only a commercial divi-
dend that he embodies the stability against which Billie Holiday is then
judged.

The assumption is that the basic audience will be black, and so the
movie plays a few get-Whitey games: you never see Billie with any of her
white lovers, or in her quarrels with blacks (including her own mother),
and she's turned onto dope by a smiling white dude (platinum-blond Paul
Hampton, who overdoes the white sliminess). Operating on a scrambled
calendar of events, the movie avoids the complexity of the race issues in
her life, making her strictly a victim. Her tour with Artie Shaw's band has
been turned into the road to ruin for a little black girl who should have
stayed with her own people. And with this approach Billie Holiday seems
so weak a person that we can't see how she ever made it to the peak of her
profession. For reasons that are obscure—possibly in order to sustain the
victim image—her records, by which the whole world came to know her,
are omitted. One would never suspect that she began to record at the age
of eighteen and that by her early twenties she was an important figure in

the world of jazz. How shrewd it is, consciously or unconsciously, to show us not the woman who had made over a hundred recordings by the time she was twenty-five, not the embattled woman who broke down racial barriers while creating a new musical style, but a junkie girl who makes it to the top—the stage of Carnegie Hall—yet at too great a price. A loser. A movie that dealt with Billie Holiday's *achievements* wouldn't be hip; what's hip is the zingy romanticism of failure. *Lady Sings the Blues* is about a junkie who has it made but keeps pulling herself down.

Diana Ross, a tall, skinny goblin of a girl, intensely likable, always in motion, seemed an irrational choice for the sultry, still Billie Holiday, yet she's like a beautiful bonfire: there's nothing to question—you just react with everything you've got. You react in kind, because she has given herself to the role with an all-out physicality, not holding anything back. At times, she reminded me a little of the way Carole Lombard used to throw herself into a role; Lombard wasn't a great comedienne, but she had such zest and vitality that you liked her better than mere comediennes. She was striking and special—an original. So is Diana Ross, and with gifts that can't be defined yet. She couldn't have won us over so fast if the director hadn't shaped and built our interest in her from the childhood scenes. She's knockabout, tomboy angular as an adolescent, and a little later she has a harlequin beauty: huge eyes and a pointed chin and an impishly pretty smile. When she wears ruby lipstick, it's so absolutely right it looks like part of her. She's made up to look uncannily like Billie Holiday in flashes in the latter part of the film, but she's most appealing in the early scenes, when she's least like Billie. The elements of camp and self-parody in Diana Ross's performances with the Supremes and in her TV solo appearances are gone, but, in her whore's orange dress with ruffles at the shoulders and a snug fit over her wriggly, teasing little bottom, she still has her impudence. She's scat-fast with a funny line, she's inventive when she delivers her dialogue like lyrics, and she has a sneaky face for the times when Billie is trying to put something over on Louis. The drugs act like a dimmer: the lights in her voice go down. She differentiates the stoned singing from the "clean" singing by a slight slippery uncertainty (though there's a kitchen scene when she's clean but depressed and she sings—inappropriately, I thought—in this desultory way).

In the established Hollywood tradition, Billie Holiday doesn't have to become Billie Holiday, musically speaking; the first time she sings in public, she has the full Holiday style. But, of course, Diana Ross doesn't pierce us the way Holiday does. She's strong in everything but her singing; as a singer, she's caught in the trap of this bio-melodrama form. *Funny Girl* was a stylized musical comedy, and so no one expected Streisand to sing like Fanny Brice; besides, Fanny Brice isn't on many jukeboxes. But the star of *Lady Sings the Blues* is expected to sound like Billie Holiday. And the key problem for me with the movie is that Diana Ross's singing is *too* close. Her voice is similar—small and thin and reedy, and suspended in air, like a little girl's—and when she sings the songs that Holiday's phrasing fixed in our minds and imitates that phrasing, our memories are blurred. I felt as if I were losing something. I could hear Billie Holiday in my head perfectly clearly as Ross sang each number, but by the time she had finished it, I could no longer be certain of the exact Holiday sounds. What's involved here isn't quite like the vandalism that Stokowski and Disney committed in *Fantasia*, with cupids and winged horses cavorting to the "Pastoral" and volcanoes erupting to Stravinsky—wrecking music for us by forcing us to hear it forever after with incongruous images welded to it—or like the way Kubrick played droog to Beethoven, and even to "Singin' in the Rain." But something similar is at work: Kubrick left Moog-synthesized versions of classics echoing in our skulls, and I think *Lady Sings the Blues*, by its pop versions of Billie Holiday's numbers, will deprive people of the originals. Yes, of course, they still exist, just as the originals of the Benny Goodman and Duke Ellington records that Time-Life has had imitated by modern bands still exist, but new generations are effectively deprived of them just the same. Movies never use the original records in these bios, because the contemporary sound always sells better, and so movies use art as grist.

With Holiday, it was as if everything extra—the padding, all the resonances—had been pared away by troubles: just this thin, wounded sound was left. She made her limited voice yield pure emotion—what jazz horn players sought to do. And her plaintiveness made even her vivacious numbers hurt. There's no pain in Diana Ross's voice, and none of that lazy, sullen sexiness that was a form of effrontery and a turn-on. In song after song in *Lady Sings the Blues*, the phrasing has been split off from its emotional meaning. Diana Ross's "Them There Eyes" comes at the happiest moment in the movie and she's charming on it, but it works on a simple, pop level. She sings the showpiece number, "Strange Fruit," very well, and it's pretty, but it lacks Holiday's chilling tautness that keeps you silent until the final word, "crop," flicks you like a whip. Holiday's acrid edge is missing, and her authority. Ross gives you the phrasing without the intensity that makes it dramatic and memorable, and fresh each time you hear it.

What one always knew, with Billie Holiday, was that there was one thing her voice could never do: heal, the way a rich, full voice can—as Bessie Smith could and Aretha Franklin can. Maybe Billie Holiday willed that effect of being a lone, small voice in the wilderness—isolation rooted in the sound—because that was the only way she could make a great instrument out of her limited voice, and because she meant to wound, not to heal. She wasn't hiding anything: her voice was a direct line from her to us, hurting us (exquisitely, of course) because she'd been hurt (and not exquisitely at all). She was a jazz singer; Ross is a pop singer singing in the Holiday manner. It's imitation soul. That was the letdown of Billie Holiday's later singing—her creativity gave out and she was imitating her own style. Diana Ross's imitation may be an act of homage as much as a requirement of the role, but what she had with the Supremes—which was freaky and as commercial as hell—was recognizably hers. Singing in the style of someone else kills her spark, though she has it here as an actress. Perhaps the decision to spare us the dregs of Billie Holiday's life—the club appearances when her voice was shot and she could barely be heard and the scattering of audience was mostly narcotics agents anyway—was based on a recognition that it wouldn't jibe with Diana Ross's lively, quick spirit. She doesn't have the punishing personality of Billie Holiday; she wants to give pure, crazy, hip pleasure.

So, in his own way, does the director, Sidney J. Furie, the young Canadian with a mottled career of hits and flops (*The Leather Boys, The Ipcress File, The Appaloosa, The Naked Runner, The Lawyer, Little Fauss and Big Halsy*). Furie is wily and talented in small ways that count, but sometimes in his pictures it's *only* the small ways that count—the marginal details and minor characters. He hammers out the heavy stuff, such as the hokey-powerful opening scene, under the titles, with Holiday being hauled into jail and tied in a straitjacket while Michel Legrand's hyperactive crime-suspense music cues us in to the overwrought genre, but he also disposes of a lot of second-rate dialogue by fast throwaway delivery and overlaps, and his best sequences are unusually loose. In one, a scene of gruesome comic confusion, Billie and Richard Pryor, as her accompanist, Piano

Man, are backstage at a club, with her connection waiting to give her a shot, when she learns of her mother's death; they're in no shape to deal with the situation, and the talk dribbles on in a painfully lifelike way. Pryor, a West Coast coffeehouse comic, has such audience rapport that a shot of him in Los Angeles in fancy clothes and a beret is enough to bring down the house. Billie and Piano Man have a sequence that feels improvised, on a California beach, when she asks him to get her some dope, and then a long unstructured "high" scene together, when they're like two innocently obscene junkie babies. Elsewhere, Furie's direction is often crude (as with the Smilin' Jack villain, and Black Beauty Billy Dee Williams), but he has a sense of pace and a knack for letting the audience know that he wants us to have a good time. The bad side of his hardboiled expertise — the insistence on being modern and tough by not showing too much compassion — is that though Diana Ross wins you and holds you, your feelings about Billie Holiday become uncertain and muddy as the film progresses. The keys to her life are in her art, and that's not in the movie. (It almost never is in movies, because how do you re-create the processes of artistic creation?) *Lady Sings the Blues* is as good as one can expect from the genre — better, at times — and I enjoyed it hugely, yet I don't want Billie Holiday's hard, melancholic sound buried under this avalanche of pop. When you get home, you have to retrieve her at the phonograph; you have to do restoration work on your own past.

{*The New Yorker*, November 4, 1972}

:: *The Fred Astaire &*
    Ginger Rogers Book

The Fred Astaire & Ginger Rogers Book, by Arlene Croce, has verve and wit, like the series of musicals it covers. Movie criticism suffered a loss when, in the mid-sixties, Miss Croce abandoned the field and gave most of her energies to dance criticism; now she has joined her two major talents. No one has ever described dance in movies the way she does: she's a slangy, elegant writer; her compressed descriptions are evocative and analytic at the same time, and so precise and fresh that while bringing the pleasure of the dances back she adds to it. There is a sense of pressure in her style that has something like the tension and pull of the dances themselves. Her descriptions are original and imperially brusque in a way that keeps the reader alert; one responds to her writing kinesthetically, as if it were dance. This small book, published this week by Outerbridge & Lazard, and about half text, half photographs (with two flip-page dances, of which one is effective, the other badly cropped), is a history of the team and an assessment of its place in dance and movie history, and also an acute examination of how movies were made in the factory-system days. We learn who did what on those musicals and how they "happened," and yet, just as Astaire never lets you see the hard work, so that his dances appear to be spontaneous, Miss Croce doesn't present the history as history; she lets it come in casually, jauntily, as she covers the series of films, fitting the background material to the illustrated section on each movie. There are times when one may want her to expand on a point or explain, but the reward of her brevity is the same achieved nonchalance that she prizes in these movies; it comes out of her controlled ecstatic response to the dances. Here is a sentence of Miss Croce's on Astaire in the "I Won't Dance" number from *Roberta*:

> Two big Cossacks have to carry him protesting onto the dance floor, and there he does his longest and most absorbing solo of the series so far, full of stork-legged steps on toe, wheeling pirouettes in which he seems to be winding one leg around the other, and those ratcheting tap clusters that fall like loose change from his pockets.

And here a fragment on Astaire's singles:

> With him, a dance impulse and a dramatic motive seem to be indivisible and spontaneous, so that we get that little kick of imaginative sympathy every time he changes the rhythm or the speed or the pressure of a step. And though we don't perceive the dance as "drama," the undertone of motivation continually sharpens and refreshes our interest in what we do see.

And, on the pair in "Let's Face the Music and Dance," from *Follow the Fleet*:

> The mood is awesomely grave. The dance is one of their simplest and most daring, the steps mostly walking steps done with a slight retard. The withheld impetus makes the dance look dragged by destiny, all the quick little circling steps pulled as if on a single thread.

Every few sentences, you're stopped by the audacity of a description or by some new piece of information; we learn what that mysterious name Van Nest Polglase in the credits actually meant, and of the writing contribution of Laurette Taylor's son, Dwight Taylor, and we get such footnotes to social history as this, from the section on *Top Hat*:

> The most quoted line in the film is the motto of the House of Beddini, delivered with supreme flourish by Erik Rhodes: "For the women the kiss, for the men the sword." This was originally written, "For the men the sword, for the women the whip," and was changed when the Hays office objected.

I doubt if anyone else will ever love Astaire the dancer and creator as fully as this author: the book is a homage to him and the simplicity and mastery he represents. Miss Croce documents how he choreographed the dances—improvising them with Hermes Pan, with Pan doing Rogers' steps and later training her to do them. ("With Fred I'd be Ginger," Pan says, "and with Ginger I'd be Fred." After the dances were photographed, Hermes Pan usually dubbed in the taps for her as well.) It was Astaire himself who controlled the shooting, and he insisted that each dance be recorded in a single shot, without fakery, and without the usual cuts to the reactions of onlookers. But sometimes the ideal of "perfection within a single shot"—the dance just as it would be done for a live audience, so that moviegoers would see it as if from the best seats in a theater—wasn't attained. There is a cut toward the close of the "Never Gonna Dance" number, in *Swing Time*; Miss Croce explains that it "may have been one of the few Astaire-Rogers dances that couldn't be filmed entirely in one continuous shot, for its climax, a spine-chilling series of pirouettes by Rogers, took forty takes to accomplish, and in the middle of shooting Rogers' feet began to bleed."

For Miss Croce, in the best Astaire-and-Rogers films *(The Gay Divorcée, Roberta, Top Hat, Follow the Fleet, Swing Time)* something happened that "never happened in movies again"—"dancing was transformed into a vehicle of serious emotion between a man and a woman." And from this, I think, flow my disagreements with her. We have had many happy arguments about dance and movies; I suspect that they hinge on temperament. Miss Croce (she is the editor of *Ballet Review*) is a perfectionist—a romantic perfectionist. I, too, find Astaire and Rogers rapturous together, but Miss Croce's romanticism about the two leads her to ascribe a *dance* perfection to them. I think that Astaire's dry buoyancy comes through best in his solos, which are more exciting dances than the romantic ballroom numbers with Rogers. Miss Croce says Rogers' "technique became exactly what she needed in order to dance with Fred Astaire, and, as no other woman in movies ever did, she created the feeling that stirs us so deeply when we see them together: Fred need not be alone." Well, that's maybe a bit much. Of Rogers in a rare tap solo (on "Let Yourself Go," in *Follow the Fleet*), she writes, "It's easy to underrate Rogers' dancing because she never appeared to be working hard. . . . She avoided any suggestion of toil or inadequacy. She was physically incapable of ugliness." But she was certainly capable of *clumsiness* when she danced with Astaire, and you can see that she *is* working hard. She doesn't always look comfortable doing the steps—her arms are out of kilter, or she's off balance. And, from Miss Croce's own account of how the dances were devised, you can see why: If Astaire had improvised the choreography with Rogers instead of with Hermes Pan, Rogers would probably have worked out things that came more easily and naturally to her, and you wouldn't have the sense you often get—that it's too difficult for her and she's doing her damnedest just to get the steps right. Rogers, of course, who was making three pictures to each one of Astaire's, was too valuable a property of R.K.O.'s to be spared for these sessions (even if the men had wanted her, which is doubtful). A ballet dancer, whose technique is set in training, can accept the choreography of others far more easily than a pop dancer. In the case of this team, Astaire, with his winged body, his weightless, essentially bodiless style, devised his own personal balletistic jazz form of dance, and then Ginger Rogers had to try to fit into it. But her clumsiness is rather ingratiating; it isn't *bad*, and the choreography and the whole feeling of their dances is so romantically appealing that you don't *mind* Ginger's dancing. We don't care if Ginger Rogers isn't a *superb* dancer. (The team might be boringly ethereal if she were.) It's part of Ginger's personality that she's a tiny bit klutzy. Yes, she has that beautiful figure, which Miss Croce rightly admires, but there is also the slight grossness of her face and her uncultivated voice. What makes Ginger Rogers so unsettling, so *alive*, on the screen is the element of insensitivity and the happy, wide streak of commonness in a person of so much talent. Maybe it's her greatest asset that she always seems to have a wad of gum in her mouth. I don't mean to suggest that Miss Croce is unaware of this side of Ginger Rogers (she's at her satirical best on Rogers as an actress, and there really isn't much that Arlene Croce is unaware of)—only that she and I view it differently. Miss Croce sees it as what was *overcome* in the dance—"Astaire would turn her into a goddess"; she believes Rogers was transformed, that she "turned from brass to gold under his touch." Sure, she was Cinderella at the ball, but we still thought of her as the spunky, funny, slightly pie-faced chorus girl trying to keep up with him. Rogers seems most fully herself to me in the comic hoofing showing-off numbers, and that's when I love her dancing best; in the more decorous simulated passion of the dramatic dances with Astaire, she's not that different from other fancy ballroom dancers—she's not quite Ginger.

Miss Croce takes their dancing perhaps a bit too seriously, seeing it not just as heavenly romance or—as perhaps many of us did—as a dream of a date but as something more: "Astaire in his flying tails, the pliant Rogers in one of her less-is-more gowns, were an erotic vision that audiences beheld in the electric silence of the dance. Everyone knew what was happening in these dances." But how could Fred Astaire be erotic? Fred Astaire has no flesh, and I think the only conceivable "eroticism" in their dances is a sort of transfigured view of courtship and romance, a fantasy of being swept off one's feet.

I suspect it is this *Camelot* view that leads Miss Croce to be rather unfair to Gene Kelly. She says, "The major difference between Astaire and Kelly is a difference, not of talent or technique, but of levels of sophistication." I should say the difference starts with their bodies. If you compare Kelly to Astaire, accepting Astaire's debonaire style as perfection, then, of course, Kelly looks bad. But in popular dance forms, in which movement is not rigidly codified, as it is in ballet, perfection is a romantic myth or a figure of speech, nothing more. Kelly isn't a winged dancer; he's a hoofer, and more earthbound. But he has warmth and range as an actor. Kelly's "natural," unaffected line readings, in a gentle, unactorish voice, probably come from the same basic sense of timing that leads Astaire to the clocked, tapped-out readings. Kelly's inflections are subtle and delicate, while his acting is slightly larger than life. He leaps into a simple scene, always "on" (as "on" as Cagney), distinctively eager and with a chesty, athletic, over-dramatic exuberance that makes audiences feel good. Though there was something moist and too exposed in the young Judy Garland, Kelly and Garland, both emotional performers, had a special rapport based on tenderness. They could bring conviction to banal love scenes (as in *Summer Stock*) and make them naïvely fresh. They balanced each other's talents: she joined her odd and undervalued cakewalker's prance to his large-spirited hoofing, and he joined his odd, light, high voice to her sweet, good, deep one. Their duets (such as "You Wonderful You," in *Summer Stock*, and the title song in *For Me and My Gal*) have a plaintive richness unlike anything in the Astaire-Rogers pictures. They could really sing together; Astaire and Rogers couldn't, despite Astaire's skill and charm when he sang alone. Astaire's grasshopper lightness was his limitation as an actor—confining him to perennial gosh-oh-gee adolescence; he was always and only a light comedian and could function only in fairy-tale vehicles. Miss Croce, for whom ballet is the highest form of dance, sees the highest, subtlest emotional resonances in the most stylized forms. I don't think she's wrong in her basic valuation of Astaire and Rogers, but she's too exclusive about it: she has set up an ideal based on Astaire which denies the value of whatever he didn't have.

What it comes down to is that Miss Croce, as in her discussion of Astaire and Rogers in *Swing Time*, sees "the dance as love, the lovers as dancers"; in a funny way, Astaire and Rogers are both too likable for that, and it's the wrong kind of glorification of their frivolous mixture of romance and comedy—a fan's deification. Astaire and Rogers were fortunate: they embodied the swing-music, white-telephone, streamlined era before the Second World War, when frivolousness wasn't decadent and when adolescents dreamed that "going out" was dressing up and becoming part of a beautiful world of top hats and silver lamé. It was a lovely dream, and perhaps Miss Croce still dreams it. A possible indication of the degenerative effects of movies on our good sense is that a writer with a first-class mind can say of Astaire, after the partnership ended, "He never ceased to dance wonderfully and he has had some good dancing partners. But it is a world of sun without a moon." However, it is also because of such swoony romanticism that this writer has brought her full resources to bear on the kind of subject that generally attracts pinheads. I think it's perfectly safe to say that this is the best book that will ever be written about Astaire and Rogers.

{*The New Yorker*, November 25, 1972}

:: *Days and Nights in the Forest*

"It adds years to your life," the young men from Calcutta in Satyajit Ray's *Days and Nights in the Forest* say of the country quiet, and it's easy to believe. Ray's images are so emotionally saturated that they become suspended in time and, in some cases, fixed forever. Satyajit Ray's films can give rise to a more complex feeling of happiness in me than the work of any other director. I think it must be because our involvement with his characters is so direct that we are caught up in a blend of the fully accessible and the inexplicable, the redolent, the mysterious. We accept the resolutions he effects not merely as resolutions of the stories but as truths of human experience. Yet it isn't only a matter of thinking, Yes, this is the way it is. What we assent to is only a component of the pattern of associations in his films; to tell the stories does not begin to suggest what the films call to mind or why they're so moving. There is always a residue of feeling that isn't resolved. Two young men sprawled on a porch after a hot journey, a drunken group doing the Twist in the dark on a country road, Sharmila Tagore's face lit by a cigarette lighter, her undulating walk in a sari—the images are suffused with feeling and become overwhelmingly, sometimes unbearably beautiful. The emotions that are imminent may never develop, but we're left with the sense of a limitless yet perhaps harmonious natural drama that the characters are part of. There are always larger, deeper associations impending; we recognize the presence of the mythic in the ordinary. And it's the mythic we're left with after the ordinary has been (temporarily) resolved.

When *Days and Nights in the Forest*, which was made in 1969, was shown at the New York Film Festival in 1970, it received a standing ovation, and it seemed so obvious that a film of this quality—and one more immediate in its appeal than many of Ray's works—would be snapped up by a distributor that I waited to review it upon its theater opening. But distributors are often lazy men who don't bother much with festivals, least of all with films that are shown at the dinner hour (it went on at six-thirty); they wait for the *Times*. The review was condescendingly kindly and brief—a mere five and a half inches, and not by the first-string critic—and *Days and Nights in the Forest*, which is a major film by a major artist, is finally opening, two and a half years later, for a week's run at a small theater. On the surface, it is a lyrical romantic comedy about four educated young men from Calcutta driving together for a few days in the country, their interrelations, and what happens to them in the forest, which is both actual and metaphorical. As the men rag each other and bicker, we quickly sort them out. Ashim is a rising executive and the natural leader of the group. Lordly and disdainful to underlings, he is the worst-behaved; the most intelligent, he is also the most dissatisfied with his life and himself—he feels degraded. He and Sanjoy, who is more polite and reticent, used to slave on a literary magazine they edited, but they have settled down. Ashim is much like what Apu might have turned into if he had been corrupted, and he is played by Soumitra Chatterji, who was Apu in *The World of Apu*. On this holiday in the forest, Ashim meets Aparna, played by the incomparably graceful Sharmila Tagore (who ten years before, when she was fourteen, played Aparna, Apu's exquisite bride). In his fine book on the Apu Trilogy, Robin Wood wrote that the physical and spiritual beauty of Soumitra Chatterjee and Sharmila Tagore seems "the ideal incarnation of Ray's belief in human potentialities." And I think they represent that to Ray, and inspire him to some of his finest work (he used them also in *Devi*) because they are modern figures with overtones of ancient deities. Unlike the other characters in *Days and Nights in the Forest*, they bridge the past and the future and—to some degree—India and the West. As Ray uses them, they embody more than we can consciously grasp. But we feel it: when Sharmila Tagore in her sunglasses and white slacks stands still for a second, she's a creature of fable—the image carries eternity. Even her melodious voice seems old and pure, as if it had come through fire.

Ashim has been strangling in the business bureaucracy of Calcutta; frustrated, he has become an egotist, and confidently condescending to women. Aparna, a city girl vacationing at her father's house in the forest along with her widowed sister-in-law, is not impressed by his big-city line. Her irony and good sense cut through his arrogance, and, made to feel foolish, he rediscovers his humanity. Underneath their love story, and the stories of Ashim's companions, there's the melancholy and corruption of their class and country. In a quiet way, the subtext is perhaps the subtlest, most plangent study of the cultural tragedy of imperialism the screen has ever had. It is the tragedy of the bright young generation who have internalized the master race (like many of the refugees from Hitler who came to America); their status identity is so British that they treat all non-Anglicized Indians as non-persons. The caste system and the British attitudes seem to have conspired to turn them into self-parodies—clowns who ape the worst snobberies of the British. The highest compliment the quartet can bestow on Aparna's father's cottage is to say, "The place looks absolutely English." We don't laugh at them, though, because they're achingly conscious of being anachronistic and slightly ridiculous. When we see them playing tennis in the forest, the image is so ambiguous that our responses come in waves.

Ray not only directed but did the screenplay (from a novel by Sunil Ganguly), drew the credit titles, and wrote the music. His means as a director are among the most intuitively right in all moviemaking: he knows when to shift the camera from one face to another to reveal the utmost, and he knows how to group figures in a frame more expressively than anyone else. He doesn't butt into a scene; he seems to let it play itself out. His understatement makes most of what is thought of as film technique seem unnecessary, and even decadent, because he does more without it. (No Western director has been able to imitate him.) The story is told with great precision at the same time that the meanings and associations multiply. Ray seems to add something specifically Eastern to the "natural" style of Jean Renoir. Renoir, too, put us in unquestioning and total—yet discreet—contact with his people, and everything seemed fluid and easy, and open in form. But Renoir's time sense is different. What is distinctive in Ray's work (and it may be linked to Bengali traditions in the arts, and perhaps to Sanskrit) is that sense of imminence—the suspension of the images in a larger context. The rhythm of his films seems not slow but, rather, meditative, as if the viewer could see the present as part of the past and could already reflect on what is going on. There is a rapt, contemplative quality in the beautiful intelligence of his ideal lovers. We're not at all surprised in this film that both Ashim and Aparna have phenomenal memories; we knew that from looking at them.

Ray takes a risk when he contrasts his poetic sense of time against the hasty Western melodramatic tradition. One of the four young men is a figure in the sporting world—Hari, who is quick-tempered and rash. He has just been jilted by a dazzler of a girl for his insensitivity. (He answered a six-page letter from her in a single curt sentence.) Hari picks up a local "tribal" girl in the forest for some fast sex, and he is also attacked and almost killed by a servant he has wrongly accused of stealing. The scenes relating to Hari (especially those dealing with the equally thoughtless local girl) feel very thin and unconvincing, because they are conventional. They have no mystery, no resonance, and though this is surely deliberate, the contrast doesn't succeed; the scenes seem more contrived than they would in an American movie. In a scene by a river, Sharmila Tagore's glance brings Hari back into the film's harmony, but he goes out again. The fourth young man, Sekhar, has no subplot; he's a plump buffoon, a fawning hanger-on, who drops pidgin-English phrases into his conversation as if they were golden wit. Like Joyce Cary's Mr. Johnson in Africa, he's a joke the British left behind. Nothing happens to him; spinelessly affable, he behaves in the country as he does in the city.

It is the shy Sanjoy who has the worst experience. Aparna's sister-in-law, the young, heavily sensual widow, makes a physical overture to him. She has been flirting with him for days, and we have observed the ordinariness of her middle-class character, listened to the coyness in her slightly disagreeable voice; we know that he is flattered by her attention and oblivious of the import of her broad smiles and provocative, teasing manner. When she lures him in at night with an offer of real coffee and puts her hand on his chest, we see his stricken face, and we are torn in half. She hadn't seen in him what we had, or he in her. Ray, without our full awareness, has prepared us, and now we are brought closer to them both than we had ever anticipated. This desperately lonely woman might be too much for most men, and this man is less secure than most. The moment of his petrified indecision about how to retreat and her realization of the rejection is a fully tragic experience. Ray is a master psychologist: the pain for us is the deeper because Ray had made her so coarse-grained that we hadn't cared for her; now her humiliation illuminates what was going on in her while we were dismissing her for her middle-classness and the tension in her voice. No artist has done more than Satyajit Ray to make us reëvaluate the commonplace. And only one or two other film artists of his generation—he's just past fifty—can make a masterpiece that is so lucid and so inexhaustibly rich. At one point, the four young blades and the two women sit in a circle on picnic blankets and play a memory game that might be called Let Us Now Praise Famous Men; it's a pity that James Agee didn't live to see the films of Satyajit Ray, which fulfill Agee's dreams.

{*The New Yorker*, March 17, 1973}

:: A Rip-off with Genius

It's the glossiest of glossy books—the sexy waif-goddess spread out in over 100 photographs by two dozen photographers plus the Mailer text and all on shiny coated paper. It's a rich and creamy book, an offensive physical object, perhaps even a little sordid. On the jacket, her moist lips parted, in a color photograph by Bert Stern taken just before her death in 1962, Marilyn Monroe has that blurry, slugged look of her later years; fleshy but pasty. A sacrificial woman—*Marilyn* to put beside *Zelda*. This glassy-eyed goddess is not the funny bunny the public wanted, it's Lolita become Medusa. The book was "produced" by the same Lawrence Schiller who packaged the 1962 Hedda Hopper story congratulating 20th Century-Fox for firing Monroe from her last picture; now there are new ways to take her. The cover-girl face on *Marilyn* is disintegrating; and the astuteness of the entrepreneurs in exploiting even her disintegration, using it as a Pop icon, gets to one. Who knows what to think about Marilyn Monroe or about those who turn her sickness to metaphor? I wish they'd let her die.

In his opening, Mailer describes Marilyn Monroe as "one of the last of cinema's aristocrats" and recalls that the sixties, which "began with Hemingway as the monarch of American arts, ended with Andy Warhol as its regent." Surely he's got it all wrong? He can't even believe it; it's just a conceit. Hemingway wasn't the monarch of American arts but our official literary celebrity—our big writer—and by the end of the sixties, after *An American Dream* and *Cannibals and Christians* and *The Armies of the Night* and *Miami and the Siege of Chicago*, the title had passed to Mailer. And Marilyn Monroe wasn't a cinema aristocrat (whatever nostalgic reverie of the "old stars" is implied); a good case could be made for her as the first of

the Warhol superstars (funky caricatures of sexpot glamour, impersonators of stars). Jean Harlow with that voice of tin may have beat her to it,
but it was Monroe who used her lack of an actress's skills to amuse the
public. She had the wit or crassness or desperation to turn cheesecake into
acting—and vice versa; she did what others had the "good taste" not to do,
like Mailer, who puts in what other writers have been educated to leave
out. She would bat her Bambi eyelashes, lick her messy suggestive open
mouth, wiggle that pert and tempting bottom, and use her hushed voice
to caress us with dizzying innuendos. Her extravagantly ripe body bulging
and spilling out of her clothes, she threw herself at us with the off-color
innocence of a baby whore. She wasn't the girl men dreamed of or wanted
to know but the girl they wanted to go to bed with. She was Betty Grable
without the coy modesty, the starlet *in flagrante delicto* forever because
that's where everybody thought she belonged.

Her mixture of wide-eyed wonder and cuddly drugged sexiness seemed
to get to just about every male; she turned on even homosexual men. And
women couldn't take her seriously enough to be indignant; she was funny
and impulsive in a way that made people feel protective. She was a little
knocked out; her face looked as if, when nobody was paying attention to
her, it would go utterly slack—as if she died between wolf calls.

She seemed to have become a camp siren out of confusion and ineptitude; her comedy was self-satire, and apologetic—conscious parody that
had begun unconsciously. She was not the first sex goddess with a trace of
somnambulism; Garbo was often a little out-of-it, Dietrich was numb
most of the time, and Hedy Lamarr was fairly zonked. But they were exotic
and had accents, so maybe audiences didn't wonder why they were in a
daze; Monroe's slow reaction time made her seem daffy, and she tricked
it up into a comedy style. The mystique of Monroe—which accounts for
the book *Marilyn*—is that she became spiritual as she fell apart. But as an
actress she had no way of expressing what was deeper in her except in
moodiness and weakness. When she was "sensitive" she was drab.

Norman Mailer inflates her career to cosmic proportions. She becomes
"a proud, inviolate artist," and he suggests that "one might literally have
to invent the idea of a soul in order to approach her." He pumps so much
wind into his subject that the reader may suspect that he's trying to make
Marilyn Monroe worthy of him, a subject to compare with the Pentagon
and the moon. Laying his career calibrations before us, he speculates that

"a great biography might be constructed some day" upon the foundation of Fred Lawrence Guiles's *Norma Jean* and proceeds to think upon himself as the candidate for the job: "By the logic of transcendence, it was exactly in the secret scheme of things that a man should be able to write about a beautiful woman, or a woman to write about a great novelist—that would be transcendence, indeed!" Has he somehow forgotten that even on the sternest reckonings the "great" novelists include Jane Austen and George Eliot?

But no he decides that he cannot give the years needed for the task; he will write, instead, a "novel biography." "Set a thief to catch a thief and put an artist on an artist," he hums, and seeing the work already in terms to give Capote shivers, he describes it as "a *species* of novel ready to play by the rules of biography." The man is intolerable; he works out the flourishes of the feat he's going to bring off before allowing his heroine to be born. After all this capework and the strain of the expanding chest on the buttons of his vest, the reader has every right to expect this blowhard to take a belly flop, and every reason to want him to. But though it's easy—in fact, natural—to speak of Mailer as crazy (and only half in admiration) nobody says dumb. *Marilyn* is a rip-off all right but a rip-off with genius.

Up to now we've had mostly contradictory views of Monroe. Those who have taken a hard line on her (most recently Walter Bernstein in the July *Esquire*) never accounted for the childlike tenderness, and those who have seen her as shy and loving (like the Strasbergs or Diana Trilling or Norman Rosten) didn't account for the shrill sluttiness. Arthur Miller had split her into *The Misfits* and the scandalous *After the Fall*, and since each was only a side of her, neither was believable. With his fox's ingenuity, Mailer puts her together and shows how she might have been torn apart, from the inside by her inheritance and her childhood, by the outside pressures of the movie business. But it's all conjecture and sometimes pretty wild conjecture; he's a long way from readiness "to play by the rules of biography" since his principal technique—how could the project interest him otherwise?—is to jump inside everyone's head and read thoughts.

He acknowledges his dependence for the putative facts on the standard biographies—principally Guiles's *Norma Jean*, and also Maurice Zolotow's *Marilyn Monroe*—but deciding to interpret the data researched and already presented by others is a whopping putdown of them; their work thus becomes grist for his literary-star mill. Some of his milling is not so stellar. He quotes trashy passages (with a half-smile) and uses them for their same trashy charge. And his psychoanalytic detective work is fairly mawkish; we don't need Norman Mailer to tell us about Marilyn Monroe's search for parent figures — even fan magazines have become adept at this two-bit stuff about her claiming to her schoolmates that Clark Gable was her father and then winding up in Gable's arms in *The Misfits*.

Mailer explains her insomnia and her supposed attraction to death by her own account of someone's attempt to suffocate her when she was thirteen months old. But since there's no evidence for her account (except hindwise, in her insomnia) and since she apparently didn't start telling the story until the mid-fifties, when she was embroidering that raped and abused Little Nell legend that *Time* sent out to the world in a cover story, isn't it possible that before building a house of cards on the murderous incident one should consider if it wasn't linked to her having played (in *Don't Bother to Knock* in 1952) a psychopathic babysitter who blandly attacks a little girl? (The faintly anesthetized vagueness of her babysitter prefigured the ethereal vacuity of the face in the last photos.)

When the author says that it was his "prejudice that a study of Marilyn's movies might offer more penetration into her early working years in film than a series of interviews . . ." one may guess that his model is Freud's book on Leonardo da Vinci, which is also an ecstasy of hypothesis. But surprisingly, Mailer makes only perfunctory use of her movies. He can't be much interested: he doesn't even bother to discuss the tawdriness of *Niagara* (made in 1953, just before she won Hollywood over with *Gentlemen Prefer Blondes*), in which her amoral destructive tramp — carnal as hell — must surely have represented Hollywood's lowest estimate of her.

Nor is he very astute about her career possibilities: He accepts the pious view that she should have worked with Chaplin and he says, complaining of Twentieth Century-Fox's lack of comprehension of her film art, that she could "have done *Nana*, *The Brothers Karamazov*, *Anna Christie* or *Rain* to much profit, but they gave her *Let's Make Love*." Who would quarrel with his judgment of *Let's Make Love*, but do the other titles represent his idea of what she should have done? (To *her* profit, he must mean, surely not the studio's.) Yes, probably she could have played a Grushenka (though not a Russian one), but does Mailer want to look at a Hollywood

Karamazov or new versions of those other clumping war-horses? (Not a single one of those girls is American, and how could Monroe play anything else?)

Monroe might have "grown" as an actress but she would have died as a star. (Isn't the vision of the Reverend Davidson kneeling to her Sadie Thompson the purest camp?) The pity is that she didn't get more of the entertaining roles that were in her range; she hardly had the stability to play a mother or even a secretary and she was a shade too whorey for Daisy Miller or her descendants, but she was the heroine of every porny-spoof like *Candy* come to life, and she might have been right for *Sweet Charity* or for *Lord Love a Duck* or *Born Yesterday* or a remake of the Harlow comedy *Bombshell* or another *Red Dust*. She might have had a triumph in *Breakfast at Tiffany's* and she probably could have toned down for Tennessee Williams's *Period of Adjustment* and maybe even *Bonnie and Clyde*. Plain awful when she suffered, she was best at demi-whores who enjoyed the tease, and she was too obviously a product of the movie age to appear in a period picture.

It isn't enough for Mailer that people enjoyed her; he cranks her up as great and an "angel of sex" and, yes, "Napoleonic was her capture of the attention of the world." Monroe the movie star with sexual clout overpowers Norman Mailer. But most of her late pictures (such as *The Prince and the Showgirl*, *Let's Make Love* and *The Misfits*) didn't capture the public. Audiences didn't want the nervous, soulful Monroe—never so dim as when she was being "luminous"; they wanted her to be a mock-dumb snuggly blonde and to have some snap. When Mailer writes about her "artist's intelligence" and "superb taste" and about the sort of work she did in *The Misfits* as "the fulfillment of her art," he just seems to be getting carried away by the importance of his subject. Back in 1962, he wrote that "she was bad in *The Misfits*, she was finally too vague, and when emotion showed, it was unattractive and small," and he was right. It was already the Marilyn legend in that role—the baffled, vulnerable child-woman; she didn't have the double-edged defenselessness of her comedy hits, she looked unawakened yet sick—anguished.

But Mailer understands how Hollywood uses its starlets and how Marilyn Monroe the star might have reacted to that usage, and that is the key understanding that most commentators on her have lacked (though Clifford Odets's obit of her had it, also the story Ezra Goodman wrote for

Time in 1956, which *Time* didn't print but which appears in his *The Fifty Year Decline and Fall of Hollywood*). And who but Norman Mailer could have provided the analysis (that starts on page 35, the real beginning of the book) of the effect on Monroe of the torpor of her twenty-one months in an orphanage and why it probably confirmed her into a liar and reinforced "everything in her character that was secretive"? And who else, writing about a Pop figure, would even have thought about the relation of narcissism to institutional care? His strength—when he gets rolling—isn't in Freudian guesses but in his fusing his knowledge of how people behave with his worst suspicions of where they really live.

His best stuff derives from his having been on the scene, or close enough to smell it out. When it comes to reporting the way American rituals and institutions operate, Mailer's low cunning is maybe the best tool anyone ever had. He grasps the psychological and sexual rewards the studio system offered executives. He can describe why Zanuck, who had Monroe under contract, didn't like her; how she became "a protagonist in the great American soap opera" when her nude calendar was "discovered"—i.e., leaked to the press by Jerry Wald to publicize *Clash by Night*; and what it may have meant to her to date DiMaggio, "an American king—her first. The others have been merely Hollywood kings." He's elegantly cogent on the Method and his paragraphs on Lee Strasberg as a critic of acting are a classic.

About half of *Marilyn* is great as only a great writer, using his brains and feelers, could make it. Just when you get fed up with his flab and slop, he'll come through with a runaway string of perceptions and you have to recognize that, though it's a bumpy ride, the book still goes like a streak. His writing is close to the pleasures of movies; his immediacy makes him more accessible to those brought up with the media than, say, Bellow. You read him with a heightened consciousness because his performance has zing. It's the star system in literature; you can feel him bucking for the big time, and when he starts flying it's so exhilarating you want to applaud. But it's a good-bad book. When Mailer tries to elevate his intuitions into theories, the result is usually verbiage. (His theory that men impart their substance and qualities into women along with their semen is a typical macho Mailerism; he sees it as a one-way process, of course. Has no woman slipped a little something onto his privates?) There are countless bits of literary diddling: "—she had been alive for twenty years but not yet named!—"; the exclamation points are like sprinkles. Mailer the soothsayer with his rheumy metaphysics and huckster's magick is a carny quack, and this Hollywood milieu seems to bring out his fondness for the slacker reaches of the occult—reincarnation and sob-sister omens ("a bowl of tomato sauce dropped on her groom's white jacket the day of her first wedding"). We know his act already and those words (dread, existential, ontology, the imperatives) that he pours on like wella balsam to tone up the prose. And there's his familiar invocation of God, i.e., mystery. But it's less mysterious now because it has become a weapon: the club he holds over the villain of the book—respectable, agnostic Arthur Miller, a writer of Mailer's own generation (and closer than that) who won Marilyn Monroe. Set a thief to catch a thief, an artist on an artist, and one nice Jewish boy from Brooklyn on another.

It's not just a book about Monroe, it's Mailer's show. "Feedback has become the condition of our lives," he said in an interview in 1972. "It's the movies. We've passed the point in civilization where we can ever look at anything as an art work. There is always our knowledge of it and of the making of it." Whether true or false, this applies to Mailer, and he has made us more aware than we may want to be of his titles and campaigns, his aspiration to be more than a writer, to conquer the media and be monarch of American arts—a straight Jean Cocteau who'd meet anybody at high noon. Something has been withheld from Norman Mailer: his crown lacks a few jewels, a star. He has never triumphed in the theater, never been looked up to as a Jewish Lincoln, and never been married to a famous movie queen—a sex symbol. (He's also not a funny writer; to be funny you have to be totally unfettered, and he's too ambitious.) Mailer's waddle and crouch may look like a put-on, but he means it when he butts heads. *Marilyn* is his whammy to Arthur Miller.

In 1967, in an article written to promote the off-Broadway version of *The Deer Park*, Mailer said of himself, "There were too many years when he dreamed of *The Deer Park* on Broadway and the greatest first night of the decade, too many hours of rage when he declaimed to himself that his play was as good as *Death of a Salesman*, or even, and here he gulped hard, *A Streetcar Named Desire*." The sly sonuvabitch coveted Miller's success and cut him down in the same sentence. (*The Deer Park* wasn't Mailer's *Salesman*; based on Mailer's own second marriage and dealing with integrity and the McCarthy period and sex and love, it was more like Mailer's *After the Fall*.) In his warm-up in *Marilyn* Mailer points out that though he'd never met Marilyn Monroe, she had for a time lived with Miller in Connecticut "not five miles away from the younger author, who [was] not yet aware of what his final relation to Marilyn Monroe would be. . . ." It appears to be destiny's decree that he should take her over. Mailer isn't the protagonist of this book; Marilyn is. But Mailer and God are waiting in the wings.

How can we readers limit ourselves to the subject when he offers us this name-play: "it was fair to engraved coincidence that the letters in Marilyn Monroe (if the 'a' were used twice and 'o' but once) would spell his own name leaving only the 'y' for excess, a trifling discrepancy, no more calculated to upset the heavens than the most miniscule diffraction of the red shift"? (What would happen to any other serious writer trying to foist his giddy acrostics on us?) He fails to record that both Miller and Mailer probably derive from Mähler. Siblings. He had said in *The Armies of the Night* that he dreaded winding up "the nice Jewish boy from Brooklyn," that that was the one personality he considered "absolutely insupportable," but it was clearly a love-hate game — or why dread it? Actually he's in no danger. He's cut off from respectability, like our country; the greatest American writer is a bum, and a bum who's starting not to mind it. The time to begin worrying is when both he and the U. S. start finding virtues in this condition; we could all wind up like drunks doing a music-hall turn.

He can't get Arthur Miller's long bones, but he's busy trying to take off his skin; he wouldn't do it to Robert Lowell. But Miller and Mailer try for the same things: he's catching Miller's hand in the gentile cookie jar. Mailer doesn't get into confessional self-analysis on Miller as he did with Lowell; he writes as if with lordly objectivity — but the reader can feel what's going on. He says of Miller's possible fear of the marriage's failing, "a man who has lost confidence in his creative power sees ridicule as the broom that can sweep him to extinction" and then proceeds to make every kind of fool of him, attributing to him the impulses and motives that Mailer considers most contemptible. Ultimately what he's saying is that Miller wasn't smart enough to get any more out of Monroe than *After the Fall*. With Mailer, if you're going to use, use big. The second half of the book is supremely cruel to Miller — and it infects and destroys one's pleasure in the good parts. The "novel biography" becomes Mailer's way to perform character assassination with the freedom of a novelist who has created fictional characters. He's so cold-blooded in imputing motives to others that he can say of Yves Montand, for example, that Marilyn Monroe was "his best ticket to notoriety." Is this how Mailer maneuvers—is Marilyn Monroe Norman Mailer's surefire subject after a few box-office flops? Is that why he shoots the works in his final orgies of gossipy conjecture and turns her death into another Chappaquiddick—safe in the knowledge no one is left to call him a liar?

He uses his gifts meanly this time—and that's not what we expect of Mailer, who is always billed as generous. This brilliant book gives off bad vibes—and vibes are what Mailer is supposed to be the master of. *Marilyn* is a feat all right: matchstick by matchstick, he's built a whole damned armada inside a bottle. (Surely he's getting ready to do *Norman*? Why leave it to someone who may care less?) But can we honor him for this book when it doesn't sit well on the stomach? It's a metaphysical cocktail-table book, and probably not many will be able to resist looking for the vicious digs and the wrap-up on the accumulated apocrypha of many years, many parties. To be king of the bums isn't really much. What are we actually getting out of *Marilyn*? Good as the best parts of it are, there's also malevolence that needs to be recognized. Is the great reporter's arrogance so limitless that he now feels free to report on matters to which he's never been exposed? Neither the world nor Marilyn Monroe's life should be seen in Norman Mailer's image.

{*The New York Times Book Review*, July 22, 1973}

:: After Innocence

The Watergate hearings have overshadowed the movies this summer, yet the corruption that Watergate has come to stand for can be seen as the culmination of what American movies have been saying for almost a decade. The movies of the thirties said that things would get better. The post-Second World War movies said that villainy would be punished and goodness would triumph; the decencies would be respected. But movies don't say that anymore; the Vietnamization of American movies is nearly complete. Today, movies say that the system is corrupt, that the whole thing stinks, and they've been saying this steadily since the mid-sixties. The Vietnam war has barely been mentioned on the screen, but you could feel it in *Bonnie and Clyde* and *Bullitt* and *Joe*, in *Easy Rider* and *Midnight Cowboy* and *The Last Picture Show*, in *They Shoot Horses, Don't They?* and *The Candidate* and *Carnal Knowledge* and *The French Connection* and *The Godfather*. It was in good movies and bad, flops and hits, especially hits—in the convictionless atmosphere, the absence of shared values, the brutalities taken for granted, the glorification of loser-heroes. It was in the harshness of the attitudes, the abrasiveness that made you wince—until, after years of it, maybe you stopped wincing. It had become normal.

In earlier action and adventure films, strength—what the strapping American hero was physically and what he embodied as the representative of the most powerful nation on earth—had to triumph. The American in those movies was the natural leader of men; he had to show the natives of any other country how to defend themselves. Even little Alan Ladd used to show them how to fight. Of course, it was a fantasy world, but this set of fantasies must have satisfied something deep down in the audience; it didn't come out of nowhere. Now the American man of action has become

367

the enemy of all men—a man out for his own good only, and, very likely, a psychotic racist. In recent films, if a character spoke of principles or ideals the odds were he would turn out to be a ruthless killer, or at least a con artist; the heroes didn't believe in anything and didn't pretend they did. American history was raked over and the myths of the Old West were turned upside down; massacre scenes, indicting our past as well as our present, left us with nothing. Just jokes and horror. Whatever the period—in *Little Big Man* or *Butch Cassidy and the Sundance Kid* or *The Wild Bunch*—you could be sure nobody was going to amount to much. The air wasn't right for achievement.

In action pictures, there was no virtuous side to identify with and nobody you really felt very good about cheering for. Both sides were unprincipled; only their styles were different, and it was a matter of preferring the less gross and despicable characters to the total monsters. In cops-and-robbers movies, the cops were likely to be no better than the crooks; sometimes they'd be worse crooks. The freshest, most contemporary element in the current movie *Cops and Robbers* is that the cops commit a robbery to get away from the hell and hopelessness of trying to keep law and order. There was a cycle of movies about drugs, and, of all those addicts sinking down and down, was there one who got himself together? In some of the most popular films, the heroes were helpless losers, self-destructive, or drifters, mysteriously defeated. Defeated just in the nature of things. Sometimes, as in *Five Easy Pieces*, the hero was so defeated he was morally superior. There were few happy endings; when a comedy such as *The Owl and the Pussycat* or *Made for Each Other* wound up with a matched pair, the characters were so knocked out that if they didn't want each other who would? It wasn't exactly as if they'd taken first place in a contest; it was more like the last stand of bedraggled survivors. And it was emotionally satisfying just because it wasn't the sort of upbeat finish that you'd have to put down as a Hollywood ending.

Though it was exhilarating to see the old mock innocence cleared away, a depressive uncertainty has settled over the movies. They're seldom enjoyable at a simple level, and that may be one of the reasons older people no longer go; they watch TV shows, which are mostly reprocessed versions of old movies—the same old plots, characters, and techniques, endlessly recombined. The enjoyment has been squeezed out, but not the reassuring simplicity. Almost three-fourths (73 percent) of the movie audience is under twenty-nine; it's an audience of people who grew up with TV and began going out to theaters when they became restless and started dating. Chances are that when they have children of their own they'll be back with the box. But while they're going out to the movies they want something different, and this demand—in the decade of Vietnam—has created a fertile chaos, an opportunity for artists as well as for the bums who pile on the meat-cleaver brawls, and for those proud of not giving a damn. Maybe the effects of the years of guilt can be seen in the press's inability to be disgusted by the witless, desiccated *The Last of Sheila*, with its pinched little dregs of chic, its yearning for Weimar. Often even the fairy-tale films are indecisive and not quite satisfying, as if the writers and directors were afraid of showing any feeling. If *Paper Moon* had been made in an earlier decade, the con man (Ryan O'Neal) would have embraced the child (Tatum O'Neal) at the end and maybe he'd have told her he was her father (whether he was or not), and the audience would have had some emotional release. The way Peter Bogdanovich did it, it's pleasant while you're watching, but you're waiting for something that never comes; it's finally a little flat and unfulfilled. But if the story had been carried to the classic tearful father-daughter embrace, mightn't the audience—or, at least, part of it—have been turned off by the unabashed sweetness? By the hope for a better future? (In movies now, people don't talk about the future; they don't make plans; they don't expect much.) Possibly the very flatness makes it easier for audiences to accept the movie.

American movies didn't "grow up"; they did a flipover from their prolonged age of innocence to this age of corruption. When Vietnam finished off the American hero as righter of wrongs, the movie industry embraced corruption greedily; formula movies could be energized by infusions of brutality, cynicism, and Naked Apism, which could all be explained by Vietnam and called realism. Moviemakers could celebrate violence and pretend, even to themselves, that they were doing the public a service. Even though some writers and directors have probably been conscientious in their attempts to shock the audience by exposing the evils of the past, the effect has not been like that of Costa-Gavras's *State of Siege*, which is literally an SOS, and makes one want to find out what's going on and do something about it. And not like the effects of *I Am a Fugitive from a Chain Gang*, which outraged people, or Fred Wiseman's *Titicut Follies* and *High*

School, which shook things up and led to reforms. Outrage isn't the aim of our most violent films; outrage isn't expected. When movie after movie tells audiences that they should be against themselves, it's hardly surprising that people go out of the theaters drained, numbly convinced that, with so much savagery and cruelty everywhere, nothing can be done. The movies have shown us the injustice of American actions throughout our history, and if we have always been rotten, the effect is not to make us feel we have the power to change but, rather, to rub our noses in it and make us accept it. In this climate, Watergate seems the most natural thing that could happen. If one were to believe recent movies, it was never any different in this country: Vietnam and Watergate are not merely where we got to but where we always were. The acceptance of corruption and the sentimentalization of defeat—that's the prevailing atmosphere in American movies, and producers, writers, and directors now make their choices in terms of a set of defeatist conventions.

When Tom Wolfe wrote about stock-car racing in *Esquire* in March, 1965 ("The Last American Hero Is Junior Johnson. *Yes!*"), he tried to evoke the physical sensations of this motor-age sport, with its rural speed-demon kings. Wolfe used the youth culture for excitement just as the movies did. Movies hit us in more ways than we can ever quite add up, and that's the kind of experience that Tom Wolfe tried to convey in prose. He described the sensations without attempting to add them up or theorize about them, and, because he had a remarkable gift for hyperactive, evocative writing, the effect was an impassioned turn-on. And, because in this article and others he didn't make his obeisances to the higherness of the traditional arts, he ran into the sort of disapproval that movies get. It was a compliment, of course—recognition from the enemy, because he had set up a great polemical target: the genteel, condescending press, which had ignored the new sports or treated them marginally. When Wolfe reprinted the racing article, which became the largest section of *The Kandy-Kolored Tangerine-Flake Streamline Baby*, he shortened the title to "The Last American Hero," and that's the name of the film based on it.

As journalism, Wolfe's charged-up pieces had the impact of an explorer's excited report on new terrain. But the youth culture that he brought into star journalism was already in the movies (just as the movies were in it). That culture was partly created by the movies, and his surfers and rockers and racers had been the lifeblood of the Grade B pop-genre films of the fifties. The car and the movie came along together, and chases, usually involving cars, have been surefire for so long that there was a time when the chase used to be called "pure movie"; there's barely a male star who hasn't served his days as a racer. The first demolition derby wasn't held until 1961, but moviemakers had always known about people's loving to see cars bashed. Demolition scenes were the primeval laugh-getters of silent pictures, and smashed cars and planes still get the biggest laughs in a new primeval picture like *Live and Let Die*. (Geoffrey Holder's leering wickedness as the impresario of the revels in the picture is kiddie camp.)

In the introduction to his book, Wolfe recorded the discovery that a builder of baroque custom cars he talked with "had been living like the *complete artist* for years," and went on, "He had starved, suffered—the whole thing—so he could sit inside a garage and create these cars which more than 99 percent of the American people would consider ridiculous, vulgar and lower-class-awful beyond comment almost." That's a strange overestimate of the number of people with good taste arrayed against the car builder; racing pictures were made for audiences to whom such a man had been an artist all along. So when you make a movie out of Tom Wolfe's reports on the world outside the class biases of Eastern-establishment prudery, you're taking the material back where it came from, and there's no occasion for whoops of revelation. The movie of "The Last American Hero" isn't startling, the way Wolfe's pieces were; but, with a script that uses Wolfe as the source for most of the story elements, Lamont Johnson, who directed, has done the Southern racing scene and the character of the people caught up in it better, perhaps, than they've ever been done before. The movie has everything *but* originality.

The title (which is a tired one anyway) no longer means what it did for Tom Wolfe. The Junior Johnson that Wolfe wrote about beat the system and won on his own terms; that was what made him a hero and a legend. Driving whatever he could stick together, he won out over the cars sponsored and specially built by the motor industry. He won even when his own car couldn't go as fast, by tricks such as catching free rides—by tailgating and being sucked along by the vacuum of the faster cars. A Southern country boy who became a hot-rod genius by running his father's moonshine whiskey in the middle of the night, he beat the big pros by ingenuity, skill, and blind impudence, and he beat them over and over—seven times, even though he was out for a couple of seasons when he was sent to federal prison for helping his daddy with some of the heavy labor at the still. (The agents were gunning for him, because he'd made them look ridiculous on the back roads years before.) That's the stuff of legend, all right. By the time Junior Johnson made his peace with Detroit and started to drive the factory-built racing cars, he was too much of a hero to be judged a sellout. He had already proved himself and then some, so it was all right for him to settle down, like a man of sense.

But between the publication of the Wolfe article and the making of the movie there was Vietnam. The hero of the movie—called Junior Jackson—starts out by cheating to win a demolition derby, and when he moves on to racing he can't make it with his own car. He wins his first big race *after* he starts driving as a hired hand for a big-money man, Colt (Ed Lauter). Even the steady girl the real Junior had gone with since high school, and later married, is replaced by a track follower (Valerie Perrine), who floats along with the winners. So there's sex without romance, sex without a future. The movie also avoids the easy possibilities for sympathy; it doesn't make Junior's path as hard as it was. He doesn't go to prison in the movie—it's his father who is busted as a result of Junior's bravado at the wheel. Colt, rather like George C. Scott in *The Hustler*, suggests a personification of the power of money, rather than just a representative of Detroit. Colt is almost lascivious about winning, and his winning is evil (but we never learn what winning gets him, or what it did for the diabolical Scott character). In *The Last American Hero*, corruption seems to be inescapable: if you want to win, you learn to take orders even from people whose idea of winning you don't understand. And at the end Junior Jackson is growing up—which is to say, learning the price of success in the real world. He is forced to sacrifice his friendships and his principles. The film says that to win you give up everything you care about except winning. It tells the story not of a man who fights for his independence but of a man who is smart enough not to sell himself too cheap.

Who would believe the actual story of Junior Johnson now—how hard it really was for him, and that he made it? This version will seem far more honest to movie audiences, because the new conventions are that you can't win and that everybody's a sellout. Even the absence of romance makes the movie more convincing—tougher, cool. And since Junior, played by Jeff Bridges, has a visible capacity for tenderness, the absence of romance is cruelly felt by the audience. By turning Junior Johnson's story around, the director, Lamont Johnson (and his writer, William Roberts, with a sizable, though uncredited, assist from William Kerby, who wrote the best scenes), has been able to make a hip, modern movie. It is, ironically, the most honest and gifted and tough-minded people in Hollywood who are fighting for defeat. The picture has total fidelity to its own scrupulous, hard-edged vision: the hero pays a price. It costs Junior Jackson something to win races; you can see that in Jeff Bridges' face.

Lamont Johnson doesn't exploit the backwoods people for the folksy touches that can make urban audiences laugh; he perceives the values in Junior Jackson's family life—in his affection for his mother (Geraldine Fitzgerald) and his vacuously grinning brother (Gary Busey), and, especially, in his bond to his father (Art Lund, in a towering performance). The picture was shot in Virginia and the Carolinas, using footage from actual races and derbies, and the crowds and details, the excited Southern faces at the stock-car tracks—everything feels right. Lamont Johnson has the feel for the South that John Boorman (who is English) couldn't get in *Deliverance*. Boorman is such an aestheticizing director—alienated, inhuman, yet the more gripping for the distance he keeps—that *Deliverance* held audiences by its mannered, ghastly-lovely cumulative power. It had the formality of a nightmare. (There was a hush in the theater when it was over.) *Deliverance* demonstrated that a movie can be effective even if you are always aware of the actors' acting and don't really believe in a single character, down to the bit players (except maybe James Dickey as the sheriff). But there is a special elation about a movie when the casting and the acting and the milieu seem effortlessly, inexplicably right. Paul Mazursky can get Los Angeles (*Alex in Wonderland*, *Blume in Love*) but can't get Venice (*Blume in Love*). Lamont Johnson's feeling for the milieu here amounts to an unusual sensibility: a gift for bringing all the elements of film together so that the people breathe right for where they live. He isn't an original—not in the way that, say, Mazursky, manic poet of middle-class quirk, is. (Has there ever been another self-satirist like Mazursky—humanly understanding and utterly freaked out?) But Lamont Johnson's work is attentive and satisfying. He's a far better movie man than many of the more original talents, and this film, if one sees the version he made, has everything going for it. (Twentieth Century-Fox tampered with the film, cutting a couple of the best scenes and then opening it in the South as an action racing picture. Since it isn't, it bombed out. And then the Fox executives decided it was a dog that wouldn't go in the big cities, because they knew that sophisticated people don't go to racing pictures. It opened in New York for a week in the summer as a "Showcase" presentation—that is to say, it got a second run without a first run—and its failure was the movie company's self-fulfilling prophecy. Though the reviews were excellent, they came out too late to attract an audience; Fox hadn't bothered with advance press screenings for a racing picture. But this movie transcends its genre; *The Last American Hero*, which is coming back next week, isn't just about stock-car racing, any more than *The Hustler* was only about shooting pool, and in terms of presenting the background of a sports hero it goes far beyond anything in *Downhill Racer*. If *The Last American Hero* finds a fraction of its rightful audience now, perhaps someone in the head office at Fox could do the sane, decent thing and restore the cuts?)

Sometimes, just on his own, Jeff Bridges is enough to make a picture worth seeing, and he's never before been used so fully, or in a way so integral to a film's conception. Only twenty-two when this picture was shot, he may be the most natural and least self-conscious screen actor who ever lived; physically, it's as if he had spent his life in the occupation of each character. He's the most American—the loosest—of all the young actors, unencumbered by stage diction and the stiff, emasculated poses of most juveniles. If he has a profile, we're not aware of it. He probably can't do the outrageous explosive scenes that Robert De Niro brings off in *Mean Streets* or the giddy-charming romantic clowning that De Niro did in the otherwise forgettable *The Gang That Couldn't Shoot Straight*, but De Niro—a real winner—is best when he's coming on and showing off. Jeff Bridges just moves into a role and lives in it—so deep in it that the little things seem to come straight from the character's soul. His brother Beau shares this infallible instinct, but Beau's effects don't seem to come from as far down; Beau Bridges has a lighter presence, an easier smile. Jeff Bridges' Junior Jackson is a cocky Huck Finn in the age of Detroit: impulsive, dogged, and self-sufficient; sure enough of himself to show his rank, shrewd enough to know where he's outranked. In a monologue scene (possibly suggested by Godard's *Masculine Feminine*), Junior, away from home for a race and feeling sentimental, uses a make-your-own-record machine to tell his family he's thinking of them and loves them; then, realizing he's beyond this kind of kid stuff, he throws the record away. The quality of Bridges' acting in this scene enlarges the meaning of the movie, yet he doesn't seem to be using anything more than a few shrugs and half-smothered words.

The Last American Hero never goes soft, and maybe that's why the picture felt so realistic to me; it wasn't until I reread the Wolfe piece that I realized what a turnaround it was. But we believe the worst now—maybe *only* the worst. When we see a picture from the age of happy endings, the conventions may stick out as antiquated and ludicrous (and often they did when the picture was new), but the conventions that flow from the acceptance of corruption are insidiously believable, because they seem smart, while the older ones seem dumb. We will never know the extent of the damage movies are doing to us, but movie art, it appears, thrives on moral chaos. When the country is paralyzed, the popular culture may tell us why. After innocence, winners become losers. Movies are probably inuring us to corruption; the sellout is the hero-survivor for our times.

{*The New Yorker*, October 1, 1973}

:: Everyday Inferno

Martin Scorsese's *Mean Streets* is a true original of our period, a triumph of personal filmmaking. It has its own hallucinatory look; the characters live in the darkness of bars, with lighting and color just this side of lurid. It has its own unsettling, episodic rhythm and a high-charged emotional range that is dizzyingly sensual. At the beginning, there's a long, fluid sequence as the central character, Charlie, comes into a bar and greets his friends; there's the laying on of hands, and we know that he is doing what he always does. And when the camera glides along with him as he's drawn toward the topless dancers on the barroom stage, we share his trance. At the end of the scene, when he's up on the stage, entering into the dance, he's not some guy who's taken leave of his senses but a man going through his nightly ritual. Movies generally work you up to expect the sensual intensities, but here you may be pulled into high without warning. Violence erupts crazily, too, the way it does in life—so unexpectedly fast that you can't believe it, and over before you've been able to take it in. The whole movie has this effect; it psychs you up to accept everything it shows you. And since the story deepens as it goes along, by the end you're likely to be open-mouthed, trying to rethink what you've seen. Though the street language and the operatic style may be too much for those with conventional tastes, if this picture isn't a runaway success the reason could be that it's so original that some people will be dumbfounded—too struck to respond. It's about American life here and now, and it doesn't look like an American movie, or feel like one. If it were subtitled, we could hail a new European or South American talent—a new Buñuel steeped in Verdi, perhaps—and go home easier at heart. Because what Scorsese, who is thirty, has done with the experience of growing up in New York's Little Italy has a thicker-textured rot and violence than we have ever had in an American movie, and a riper sense of evil.

The zinger in the movie—and it's this, I think, that begins to come together in one's head when the picture is over—is the way it gets at the psychological connections between Italian Catholicism and crime, between sin and crime. Some editorial writers like to pretend this is all a matter of prejudice; they try to tell us that there is no basis for the popular ethnic stereotypes—as if crime among Italians didn't have a different tone from crime among Irish or Jews or blacks. Editorial writers think they're serving the interests of democracy when they ask us to deny the evidence of our senses. But all crime is not alike, and different ethnic groups have different styles of lawlessness. These Mafiosi loafers hang around differently from loafing blacks; in some ways, the small-time hoods of *Mean Streets* (good Catholics who live at home with their parents) have more in common with the provincial wolf pack of Fellini's *I Vitelloni* (cadging, indulged sons of middle-class families) than with the other ethnic groups in New York City. And these hoods live in such an insulated world that anyone outside it—the stray Jew or black they encounter—is as foreign and funny to them as a little man from Mars.

Many people interpreted the success of *The Godfather* to mean that the film glorified the gangsters' lives. During the Second World War, a documentary showing the noise and congestion of New York City was cheered by nostalgic American soldiers overseas; if audiences were indeed attracted to the life of the Corleone family (and I think some probably were), the reaction may be just as aberrant to the intentions of *The Godfather*, the best gangster film ever made in this country. It's likely that Italian, or Sicilian, Catholicism has a special, somewhat romantic appeal to Americans at this time. Italians appear to others to accept the fact that they're doomed; they learn to be comfortable with it—it's what gives them that warm, almost tactile glow. Their voluptuous, vacant-eyed smiles tell us that they want to get the best out of this life: they know they're going to burn in eternity, so why should they think about things that are depressing? It's as if they were totally carnal: everything is for their pleasure. Maybe it is this relaxed attitude that gave the Mafiosi of *The Godfather* their charm for the American audience. Was the audience envying them their close family ties and the vitality of their lawlessness? Was it envying their having got used to a sense of sin? It's almost as if the non-Catholic part of America wanted to say that *mea culpa* is *nostra culpa*.

Before *Mean Streets* is over, that glow gets very hot and any glamour is sweated off. The clearest fact about Charlie (Harvey Keitel), junior member of a Mafia family—and, in a non-literal sense, the autobiographical central figure—is that whatever he does in his life, he's a sinner. Behind the titles you see him smiling his edgy, jocular smile and shaking hands with a priest, as if sealing a pact, while the words appear: "Directed by Martin Scorsese." Charlie, you can see in his tense ferret's face, feels he was born to be punished. Like his friends, round-faced, jovial Tony the barkeep (David Proval) and pompous Michael (Richard Romanus), a chiseling dude, he basks in the life. Running numbers, gambling, two-bit swindles: they grew up in this squalor and it's all they've ever known or wanted. To them, this is living it up. But Charlie isn't a relaxed sinner; he torments himself, like a fanatic seminarian. He's so frightened of burning he's burning already. Afraid of everything, he's everybody's friend, always trying to keep the peace. He's a dutiful toady to his Uncle Giovanni (Cesare Danova), the big man in the Mafia, and he fails those he really cares about: his girl, Teresa (Amy Robinson), and his friend Johnny Boy (Robert De Niro), a compulsive gambler—more than compulsive, irrational, a gambler with no sense of money. Charlie is too vain and sycophantic not to give in to social pressure. Teresa isn't rated high enough by his uncle; and his uncle, his king, the source of the restaurant he hopes to get, has told him not to be involved with Johnny Boy. Johnny Boy was named after Giovanni, but the family protects you only if you truckle to the elder statesmen and behave yourself—if you're a good timeserver.

Johnny Boy isn't; he flouts all the rules, he just won't "behave." He's fearless, gleefully self-destructive, cracked—moonstruck but not really crazy. His madness isn't explained (fortunately, since explaining madness is the most limiting and generally least convincing thing a movie can do). When you're growing up, if you know someone crazy-daring and half-admirable (and maybe most of us do), you don't wonder how the beautiful nut got that way; he seems to spring up full-blown and whirling, and you watch the fireworks and feel crummily cautious in your sanity. That's how it is here. Charlie digs Johnny Boy's recklessness. De Niro's Johnny Boy is the only one of the group of grifters and scummy racketeers who is his own man; he is the true hero, while Charlie, through whose mind we see the action, is the director's worst vision of himself.

The story emerges from the incidents without dominating them; it's more like a thread running through. The audience isn't propelled by suspense devices, nor is the cataclysmic finish really an end—it's only a stop. Johnny Boy needs help. He owes Michael, the dude, a lot of money, and it hurts Michael's self-esteem that he can't collect; nagging and spiteful, he threatens violence. But Charlie doesn't save Johnny Boy by going to his big-shot uncle for help, because he just can't risk taking a problem to his uncle. A good Mafia boy is not only subservient; unless something important is happening to him, he maintains his visibility as near to invisibility as possible. Uncle Giovanni, a dignified, dull, dull man, doesn't really see Charlie—doesn't register his existence—and that's what keeps Charlie in his good graces. But if Charlie asks for help for a crazy friend in trouble, he loses his low visibility. So Charlie talks a lot to Johnny Boy about friendship and does nothing. He's Judas the betrayer because of his careful angling to move up the next rung of the ladder. How can a man show his soul to be pettier than that? Charlie, the surrogate for the director, is nobody's friend, and—as the movie itself proves—least of all his own. Charlie knows from the beginning that he pays for everything. Scorsese isn't asking for expiation of Charlie's sins in the movie; sins aren't expiated in this movie. (The director has cast himself in the bit part of Michael's helper; when Johnny Boy makes Michael look so bad that Michael decides to get satisfaction, it is Scorsese who, as the gunman, pulls the trigger.)

It's twenty years since Fellini's *I Vitelloni* planted the autobiographical hero on the screen. Fellini did it in a fairly conventional way: his Moraldo (Franco Interlenghi) was the sensitive, handsome observer who looked at the limitations of small-town life and, at the end, said goodbye to all that. In *La Dolce Vita*, the Fellini figure was the seduced, disillusioned journalist (Marcello Mastroianni) to whom everything happened, and in *8½* Mastroianni, again standing in for Fellini, was the movie director at the center of a multi-ring circus, the man sought after by everyone. In *Roma*, Fellini threw in new versions of several of his earlier representatives, and himself to boot. No other movie director, except among the "underground" filmmakers, has been so explicitly autobiographical. But in *I Vitelloni* we never caught a glimpse of the actual Fellini who emerged later; we never saw the fantasist as a young man, or the energy and will that drove him on. Movie directors have not yet learned the novelists' trick of throwing themselves into the third person, into the action, as Norman Mailer does even in his reporting; directors tend to make their own representatives passive, reflective figures, with things happening to them and around them, like Curt (Richard Dreyfuss) in George Lucas's nice (though overrated) little picture *American Graffiti*. Scorsese does something far more complex, because Charlie's wormy, guilt-ridden consciousness is made abhorrent to us at the same time that we're seeing life through it. Charlie is so agitated because he is aware of his smallness.

Scorsese's method is more like that of the Montreal filmmaker Claude Jutra, who, playing himself in *À Tout Prendre*, masochistically made himself weak, like those chinless self-portraits with traumatic stares which painters put at the edges of their canvases. Jutra left out the mind and energies that made him a movie director, and apparently put on the screen everything in himself he loathed, and this is what Scorsese does, but Scorsese also puts in the tensions of a man in conflict, and a harlequin externalization of those tensions. He's got that dervish Johnny Boy dancing around Charlie's fears, needling Charlie and exposing him to danger despite all his conciliatory nice-guyism. Johnny Boy's careless, contemptuous explosions seem a direct response to Charlie's trying to keep the lid on everything—it's as if Charlie's id were throwing bombs and laughing at him. When Johnny Boy has finally loused everything up, he can say to Charlie, "You got what you wanted."

While an actor like Jeff Bridges in *The Last American Hero* hits the true note, De Niro here hits the far-out, flamboyant one and makes his own truth. He's a bravura actor, and those who have registered him only as the grinning, tobacco-chewing dolt of that hunk of inept whimsey *Bang the Drum Slowly* will be unprepared for his volatile performance. De Niro does something like what Dustin Hoffman was doing in *Midnight Cowboy*, but wilder; this kid doesn't just act—he takes off into the vapors. De Niro is so intensely appealing that it might be easy to overlook Harvey Keitel's work as Charlie. But Keitel makes De Niro's triumph possible; Johnny Boy can bounce off Charlie's anxious, furious admiration. Keitel, cramped in his stiff clothes (these Mafiosi dress respectable—in the long, dark overcoats of businessmen of an earlier era), looks like a more compact Richard Conte or Dane Clark, and speaks in the rhythms of a lighter-voiced John Garfield, Charlie's idol; it's his control that holds the story together. The whole world of the movie—Catholicism as it's actually practiced among these people, what it means on the street—is in Charlie's mingy-minded face.

The picture is stylized without seeming in any way artificial; it is the only movie I've ever seen that achieves the effects of Expressionism without the use of distortion. *Mean Streets* never loses touch with the ordinary look of things or with common experience; rather, it puts us in closer touch with the ordinary, the common, by turning a different light on them. The ethnic material is comparable to James T. Farrell's Studs Lonigan trilogy and to what minor novelists like Louis Golding did in the street-and-tenement novels of the thirties, but when this material is written on the screen the result is infinitely more powerful. (In a film review in 1935, Graham Greene—a Catholic—said that "the camera . . . can note with more exactitude and vividness than the prose of most living playwrights the atmosphere of mean streets and cheap lodgings.") And though *Mean Streets* has links to all those Richard Conte Italian-family movies, like *House of Strangers*, and to the urban-feudal life of *The Godfather*, the incidents and details are far more personal. Scorsese, who did the writing with Mardik Martin, knows the scene and knows how it all fits together; it's his, and he has the ability to put his feelings about it on the screen. All this is what the Boston Irish world of *The Friends of Eddie Coyle* lacked; the picture was shallow and tedious, because although we could see how the gangsters victimized each other, the police and the gangsters had no roots—and intertwined roots were what it was meant to be about. It was a milieu picture without milieu. In *Mean Streets*, every character, every sound is rooted in those streets. The back-and-forth talk of Charlie and Johnny Boy isn't little-people empty-funny (as it was in *Marty*); it's a tangle of jeering and joshing, of mutual goading and nerves getting frayed. These boys understand each other too well. Charlie's love for Johnny Boy is his hate for himself, and Johnny Boy knows Charlie's flaw. No other American gangster-milieu film has had this element of personal obsession; there has never before been a gangster film in which you felt that the director himself was saying, "This is my story." Not that we come away thinking that Martin Scorsese is or ever was a gangster, but we're so affected because we know in our bones that he has walked these streets and has felt what his characters feel. He knows how natural crime is to them.

There is something of the Carol Reed film *The Third Man* in the way the atmosphere imposes itself, and, like Reed, Scorsese was best known as an editor (on *Woodstock*, *Medicine Ball Caravan*, *Elvis on Tour*, C.B.S. documentaries, etc.) before he became a director *(Who's That Knocking at My Door?, Boxcar Bertha)*. Graham Greene, the screenwriter of *The Third Man*, wrote a prescription for movies that fits this one almost perfectly. "The cinema," Greene said, "has always developed by means of a certain low cunning. . . . We are driven back to the 'blood,' the thriller. . . . We have to . . . dive below the polite level, to something nearer to the common life. . . . And when we have attained to a more popular drama, even if it is in the simplest terms of blood on a garage floor ('There lay Duncan laced in his golden blood'), the scream of cars in flight, all the old excitements at their simplest and most sure-fire, then we can begin—secretly, with low cunning—to develop our poetic drama." And, again, "If you excite your audience first, you can put over what you will of horror, suffering, truth." However, Scorsese's atmosphere is without the baroque glamour of evil that makes *The Third Man* so ambiguous in its appeal. There's nothing hokey here; it is a low, malign world Scorsese sees. But it's seen to the beat of an exuberant, satiric score. Scorsese has an operatic visual style (the swarthy, imaginative cinematography is by Kent Wakeford), and, with Jonathan T. Taplin, the twenty-six-year-old rock-record impresario, as producer, he has used a mixture of records to more duplicit effect than anyone since Kenneth Anger in *Scorpio Rising*. It's similar to Bertolucci's use of a motley score in *Before the Revolution* and *The Conformist* and to the score in parts of *The Godfather*, but here the music is a more active participant. The score is the background music of the characters' lives—and not only the background, because it enters in. It's as if these characters were just naturally part of an opera with pop themes. The music is the electricity in the air of this movie; the music is like an engine that the characters move to. Johnny Boy, the most susceptible, half dances through the movie, and when he's trying to escape from Michael he does a jerky frug before hopping into the getaway car. He *enjoys* being out of control—he revels in it—and we can feel the music turning him on. But *Mean Streets* doesn't use music, as *Easy Rider* sometimes did, to do the movie's work for it. (In *American Graffiti*, the old-rock nostalgia catches the audience up before the movie even gets going.) The music here isn't our music, meant to put us in the mood of the movie, but the characters' music. And bits of old movies become part of the opera, too, because what the characters know of passion and death, and even of big-time gangster-ism, comes from the movies. In Scorsese's vision, music and the movies work within us and set the terms in which we perceive ourselves. Music and the movies and the Church. A witches' brew.

Scorsese could make poetic drama, rather than melodrama laced with decadence, out of the schlock of shabby experience because he didn't have to "dive below the polite level, to something nearer to the common life" but had to do something much tougher—descend into himself and bring up what neither he nor anyone else could have known was there. Though he must have suspected. This is a blood thriller in the truest sense.

{*The New Yorker*, October 8, 1973}

:: Movieland—The Bums' Paradise

Edmund Wilson summed up Raymond Chandler convincingly in 1945 when he said of *Farewell, My Lovely*, "It is not simply a question here of a puzzle which has been put together but of a malaise conveyed to the reader, the horror of a hidden conspiracy which is continually turning up in the most varied and unlikely forms. . . . It is only when I get to the end that I feel my old crime-story depression descending upon me again—because here again, as is so often the case, the explanation of the mysteries, when it comes, is neither interesting nor plausible enough. It fails to justify the excitement produced by the picturesque and sinister happenings, and I cannot help feeling cheated." Locked in the conventions of pulp writing, Raymond Chandler never found a way of dealing with that malaise. But Robert Altman does, in *The Long Goodbye*, based on Chandler's 1953 Los Angeles-set novel. The movie is set in the same city twenty years later; this isn't just a matter of the private-detective hero's prices going from twenty-five dollars a day to fifty—it's a matter of rethinking the book and the genre. Altman, who probably works closer to his unconscious than any other American director, tells a detective story, all right, but he does it through a spree—a high-flying rap on Chandler and the movies and that Los Angeles sickness. The movie isn't just Altman's private-eye movie—it's his Hollywood movie, set in the mixed-up world of movie-influenced life that is L.A.

In Los Angeles, you can live any way you want (except the urban way); it's the fantasy-brothel, where you can live the fantasy of your choice. You can also live well without being rich, which is the basic and best reason people swarm there. In that city—the pop amusement park of the shifty and the uprooted, the city famed as the place where you go to sell out—

Raymond Chandler situated his incorruptible knight Philip Marlowe, the private detective firmly grounded in high principles. Answering a letter in 1951, Chandler wrote, "If being in revolt against a corrupt society constitutes being immature, then Philip Marlowe is extremely immature. If seeing dirt where there is dirt constitutes an inadequate social adjustment, then Philip Marlowe has inadequate social adjustment. Of course Marlowe is a failure, and he knows it. He is a failure because he hasn't any money. . . . A lot of very good men have been failures because their particular talents did not suit their time and place." And he cautioned, "But you must remember that Marlowe is not a real person. He is a creature of fantasy. He is in a false position because I put him there. In real life, a man of his type would no more be a private detective than he would be a university don." Six months later, when his rough draft of *The Long Goodbye* was criticized by his agent, Chandler wrote back, "I didn't care whether the mystery was fairly obvious, but I cared about the people, about this strange corrupt world we live in, and how any man who tried to be honest looks in the end either sentimental or plain foolish."

Chandler's sentimental foolishness is the taking-off place for Altman's film. Marlowe (Elliott Gould) is a wryly forlorn knight, just slogging along. Chauffeur, punching bag, errand boy, he's used, lied to, double-crossed. He's the gallant fool in a corrupt world—the innocent eye. He isn't stupid and he's immensely likable, but the pulp pretense that his chivalrous code was armor has collapsed, and the romantic machismo of Bogart's Marlowe in *The Big Sleep* has evaporated. The one-lone-idealist-in-the-city-crawling-with-rats becomes a schlemiel who thinks he's tough and wise. (He's still driving a 1948 Lincoln Continental and trying to behave like Bogart.) He doesn't know the facts of life that everybody else knows; even the police know more about the case he's involved in than he does. Yet he's the only one who *cares*. That's his true innocence, and it's his slack-jawed crazy sweetness that keeps the movie from being harsh or scabrous.

Altman's goodbye to the private-eye hero is comic and melancholy and full of regrets. It's like cleaning house and throwing out things that you know you're going to miss—there comes a time when junk dreams get in your way. *The Long Goodbye* reaches a satirical dead end that kisses off the private-eye form as gracefully as *Beat the Devil* finished off the cycle of the international-intrigue thriller. Altman does variations on Chandler's theme the way the John Williams score does variations on the title song, which is a tender ballad in one scene, a funeral dirge in another. Williams' music is a parody of the movies' frequent overuse of a theme, and a demonstration of how adaptable a theme can be. This picture, less accidental than *Beat the Devil*, is just about as funny, though quicker-witted, and dreamier, in soft, mellow color and volatile images—a reverie on the lies of old movies. It's a knockout of a movie that has taken eight months to arrive in New York because after opening in Los Angeles last March and being badly received (perfect irony) it folded out of town. It's probably the best American movie ever made that almost didn't open in New York. Audiences may have felt they'd already had it with Elliott Gould; the young men who looked like him in 1971 have got cleaned up and barbered and turned into Mark Spitz. But it actually adds poignancy to the film that Gould himself is already an anachronism.

Thinner and more lithe than in his brief fling as a superstar (his success in *Bob & Carol & Ted & Alice* and *M*A*S*H* led to such speedy exploitation of his box-office value that he appeared in seven films between 1969 and 1971), Gould comes back with his best performance yet. It's his movie. The rubber-legged slouch, the sheepish, bony-faced angularity have their grace; drooping-eyed, squinting, with more blue stubble on his face than any other hero on record, he's a loose and woolly, jazzy Job. There's a skip and bounce in his shamble. Chandler's arch, spiky dialogue—so hardboiled it can make a reader's teeth grate—gives way to this Marlowe's muttered, befuddled throwaways, his self-sendups. Gould's Marlowe is a man who is had by everybody—a male pushover, reminiscent of Fred MacMurray in *Double Indemnity*. He's Marlowe as Miss Lonelyhearts. Yet this softhearted honest loser is so logical a modernization, so "right," that when you think about Marlowe afterward you can't imagine any other way of playing him now that wouldn't be just fatuous. (Think of Mark Spitz as Marlowe if you want fatuity pure.) The good-guys-finish-last conception was implicit in Chandler's L.A. all along, and Marlowe was only one step from being a clown, but Chandler pulped his own surrogate and made Marlowe, the Victorian relic, a winner. Chandler has a basic phoniness that it would have been a cinch to exploit. He wears his conscience right up front; the con trick is that it's not a writer's conscience. Offered the chance to break free of the straitjacket of the detective novel, Chandler declined. He clung to the limiting stereotypes of pop writing and blamed "an age whose dominant note is an efficient vulgarity, an unscrupulous scramble for the dollar." Style, he said, "can exist in a savage and dirty age, but it cannot exist in the Coca-Cola age . . . the Book of the Month, and the Hearst Press." It was Marlowe, the independent man, dedicated to autonomy—his needs never rising above that twenty-five dollars a day—who actually lived like an artist. Change Marlowe's few possessions, "a coat, a hat, and a gun," to "a coat, a hat, and a typewriter," and the cracks in Chandler's myth of the hero become a hopeless split.

Robert Altman is all of a piece, but he's complicated. You can't predict what's coming next in the movie; his plenitude comes from somewhere beyond reason. An Altman picture doesn't have to be great to be richly pleasurable. He tosses in more than we can keep track of, maybe more than *he* bothers to keep track of; he nips us in surprising ways. In *The Long Goodbye*, as in *M*A*S*H*, there are climaxes, but you don't have the sense of waiting for them, because what's in between is so satisfying. He underplays the plot and concentrates on the people, so it's almost all of equal interest, and you feel as if it could go on indefinitely and you'd be absorbed in it. Altman may have the most glancing touch since Lubitsch, and his ear for comedy is better than anybody else's. In this period of movies, it isn't necessary (or shouldn't be) to punch the nuances home; he just glides over them casually, in the freest possible way. Gould doesn't propel the action as Bogart did; the story unravels around the private eye—the corrupt milieu wins. Maybe the reason some people have difficulty getting onto Altman's wavelength is that he's just about incapable of overdramatizing. He's not a pusher. Even in this film, he doesn't push decadence. He doesn't heat up angst the way it was heated in *Midnight Cowboy* and *They Shoot Horses, Don't They?*

Pop culture takes some nourishment from the "high" arts, but it feeds mainly on itself. *The Long Goodbye* had not been filmed before, because the book came out too late, after the private-eye-movie cycle had peaked. Marlowe had already become Bogart, and you could see him in it when you read the book. You weren't likely to have kept the other Marlowes of the forties (Dick Powell, Robert Montgomery, George Montgomery) in your mind, and you had to see somebody in it. The novel reads almost like a parody of pungent writing—like a semiliterate's idea of great writing. The detective-novel genre always verged on self-parody, because it gave you nothing under the surface. Hemingway didn't need to state what his characters felt, because his external descriptions implied all that, but the pulp writers who imitated Hemingway followed the hardboiled-detective pattern that Hammett had invented; they externalized everything and implied nothing. Their gaudy terseness demonstrates how the novel and the comic strip can merge. They described actions and behavior from the outside, as if they were writing a script that would be given some inner life by the actors and the director; the most famous practitioners of the genre were, in fact, moonlighting screenwriters. *The Long Goodbye* may have good descriptions of a jail or a police lineup, but the prose is alternately taut and lumpy with lessons in corruption, and most of the great observations you're supposed to get from it are just existentialism with oil slick. With its classy dames, a Marlowe influenced by Marlowe, the obligatory tension between Marlowe and the cops, and the sentimental bar scenes, *The Long Goodbye* was a product of the private-eye films of the decade before. Chandler's corrupt milieu—what Auden called "The Great Wrong Place"—was the new-style capital of sin, the city that made the movies and was made by them.

In Chandler's period (he died in 1959), movies and novels interacted; they still do, but now the key interaction may be between movies and movies—and between movies and us. We can no longer view ourselves—the way Nathanael West did—as different from the Middle Westerners in L.A. lost in their movie-fed daydreams, and the L.A. world founded on pop is no longer the world *out there*, as it was for Edmund Wilson. Altman's *The Long Goodbye* (like Paul Mazursky's *Blume in Love*) is about people who live in L.A. because they like the style of life, which comes from the movies. It's not about people who work in movies but about people whose lives have been shaped by them; it's set in the modern L.A. of the stoned sensibility, where people have given in to the beauty that always looks unreal. The inhabitants are an updated gallery of California freaks, with one character who links this world to Nathanael West's—the Malibu Colony gatekeeper (Ken Sansom), who does ludicrous, pitiful impressions of Barbara Stanwyck in *Double Indemnity* (which was Chandler's first screenwriting job), and of James Stewart, Walter Brennan, and Cary Grant (the actor Chandler said he had in mind for Marlowe). In a sense, Altman here has already made *Day of the Locust*. (To do it as West intended it, and to have it make contemporary sense, it would now have to be set in Las Vegas.) Altman's references to movies don't stick out—they're just part of the texture, as they are in L.A.—but there are enough so that a movie pedant could do his own weirdo version of *A Skeleton Key to Finnegans Wake*.

The one startlingly violent action in the movie is performed by a syndicate boss who is as rapt in the glory of his success as a movie mogul. Prefigured in Chandler's description of movie producers in his famous essay "Writers in Hollywood," Marty Augustine (Mark Rydell) is the next step up in paranoid self-congratulation from the Harry Cohn-like figure that Rod Steiger played in *The Big Knife*; he's freaked out on success, L.A.-Las Vegas style. His big brown eyes with their big brown bags preside over the decaying pretty-boy face of an Eddie Fisher, and when he flashes his ingenuous Paul Anka smile he's so appalling he's comic. His violent act is outrageously gratuitous (he smashes a Coke bottle in the fresh young face of his unoffending mistress), yet his very next line of dialogue is so comic-tough that we can't help laughing while we're still gasping, horrified—much as we did when Cagney shoved that half grapefruit in Mae Clarke's nagging kisser. This little Jewish gangster-boss is a mod imp—offspring of the movies, as much a creature of show business as Joel Grey's m.c. in *Cabaret*. Marty Augustine's bumbling goon squad (ethnically balanced) are the illegitimate sons of Warner Brothers. In the Chandler milieu, what could be better casting than the aristocratic Nina van Pallandt as the rich dish—the duplicitous blonde, Mrs. Wade? And, as her husband, the blocked famous writer Roger Wade, Sterling Hayden, bearded like Neptune, and as full of the old mach as the progenitor of tough-guy writing himself. The most movieish bit of dialogue is from the book: when the police come to question Marlowe about his friend Terry Lennox, Marlowe says, "This is where I say, 'What's this all about?' and you say, 'We ask the questions.'" But the resolution of Marlowe's friendship with Terry isn't from Chandler, and its logic is probably too brutally sound for Bogart-lovers to stomach. Terry Lennox (smiling Jim Bouton, the baseball player turned broadcaster) becomes the Harry Lime in Marlowe's life, and the final sequence is a variation on *The Third Man*, with the very last shot a riff on the leave-taking scenes of the movies' most famous clown.

The movie achieves a self-mocking fairy-tale poetry. The slippery shifts within the frames of Vilmos Zsigmond's imagery are part of it, and so are the offbeat casting (Henry Gibson as the sinister quack Dr. Verringer; Jack Riley, of the Bob Newhart show, as the piano player) and the dialogue.

(The script is officially credited to the venerable pulp author Leigh Brackett; she also worked on *The Big Sleep* and many other good movies, but when you hear the improvised dialogue you can't take this credit literally.) There are some conceits that are fairly precarious (the invisible-man stunt in the hospital sequence) and others that are waywardly funny (Marlowe trying to lie to his cat) or suggestive and beautiful (the Wades' Doberman coming out of the Pacific with his dead master's cane in his teeth). When Nina van Pallandt thrashes in the ocean at night, her pale-orange butterfly sleeves rising above the surf, the movie becomes a rhapsody on romance and death. What separates Altman from other directors is that time after time he can attain crowning visual effects like this and they're so elusive they're never precious. They're like ribbons tying up the whole history of movies. It seems unbelievable that people who looked at this picture could have given it the reviews they did.

The out-of-town failure of *The Long Goodbye* and the anger of many of the reviewers, who reacted as if Robert Altman were a destroyer, suggest that the picture may be on to something bigger than is at first apparent. Some speculations may be in order. Marlowe was always a bit of a joke, but did people take him that way? His cynical exterior may have made it possible for them to accept him in Chandler's romantic terms, and really—below the joke level—believe in him. We've all read Chandler on his hero: "But down these mean streets a man must go who is not himself mean, who is neither tarnished nor afraid." He goes, apparently, in our stead. And as long as he's there—the walking conscience of the world—we're safe. We could easily reject sticky saviors, but a cynical saviour satisfies the Holden Caulfield in us. It's an adolescent's dream of heroism—someone to look after you, a protector like Billy Jack. And people cleave to the fantasies they form while watching movies.

After reading *The Maltese Falcon*, Edmund Wilson said of Dashiell Hammett that he "lacked the ability to bring the story to imaginative life." Wilson was right, of course, but this may be the basis of Hammett's appeal; when Wilson said of the detective story that "as a department of imaginative writing, it looks to me completely dead," he was (probably intentionally) putting it in the wrong department. It's precisely the fact that the detective novel is engrossing but does not impinge on its readers' lives or thoughts that enables it to give a pleasure to some which is distinct from the pleasures of literature. It has no afterlife when they have closed the covers; it's completely digested, like a game of casino. It's a structured time killer that gives you the illusion of being speedy; *The Long Goodbye* isn't a fast read, like Hammett, but when I finished it I had no idea whether I'd read it before. Essentially, we've all read it before.

But when these same stories were transferred to the screen, the mechanisms of suspense could strike fear in the viewer, and the tensions could grow almost unbearable. The detective story on the screen became a thriller in a much fuller sense than it had been on the page, and the ending of the movie wasn't like shutting a book. The physical sensations that were stirred up weren't settled; even if we felt cheated, we were still turned on. We left the theater in a state of mixed exhilaration and excitement, and the fear and guilt went with us. In our dreams, we were menaced, and perhaps became furtive murderers. It is said that in periods of rampant horrors readers and moviegoers like to experience imaginary horrors, which can be resolved and neatly put away. I think it's more likely that in the current craze for horror films like *Night of the Living Dead* and *Sisters* the audience wants an intensive dose of the fear sickness—not to confront fear and have it conquered but to feel that crazy, inexplicable delight that children get out of terrifying stories that give them bad dreams. A flesh-crawler that affects as many senses as a horror movie can doesn't end with the neat fake solution. We are always aware that the solution will not really explain the terror we've felt; the forces of madness are never laid to rest.

Suppose that through the medium of the movies pulp, with its five-and-dime myths, can take a stronger hold on people's imaginations than art, because it doesn't affect the conscious imagination, the way a great novel does, but the private, hidden imagination, the primitive fantasy life—and with an immediacy that leaves no room for thought. I have had more mail from adolescents (and post-adolescents) who were badly upset because of a passing derogatory remark I made about *Rosemary's Baby* than I would ever get if I mocked Tolstoy. Those adolescents think *Rosemary's Baby* is great because it upsets them. And I suspect that people are reluctant to say goodbye to the old sweet bull of the Bogart Marlowe because it satisfies a deep need. They've been accepting the I-look-out-for-No. 1 tough guys of recent films, but maybe they're scared to laugh at Gould's out-of-it Marlowe because that would lose them their Bogart icon. At the moment, the shared pop culture of the audience may be all that people feel they have left. The negative reviews kept insisting that Altman's movie had nothing to do with Chandler's novel and that Elliott Gould wasn't Marlowe. People still want to believe that Galahad is alive and well in Los Angeles — biding his time, perhaps, until movies are once again "like they used to be."

The jacked-up romanticism of movies like those featuring Shaft, the black Marlowe, may be so exciting it makes what we've always considered the imaginative artists seem dull and boring. Yet there is another process at work, too: the executive producers and their hacks are still trying to find ways to make the old formulas work, but the gifted filmmakers are driven to go beyond pulp and to bring into movies the qualities of imagination that have gone into the other arts. Sometimes, like Robert Altman, they do it even when they're working on pulp material. Altman's isn't a pulp sensibility. Chandler's, for all his talent, was.

{*The New Yorker*, October 22, 1973}

:: Moments of Truth

The Iceman Cometh is a great, heavy, simplistic, mechanical, beautiful play. It is not the Eugene O'Neill masterpiece that *Long Day's Journey Into Night*, the finest work of the American theater, is, but it is masterpiece enough—perhaps the greatest thesis play of the American theater—and it has been given a straightforward, faithful production in handsome dark-toned color in the subscription series called the American Film Theatre. A filmed play like this doesn't offer the sensual excitement that movies *can* offer, but you don't go to it for that. You go to it for O'Neill's crude, prosaic virtuosity, which is also pure American poetry, and, as with most filmed dramas, if you miss the "presence" of the actors, you gain from seeing it performed by the sort of cast that rarely gathers in a theater. John Frankenheimer directed fluently and unobtrusively, without destroying the conventions of the play. The dialogue is like a ball being passed from one actor to the next; whenever possible (when the speakers are not too far apart), the camera pans smoothly from one to another. We lose some of the ensemble work we'd get from a live performance, but we gain a closeup view that allows us to see and grasp each detail. The play here is less broad than it would be on the stage, and Frankenheimer wisely doesn't aim for laughs at the characters' expense (even those that O'Neill may have intended), because the people are so close to us. The actors become close to us in another way. Actors who have been starved for a good part get a chance to stretch and renew themselves. In some cases, we've been seeing them for years doing the little thing that passes for acting on TV and in bad movies, and their performances here are a revelation; in a sense, the actors who go straight for the occasion give the lie to the play's demonstration that bums who live on guilt for what they don't do can't go back and do it.

Set in 1912 in a waterfront saloon, much like the one in which O'Neill had attempted suicide that year, the play was written in the late thirties and was first produced in 1946, on Broadway, under his supervision, but it achieved its present eminence from the Circle in the Square revival in 1956, starring Jason Robards, who then appeared in the celebrated television version of 1960, directed by Sidney Lumet. The characters are drunken bums and whores who have found sanctuary in Harry Hope's flophouse saloon; each has a "pipe dream" that sustains him until Hickey the salesman, the "iceman," who attempts to free them all by stripping them of their lies and guilt, takes the life out of them. It is both a pre-Freudian play and a post-Freudian one, and that may be the source of the trouble people have "placing" it; you can't call this play dated, and you can't quite call it modern, either. The thesis is implicitly anti-Freudian: the play says that the truth destroys people—that it wipes them out. Like most thesis plays, this one rigs the situation to make its points. There are no planned surprises in O'Neill's world—no freak characters who go out and make good. The people forced by Hickey to rid themselves of illusions are such ruins that they can live only on false hopes; without illusions they have nothing. O'Neill has rather cruelly—and comically (which is the most cruel, I think, though others may say the most human)—designed the play to demonstrate that they're better off as lying, cadging bums. With his stageproof craft, O'Neill sets in motion a giant game of ten little Indians. Each of the many characters has his lie, and each in turn has it removed and must face his truth, and we look to see who's next. It's as if illusion were a veil, and under it lay truth. This simplistic view of illusion and reality is the limiting thesis device of the play, and O'Neill's demonstration that mankind is too weak to live without the protective veil is—well, maudlin. But O'Neill was too powerful and too instinctual a dramatist to stay locked within the thesis structure. Not quite all of mankind is reconciled to wearing the veil that protects the weak, and that's where the ambiguities burst through the mechanics of *The Iceman Cometh*.

The play is essentially an argument between Larry, an aging anarchist (Robert Ryan), and Hickey (Lee Marvin); they speak to each other as equals, and everything else is orchestrated around them. Larry speaks for pity and the necessity of illusions, Hickey for the curative power of truth.

They're the two poles of consciousness that O'Neill himself is split between. Larry, a self-hating alcoholic, is a weak man and a windbag, but Robert Ryan brings so much understanding to Larry's weakness that the play achieves new dimensions. In the most difficult role he ever played on the screen, Ryan is superb. Larry's dirty "truth" is hidden under a pile of philosophizing, and the actor is stuck with delivering that philosophizing, which rings like the fakery it's meant to be but which we know O'Neill half believes. Ryan becomes O'Neill for us, I think. George Jean Nathan said that O'Neill carefully selected the photographs of himself that were to be published, and "always made sure that the photographs were not lacking in that impressive look of tragic handsomeness which was his." Ryan has that tragic handsomeness here and O'Neill's broken-man jowls, too, and at the end, when Larry is permanently "iced"—that is, stripped of illusion—we can see that this is the author's fantasy of himself: he alone is above the illusions that the others fall back on; he is tragic, while the others, with their restored illusions, have become comic. Yes, it's sophomoric to see yourself as the one who is doomed to live without illusions, but then so is the idea of the play sophomoric, and yet what O'Neill does with that sophomoric idea is masterly. And Ryan gets right to the boozy, gnarled soul of it. According to his associates, Ryan did not know he was dying until after the picture was finished, but he brought to this role the craft that he had perfected in his fifty-nine years and that he certainly knew he might never be able to exercise to its fullest again. The man who had tested himself against such uncompromisingly difficult roles on the stage as Coriolanus and the father in *Long Day's Journey* and on the screen as the depraved Claggart of *Billy Budd* got a last chance to show his stature, and he was ready. Ryan is so subtle he seems to have penetrated to the mystery of O'Neill's gaunt grandeur—to the artist's egotism and that Catholic Cassandra's pride in tragedy which goes along with the fond pity for the foolish clowns lapping up their booze.

Lee Marvin's Hickey is another matter. The characters have been waiting for Hickey, as for Godot, and his entrance is preceded by a whore who acts as herald; it's an unparalleled opportunity for an actor, as Jason Robards demonstrated so memorably in the TV version. I remember that during his long, scarily self-lacerating monologue I felt as if I couldn't breathe until it was finished. Suddenly, you knew that Hickey had been punishing the others for what he had been trying to live with, and that he was totally indifferent to them as people, and the play rose to heights you hadn't anticipated. But Hickey, with his edgy, untrustworthy affability, is a part for a certain kind of actor, and Lee Marvin isn't it. Marvin has a jokester's flair for vocal tricks and flip gestures; he can project the tough guy's impassive strength that is needed for the films he's generally in, and I don't think I've ever seen him give a bad performance in an action film. Here it's a matter not just of his not being up to it but of his being all wrong for it. We need to see the man under the salesman's exterior, and instead we realize how little interior life Marvin's action-film characters have had and how few expressive resources he has had besides a gleam in the eye. With his snub nose and long upper lip, he has a great camera face, but he's been acting for a long time now on star presence, and though that may be what you attract backers with, it's not what you play O'Neill with. What Marvin does is all on one level. At first, he's like a pudgy, complacent actor having a go at Mr. Scratch in *The Devil and Daniel Webster*, and then he just seems to coast. Hickey needs an element of irony and an awareness of horror; Marvin's Hickey exudes hostile, stupid arrogance—the impatience of the prosperous, well-fed, insensitive man with the sick. Marvin is so poorly equipped for the kind of acting required for Hickey that as the monologue approached I began to dread it. As it turns out, the monologue goes by without really being experienced by the viewer. Marvin's best recourse is to shout, because when he doesn't shout there's nothing going on. We don't seem to see this Hickey's eyes; Marvin offers us a blank face. He's thick, somehow, and irrelevantly vigorous. Marvin doesn't appear to have found anything in himself to draw on for the role. The film isn't destroyed by this performance, but it's certainly marred; yet who knows whether we will ever get a definitive version on film? We're lucky to get as much as we get here, even though the film never rises to the intensity that O'Neill put into the play. Frankenheimer has directed tactfully but not very probingly.

O'Neill is such an orderly madman: he neatly constructs a massive play around a weird conceit—the sexual wordplay on "come" in the title, which refers to Hickey's murderous explosion when he kills his wife. What we don't get, because of Marvin's one-level performance, are the terrifying intimations in this Strindbergian monologue that O'Neill is talking about himself and his wife—that he is giving Hickey the kind of raging emotion that is in *Long Day's Journey Into Night*, the kind that transcended O'Neill's ideas, yet that in this play he used to fuel his thesis. The intensity of the monologue should blow the play sky-high. Maybe O'Neill's conscious plan had become too easy to fulfill, and, as sometimes happened in Ibsen's greatest thesis plays, what was underneath the choice of subject suddenly boiled up. How, one may wonder, did Carlotta O'Neill take it as Hickey talked about the peace he found after he killed his wife? The play has a subtext that fuses with the thesis at this point, and the subtext is the hell and horror of marriage. Every character in the saloon who has talked about marriage has given us a variation on Hickey's murderous solution, and his monologue awakens Harry Hope (Fredric March) to expose his own loathing of the dead wife he's been sentimentalizing about for twenty years. O'Neill twists this male-female hatred in and out of his they-need-their-illusions thesis. It is he as dramatist who furiously, yet icily, tears away the sentimental illusions; that's what gives his kind of playwriting its power. It's not polite entertainment—not a show—but an exploration; he digs down as far as he can go. That he is the worst sentimentalist—the man who needs his illusions the most—is what makes him, like Tennessee Williams, so greatly to be felt for, and respected.

What this play seems to say, in the end, is that O'Neill the man of pity is the illusion, and that the only man he respects is the man without illusions. (I think one could say that it is just the opposite for Williams—that he abandons the man without illusions.) It's Larry, the man too full of self-loathing even to get drunk—Larry the man of pity—who refuses to offer the eighteen-year-old Parritt (Jeff Bridges) any comfort or hope, who judges him pitilessly and sends him to his death. Parritt has come to see Larry, the one person who was ever kind to him, asking to be helped. And Larry, the kindly spokesman for the necessity of illusion, doesn't want to help Parritt lie to himself; he wants him dead. It's a cruel, ambiguous kicker in the neat-looking finish. Larry's compassion, it seems, extends only to those he's not emotionally involved with. O'Neill makes Larry a hard man, finally, and desolate and unyielding, like himself. And though the bums are restored to their illusions, it's a fools' paradise regained; there's a streak of contempt in O'Neill's final view of them. O'Neill gives the lie to his own thesis: the bums need illusions not in order to be fully human (as would be the case in Tennessee Williams) but because they're weak. Those who find life without illusions insupportable are poor slobs— not strong enough to face truth and be broken by it. Hickey deceived himself about why he killed his wife; Larry, the self-hater, the only man Hickey succeeded in stripping of illusions, is, at the end, the iceman. He's stone sober, like the O'Neill of the photographs. How could anyone look at O'Neill's face and believe that he's telling people to be happy with their illusions? Sure, O'Neill is destroyed by "the truth," but he thinks he lives with "truth"; that's the secret in that haunted, sunken-jawed, angry face. And if he didn't linger on the implications of Larry's position at the end, maybe it's because he didn't dare to examine the false glory in it. It's hubris if ever there was hubris in an American play; it's also a common delusion of the mad.

It was only when, in *Long Day's Journey Into Night*, O'Neill abandoned the mechanistic dualisms (such as illusion and truth here) which he used as the underpinnings of his plays—and which make them look dated yet give them structural clarity and easy-to-take-home "serious" themes— that he could see people whole. But though the characters in *Iceman* are devised for a thesis, and we never lose our consciousness of that, they are nevertheless marvellously playable. Fredric March, like Ryan, can let the muscles in his face sag to hell to show a character falling apart. He interprets Harry Hope (who could be a dismal bore) with so much quiet tenderness and skill that when Harry regains his illusions and we see March's muscles tone up we don't know whether to smile for the character or for the actor. March is such an honorable actor; he's had a long and distinguished career. On the stage since 1920, in movies since 1929, and at seventy-six he goes on taking difficult roles; he's not out doing TV commercials or grabbing a series. At a press conference just before the 1946 opening of *The Iceman Cometh*, Eugene O'Neill said that the secret of happiness was contained in one simple sentence: "For what shall it profit a man if he shall gain the whole world and lose his own soul?" I think that once again he was being simplistic (O'Neill didn't sell his own soul, and I seriously doubt he was a happy man), but what he said has a basic truth in terms of the life of theater people. Taking on a role in *The Iceman Cometh* is a moment of truth for an actor. One of the pleasures is the way Bradford Dillman (a hole in the screen in *The Way We Were*) passes the test here. As Willie, singing his Harvard drinking song and shaking from the DTs, Dillman is funny and lively—like a Rip Torn without pent-up aggression. It's a small but flawless performance; you can almost taste the actor's joy in the role—in *working* again. Jeff Bridges has been working all along;

he's one of the lucky ones in Hollywood—so fresh and talented that just about every movie director with a good role wants him for it. But he has been cast as a country boy (*The Last Picture Show*, *Fat City*, *Bad Company*, *The Last American Hero*) and used for his "natural" ease on the screen—used, that is, for almost the opposite of what a stage actor needs. What he does here as the kid Parritt (it's the role that Robert Redford played in the TV version) is a complete change from the improvisational style he has developed, and initially it is a thankless role, a pain, really—one of those hideously-obvious-guilty-secret roles that you wish weren't in the play. Every line Parritt utters tells of his guilt. But, of course, O'Neill knew what he was doing; the obviousness turns out to be necessary, and when it pays off in Parritt's big scenes with Larry, Bridges, looking as young as the role requires, and so powerfully built that his misery has physical force, comes through. He is convincing-looking as a boy of that period, and he makes an almost impossibly schematic role believable. Toward the end, there is an instant while he's looking at Larry when his face is childishly soft and vulnerable; it's this instant that reminds us to be grateful for what a camera can add to the experience of a play.

We may think we could do without the irritating repetition of the term "pipe dream," and I know that at times I felt I could do without the three painted whores and maybe without the captain and the general who are still fighting the Boer War (though not without the actors who play them—Martyn Green and George Voskovec). But in O'Neill the laborious and the mysterious are peculiarly inextricable, and, with actors like Sorrell Booke as Hugo (which he played in the 1960 TV version), and Moses Gunn as Joe, and Tom Pedi as Rocky (which he played on Broadway in 1946 and again on TV in 1960), and John McLiam as a lyrically sad Jimmy Tomorrow, the four hours less a minute have a special grace. It was O'Neill's genius to discover what no other dramatist has—that banality in depth can let loose our common demons.

{*The New Yorker*, November 5, 1973}

:: Politics and Thrills

Gian Maria Volonté, a great actor, is a political star the way Germaine Greer, with her Gypsy Rose Lee smile and her Bankhead bravura, is a political star. When Volonté as Vanzetti in *Sacco and Vanzetti* marched to his death, you felt that it would take a lot of juice to kill him. Mastroianni can play a good man but can't play a great man. Volonté can; he isn't smoothly handsome—he's so full of life he's beautiful. As Mattei in *The Mattei Affair*, he had those Laurence Olivier-James Cagney zingylion eyes and the foxy intensity that Martin Kosleck patented in his Nazi roles. His Mattei even had a bit of Ralph Nader in the facial contours; in other roles, such as the megalomaniac chief of Rome's homicide squad in *Investigation of a Citizen Above Suspicion*, Volonté often recalls the Paul Muni of *Scarface* and *I Am a Fugitive from a Chain Gang*. The man is a chameleon-star, a fiery Italian Olivier, with the suggestion that he might have Olivier's impudent wit, too. But from a movie like *The French Conspiracy*, how will we ever know? Volonté plays Sadiel, the hero-victim—a character based on the Moroccan revolutionary Ben Barka—and he has the commanding presence for it; he has conscious magnetism, and the ability to project intelligence. (The absence of this ability has often made Hollywood actors grimly pathetic when they impersonated men of historical significance. I don't know anything at all about the late Robert Taylor's intelligence—it may have been enormous—but as an actor he couldn't project brains. Paul Newman has the same incapacity; so has Steve McQueen, and so had Clark Gable.) But in this movie Volonté, with the virile curly white hair of a people's leader, speaks heroic hogwash, while his enemies, smiling their thin, slimy smiles and plotting in their fur-collared overcoats—as if Cecil B. De Mille had coached them in intrigue—are fully aware of the dirtiness of their deeds. They know they're the villains, just as the mustache-twirlers in two-reelers did, and they know that Sadiel is honest and dedicated and incorruptible, and that that's why they have to kill him. This is politics? No, it's show-business politics. *The French Conspiracy* takes the revolutionary political thriller backward about as far as it can go—to the Hollywood historical movies in which the sinister-high-and-powerful (Douglass Dumbrille, in all his evil splendor) schemed against the poor-and-virtuous. The title *The French Conspiracy*, with its echoes of *The French Connection* (Roy Scheider, Popeye's police partner in that, is a C.I.A. agent here), is an attempt to cash in on other movies' success; the original French title is *L'Attentat*—that is, *The Assassination*. The method of this picture could stand as a textbook demonstration of how not to make a political movie.

The other new assassination film—*Executive Action*, a fictionalization of how President Kennedy *might* have been the victim of a large-scale right-wing plot—is so graceless it's beyond using even as a demonstration of ineptitude. The failures of *The French Conspiracy* are the result of commercialization and so are instructive; the failures of *Executive Action* might be the result of sleeping sickness. In this account, the big, big businessmen who plot Kennedy's death find an Oswald look-alike in order to frame Oswald—for reasons no one will ever understand. The picture, written by Dalton Trumbo from a story by Donald Freed and Mark Lane, and directed by David Miller (the low-budget Richard Fleischer), ends in perhaps the most ludicrous dénouement in thriller history. We are presented with the faces of eighteen "material witnesses" who, we are told, have died, against odds of "one hundred thousand trillion to one." But the movie has failed to introduce those witnesses into the action; we haven't discovered what a single one of them witnessed or how he happened to get involved, so the end is as flat as the beginning and the middle. It's a dodo bird of a movie, the winner of the *Tora! Tora! Tora!* prize—in miniature—for 1973, with matchlessly dull performances from a cast that includes Burt Lancaster (looking very depressed), Robert Ryan, and Will Geer. *Executive Action* could hardly be called a thriller, and it's so worshipful of Kennedy (while treating him insensitively) as to seem to have no politics. David Miller, whose direction is merely halfhearted traffic management, has made a couple of dozen movies (such as *Love Happy*, *Captain Newman, M.D.*, *Hail,*

Hero!, and, with Trumbo, the thickly ironic, overrated *Lonely Are the Brave*), so he doesn't even have the freshness of amateurism. His approach appears to be low-key not by choice but by default; he gives no inkling that he has seen what other directors have been doing lately in the political-thriller form. *The French Conspiracy* is bad, but it isn't stone-dead on the screen; it's bad because it's an ersatz political thriller. One can at least perceive what it aspires to be.

The first wave of revolutionary politics on film came from the newly formed Soviet Union; its masters were Eisenstein, Dovzhenko, and Pudovkin. The second wave broke in 1966, with Gillo Pontecorvo and *The Battle of Algiers*, probably the most emotionally stirring revolutionary epic since Eisenstein's *Potemkin* (1925) and Pudovkin's *Mother* (1926). After him have come Costa-Gavras—with the modern classic political thriller *Z*, in 1969, and then *The Confession*, and *State of Siege*, all three starring Yves Montand—and Pontecorvo again, with *Burn!*, in 1970, and Francesco Rosi, with *The Mattei Affair*, in 1973. Approaching filmmaking as a political act and trying to reach a large audience by putting political material into popular forms, the writers and directors have found themselves sacrificing meaning to thrills, or thrills to meaning. Yet their work has had a potency that ordinary films haven't; their subjects were new to the screen and made restorative contact with the actual world. And even though most of the films weren't imaginatively satisfying, they raised political and aesthetic questions, and showed the intelligence of directors aware of the problems they'd got into.

Like *Potemkin*, *The Battle of Algiers* is an epic in the form of a "created documentary," with the oppressed, angry masses as the hero. The imperialist enemy and class enemy of the Algerian National Liberation Front—the hyperintelligent French colonel played by Jean Martin—isn't really a character; he represents the cool, inhuman manipulative power of imperialism versus the animal heat of the multitudes rushing toward us as they rise against their oppressors. Pontecorvo and his writer, Franco Solinas, were almost too clever in their use of this device of the colonel—yet it works, and brilliantly. The revolutionaries forming their pyramid of cells didn't need to express revolutionary consciousness, because the French colonel was given such a full counter-revolutionary consciousness that he said it all for them. He even expressed the knowledge that history was on the side of the oppressed colonial peoples, who would win; he himself was merely part of a holding action, preserving imperialism a little longer but bound to fail. To put it satirically but, in terms of the movie, accurately, the Algerian people were spontaneously turned into revolutionaries by historical events, and if they hadn't studied Marx, the counter-revolutionaries had, and knew they were on the wrong side and were doomed by history. In Eisenstein's revolutionary "documentaries," his technique—the formal design of the images, the dynamics of their interaction—had visceral impact, but the films were like giant posters in motion, and the harshly simplified contrasts (the inhumanity of the officers versus the generous camaraderie of the common sailors and soldiers) made one completely aware of the loaded message. In *The Battle of Algiers*, the movie hardly seems to be "saying" anything, yet the historical-determinist message seeps right into your bones. As a propaganda film, it ranks with Leni Riefenstahl's big-game rally, the 1935 *Triumph of the Will*, and it's the one great revolutionary "sell" of modern times.

The Battle of Algiers has a firebrand's fervor; it carries you with it, and doesn't give you time to think. Since the colonel provides the Marxist ideology of the picture, the revolutionaries are spared any taint of ideology (even though you observe how the N.L.F. leadership serves as a spearhead), and the inevitability of the ultimate victory of revolution is established to your—almost ecstatic—emotional relief. You may even accept the movie's implicit message that the N.L.F.'s violent methods are the only way to freedom. Pontecorvo's inflammatory passion works directly on your feelings, saying that both sides kill in a revolution and that it's unavoidable, saying that the bombs set in a city by revolutionaries—resulting in the death of men and women and children—are regrettable but justified, because this movement toward freedom is natural and unstoppable and good. The special genius of Pontecorvo as a Marxist filmmaker is that, though the masses are the hero, he has a feeling for the beauty and primitive terror in faces, and you're made to care for the oppressed people—to think of them not as masses but as people. Pontecorvo—the most dangerous kind of Marxist, a Marxist poet—shows us the raw strength of the oppressed, and the birth pangs of freedom. He gives us a portrait of a revolution that explains it and justifies whatever is done in its name, and serves as the most impassioned, most astute call to revolution ever. (The film, an Italian and Algerian co-production, is said to be the first feature ever made in Algeria; born in Italy, Gillo Pontecorvo is a younger brother of the famous Bruno Pontecorvo, the atomic physicist, part of Fermi's team, who worked in this country and then at Harwell, and disappeared into Russia in 1950, subsequently winning the Lenin Prize.)

No one has carried "immediacy" farther than Pontecorvo—neither Rossellini, from whose post–Second World War films, such as *Open City* (1945) and *Paisan* (1946), he learned so much, nor Francesco Rosi, who had experimented in a similar direction in *Salvatore Giuliano*, a 1962 political "created documentary" that Franco Solinas worked on. *The Battle of Algiers* is probably the only film that has ever made middle-class audiences believe in the necessity of bombing innocent people—perhaps because Pontecorvo made it a *tragic* necessity. In none of the political melodramas that were to follow from his epic is there any sequence that comes near to the complex overtones of the sorrowful acceptance with which each of the three bomb-planting women looks to see who will be killed by her bomb. Pontecorvo produces these mixed emotions in us and *still* is able to carry most of us with him. I think people's senses are so overwhelmed by the surging inevitability of the action that they are prepared to support what in another context—such as newsprint—they would reject. It's practically rape of the doubting intelligence. In *The Battle of Algiers*, music becomes a form of agitation: at times, the strange percussive sound is like an engine that can't quite start; pounding music gives the audience a sense of impending horror at each critical point; the shrill, rhythmic, birdlike cries from the Casbah tell us that all life is trilling and screaming for freedom.

The Battle of Algiers has been the inspiration for other filmmakers—and they have been influenced by its techniques—but it was Costa-Gavras's *Z*, a French and Algerian co-production, set in Salonika but also shot in Algeria, that updated the brutal American thriller of the forties and put it to new—and easily imitable—political use. Jorge Semprun, who adapted *Z*, had written an earlier political film, *La Guerre Est Finie*, with Yves Montand as a Spanish Communist in exile, but that was reflective, elegiac. *Z* is a victimizers-and-victims crime thriller in which the Greek government is the crime ring—and, despite one's queasiness about the thriller techniques, in its own terms *Z* works. Maybe it works so well because we could respond to the high-pressure urgency of the Greek situation which had dictated the daring method, and also because Costa-Gavras, born in Greece, must have felt that the Lambrakis case (on which the film was based) took place on the blood-and-fear-and-bribery level of corrupt politics—that it was the stuff of conspiratorial thrillers.

Costa-Gavras, the suspense storyteller as investigative journalist, uses the form of melodrama to dramatize political injustice as speedily and vividly as possible, in a way that can't be ignored. But a moviemaker who tries to deal with ongoing political situations antagonizes just about everybody in one way or another (and, when he doesn't provide thrills, bores the rest). Probably the more sensitive he is to the problems the more difficulties he faces—and this seems to be what has been happening with Costa-Gavras. Filmmakers who try to combine serious content with a popular form land in trouble. (*Z* only *feels* like an exception.) When Pontecorvo and Solinas carried their French-colonel idea a step farther, in the historical-adventure film *Burn!*, by having Marlon Brando, as a British *agent provocateur*, embody and express the imperialist manipulative role throughout colonial history, they pushed their brilliant ploy over the edge; this cynical oppressor, so conscious of his role that he seemed to have studied Frantz Fanon, became as unconvincing as the villain in an antique swashbuckler. The message was again that revolution was inevitable and that freedom is worth all the suffering it takes—and, in addition, that black men should never trust white men (a message one hopes blacks will extend to the white men who made the movie)—but the didacticism kept sticking out. Pontecorvo was romantic in *The Battle of Algiers* and it worked; here he became obviously romantic. Costa-Gavras is a less gifted artist—his talents appear to be rather shallow—but he's probably a more thoughtful man. He moved away from explosive, morally questionable technique in *The Confession*, and then, moving back—though only part way—in *State of Siege*, with a script by Solinas (Semprun, his collaborator on *Z* and *The Confession*, being busy on *The French Conspiracy*), he was caught in several splits.

At the outset of *State of Siege*, Costa-Gavras worked up so much ingratiating comedy and ominous excitement about the mechanical details of how the Tupamaros (urban guerrillas in Uruguay) kidnapped some officials that those who were turned on felt let down and bored when the film got into its subject—the political meaning of these kidnappings and a demonstration of the why and how of terrorism. For American audiences, the crux of the demonstration was our complicity in the repression that brought on the terrorism. According to the film, Santore, the character

Montand plays—which is based on Dan Mitrione, the American A.I.D. official executed by the Tupamaros—was there as a police technician training the native police in torture and counter-revolution. *State of Siege* had a mixed form, and the part of the audience that enjoyed the early action didn't care for the rest, and vice versa. And it had a mixed consciousness, too: the picture succeeds in most of its political intentions—despite those who complained that it was "tiresome" (as one TV reviewer called it), it broke through public indifference to Latin American affairs—but emotionally it doesn't add up right. I think that Solinas is using the unprincipled Santore as he used Jean Martin's colonel and Marlon Brando's *agent provocateur*, to represent imperialism abroad, while Costa-Gavras sees the situation in more specific terms, and perhaps doesn't see the United States' role as so monolithically imperialist throughout Latin America. And Costa-Gavras seems too skeptical to achieve the cumulative power that Solinas is driving toward. Costa-Gavras's theme is justice. He's more tentative than Pontecorvo, perhaps because of his doubts about whether Party-spearheaded movements achieve "freedom." After all, he made *The Confession*, which Solinas has condemned as anti-Communist. Costa-Gavras is full of reservations, and even in the thriller form of *State of Siege*, in which the youthful, idealistic Tupamaros and the old fat-cat government men and businessmen are almost cartoons of good and evil, he presents the political argument on a conscious level. His movies can be as confused as political arguments usually are (and we come out and continue the argument), and so it's easy to pick quarrels with him—and easy to disparage the films because of those quarrels.

Pontecorvo celebrates the proletarian strength of Third World faces; the Algerians and the black slaves in *Burn!* are figures of love and nobility. When he needs to introduce some French troops in *The Battle of Algiers*, the documentary texture falls apart and everything looks set up; the French who man the roadblocks are well handled, but they leave no imprint on one's memory. Pontecorvo's passion vitalizes the scenes of oppressed natives and makes the people seem "real" in a way that the French troops aren't "real." In *Burn!* the treatment of the colonial masters and the mulattoes who side with them is as stilted and visually dead as in a standard swashbuckler. We respond emotionally to the revolutionary message in Pontecorvo's films because even his erotic-aesthetic sense is unified with his revolutionary purpose. Costa-Gavras, not a poet of the masses and hence not an ideal collaborator for Solinas, has a respect for those consciously caught in political dilemmas, even if they're middle-class or professional people, and a respect and sympathy for ineffectual people. It's no accident that Montand, with his sagging, tired face, is Costa-Gavras's hero, and is used even for Santore-Mitrione; that game but already defeated face is the key to the mood. In Costa-Gavras's films, people talk politics. In Pontecorvo's films, people talk history; that is, destiny. Costa-Gavras makes melodramas with thin characters, but he works on the pragmatic short-run political situation as he sees it, and his melodramas are tragic. Pontecorvo works on the visionary's long run and makes heroic epics—triumphant, blinding, incendiary myths.

The world of political movies has been incestuous—partly, I imagine, because some committed actors have been eager to work on these projects, and partly because the actors could confer their own movie backgrounds on the shorthand storytelling methods of these fast, complicated, infor-mation-packed thrillers. The actors have commuted from one revolution-ary situation to another, and to other kinds of political films, and to commercial thrillers. *The French Connection* borrowed its villain, Marcel Bozzuffi, from *Z*; *The Day of the Jackal* took for its right-wing Algerian agent Jean Martin, the French colonel of *The Battle of Algiers*; *The Inheritor* put Charles Denner in a role similar to the one he'd played in *Z*; and so on. *The French Conspiracy*, directed by Yves Boisset, raids them all—the bor-rowers and the originals. It is a colossal job of vandalism. In a sense, it does what Hollywood did in the late forties and early fifties: after the Italian neo-realists had shot their films on the streets, Hollywood "discovered" the documentary look and shot cloak-and-dagger movies on location. What *The French Conspiracy* does is what that television reviewer who was bored by *State of Siege* really wanted. *Z*, by its success in combining thrills and politics, worked against Costa-Gavras when he attempted the morally more complex *The Confession* and *State of Siege*; some of the audience now regards a political film as a failure if it isn't as thrilling as *Z*. *The French Conspiracy* separates the thrills from the politics. That is, it uses the politics as a stage set for the thrills, and it uses all those other political thrillers as part of the stage set. The Ben Barka kidnapping, which took place in Paris in 1965, also figured in the events dramatized in *The Battle of Algiers*, and Boisset simulates the sense of urgency of *Z*; the score (a muddy hype) is by Ennio Morricone, who did the hypes for *Sacco and Vanzetti* and *Investigation of a Citizen Above Suspicion*; Jorge Semprun is one of the writers (the script is almost worthy of Trumbo); Jean-Louis Trintignant, the investigator of *Z*, is the journalist caught in the plot here; Jean Bouise, from *Z* and *The Confession* and *La Guerre Est Finie*, is the vicious cop; Michel Piccoli, from *La Guerre Est Finie*, is the political villain; François Périer, the public prosecutor from *Z*, is the Paris chief of police. And in the middle of this echo chamber there's the great Left hero-star, Volonté, burning with indignation and revolutionary fervor. The actors bring so many associations that it's almost a satire: Trintignant twists his face to look cowardly, and grimaces at Jean Seberg's glazed, inexpressive, non-actress face, while Michel Bouquet twitches his pursed lips and connives with Philippe Noiret. All the film's energy must have gone into meeting the payroll.

It's got everything and everybody, and it's totally empty—not just because Boisset is a mediocre director, and not just because the concentration of attention on the high-level plotters turns the movie into silly melodrama, but because it has no real political content. One can forgive a political thriller a lack of thrills if the picture has something to say. (By now, many of us may prefer the absence of thrills—the razzle-dazzle beginning of *State of Siege* was a little insulting, a lollipop offered to the audience.) But when politics becomes decorative—when revolutionary heroes are used because they're commercially à la mode—then the filmmaker has to be a damned good director to hack it. If you haven't anything to say, you sure as hell better know how to say it. *The French Conspiracy* hasn't and doesn't.

{*The New Yorker*, November 19, 1973}

:: Survivor

Woody Allen appears before us as the battered adolescent, scarred forever, a little too nice and much too threatened to allow himself to be aggressive. He has the city-wise effrontery of a shrimp who began by using language to protect himself and then discovered that language has a life of its own. The running war between the tame and the surreal—between Woody Allen the frightened nice guy trying to keep the peace and Woody Allen the wiseacre whose subversive fantasies keep jumping out of his mouth—has been the source of the comedy in his films. Messy, tasteless, and crazily uneven (as the best talking comedies have often been), the last two pictures he directed—*Bananas* and *Everything You Always Wanted to Know About Sex*—had wild highs that suggested an erratic comic genius. The tension between his insecurity and his wit makes us empathize with him; we, too, are scared to show how smart we feel. And he has found a nonaggressive way of dealing with urban pressures. He stays nice; he's not insulting, like most New York comedians, and he delivers his zingers without turning into a cynic. We enjoy his show of defenselessness, and even the I-don't-mean-any-harm ploy, because we see the essential sanity in him. We respect that sanity—it's the base from which he takes flight. At his top, in parts of *Bananas* and *Sex*, the inexplicably funny took over; it might be grotesque, it almost always had the flippant, corny bawdiness of a frustrated sophomore running amok, but it seemed to burst out—as the most inspired comedy does—as if we had all been repressing it. We laughed as if he had let out what we couldn't hold in any longer.

The surreal is itself tamed in Woody Allen's *Sleeper*, the most stable and most sustained of his films. (It also has the best title.) Easily the slapstick comedy of the year—there hasn't been any other—*Sleeper* holds together, as his sharpest earlier films failed to do; it doesn't sputter and blow fuses, like *Bananas* and *Sex*. It's charming—a very even work, with almost no thudding bad lines and with no low stretches. I can't think of anything much the matter with it; it's a small classic. But it doesn't have the loose, manic highs of those other films. You come out smiling and perfectly happy, but not driven crazy, not really turned on, the way his messier movies and some musicals (*Singin' in the Rain*, *Cabaret*) and some comic movies (*M*A*S*H*, *The Long Goodbye*) and parts of Paul Mazursky's movies can turn one on. I had a wonderful time at *Sleeper*, and I laughed all the way through, but it wasn't exhilarating. Allen's new sense of control over the medium and over his own material seems to level out the abrasive energy. You can be with it all the way, and yet it doesn't impose itself on your imagination—it dissolves when it's finished. If it sounds like a contradiction to say that *Sleeper* is a small classic and yet not exhilarating—well, I can't completely explain that. Comedy is impossibly mysterious; this is a beautiful little piece of work—it shows a development of skills in our finest comedy-maker—and yet it's mild, and doesn't quite take off.

Woody Allen plays a Rip Van Winkle who wakes up in 2173—and that's all I'm going to say about the story, because I don't want to squeeze the freshness out of the jokes. His girl is Diane Keaton (who was practically the only good thing in *Play It Again, Sam*), and she has a plucky, almost Jean Arthur quality. She's very appealing, and in *Sleeper* you want to like her; I always felt right on the verge of responding to her (as a broad-faced, Slavic-looking poet of the future), but she isn't quite funny enough. She has good bits (like her Brando parody), but her timing is indefinite, and so is the character she plays. She's really just there to be Woody's girl, and there's nobody else—other than Allen himself—you remember from the movie. *Sleeper* could really use a *cast*. In a Preston Sturges comedy, the various characters' madnesses and obsessions bounced off each other and got all scrambled up; Chaplin and Keaton had their big fellows to contend with; the Marx Brothers had each other, plus Margaret Dumont and Walter Woolf King and Sig Rumann and those blondes wriggling in satin. But Woody Allen has no set characters to respond to. He needs a great stock company, like Carol Burnett's (Who wants to be a crazy alone? That leads to melancholy), but so far in his movies he's the only character, because his conception of himself keeps him alone.

The Woody Allen character suffers, in all his films, from sex in the head which he figures his body can't get for him. It's the comedy of sexual inadequacy; what makes it hip rather than masochistic and awful is that he thinks women want the media macho ideal, and we in the audience are cued to suspect, as he secretly does, that that's the real inadequacy (social even more than sexual). Woody Allen is a closet case of potency; he knows he's potent, but he's afraid to tell the world—and adolescents and post-adolescents can certainly identify with that. His shrimp-hero's worst fear may be that he would be attractive only to women who feel sorry for him (or want to dominate him). The latter is parenthetical because Allen hasn't explored that possibility; the thought of him with, say, Anne Bancroft suggests the sort of gambit he hasn't tried. When we see his films, all our emotions attach to him; his fear and his frailty are what everything revolves around. No one else in his pictures has a vivid presence, or any particular quality except being a threat to him, and even that quality isn't really characterized. Maybe the reason he doesn't invest others with comic character (or even villainous character) is that he's so hung up that he has no interest in other people's hangups; that could be why his stories never really build to the big climactic finish one expects from a comedy. His plots don't tie a gigantic knot and then explode it, because the other characters aren't strong enough to carry the threads. The end of *Sleeper* is just a mild cut-off point—not bad but unexciting. The movie has a more conventional slapstick-comedy structure than *Bananas*, and slapstick isn't something you can do with a pickup cast. The comedy isn't forced, it looks relaxed and easy, but the routines don't gather momentum—they slide off somewhere. Woody Allen loses his supporting players along the way, and one hardly notices. It's likely that he sees his function as being all of us, and since he's all of us, nobody else can be anything.

But, being all of us, he can get too evenly balanced, he can lose his edge. Nobody else could have made *Bananas* or parts of *Sex*, but others could conceivably make a movie like *Sleeper*, just as others are beginning to write in the Woody Allen manner—and one of the most gifted of them, Marshall Brickman, is co-author of the *Sleeper* script. The humor here doesn't tap the mother lode; it's strip-mining. The movie is in the Woody Allen style, but it doesn't have the disruptive inspiration that is the unbalanced soul of Woody Allen. In interviews, Allen has often been quoted as saying that he wants to stay rough in his movie technique; I used to enjoy reading those quotes, because I thought he was right, and in *Bananas* his instinct to let the jokes run shapelessly loose instead of trimming them and making them tidy paid off. The effect was berserk, in an original way. But he tailored his play *Play It Again, Sam* in the smooth George S. Kaufman-Broadway style, and the movie version, which Herbert Ross directed even more smoothly (I hated it), turned out to be Woody Allen's biggest box-office success up to that time, and made him a mass-audience star. How could a man who really trusted the free and messy take up the clarinet, an instrument that appeals to controlled, precise people? You can't really goof around with a clarinet. (The group he plays with, the New Orleans Funeral and Ragtime Orchestra, can be heard on the *Sleeper* track, along with the Preservation Hall Jazz Band.) I think he knows that the free and messy is the right, great direction for his comedy, but he's very well organized, and, like most comedians, he really trusts success. He trusts laughs, and how can a comedian tell when they're not earned? He's a romantic comedian — he goes on believing in love and the simple, good things in life. He's also a very practical-man comedian — he's the harried, bespectacled nice guy who just wants to stay nice and be a success and get the girl. In terms of his aspirations, he's rather like Truffaut's Antoine Doinel — the unpretentious, hopeful joiner of the bourgeoisie — as a jester. In American terms, he's Harold Lloyd with Groucho's tongue.

To have found a clean visual style for a modern slapstick comedy in color is a major victory; Woody Allen learns with the speed of a wizard. *Sleeper* has a real look to it, and simple, elegant design. (The robot servants of the future, in their tuxedos, might be windup dandies by Elie Nadelman.) Physically, Woody Allen is much more graceful in *Sleeper*; he's turning into that rarity, a verbal comedian who also knows how to use his body. And his acting has developed; he can register more emotions now, and his new silly beatific look — the look of a foolish sage — goes with the wonderful infantile jokes that don't make sense. But one might say that *Sleeper* is a sober comedy; it doesn't unhinge us, we never feel that our reason is being shredded. It has a businesslike, nine-to-five look about it, and a faint nine-to-five lethargy. For a comedian, the price of stability may be the loss of inspiration. (Our most inspired comedian, Jonathan Winters, has never found his forms. But then he doesn't have that base of sanity, either.) What's missing is the wild man's indifference to everything but the joke. In Woody Allen's case, this out-of-control edge went way past Groucho's effrontery and W. C. Fields' malice into a metaphysical outrageousness, but the impulse was similar: finally, the pleasure in the joke was all that mattered. That's what put him among the great ones.

Woody Allen has become our folk hero because we felt that if we stuck with him failure could succeed; this was, in a sense, his pact with us to get our loyalty, and it worked. We don't want to have to go through failure; we want to watch him go through it—and come out the other side. I always thought the danger for him was that he wanted to be a universal little fellow—a Chaplin—and that he might linger too long on the depressive, misfit side of his character and let the schleppy pathos take over (as he did in *Take the Money and Run*). And I thought that if he ever convinced us that he was really failing he'd lose us—who wants to watch a wispy schlep? He may not fully know it, but he doesn't need our sympathy; he's got much more than that already. What Woody Allen probably doesn't realize is that when he uses his wit he becomes our D'Artagnan. He isn't a little fellow for college students; he's a *hero*. They want to be funny, like him.

What I had underestimated was another danger. Woody Allen tips the scales toward winning in *Sleeper*, all right, but he overvalues normality; the battered adolescent still thinks that that's the secret of happiness. He hasn't come to terms with what his wit is telling him. He's dumped Chaplin (blessings) and devised a Buster Keaton-style story, but Keaton's refined physical movements were a clown's poetry, while when Allen does physical comedy—even when he's good at it—he's a very ordinary person. His gift is upstairs. It's really lucky that he cares about himself as much as he does, or he might get so balanced out that his jokes would become monotonous, like those of his imitators. If only he can begin to take control for granted, now that he's improving as a physical comedian and gaining infinitely greater skill as a director. Surreal comedy is chaos; to be really funny, you have to be willing to let your unconscious take over. That's what doesn't happen in *Sleeper*.

{*The New Yorker*, December 31, 1973}

:: Killing Time

Clint Eastwood isn't offensive; he isn't an actor, so one could hardly call him a bad actor. He'd have to *do* something before we could consider him bad at it. And acting isn't required of him in *Magnum Force*, which takes its name from the giant's phallus — the long-barreled Magnum .44 — that Eastwood flourishes. Acting might even get in the way of what the movie is about — what a big man and a big gun can do. Eastwood's wooden impassivity makes it possible for the brutality in his pictures to be *ordinary*, a matter of routine. He may try to save a buddy from getting killed, but when the buddy gets hit no time is wasted on grief; Eastwood couldn't express grief any more than he could express tenderness. With a Clint Eastwood, the action film can — indeed, must — drop the pretense that human life has any value. At the same time, Eastwood's lack of reaction makes the whole show of killing seem so unreal that the viewer takes it on a different level from a movie in which the hero responds to suffering. In *Magnum Force*, killing is dissociated from pain; it's even dissociated from life. The killing is totally realistic — hideously, graphically so — yet since it's without emotion it has no impact on us. We feel nothing toward the victims; we have no empathy when they get it, and no memory of them afterward. As soon as one person gets it, we're ready for the next. The scenes of carnage are big blowouts — parties for the audience to gasp at in surprise and pleasure.

At an action film now, it just doesn't make much difference whether it's a good guy or a bad guy who dies, or a radiant young girl or a double-dealing chippie. Although the plots still draw this distinction, the writers and the directors no longer create different emotional tones for the deaths of good and bad characters. The fundamental mechanism of melodrama has broken down, I think: the audience at action pictures reacts to the killing scenes simply as spectacle. A tall, cold cod like Eastwood removes the last pretensions to humane feelings from the action melodrama, making it an impersonal, almost abstract exercise in brutalization. Eastwood isn't very different from many of the traditional inexpressive, stalwart heroes of Westerns and cops-and-robbers films—actors notoriously devoid of personality—but the change in action films can be seen in its purest form in him. He walks right through the mayhem without being affected by it—and we are not cued to be affected, either. The difference is a matter of degree, but it's possible that this difference of degree has changed the nature of the beast—or, to put it more accurately, the beast can now run wild. The audiences used to go mainly for the action but also to hate the ruthless villains, sympathize with the helpless victims, and cheer on the protector-of-the-weak heroes. It was the spaghetti Westerns (which made Clint Eastwood a star) that first eliminated the morality-play dimension and turned the Western into pure violent reverie. Apart from their aesthetic qualities (and they did have some), what made these Italian-produced Westerns popular was that they stripped the Western form of its cultural burden of morality. They discarded its civility along with its hypocrisy. In a sense, they liberated the form: what the Western hero stood for was left out, and what he embodied (strength and gun power) was retained. Abroad, that was probably what he had represented all along. In the figure of Clint Eastwood, the Western morality play and the myth of the Westerner were split. Now American movies treat even the American city the way the Italians treated the Old West; our cops-and-robbers pictures are like urban spaghetti Westerns. With our ethical fabric torn to shreds in this last decade, American action films such as *Magnum Force* and *The Laughing Policeman* are becoming daydream-nightmares of indiscriminate mayhem and slaughter.

The John Wayne figure—the man who stood for the right (in both senses, I fear, and in both senses within the movies themselves)—has been replaced by a man who essentially stands for nothing but violence. Eastwood has to deliver death, because he has no other appeal. He can barely speak a line of dialogue without making an American audience smile in disbelief, but his big gun speaks for him. The concept of the good guy has collapsed simultaneously in our society and in our movies. Eastwood isn't really a good guy; you don't *like* him, the way you liked Wayne. You don't even enjoy him in the way you could enjoy a scoundrel. He's simply *there*, with his Magnum force. For a hero who can't express himself in words or by showing emotion, shooting first and asking questions later has got to be the ultimate salvation. In *Dirty Harry*, Eastwood said to the hippie psychotic, "This is the most powerful handgun in the world, punk. It can blow your head off." The strong, quiet man of the action film has been replaced by the emotionally indifferent man. He's the opposite of Bogart, who knew pain. Perhaps the top box-office star in the movie business, Eastwood is also the first truly stoned hero in the history of movies. There's an odd disparity between his deliberate, rather graceful physical movements and his practically timberless voice. Only his hands seem fully alive. In the Italian movies, the character he played was known as the Man with No Name, and he speaks in a small, dead, non-actor's voice that drops off to nowhere at the end of a line and that doesn't tell us a thing about him. While actors who are expressive may have far more appeal to edu-cated people, Eastwood's inexpressiveness travels preposterously well. What he does is unmistakable in any culture. He's utterly unbelievable in his movies—inhumanly tranquil, controlled, and assured—and yet he seems to represent something that isn't so unbelievable. He once said of his first Italian Western, *A Fistful of Dollars*, that it "established the pat-tern," that it was "the first film in which the protagonist initiated the action—he shot first." Eastwood stands melodrama on its head: in his world nice guys finish last. This is no longer the romantic world in which the hero is, fortunately, the best shot; instead, the best shot is the hero. And that could be what the American audience for action films, grown derisive about the triumph of the good, was waiting for. Eastwood's gun power makes him the hero of a totally nihilistic dream world.

Hollywood's flirtation with the ideology of the law-and-order advocates reached its peak two years ago with the release of *Dirty Harry*, a Warner Brothers picture directed by Don Siegel and starring Eastwood as the saintly tough cop Harry Callahan. A right-wing fantasy about the San Fran-cisco police force as a helpless group, emasculated by the liberals, the picture propagandized for para-legal police power and vigilante justice. The only way Harry could protect the city against the mad hippie killer who was terrorizing women and children was by taking the law into his own hands; the laws on the books were the object of his contempt, because he knew what justice was and how to carry it out. The political climate of the country has changed, of course, and, besides, Hollywood is, in its own cheaply Machiavellian way, responsive to criticism. In *Magnum Force*, the sequel to *Dirty Harry*, and also from Warner Brothers, Clint Eastwood, again playing Harry Callahan, is just as contemptuous of the laws on the books, but he believes in enforcing them. John Milius, who had an uncredited paw in *Dirty Harry*, and who gets the screenwriting credit here, along with Michael Cimino, twists the criticism of the earlier film to his own purposes: he takes his plot gimmick from those of us who attacked *Dirty Harry* for its fascist medievalism. The villains now are a Nazi-style élite cadre of clean-cut, dedicated cops who have taken the law into their own hands and are cleaning out the scum of the city—assassinating the labor racketeers, the drug dealers, the gangsters and their groupies. They are explicit versions of what we accused Harry of being; they might be the earlier Harry's disciples, and the new Harry wipes them all out. "I hate the goddam system," he says, "but I'll stick with it until something better comes along." *Magnum Force* disarms political criticism and still delivers the thrills of brutality. Harry doesn't bring anyone to court; the audience understands that Harry *is* the court. The picture is so sure it can get away with its political switch that before it allows Harry to spout his new defender-of-the-system line it actually tweaks the audience (and the movie press) by implying that he is the assassin who's mowing down the gangsters. But the movie—and this is what is distinctively new about it—uses the same tone for the Storm Troopers' assassination orgies that is used for Harry's killing of the Storm Troopers. At no point are we asked to be appalled by homicide. We get the shocks without any fears for the characters' safety or any sadness or horror at their gory deaths. The characters aren't characters in any traditional sense; they're not meant to be cared about.

Studio-machine-made action pictures have the speedy, superficial adaptability of journalism. One can measure some of the past two years' changes in the society by comparing the two films. In *Dirty Harry*, the sniper villain (wearing a peace symbol on his belt) idly picked off an innocent girl in a bikini while she was swimming, and the pool filled with her blood. In *Magnum Force*, one of the young Storm Troopers machine-guns everyone at a gangland swimming-pool party, and you get the impression that the girls prove their corruption and earn their deaths by being braless. Generally speaking, the victims now are all guilty of something, even if only of taking drugs, so you're exonerated—you don't have to feel anything. You can walk out and pretend you didn't see what went on. If the élite cadre and their prim Führer (Hal Holbrook) represent what Harry the hero represented the first time around, and if it's now right for Harry the hero to kill them, what of the writers who confect one position and then the next? Do they believe in anything? I think they do. Despite the superficial obeisance to the rule of law, the underlying content of *Magnum Force*—the buildup of excitement and pleasure in brutality—is the same as that of *Dirty Harry*, and the strong man is still the dispenser of justice, which comes out of his gun. Harry says it: "Nothing's wrong with shooting as long as the right people get shot." He's basically Paul Newman's Judge Roy Bean—another Milius concoction—all over again. Although Ted Post's direction of *Magnum Force* is mediocre, the picture isn't as numbing as *The Life and Times of Judge Roy Bean*, because it stays on its own coarse, formula-entertainment level, trying to turn on the audience to the garish killings and sustaining a certain amount of suspense about what's coming next. It sticks to its rationale. In *Magnum Force*, Dirty Harry is still the urban garbage man, cleaning up after us. His implicit justification is "You in the audience don't have the guts to do what I do, so don't criticize me." He says he does our dirty work for us, and so he invokes our guilt, and we in the audience don't raise the question "Who asked you to?" If Milius were a real writer instead of a hero-idolater, he might begin to raise questions about whether Harry unconsciously manipulates himself into these situations because he likes to kill, and about whether he keeps his face stony so as not to reveal this. But *Magnum Force*, the new city Western, has no mind and no class; the moviemakers seem unaware that their hero lives and kills as affectlessly as a psychopathic personality.

"A man's got to know his limitations," Harry keeps saying, and it's a comment not on himself but on his enemies' failure to recognize that he's the better man. Harry is tougher than the élite cadre, just as he was tougher than the mad hippie killer. The Nazis look like a troupe of juveniles in training for stardom in the old studio days, and are suspected by other cops of being homosexual, so Harry's weathered face and stud reputation (which is all hearsay as far as the audience goes) are like additional equipment for destroying them. But Eastwood is not a lover: women flock to him, but he makes no moves toward them. From what we see, they have to do all the work; he accepts one as dispassionately as he declines another. In one sequence, a woman bares her feelings and tells Harry of her desire for him while he just sits there, as unconcerned as ever; he's not going to get involved. Like the Western loner, he's almost surreally proper—lunatically so, considering what he does with his gun and fists. The only real sex scene in *Magnum Force* is a black pimp's murder of a black whore, which is staged for a turn-on erotic effect that I found genuinely shocking and disgusting. But the movie is full of what in a moral landscape would be sickening scenes of death: a huge metal girder smashes right into a man's face, and the audience is meant not to empathize and to hide from the sight but to say "Wow!"

The right-wing ideology functioned in *Dirty Harry*; here the liberalized ideology is just window dressing. What makes Harry the sharpshooter a great cop is that he knows the guilty from the innocent, and in this action world there's only one thing to be done with the guilty—kill them. Alternatives to violence are automatically excluded. If we talk to Harry, if after he dispatches his thirty-fifth or eightieth criminal one of us says "Harry, could you maybe ask the guy's name before you shoot, to make sure you've got the right man?" Harry's answer *has* to be "All criminals are liars anyway," as he pulls the trigger. Because that's what he wants to do: pull the trigger. What keeps the audience watching is one round of killings after another. *Magnum Force* is a far less skillful fantasy than *Dirty Harry*, and so is less involving, and it isn't likely to be as big a hit, yet my hunch is that the audience, after these last couple of years, rather likes its fantasies to be uninvolving.

It's the emotionlessness of so many violent movies that I'm becoming anxious about, not the rare violent movies (*Bonnie and Clyde*, *The Godfather*, *Mean Streets*) that make us care about the characters and what happens to them. A violent movie that intensifies our experience of violence is very different from a movie in which acts of violence are perfunctory. I'm only guessing, and maybe this emotionlessness means little, but, if I can trust my instincts at all, there's something deeply wrong about anyone's taking for granted the dissociation that this carnage without emotion represents. Sitting in the theater, you feel you're being drawn into a spreading nervous breakdown. It's as if pain and pleasure, belief and disbelief had got all smudged together, and the movies had become some schizzy form of put-on.

{*The New Yorker*, January 14, 1974}

:: Cicely Tyson Goes to the Fountain

At American movies now, black people are just about the only ones looking to find heroes for themselves. Films made for whites are curdled by guilt and confusion; the heroes are corrupted, they fail, they live or die meaninglessly. But the black pictures feature winners, sometimes even non-racist winners — like the heroine of *Cleopatra Jones*. Played by Tamara Dobson, who is six feet two in her stocking feet and looks like a powerful, elongated Eartha Kitt, Cleopatra Jones is a female version of Robin Hood crossed with James Bond. She's protecting her people against the poppy growers and drug pushers, and audiences cheer for her as happily as audiences ever cheered for Robin Hood. Like him, she is guiltlessly heroic, a champion, fighting for the abused and mistreated. In the recent film *Gordon's War*, Gordon, a Green Beret (Paul Winfield), comes back from Vietnam to learn that the dope plague in the cities has taken his wife, and he organizes an army to clean the dope out of Harlem. The picture's celebration of vigilante justice may have been frightening to a white viewer, but the black movie audiences don't need to have it explained that the white-controlled system of authority is imposed on them and is corrupt. For them, Gordon's group represented an attempt by blacks to create their own system of authority. And the audiences could identify with Gordon's army just as at the Second World War movies the audiences identified with the ruthless American heroes — such as Bogart, or Dick Powell in *Cornered*, also avenging his dead wife — who were cleaning out the Nazis. Gordon's dedicated buddies, united by shared ideals, have the camaraderie that white movies used to feature. The shabbily constructed script made it impossible for the director, Ossie Davis, to bring his special gifts to *Gordon's War*—it has none of his feeling for comedy or for joy—and it hasn't been a hit, but it has something that unites the audience, something that one no longer gets out of white movies. Most of the films made for black audiences are exploitation jobs, as cynical and brutal as the current action films made for general audiences (if not more so). But the audiences at black films react more: with more gusto to the killings but also with more disgust to certain kinds of routine phoniness—like weak blacks pleading for their lives, or too much cant from the women characters. The audience seems to want its action, its heroism—even its sex—*pure*, not doctored with cowardice or a lot of bulling around. And if the audience reacts to the victories of Shaft or his progeny with the same pleasure as to the victories of a Cleopatra Jones, this is clearly because the audience enjoys feeling victorious.

To put it bluntly: While white audiences can laugh together at the same things—mainly at evidence of American stupidity and rot—there is nothing positive that they share. (I don't mean to suggest that this is necessarily bad, and I certainly don't mean to suggest that we should have clung to our myths of American heroism, or to that worst myth of all—the self-righteous union of strength and virtue. I'm just trying to pin down a distinction.) The movies for blacks have something that white movies have lost or grown beyond. I point this out because I think it's something that whites miss; it's what they mean when they say that there's nothing to take their children to. It's a lost innocence, a lost paradise of guiltlessness, and some of the black movies have it. A few months ago, when some friends asked me what they could take their kids to that their kids would have a good time at—something like the old Errol Flynn swashbucklers—the only picture I could think of was *Cleopatra Jones*. They told me later that the whole family had enjoyed it. We may have reached such a strange impasse in this country that whites need to go to black movies to relax and partake of guiltlessness.

The ironic miracle of *Sounder* was that whites could respond to its black family far more intensely than they could conceivably now respond to a white family. The blacks of *Sounder* live in hardship circumstances in which their sheer endurance is a victory—their endurance and their ability to sustain their feeling for each other. In the past, American movies celebrated white-pioneer courage and endurance; now the black movies take us back to those satisfying hopeful qualities, but, for whites, with a difference. Implicit in *Sounder* and in the new *The Autobiography of Miss Jane Pittman* is a sense of moral complexity—of a redressing of the balance, of justice at work within the mythology of popular culture. What we can no longer accept about white heroes and heroines we surrender to when the characters are black. I think we absolutely need to; this has nothing to do with the formal aesthetics of a particular piece of popular culture but everything to do with how popular culture works in a society. And we have been lucky. The beautifully made *Sounder* spared us the embarrassments of maudlin emotions; and *The Autobiography of Miss Jane Pittman*, which was produced for television by Tomorrow Entertainment and will be on C.B.S. on Thursday, January 31st (and will run in theaters in other countries), stars Cicely Tyson and was made by John Korty, a self-effacing director who has what might be described as an aesthetics ruled by morality. His past work (such films as *The Crazy Quilt* and *Funnyman*, and the TV film *Go Ask Alice*) shows his principled unwillingness to push for dramatic effect; this makes him the ideal director for *The Autobiography of Miss Jane Pittman*. One shove and we would say, "Oh, here it comes—more guilt piled high on us." But as *Jane Pittman* has been directed, her story, of how a black woman lived and what she went through, with major historical events seen through her eyes, has a far greater meaning than if white viewers were browbeaten into a defensive reaction. The full force of *The Autobiography of Miss Jane Pittman* is that no defense is possible, so none is called for.

Cicely Tyson plays a woman who was born in slavery and lived to take part in a civil-rights demonstration in 1962; the role spans Jane Pittman's life from the age of twenty to the age of a hundred and ten, and Cicely Tyson knows what she's doing every inch of the way. Her Jane Pittman does not have the Biblical strength or the emotional depth of her Rebecca in *Sounder*. Jane isn't a deep woman; childless, uneducated, she's an enjoyer of life. It isn't until extreme old age gives her a privileged status that she loses her fear and becomes—briefly, just before her death—politically active. Old age brings her out in other ways, too; it's as if her life were a series of liberations, so that only at the end is she free enough to speak her mind and to crack a joke and to find herself. When she walks up to a whites-only drinking fountain in front of a Southern courthouse, and drinks from it, all of us in the audience can taste the good water.

Tyson is an extraordinarily controlled actress, and perhaps this control has some relationship to the history of black people in this country. I used to watch her sometimes in the old George C. Scott TV series *East Side, West Side*, and I found her control and her tight reserve slightly antipathetic; she seemed to be holding back from us—not yielding her personality, not relaxing within the minuscule demands of the role. Now I think I can see why. It was a role in which a beautiful pinheaded actress might have been perfectly content, and her contentment might have made her seem delectable. Those secretary roles, black and white, are generally played for comedy or for sex; the black girls are plumped down in an office—to fill the quotas—but they're playing classy maids. What Tyson's strained manner in that series was saying to us was "I can't give myself to this role—I have more than this in me." And, despite her magnetic glamour, she wouldn't give us more than the cold efficiency of the secretary she played—which could only make a viewer slightly uncomfortable. In small, empty roles, this New York-born actress who had sold shopping bags on the streets when she was nine years old seemed aloof. She *felt* aloof from the roles, and she had too much in her to sell herself cheap. She still refuses to sell herself; in her performances as Rebecca and here as Jane, she never bathes us in the ravishing smile of her modeling years or her TV talk-show appearances. She has the haughtiness of the enormously gifted—of those determined to do everything the most difficult way, because they know they can. Her refusal to melt us with her smile is like Streisand's refusal to sing; there's some foolishness in these refusals, but also hard-won pride. In every breath, Cicely Tyson says to us, "I'm not going to make Jane a cute, feisty old darling for you to condescend to. I'm not going to warm the cockles of your heart. And don't treat me kindly as a great black actress; I'm an actress or nothing." She's an actress, all right, and as tough-minded and honorable in her methods as any we've got. You feel you're inside skinny old Jane's head: you get to understand her mixture of shallowness and superstition and pop culture and folk wisdom. And through knowing Jane Pittman you feel closer to a recognition of black experience in this country; at an ironic level Jane's story is the story of how it takes a hundred and ten years to make an activist out of an ordinary black woman. Tyson won't allow her beauty to carry her; she plays Jane with supreme integrity. Jane's charm seems all to belong to Jane; Tyson doesn't shove any of her own onto her. She doesn't yet have the fluidity of an actress who can turn the character into herself, and vice versa; she is still in conscious control.

She hasn't made that leap to unconscious control which separates the "divine" legendary actresses from the superlative technicians. I'm comparing Tyson to the highest, because that's the comparison she invites and has earned. She isn't there, but she's on her way. She's great, but she will be even greater when she can relax and smile without feeling she's Uncle Tomming, as Streisand will be a greater artist when she can accept all her gifts and use them together.

The subject of the Ernest J. Gaines novel on which *Jane Pittman* is based is so good that everyone connected with the movie seems to have respected it. There are inevitable losses. The incendiary preaching that, in the novel, leads to one character's murder has been softened, and events sometimes lose their repercussions—no doubt because a novel more sprawling in time than *Gone with the Wind* is being attempted on a TV shooting schedule and budget, to fit a two-hour slot. There are almost eighty speaking parts, and some of the casting and acting—though not blatantly bad—are nondescript. (A Cajun character certainly doesn't help; no Cajun on the screen ever does.) Yet none of this does serious damage. There's one unfortunate change. In the novel, Jane dreads a black stallion that she thinks will kill Joe Pittman (the one man she loves enough to carry his name). For photographic reasons (the sequence was being shot using day for night), an albino was used instead; the eerie white horse, with a ghastly pink look around the eyes, is mystically effective, but the color switch suggests a racial symbolism that doesn't quite fit the situation. The clumsiest addition is the device of using Michael Murphy as a journalist interviewing the ancient Miss Pittman to link the episodes; toward the end, we feel the shift to amateurishness each time he appears. But Cicely Tyson is, I think, all that a reader of the book could ask for, and her performance and the director's tact are more than enough to compensate for these flaws, and for the anachronisms and naïveté in parts of Tracy Keenan Wynn's adaptation.

John Korty tells the story at a satisfyingly leisurely pace, befitting a woman who accumulates a hundred and ten years. Korty is a director who has never quite come into his own; his loose, unlabored style was probably at its best in the charming, neglected 1966 comedy *Funnyman*, starring Peter Bonerz (the dentist of *The Bob Newhart Show*) as a member of The Committee, the improvisational-revue troupe in San Francisco. This hero is wry and self-conscious, and automatically turns human relations into put-ons; he works up whatever situations he's in into routines—his "life situations" have the rhythm of revue acts, and vice versa. Korty didn't make a big thing of his funnyman hero; the movie just skipped along, and in places dawdled along, without solemnity. Probably Korty's movies suffered commercially from his honesty and tentativeness and his refusal to heighten emotions, but those same qualities showed to great advantage in his direction of the TV film about teen-age drug addiction *Go Ask Alice*. The contrast with the usual TV director's hysterically manipulative approach made Korty's work shine. Some of Korty's virtues are dimmed in *The Autobiography of Miss Jane Pittman*, because he's not working as flexibly as he did on his own movies (which he also photographed himself)—the direction here is more stilted—but the movie is still so much cleaner and simpler than just about any other movie made for TV (or any TV series show, either) that the fictional Jane Pittman has the singularity and dignity of a person in a documentary. There never was a Jane Pittman; the character is synthesized from stories that Gaines heard while growing up on a plantation in Louisiana, but, watching the film (which was all shot in Louisiana), one literally forgets (as readers of the novel did) that it is fiction. It seems to be a slightly awkward reënactment of the life of an actual person.

Beauty is almost unknown in movies shot for TV, but Korty has brought his compositional sense and his own unassertive lyricism to this mixture of folk history and agitprop. Visually, the interiors and the closeups of people making polemical speeches are only serviceable, but the exteriors and the closeups of Jane show the sane affection of an artist with no fakery about him. John Korty has no show business in his soul, and sometimes we really need to get away from the show-business hype. *The Autobiography of Miss Jane Pittman* isn't a great movie, though with more directorial freedom and a better script it might have been. But it's quite possibly the finest movie ever made for American television. Would a story about the endurance of an ancient white woman be this effective? There's no way for it to be comparable. There is probably no imaginable way that at this point in American history we could be as deeply moved by a white woman's story—no matter how much truth there was in it—as we are by this black woman's story.

{*The New Yorker*, January 28, 1974}

:: The Used Madonna

The Mother and the Whore is made from inside the state of mind that is thought of as Village or Berkeley-graduate-school or, as in this case, Left Bank. It's about the attitudes of educated people who use their education as a way of making contact with each other rather than with the larger world. Their manner of dress and behavior is a set of signals; they're telling each other that they're illusionless. Their way of life is a group courtship rite, though they court each other not in order to find someone to love but in order to be loved—that is, admired. They live in an atmosphere of apocalyptic narcissism. The characters in *The Mother and the Whore* belong to the café life of St.-Germain-des-Prés, and so does the film, which can be said to represent the dead hopes of a decade and a generation. The Don Juans of this group hardly need to be ambulatory; they cruise from their coffee-house chairs. The hero, Alexandre (Jean-Pierre Léaud), is a thirty-year-old puppy; in his milieu the less you do the cooler you appear. Alexandre has the glib, attitudinizing male-intellectual vanity that is the educated bum's form of machismo. He's a harmless, light-weight liar; he cultivates his whims; he lies for the fun of it. He's an amusing put-on artist, with no visible convictions or depth of feeling. When he sees an old girl friend who's about to be married (Isabelle Weingarten), he makes a declaration of undying passion merely for the pleasure of hearing himself sound passionate. She's smart enough not to take him any more seriously than he takes himself.

Alexandre has no interest in a profession; he's just a professional charmer. He's able to live without working because he has found a "mother" —a mistress who takes care of him. Tough, good-natured Marie (Berna-dette Lafont) runs a dress shop, but she's far from being a bourgeoise. She's a coarse, unpretentious working-class woman trying to enjoy herself; she's the solid world that Alexandre returns to from the hours of preening at the café. All his energy goes into his poses and paradoxes, and the strategies of coolness. But when he plots a little campaign to make himself important to Veronika—a new girl he spots—it's wasted effort. Veronika (Françoise Lebrun), a young, bone-poor nurse, has a tired, stolid madonna face, but she's so whorishly available that, as she says, "it turns a lot of people off." The movie is a fugal series of monologues and dialogues among Alexandre, Marie, and Veronika, almost entirely on the subject of sex. It was shot in grainy black-and-white that's deliberately dark and streaked; there's no musical score—only "natural" sounds and an occasional scratchy record played on a phonograph—and it's three hours and thirty-five minutes long. A viewer's response to this debauch of talk will be determined by whether he can accept the whorish madonna Veronika's monologues as revealing the truth or thinks they're the familiar rant of Catholic women on the sauce. If the former, the film, which was written and directed by Jean Eustache, may seem a depressive-generation masterpiece; if the latter, a sour conceit. I think it's part one and part the other—but the parts are inseparable.

The rough-and-tumble Marie is warmly played. Bernadette Lafont, whose large, generous features make her a natural for working-class women, is open-hearted in the role—crass and likable. The filmmaker goes in for paradoxes, too: Marie, the "mother," resembles the traditional understanding whore of French films (such as Arletty in *Le Jour Se Lève*), and her relationship with Alexandre is an updating of the whore-pimp relationship. Alexandre (and the graduate-school little bohemias of the world are full of Alexandres, though generally they sponge off their parents as well as friends and girl friends) is, in fact, a spoiled-infant pimp, who lives off Marie and doesn't even provide a pimp's protection. He has nothing to offer but his taste, his classy prattle, and some body warmth. He considers that his presence—when he's around—is gift enough. Léaud doesn't just walk through his role (as he sometimes does); he projects the shallow Alexandre's emotional states, and he gives what is probably his most deeply felt performance as an adult. Alexandre is onscreen throughout, reacting to the women, cajoling them, trying on attitudes—so infatuated with his own pranks he hardly cares what effect they have on others. Alexandre likes to perform, and his dry facetiousness is often funny (probably considerably funnier if one knows French well enough to get the slang). Though Jean Eustache has said that he wrote the roles specifically for the performers, Léaud's performance is nevertheless a feat of giving oneself over to a role. He never drops the mask, he never slips away from Alexandre.

However, the picture stands or falls with the character of Veronika (and she's a very creepy, dolorous character), because it's Veronika who carries the burden of Eustache's emotionalism. She looks Slavic (she says she is of Polish origin), and she appears to be Eustache's holy-whory Sonia, an updated version of the heroine of *Crime and Punishment*; she's there to awaken silly Alexandre's soul, though he's no Raskolnikov. The only thing that keeps Alexandre from being the Léaud specialty—a pet—is that he's forced to listen to Veronika's recital of her ugly, seamy deprivations and her nausea. She's drunken and insistent; once Alexandre has gone to bed with her, he can't get rid of her. She hounds him; she comes to Marie's apartment and climbs into bed with them. Veronika, who wears her hair saint-style, braided around her head, is a sexually abused character; her tiny garret room in the nurses' quarters of a hospital is like a penitential chamber. She volunteers for abuse; she seeks sex and feels humiliated by it. She's the biggest bundle of guilt ever to be hurled on the screen, and once she stops listening to Alexandre and starts talking she never shuts up—except to vomit up all the sex-without-love that she has subjected herself to.

Bernadette Lafont, who made her first screen appearance in the leading role of Truffaut's short *Les Mistons* (1957), and Léaud, whose long scarves here stretch back to his appearance as the twelve-year-old boy in *The 400 Blows* (1959), have been the emblematic New Wave performers; and the characters they play here are further extensions of the characters they've developed over the intervening years. (Even Isabelle Weingarten, who played the lead in Bresson's *Four Nights of a Dreamer*, carries that credential.) But Françoise Lebrun, a graduate student in modern literature who has never acted on the screen before, is completely Eustache's; she gives the picture its sullen, scratched soul. One may guess that her sad, deceptively placid face, with its suggestion of a badly used madonna, inspired Eustache. She has the sort of young-old face that a moviemaker could easily project onto; she's like a beat-out version of the young Dietrich, with her pale-gold braid around her head, as the innocent peasant, soon to be a fallen woman, in *The Song of Songs*, the hokey old Mamoulian-Sudermann film of innocence betrayed. Lebrun's wide-eyed face is blankly opaque—the face of a woman locked in her miseries. She keeps a sullen, suffering deadpan, and as the torrent of obscenities and complaints pours out, we can all project onto that face. *The Mother and the Whore* is a psychodrama that keeps shifting and redefining its terms; those terms are ironic until the last hour, when Veronika is exempted from irony and we are asked to identify with her and to see her as an icon of modern loneliness and suffering and degradation. She's a martyr to callous sex.

Eustache has no distance from Veronika. That's why the movie seems so arbitrary—you may feel that you've been a good sport to sit through it, that it's been an endurance contest—but it's also what gives the film its distinction. Eustache is right in there. His method is rather like that of a French Cassavetes; he's trying to put raw truth on the screen, and this film might be his *Lovers* to set next to Cassavetes' *Husbands*. Cassavetes tries to give acted material the look and sound of *cinéma vérité*; Eustache goes even further. He puts in dead stretches and trivia, building in boredom so that the material will seem lifelike; he prolongs the movie after one thinks it's finished—the prolongation seems almost like a director's joke. Eustache's method resembles the static randomness of the Warhol-Morrissey pictures, yet the randomness here is not a matter of indifference but a conscious goal. Chance is the illusion that Eustache seeks. He didn't allow the actors to deviate from the three-hundred-page script, but he keeps the framing a little rough and insecure, as if the cameraman were looking for the action, and it took three months of editing to make this film seem unedited. Eustache wants the look of chance because he's determined not to be ingratiating. It's as if he felt that only by pushing us beyond patience, only by taking us away from the surface pleasures of cinematographic elegance and a full score, only by rubbing our noses in his view of reality, can he make us *feel*. (He may equate us with the infantile, pleasure-seeking Alexandre.)

It's true that films tend to look too rich and that they're often rotten with meaningless "production values"—and sometimes rotten with "beauty." But those who try to strip them down to naked fundamentals usually seem to be puritan aesthetes—and a pain. *The Mother and the Whore* proclaims its honesty and its purity in a way I can't stomach—as if its messiness and its characters' messy lives were holy. The religiously inspired polarity of the title suggests that Eustache sees himself as Alexandre, divided, torn between the mother and the whore. And it's part of the emotional tone of this period to reject the mother and to identify with the whore. Like Veronika, Eustache is saying, "I'm going to show you more of the tormented soul than anybody has ever shown you," and, like Veronika, he confuses rag-chewing and revulsion with holy revelation.

Art and disgust are closely related in the thinking of a number of modern filmmakers of religious background. Paul Morrissey's films seem to be made by a dirty-minded altar boy, and the concept that messy anguish sanctifies is at the very heart of Cassavetes' films. *The Mother and the Whore* is not a negligible film: it's unmistakably a personal expression, and it does achieve moments of intensity. No doubt some people will say more than moments, and some will consider Veronika's ultimate monologue cathartic, though the fact that it signals reprieve for the exhausted viewer may contribute to that feeling. (The three hours and thirty-five minutes feel so long that you want to think you've had something to show for it, and catharsis is big stuff—worth squirming for.) But is Alexandre ultimately moved to ask Veronika to marry him because he's a fool who loves grand gestures, or are we really meant to believe in the authenticity of what she represents? For me, it was as if Alexandre were pressured into confessing a crime he hadn't committed. Veronika rants so much that finally he assumes the guilt for all the men whom this obsessive woman has landed in bed with and then felt lacerated by. He assumes the guilt for the whole world's failure to love. Alexandre may be just trying on his new deep feelings, but she, I'm afraid, is intended to be the real thing. It turns out that Eustache is a sin-ridden bohemian of an earlier school and that the movie is about the penance that must be done for sex-without-love. He has welded together the disaffection of a generation and his own sexual disgust. Isn't that really what Veronika's diatribe is all about? Isn't she really saying "I want to be loved"? I suspect that that's why the movie will appeal to people who feel stranded in a confusion of personal freedom and social hopelessness. Antonioni explored the theme of sex without love, but he placed it among the affluent; in placing this theme among the students and those who go on living like students, Eustache makes direct contact with the movie audience. Antonioni's bleak atmosphere spoke of spiritual emptiness; Eustache's atmosphere is like a spiritual mange, and probably many people in the aging-young movie audience feel mangy and lost and degraded, and have had their share of miserable sex experiences. They may be willing to embrace Veronika's loathing of her life, and perhaps willing to look to the healing power of Christian love. The film is designed to be a religious experience, but the musty answer it offers to the perils of sexual freedom is actually a denial of sexual freedom. In *The Mother and the Whore*, the New Wave meets the Old Wave.

{*The New Yorker*, March 4, 1974}

:: When the Saints
Come Marching In

Lenny, the Bob Fosse film starring Dustin Hoffman, is for audiences who want to believe that Lenny Bruce was a saintly gadfly who was martyred for having lived before their time. Julian Barry, who wrote the Tom O'Horgan 1971 stage show, starring Cliff Gorman, has written the screenplay, and the material is conceived for well-meaning innocents who never saw Lenny Bruce and who can listen to Dustin Hoffman delivering bits of Bruce routines and think, People just didn't understand him then—he isn't shocking at all. There was every reason to believe that O'Horgan knew the difference between Lenny Bruce the performer he'd been on the same bill with back in the late fifties and the Lenny Bruce turn-on myth he helped whip up. His *Lenny*, which came between his *Hair* and his *Jesus Christ Superstar*, was part of an effort to create a youth theater; the show dealt with Bruce not as a man but as a sacrificial symbol surrounded by tribal symbols on stilts and decked out in papier-mâché heads and grass skirts. It was James Dean updated—Lenny Bruce as a misunderstood kid, the way *Jesus Christ Superstar* was to be Jesus as a misunderstood kid. Taking over the O'Horgan-Barry material, Bob Fosse has eliminated the totemic haberdashery. His staging goes all the way in the opposite direction: the film is in black and white, in a semi-documentary style. But Julian Barry hasn't rethought Bruce's life or fleshed out the characters, and the closer Fosse gets to them, the more abstract they become. Lenny's wife, the stripper Honey Harlow (Valerie Perrine); his mother, Sally Marr (Jan Miner); a fictitious manager (Stanley Beck); and Lenny himself are still no more than symbolic figures, and they inhabit an abstract, stage-bound world that doesn't seem to relate to a specific period or to the cities where the key events of Bruce's life actually took place.

Fosse has learned a phenomenal amount about film technique in a short time; *Lenny* is only his third movie (after *Sweet Charity* and *Cabaret*), and it's a handsome piece of work. I don't know of any other director who entered moviemaking so late in life and developed such technical proficiency; Fosse is a true prodigy. *Lenny* is far removed in style from *Cabaret*, yet it's controlled and intelligent. But the script is simply too thin for the method Fosse uses. A searching, close-in documentary technique can sometimes provide glimpses of the riches of people's interior lives, but it is rarely effective with actors: their controls are exposed, and we become more conscious of their acting than in a conventionally dramatized work. The idea here seems to be that what the writer has failed to provide, the camera will somehow probe. But since the characters have nothing to yield up, it probes superficiality. Essentially, the method is to cut from episodes recalled by Lenny's family and associates to Lenny performing a sliver of a routine that seems to have developed out of each episode. However, the film never quite achieves a "present": we might almost be watching him perform after the survivors were interviewed. The crosscutting between present and past is smoothly engineered, but it doesn't really do anything for us. I get the impression that, unlike O'Horgan, Fosse thought he was really getting at truth, and that he got so caught up in the complicated structure he didn't see that it surrounded a void. Despite the fluent editing and sophisticated graphics, the picture is the latest version of the one-to-one correlation of an artist's life and his art which we used to get in movies about painters and songwriters. Lenny's life becomes footnotes to his night-club acts — as if the acts needed footnotes! — and often the biographical account has the odd effect of making his stage acts seem like simple rationalizations of what was going on in his life. In the traditional movie, life is transmuted into art; here the hero's routines are so unfunny that no transmutation seems to have taken place.

Fosse may have tried so hard to stretch himself that he lost perspective (and his sense of humor) on this project. Within its serious conception, *Lenny* is very well made. But why does it take itself so insufferably seriously? Why the sociological black-and-white investigatory style for a subject like Lenny Bruce? The style says, Listen, kids, this is going to be about a very important man; be quiet, now — remember you're in church. The movie turns out to be the earnest story of a Jewish prophet who shouldn't have got involved with a shiksa junkie.

There really is no script. There was no play inside O'Horgan's production, either, but there were so many dervishes whirling that most of the audience didn't seem to mind. Gorman delivered large chunks of Bruce's material, and though he lacked the spiv comic's jabbing hostility, he was able to build up a rhythm with the audience. His actor's exertion and the sweetness he brought to the material fitted O'Horgan's sacrificial-lamb concept: the audience could appreciate the humor without feeling the danger that made Bruce's audiences prickle with nervous pleasure. Gorman seemed like such a nice boy up there, harried, and working hard. So does Dustin Hoffman, but he can't even work up a performing rhythm, because in the movie the shticks have been reduced to snippets and high points.

Hoffman makes a serious, honorable try, but he's the wrong kind of actor to play Bruce. Hoffman ingratiates himself with an audience by his shy smile, his gentleness, and his insecurity. He wins people over by his lack of physical confidence; you pull for him because he's so non-threatening—you hope that he isn't actually weak and that he'll prove himself. But that clenched, nasal voice of his is the voice of someone trying to get along in the nervous straight world Bruce fled; his putziness is just what Bruce despised. Hoffman is touchingly childlike (he was at his best on the TV show *Free to Be . . . You and Me*, when he read Herb Gardner's monologue about a child's first crossing a street by himself); there was nothing childlike about Lenny Bruce. He vamped the audience with a debauched, deliberately faggy come-hither that no one quite knew how to interpret; he was uncompromisingly not nice.

Who would be right to play him? Is there an actor with the hooded eyes and sensual come-on of a Persian hipster prince? Lenny Bruce had a treacherous glint under those heavy lids, and his cool pimp's mask of indifference was almost reptilian. He took off on the whole straight world, and that certainly meant the Dustin Hoffmans and it could mean you, because he was more of a hipster than anybody, and it was his vision and his rules (no rules at all) he played by. Hoffman's Lenny Bruce, like Gorman's, is on your side. Lenny Bruce was on nobody's side. The farthest-out hipster, like the farthest-out revolutionary, has an enormous aesthetic advantage over everybody else: he knows how to play his hand to make us all feel chicken.

Bruce's hostility and obscenity were shortcuts to audience response; he could get and hold audiences' attention because they didn't know what or whom he was going to attack and degrade next, and they could sense that he wasn't sure himself. He was always open to darts of inspiration, so suspense was built in. He dropped the barrier between the vagrant obscene jokes that club comics, jazz musicians, and assorted con artists might exchange offstage and what was said publicly onstage. Educated left-wingers were probably his natural audience, because his gutter shpritz was often a more extreme and nihilistic form of what they were thinking, and the maggoty vitality of his language was a heady revelation to them. Words whizzed by that you'd never heard before and that may not have existed in any argot but his own, yet their sound was so expressive that the meaning got across. He flew recklessly low, and the audience, awed and delighted, howled at feeling so ridiculously dirty-minded, howled at the joke of how good it felt to be shameless. We hadn't known how many taboos we were living with, and how many humiliations and embarrassments we were hiding, until we heard him pop them one after another, like a string of firecrackers. That's what a Bruce routine did, and why it felt liberating. Bruce's gleeful, surreal, show-biz Yiddish-jive dirtiness was a mind-opener. He was always testing the audience and himself, and for religious people his blasphemy could only be a whack in the face. He wanted to reach audiences and hold them, yet the only way he knew how was to assault them with obscene jokes about everything that could conceivably be sacred to them. For the people sitting there, complacency was impossible. No matter how hip they thought they were, he would find ways to shock them. The prudish were almost forced to walk out.

Bruce's material is practically indelible for many of us who heard him, and his records stay in the mind for a decade, yet some of Bruce's best stuff is in the movie and we don't remember it ten minutes later, because the man who delivers the bits doesn't know why Bruce said them. The scriptwriter of *Lenny* must think that Bruce's material is so good that an actor can say it and that this will be enough. But those routines don't work without Bruce's teasing, seductive aggression and his delirious amorality. If they are presented as the social criticism of a man who's out to cleanse society of hypocrisy, the material goes flat. When Hoffman's Lenny tells the people in a club that he feels like urinating on them, Hoffman's tone is uncertain and his blank face says that he doesn't understand why Bruce felt that way. The screen never ignites: you're listening to Lenny Bruce's shticks and you don't even feel like laughing.

This Lenny, with his flower child's moral precepts, is a drag. When he does the famous Bruce bit about Jacqueline Kennedy trying to climb out of the assassination car, he attaches the moral that it's important to tell the truth about it in order to help other girls who might be in similar situations. When he assaults his night-club audience, singling out individuals as niggers, kikes, and greaseballs, he expounds on how much better the world would be if those words were freely shouted. Apart from the idiocy of the picture's endorsing this dubious theory and trying to wring applause for it, there's the gross misunderstanding of Bruce's methods. If Bruce did in fact stoop that low upon occasion, gathering sanctity around himself, the moviemakers should have had the brains to know that those explanations were false. I certainly don't recall Bruce's smiling at black patrons (as Hoffman does) to take the sting out of having called them niggers, but if he ever did, that wasn't Bruce the comic, it was Bruce the phony. His cruel jokes may have been a release for the audience (I think they were), but that's not why he did them. He didn't ridicule Jackie Kennedy's actions in order to help women, and he didn't use racial slurs in order to cleanse the national air. He did heartlessly cynical bits because there were only two possible audience reactions—to be outraged or to laugh. And either way he was the winner. But when he drove people out, he was the loser, too. He didn't want them to be outraged only: he was a comic, and he wanted them to laugh at what outraged them. Yet some people couldn't laugh at Bruce, because laughter was an admission that the ideas he was shocking you with weren't altogether new to you—or that, if you hadn't entertained them, you knew that you could. There was a good reason for him to become a counterculture hero: his scabrous realism never seemed a matter of choice. However, he went to the farthest lengths he could dream up, not out of missionary motives but out of a performer's zeal.

There are two views of Bruce competing for public acceptance now, and though a major-studio movie like *Lenny* is bound to set the pattern in which most people will think of Bruce for years to come, this movie suffers in just about every imaginable way by comparison with the Albert Goldman book *Ladies and Gentlemen Lenny Bruce!!* Goldman's greatest value is probably in supplying the show-business milieu that Bruce's humor came from. He provides a sense of how Bruce's act developed, and of who the audiences were, what the clubs were like, and what the other comics were doing. Goldman argues against the saintly view of Bruce, yet in his own way he falls into it—glorifying Bruce the junkie and putting down those who stayed clear of drugs. The book is brilliant, but it made me uneasy, as if Goldman were working off something on Bruce—maybe his own *not* being a junkie. Lenny Bruce got to him—Goldman admires him so much that he feels chicken for his own traces of cautious sanity.

The book has the involvement that is missing from the movie. I felt cold and remote while watching *Lenny*, with its plaster saint; the Goldman book, with its saint junkie, has overheated perils. The book is show business. Goldman gets the hype going and then doesn't go underneath it; the book stays hyped up, and the reader tires. You may begin to feel that Goldman wants the highs of a junkie without really getting hooked, and that he creates the hysterical hero to which his own prose is appropriate. He's so addictively involved that he assumes he's inside Bruce's head, and the interior view he gives is suspect. Goldman doesn't really see Bruce's suffering, because he thinks Lenny Bruce should know he's the great Lenny Bruce. He denies Bruce his pain. In his own way, Goldman competes with Bruce. He isn't just writing a biography; he does what Bruce did—he works the room.

The movie isn't show-biz enough; it's so busy with travail that it never gets any hype going—though Bruce was a hype artist. His view of the world came from the cruddiness and corruption of show business. Bruce spent his youth on the bottom rungs of the sordid club world, guided by his tough, lively mother, Sally Marr, also known as Boots Malloy, who worked as a comic in burlesque joints, managed comedians, and trained strippers. (In *Harry & Tonto*, Sally Marr plays the friendly old broad at the end who suggests to Art Carney that they get together.) And Bruce's seeing the world in show-biz terms was the key to his wit. In his "Religions, Inc." number, the Oral Roberts-type preacher greets Pope John on the phone with "Hey, Johnny, what's shakin', baby?" (This amiable near-obscenity isn't in the movie; if it were, Hoffman's Bruce might explain that it's not good for people to believe in the superstition that the Pope is holier than other men.) Many other comics have lifted Bruce's put-down style of treating the leaders of church and state as cheap hustlers, but when Bruce used show biz as the metaphor for everything squalid and hateful—and lively—in the world, it had a special impact. He was obsessed with bringing everything down to his own terms. Maybe most people who grow up in show business begin to see the world as an extension of it ("Life is a cabaret"), but the traditional performer glosses over the sleaziness with show-biz sentimentality. Even an insult comedian like Don Rickles lays on the sentimental shock absorbers; he titillates the audience by his naughtiness and then asks acceptance as a good boy. Bruce wouldn't play that show-biz game; he despised theatrical sentimentality as the worst form of sleaze (as in his great "Palladium" number). Sentimentality was a rotten, wet show; it disgusted him. Flattering the audience, squeezing for approval, offended his performer's instinct, which was far deeper in him than any social morality and was the base of his satirical outlook. It wasn't until late in his life that he got told that it was a moral base—and after that his instinct began to play him false.

Bob Fosse could have made a sensational movie if he had shown the backstage life that shaped Bruce's awareness, if he had given us a Lenny Bruce who enlarged his satirical perceptions of show biz to include the world—going from imitations of other performers and parodies of movies to parodies of religious show biz and, ultimately, to those labyrinthine, bebop satires of the law in which he was entangled. Maybe for Fosse that approach seems too close to home and too easy. He may devalue the show-biz sensationalism that he's practically a genius at, but the best bit in the movie is Gary Morton's performance as Sherman Hart, a comic based on Milton Berle (who pitched in for Bruce's funeral expenses), and Valerie Perrine's early striptease number has high theatrical dazzle. It's out of character for Honey, because Honey wasn't a top headliner, but if Fosse couldn't resist shooting the works and outblazing Blaze Starr, who will complain? Nothing in Honey's personality ties in with that high-powered strip, but Valerie Perrine gives an affecting, if limited, performance, and her Honey comes closer than Hoffman's Lenny to being a character. Hoffman has his moments; he looks better (and acts less gawky) when he's bearded, and he gets a jazzy performing style going on one piece of tape we hear, but he's respectable, like Paul Muni when he impersonated historical characters. No matter what he does, Hoffman never manages to suggest a hipster.

Lenny Bruce's story is a show-biz story. That's what the Julian Barry script, with its already dated leching-after-youth liberalism, fails to get at.

Before his death, in 1966, Bruce himself began the moist process of canonization; it was his amorality that had shocked people, but now he began to claim that it was his morality. This movie swallows the lie that his motivating force was to make the audience well, and, having swallowed that, it can only defuse his humor. The moviemakers are working something off on Bruce, too: they're staking higher claims for themselves, trying to go beyond show business. The black-and-white earnestness of this movie and the youth-culture saintliness laid on Lenny Bruce are the ultimate in modern show-biz sentimentality.

{*The New Yorker*, November 18, 1974}

:: Fathers and Sons

At the close of *The Godfather*, Michael Corleone has consolidated his power by a series of murders and has earned the crown his dead father, Don Vito, handed him. In the last shot, Michael—his eyes clouded—assures his wife, Kay, that he is not responsible for the murder of his sister's husband. The door closes Kay out while he receives the homage of subordinates, and if she doesn't know that he lied, it can only be because she doesn't want to. *The Godfather, Part II* begins where the first film ended: before the titles there is a view behind that door. The new king stands in the dark, his face lusterless and dispassionate as his hand is being kissed. The familiar *Godfather* waltz theme is heard in an ambiguous, melancholy tone. Is it our imagination, or is Michael's face starting to rot? The dramatic charge of that moment is Shakespearean. The waltz is faintly, chillingly ominous.

By a single image, Francis Ford Coppola has plunged us back into the sensuality and terror of the first film. And, with the relentlessness of a master, he goes farther and farther. The daring of Part II is that it enlarges the scope and deepens the meaning of the first film; *The Godfather* was the greatest gangster picture ever made, and had metaphorical overtones that took it far beyond the gangster genre. In Part II, the wider themes are no longer merely implied. The second film shows the consequences of the actions in the first; it's all one movie, in two great big pieces, and it comes together in your head while you watch. Coppola might almost have a pact with the audience; we're already so engrossed in the Corleones that now he can go on to give us a more interior view of the characters at the same time that he shows their spreading social influence. The completed work is an epic about the seeds of destruction that the immigrants brought to the new land, with Sicilians, Wasps, and Jews separate socially but joined together in crime and political bribery. This is a bicentennial picture that doesn't insult the intelligence. It's an epic vision of the corruption of America.

After the titles, the action begins in Sicily in 1901, with the funeral procession of Michael's murdered grandfather, and we realize that the plaintive tone that was so unsettling in the opening music is linked to funeral drums and to a line of mourning women. The rot in Michael's face starts here, in his legacy from his father. The silent nine-year-old boy walking behind the coffin with his strong, grief-hardened mother is Vito, who will become the Don, the Godfather (the role played in the first film by Marlon Brando). Shots are heard, the procession breaks up—Vito's older brother has just been killed. And in a few minutes Vito, his mother dead, too, is running for his life. The waltz is heard again, still poignant but with a note of exaltation, as a ship with the wide-eyed child among the hordes in steerage passes the Statue of Liberty. The sallow, skinny boy has an almost frightening look of guarded intelligence; not understanding a word of English, he makes no sound until he's all alone, quarantined with smallpox on Ellis Island. Then, in his hospital cell, he looks out the barred window and, in a thin, childish soprano, sings a Sicilian song. As he sings, we see the superimposed face of another dark-eyed little boy, a shining princeling in white with a pretty flower-face—Michael's son, the little boy who had been playing in the garden with the old Don Vito when he died. It is the rich princeling's First Communion, and there is a lavish celebration at the Corleone estate on the shore of Lake Tahoe. The year is 1958, and the surviving members of the Corleone family, whose base of operations is now in Nevada, are gathered for the occasion.

The first film covered the period from 1945 to the mid-fifties. Part II, contrasting the early manhood of Vito (played by Robert De Niro) with the life of Michael, his inheritor (Al Pacino), spans almost seventy years. We saw only the middle of the story in the first film; now we have the beginning and the end. Structurally, the completed work is nothing less than the rise and decay of an American dynasty of unofficial rulers. Vito rises and becomes a respected man while his son Michael, the young king, rots before our eyes, and there is something about actually seeing the generations of a family in counterpoint that is emotionally overpowering. It's as if the movie satisfied an impossible yet basic human desire to see what our parents were like before we were born and to see what they did that affected what we became—not to hear about it, or to read about it, as we can in novels, but actually to see it. It really is like the past recaptured. We see the characters at different points in their lives, with every scene sharpening our perception of them; at one moment Michael embraces his young son, at another Vito cradles young Michael in his arms. The whole picture is informed with such a complex sense of the intermingling of good and evil—and of the inability to foresee the effects of our love upon our children—that it may be the most passionately felt epic ever made in this country.

Throughout the three hours and twenty minutes of Part II, there are so many moments of epiphany—mysterious, reverberant images, such as the small Vito singing in his cell—that one scarcely has the emotional resources to deal with the experience of this film. Twice, I almost cried out at acts of violence that De Niro's Vito committed. I didn't look away from the images, as I sometimes do at routine action pictures. I wanted to see the worst; there is a powerful need to see it. You need these moments as you need the terrible climaxes in a Tolstoy novel. A great novelist does not spare our feelings (as the historical romancer does); he intensifies them, and so does Coppola. On the screen, the speed of the climaxes and their vividness make them almost unbearably wounding.

Much of the material about Don Vito's early life which appears in Part II was in the Mario Puzo book and was left out of the first movie, but the real fecundity of Puzo's mind shows in the way this new film can take his characters further along and can expand (and, in a few cases, alter) the implications of the book. Puzo didn't write the novel he probably could have written, but there was a Promethean spark in his trash, and Coppola has written the novel it might have been. However, this second film (the script is again by Coppola and Puzo) doesn't appear to derive from the book as much as from what Coppola learned while he was making the first. In Part II, he has had the opportunity to do what he was prevented from doing before, and he's been able to develop what he didn't know about his characters and themes until after he'd made the first picture. He has also been able to balance the material. Many people who saw *The Godfather* developed a romantic identification with the Corleones; they longed for the feeling of protection that Don Vito conferred on his loving family. Now that the full story has been told, you'd have to have an insensitivity bordering on moral idiocy to think that the Corleones live a wonderful life, which you'd like to be part of.

The violence in this film never doesn't bother us — it's never just a kick. For a movie director, Coppola has an unusual interest in ideas and in the texture of feeling and thought. This wasn't always apparent in the first film, because the melodramatic suspense was so strong that one's motor responses demanded the resolution of tension (as in the restaurant scene, when one's heart almost stopped in the few seconds before Michael pulled out the gun and fired). But this time Coppola controls our emotional responses so that the horror seeps through everything and no action provides a melodramatic release. Within a scene Coppola is controlled and unhurried, yet he has a gift for igniting narrative, and the exploding effects keep accumulating. About midway, I began to feel that the film was expanding in my head like a soft bullet.

The casting is so close to flawless that we can feel the family connections, and there are times when one could swear that Michael's brother Fredo (John Cazale), as he ages, is beginning to look like a weak version of his father, because we see Marlon Brando in the wide forehead and receding hair. Brando is not on the screen this time, but he persists in his sons, Fredo and Michael, and Brando's character is extended by our seeing how it was formed. As Vito, Robert De Niro amply convinces one that he has it in him to become the old man that Brando was. It's not that he looks exactly like Brando but that he has Brando's wary soul, and so we can easily imagine the body changing with the years. It is much like seeing a photograph of one's own dead father when he was a strapping young man; the burning spirit we see in his face spooks us, because of our knowledge of what he was at the end. In De Niro's case, the young man's face is fired by a secret pride. His gesture as he refuses the gift of a box of groceries is beautifully expressive and has the added wonder of suggesting Brando, and not from the outside but from the inside. Even the soft, cracked Brando-like voice seems to come from the inside. When De Niro closes his eyes to blot out something insupportable, the reflex is like a presentiment of the old man's reflexes. There is such a continuity of soul between the child on the ship, De Niro's slight, ironic smile as a cowardly landlord tries to appease him, and Brando, the old man who died happy in the sun, that although Vito is a subsidiary character in terms of actual time on the screen, this second film, like the first, is imbued with his presence.

De Niro is right to be playing the young Brando because he has the physical audacity, the grace, and the instinct to become a great actor— perhaps as great as Brando. In *Mean Streets*, he was a wild, reckless kid who flaunted his being out of control; here he's a man who holds himself in— and he's just as transfixing. Vito came to America to survive. He brought nothing with him but a background of violence, and when he believes the only choice is between knuckling under to the gangsters who terrorize the poor in Little Italy—just as gangsters terrorized his family in Sicily—and using a gun, he chooses the gun. In his terms, it's a simple matter of self-preservation, and he achieves his manhood when he becomes a killer. Vito has a feudal code of honor. To the Italians who treat him with respect he's a folk hero—a Robin Hood you can come to in times of trouble. No matter what he does, he believes he's a man of principle, and he's wrapped in dignity. The child's silence is carried forward in the adult. De Niro's performance is so subtle that when he speaks in the Sicilian dialect he learned for the role he speaks easily, but he is cautious in English and speaks very clearly and precisely. For a man of Vito's character who doesn't know the language well, precision is important—sloppy talk would be unthinkable. Like Brando's Vito, De Niro's has a reserve that can never be breached. Vito is so secure in the knowledge of how dangerous he is that his courtliness is no more or less than noblesse oblige.

The physical contrasts between De Niro's characterization and Pacino's give an almost tactile dimension to the theme. Driving through the streets of Batista's Havana, which he's buying into—buying a piece of the government—Michael sees the children begging, and he knows what he is: he's a predator on human weakness. And that's exactly what he looks like. He wears silvery-gray nubby-silk suits over a soft, amorphous body; he's hidden under the price tag. The burden of power sits on him like a sickness; his expression is sullen and withdrawn. He didn't have to be what he is: he knew there were other possibilities, and he chose to become a killer out of family loyalty. Here in Part II he is a disconsolate man, whose only attachment is to his children; he can never go back to the time before that moment in the restaurant when he shot his father's enemies. In the first film, we saw Don Vito weep when he learned that it was Michael who had done the killing; Michael's act, which preserved the family's power, destroyed his own life. Don Vito had recoiled from the sordid drug traffic, but since crime is the most competitive business of all (the quality of what you're peddling not being a conspicuous factor), Michael, the modernist, recoils from nothing; the empire that he runs from Nevada has few links with his young father's Robin Hood days. It's only inside himself that Michael recoils. His tense, flaccid face hovers over the movie; he's the man in power, trying to control the lives around him and feeling empty and betrayed. He's like a depressed Brando.

There are times when Pacino's moodiness isn't particularly eloquent, and when Michael asks his mother (Morgana King) how his father felt deep down in his heart the question doesn't have enough urgency. However, Pacino does something very difficult: he gives an almost immobile performance. Michael's attempt to be the man his father was has aged him, and he can't conceal the ugliness of the calculations that his father's ceremonial manner masked. His father had a domestic life that was a sanctuary, but Michael has no sanctuary. He cannot maintain the traditional division of home and business, and so the light and dark contrasts are not as sharp as in the first picture. His wife knows he lied to her, just as he lies to a Senate investigating committee, and the darkness of his business dealings has invaded his home. Part II has the same mythic and operatic visual scheme as the first; once again the cinematographer is Gordon Willis. Visually the film is, however, far more complexly beautiful than the first, just as it's thematically richer, more shadowed, more full. Willis's workmanship has developed, like Coppola's; even the sequences in the sunlight have deep tones—elegiac yet lyrical, as in *The Conformist*, and always serving the narrative, as the Nino Rota score also does.

Talia Shire had a very sure touch in her wedding scenes in the first film; her Connie was like a Pier Angeli with a less fragile, bolder nature—a spoiled princess. Now, tight with anger, dependent on her brother Michael, who killed her husband, Connie behaves self-destructively. She once had a dream wedding; now she hooks up with gigolo playboys. (Troy Donahue is her newest husband.) Talia Shire has such beauty and strength that she commands attention. It's possible that she didn't impose herself more strongly in the first film because Coppola, through a kind of reverse nepotism (Miss Shire is his sister), deëmphasized her role and didn't give her many closeups, but this time—pinched, strident, whory—she comes through as a stunningly controlled actress. Kay (Diane Keaton), Michael's New England-born wife, balks at becoming the acquiescent woman he requires, so he shows her what his protection means. It's dependent on absolute fealty. Any challenge or betrayal and you're dead—for men, that is. Women are so subservient they're not considered dangerous enough to kill—that's about the extent of Mafioso chivalry. The male-female relationships are worked out with a Jacobean splendor that goes far beyond one's expectations.

There must be more brilliant strokes of casting here (including the use of a batch of Hollywood notables—Phil Feldman, Roger Corman, and William Bowers—as United States senators), and more first-rate acting in small parts, than in any other American movie. An important new character, Hyman Roth, a Meyer Lansky-like businessman-gangster, as full of cant and fake wisdom as a fund-raising rabbi, is played with smooth conviction by the near-legendary Lee Strasberg. Even his breath control is impeccable: when Roth talks too much and gets more excited than he should, his talk ends with a sound of exertion from his chest. As another new major character, Frankie Pentangeli, an old-timer in the rackets who wants things to be as they were when Don Vito was in his heyday, Michael V. Gazzo (the playwright-actor) gives an intensely likable performance that adds flavor to the picture. His Pentangeli has the capacity for enjoying life, unlike Michael and the anonymous-looking high-echelon hoods who surround him. As the bland, despicably loyal Tom Hagen, more square-faced and sturdy now, Robert Duvall, a powerful recessive actor, is practically a genius at keeping himself in the background; and Richard Bright as Al Neri, one of Michael's henchmen, runs him a close second.

Coppola's approach is openhanded: he doesn't force the situations. He puts the material up there, and we read the screen for ourselves. But in a few places, such as in the double-crossing maneuvers of Michael Corleone and Hyman Roth, his partner in the Cuban venture, it hasn't been made readable enough. There's a slight confusion for the audience in the sequences dealing with Roth's bogus attempt on the life of Pentangeli, and the staging is a little flatfooted in the scenes in which the Corleone assassin first eliminates Roth's bodyguard and then goes to kill Roth. Also, it's a disadvantage that the frame-up of Senator Geary (which is very poorly staged, with more gory views of a murdered girl than are necessary) comes so long after the provocation for it. Everywhere else, the contrapuntal cutting is beautifully right, but the pieces of the Senator Geary story seem too slackly spaced apart. (The casting of G. D. Spradlin in the role is a juicy bit of satire; he looks and acts like a synthesis of several of our worst senators.) These small flaws are not failures of intelligence; they're faults in the storytelling, and there are a few abrupt transitions, indicating unplanned last-minute cuts. There may be too many scenes of plotting heads, and at times one wishes the sequences to be more fully developed. One never wants less of the characters; one always wants more — particularly of Vito in the 1917 period, which is recreated in a way that makes movies once again seem a miraculous medium.

This film wouldn't have been made if the first hadn't been a hit—and the first was made because the Paramount executives expected it to be an ordinary gangster shoot-'em-up. When you see this new picture, you wonder how Coppola won the fights. Maybe the answer is that they knew they couldn't make it without him. After you see it, you feel they can't make *any* picture without him. He directs with supreme confidence. Coppola is the inheritor of the traditions of the novel, the theater, and—especially— opera and movies. The sensibility at work in this film is that of a major artist. We're not used to it: how many screen artists get the chance to work in the epic form, and who has been able to seize the power to compose a modern American epic? And who else, when he got the chance and the power, would have proceeded with the absolute conviction that he'd make the film the way it should be made? In movies, that's the inner voice of the authentic hero.

{*The New Yorker*, December 23, 1974}

:: Beverly Hills as a Big Bed

When George (Warren Beatty), the hairdresser hero of *Shampoo*, asks Jackie (Julie Christie), "Want me to do your hair?", it's his love lyric. George massages a neck and wields a blower as if he would rather be doing that than anything else in the world. When he gets his hands in a woman's hair, it's practically sex, and sensuous, tender sex—not what his Beverly Hills customers are used to. Their husbands and lovers don't have professionally caressing hands like the dedicated George's. Some ideas for films are promising, some are cocksure audacious, but a film about the movie colony featuring the lives of the rich, beautiful women who have a yen for their handsome hairdresser is such a yummy idea that it almost sounds like something a smart porno filmmaker would come up with. Exploited for gags, it might have been no more than a saucy romp, a modernized *Fanfan the Tulip*, and that may be what audiences expect—maybe even what some audiences want. But the way it has been done, the joke expands the more you think about it. *Shampoo* is light and impudent, yet, like the comedies that live on, it's a bigger picture in retrospect.

The attention George gives women is so exciting to him and to them that he's always on the go. He works in a fashionable salon, commutes to his assignations on a motorbike, and tells himself and his girl, Jill (Goldie Hawn), that they'll settle down as soon as he gets his own shop. The movie deals with his frantic bed-hopping during the forty-odd hours in which he tries to borrow the stake he needs from Lester (Jack Warden), the shyster tycoon who is married to Felicia (Lee Grant), a rapacious customer. Lester is also keeping Jackie, George's old girl friend, who is Jill's closest friend. *Shampoo* opens on Election Eve, November 4, 1968, when the hero's life has begun to boil over. The characters whirl in and out of bed with each other through Election Day and Night, watching the returns at a party at The Bistro, acknowledging Nixon and Agnew's victory by seeing in the dawn at another party, and preparing for the new era by shifting partners. The picture is a sex roundelay set in a period as clearly defined as the Jazz Age. (It's gone, all right, and we know that best when we catch echoes from it.) Maybe we've all been caught in a time warp, because the Beatles sixties of miniskirts and strobe lights, when people had not yet come down from their euphoria about the harmlessness of drugs, is already a period with its own bubbly potency. The time of *Shampoo* is so close to us that at moments we forget its pastness, and then we're stung by the consciousness of how much has changed.

Shampoo is set in the past for containment, for a formalized situation, just as Ingmar Bergman set his boudoir farce, *Smiles of a Summer Night*, in the operetta past of the *Merry Widow* period. What the turn-of-the-century metaphor did for Bergman the 1968 election, as the sum of an era, does for *Shampoo*. The balletic, patterned confusion of *Shampoo* is theatrical, and Los Angeles—more particularly, Beverly Hills, the swankest part of it, a city within a city—is, indisputably, a stylized, theatrical setting. But a bedroom-chase construction isn't stagey in Beverly Hills: *Shampoo* has a mathematically structured plot in an open society. Los Angeles itself, the sprawl-city, opens the movie up, and the L.A. sense of freedom makes its own comment on the scrambling characters. Besides, when you play musical chairs in the bedrooms of Beverly Hills, the distances you have to cover impose their own comic frenzy. As in a Feydeau play or some of the René Clair and Lubitsch films, the more complicated the interaction is, the more we look forward to the climactic muddle and the final sorting out of couples. The whirring pleasures of carnal farce require our awareness of the mechanics, and the director, Hal Ashby, has the deftness to keep us conscious of the structure and yet to give it free play. The plot isn't arbitrary; it's what George, who can never really get himself together, is caught in. The mixed pairs of lovers don't get snarled at the same parties by coincidence; they go knowing who else is going to be there, wanting the danger of collisions.

Shampoo expresses the emotional climate of the time and place. Los Angeles has become what it is because of the bright heat, which turns people into narcissists and sensuous provocateurs. The atmosphere seems to infantilize sex: sexual desire is despiritualized; it becomes a demand for immediate gratification. George's women have their status styles—money and sun produce tough babies—but George, the sexual courier, servicing a garden apartment as ardently as a terraced estate, is a true democrat. The characters are all linked by sex—and dissatisfaction. They're passionate people from minute to minute. They want to have something going for them all the time, and since they get it only part of the time, and it doesn't last long, they feel upset and frustrated. They're so foolish, self-absorbed, and driven that the film can easily seem a trifle—and at one level it is—but it's daringly faithful to the body-conscious style of life that is its subject, and it never falls into low farce by treating the characters as dum-dums. They're attractively, humanly, greedily foolish, and some of their foolishness is shared by people much more complex. The movie gets at the kink and willfulness of the Beverly Hills way of life (which magnetizes the whole world), but it doesn't point any comic fingers. It's too balanced and Mozartean for that.

The scenarist, Robert Towne (Beatty, who shares the screenplay credit, contributed ideas and worked on the structuring with him), has brought something new to bedroom farce. The characters have more than one sex object in mind, and they're constantly regrouping in their heads. No one is romantically in love or devoted in the sense in which Bergman's characters are in *Smiles of a Summer Night*. *Shampoo* isn't about the bondage of romantic pursuit, it's about the bondage of the universal itch among a group primed to scratch. Ready and waiting, the characters keep all possibilities open. This variation on the usual love comedy is the trickiest, funniest, truest-to-its-freeway-love-environment ingredient of the movie. Except for George, who doesn't plan ahead, everyone is always considering alternatives. It's a small, rich, loose society, and its members know each other carnally in a casual way; it's in the nature of things that they take turns in the one big bed that is their world. Since the characters hold multiple goals, when they look depressed you're never sure who exactly is the object of their misery. The actors are much more free than in the confines of classic farce. They're free, too, of the stilted witticisms of classic farce: Towne writes such easy, unforced dialogue that they might be talking in their own voices.

Julie Christie's locked-in, libidinous face has never been harder, more petulant, or more magical than in her role as Lester's kept woman, who hates her position because she never gets to go anywhere with him. Jackie is coarse and high-strung (a true L.A. combo); she's a self-destructive win-ner, and Julie Christie plays her boldly, with a moody ruthlessness that I find uncanny. This is the first time Christie and Beatty have acted together since *McCabe & Mrs. Miller*, and each of them gains. Julie Christie is one of those screen actresses whose every half-buried thought smashes through; she's so delicate an actress that when she plays a coarse girl like Jackie there's friction in each nuance. On the stage last year in *Uncle Vanya* she was a vacuum; in *Shampoo* she's not only an actress, she is—in the high-class-hooker terms of her role—the sexiest woman in movies right now. She has the knack of turning off her spirituality totally; in this role she's a gorgeous, whory-lipped little beast, a dirty sprite.

Goldie Hawn, who began to come into her own as a screen actress in last year's *The Sugarland Express*, is probably going to be everything her admirers have hoped for. As the hysterical young Jill, she isn't allowed to be too hysterical; Hal Ashby doesn't let her go all frilly and wistful, either. She used to be her own best audience; now that she has stopped breaking up infectiously, we're free to judge her for ourselves. She has calm moments here—we see Jill's mind working without Goldie Hawn's goldfish eyes batting—and I think it's the first time I've noticed that she has a speaking voice. (She's always been a screamer.) She looks great in her baby dolls and minis, and it's a relief that her Jill doesn't have a mini baby-doll head. Lee Grant, who worked with Ashby in *The Landlord*, the film of his that *Shampoo* most resembles (though he was a beginner then, with nothing like the assurance he shows now), is such a cool-style comedienne that she's in danger of having people say that she's good, as usual. But she carries off the film's most sexually brutal scene: Felicia comes home late for an assig-nation with George and discovers that while he was waiting for her he has been occupied with her teenage daughter (Carrie Fisher), and she *still* wants to go to bed with him. She wants it more than ever. As her husband, Jack Warden is the biggest surprise in the cast. He's both a broad cartoon and an appealing character. Lester is triply cuckolded—George commutes between Lester's mistress and wife and daughter—and he's a heavy con-tributor to the Nixon-Agnew campaign, for business purposes. And yet he has more depth than anyone else in the movie. He's ready to investigate anything: invited to join a nymphs-and-satyrs bathing orgy, he considers getting into the water as he would a new investment, and thinks, Why not? Warden shows us Lester's pragmatic ruminations; we see that he's a business success because he's learned to make compromises in his own favor. While Nixon is on TV making his victory speech, Lester and George have it all out, in a final confrontation scene, and the astute Lester realizes that, despite the wear and tear on George's zipper, the hairdresser is no threat to him.

The central performance that makes it all work is Beatty's. George, who wears his hair blower like a Colt .45, isn't an easy role; I don't know anyone else who could have played it. Because of Beatty's offscreen reputation as a heterosexual dynamo, audiences may laugh extra hard at the scenes in which Lester assumes that a male hairdresser can't be straight, but that joke is integral to the conception anyway. Beatty makes George's impulsive warmth toward his customers believable. An uncomplicated Don Juan, George gets pleasure from giving pleasure. He doesn't smoke tobacco or dope; he doesn't pop pills; outside of soft drinks, the only beverage he takes in the whole film is a little white wine. George doesn't need to be raised high or brought down, and he has nothing to obliterate. Maybe when he's older, if he's still working in someone else's shop, he'll be embittered, and he'll be one of the garden-variety narcissists who must have attention from women (and secretly hate them). But at this point in his life, jumping happily to oblige any woman who wants him, he has the pagan purity of an adolescent. At the start of the film, George is in the middle of the whirligig, but by the end the game has moved on, and he's left behind, dreaming of a simpler life and longing for a sexual playmate from the past. "You're the only one I trust," he tells Jackie. The others are upward-mobile and moving fast, and they live as if upward mobility were a permanent condition. George wants something to hang on to, and he can't get it, because he's too generous. He lives in constant excitation, and so he's the closest to exhaustion. George is the only one of the characters who isn't completely selfish; he's the only one who doesn't function successfully in the society. The others know how to use people, but George, the compleat lover, does everything for fun. Making love to a beautiful woman is an aesthetic thing with him, and making her look beautiful is an act of love for him. He's almost a sexual saint.

Shampoo doesn't seem inspired the way Renoir's roundelay *Rules of the Game* does. It doesn't have the feeling that one gets from the Renoir film — that the whole beautiful, macabre chaos is bubbling up right this minute. And *Shampoo* is not as lyrical — or as elegantly moldy to the taste — as parts of Bergman's *Smiles*. It doesn't give the lunatic delight of *Bringing Up Baby*, which in its homegrown, screwball style also suggested an equivalent of Restoration comedy. But it's the most virtuoso example of sophisticated, kaleidoscopic farce that American moviemakers have ever come up with. And, as in *Rules of the Game*, the farce movement itself carries a sense of heedless activity, of a craze of dissatisfaction. In this game, George, who loves love too much to profit from it, has to be the loser. He's a fool (that's why Lester doesn't have him beaten up), but he's a pure fool (and Lester can appreciate that). George isn't a negligible dramatic creation. For the moviemakers, he's the foolish romanticism of youth incarnate, but some people may see him as a jerk and resent him. To them, possibly, the new romantic hero would be a cynical stud who gets it all and wins out. In its own way, *Shampoo* is a very uncompromising film, and it's going to cause dissension. People who are living the newer forms of the *Blow-Up* style, or want to, won't like this view of it. *Shampoo* may be put down as frivolous just because it really isn't; to lift a line from *The Earrings of Madame de* . . . , it's "only superficially superficial." Was it Osbert Sitwell who said that life might be considered a comedy only if it were never to end? *Shampoo* tosses the fact of death into the midst of the beauty shop; we suddenly learn that Norman (Jay Robinson), the languid, pettish proprietor, whom we'd assumed to be strictly homosexual, has just lost his teenage son in a car crash. It's an artifice—reality intruding upon the clowns at their revels, death as an interruption to the babble and trivial bickering of the beauty-salon world. But it's needed, and it's the right death—the accidental death of someone young, the only event, maybe, that can't be converted into gossip.

There are minds at work in this film: three principal ones—Ashby, Beatty, who produced it (it is his second production; the first was *Bonnie and Clyde*), and Towne. Hal Ashby says that he had fifty or sixty jobs (starting when he was ten years old) before he landed as a Multilith operator at the old Republic Studios in L.A., and decided he wanted to become a director. As the first step, he went to work in the cutting room, where he spent the standard eight years as an apprentice before he was allowed (by feudal union regulation) to edit a film. Afterward, he edited Norman Jewison's *The Cincinnati Kid*, *The Russians Are Coming, The Russians Are Coming*, *In the Heat of the Night*, and *The Thomas Crown Affair*, and then, in 1968, Jewison, who was supposed to direct *The Landlord*, arranged with the moneymen to turn it over to Ashby. (*Shampoo* should cause *The Landlord* to get the attention it deserves.) His new film is only his fourth (*Harold and Maude* and *The Last Detail* came between), but he's developed quickly. Ashby's control keeps *Shampoo* from teetering over into burlesque. His work doesn't have the flash of an innovative, intuitive film artist, but for the script Towne has prepared, Ashby, the craftsman who serves the material, is probably the only kind of director.

Robert Towne didn't write a screenplay a director can take off from. *Shampoo* is conceived for the movies, and it's porous, yet the development of the themes is completely conceived. It isn't the basis for a director to work out his own conception; it *is* a conception. (Tall, his long face dark-bearded, Towne appears in one party shot in *Shampoo*, looking a little like Albrecht Dürer.) It's more apparent now why Towne collided with Polanski over his script (also an original) for *Chinatown*. He provided a script that culminated—logically—with the heroine's killing her lover-father in order to save her daughter. A Gothic-minded absurdist, Polanski didn't see why he shouldn't end it with the death of the heroine and the triumph of the father, who had raped the land, raped his daughter, and would now proceed to corrupt the child he'd had by her. Towne doesn't pull everything down like that. It has taken a while to get a fix on his talent, because he's not a published writer, and because he didn't receive credit for some of the films he worked on, and didn't take blame for others (*The New Centurions*). His earliest screen credits are for *Villa Rides* and *The Tomb of Ligeia*, but even before those, in 1964, he wrote an episode for TV's *Breaking Point*, called "So Many Pretty Girls, So Little Time," about a Don Juan. Beatty brought him in to do the rewriting on *Bonnie and Clyde* (he was listed as "Special Consultant"), and when Coppola accepted his Academy Award for the screenplay of *The Godfather* he acknowledged Towne's contribution (he wrote one scene and tinkered with a few others). Towne also did a major rewrite on *Cisco Pike* (the film has certain similarities to *Shampoo*) and on *The Yakuza*, which hasn't opened yet, and he wrote the script (an adaptation) of *The Last Detail*.

Towne's heroes, if we can take Gittes, of *Chinatown*, and George, here, as fair examples, are hip to conventional society, and they assume that they reject its dreams. But in some corner of their heads they think that maybe the old romantic dream can be made to work. Gittes is basically a very simple man. He wants the woman he loves to tell him the truth about herself; the truth is very important to him. And George is even simpler. Towne's heroes are like the heroes of hardboiled fiction: they don't ask much of life, but they are also romantic damn fools who ask just what they can't get. His characters are so effective on the screen because they have sides you don't expect and—a Towne idiosyncrasy—they tell anecdotes, mostly inane, backslapping ones (Jack Nicholson has several in *The Last Detail* and *Chinatown*, and Jack Warden gets off a real puzzler). With his ear for unaffected dialogue, and with a gift for never forcing a point, Towne may be a great new screenwriter in a structured tradition—a flaky classicist.

{*The New Yorker*, February 17, 1975}

:: Coming: *Nashville*

Is there such a thing as an orgy for movie-lovers—but an orgy without excess? At Robert Altman's new, almost-three-hour film, *Nashville*, you don't get drunk on images, you're not overpowered—you get elated. I've never before seen a movie I loved in quite this way: I sat there smiling at the screen, in complete happiness. It's a pure emotional high, and you don't come down when the picture is over; you take it with you. In most cases, the studio heads can conjecture what a director's next picture will be like, and they feel safe that way—it's like an insurance policy. They can't with Altman, and after United Artists withdrew its backing from *Nashville*, the picture had to be produced independently, because none of the other major companies would take it on. U.A.'s decision will probably rack up as a classic boner, because this picture is going to take off into the stratosphere—though it has first got to open. (Paramount has picked up the distribution rights but hasn't yet announced an opening date.) *Nashville* is a radical, evolutionary leap.

Altman has prepared us for it. If this film had been made earlier, it might have been too strange and new, but in the five years since he broke through with *M*A*S*H* he's experimented in so many directions that now, when it all comes together for him, it's not really a shock. From the first, packed frames of a recording studio, with Haven Hamilton (Henry Gibson), in bespangled, embroidered white cowboy clothes, like a short, horseless Roy Rogers, singing, "We must be doing somethin' right to last two hundred years," the picture is unmistakably Altman—as identifiable as a paragraph by Mailer when he's really racing. *Nashville* is simply "the ultimate Altman movie" we've been waiting for. Fused, the different styles of prankishness of *M*A*S*H* and *Brewster McCloud* and *California Split*

become Jovian adolescent humor. Altman has already accustomed us to
actors who don't look as if they're acting; he's attuned us to the comic
subtleties of a multiple-track sound system that makes the sound more
live than it ever was before; and he's evolved an organic style of moviemaking that tells a story without the clanking of plot. Now he dissolves the
frame, so that we feel the continuity between what's on the screen and life
off-camera.

Nashville isn't organized according to patterns that you're familiar with,
yet you don't question the logic. You get it from the rhythms of the scenes.
The picture is at once a *Grand Hotel*–style narrative, with twenty-four
linked characters; a country-and-Western musical; a documentary essay
on Nashville and American life; a meditation on the love affair between
performers and audiences; and an Altman party. In the opening sequences,
when Altman's people — the performers we associate with him because he
has used them in ways no one else would think of, and they've been filtered
through his sensibility — start arriving, and pile up in a traffic jam on the
way from the airport to the city, the movie suggests the circus procession
at the non-ending of *8½*. But Altman's clowns are far more autonomous;
they move and intermingle freely, and the whole movie is their procession.
Nashville is, above all, a celebration of its own performers. Like Bertolucci,
Altman (he includes a homage to *Last Tango in Paris*) gives the actors a
chance to come out — to use more of themselves in their characters. The
script is by Joan Tewkesbury, but the actors have been encouraged to work
up material for their roles, and not only do they do their own singing but
most of them wrote their own songs — and wrote them in character. The
songs distill the singers' lives, as the mimes and theatrical performances
did for the actors in *Children of Paradise*. The impulse behind all Altman's
innovations has been to work on more levels than the conventional film
does, and now — despite the temporary sound mix and the not-quite-final
edit of the print he ran recently, informally, for a few dozen people in New
York, before even the Paramount executives had seen the picture — it's
apparent that he needed the technical innovations in order to achieve this
union of ideas and feelings. *Nashville* coalesces lightly and easily, as if it
had just been tossed off. We float while watching, because Altman never
lets us see the sweat. Altman's art, like Fred Astaire's, is the great American
art of making the impossible look easy.

Altman does for Nashville what he was trying to do for Houston in

Brewster McCloud, but he wasn't ready to fly then, and the script didn't have enough layers — he needs ideas that mutate, and characters who turn corners. Joan Tewkesbury has provided him with a great subject. Could there be a city with wilder metaphoric overtones than Nashville, the Hollywood of the C. & W. recording industry, the center of fundamentalist music and pop success? The country sound is a twang with longing in it; the ballads are about poor people with no hope. It's the simplistic music of the conquered South; the songs tell you that although you've failed and you've lived a terrible, degrading life, there's a place to come home to, and that's where you belong. Even the saddest song is meant to be reassuring to its audience: the insights never go beyond common poverty, job troubles, and heartaches, and the music never rises to a level that would require the audience to reinterpret its experience. Country stars are symbolic ordinary figures. In this, they're more like political demagogues than artists. The singer bears the burden of what he has become, and he keeps saying, "I may be driving an expensive car, but that doesn't mean I'm happier than you are." Neither he nor the politician dares to come right out and confess to the audience that what he's got is what he set out for from the beginning. Instead, he says, "It's only an accident that puts me here and you there — don't we talk the same language?" Listening to him, people can easily feel that he owes them, and everybody who can sing a little or who has written a tune tries to move in close to the performers as a way of getting up there into the fame business.

Nashville is about the insanity of a fundamentalist culture in which practically the whole population has been turned into groupies. The story spans the five days during which a political manager, played by Michael Murphy, lines up the talent for a Nashville rally to be used as a TV show promoting the Presidential candidacy of Hal Phillip Walker. Walker's slogan is "New Roots for the Nation" — a great slogan for the South, since country music is about a longing for roots that don't exist. Because country singing isn't complex, either musically or lyrically, Altman has been able to create a whole constellation of country stars out of actors. Some of them had actually cut records, but they're not primarily country singers, and their songs are never just numbers. The songs are the story being told, and even the way the singers stand — fluffing out a prom-queen dress, like Karen Black, or coolly staring down the audience, like the almond-eyed, slightly withdrawn Cristina Raines — is part of it. During this movie, we begin to realize that all that the people are is what we see. Nothing is held back from us, nothing is hidden.

When Altman—who is the most atmospheric of directors—discusses what his movies are about, he makes them sound stupid, and he's immediately attacked in the press by people who take his statements literally. (If pinned to the wall by publicity men, how would Joyce have explained the "Nighttown" sequence of *Ulysses*?) The complex outline of *Nashville* gives him the space he needs to work in, and he tells the story by suggestions, echoes, recurrences. It may be he's making a joke about how literally his explanations have been taken when in this picture the phony sentiments that turn up in the lyrics recur in other forms, where they ring true. Haven Hamilton, the bantam king of Nashville, with a red toupee for a crown, sings a maudlin piece of doggerel, with a heavy, churchy beat, about a married man's breaking up with his girl friend ("For the sake of the children, we must say goodbye"). Later, it's almost a reprise when we see Lily Tomlin, as the gospel-singing wife of Haven's lawyer, Ned Beatty, leave Keith Carradine (the hot young singer in a trio) for exactly that reason. Throughout, there are valid observations made to seem fake by a slimy inflection. Geraldine Chaplin, as Opal, from the BBC, is doing a documentary on Nashville; she talks in flights of poetic gush, but nothing she says is as fatuous as she makes it sound. What's funny about Opal is that her affectations are all wasted, since the hillbillies she's trying to impress don't know what she's talking about. Opal is always on the fringe of the action; her opposite is the figure that the plot threads converge on—Barbara Jean (Ronee Blakley), whose ballads are her only means of expressing her yearnings. Barbara Jean is the one tragic character: her art comes from her belief in imaginary roots.

The movies often try to do portraits of artists, but their artistry must be asserted for them. When we see an actor playing a painter and then see the paintings, we don't feel the relation. And even when the portrait is of a performing artist, the story is almost always of how the artist achieves recognition rather than of what it is that has made him an artist. Here, with Ronee Blakley's Barbara Jean, we perceive what goes into the art, and we experience what the unbalance of life and art can do to a person. When she was a child, Barbara Jean memorized the words on a record and earned fifty cents as a prize, and she's been singing ever since; the artist has developed, but the woman hasn't. She has driven herself to the point of having no identity except as a performer. She's in and out of hospitals, and her manager husband (Allen Garfield) treats her as a child, yet she's a true folk artist; the Nashville audience knows she's the real thing and responds to the purity of her gift. She expresses the loneliness that is the central emotion in country music. But she isn't *using* the emotion, as the other singers do: it pours right out of her—softly. Arriving at the airport, coming home after a stretch of treatment—for burns, we're told—she's radiant, yet so breakable that it's hard to believe she has the strength to perform. A few days later, when she stands on the stage of the Opry Belle and sings "Dues," with the words "It hurts so bad, it gets me down," her fragility is so touching and her swaying movements are so seductively musical that, perhaps for the first time on the screen, one gets the sense of an artist's being consumed by her gift. This is Ronee Blakley's first movie, and she puts most movie hysteria to shame; she achieves her effects so simply that I wasn't surprised when someone near me started to cry during one of her songs. She has a long sequence on the stage of the Opry Belle when Barbara Jean's mind starts to wander and, instead of singing, she tells out-of-place, goofy stories about her childhood. They're the same sort of stories that have gone into her songs, but without the transformation they're just tatters that she clings to—and they're all she's got. Ronee Blakley, who wrote this scene, as well as the music and lyrics of all her songs, is a peachy, dimpled brunette, in the manner of the movie stars of an earlier era; as Barbara Jean, she's like the prettiest girl in high school, the one the people in town say is just perfect-looking, like Linda Darnell. But she's more delicate; she's willowy and regal, tipping to one side like the Japanese ladies carved in ivory. At one point, she sings with the mike in one hand, the other hand tracing the movements of the music in the air, and it's an absolutely ecstatic moment.

Nashville isn't in its final shape yet, and all I can hope to do is suggest something of its achievement. Altman could make a film of this magnitude for under two million dollars* because he works with actors whose range he understands. He sets them free to give their own pulse to their characters; inspired themselves, they inspire him. And so we get motifs that bounce off each other—tough-broad Barbara Baxley's drunken fix on

---

*The final cost, after the prints were made, was about two million, two hundred thousand.

the murdered Kennedys, Shelley Duvall's total absorption in celebrity, a high-school band of majorettes twirling rifles, and Robert Doqui's anger at a black singer for not being black enough. All the allusions tell the story of the great American popularity contest. Godard was trying to achieve a synthesis of documentary and fiction and personal essay in the early sixties, but Godard's Calvinist temperament was too cerebral. Altman, from a Catholic background, has what Joyce had: a love of the supreme juices of everyday life. He can put unhappy characters on the screen (Keenan Wynn plays a man who loses the wife he's devoted to) and you don't wish you didn't have to watch them; you accept their unhappiness as a piece of the day, as you do in *Ulysses*. You don't recoil from the moody narcissism of Keith Carradine's character: there he is in his bedroom, listening to his own tapes, with one bed partner after another—with Geraldine Chaplin, whom he'll barely remember the next day, and with Lily Tomlin, whom he'll remember forever. You don't recoil, as you do in movies like *Blow-Up* or *Petulia*, because Altman wants you to be part of the life he shows you and to feel the exhilaration of being alive. When you get caught up in his way of seeing, you no longer anticipate what's coming, because Altman doesn't deliver what years of moviegoing have led you to expect. You get something else. Even when you feel in your bones what has to happen—as you do toward the climax of *Nashville*, when the characters assemble for the rally at the Parthenon and Barbara Jean, on the stage, smiles ravishingly at her public—he delivers it in a way you didn't expect. Who watching the pious Haven Hamilton sing the evangelical "Keep A' Goin'," his eyes flashing with a paranoid gleam as he keeps the audience under surveillance, would guess that the song represented his true spirit, and that when injured he would think of the audience before himself? Who would expect that Barbara Harris, playing a runaway wife—a bombed-out groupie hovering around the action—would finally get her chance onstage, and that her sexy, sweetly shell-shocked look would, at last, fit in perfectly? For the viewer, *Nashville* is a constant discovery of overlapping connections. The picture says, This is what America is, and I'm part of it. *Nashville* arrives at a time when America is congratulating itself for having got rid of the bad guys who were pulling the wool over people's eyes. The movie says that it isn't only the politicians who live the big lie—the big lie is something we're all capable of trying for. The candidate, Hal Phillip Walker, never appears on the screen; he doesn't need to—the screen is full of candidates. The name of Walker's party doesn't have to stand for anything: that's why it's the Replacement Party.

Nashville isn't full of resolutions, because Altman doesn't set up conflicts; the conflicts, as in Lily Tomlin's character, are barely visible. Her deepest tensions play out in the quietest scenes in the movie; she's a counterbalance to the people squabbling about whatever comes into their heads. There's no single reason why anybody does anything in this movie, and most of the characters' concerns are mundane. Altman uses a *Grand Hotel* mingling of characters without giving false importance to their unions and collisions, and the rally itself is barely pivotal. A lot happens in the five days, but a lot happens in any five days. There are no real dénouements, but there are no loose ends, either: Altman doesn't need to wrap it all up, because the people here are too busy being alive to be locked in place. Frauds who are halfway honest, they're true to their own characters. Even the stupidest among them, the luscious bimbo Sueleen (Gwen Welles), a tone-deaf waitress in the airport coffee shop, who wiggles and teases as she sings to the customers, and even the most ridiculous—Geraldine Chaplin's Opal—are so completely what they are that they're irresistible. At an outdoor party at Haven Hamilton's log-cabin retreat, the chattering Opal remarks, "Pure, unadulterated Bergman," but then, looking around, she adds, "Of course, the people are all wrong for Bergman, aren't they?" *Nashville* is the funniest epic vision of America ever to reach the screen.

{*The New Yorker*, March 3, 1975}

from
WHEN THE LIGHTS GO DOWN

:: The Man from Dream City

"You can be had," Mae West said to Cary Grant in *She Done Him Wrong*, which opened in January, 1933, and that was what the women stars of most of his greatest hits were saying to him for thirty years, as he backed away—but not too far. One after another, the great ladies courted him—Irene Dunne in *The Awful Truth* and *My Favorite Wife*, Katharine Hepburn in *Bringing Up Baby* and *Holiday*, Jean Arthur and Rita Hayworth in *Only Angels Have Wings*, Ingrid Bergman in *Notorious*, Grace Kelly in *To Catch a Thief*, Eva Marie Saint in *North by Northwest*, Audrey Hepburn in *Charade*. Willing but not forward, Cary Grant must be the most publicly seduced male the world has known, yet he has never become a public joke—not even when Tony Curtis parodied him in *Some Like It Hot*, encouraging Marilyn Monroe to rape. The little bit of shyness and reserve in Grant is pure box-office gold, and being the pursued doesn't make him seem weak or passively soft. It makes him glamorous—and, since he is not as available as other men, far more desirable.

Cary Grant is the male love object. Men want to be as lucky and enviable as he is—they want to be like him. And women imagine landing him. Like Robert Redford, he's sexiest in pictures in which the woman is the aggressor and all the film's erotic energy is concentrated on him, as it was in *Notorious*: Ingrid Bergman practically ravished him while he was trying to conduct a phone conversation. Redford has never been so radiantly glamorous as in *The Way We Were*, when we saw him through Barbra Streisand's infatuated eyes. But in *The Great Gatsby*, when Redford needed to do for Mia Farrow what Streisand had done for him, he couldn't transcend his immaculate self-absorption. If he had looked at her with desire, everything else about the movie might have been forgiven. Cary Grant would

465

not have failed; yearning for an idealized love was not beyond his resources. It may even be part of his essence: in the sleekly confected *The Philadelphia Story*, he brought conviction to the dim role of the blue blood standing by Katharine Hepburn and waiting on the sidelines. He expressed the very sort of desperate constancy that Redford failed to express. Grant's marital farces with Irene Dunne probably wouldn't have been as effective as they were if he hadn't suggested a bedevilled constancy in the midst of the confusion. The heroine who chases him knows that deep down he wants to be caught only by her. He draws women to him by making them feel he needs them, yet the last thing he'd do would be to come right out and say it. In *Only Angels Have Wings*, Jean Arthur half falls apart waiting for him to make a move; in *His Girl Friday*, he's unabashed about everything in the world except why he doesn't want Rosalind Russell to go off with Ralph Bellamy. He isn't weak, yet something in him makes him hold back—and that something (a slight uncertainty? the fear of a commitment? a mixture of ardor and idealism?) makes him more exciting.

The romantic male stars aren't necessarily sexually aggressive. Henry Fonda wasn't; neither was James Stewart, or, later, Marcello Mastroianni. The foursquare Clark Gable, with his bold, open challenge to women, was more the exception than the rule, and Gable wasn't romantic, like Grant. Gable got down to brass tacks; his advances were basic, his unspoken question was "Well, sister, what do you say?" If she said no, she was failing what might almost be nature's test. She'd become overcivilized, afraid of her instincts—afraid of being a woman. There was a violent, primal appeal in Gable's sex scenes: it was all out front—in the way he looked at her, man to woman. Cary Grant doesn't challenge a woman that way. (When he tried, as the frontiersman in *The Howards of Virginia*, he looked thick and stupid.) With Gable, sex is inevitable: What is there but sex? Basically, he thinks women are good for only one thing. Grant is interested in the qualities of a particular woman—her sappy expression, her non sequiturs, the way her voice bobbles. She isn't going to be pushed to the wall as soon as she's alone with him. With Grant, the social, urban man, there are infinite possibilities for mutual entertainment. They might dance the night away or stroll or go to a carnival—and nothing sexual would happen unless she wanted it to. Grant doesn't assert his male supremacy; in the climax of a picture he doesn't triumph by his fists and brawn—or even by outwitting anybody. He isn't a conqueror, like Gable. But he's a winner. The game, however, is an artful dodge. He gets the blithe, funny girl by maneuvering her into going after him. He's a fairy-tale hero, but she has to pass through the trials: She has to trim her cold or pompous adversaries; she has to dispel his fog. In picture after picture, he seems to give up his resistance at the end, as if to say, What's the use of fighting?

Many men must have wanted to be Clark Gable and look straight at a woman with a faint smirk and lifted, questioning eyebrows. What man doesn't—at some level—want to feel supremely confident and earthy and irresistible? But a few steps up the dreamy social ladder there's the more subtle fantasy of worldly grace—of being so gallant and gentlemanly and charming that every woman longs to be your date. And at that deluxe level men want to be Cary Grant. Men as far apart as John F. Kennedy and Lucky Luciano thought that he should star in their life story. Who but Cary Grant could be a fantasy self-image for a President and a gangster chief? Who else could demonstrate that sophistication didn't have to be a sign of weakness—that it could be the polished, fun-loving style of those who were basically tough? Cary Grant has said that even he wanted to be Cary Grant.

And for women, if the roof leaks, or the car stalls, or you don't know how to get the super to keep his paws off you, you may long for a Clark Gable to take charge, but when you think of going out, Cary Grant is your dream date—not sexless but sex with civilized grace, sex with mystery. He's the man of the big city, triumphantly suntanned. Sitting out there in Los Angeles, the expatriate New York writers projected onto him their fantasies of Eastern connoisseurship and suavity. How could the heroine ever consider marrying a rich rube from Oklahoma and leaving Cary Grant and the night spots? Los Angeles itself has never recovered from the inferiority complex that its movies nourished, and every moviegoing kid in America felt that the people in New York were smarter, livelier, and better-looking than anyone in his home town. The audience didn't become hostile; it took the contempt as earned. There were no Cary Grants in the sticks. He and his counterparts were to be found only in the imaginary cities of the movies. When you look at him, you take for granted expensive tailors, international travel, and the best that life has to offer. Women see a man they could have fun with. Clark Gable is an intensely realistic sexual presence; you don't fool around with Gable. But with Grant there are no pressures, no demands; he's the sky that women aspire to. When he and a woman are together, they can laugh at each other and at themselves. He's a slapstick Prince Charming.

Mae West's raucous invitation to him—"Why don't you come up sometime and see me?"—was echoed thirty years later by Audrey Hepburn in *Charade*: "Won't you come in for a minute? I don't bite, you know, unless it's called for." And then, purringly, "Do you know what's wrong with you? Nothing." That might be a summary of Cary Grant, the finest romantic comedian of his era: there's nothing the matter with him. Many of the male actors who entered movies when sound came in showed remarkable powers of endurance—James Cagney, Bing Crosby, Charles Boyer, Fred Astaire—but they didn't remain heroes. Spencer Tracy didn't, either; he became paternal and judicious. Henry Fonda and James Stewart turned into folksy elder statesmen, sagacious but desexed. Cary Grant has had the longest romantic reign in the short history of movies. He might be cast as an arrogant rich boy, an unscrupulous cynic, or a selfish diplomat, but there was nothing sullen or self-centered in his acting. Grant never got star-struck on himself; he never seemed to be saying, Look at me. The most obvious characteristic of his acting is the absence of narcissism—the outgoingness to the audience.

Cary Grant was a knockout in his dapper young days as a Paramount leading man to such suffering sinners as Sylvia Sidney, Carole Lombard, Tallulah Bankhead, Marlene Dietrich, Nancy Carroll. He appeared with this batch in 1932; Paramount threw him into seven pictures in his first year. In some two dozen roles in four years, he was a passable imitation of Noël Coward or Jack Buchanan, though not as brittle as Coward or as ingratiatingly silly as Buchanan. He played a celebrated javelin thrower in *This Is the Night*, a rotten rich roué in *Sinners in the Sun*, the husband of a diva in *Enter Madam* and of another diva in *When You're in Love*. He was a flier who went blind in *Wings in the Dark*; he wore a dinky mustache and was captured by the Kurds in *The Last Outpost*; he used a black bullwhip on the villainous Jack La Rue in *The Woman Accused*. But that's all a blur. He didn't have a strong enough personality to impose himself on viewers, and most people don't remember Cary Grant for those roles, or even much for his tall-dark-and-handsome stints with Mae West. He might never have become a star if it had not been for the sudden onset of screwball comedy in 1934—the year when *The Thin Man* and *Twentieth Century* and *It Happened One Night*

changed American movies. His performances in screwball comedies—
particularly *The Awful Truth*, in 1937, his twenty-ninth picture—turned
him into the comedian-hero that people think of as Cary Grant. He was
resplendent before but characterless, even a trace languid—a slightly
wilted sheik. He was Mae West's classiest and best leading man, but he did
more for her in *She Done Him Wrong* and *I'm No Angel* than she did for him.
She brought out his passivity, and a quality of refinement in him which
made her physical aggression seem a playful gambit. (With tough men
opposite her, she was less charming, more crude.) Sizing him up with her
satyr's eyes and deciding he was a prize catch, she raised our estimate
of him. Yet Grant still had that pretty-boy killer look; he was too good-
looking to be on the level. And although he was outrageously attractive
with Mae West, he was vaguely ill at ease; his face muscles betrayed him,
and he looked a little fleshy. He didn't yet know how the camera should
see him; he didn't focus his eyes on her the way he learned to use his eyes
later. No doubt he felt absurd in his soulful, cow-eyed leading-man roles,
and tried to conceal it; when he had nothing to do in a scene, he stood
lunged forward as if hoping to catch a ball. He became Cary Grant when
he learned to project his feelings of absurdity through his characters and
to make a style out of their feeling silly. Once he realized that each movement could be stylized for humor, the eyepopping, the cocked head, the
forward lunge, and the slightly ungainly stride became as certain as the
pen strokes of a master cartoonist. The new element of romantic slapstick in the mid-thirties comedies—the teasing role reversals and shifts of
mood—loosened him up and brought him to life. At last, he could do on
the screen what he had been trained to do, and a rambunctious, springy
side of his nature came out. Less "Continental" and more physical, he
became funny and at the same time sexy. He was no longer effete; the
booming voice had vitality.

It was in 1935, when the director George Cukor cast him as a loud-
mouthed product of the British slums—a con man and strolling player—
in the Katharine Hepburn picture *Sylvia Scarlett*, that Grant's boisterous
energy first broke through. He was so brashly likable that viewers felt
vaguely discomfited at the end when Brian Aherne (who had given an
insufferably egotistic performance) wound up with Hepburn. Grant, on
loan from Paramount to RKO, doesn't play the leading-man role, yet his
con man is so loose and virile that he has more life than anything else in

the picture. Grant seemed to be enjoying himself on the screen in a way he never had before. Cukor said that Grant suddenly "felt the ground under his feet." Instead of hiding in his role, as usual, he expanded and gave his scenes momentum. *Sylvia Scarlett* was a box-office failure, but Grant knew now what he could play, and a year later, free to pick his own projects, he appeared in *Topper* and his fan mail jumped from two hundred letters a week to fourteen hundred. A few months after that, he got into his full stride with *The Awful Truth*.

What makes Grant such an uncannily romantic comedian is that with the heroine he's different from the way he is with everybody else; you sense an affinity between them. In *The Awful Truth*, he's a hearty, sociable businessman when he's with other people, but when he's with Irene Dunne you feel the tenderness that he conceals from others. The conventional bedroom-farce plot (filmed twice before) is about a couple who still love each other but have a tiff and file for divorce; during the period of the interlocutory decree, the husband has visiting rights to see their dog, and this cunning device enables Grant to hang around, romping affectionately with the dog while showing his (unstated) longing for his wife. Grant is a comic master at throwaway lines, and he turns them into a dialogue, as if he were talking to himself. The husband can't quite straighten out his marriage, yet every muttered, throwaway word expresses how badly he wants to. Grant's work with Irene Dunne in *The Awful Truth* is the most gifted stooging imaginable. She was betrayed by the costume designer: she's shrilly dressed. And though she is often funny, she overdoes the coy gurgles, and that bright, toothy smile of hers — she shows both rows of teeth, prettily held together — can make one want to slug her. The ancestor of Julie Andrews, Irene Dunne has a bad habit of condescending to anything oddball her character does — signalling the audience that she's really a lady playacting. But Grant stabilizes her and provides the believability. He's forceful and extroverted, yet he underplays so gently that his restraint enables her to get by with her affectations. Grant uses his intense physical awareness to make the scenes play, and never to make himself look good at the expense of someone else — not even when he could waltz away with the show. He performs the gags with great gusto, but he never lets us forget that the character is behaving like an oaf because he doesn't want to lose his wife, and that he's trying to protect his raw places.

Henry Fonda played roles similar to Grant's, and it isn't hard to imagine

Fonda as the husband in *The Awful Truth* or as the paleontologist hero of *Bringing Up Baby*, but Fonda would have been more of a hayseed, and lighter-weight. And if Grant had played Fonda's role in *The Lady Eve* Grant wouldn't have been the perfect, pratfalling innocent that Fonda was: Fonda, with his saintly bumpkin's apologetic smile and his double-jointed gait, could play bashful stupes more convincingly than any other romantic star. However, it's part of the audience's pleasure in Grant that he isn't a green kid—he's a muscular, full-bodied man making a fool of himself. There were other gifted urbane *farceurs*. The best of them, William Powell, with his skeptical, tolerant equanimity, was supremely likable; he got the most out of each blink and each twitch of his lips, and he had amazing dimples, which he could invoke without even smiling. But Powell and the others didn't have romantic ardor hidden inside their jokes. And although there were other fine romantic actors, such as Charles Boyer, their love scenes often turned mooshy, while Grant's had the redeeming zest of farce.

Perfection in drawing-room comedy was almost certainly Grant's dream of glory (it appears to have remained so), but he had, as a young vaudeville comedian, acquired the skills that were to turn him into an idol for all social classes. Drawing-room-comedy stars—no matter how artful—don't become that kind of idol. When we in the audience began to sense the pleasure he took in low comedy, we accepted him as one of us. Ray Milland, Melvyn Douglas, and Robert Young acted the screwball-comedy heroes proficiently, but the roles didn't release anything in their own natures—didn't liberate and complete them, the way farce completed Grant. Afterward, even when he played straight romantic parts the freedom and strength stayed with him. And never left him: he gave some embarrassed, awful performances when he was miscast, but he was never less than a star. He might still parade in the tuxedos and tails of his dashing-young-idiot days, but he was a buoyant, lusty performer. The assurance he gained in slapstick turned him into the smoothie he had aspired to be. He brought elegance to low comedy, and low comedy gave him the corky common-man touch that made him a great star. Grant was English, so Hollywood thought he sounded educated and was just right for rich play-boys, but he didn't speak in the gentlemanly tones that American movie-goers think of as British; he was a Cockney. In the early sixties, when he was offered the role of Henry Higgins in the big movie version of *My Fair*

Lady, he laughed at the idea. "The way I talk *now*," he said, "is the way Eliza talked at the beginning." Cary Grant's romantic elegance is wrapped around the resilient, tough core of a mutt, and Americans dream of thoroughbreds while identifying with mutts. So do moviegoers the world over. The greatest movie stars have not been highborn; they have been strongwilled (often deprived) kids who came to embody their own dreams, and the public's.

Archibald Alexander Leach, born in Bristol on January 18, 1904, was the only child of Elias James Leach and Elsie Kingdom Leach, their firstborn son having died in infancy. Elias Leach was tall, and in photographs he seems almost reprehensibly handsome, with a cavalier's mustache, soft, flashing dark eyes, and a faintly melancholy look of resignation. He is said to have been convivial and fond of singing—a temperament his wife definitely did not share. There wasn't much they did share. He came, probably, from a Jewish background, but went along with his wife's Anglicanism. He couldn't live up to her middle-class expectations, however. Elias Leach pressed men's suits in a garment factory, and although he worked hard in the first years of the marriage, he never rose far or made much of a living. Mrs. Leach pampered their protesting child, keeping him in baby dresses, and then in short pants and long curls. A domineering woman with an early history of mental instability, she was married to a pants-presser but she wanted her son to be a cultured, piano-playing little gentleman. The parents were miserable together, and the boy was caught in the middle. When Archie was nine, he returned home from school one day to find that his mother was missing; he was led to think she had gone to a local seaside resort, and it was a long time before he learned that she had broken down and been taken to an institution. In a series of autobiographical articles published in the *Ladies' Home Journal* in 1963, he wrote, "I was not to see my mother again for more than twenty years, by which time my name was changed and I was a full-grown man living in America, thousands of miles away in California. I was known to most people of the world by sight and by name, yet not to my mother."

After Mrs. Leach's removal, Leach and his son took up quarters in the same building as Leach's mother, but the boy was left pretty much on his own, fixing meals for himself most of the week, and trying to live up to his absent mother's hopes for him. He went to Boy Scout meetings, studied hard, and won a school scholarship; he planned to try for a further scholarship, which would take him to college, but found out that even with a scholarship college would be too expensive. From early childhood, he had been going to the children's Saturday movie matinées, and he later said that the sessions with Chaplin, Ford Sterling and the Keystone Cops, Fatty Arbuckle, Mack Swain, John Bunny and Flora Finch, and Broncho Billy Anderson were the high point of his week. When his mother was still at home, he had a party (the only children's party he remembers attending) that featured a candle-powered magic lantern with comic slides, to which he added his own joking commentary. His first contact with music hall came quite by chance. At school, he liked chemistry, and he sometimes hung around the lab on rainy days; the assistant science teacher was an electrician, who had installed the lighting system at the Bristol Hippodrome, and one Saturday matinée he took Archie, just turned thirteen, backstage.

It was probably the only free atmosphere the boy had ever experienced. He wrote later that backstage, in a "dazzling land of smiling, jostling people," he *knew*. "What other life could there *be* but that of an actor? . . . They were classless, cheerful, and carefree." He was lonely enough and had enough hustle to start going to the Hippodrome, and another theatre, the Empire, in the early evenings, making himself useful; he helped with the lights, ran errands, and began to pick up the show-business vernacular. When he learned that Bob Pender, a former Drury Lane clown, had a troupe of young knockabout comedians that suffered attrition each time a boy came of military age, he wrote, in the guise of his father, asking that Archibald be taken for training. Pender replied offering an interview and enclosing the railway fare to Norwich, and Archie ran away from home to become an apprentice. He was so tall that Pender accepted him, not realizing that he wasn't yet fourteen—the legal age for leaving school. It took a few days before Leach noticed that his son was gone. Earlier that year, Archie had taken a spill on an icy playground and broken an upper front tooth. Rather than tell his father, he had gone to a dental school and had the remainder of the tooth pulled out. His other teeth had closed together over the gap (giving him his characteristic upper-lip-pulled-down, tough-urchin grin) without his father's ever noticing. But, whatever Leach's failings, he appears to have meant well, and when it registered with him that the boy had run off, he tracked him down and brought him back. He might as well have saved himself the effort. Having given up his dream of college, Archie no longer cared about school, and he concentrated on acrobatics, so he'd be in shape to rejoin Pender as soon as he could. It was soon. Just after he turned fourteen, he and another boy attempted to explore the girls' lavatories, and he was expelled from school. Three days later, with his father's consent, he was a member of Pender's troupe. Only three months passed before he returned to Bristol in triumph—on the stage at the Empire, his old schoolmates in the audience.

Archie Leach found his vocation early and stuck to it. He studied dancing, tumbling, stilt-walking, and pantomime, and performed constantly in provincial towns and cities and in the London vaudeville houses. In the Christmas season, the troupe appeared in the traditional entertainments for children—slapstick musical-comedy versions of such stories as "Cinderella" and "Puss in Boots." Living dormitory-style, exercising and rehearsing, Archie had left his parents' class-ridden world behind. Once he'd joined up with Pender, he never lived with his father again, and he lost track of him over the years. The music-hall theatre became his world; he has said that at each theatre, when he wasn't onstage, he was watching and studying the other acts from the wings. In July, 1920, when Pender selected a group of eight boys for an engagement in New York City, the sixteen-year-old Archie was among them. They sailed on the S.S. Olympic, which was also carrying the celebrated honeymooners Douglas Fairbanks, Sr., and Mary Pickford. More than forty years later, Cary Grant described his reaction to Fairbanks: "Once even I found myself being photographed with Mr. Fairbanks during a game of shuffleboard. As I stood beside him, I tried with shy, inadequate words to tell him of my adulation. He was a splendidly trained athlete and acrobat, affable and warmed by success and well-being. A gentleman in the true sense of the word. . . . It suddenly dawns on me as this is being written that I've doggedly striven to keep tanned ever since, only because of a desire to emulate his healthful appearance." He and Fairbanks had much in common: shattered, messy childhoods, and fathers who drifted away and turned to drink. It appears that they were both part Jewish but were raised as Christians; and they both used acrobatics in their careers—though Fairbanks, a narrowly limited actor but a fine acrobat, was a passionate devotee, while Grant used acrobatics only as a means of getting into theatrical life. And, though they

represented different eras, they were loved by the public in similar ways—
for their strapping health and high spirits, for being *on* and giving out
whenever they were in front of an audience, for grinning with pleasure at
their own good luck. Grant's later marriage to Barbara Hutton—Babs, the
golden girl, "the richest girl in the world"—had a fairy-tale resemblance
to the Fairbanks-Pickford nuptials.

In New York City, the Bob Pender boys were a great success at the Hippodrome, which was considered the world's largest theatre. After the
engagement was over, they got booked in the major Eastern cities and
wound up back in New York at the top—the Palace. When the American
tour ended, in 1922, and it was time to go home, Archie Leach and several
of the other boys decided to stay. He had four solid years of performing
behind him, but he had never actually been in a play, and though he'd been
singing on the stage, he'd never spoken dialogue. The Pender troupe had
been big time, but on his own he wasn't even small time—he had no act.
In the first summer of job-hunting in New York, his savings went and he
ate into the return fare Pender had given him for an emergency retreat.
He must, however, have been an incredible charmer (it isn't hard to imagine), because, although he was only eighteen, he was invited to fill in at
dinner parties, where he sat among the wealthy and famous—on one occasion, he was delegated to be the escort of the great soprano Lucrezia Bori.
By day, after he finally landed work, he was a stilt-walker on the boardwalk
at Coney Island, advertising Steeplechase Park. (It was many years before
his status in life was commensurate with the regard people had for him.)
In the fall, he shared quarters with a young Australian, who later became
known as the costume designer Orry-Kelly; in those days, Kelly made and
tried to sell hand-painted neckties, and Archie Leach peddled them along
Sixth Avenue and in Greenwich Village. Around the same time, Leach and
other ex-members of the Pender troupe got together in the new Hippodrome show, and joined up with some Americans and organized a vaudeville act. After trying it out in small towns in the East, they played the
lesser vaudeville circuits through Canada and back across the country
from California to New York. In 1924, having saved enough money to go
their separate ways, the boys disbanded, some of them returning to
England, Archie Leach to job-hunting in New York again.

He worked in juggling acts, and with unicycle riders, and with dancers;
he was the audience plant with a mind-reading act. As a straight man for

comics, he got one-night stands at churches and lodges, and brief engagements in the stage shows that movie theatres used to put on before the film. As his timing improved and he became more experienced, he got more bookings; he says that eventually he played "practically every small town in America." Then, when he was working in New York, a friend who was a musical-comedy juvenile suggested that instead of going on with his vaudeville career he should try to get into Broadway musical comedy, and introduced him to Reggie Hammerstein, who took him to his uncle, the producer Arthur Hammerstein. At the end of 1927, Archie Leach appeared in the role of an Australian—the second male lead—in the Otto Harbach–Oscar Hammerstein II show *Golden Dawn*, which opened the new Hammerstein's Theatre and ran there until the late spring. He'd got onto Broadway, all right—and Broadway was then in its frivolous heyday—but he hadn't got into musical comedy. It was operetta he was caught in, and, having signed a contract with the Hammersteins, that's where he stayed. Marilyn Miller wanted him as a replacement for Jack Donahue, her leading man in the Ziegfeld hit *Rosalie*, but Arthur Hammerstein and Ziegfeld were enemies, and instead (despite his pleas) his contract was turned over to the Shuberts—for three full years of operetta.

Archie Leach's first Shubert show was *Boom Boom*, a 1929 hit, starring Jeanette MacDonald. (*The New Yorker*'s reviewer, Charles Brackett, wrote that "*Boom Boom* can teach one more about despair than the most expert philosopher.") During its run, he and Jeanette MacDonald were both tested at Paramount's Astoria studio. She was immediately signed up to be the bubbly Maurice Chevalier's petulant, coy co-star in Ernst Lubitsch's *The Love Parade*; he was rejected, because he had a thick neck and bowlegs. Had he been signed as a singing star, he might have been stuck in a Mountie's hat, like Nelson Eddy. He did become a singing star on the stage. He played a leading role in a lavish and, apparently, admirable version of *Die Fledermaus* called *A Wonderful Night*, but it opened on October 31, 1929, two days after the stock-market crash, and it crashed too; for months it was performed to near-empty houses. In the summer of 1931, the Shuberts sent him to St. Louis for the open-air Municipal Opera season, where he was a great success in such shows as *Irene*, *Rio Rita*, *Countess Maritza*, *The Three Musketeers*, and the Broadway casualty *A Wonderful Night*. After that, he got a temporary release from the Shuberts and appeared on Broadway in the role of Cary Lockwood, supporting Fay Wray (who was already a popular movie actress) in *Nikki*, a musical play by her husband, John Monk Saunders, which flopped.

In 1931, Leach also appeared in *Singapore Sue*, a ten-minute movie short, starring Anna Chang, that Casey Robinson made for Paramount in Astoria; Leach, Millard Mitchell, and two other actors played American sailors in an Oriental café. Leach is striking; he grabs the screen—but not pleasantly, and he does have a huge neck. He's rather gross in general—heavy-featured, and with a wide, false smile. His curly-lipped sailor is excessively handsome—overripe, like the voluptuous young Victor Mature. Some of the early-thirties Hollywood publicity photographs of Grant are like that, too; the images have the pop overeagerness one often sees in graduation and wedding poses in photographers' shopwindows. Self-consciousness and bad makeup must have overcome him on that first bout with the movie camera, because photographs of him in his stage performances show a far more refined handsomeness, and the Leach of *Singapore Sue* doesn't fit the image of him in accounts by his contemporaries.

Although Leach didn't appear in the smart shows, he was something of a figure in the New York smart set, and he was known to the Algonquin group in that period when the theatrical and literary worlds were one. Some people considered him an intellectual and a powerhouse talent of the future. Moss Hart later described him as disconsolate in those years; Hart and Leach were among a group of dreamers talking of changing the theatre (the circle also included Edward Chodorov and Preston Sturges) who met daily in the Rudley's Restaurant at Forty-first Street and Broadway. It was a hangout where one got leads about possible jobs, and many performers frequented the place—Jeanette MacDonald, George Murphy, Humphrey Bogart. But Archie Leach was the only actor who was a regular at the Rudley rebels' table. The Anzac role he'd played in *Golden Dawn* must have clung to him, or perhaps, since he never talked much about his background, some of the others mistook his Cockney for an Australian accent, because they called him Kangaroo, and sometimes Boomerang. "He was never a very open fellow," Chodorov says, "but he was earnest and we liked him." "Intellectual" was probably the wrong word for Leach. They talked; he listened. He doesn't appear to have been much of a reader (except later on, during his marriage to Betsy Drake, when he became immersed in the literature of hypnotism and the occult), but there's no indication that anyone ever doubted his native intelligence. It's a wide-awake intelligence, though this may not be apparent from his public remarks of the sixties, which had a wholesome Rotarian tone he adopted during LSD treatments with a medical guru. In his youth, Leach liked to hang around people who were gifted and highly educated; always looking for ways to improve himself, he probably hoped that their knowledge would rub off on him. But there must have been more to it than that; he must have looked up to the brilliant young Rudley's group because the theatre he worked in didn't fully satisfy his mind. Uneducated outside the theatre, he was eager for spiritual leadership—for wisdom. In Hollywood, he was to sit at the feet of Clifford Odets, the leading wisdom merchant of the theatrical left (the sagacity was what marred Odets' plays). And during his many years of LSD sessions he was euphoric about how the drug had enabled him to relax his conscious controls and reach his subconscious, thus making him a better man—less selfish, fit at last for marriage, and so on. Obviously, he felt that he'd found a scientific route to wisdom.

When *Nikki* closed, on October 31, 1931, Leach decided to take a "vacation," and set out with a composer friend to drive to Los Angeles. He knew what he was after; many of the people he'd been working with were already in the movies. He had the situation cooled: he'd been earning from three hundred dollars to four hundred and fifty dollars a week for several years, and the Shuberts were eager to employ him if he returned. He had barely arrived in Hollywood when he was taken to a small dinner party at the home of B. P. Schulberg, the head of Paramount, who invited him to make a test (*Singapore Sue* had not yet been released), and after seeing it Schulberg offered him a contract. The studio executives wanted his name changed, and his friends Fay Wray and John Monk Saunders suggested that he use "Cary Lockwood." He proposed it when he went back to discuss the contract, but he was told that "Lockwood" was a little long. Someone went down a list of names and stopped at "Grant." He nodded, they nodded, and the contract went into effect on December 7th. He wasn't ever "discovered." Movies were simply the next step.

If Archie Leach's upward progress seems a familiar saga, it is familiar in the rags-to-riches mode of a tycoon or a statesman. What is missing from his steady climb to fame is tension. He became a performer in an era in which learning to entertain the public was a trade; he worked at his trade, progressed, and rose to the top. He has probably never had the sort of doubts about acting which have plagued so many later performers, and he didn't agonize over choices, as actors of his stature do now. A young actor now generally feels that he is an artist only when he uses his technique for personal expression and for something he believes in. And so he has a problem that Archie Leach never faced: When actors became artists in the modern sense, they also became sellouts. They began to feel emasculated when they played formula roles that depended on technique only, and they had to fight themselves to retain their belief in the audience, which often preferred what they did when they sold out. They were up against all the temptations, corruptions, and conflicts that writers and composers and painters had long been wrestling with. Commerce is a bind for actors now in a way it never was for Archie Leach; art for him was always a trade.

He was unusually long-sighted about his career, and prodigiously disciplined, and so he got into a position in which he didn't have to take any guff from anybody. The Hammersteins had sold him to the Shuberts when he wanted to go to Ziegfeld; and to get movie roles he had to commit himself to a five-year contract with Paramount. But that was the last time he let others have the power to tell him what to do. He was twenty-seven when he signed the contract—at a starting salary of four hundred and fifty dollars a week. Paramount didn't know what it had. It used him as a second-string Gary Cooper, putting him in the pictures Cooper was too busy for—or, even worse, in imitations of roles that Cooper had just scored in. In between, Paramount lent him out to other studios and collected the fees. He was no more than a pawn in these deals. M-G-M requested him for one of the top roles in *Mutiny on the Bounty*, a role he desperately wanted, but Paramount refused, and Franchot Tone won the part. A little later, Paramount lent him to M-G-M to support Jean Harlow in the piddling *Suzy*.

When that contract ended, in February, 1937, Cary Grant, just turned thirty-three, was raring to go. He never signed another exclusive contract with a studio; he selected his scripts and his directors, and this is probably what saved him from turning into a depressingly sentimental figure, like the later, tired Gary Cooper, or a drudge, like the big M-G-M stars. It was in his first year on his own, free of studio orders, that he became a true star. In comedy, Cary Grant just might be the greatest straight man in the business, and his specialty is to apply his aplomb as a straight man to romance.

The "lunatic" thirties comedies that made him a star are still enjoyed, but their rationale has dropped from sight. In essence, they turned love and marriage into vaudeville acts and changed the movie heroine from sweet clinging vine into vaudeville partner. Starting in 1934, when things were still bad but Roosevelt and the New Deal had created an upswing spirit, the happy screwball comedies were entertainment for a country that had weathered the worst of the Depression and was beginning to feel hopeful. Yet people had been shaken up. The new comedies suggested an element of lunacy and confusion in the world; the heroes and heroines rolled with the punches and laughed at disasters. Love became slightly surreal; it became stylized—lovers talked back to each other, and fast. Comedy became the new romance, and trading wisecracks was the new courtship rite. The cheerful, wacked-out heroes and heroines had abandoned sanity; they were a little crazy, and that's what they liked in each other. They were like the wisecracking soldiers in service comedies: if you were swapping quips, you were alive—you hadn't gone under. The jokes were a national form of gallantry—humor for survival. Actual lunatics in these movies became enjoyable eccentrics, endearing nuts who often made better sense than anybody else (or at least as much sense), while the butts of screwball humor were the prigs and phonies, the conventional go-getters, the stick-in-the-mud conformists. Ralph Bellamy, the classic loser and opposite number to Cary Grant in *The Awful Truth* and again in *His Girl Friday*, still thought in the strict, stuffed-shirt terms of the Babbitty past. The word "square" wasn't yet in slang use, but that's the part Bellamy played—the man who didn't get the joke. Obliging and available, always around when you didn't want him (there was really no time when you did), he was the man to be jilted.

The comedies celebrated a change in values. In the movies of the twenties and the early thirties, girls who chased after riches and luxury learned the error of their ways, but after 1934 sin wasn't the big movie theme it had been. Adultery was no longer tragic; the unashamed, wisecracking gold diggers saw to that. Glenda Farrell, one of the toughest and most honestly predatory of the millionare-hunters, put it this way in *Gold Diggers of 1937*: "It's so hard to be good under the capitalistic system." Impudence became a virtue. Earlier, the sweet, archly virginal heroine had often had a breezy, good-hearted confidante; now the roles were reversed, and the lively, resilient heroine might have an innocent kid sister or a naïve little friend from her home town who needed looking after. What man in the Depression years would welcome a darling, dependent girl? Maybe the hero's shy buddy, but not the hero. He looked for the girl with verve; often she was so high and buoyant she could bounce right over trouble without noticing it. It was Carole Lombard's good-hearted giddiness that made her lovable, Jean Arthur's flightiness, Myrna Loy's blithe imperviousness — and in *Bringing Up Baby* Katharine Hepburn was so light-headed, so out of it, that she was unbeatable. The mistreated, masochistic women who had been moping through the confessional movies, pining for the men who had ruined them and looking tenderly at their fatherless offspring, either faded (like Ann Harding, Ruth Chatterton, and Helen Hayes) or changed their styles (like Constance Bennett in *Topper*, Lombard in *Twentieth Century*, and, of course, Claudette Colbert in *It Happened One Night* and Irene Dunne in *Theodora Goes Wild* and *The Awful Truth*). The stars came down to earth in the middle and late thirties — and became even bigger stars. Marlene Dietrich, who had turned into a lolling mannequin, reëmerged as the battling floozy of *Destry Rides Again*. Just as in the late sixties some of the performers loosened up and became hip, thirties performers such as Joel McCrea and Fredric March became lighter-toned, gabby, and flip. An actor who changes from serious to comic roles doesn't have problems with the audience (the audience loves seeing actors shed their dignity, which has generally become a threadbare pose long before it's shed); it's the change from comic to serious that may confound the audience's expectations.

The speed and stylization of screwball humor were like a stunt, and some of the biggest directors of the thirties had come out of two-reel comedy and had the right training. Leo McCarey, who directed *The Awful Truth*, had directed the Marx Brothers in *Duck Soup* and, before that, Laurel & Hardy comedies for Hal Roach. George Stevens, who directed Grant in *Gunga Din*, was also a Hal Roach alumnus — cameraman on Laurel & Hardy and Harry Langdon shorts, and then a Roach director. *Topper*, with its sunny hocus-pocus and Grant as a debonair ghost, was actually a Hal Roach production; it was considered Roach's most ambitious project. Movies in the thirties were still close to their beginnings. Wesley Ruggles, who directed Grant in *I'm No Angel*, had been one of Mack

Sennett's Keystone Cops; Howard Hawks, who directed Grant in several of his best thirties films, had started as a director by writing and directing two comedy shorts. The directors had graduated from slapstick when sound came in and Hollywood took over Broadway's plays, but after a few years all that talk without much action was becoming wearying.

The screwball movies brought back the slapstick tradition of vaudeville and the two-reelers, and blended it into those brittle Broadway comedies. When it was joined to a marital farce or a slightly daring society romance, slapstick no longer seemed like kid stuff: it was no longer innocent and was no longer regarded as "low" comedy. The screwball movies pleased people of all ages. (The faithful adaptations of stage plays had often been a little tepid for children.) And the directors, who had come out of a Hollywood in which improvising and building gags were part of the fun of moviemaking, went back—partly, at least—to that way of working. No longer so script-bound, movies regained some of the creative energy and exuberance—and the joy in horseplay, too—that had been lost in the early years of talkies. The new freedom can be seen even in small ways, in trivia. Grant's screwball comedies are full of cross-references, and gags from one are repeated or continued in another. In *The Awful Truth*, Irene Dunne, trying to do in her (almost) ex-husband—Grant—refers to him as Jerry the Nipper; in *Bringing Up Baby*, Hepburn, pretending to be a gun moll, tells the town constable that Grant is the notorious Jerry the Nipper. And the same dog trots through the pictures, as Mr. Smith in *The Awful Truth*, as George in *Bringing Up Baby* (and as Mr. Atlas in *Topper Takes a Trip* and Asta in the *Thin Man* movies). That dog was a great actor: he appeared to adore each master in turn.

Once Grant's Paramount contract ended, there seemed no stopping him. As long as the screwball-comedy period lasted, he was king. After *The Awful Truth*, in 1937, he did two pictures with Katharine Hepburn in 1938—*Bringing Up Baby* and *Holiday*. It was a true mating—they had the same high-energy level, the same physical absorption in acting. In 1939 he did *Gunga Din* and *Only Angels Have Wings*, and in 1940 *His Girl Friday*, *My Favorite Wife*, and *The Philadelphia Story*.

During those peak years—1937 to 1940—he proved himself in romantic melodrama, high comedy, and low farce. He does uproarious mugging in the knockabout jamboree *Gunga Din*—a moviemakers' prank, like *Beat the Devil*. Ben Hecht and Charles MacArthur stole the adolescent boys' fantasy atmosphere from *Lives of a Bengal Lancer*, then took the plot from their own *The Front Page*, mixed it with a slapstick *The Three Musketeers*, and set it in a Hollywood Kipling India. Douglas Fairbanks, Jr., plays the Hildy Johnson role—he plans to leave the British Army to get married and go into the tea business—and Victor McLaglen, in the Walter Burns role, and Grant, as the Cockney bruiser Archibald Cutter, scheme to get him to reënlist. When the three comrades fight off their enemies, they're like three Fairbankses flying through the air. Grant looks so great in his helmet in the bright sunshine and seems to be having such a marvellous time that he becomes the picture's romantic center, and his affection for the worshipful Gunga Din (Sam Jaffe) becomes the love story. The picture is both a stirring, beautifully photographed satiric colonial-adventure story and a walloping vaudeville show. Grant's grimaces and cries when Annie the elephant tries to follow him and Sam Jaffe onto a rope bridge over a chasm are his broadest clowning. (The scene is right out of Laurel & Hardy.) And he's never been more of a burlesque comic than when he arrives at the gold temple of the religious cult of thugs and whinnies with greedy delight at the very moment he's being shot at. The thug guru is shaven-headed Eduardo Ciannelli (the original Diamond Louis of *The Front Page*), who wears a loincloth and chants "Kill! Kill! Kill for the love of Kali!" Perhaps because the picture winds up with a bit of pop magic—an eye-moistening, Kiplingesque tribute to Gunga Din, shown in Heaven in the British Army uniform he longed to wear—the press treated it rather severely, and George Stevens, the director, was a little apologetic about it. He may have got in over his head. He had replaced Howard Hawks as director, and when he added his Stan Laurel specialties to the heroic flourishes Hawks had prepared, and after the various rewrite men (William Faulkner and Joel Sayre were among them) built on to the gags, the result was a great, bounding piece of camp. Grant has always claimed that he doesn't like to exert himself, and that his ideal role would be a silent man in a wheelchair, but his performance here tells a different story. (All his performances tell a different story.) The following year, when Grant played Walter Burns in *His Girl Friday* (this time an acknowledged remake of *The Front Page*, and, with Charles Lederer's additions, a spastic explosion of dialogue), he raised mugging to a joyful art. Grant obviously loves the comedy of monomaniac egotism: Walter Burns' callousness and unscrupulousness are expressed in some of the best farce lines ever written in this country, and

Grant hits those lines with a smack. He uses the same stiff-neck, cocked-head stance that he did in *Gunga Din*: it's his position for all-out, unsubtle farce. He snorts and whoops. His Walter Burns is a strong-arm performance, defiantly self-centered and funny.

When Grant was reunited with Irene Dunne in *My Favorite Wife*, they had another box-office smash, but his playing wasn't as fresh as in *The Awful Truth*. This marital farce was really moldy (it was based on Tennyson's *Enoch Arden*, filmed at least a dozen times, starting in 1908), and Grant's performance as the rattled husband is a matter of comic bewilderment and skittish double takes. The presence in the cast of his close friend Randolph Scott (they shared a house for several years) as the rival for Irene Dunne's affections may have interfered with his concentration; he doesn't provide an underlayer of conviction. He's expert but lightweight, and the role and the bustling plot don't bring anything new out of him.

The Hollywood comedy era was just about over by then. The screwball comedies, in particular, had become strained and witless; the spoiled, headstrong runaway heiresses and the top-hatted playboy cutups had begun to pall on the public, and third-rate directors who had no feeling for slapstick thought it was enough to have players giggling and falling over the furniture. Right from the start, screwball comedy was infected by the germ of commercial hypocrisy. The fun-loving rich, with their glistening clothes, whitewall tires, mansions in the country, and sleek Art Deco apartments, exalted a carefree contempt for material values. The heroes and heroines rarely had any visible means of support, but they lived high, and in movie after movie their indifference to such mundane matters as food and rent became a self-admiring attitude — the attitude that is still touted in *Travels with My Aunt* and *Mame*. Like Mame, the unconventional heroines of the thirties were beloved by their servants. Irene Dunne in white fox and a trailing evening gown would kick her satin train impatiently to tell us that it was not money but love and laughter that mattered. The costume designers often went in for sprightly effects: Irene Dunne and Katharine Hepburn would be put into pixie hats that clung on the side of the head, dipping over one eye, while on top there were pagodas that shot up six or seven inches to a peak. All too often, the villains were stuffy society people or social climbers (as in *Mame*), and the heroes and heroines just too incorrigibly happy-go-lucky. Love seemed to mean making a fool of yourself. The froth hung heavy on many a screwball comedy, and as the pictures got worse and the Cary Grant parts began to be played by Lee Bowman and David Niven the public got fed up. The movement had already run down before the war started. In the forties, there were still some screwball comedies, but they were antic and shrill, except for a few strays: some of the Tracy-Hepburn pictures, and the comedies in which Preston Sturges reinvented slapstick in a more organic form— creating an image of Americans as a people who never stopped explaining themselves while balling up whatever they were trying to do.

Though he remained a top box-office star, Cary Grant fell on evil days. After 1940, he didn't seem to have any place to go—there were no longer Cary Grant pictures. Instead, he acted in pictures that nobody could have been right for—abominations like the 1942 anti-Nazi romantic comedy *Once Upon a Honeymoon*, in which he was an American newsman in Warsaw trying to rescue the American stripper Ginger Rogers from her Nazi husband (Walter Slezak). From the first frame, it was as clammily contrived as anything that Paramount had shoved him into, and in one pathetically insensitive sequence Grant and Rogers are mistaken for Jews and held in a concentration camp. His performance is frequently atrocious: he twinkles with condescending affection when the nitwit stripper develops a political consciousness and helps a Jewish hotel maid escape from danger. Mostly, he acted in stock situation comedies—comedies with no comic roots, like *The Bachelor and the Bobby-Soxer* (1947), in which Myrna Loy is a judge who works out a deal. Grant, a philandering artist, will go to jail unless he dates her schoolgirl sister (Shirley Temple) until the teen-ager's crush on him wears off. Escorting Shirley Temple—wearing his shirt open and acting like an adolescent—Cary Grant is degradingly unfunny. There's no core of plausibility in his role. Grant doesn't have the eyes of a Don Juan, or the temperament. When Grant is accused of being a skirt-chaser, it seems like some kind of mistake.

In the thirties, Grant would sometimes appear in a role, such as the despondent husband of a mercenary, coldhearted woman (Kay Francis) in the 1939 *In Name Only*, that suggested that he had unexplored dimensions. They remained unexplored. In 1941, when he departed from comedy, it was in just the sort of sincere tearjerker that Hollywood was always proudest of—*Penny Serenade*, with Irene Dunne again. The unrealistic casting of this inert, horribly pristine film is the trick: the appeal to the audience is that these two glamorous stars play an ordinary couple and suffer the calamities that do in fact happen to ordinary people. When tragedy strikes Cary Grant and Irene Dunne, it hurts the audience in a special way—*Penny Serenade* is a sweet-and-sour pacifier. Grant, who got an Academy Award nomination, could hardly have been better. Using his dark eyes and his sensuous, clouded handsomeness as a romantic mask, he gave his role a defensive, not quite forthright quality, and he brought out everything that it was possible to bring out of his warmed-over lines, weighting them perfectly, so that they almost seemed felt.

Nearly all Grant's seventy-two films have a certain amount of class and are well above the Hollywood average, but most of them, when you come right down to it, are not really very good. Grant could glide through a picture in a way that leaves one indifferent, as in the role of a quaint guardian angel named Dudley in the bland, musty Goldwyn production *The Bishop's Wife* (1947), and he could be the standard put-upon male of burbling comedy, as in *Every Girl Should Be Married* (1948) and the pitifully punk *Room for One More* (1952)—the nice-nice pictures he made with Betsy Drake, who in 1949 became his third wife. He could be fairly persuasive in astute, reflective parts, as in the Richard Brooks thriller *Crisis* (1950), in which he plays a brain surgeon forced to operate on a Latin-American dictator (José Ferrer). He's a seasoned performer here, though his energy level isn't as high as in the true Grant roles and he's a little cold, staring absently when he means to indicate serious thought. What's missing is probably that his own sense of humor isn't allowed to come through; generally when he isn't playing a man who laughs easily he isn't all there.

He was able to keep his independence because he had a good head for business. Within a short time of leaving Paramount, he could command a hundred and fifty thousand dollars a picture, and that was only the beginning. Later, he formed partnerships and produced his pictures through his own corporations—Grandon, Granart, Granley, and Granox. He didn't do what stars like Kirk Douglas did when they gained control over their productions: he didn't appear in Westerns, for the virtually guaranteed market. He was too self-aware for that; he was a lonely holdout in the period when even Frank Sinatra turned cowpoke. From the thirties on, Grant looked for comedies that would be mass-oriented versions of the Noël Coward and Philip Barry and Frederick Lonsdale drawing-room and boudoir farces that Broadway theatregoers admired in the twenties. And so he settled for Sidney Sheldon (*The Bachelor and the Bobby-Soxer*, *Dream Wife*), or Stanley Shapiro (*Operation Petticoat*, *That Touch of Mink*), for Norman Panama and Melvin Frank (*Mr. Blandings Builds His Dream House*), or for Melville Shavelson and Jack Rose (*Room for One More*, *Houseboat*). He sought the best material and got the second-rate and synthetic, because good writers wouldn't (and couldn't) write that way anymore. His taste didn't change, but he didn't do the real thing—not even the real Lonsdale. His friends say he believes that the world doesn't understand fine language. With *People Will Talk* and *The Talk of the Town*, he was probably reaching toward Shaw. He got the loquacity without the wit.

Considering that he selected his roles, these choices indicate one of the traps of stardom. When actors are young, they're eager for great roles, but when they become stars they generally become fearful that the public won't accept them in something different. They look for roles that seem a little more worthwhile than the general run. With one exception—*None but the Lonely Heart*—Cary Grant appeared to be content throughout his career to bring savoir-faire to pratfalls, romantic misunderstandings, and narrow escapes. It seems reasonable to assume that he attained something so close to the highest aspirations of his youth that, as far as acting was concerned, he had no other goals—and no conflicts. Moss Hart said that Archie Leach's gloom vanished when he became Cary Grant.

The only trace of gloom in Grant's movies is in *None but the Lonely Heart*, which he made in association with Clifford Odets (as writer and director) in 1944. The film was an ironic interlude in Grant's career, coming, as it did, between the cloying whimsey of *Once Upon a Time*, in which he was a Broadway sharpie exploiting a boy who had a pet dancing caterpillar, and *Night and Day*, the ten-ton Cole Porter musical bio, in which he skittered about as a youthful Yalie before facing life with stoic courage and inscrutable psychic hangups. In *None but the Lonely Heart*, set in the East End of London, he plays Ernie Mott, a young Cockney—a restless drifter who lacks the will to leave the ghetto for good. Ernie grew up in oppressive poverty, but he wants to make life better for his mother, who runs a grubby antiques and secondhand-furniture shop. Made at Grant's instigation (he acquired the rights to the book), the film was a gesture toward the ideas he shared with the other dissidents at Rudley's, and, even more, a gesture toward his own roots—toward the grimness of his life before he apprenticed himself to the theatre. His mother was released from confinement in 1933 (that same year, his father died of "extreme toxicity"), and he established a surprisingly close relationship with her. Eccentric but hardy and self-sufficient, she had a whole new life after that twenty-year incarceration. She lived into her mid-nineties, and until she was in her late eighties she did all her own shopping and housework, and occupied her days with antiquing—driving fierce bargains when she spotted something she wanted. Grant has described her as "extremely good company." He wrote that "sometimes we laugh together until tears come into our eyes." In the thirties, he went to England several times a year to see her, and he took the socialite beauty Virginia Cherrill (Chaplin's leading lady in *City Lights*) to meet his mother before they were married, in London, in 1934—his first marriage, which was dissolved the following year. The outbreak of the Second World War must have brought his English past even closer to him; he was still a British subject, and in 1939 he became involved in activities to aid the British. Later, when the United States was in the war, he went on trips to entertain the troops and on bond-selling tours. (In one routine, he played straight man to Bert Lahr.) In June, 1942, less than two weeks before his marriage to Barbara Hutton, he legally changed his name and became an American citizen.

Grant's old name had long been a joke—to the public and to him. He had named his pet Sealyham Archibald, and when the dog ran away from his Los Angeles home (it is said that the dog ran out the door while Grant was carrying Virginia Cherrill over the threshold), he took large ads in the papers giving the dog's name. In *Gunga Din*, when Grant, as the soldier Cutter, receives an invitation to a regimental ball, he reads the salutation aloud—"Arch-i-bald Cutter"—chewing the syllables and savoring their preposterousness. As the editor in *His Girl Friday*, when Grant is threatened with prison by the mayor and the sheriff, he yammers out, "The last man to say that to me was Archie Leach, just a week before he cut his throat."

Yet when he played Ernie Mott in *None but the Lonely Heart* he became Archie Leach again; even the names are similar. *None but the Lonely Heart* was the first movie Clifford Odets had ever directed, and although the original material was not his but a best-selling novel by Richard Llewellyn, Odets gave it the rich melancholy of his best plays. Too much of it, however: the dirgelike, mournful, fogged-up atmosphere seemed fake and stagy. Odets worked up each scene (almost as one develops scenes in the theatre) and didn't get them to flow thematically, but he went all out. He brought off some hard-earned effects with an élan that recalled Orson Welles' first films, and there were unexpected crosscurrents. (Ernie's girl, played by June Duprez, was plaintive and distressed, and turned out not to be Ernie's girl at all.) It was an extraordinary début film, and it is an indication of the movie industry's attitude toward talent that Odets got only one other chance to direct—fifteen years later (*The Story on Page One*, in 1959). The complicated texture of *None but the Lonely Heart* made a pervasive, long-lasting impression. What can one remember of such Grant films as *Room for One More* or *Dream Wife* or *Kiss Them for Me* or *Houseboat*? But from *None but the Lonely Heart* one retains June Duprez's puzzlingly perverse face and voice; a scene of Grant and a buddy (Barry Fitzgerald) drunk in a tunnel, letting out their voices and teasing their echoes; and—especially—Grant and Ethel Barrymore together. She played his mother, and her great, heavy eyes matched up with his. In her screen roles, this statuesque, handsome woman usually substituted presence and charm and hokum for performance; she wasn't tedious, like her brother Lionel, but she was a hollow technician. Not this time, though. In a few scenes, she and Grant touched off emotions in each other which neither of them ever showed on the screen again. When Ernie, who has become a petty racketeer, is told that his mother has been arrested for trafficking in stolen goods, he has an instant's disbelief: "They got her inside, you mean—pinched?" Grant says that line with more fervor than any other line he ever delivered. And there are viewers who still—after three decades—recall the timbre of Ethel Barrymore's voice in the prison hospital when she cries, "Disgraced you, Son."

Grant is not as vivid in the memory as Ethel Barrymore is. Of the profusion of themes in the film, the deeply troubled bond of love between the mother and the son must have been a strong factor in his original decision to buy the book. Yet he didn't fully express what had attracted him to the material. His performance was finer than one might have expected, considering that in all his years on the stage he'd never actually done a play without music, and that he couldn't use the confident technique that made him such a dynamo in screen comedy, or the straightforward, subdued acting he depended on in the war film *Destination Tokyo*. Grant was always desperately uncomfortable when he played anyone who wasn't close to his own age, and though he may have felt like the Ernie of the novel (a dreamy nineteen-year-old, an unformed artist-intellectual), as an actor he was too set in his ways. The slight stylization of his comic technique—the deadpan primed to react, the fencer's awareness of the camera, all the self-protective skills he'd acquired—worked against him when he needed to be expressive. Cary Grant acts from the outside; he's the wrong kind of actor to play a disharmonious character, a precursor of the fifties rebel-hero. Grant isn't totally on the surface: there's a mystery in him—he has an almost stricken look, a memory of suffering—but he's not the modern kind of actor who taps his unconscious in his acting. Part of his charm is that his angers are all externally provoked; there are no internal pressures in him that need worry us, no rage or rebelliousness to churn us up. If he reacts with exasperation or a glowering look, we know everything there is to know about his reaction. When we watch Brando, the dramatic stage is *in* him, and the external aggressions against him are the occasions for us to see the conflicts within; the traditional actor's distance and his perfect clarity are gone. Life seemed simpler with Cary Grant's pre-Freudian, pre-psychological acting-as-entertaining. But he couldn't split Ernie Mott apart effectively, and he couldn't hold him together, either. And—it was nobody's fault—one reason Ernie wasn't as vivid a character as he needed to be was that it was Cary Grant trying to be grubby Ernie Mott. A movie star like Cary Grant carries his movie past with him. He becomes the sum of his most successful roles, and he has only to appear for our good will to be extended to him. We smile when we see him, we laugh before he does anything; it makes us happy just to look at him. And so in *None but the Lonely Heart*, in the role that was closest to Grant's own buried feelings—the only character he ever played that he is known to have consciously identified with—he seemed somewhat miscast.

It's impossible to estimate how much this failure meant to him, but more than a year passed before he plunged into the inanities of *Night and Day*—the only year since he had entered movies in which he made no pictures, and a bad year in other ways, too, since his marriage to Barbara Hutton broke up. However, Cary Grant appears to be a profoundly practical man; after the disappointing box-office returns from *None but the Lonely Heart* (he did get an Academy Award nomination for it, but the award was given to Bing Crosby for *Going My Way*), he never tried anything except Cary Grant roles. As far as one can judge, he never looked back.

He remained a lifelong friend of Clifford Odets; he was proud to be accepted by Odets, and Odets was proud that the handsome, tanned idol was there at his feet. But Odets' passion no longer fired Cary Grant to make business decisions. When Odets was trying to set up picture deals and needed him as a star, he didn't return the calls. This didn't spoil their friendship—they had both been living in Los Angeles a long time.

No doubt Grant was big enough at the box office to have kept going indefinitely, surviving fables about caterpillars, and even such mournful mistakes as hauling a cannon through the Napoleonic period of *The Pride and the Passion*. But if Alfred Hitchcock, who had worked with him earlier on *Suspicion*, hadn't rescued him with *Notorious*, in 1946, and again, in 1955, with *To Catch a Thief* (a flimsy script but with a show-off role for him) and in 1959 with *North by Northwest*, and if Grant hadn't appeared in the Stanley Donen film *Charade* in 1963, his development as an actor would have essentially been over in 1940, when he was only thirty-six. In all four of those romantic suspense comedies, Grant played the glamorous, worldly figure that "Cary Grant" had come to mean: he was cast as Cary Grant, and he gave a performance as Cary Grant. It was his one creation, and it had become the only role for him to play—the only role, finally, he *could* play.

Had he made different choices, had he taken more risks like *None but the Lonely Heart*, he might eventually have won acceptance as an actor with a wide range. He might have become a great actor; he had the intensity, and the command of an audience's attention. But how can one tell? One thinks of Cary Grant in such a set way it's difficult even to speculate about his capacities. Yet, considering his wealth and his unusually independent situation, it's apparent that if he was constricted, it wasn't just Hollywood's doing but his own. Working within the framework of commercial movies, James Mason, who at one time also seemed a highly specialized star, moved on from romantic starring roles to a series of deeper character portraits. However, Mason had to move away from the sexual center of his movies to do it, and it's doubtful if Grant would have sacrificed—or even endangered—the type of stardom he had won. His bargaining power was probably more important to him than his development as an actor; he *was* a tycoon. Whatever his reasons were, they're concealed now by his brisk businessman's manner. He doesn't seem to know or to care whether his pictures were good or bad; he says that if they did well at the box office, that's all that matters to him, and this doesn't appear to be an affectation. He made a gigantic profit on the gagged-up *Operation Petticoat*, which he produced in 1959; his friends say that he makes no distinction between that and *Notorious*.

Cary Grant always looks as if he'd just come from a workout in a miracle gym. And it's easy for audiences to forget about his stinkers (they're not held against him), because he himself isn't very different in them from the way he is when he has a strong director and a script with some drive. It's his sameness that general audiences respond to; they may weary of him, but still he's a guaranteed product. (It's the pictures that aren't.) And if he didn't grow as an actor, he certainly perfected "Cary Grant." One does not necessarily admire an icon, as one admires, say, Laurence Olivier, but it can be a wonderful object of contemplation. (If Olivier had patented the brand of adorable spoiled-boy charm he exhibited on the stage in *No Time for Comedy*, he might have had a career much like Grant's—and, indeed, in *Sleuth* Olivier played the sort of role which would then have been all that could be expected of him.)

As a movie star, Grant is so much a man of the city that he couldn't play a rural hero or a noble, rugged man of action, and so much a modern man that he couldn't appear in a costume or period picture without looking obstreperous—as if he felt he was being made a fool of. In *The Howards of Virginia*, it wasn't just the hot-blooded fighter-lover role that threw him, it was also wearing a Revolutionary uniform and a tricornered hat, with his hair in a chignon; he waddled through the picture like a bowlegged duck. The thought of him in Biblical sackcloth or in a Roman toga or some Egyptian getup is grisly-funny. And he's inconceivable in most of the modern urban films: how could Cary Grant play a silent stud or a two-fisted supercop? Grant never quite created another character—not even in the limited sense that screen stars sometimes do, using their own bodies and personalities as the base for imaginative creations. There are no Fred C. Dobbses or Sam Spades in his career. It's doubtful if he could even play a biographical character without being robbed of his essence. As Cole Porter, he wanders around in *Night and Day* looking politely oblivious; he's afraid to cut loose and be himself, yet he's too constrained to suggest anything resembling Cole Porter, so the hero seems to have a sickly, joyless nature. Composing song after song, his Cole Porter appears to have less music in his soul than any other living creature. Grant relaxes a little just once, while singing "You're the Top" with Ginny Simms.

He sings quite often in movies—as in *The Awful Truth*, when he parodies Ralph Bellamy's version of "Home on the Range," or in *Suzy*, in which he does the number that is included in *That's Entertainment*, and he replaced Bing Crosby as the Mock Turtle in the 1933 *Alice in Wonderland*, and sang "Beautiful Soup"—but he played an actual singing role in only one movie, early in his career: the disarmingly frilly 1934 *Kiss and Make Up*, one of Paramount's many imitations of the Lubitsch musical-comedy style. A sense of fun breaks through when he shows off his vaudeville skills—a confident, full-hearted exhibitionism. He frequently plays the piano in movies—happily and enthusiastically—and he does off the screen, too. For the past decade, since the breakup of his fourth marriage—to Dyan Cannon—following the birth of a daughter (his first child), he's been in retirement from the screen, but he's been active as an executive with Fabergé, whose president, George Barrie, used to play the saxophone for a living (Barrie composed the title song for *A Touch of Class*, produced by Brut, a subsidiary of Fabergé); they sometimes have jam sessions after board meetings, with Grant playing piano or organ. It's a corporate business right out of a thirties Cary Grant movie: in *Kiss and Make Up*, he actually ran a swank beauty salon. Grant belongs to the tradition of the success-worshipping immigrant boy who works his way to the top, but with a difference: the success he believes in is in the international high style of the worldly, fun-loving men he played—he's got Rolls-Royces stashed away in key cities. He has lived up to his screen image, and then some; welcome everywhere, more sought after than the Duke of Windsor was, in his seventies he's glitteringly—almost foolishly—hale.

Grant has had an apparently wide range of roles, but only apparently. Even in the era when he became a star, his sexual attraction worked only with a certain type of co-star—usually playing a high-strung, scatter-brained heroine, dizzy but not dumb. He would have been a disaster opposite Joan Crawford. With her gash smile, thick-syrup voice, and enormous tension, she required a roughneck titan like Gable to smite her; she would have turned Cary Grant into Woody Allen. A typical fan-magazine quote from Joan Crawford in her big-box-office youth was "Whatever we feel toward the man of the moment, it is he who is our very life and soul." It hardly matters whether Crawford herself was the author of those sentiments; that was the kind of woman she represented on the screen. It's easy to visualize Cary Grant's panic at the thought of being somebody's "very life and soul." He wanted to have a good time with a girl. It was always implicit that she had something going on her own; she was a free lance. She wasn't going to weigh him down—not like Crawford, who was all character armor and exorbitant needs. Crawford actually intended to take over the man of the moment's life and soul; that was what love meant in her pictures, and why she was so effective with skinny, refined, rich-hero types, like Robert Montgomery and Franchot Tone, whom she could scoop up. She gave the same intensity to everything she did; she inspired awe. But Grant didn't want to be carried away—nobody scoops up Cary Grant—and he didn't want an electrical powerhouse. (He's unthinkable with Bette Davis.) Once Grant became a star, there was a civilized equality in his sex partnerships, though his co-star had to be not only a pal but an ardent pal. When he appeared with Myrna Loy, they were pleasant together, but they didn't really strike sparks. Loy isn't particularly vulnerable, and she isn't dominant, either; she's so cool and airy she doesn't take the initiative, and since he doesn't either (except perfunctorily), nothing happens. They're too much alike—both lightly self-deprecating, both faintly reserved and aloof.

In dramatic roles, the women stars of the thirties and forties could sometimes triumph over mediocre material. This has been one of the saving aspects of the movie medium: Garbo could project so much more than a role required that we responded to her own emotional nature. Her uniquely spiritual eroticism turned men into willing slaves, and she was often at her best with rather passive men—frequently asexual or unisexual or homosexual (though not meant to be in the course of the films). Garbo's love transcended sex; her sensuality transcended sex. She played opposite Clark Gable once, and the collision, though heated, didn't quite work; his macho directness—and opacity—reduced her from passionate goddess to passionate woman. And Garbo seemed to lose her soul when she played mere women—that's why she was finished when the audience had had enough of goddesses. But for a time in the late twenties and early thirties, when she leaned back on a couch and exposed her throat, the whole audience could dream away—heterosexual men as much as the homosexuals (whom she was, indeed, generally seducing in her movies). Something similar operated, to a lesser extent, with Katharine Hepburn. In the thirties, she was frequently most effective with the kind of juveniles who were called boys: they were male versions of sensitive waifs, all cheekbone. She was effective, but there wasn't much sexual tension in those movies. And, despite the camaraderie and marvellous byplay of her later series with Spencer Tracy, she lost some of her charge when she acted with him. She was humanized but maybe also a little subjugated, and when we saw her through his eyes there seemed to be something the matter with her—she was too high-strung, had too much temperament. Tracy was stodgily heterosexual. She was more exciting with Cary Grant, who had a faint ambiguity and didn't want her to be more like ordinary women: Katharine Hepburn was a one-of-a-kind entertainment, and he could enjoy the show. The element of Broadway conventionality that mars *The Philadelphia Story* is in the way she's set up for a fall—as a snow maiden and a phony. Grant is cast as an élitist variation of the later Spencer Tracy characters.

Cary Grant could bring out the sexuality of his co-stars in comedies. Ingrid Bergman, a powerful presence on the screen, and with a deep, emotional voice (her voice is a big part of her romantic appeal in *Casablanca*), is a trifle heavy-spirited for comedy. She was never again as sexy as in that famous scene in *Notorious* when she just keeps advancing on Grant; you feel that she's so far gone on him that she can't wait any longer—and it's funny. Although Grant is a perfectionist on the set, some of his directors say that he wrecks certain scenes because he won't do fully articulated passages of dialogue. He wants always to be searching for how he feels; he wants to waffle charmingly. This may be a pain to a scenarist or a director, but in his own terms Grant knows what he's doing. He's the greatest sexual stooge the screen has ever known: his side steps and delighted stares turn his co-stars into comic goddesses. Nobody else has ever been able to do that.

When the sexual psychology of a comedy was right for Grant, he could be sensational, but if it was wrong and his energy still came pouring out, he could be terrible. In Frank Capra's *Arsenic and Old Lace* (made in 1941 but not released until 1944, because, by contract, it couldn't open until the Broadway production closed) he's more painful to watch than a normally bad actor—like, say, Robert Cummings—would be, because our affection for Grant enters into our discomfort. As it was originally written, the Mortimer Brewster role—an acerbic theatre critic being pursued by his aggressive, no-nonsense fiancée—wouldn't have been bad for Grant, but the Capra film sweetened the critic and turned the fiancée into a cuddly, innocuous little dear (Priscilla Lane). Capra called Grant Hollywood's greatest *farceur*, but the role was shaped as if for Fred MacMurray, and Grant was pushed into frenzied overreacting—prolonging his stupefied double takes, stretching out his whinny. Sometime after the whopping success of *It Happened One Night*, Frank Capra had lost his instinct for sex scenes, and his comedies became almost obscenely neuter, with clean, friendly old grandpas presiding over blandly retarded families. Capra's hick jollity was not the atmosphere for Cary Grant, and he was turned into a manic enunch in *Arsenic and Old Lace*.

In drag scenes—even in his best movies—Grant also loses his grace. He is never so butch—so beefy and clumsy a he-man—as in his female impersonations or in scenes involving a clothes switch. In *Bringing Up Baby*, Katharine Hepburn takes his suit away, and he has nothing to wear but a flouncy fur-trimmed negligee. When Hepburn's aunt (May Robson) arrives and demands crossly, querulously, "Why are you wearing a robe?" Grant, exasperated, answers "Because I just went gay all of a sudden." It doesn't work: he goes completely out of character. Burt Lancaster was deliriously, unself-consciously funny in a long drag sequence in *The Crimson Pirate* (a parody adventure picture roughly comparable to *Gunga Din*); he turned himself into a scrambled cartoon of a woman, as Harry Ritz had done in *On the Avenue*. That's what Tony Curtis and Jack Lemmon did in *Some Like It Hot*—only they did it by yielding to their feminine disguises and becoming their own versions of gorgeous, desirable girls. Bert Remsen does it that way in *California Split*, anxiously seeing himself as a gracious lady of quality. But Grant doesn't yield to cartooning femininity or to enjoying it; he doesn't play a woman, he threatens to—flirting with the idea and giggling over it. His sequence in a skirt and a horsehair wig in the stupid, humiliating *I Was a Male War Bride* was a fizzle. He made himself brusque and clumsy to call attention to how inappropriate the women's clothes were on him—as if he needed to prove he was a big, burly guy.

The beautifully tailored clothes that seem now to be almost an intrinsic part of the Cary Grant persona came very late in his career. Decked out in the pinstripes, wide lapels, and bulky shoulders of the early forties, Grant, with his thick, shiny black hair, often suggested a race-track tout or a hood. He was a snappy dresser, and when he was playing Ivy League gentlemen, his clothes were often kingpin flashy, in the George Raft manner. Happy and hearty, he looked terrific in those noisy clothes; he wore baggy pants in *Only Angels Have Wings* and was still a sexual magnet. But sometimes his slouch hats and floppy, loose-draped jackets seemed to dominate the actor inside. His strutting appearance was distracting, like a gaudy stage set. As he got older, however, he and his slim-line clothes developed such an ideal one-to-one love affair that people could grin appreciatively in the sheer pleasure of observing the union. In *North by Northwest*, the lean-fitting suit he wore through so many perils seemed the skin of his character; and in *Charade*, when for the sake of a dim joke about drip-dry he got under the shower with his suit on, he lost the skin of his character—even though that character was "Cary Grant."

It's a peerless creation, the "Cary Grant" of the later triumphs—*Notorious, To Catch a Thief, North by Northwest*, and *Charade*. Without a trace of narcissism, he appears as a man women are drawn to—a worldly, sophisticated man who has become more attractive with the years. And Grant really had got better-looking. The sensual lusciousness was burned off: age purified him (as it has purified Paul Newman). His acting was purified, too; it became more economical. When he was young, he had been able to do lovely fluff like *Topper* without being too elfin, or getting smirky, like Ray Milland, or becoming a brittle, too bright gentleman, like Franchot Tone. But he'd done more than his share of arch mugging—lowering his eyebrows and pulling his head back as if something funny were going on in front of him when nothing was. Now the excess energy was pared away; his performances were simple and understated and seamlessly smooth. In *Charade*, he gives an amazingly calm performance; he knows how much his presence does for him and how little he needs to do. His romantic glamour, which had reached a high peak in 1939 in *Only Angels Have Wings*, wasn't lost; his glamour was now a matter of his resonances from the past, and he wore it like a mantle.

Some stars (Kirk Douglas, for one) don't realize that as they get older, if they continue to play the same sort of parts, they no longer need to use big, bold strokes; they risk self-caricature when they show their old flash, and they're a bit of a joke when they try to demonstrate that they're as good as they ever were. But if they pare down their styles and let our memories and imaginations fill in from the past, they can seem masters. Sitting in an airport V.I.P. lounge a few years ago, Anthony Quinn looked up from the TV set on which he was watching *To Catch a Thief* and said, "That's the actor I always wanted to be"—which is fairly funny, not only because Quinn and Grant are such contrasting types but because Quinn has never learned the first thing from Cary Grant. He's never understood that he needs to dry out a little. Some actors are almost insultingly robust. If you should ask Anthony Quinn "Do you know how to dance?" he would cry "Do I know how to dance?" and he'd answer the question with his whole body—and you'd probably wind up sorry that you'd asked. Cary Grant might twirl a couple of fingers, or perhaps he'd execute an intricate, quick step and make us long for more. Unlike the macho actors who as they got older became strident about their virility, puffing their big, flabby chests in an effort to make themselves look even larger, Grant, with his sexual diffidence, quietly became less physical—and more assured. He doesn't wear out his welcome: when he has a good role, we never get enough of him. Not only is his reserve his greatest romantic resource—it is the resource that enables him to age gracefully.

What the directors and writers of those four suspense films understood was that Cary Grant could no longer play an ordinary man—he had to be what he had become to the audience. In box-office terms, he might get by with playing opposite Doris Day in *That Touch of Mink*, but he was interchangeable with Rock Hudson in this sort of picture, and the role was a little demeaning—it didn't take cognizance of his grace or of the authority that enduring stardom confers. The special charm of *Notorious*, of the piffle *To Catch a Thief*, and of *North by Northwest* and *Charade* is that they give him his due. He is, after all, an immortal—an ideal of sophistication forever. He spins high in the sky, like Fred Astaire and Ginger Rogers. He may not be able to do much, but what he can do no one else has ever done so well, and because of his civilized nonaggressiveness and his witty acceptance of his own foolishness we see ourselves idealized in him. He's self-aware in a charming, non-egotistic way that appeals to the very people we'd want to appeal to. Even when he plays Cockneys, he isn't English or foreign to us—or American, either, exactly. Some stars lose their nationality, especially if their voices are distinctive. Ronald Colman, with his familiar cultivated, rhythmic singsong, seemed no more British, really, than the American Douglas Fairbanks, Jr.; they were both "dashing" men of the world. Ingrid Bergman doesn't sound Swedish to us but sounds simply like Ingrid Bergman. Cary Grant became stateless early: he was always Cary

Grant. Making love to him, the heroines of the later movies are all aware that he's a legendary presence, that they're trying to seduce a legend. "How do you shave in there?" Audrey Hepburn asks bemusedly in *Charade*, putting her finger up to the cleft in his chin. Her character in the movie is to be smitten by him and to dote on him. Actually, he had begun to show his age by that time (1963); it was obvious that he was being lighted very carefully and kept in three-quarter shots, and that his face was rounder and a little puffy. And although lampblack may have shielded the neck, one could tell that it was being shielded. But we saw him on Audrey Hepburn's terms: Cary Grant at his most elegant. He didn't need the show-stopping handsomeness of his youth; his style, though it was based on his handsomeness, had transcended it.

Everyone likes the idea of Cary Grant. Everyone thinks of him affectionately, because he embodies what seems a happier time—a time when we had a simpler relationship to a performer. We could admire him for his timing and nonchalance; we didn't expect emotional revelations from Cary Grant. We were used to his keeping his distance—which, if we cared to, we could close in idle fantasy. He appeared before us in his radiantly shallow perfection, and that was all we wanted of him. He was the Dufy of acting—shallow but in a good way, shallow without trying to be deep. We didn't want depth from him; we asked only that he be handsome and silky and make us laugh.

Cary Grant's bravado—his wonderful sense of pleasure in performance, which we respond to and share in—is a pride in craft. His confident timing is linked to a sense of movies as popular entertainment: he wants to please the public. He became a "polished," "finished" performer in a tradition that has long since atrophied. The suave, accomplished actors were usually poor boys who went into a trade and trained themselves to become perfect gentlemen. They're the ones who seem to have "class." Cary Grant achieved Mrs. Leach's ideal, and it turned out to be the whole world's ideal.

{*The New Yorker*, July 14, 1975}

:: All for Love

After a two-year break to read and to write, François Truffaut has come back to moviemaking with new assurance, new elation. *The Story of Adèle H.* (the closing-night selection of the New York Film Festival) is a musical, lilting film with a tidal pull to it. It's about a woman who is destroyed by her passion for a man who is indifferent to her—a woman who realizes herself in self-destruction. The only surviving daughter of the writer Victor Hugo, Adèle was sharing his exile in the Channel Islands during the reign of Louis Napoleon when she met the English Lieutenant Pinson, with whom she had a brief affair. When Pinson was transferred to Nova Scotia, she followed him. The film, based on her journals, begins with her arrival in Halifax in 1863—at the high point in her life, when she has had the courage to defy her family and cross the ocean.

A composer as well as a writer, Adèle (Isabelle Adjani) is educated, perceptive, wily; she's not taken in by Lieutenant Pinson (Bruce Robinson). She knows that he's essentially worthless—selfish, mercenary, fickle—and that he doesn't want her. But she constructs an altar to his photograph in the rented room where she waits out months, years. "Love is my religion," she writes in her journal. It may be necessary to this neurotic conception that the love object be himself negligible, even contemptible. How else can she—the gifted daughter of the most famous man in the world—know the full grandeur of self-abasement but with a tinhorn in a flashy uniform? How better punish her father for being a man of great accomplishments than to declare that she cares for nothing but love? By throwing herself in the dirt at the feet of a good-for-nothing, she proves her moral superiority to her father and all his worldly honors. You can see the pride she takes in being the lowliest of the low. With nothing to lose (she has already lost Pinson, before the start of the picture), there's nothing she won't stoop to. He's a gambler, so she bribes him with money. He's a womanizer, so she sends him a whore. All her waking moments are given to planning the blackmailing pressures that the unloved exert on those they claim to love. "Do with me whatever you will!" she cries, but the only thing he wants to do with her is to get rid of her. Spying on him, claiming to be his wife, breaking up an advantageous match he has arranged, turning up to make a scene when he's on maneuvers with his unit, she has him surrounded.

She's an appallingly devious woman, and as it becomes clear that she doesn't care anything about him, that all that matters to her is the purity of *her* feeling toward him, you begin to relate to the hounded Pinson, not because you're concerned for his career but because you can't help recognizing that it's only an accident—a joke, really—that he is the recipient of all this unwanted passionate attention. Weakly ladylike in appearance, Adèle looks a mere maiden—the sort of frail gentlewoman that men would help across the street in bad weather. But out of nowhere some hidden spring will snap, and she'll be rude and peremptory. Truffaut has one gasping at this dainty woman's fearless outrageousness. Adèle isn't a charmer, like Jeanne Moreau's Catherine in *Jules and Jim*; she's a limp, strung-out madwoman, so obsessed with love that she isn't even very sexy. The film doesn't have the raw, playful, sensual lyricism of *Jules and Jim*; it doesn't shift moods in that young, iridescent way. *Adèle H.* is damnably intelligent —almost frighteningly so, like some passages in Russian novels which strip the characters bare. And it's deeply, disharmoniously funny—which Truffaut has never been before. This picture is so totally concentrated on one character that it's a phenomenon: we become as much absorbed in Adèle as she is in Lieutenant Pinson. And our absorption extends from the character to a larger view of the nature of neurotically willed romanticism. The subject of the movie is the self-destructive love that everyone has experienced in one form or another. Adèle is a riveting, great character because she goes all the way with it.

One never for an instant condemns her or pities her. The triumph of *Adèle H.* is that she is a heroine. And, because of that, an archetypal creation. Her unshakable conviction that this one man—Lieutenant Pinson —is the only man for her may be woman's inverse equivalent of the Don Juan, forever chasing. Woman's mania transcends sex; the male mania centers on physical conquest. The woman values the dream of what she's almost had, or what she's had and lost; the Don Juan values only what he's never had. You could draw the connections geometrically: Adèle does what a woman can do to carry her social and biological position to maniacal extremes, and that's what—in male terms—a Don Juan does. Perhaps the one obsessive could intuitively understand the other. (Victor Hugo was an insatiable sexual prodigy right up to the end—a white-bearded satyr, tumbling new women each day.) Don Juanism has often been dealt with on the screen, but no one before Truffaut has ever treated a woman's crippling romantic fixation with such understanding, black humor, and fullness. Truffaut has found an exact visual metaphor for her neurosis. Toward the end of the film, Adèle, still dogging Pinson's footsteps, has followed him to Barbados. Living in the native quarter under the name Mrs. Pinson, she's a wintry wraith, out of place, belonging nowhere. The Lieutenant, now a captain, married, and fearful that her use of his name will cause more trouble for him, confronts her on the street. And she sails by him, as if she were from another world; she seems at peace, insensible to pain, with the calm of exhaustion. She has given herself over to love so completely that the actual man doesn't exist for her anymore. She doesn't even know him. It's inevitable, perfect. She has arrived at her goal.

Only nineteen when the film was shot, Isabelle Adjani is much younger than the woman she's playing. (Adèle Hugo was in her early thirties when she took off after Pinson.) She hardly seems to be doing anything, yet you can't take your eyes off her. You can perceive why Truffaut, who had worked on the Adèle Hugo material off and on for six years, has said that he wouldn't have made this "musical composition for one instrument" without Isabelle Adjani. She has a quality similar to Jean-Pierre Léaud's in *The 400 Blows*—not a physical resemblance but a similar psychological quality. The awareness and intelligence are there, but nothing else is definite yet; the inner life has not yet taken outer form, and so in the movie you see the downy opacity of a face in process, a character taking shape. We keep staring at Adèle to see what that face *means*. She's right for the role, in the way that the young Jennifer Jones was for Bernadette: you believe her capable of anything, because you can't see yet what she is. If the planes of Isabelle Adjani's face were already set in the masklike definition of a famous movie star's face (even child stars can get it), we couldn't have this participatory excitement—the suspense of seeing what Adèle is turning into. Isabelle Adjani has been a professional actress since she was fourteen without tightening; one French director says that she's James Dean come back as a girl. Considering how young she is, her performance here is scarily smart. She knows how to alert us to what Adèle conceals; she's unnaturally quiet and passive, her blue eyes shining too bright in a pale flower face. Truffaut had the instinct not to age her with makeup in the course of the film; we can see that years are passing, but the tokens of time are no more than reddened eyes, a pair of glasses, tangled hair, a torn, bedraggled gown. Aging her would have wrecked the poetry of her final, distraught image, and it's the poetry of the whole conception—the undecorated, pared-to-the-bone poetry—that gives the movie its force. The film is concrete, simple, literal, yet it all works on a metaphorical level. It's an intense, daring vision of the passions that women have kept hidden under a meek exterior. And Isabelle Adjani's soft, plangent quality (along with her trained, outsize talent) makes it possible for Adèle's heroic insanity to seem to explode on the screen.

It's a great film, I think—the only great film from Europe I've seen since *Last Tango*. Thematic ideas that have been plaguing Truffaut have fallen into place—especially the two-sisters theme of his *Two English Girls*. In that film, the girl could not be happy with the man she loved, because he had slept with her older sister, who had died. But Truffaut couldn't seem to express what engaged him in the material, which may have been an unworked-out allusion to the deceased Françoise Dorléac, who had appeared in a Truffaut film, and her younger sister Catherine Deneuve, who subsequently starred for him. It's possible that he was attracted to the story of Adèle Hugo by the fact that Adèle also had an older sister who died. Léopoldine Hugo was drowned at nineteen, along with her young husband, who was trying to save her, and she was temporarily immortalized in commemorative poems by her father; Adèle broke off her own engagement to her sister's husband's brother when she took up with Lieutenant Pinson. This time, however, Truffaut doesn't shy away from the competitive love-hate possibilities of the subject. Adèle is so wan because her energies are spent by violent nightmares: she tosses at sea, crying out as if she were drowning, while Maurice Jaubert's slightly jangling music intensifies the turbulence. (The score is from Jaubert's unpublished compositions—he died before the Second World War.) The water imagery is very powerful throughout. Adèle wrote letters to a brother, which were then transmitted to her father, for whom they were intended, and who replied. Midway in the film, we follow the oceanic trail of these letters; there's no apparent rational motive for this break in the action, yet it's highly effective. Adèle's biggest act of independence was to cross the waters all alone—a journey in bondage to a delusion. *Adèle H.* is her trip, and her divided spirit makes the whole movie vibrate.

Truffaut quoted the Brontës in *Two English Girls*, but this is his Brontë movie—finally brought off because he has given it his own thin-skinned, analytic spirit. His Gothic heroine brought up to date might have been conceived by Edna O'Brien Brontë. Truffaut is romantic *and* ironic: he understands that maybe the only way we can take great romantic love now is as craziness, and that the craziness doesn't cancel out the romanticism— it completes it. Adèle's love isn't corrupted by sanity; she's a great crazy. She carries her love to the point where it consumes everything else in her life, and when she goes mad, it doesn't represent the disintegration of her personality; it is, rather, the final integration. *Adèle H.* is a feat of sustained acuteness, a grand-scale comedy about unrequited love, and it's Truffaut's most passionate work. There's none of the puppyish reticence of several of his recent films. You get a sense of surging happiness from the way the picture moves; the ongoingness—the feeling of being borne on a current— recalls Vigo's *L'Atalante* and the sequence in Renoir's *A Day in the Country* when the flooding river represents the passage of the years. For some time, I've thought that Sven Nykvist was a peerless cinematographer, but on the basis of this film I'd say that Nestor Almendros, who shot it, is right up there with him. Almendros' unusual consistency was memorable in Eric Rohmer's summery *Claire's Knee*, and in *The Wild Child* the radiant order-liness of the interiors was part of the theme. *Adèle H.* is in desaturated, deepened color, with the faces always clear and the bodies swathed in clothing, dark, yet distinctly outlined against the darker backgrounds. It seems to me that I wasn't aware of the sky at any time during the movie. The images are dark on dark, like a Géricault, with the characters' emo-tional lives brought luminously close.

Adèle gets so close that when you hear the voice of her father answering her letters (she writes home only to ask for money, and to reproach him), you may begin to fantasize about his tone. He is always considerate, oblig-ing, loving, yet somehow the paternal solicitude begins to weigh on one. Isn't he too humane, and impersonally so, as if he were demonstrating what a blameless father he is, and writing letters for the ages? His even-tempered voice from the other side of the ocean sounds very aloof when we're watching Adèle turn into a pile of rags: it cannot be easy to be the daughter (or son, either) of a great man. The godlike constancy of his tone recalls Cocteau's famous remark "Victor Hugo was a madman who believed himself to be Victor Hugo." Adèle Hugo used false names, her sister's name, any name but her own. Maybe she wasn't sure she had a right to it: it was rumored that her godfather, Sainte-Beuve, was actually her father. All the more reason for her to prove that, unlike her mother, and unlike her father, she was pure in her love. When Victor Hugo died, at eighty-three, he was buried like a divinity. His body was exhibited at the Arc de Triomphe, which was draped in black, and the route from the Étoile to the Panthéon, where his coffin was enshrined, was hung with crêpe and with shields bearing the titles of his works. Truffaut shows us photographs of the magnificent turnout: a procession of two million mourners followed the coffin. Adèle was not among them; she spent her last forty years in an asylum, writing in her journal, in code. Victor Hugo is said to have had no equal as a poseur and a mythmaker, but, on Truffaut's evidence, his daughter, who lived to eighty-five, burning with faith to the end, may have surpassed him.

{*The New Yorker*, October 27, 1975}

:: Walking into Your Childhood

Since the only thing about reviewing movies that makes me unhappy is that I can't get to the opera often enough, Ingmar Bergman's film version of *The Magic Flute* is a blissful present. Filmed operas generally "open out" the action or else place us as if we were spectators at a performance, looking at the entire stage. Bergman has done neither—he has moved into the stage. He emphasizes the theatricality of the piece, using space as stage space, but with the camera coming in close. We get the pixillated feeling that we're near enough to touch the person who is singing; we might be dreamers sailing invisibly among the guests at a cloud-borne party. Bergman has often delighted in including little plays (plummy satires of stage acting) within his movies, and even movies (silent slapstick comedies) within his movies. He's used them not only to comment on his characters and themes but also for the joy of re-creating different performing styles. This time, the play inside the movie has become the movie, and he's sustained his ironic juggling all the way through. He can use what he knows (and loves) about the theatre.

Although the film was actually made in a studio, it is set within the Drottningholm Court Theatre, and at the beginning we see details of the baroque décor. Bergman retains the sense of the magical theatrical machinery of Mozart's time. When the three cherubim ascend in the basket of a balloon, the ropes don't move smoothly, and all through the film he calls our attention to toy moons and suns, to trick entrances, to what's going on backstage. We get the story of the performance as well as the story of the opera. The dragon who threatens Prince Tamino prances for applause; the three flirty temptresses who compete for Tamino also compete for the audience's approval. For Bergman, who says that he usually

506

doesn't begin to write a part until he knows who's going to play it, it must have been like a game to find the singers he did, who look the roles to perfection. He must have used everything he's learned about how to get actors to trust him, because they act as if working in front of the camera were a natural thing. They don't have the wild-eyed dislocation of so many singers—that crazed stare that seems to be their amazed response to the sounds coming out of them. Those cherubim are the most winning cast members; they're three rosy-cheeked Pucks yet three child hams, and Bergman wants us to see the conscious pleasure they take in performing. They sing as if each note marked the happiest moment in their lives; you absolutely can't not grin at them.

Unlike *Don Giovanni* or *Così Fan Tutte*, *The Magic Flute*, Mozart's last opera, makes a special claim on one's affections, because its libretto is high camp. It's a peerlessly silly masterpiece: sublimely lucid music arising out of a parodistic fairy tale that celebrates in all seriousness the exalted brotherhood of the Freemasons. In most of the first act, the story seems to be a conventional romantic quest—a fairy Queen of the Night sends Prince Tamino to rescue her daughter, Pamina, from the evil sorcerer, Sarastro, who is holding her by force. But by the time the second act was written, Mozart and Schikaneder, his librettist, had shifted directions, and now Sarastro is the lord of enlightenment, High Priest of the Temple of Wisdom, and he's protecting Pamina from her demonic mother. This confusion arising from the belated decision to convert a fairy tale into a story about the mystic brotherhood (Mozart was a Mason) seems to add to rather than take away from the opera; the confusion serves as an ironic comment on the tangled stories of most librettos. In Bergman's version, Sarastro is Pamina's father—which does give the conflict between him and the Queen more substance, and even a bit of logic.

One could, if one wished, see all Bergman's themes in this opera, because it is a dream play, with many of the same motifs as *Smiles of a Summer Night*, *The Seventh Seal*, *Wild Strawberries*, and *Cries and Whispers*. In *Wild Strawberries*, the doctor, Isak Borg (I.B., like Ingmar Bergman), walked into his childhood, and that's what Bergman is doing here. But he isn't doing it realistically this time. In *The Magic Flute*, the need for love, the suicidal despair of loneliness, ambivalent feelings about one's parents, the fear of death are already ritualized, so Bergman can play with them, in mythological fantasy form. *The Magic Flute* takes place in a philosophical bubble in which you recognize your love—your other half—at once, because the names are in pairs. It's heavenly simplicity, in parody: Tamino is sent to rescue Pamina, and he's accompanied by the bird-catcher Papageno, who finds his Papagena. We know that we should identify with Prince Tamino—he's the pure-at-heart hero of legend, and Bergman has found a tenor (Josef Köstlinger) who looks like the handsome knights in the storybooks of one's childhood—but in *The Magic Flute* nothing works quite the way it's meant to, and it comes out better. Tamino goes through the trials and performs all the proper deeds, but he's a storybook stiff compared to Papageno, who flubs his tests. There's a lesson implicit in Tamino's steadfastness: he accepts his responsibilities and earns his manhood. But Papageno doesn't want responsibility—he just wants pleasure. He'll never be a "man"—he's an impetuous kid, a gamin, a folk hero. I think the reason Papageno isn't tiresome, like other buffoonish-everyman squires (and I include Sancho Panza), must be that he hasn't been burdened with practical, "earthy" wisdom; he's too goosy for that. He has his own purity—he's pure, impulsive id. Although Papageno isn't initiated into the priestly brotherhood with Tamino, and so will presumably never experience the divine wisdom of the consecrated, he is forgiven for his flimsy virtue. Papageno doesn't earn his prize, but he gets it anyway: his Papagena is easy as pie, a pushover, as carnally eager as he.

The brotherhood is clearly strictly male; like Papageno, women are considered too talkative. But Bergman tries to integrate the order by including women, from nowhere, among the men at the final ceremonial, when Sarastro retires as the leader, putting his spiritual kingdom in the hands of Tamino and Pamina. Bergman's gesture is understandable but a bit specious. The opera is based on strict polarities, turning on male-female. The Queen of the Night (Birgit Nordin) is a glittering coloratura harpy, served by witches-in-training, while Sarastro, the deep, friendly bass (Ulrik Cold, whose face belies his name), and his priests stand for sunlight, justice, and reason. Not surprisingly, the Queen and her vamps are a delight, while Bergman has to use all his ingenuity to keep the solemn priests from grinding the show to a halt. This is where his cinematographer, Sven Nykvist, turns wizard; since a film of *The Magic Flute* wasn't expected to create pandemonium at box offices around the world, it had to be shot in 16-mm., yet Nykvist got such extraordinary quality that even in the 35-mm. blowup for theatres there's a tactile dimension to the contrasting forces. This saves the dignified temple scenes, which are dull stretches in most live performances. Sarastro's dark-eyed, sympathetic face looks as if it would be warm to the touch, and Bergman's emblematic composition of two overlapping faces—used here for father and daughter—adds psychological shading to Sarastro's stepping down from his office. Though Sarastro defeats the nightmare-canary Queen (whose high trilling is a wickedly funny vocal metaphor for neurosis), the ending represents a new harmony of male and female, with joint rule by Tamino and Pamina. The melodic line of this opera, with its arias of men and women yearning for each other, is one of the rare perfect expressions of man-woman love.

The Magic Flute is a fairy tale that is also a parody of fairy tales; the libretto says that when you have your counterpart you'll never be lonely again. The working out of the story is so playful that you never forget you're in an enchanted landscape, yet the music—airily poignant—expresses the passionate desire for all this seraphic happiness to be true. The music is the distillation of our giddy longing for ideal romantic consummation; when we listen, we believe that there are partners ordained for us. The Magic Flute is a love poem that teases love; the women's costumes, cut low, show off the plushiest soft bosoms—it's all a teasing dream. The emotional quality of the music—delirium expressed in perfectly controlled, harmonious phrasing—may perhaps be compared to the flights of language in A Midsummer Night's Dream, but this music bypasses the mind altogether and goes right to the melancholy, rhapsodic core. The Magic Flute is about love as the conquest of death—and about love of the theatre as the conquest of death.

Eric Ericson conducts the Swedish State Broadcasting Network Symphony; the voices may not have the depth of feeling—that special rounded sweetness—that Dietrich Fischer-Dieskau, as Papageno, and Fritz Wunderlich, as Tamino, bring to the Deutsche Grammophon recording, with Karl Böhm conducting the Berlin Philharmonic, but they're wonderful enough, and Håkan Hagegård, who has a bright-eyed, crooked-toothed smile, is just what one wants Papageno to look like and to act like. Bergman was able to spare us the usual views of tongues and tonsils by having Ericson record the score first (in Swedish, which sounds remarkably pleasing), then playing it bit by bit while photographing the singers, who move their mouths in a more genteel manner than is feasible in actual performance. The synchronization is as close to impeccable as seems humanly possible.

The Magic Flute uses to the fullest that side of Bergman which I missed in *Scenes from a Marriage* (and I saw the complete, six-episode TV version). The telegraphic naturalism of that film seemed condescending, as if it represented Bergman's vision of how ordinary, uncreative people live; I responded most to the few minutes when Bibi Andersson was onscreen, because she appears to be closer in spirit to Bergman—she expresses the tensions of intelligence. Bergman seems more complexly involved in *The Magic Flute*, with only one exception: in the framing device, when he goes outside ironic theatricality to documentary-style shots of the "audience." During the overture and at the break between the acts, and a few times during the opera itself, he gives us family-of-man portraits of this audience, with special emphasis on a celestial-eyed little girl. The faces tell us that people of all ages, colors, and creeds enjoy Mozart; it's fiercely banal, like his sticking those modern youths in *Wild Strawberries* so we'd have something to identify with. This production, which is apparently the consummation of a dream Bergman has had for more than two decades, was financed to commemorate fifty years of Swedish broadcasting, and was presented on both Swedish and Danish television last New Year's Day. His cutting to the reactions of that princessy little girl, whom one wants to strangle, suggests that the production is designed to introduce opera to children. Some years back, I found *The Magic Flute* a wonderful first opera to take a child to, but for Bergman to institutionalize this approach—treating *The Magic Flute* as if it were *Peter and the Wolf*—devalues the opera and what he has done with it. He's undersold himself, for, apart from this visual platitudinizing, the picture is a model of how opera can be filmed. The English translation of Bergman's adaptation (he clarifies the text) is graceful, and the titles are unusually well placed on the frame. Having the titles there in front of you, you follow the libretto without losing anything; the story comes across even more directly than when you hear the opera sung in English. Bergman must have reached a new, serene assurance to have tackled this sensuous, luxuriant opera that has bewildered so many stage directors, and to have brought it off so unaffectedly. It's a wholly unfussy production, with the bloom still on it. He recently said, "Making the film was the best time of my life. You can't imagine what it is like to have Mozart's music in the studio every day." Actually, watching the movie, we can.

{*The New Yorker*, November 17, 1975}

:: Notes on the Nihilist
Poetry of Sam Peckinpah

Sam Peckinpah is a great "personal" filmmaker; he's an artist who can work as an artist only on his own terms. When he does a job for hire, he must transform the script and make it his own or it turns into convictionless self-parody (like *The Getaway*). Peckinpah likes to say that he's a good whore who goes where he's kicked. The truth is he's a very bad whore: he can't turn out a routine piece of craftsmanship—he can't use his skills to improve somebody else's conception. That's why he has always had trouble. And trouble, plus that most difficult to define of all gifts—a film sense—is the basis of his legend.

Most movie directors have short wings; few of them are driven to realize their own vision. But Peckinpah's vision has become so scabrous, theatrical, and obsessive that it is now controlling him. His new film, *The Killer Elite*, is set so far inside his fantasy-morality world that it goes beyond personal filmmaking into private filmmaking. The story, which is about killers employed by a company with C.I.A. connections, is used as a mere framework for a compressed, almost abstract fantasy on the subject of selling yourself yet trying to hang on to a piece of yourself. Peckinpah turned fifty while he was preparing this picture, and, what with booze, illness, and a mean, self-destructive streak, in recent years he has looked as if his body were giving out. This picture is about survival.

There are so many elisions in *The Killer Elite* that it hardly exists on a narrative level, but its poetic vision is all of a piece. Unlike Peckinpah's earlier, spacious movies, with Lucien Ballard's light-blue, open-air vistas, this film is intensely, claustrophobically exciting, with combat scenes of martial-arts teams photographed in slow motion and then edited in such brief cuts that the fighting is nightmarishly concentrated—almost subliminal. Shot by Phil Lathrop in cold, five-o'clock-shadow green-blue tones, the film is airless—an involuted, corkscrew vision of a tight, modern world. In its obsessiveness, with the links between sequences a matter of irrational, poetic connections, *The Killer Elite* is closer to *The Blood of a Poet* than it is to a conventional thriller made on the C.I.A.-assassins subject, such as *Three Days of the Condor*. And, despite the script by Marc Norman and Stirling Silliphant that United Artists paid for, the film isn't about C.I.A.-sponsored assassinations—it's about the blood of a poet.

With his long history of butchered films and films released without publicity, of being fired and blacklisted for insubordination, of getting ornerier and ornerier, Peckinpah has lost a lot of blood. Even *The Wild Bunch*, a great imagist epic in which Peckinpah, by a supreme burst of filmmaking energy, was able to convert chaotic romanticism into exaltation—a film comparable in scale and sheer poetic force to Kurosawa's *The Seven Samurai*—was cut in its American release, and has not yet been restored. And Peckinpah was forced to trim *The Killer Elite* to change its R rating to a PG. Why would anybody want a PG-rated Peckinpah film? The answer is that United Artists, having no confidence in the picture, grabbed the chance to place it in four hundred and thirty-five theatres for the Christmas trade; many of those theatres wouldn't have taken it if it had an R and the kids couldn't go by themselves. The film was flung into those neighborhood houses for a quick profit, without benefit of advance press screenings or the ad campaign that goes with a first-run showing. Peckinpah's career is becoming a dirty, bitter game of I-dump-on-you-because-you-dump-on-me. Increasingly, his films have reflected his war with the producers and distributors, and in *The Killer Elite* this war takes its most single-minded form.

Peckinpah's roots are in the theatre as much as they're in the West; he loves the theatricality of Tennessee Williams (early on, he directed three different stage productions of *The Glass Menagerie*), and, personally, he has the soft-spoken grandness of a Southerner in a string tie—when he talks of the way California used to be, it is in the reverent tone that Southerners use for the Old South. The hokum runs thick in him, and his years of television work—writing dozens of "Gunsmoke" episodes, "creating" the two series "The Rifleman" and "The Westerner"—pushed his thinking into good-guys-versus-bad-guys formats. The tenderness he felt for Tennessee Williams' emotional poetry he could also feel for a line of dialogue that defined a Westerner's plain principles. He loves actors, and he enjoyed the TV-Western make-believe, but that moment when the routine Western script gave way to a memorably "honest" emotion became for him what it was all about. When Peckinpah reminisces about "a great Western," it sometimes comes down to one flourish that for him "said everything." And Peckinpah lives by and for heroic flourishes; they're his idea of the real thing, and in his movies he has invested them with such nostalgic passion that a viewer can be torn between emotional assent and utter confusion as to what, exactly, he's assenting to.

As the losing battles with the moneymen have gone on, year after year, Peckinpah has—only partly sardonically, I think—begun to see the world in terms of the bad guys (the studio executives who have betrayed him or chickened out on him) and the people he likes (generally actors), who are the ones smart enough to see what the process is all about, the ones who haven't betrayed him yet. Hatred of the bad guys—the total mercenaries—has become practically the only sustaining emotion in his work, and his movies have become fables about striking back.

Many of the things that Peckinpah says in conversation began to seep into his last film, *Bring Me the Head of Alfredo Garcia* (1974), turning it into a time-machine foul-up, with modern, airborne killers functioning in the romanticized Mexico of an earlier movie era. Essentially the same assassins dominate the stylized, darkened San Francisco of *The Killer Elite*. In a *Playboy* interview with William Murray in 1972, Peckinpah was referring to movie producers when he said, "The woods are full of killers, all sizes, all colors. . . . A director has to deal with a whole world absolutely teeming with mediocrities, jackals, hangers-on, and just plain killers. The attrition is terrific. It can kill you. The saying is that they can kill you but not eat you. That's nonsense. I've had them eating on me while I was still walking around." Sam Peckinpah looks and behaves as if he were never free of their gnawing. He carries it with him, fantasizes it, provokes it, makes it true again and again. He romanticizes himself as one of the walking wounded, which is no doubt among the reasons he wanted to direct *Play It As It Lays*. (He was rejected by the businessmen as being strictly an action director.) In that Murray interview, he was referring to the making of movies when he said, "When you're dealing in millions, you're dealing with people at their meanest. Christ, a showdown in the old West is nothing compared with the infighting that goes on over money."

Peckinpah swallowed Robert Ardrey whole; it suited his emotional needs — he *wants* to believe that all men are whores and killers. He was talking to Murray about what the bosses had done to him and to his films when he said, "There are people all over the place, dozens of them, I'd like to kill, quite literally kill." He's dramatizing, but I've known Sam Peckinpah for over ten years (and, for all his ceremonial exhibitionism, his power plays, and his baloney, or maybe because of them, there is a total, physical elation in his work and in his own relation to it that makes me feel closer to him than I do to any other director except Jean Renoir) and I'm convinced that he actually feels that demonic hatred. I think Sam Peckinpah feels everything that he dramatizes — he allows himself to. He's a ham: he doesn't feel what he doesn't dramatize.

Peckinpah has been simplifying and falsifying his own terrors as an artist by putting them into melodramatic formulas. He's a major artist who has worked so long in penny-dreadful forms that when he is finally in a position where he's famous enough to fight for his freedom — and maybe win — he can't free himself from the fear of working outside those forms, or from the festering desire for revenge. He is the killer-élite hero played by James Caan in this hallucinatory thriller, in which the hirelings turn against their employers. James Caan's Mike, a No. 1 professional, is mutilated by his closest friend, George Hansen (Robert Duvall), at the order of Cap Collis (Arthur Hill), a defector within the company — Communications Integrity Associates — that they all work for. Mike rehabilitates himself, however, by a long, painful struggle, regaining the use of his body so that he can revenge himself. He comes back more determined than ever, and his enemies — Hansen and Cap Collis — are both shot. But when the wearily cynical top man in the company (Gig Young) offers Mike a regional directorship—Cap Collis's newly vacated position—he rejects it. Instead, he sails—literally—into unknown seas with his loyal friend the gunman-mechanic Mac (Burt Young).

There's no way to make sense of what has been going on in Peckinpah's recent films if one looks only at their surface stories. Whether consciously or, as I think, part unconsciously, he's been destroying the surface content. In this new film, there aren't any of the ordinary kinds of introductions to the characters, and the events aren't prepared for. The political purposes of the double-crosses are shrouded in a dark fog, and the company itself makes no economic sense. There are remnants of a plot involving a political leader from Taiwan (he sounds off about democratic principles in the manner of Paul Henreid's Victor Laszlo in *Casablanca*), but that fog covers all the specific plot points. Peckinpah can explain this disintegration to himself in terms of how contemptible the material actually is—the fragmented story indicates how he feels about what the bosses buy and what they degrade him with. He agrees to do these properties, to be "a good whore," and then he can't help turning them into revenge fantasies. His whole way of making movies has become a revenge fantasy: he screws the bosses, he screws the picture, he screws himself.

The physical rehabilitation of the hero in *The Killer Elite* (his refusal to accept the company's decision that he's finished) is an almost childishly transparent disguise for Peckinpah's own determination to show Hollywood that he's not dead yet—that, despite the tabloid views of him, frail and falling-down drunk, he's got the will to make great movies. He's trying to pick up the pieces of his career. Amazingly, Peckinpah does rehabilitate himself; his technique here is dazzling. In the moments just before violence explodes, Peckinpah's work is at its most subtly theatrical: he savors the feeling of power as he ticks off the seconds before the suppressed rage will take form. When it does, it's often voluptuously horrifying (and that is what has given Peckinpah a dubious reputation—what has made him Bloody Sam), but this time it isn't gory and yet it's more daring than ever. He has never before made the violence itself so surreally, fluidly abstract; several sequences are edited with a magical speed—a new refinement. In *Alfredo Garcia*, the director seemed to have run out of energy after a virtuoso opening, and there was a scene, when the two leads (Warren Oates and Isela Vega) were sitting by the side of a road, that was so scrappily patched together, with closeups that didn't match, that Peckinpah appeared to have run out of zest for filmmaking. Maybe it was just that in *Alfredo Garcia* his old obsessions had lost their urgency and his new one— his metaphoric view of modern corporate business, represented by the dapper, errand-boy killers (Gig Young and Robert Webber as mirror-image lovers)—had thrown him off balance. He didn't seem to know why he was making the movie, and Warren Oates, who has fine shadings in character roles, was colorless in the central role (as he was also in the title role of John Milius's *Dillinger*). Oates is a man who's used to not being noticed, and his body shows it. When he tried to be a star by taking over Peck-inpah's glasses and mustache and manner, he was imitating the outside of a dangerous person—the inside was still meek. And, of course, Peckinpah, with his feelers (he's a man who gives the impression of never missing anything going on in a room), knew the truth: that the actor in *Alfredo Garcia* who was like him, without trying at all, was Gig Young, with his weary pale eyes. In *The Killer Elite*, James Caan is the hero who acts out Peckinpah's dream of salvation, but it's Gig Young's face that haunts the film. Gig Young represents Peckinpah's idea of what he will become if he doesn't screw them all and sail away.

Peckinpah is surely one of the most histrionic men who have ever lived: his movies (and his life, by now) are all gesture. He thinks like an actor, in terms of the effect, and the special bits he responds to in Westerns are actors' gestures—corniness transcended by the hint of nobility in the actors themselves. Like Gig Young, he has the face of a ravaged juvenile, a face that magnetizes because of the suggestion that the person under-stands more than he wants to. It's a fake, this look, but Peckinpah culti-vates the whore-of-whores pose. He plays with the idea of being the best of men and, when inevitably betrayed, the worst of men. (He's got to be both the best and the worst.) Gig Young has the same air of gentleness that Peckinpah has, and the dissolute quality of an actor whose talents have been wasted. Gig Young's face seems large for his body now, in a way that suggests that it has carried a lot of makeup in its time; he looks rub-bery-faced, like an old song-and-dance man. Joel McCrea, with his humane strength, may have been Peckinpah's idealized hero in *Ride the High Coun-try*, and William Holden may have represented a real man to him in *The*

Wild Bunch, but Gig Young, who represents what taking orders from the bosses—being used—does to *a man of feeling*, is the one Peckinpah shows the most affection for now. Gig Young can play the top whore in *The Killer Elite* because his sad eyes suggest that he has no expectations and no illusions left about anything. And Peckinpah can identify with this character because of the element of pain in Gig Young, who seems to be the most naked of actors—an actor with nowhere to hide. (Peckinpah's own eyes are saintly-sly, and he's actually the most devious of men.) Peckinpah could never for an instant identify with the faceless corporate killer played by Arthur Hill. When you see Arthur Hill as Cap Collis, the sellout, you know that it didn't cost Collis anything to sell out. He's a gutless wonder, something that crawled out of the woodwork. Arthur Hill's unremarkable, company-man face and lean, tall body are already abstractions; he's a corporate entity in himself. In Peckinpah's iconography, he's a walking cipher, a man who wasn't born of woman but was cast in a mold—a man whose existence is a defeat for men of feeling.

James Caan goes through the athletic motions of heroism and acts intelligently, but he doesn't bring the right presence to the role. His stoicism lacks homicidal undercurrents, and he doesn't have the raw-nerved awareness that seems needed. The face that suggests some of what Peckinpah is trying to express—the residual humanity in killers—is that of Burt Young, as the devoted Mac. The swarthy, solid, yet sensitive face of Burt Young (he played the man looking at pictures of his faithless wife at the beginning of *Chinatown*) shows the weight of feelings. Mac's warm, gravelly croak and his almost grotesque simpleness link him to the members of the Wild Bunch. His is a face with substance, capable of dread on a friend's account. In *The Killer Elite*, his is the face that shows the feelings that have been burnt out of Gig Young's.

Peckinpah has become wryly sentimental about his own cynicism. When the Taiwanese leader's young daughter pompously tells the hero that she's a virgin, and he does a variation on Rhett Butler, saying, "To tell you the truth, I really don't give a shit," the director's contempt for innocence is too self-conscious, and it sticks out. Peckinpah wants to be honored for the punishment he's taken, as if it were battle scars. The doctor who patches up the hero says, "The scar looks beautiful"—which, in context, is a sleek joke. But when the hero's braced leg fails him and he falls helplessly on his face on a restaurant floor, Sam Peckinpah may be pushing for sympathy for his own travail. From the outside, it's clear that even his battle scars aren't all honorable—that a lot of the time he wasn't fighting to protect his vision, he was fighting for tortuous reasons. He doesn't start a picture with a vision; he starts a picture as a job and then perversely—in spite of his deal to sell out—he turns into an artist.

Much of what Peckinpah is trying to express in *The Killer Elite* is probably inaccessible to audiences, his moral judgments being based less on what his characters do than on what they wouldn't stoop to do. (In Hollywood, people take more pride in what they've said no to than in what they've done.) Yet by going so far into his own hostile, edgily funny myth—in being the maimed victim who rises to smite his enemies—he found a ferocious unity, an Old Testament righteousness that connects with the audience in ways his last few pictures didn't. At the beginning of *The Killer Elite*, the lack of sunlight is repellent; the lividness looks cheap and pulpy—were those four hundred and thirty-five prints processed in a sewer? But by the end a viewer stares fixedly, not quite believing he's seeing what he's seeing: a nightmare ballet. In the free-form murderous finale, with guns, Samurai swords, and lethal skills one has never heard of before, there are troops of Oriental assassins scurrying over the phantom fleet of Second World War ships maintained in Suisun Bay, north of San Francisco. Wrapped up in their cult garb so we can't tell one from another, the darting killers, seen in those slow-motion fast cuts, are exactly like Peckinpah's descriptions of the teeming mediocrities, jackals, hangers-on, and just plain killers that Hollywood is full of.

The film is so cleanly made that Peckinpah may have wrapped up this obsession. When James Caan and Burt Young sail away at the end, it's Sam Peckinpah turning his back on Hollywood. He has gone to Europe, with commitments that will keep him there for at least two years. It would be too simple to say that he has been driven out of the American movie industry, but it's more than half true. No one is Peckinpah's master as a director of individual sequences; no one else gets such beauty out of movement and hard grain and silence. He doesn't do the expected, and so, scene by scene, he creates his own actor-director's suspense. The images in *The*

Killer Elite are charged, and you have the feeling that not one is wasted. What they all add up to is something else—but one could say the same of *The Pisan Cantos*. Peckinpah has become so nihilistic that filmmaking itself seems to be the only thing he believes in. He's crowing in *The Killer Elite*, saying, "No matter what you do to me, look at the way I can make a movie." The bedevilled bastard's got a right to crow.

{*The New Yorker*, January 12, 1976}

:: The Artist as a Young Comedian

In the fifties, when improvisational acts were booked into night clubs and coffeehouses, and the entertainers satirized middle-class interpersonal relations, young actors had a hip edge to their conversation. Freud had got into everything, and acting was now thought of in terms of awareness. Acting coaches who had been political activists turned into psychiatric philosophers. This is the atmosphere of Paul Mazursky's new, autobiographical comedy, *Next Stop, Greenwich Village*. The hero, a twenty-two-year-old Brooklyn College graduate, Larry Lapinsky (Lenny Baker), who has never wanted to be anything but an actor, moves out of the Brownsville apartment of his parents (Shelley Winters and Mike Kellin) into an apartment of his own in the Village. The film is about Larry's acting classes and his relations with his girl, Sarah (Ellen Greene), and his friends. Mazursky knows this scene so well that every word, every hangup, every awkward, flip hesitation rings a bell. *Next Stop, Greenwich Village* gives the best portrait of Village life ever put on the screen; the casualness, the camaraderie, and the sexual freedom are balanced by glimpses of the lives of those who are in the Village because they don't fit in anywhere else. Yet there's more to the movie than that. Like Alexander Portnoy, Larry is the son in the Jewish joke, but, unlike Portnoy, he isn't crippled by it. In both *Portnoy's Complaint* and *Next Stop, Greenwich Village*, guilt is funny; but the Philip Roth book is satire from within a fixation, and Portnoy is screaming with rage. Larry Lapinsky is rather like what the young Alex Portnoy might have been if he had recovered from his complaint. He learns to live with his guilt; that's the comedy of growing up which is celebrated in *Next Stop, Greenwich Village*.

As Larry's Mom, Shelley Winters is a hysteric on the loose, barging into his apartment in the middle of a party, embarrassing him so much he wants to crawl under the furniture. It is high-mania acting, like Winters' ever-hopeful Charlotte Haze in *Lolita*. Mrs. Lapinsky pours so much brute emotion into every small detail of her life that she has lost all sense of proportion; everything to do with her becomes of world-shaking importance. Her unused brains have turned her into a howling freak, but you can recognize in her the sources of her son's talent and wit. And, even seeing her through her son's agonized-with-shame eyes, you don't get too much of her—or, rather, you can't get enough of Shelley Winters' performance. With her twinkly goo-goo eyes and flirty grin, Shelley Winters is a mother hippo charging—not at her son's enemies but at him. Fat, morose, irrepressible, she's a force that would strike terror to anyone's heart, yet in some abominable way she's likable. She's Mrs. Portnoy seen without hatred. When Larry visits his parents, she hands him a bag of apple strudel to eat on the plane taking him, first class, to a job in Hollywood. Her husband says to her, "I told you he'd get angry," but Larry says, "I'm not angry. I'm crazy, but I'm not angry." When he has said goodbye and is on his way to the subway, he stands on the Brownsville street listening to a fiddler and he eats the strudel.

Larry is crazy in a sane way: as a comedian, he puts his craziness to work for him. And that's Paul Mazursky's own greatest gift. What made his earlier films (*Bob & Carol & Ted & Alice*, *Alex in Wonderland*, *Blume in Love*, and *Harry & Tonto*) so distinctive was the acceptance of bugginess as part of the normal—maybe even the best part of it. In his films, craziness gives life its savor. When Mazursky makes fun of characters, it's not to put them down; quite the reverse—the scattier they are, the more happily he embraces them. (His quarrel is with the too controlled.) The star of *Next Stop, Greenwich Village*, the relatively unknown Lenny Baker, looks like a gangly young boy but has had almost a decade of professional experience, and he gives the central character the manic generosity that holds the film together. Starting as a runny-nosed, funny-looking kid, Larry becomes stronger and handsomer. Having survived his mother's aggression, he's got the craziness and the strength to make it as an artist.

On his own road from Brownsville through the Village and on to becoming a writer-director, Mazursky performed in improvisational cabaret theatre, wrote skits for "The Danny Kaye Show," and taught acting. Like Larry, who gets his break when he's cast as a tough punk, Mazursky got a role as one of the delinquents in *Blackboard Jungle* (1955), though he had gone West earlier, in 1951, to play a leading role as a psychopath who assaults a captive girl, in Stanley Kubrick's first feature, *Fear and Desire*. Mazursky has appeared in several of his own pictures (he was funniest as the itchy, voracious producer in *Alex in Wonderland*), and his directing style is based on the actors' intuitively taking off from each other, as they did in the coffeehouses. He does something that no other American movie director does: he writes, shapes, and edits the sequences to express the performing rhythm—to keep the actors' pulse. As a result, the audience feels unusually close to the characters—feels protective toward them. Mazursky brings you into a love relationship with his people, and it's all aboveboard.

This picture suggests that for Paul Mazursky (as for many theatre people) acting is at the basis of all judgment. Not all of Larry's friends are studying to be actors, yet one can interpret almost everything that happens to them in terms of acting. Ellen Greene's Sarah is intelligent and quick-witted, but she's already a little hard in the places where Larry is still sensitive—where you feel he'll always stay sensitive. (That's what will keep him an artist.) Sarah violates the rule that Larry's patriarchal acting teacher, Herbert (Michael Egan), says may be important "for the rest of your life": "The worst kind of joking you can do is to keep life out." According to Herbert, you shouldn't use your brain "to keep the stuff out" but "to take it in." Mazursky satirizes Herbert's litany, but very gently. (The famous acting teacher Herbert Berghof appeared in *Harry & Tonto* as Harry's New York friend the aged radical.) And Larry lives by Herbert's rule. He humors his parents, but he's really on his own; he has made the plunge—he's taking life in. Sarah, however, is still at home, and playing the lying-to-your-folks game along with the Greenwich Village game. She's a compromiser, and so elastic she doesn't know where she'll snap. Ellen Greene gives a beautiful, prickly, sensual performance; she has a big, avid mouth, which she uses for comic tics, taking us by surprise each time. The proof of her talent is that it's Sarah's hardness that makes her seem poignant. Being independent-minded has got mixed with something sharp and self-destructive; Sarah cuts herself off from people by acting sure just when she's least sure. This role is written with a respect for the ways in which savvy people with everything going for them can screw up. Mazursky keeps it all light and blowsy, yet the characters have depth, and a lot of damaging things are happening to them while they're frisking along. Sarah is attracted to Robert (Christopher Walken), a narcissistic, affectlessly calm poet-playwright. He's the sort of person who destroys a party—the one who says "Let's play the truth game." Robert is a passive sadist, who draws women to him and shrugs off any responsibility for what happens. And it's true that they've hurt themselves, but it's his passivity that has invited them to do it. Walken uses his light, high voice for an ambiguous effect, and he gives Robert an air of physical isolation that makes him seem always withdrawn from the rest of the group. When Larry, who has suffered because of him, accuses him of having nothing under his pose but more pose, it's as if Larry were using the old slang term and saying "You're a bad actor," meaning that he's untrustworthy, a crook—someone not in touch with himself. Robert might almost be the Nazi villain—he's every son of a bitch whose only interest in sex is for power. He's the only character without spontaneity, and the only one that Mazursky can't resolve his feelings about.

As a homosexual who is sick of role-playing but too frightened to stop, Antonio Fargas keeps just enough reserve to be affecting without pushing it; Lois Smith finds the archetypal Lois Smith role as the sodden Anita, a depressive who plays at suicide; Dori Brenner's Connie plays at being everybody's favorite good sport. And on the fringes of this group there's Barney (John Ford Noonan), a bearded, soft giant with a striking resemblance to Mazursky's old writing partner Larry Tucker. (Larry Lapinsky's first name may also be a nod to Tucker.) Most of these actors have been in movies before, but they didn't have Mazursky's lines to speak, or the hip timing he gets. The subsidiary characters help to form just the sort of human zoo that many of us live in. Jeff Goldblum plays a big, handsome young actor named Clyde Baxter—a goofed-up Victor Mature type. Lou Jacobi is the proprietor of a health-food lunch counter, whooping as if his whole life were vindicated when a customer comes in feeling rotten from having eaten a corned beef on rye. And Rochelle Oliver as Dr. Marsha and John C. Becher as Sid Weinberg, a casting director, contribute to making this picture Off Broadway's finest hour.

In refining his comic style, Mazursky has suffered a few losses. I miss the messy romanticism of *Blume*; there Mazursky was "too close" to the subject—he was gummed up in it, and the chaos felt good. This movie is set in his past, and the blood has cooled. But Mazursky's earlier scripts were splotchy; *Next Stop, Greenwich Village* has the intertwining of a classic American play. And if the mechanics seem a little too theatrical when Larry's Mom waddles into his apartment without knocking and pounces on him, still, in 1953 Village doors weren't always bolted. (Bolted doors wouldn't stop Shelley Winters anyway.) As in some other films shot by Arthur Ornitz, there doesn't appear to be a light source, and the color is muddy. You can't tell the blacks and browns and blues apart; Ornitz seems to get the shots to match by making them all dark. Luckily, this movie has so much else going for it that it can get along without visual beauty. Mazursky was so smitten by Fellini that his early films sometimes seemed to be commuting between cultures. But *Next Stop, Greenwich Village* isn't an imitation of *Amarcord*, it's Mazursky's own *Amarcord*. And I like it better than Fellini's. It isn't showy—Mazursky works on a small scale. Yet this satirist without bitterness and without extravagance looks to be a comic poet. His subject is the comedy of wisdom—how to become a good actor.

{*The New Yorker*, February 2, 1976}

:: Underground Man

Taxi Driver is the fevered story of an outsider in New York—a man who can't find any point of entry into human society. Travis Bickle (Robert De Niro), the protagonist of Martin Scorsese's new film, from a script by Paul Schrader, can't find a life. He's an ex-Marine from the Midwest who takes a job driving a cab nights, because he can't sleep anyway, and he is surrounded by the night world of the uprooted—whores, pimps, transients. Schrader, who grew up in Michigan, in the Christian Reformed Church, a zealous Calvinist splinter (he didn't see a movie until he was seventeen), has created a protagonist who is an ascetic not by choice but out of fear. And Scorsese, with his sultry moodiness and his appetite for the pulp sensationalism of forties movies, is just the director to define an American underground man's resentment. Travis wants to conform, but he can't find a group pattern to conform to. So he sits and drives in the stupefied languor of anomie. He hates New York with a Biblical fury; it gives off the stench of Hell, and its filth and smut obsess him. He manages to get a date with Betsy (Cybill Shepherd), a political campaigner whose blondness and white clothes represent purity to him, but he is so out of touch that he inadvertently offends her and she won't have anything more to do with him. When he fumblingly asks advice from Wizard (Peter Boyle), an older cabdriver, and indicates the pressure building up in him, Wizard doesn't know what he's talking about. Travis becomes sick with loneliness and frustration; and then, like a commando preparing for a raid, he purifies his body and goes into training to kill. *Taxi Driver* is a movie in heat, a raw, tabloid version of *Notes from Underground*, and we stay with the protagonist's hatreds all the way.

This picture is more ferocious than Scorsese's volatile, allusive *Mean*

Streets. *Taxi Driver* has a relentless movement: Travis has got to find relief. It's a two-character study—Travis versus New York. As Scorsese has designed the film, the city never lets you off the hook. There's no grace, no compassion in the artificially lighted atmosphere. The neon reds, the vapors that shoot up from the streets, the dilapidation all get to you the way they get to Travis. He is desperately sick, but he's the only one who tries to save a twelve-and-a-half-year-old hooker, Iris (Jodie Foster); the argument he invokes is that she belongs with her family and in school—the secure values from his own past that are of no help to him now. Some mechanism of adaptation is missing in Travis; the details aren't filled in— just the indications of a strict religious background, and a scar on his back, suggesting a combat wound. The city world presses in on him, yet it's also remote, because Travis is so disaffected that he isn't always quite there. We perceive the city as he does, and it's so scummy and malign we get the feel of his alienation.

Scorsese may just naturally be an Expressionist; his asthmatic bedridden childhood in a Sicilian-American home in Little Italy propelled him toward a fix on the violently exciting movies he saw. Physically and intellectually, he's a speed demon, a dervish. Even in *Alice Doesn't Live Here Anymore* he found a rationale for restless, whirlwind movement. But Scorsese is also the most carnal of directors—movement is ecstatic for him— and that side of him didn't come out in *Alice*. This new movie gives him a chance for the full Expressionist use of the city which he was denied in *Mean Streets*, because it was set in New York but was made on a minuscule budget in Southern California, with only seven shooting days in New York itself. Scorsese's Expressionism isn't anything like the exaggerated sets of the German directors; he uses documentary locations, but he pushes discordant elements to their limits, and the cinematographer, Michael Chapman, gives the street life a seamy, rich pulpiness. When Travis is taunted by a pimp, Sport (Harvey Keitel), the pimp is so eager for action that he can't stand still; the hipster, with his rhythmic jiggling, makes an eerily hostile contrast to the paralyzed, dumbfounded Travis. Scorsese gets the quality of trance in a scene like this; the whole movie has a sense of vertigo. Scorsese's New York is the big city of the thrillers he feasted his imagination on—but at a later stage of decay. This New York is a voluptuous enemy. The street vapors become ghostly; Sport the pimp romancing his baby whore leads her in a hypnotic dance; the porno theatres are like mortuaries; the congested traffic is macabre. And this Hell is always in movement.

No other film has ever dramatized urban indifference so powerfully; at first, here, it's horrifyingly funny, and then just horrifying. When Travis attempts to date Betsy, he's very seductive; we can see why she's tantalized. They're talking across a huge gap, and still they're connecting (though the wires are all crossed). It's a zinger of a scene: an educated, socially conscious woman dating a lumpen lost soul who uses one of the oldest pitches in the book—he tells her that he knows she is a lonely person. Travis means it; the gruesome comedy in the scene is how intensely he means it—because his own life is utterly empty. Throughout the movie, Travis talks to people on a different level from the level they take him on. He's so closed off he's otherworldly; he engages in so few conversations that slang words like "moonlighting" pass right over him—the spoken language is foreign to him. His responses are sometimes so blocked that he seems wiped out; at other times he's animal fast. This man is burning in misery, and his inflamed, brimming eyes are the focal point of the compositions. Robert De Niro is in almost every frame: thin-faced, as handsome as Robert Taylor one moment and cagey, ferrety, like Cagney, the next—and not just looking at the people he's talking to but spying on them. As Travis, De Niro has none of the peasant courtliness of his Vito Corleone in *The Godfather, Part II*. Vito held himself in proudly, in control of his violence; he was a leader. Travis is dangerous in a different, cumulative way. His tense face folds in a yokel's grin and he looks almost an idiot. Or he sits in his room vacantly watching the bright-eyed young faces on the TV and with his foot he slowly rocks the set back and then over. The exacerbation of his desire for vengeance shows in his numbness, yet part of the horror implicit in this movie is how easily he passes. The anonymity of the city soaks up one more invisible man; he could be legion.

Scorsese handles the cast immaculately. Harvey Keitel's pimp is slimy, all right, yet his malicious, mischievous eyes and his jumpiness are oddly winning. Jodie Foster, who was exactly Iris's age when she played the part, is an unusually physical child actress and seems to have felt out her line readings—her words are convincingly hers. Cybill Shepherd has never been better: you don't see her trying to act. She may actually be doing her least acting here, yet she doesn't have that schoolgirl model's blankness; her face is expressive and womanly. There's a suggestion that Betsy's life hasn't gone according to her expectations—a faint air of defeat. The come-dian Albert Brooks brings a note of quibbling, plump pomposity to the role of her political co-worker, and Leonard Harris, formerly the WCBS-TV arts critic, has a professionally earnest manner as Palatine, their can-didate. Peter Boyle's role is small, but he was right to want to be in this film, and he does slobby wonders with his scenes as the gently thick Wiz-ard, adjusted to the filth that Travis is coiled up to fight; Boyle gives the film a special New York–hack ambience, and, as the cabby Doughboy, Harry Northup has a bland face and Southern drawl that suggest another kind of rootlessness. Scorsese himself is sitting on the sidewalk when Travis first sees Betsy, and then he returns to play a glitteringly morbid role as one of Travis's fares—a man who wants Travis to share his rancid glee in what the Magnum he intends to shoot his faithless wife with will do to her. As an actor, he sizzles; he has such concentrated energy that this sequence burns a small hole in the screen.

As a director, Scorsese has the occasional arbitrariness and preening of a runaway talent; sometimes a shot calls attention to itself, because it serves no visible purpose. One can pass over a lingering closeup of a street musician, but when Travis is talking to Betsy on a pay phone in an office building and the camera moves away from him to the blank hallway, it's an Antonioni pirouette. The Bernard Herrmann score is a much bigger prob-lem; the composer finished recording it on December 23rd, the day before he died, and so it's a double pity that it isn't better. It's clear why Scorsese wanted Herrmann: his specialty was expressing psychological disorder through dissonant, wrought-up music. But this movie, with its suppressed sex and suppressed violence, is already pitched so high that it doesn't need ominous percussion, snake rattles, and rippling scales. These musical nudges belong back with the rampaging thrillers that *Taxi Driver* tran-scends. Scorsese got something out of his asthma: he knows how to make us experience the terror of suffocation.

Some actors are said to be empty vessels who are filled by the roles they play, but that's not what appears to be happening here with De Niro. He's gone the other way. He's used his emptiness—he's reached down into his own anomie. Only Brando has done this kind of plunging, and De Niro's performance has something of the undistanced intensity that Bran-do's had in *Last Tango*. In its own way, this movie, too, has an erotic aura. There is practically no sex in it, but no sex can be as disturbing as sex. And that's what it's about: the absence of sex—bottled-up, impacted energy and emotion, with a blood-splattering release. The fact that we experience Travis's need for an explosion viscerally, and that the explosion itself has the quality of consummation, makes *Taxi Driver* one of the few truly modern horror films.

Anyone who goes to the movie houses that loners frequent knows that they identify with the perpetrators of crimes, even the most horrible crimes, and that they aren't satisfied unless there's a whopping climax. In his essay "The White Negro," Norman Mailer suggested that when a killer takes his revenge on the institutions that he feels are oppressing him his eruption of violence can have a positive effect on him. The most shocking aspect of *Taxi Driver* is that it takes this very element, which has generally been exploited for popular appeal, and puts it in the center of the viewer's consciousness. Violence is Travis's only means of expressing himself. He has not been able to hurdle the barriers to being seen and felt. When he blasts through, it's his only way of telling the city that he's there. And, given his ascetic loneliness, it's the only real orgasm he can have.

The violence in this movie is so threatening precisely because it's cathartic for Travis. I imagine that some people who are angered by the film will say that it advocates violence as a cure for frustration. But to acknowledge that when a psychopath's blood boils over he may cool down is not the same as justifying the eruption. This film doesn't operate on the level of moral judgment of what Travis does. Rather, by drawing us into its vortex it makes us understand the psychic discharge of the quiet boys who go berserk. And it's a real slap in the face for us when we see Travis at the end looking pacified. He's got the rage out of his system—for the moment, at least—and he's back at work, picking up passengers in front of the St. Regis. It's not that he's cured but that the city is crazier than he is.

{*The New Yorker*, February 9, 1976}

:: *Sparkle*

Sparkle, the story of the three daughters of a domestic servant who become a singing group, in the style of the Supremes, opened in April and closed a few weeks later. Now, partly because of the success of the Aretha Franklin album of the Curtis Mayfield score, the picture is being reissued in some cities. This means that moviegoers have another chance to see Lonette McKee, a young singer-actress so sexy that she lays waste to the movie, which makes the mistake of killing her off in the first half. But in that first part she and Dorian Harewood show a sixth sense for being alive. The fact that nobody has picked up on these two and starred them together is just one more proof that the new studio heads don't go to the movies.

Sparkle is the first film to be directed by Sam O'Steen, the well-known editor (*The Graduate*, *Rosemary's Baby*, *Chinatown*), who also directed *Queen of the Stardust Ballroom* for TV. He must have got carried away with the black cast and the smoky theatrical milieu, because the images are sometimes irritatingly dark, but he keeps them full of atmospheric detail, and the tawdry black-vaudeville scenes have the teeming, bodies-spilling-out-the-edges quality of Toulouse-Lautrec. The crowded look of the film helps to compensate for the Joel Schumacher script, which appears to be no more than a skeleton.

The outline for *Sparkle* follows the moral scheme of the old Production Code days: the "bad" characters (Lonette McKee as Sister, the hell-bent lead singer of the trio; Harewood as the teen-age boy who nonchalantly steals a car to take her out; Tony King as the dope pusher who hooks her) die or are punished, and the "good" characters (Irene Cara as the meek Sparkle who goes on as a single, and dimply Philip M. Thomas as her hardworking young manager) are rewarded. As often happened in the old movie days, the "bad" performers are terrific and the "good" are insufferable.

Sister is a hot number, talented, smart, impudent—an inflammatory, exhibitionistic singer who wants to turn the whole world on. And as Lonette McKee plays her, Sister has the visceral beauty, the voice, and the sexual energy to do it. Sister puts the dirty fun of sex into her songs, with the raw charge of a rebellious, nose-thumbing girl making her way. She has barely had a taste of singing in public when she falls for the sadistic pusher who beats her up and degrades her; she goes downhill unbelievably fast— and the picture with her—and then she ODs. What isn't explained is the why of this relationship; instead, we move on to the way the dewy-eyed Sparkle achieves the fame Sister might have had. And in order to keep the story going the action shifts to the almost canine devotion of Sparkle's young manager; his true-hearted courage defeats the attempts of gangsters to muscle in on her career.

The subject that's passed over—why the thug wants to possess and destroy Sister, who so obviously has everything it takes to become a star, and why she's drawn to him—is a true modern subject, and not just for the rock world. Lonette McKee is the actress to drive this theme into one's consciousness, because she has the sexual brazenness that screen stars such as Susan Hayward and Ava Gardner had in their youth. You look at the sheer taunting sexual avidity of these women and you think "What man would dare?" And the answer may be: only a man with the strength to meet the challenge or a man so threatened by it that he's got to wipe the floor with the girl, and there are more of the latter. If the women who are "too much" for men fall for sharpies and rough guys who brutalize them, it probably has a lot to do with the scarcity of the other men, and something to do, too, with the women's insecurity about being too much. The stronger a woman's need to use her energy, her brains, and her talent, the more confusedly she may feel that she has a beating coming. Besides, having had to make her own way, and having—at some levels—been coarsened doing it, she may feel some rapport with the tough operators who are used to knocking people around. Whatever else these men are, they're self-made, and they instinctively know what she's gone through and how to handle her.

Movies now seem to be almost begging for this theme to come out. It's highly unlikely that a woman can become a major screen star at this time unless she has a strong personality, yet if she does—like Jane Fonda, or Barbra Streisand, or Liza Minnelli—she's likely to be experienced as threatening by some of the audience (and by women who play by the standard rules as well as by men). These stars raise the problem in their relation to the audience which is implicit in their screen roles: resentment of their dominating presence. Yet at the movies audiences are far more interested in the "bad girls" than in the ingenues, and not just because wickedness gives an actress more of a chance; these roles give an actress a better chance because there's something recognizably there in those bad girls, even when it's frustrated, soured, and self-destructive. The "bad girl" is the cheapest, easiest way for the movies to deal with the women with guts.

In *Sparkle*, we can believe in Sister but not in the rise to rock stardom of the docile, unassertive Sparkle, because, given the social and biological circumstances of women's lives, a woman who isn't called a hard-driving bitch along the way is not likely to reach any top. A movie can show us the good girls winning the fellas, mothering the kids, succoring those who have met with adversity, but a good-girl artist is a contradiction in terms.

{*The New Yorker*, September 27, 1976}

:: Notes on Evolving Heroes, Morals, Audiences

In *Jaws*, which may be the most cheerfully perverse scare movie ever made, the disasters don't come on schedule the way they do in most disaster pictures, and your guts never settle down to a timetable. Even while you're convulsed with laughter, you're still apprehensive, because the editing rhythms are very tricky, and the shock images loom up huge, right on top of you. There are parts of *Jaws* that suggest what Eisenstein might have done if he hadn't intellectualized himself out of reach—if he'd given in to the bourgeois child in himself. While having a drink with an older Hollywood director, I said that I'd been amazed by the assurance with which Steven Spielberg, the young director of *Jaws*, had toyed with the film frame. The older director said, "He must never have seen a play; he's the first one of us who doesn't think in terms of the proscenium arch. With him, there's nothing but the camera lens."

It's not only the visual technique of *Jaws* that's different. The other big disaster movies are essentially the same as the pre-Vietnam films, but *Jaws* isn't. It belongs to the pulpiest sci-fi monster-movie tradition, yet it stands some of the old conventions on their head. Though *Jaws* has more zest than a Woody Allen picture, and a lot more electricity, it's funny in a Woody Allen way. When the three protagonists are in their tiny boat, you feel that Robert Shaw, the malevolent old shark hunter, is so manly that he wants to get them all killed; he's so manly he's homicidal. It's not sharks who are his enemies; it's other men. When he begins showing off his wounds, the bookish ichthyologist, Richard Dreyfuss, strings along with him at first, and matches him scar for scar. But when the ichthyologist is outclassed in the number of scars he can exhibit, he opens his shirt, looks down at his hairy chest, and with a put-on artist's grin says, "You see that? Right there? That was Mary Ellen Moffit—she broke my heart." When Shaw squeezes an empty beer can flat, Dreyfuss satirizes him by crumpling a Styrofoam cup. The director, identifying with the Dreyfuss character, sets up bare-chested heroism as a joke and scores off it all through the movie. The third protagonist, acted by Roy Scheider, is a former New York City policeman who has just escaped the city dangers and found a haven as chief of police in a resort community on an island. There, feeling totally inadequate in his new situation, he confronts primal terror. But the fool on board the little boat isn't the chief of police who doesn't know one end of a boat from the other, or the bookman, either. It's Shaw, the obsessively masculine fisherman, who thinks he's got to prove himself by fighting the shark practically single-handed. Shaw personalizes the shark, turns him into a fourth character—his enemy. This fisherman is such a macho pain that it's harrowingly funny when he's gobbled up; a flamboyant actor like Robert Shaw, who wears a proscenium arch around him, has to be kidded.

The high point of the film's humor is in our seeing Shaw get it; this nut Ahab, with his hyper-masculine basso-profundo speeches, stands in for all the men who have to show they're tougher than anybody. The shark's cavernous jaws demonstrate how little his toughness finally adds up to. If one imagines George C. Scott or Anthony Quinn in the Robert Shaw role, these anti-macho jokes expand into a satire of movie heroism.

The actor who has put our new, ambivalent feelings about the warrior male to account is Jack Nicholson. Despite his excessive dynamism (and maybe partly because of it), this satirical actor has probably gone further into the tragicomedy of hardhat macho than any other actor. He exposes cracks in barroom-character armor and makes those cracks funny, in a low-down, grungy way. With his horny leers and his little-boy cockiness and one-upmanship, he illuminates the sources of male bravado. His whole acting style is based on the little guy coming on strong, because being a tough guy is the only ideal he's ever aspired to. This little guy doesn't make it, of course; Nicholson is the macho loser-hero. (In an earlier era, Nicholson would probably have played big guys.)

When you see the celebration of adolescent male fantasies in the film *The Yakuza*, directed by Sydney Pollack, or in a John Milius picture—

Dillinger or *The Wind and the Lion*—you may wonder of the filmmakers, "Are these boys being naughty just because they're old enough not to be scolded by their mothers?" That's the kind of naughtiness Jack Nicholson keeps us aware of; he includes it in his performances. He's the kind of actor who gives you a character and then lets you follow him around the corner and watch as he reacts to what he just pulled off back there.

The most ambiguous bumper sticker I've ever seen was "Thank God for John Wayne," though it wasn't ambiguous for the people who had put it on—they had also plastered two decals for the Patrolmen's Benevolent Association on their car windows. Yet even their assertive clinging to the old Wayne image—the very one that he can't cling to anymore himself—speaks of the changes they must feel around them. They want something that can't come back.

In recent years, John Wayne has been looking for a new image, and that great bulk has been falling flat. You can see now that, though Wayne was never much of an actor, there was a ham underneath just the same; he'd rather turn his mythic Western hero into a clown than quit. Wayne is so transparent an actor that he's foolishly likable, and so when he tries to play a Clint Eastwood city-cop role (as in *McQ*), you may feel embarrassed for him. (You don't get embarrassed by anything Clint Eastwood does; he's so hollow you don't have to feel a thing.)

In *The Shootist*, Wayne attempts to go back and complete his Western legend, but it's always dangerous when a movie sets out to be a classic, and the director, Don Siegel, who has an enjoyably trashy talent, has been so paralyzed by his high intentions that he's made a piece of solemn, unenjoyable trash. *The Shootist* has no emotional movement, despite Wayne, who has the dignity here that he'd lost in *Rooster Cogburn*. As an aged gunfighter dying of cancer, he's a noble figure; he knows the movie is trucking him out to exhibit that nobility, and he's got the farewell-tour catch in the throat. He's like an old dancer who can only do a few steps yet does them with great pride and style. The film, however, is a rigged setup. There's no conflict, no tension in his encounters with the small-minded townspeople; the old man, with his Westerner's code, is always morally superior. The bad operators in town want to get him, but he's such a nice guy you can't figure out what they've got against him, and in the climax he arbitrarily selects the three men in town who need killing without our ever understanding what they've done. In 1976, after the Western hero is dead, how can movies go on bringing us the message that he's dying? *The Shootist* digs him up to rebury him, and then has the gall to tell the story of how other people want to exploit him. Siegel has no real interest in the code; he's in his element when he stages the final shoot-out, but there's no rationale for it—no greed, no anger, and no moral drive.

The stirring, emotionally satisfying early Westerns had a narrative push forward, a belief in the future of a people. That epic spirit has—understandably—been missing from recent Westerns. It comes back in a new form in the surprising *The Return of a Man Called Horse*; in this Western, the surge of elation comes from the spiritual rebirth of an Indian tribe. The hero is John Morgan, an English lord, played by Richard Harris. In the earlier *A Man Called Horse*, Morgan was captured by the Yellow Hand, a tribe of the Sioux nation; he was accepted as a brother, and, free, returned to his own country. The new picture, directed by Irvin Kershner, is about how, once having known that brotherhood and accepted its magical religion, he is lost as a white man. We see Morgan in his English mansion, and his face shows that he's split off from the life around him; his soul has become Indian. The early part of the film, which cuts from an attack on the Yellow Hand to a foxhunt in England, has an emotional power that is almost comparable to that of the early scenes of *The Godfather, Part II*, and the sequence that replaces the usual cattle drive is of supernal landscapes—the dark shapes of buffalo running over blinding pale-green meadows. Despite a pulpy script and the sometimes awkward acting, *The Return of a Man Called Horse* may be the first Hollywood epic in which the rituals of the Indians make sense. Driven off their land, their braves killed, their young women enslaved, the Yellow Hand have become so weak that they have even lost the will to hunt buffalo. Morgan and some of the children take on themselves the burden of suffering. When, through this sacrifice, the Yellow Hand satisfy their gods, they are able to triumph over their enemies and regain their homeland, and the English lord is content to be one of the tribe. This Western, with its Old Testament mysticism, which appears to be authentically Indian as well, is a startlingly affirmative vision.

A few decades ago, if a character in a novel did something irrational—that is, out of character—the other people in the book would say, "It's so unlike

John to have done that," and we'd read on for chapters to find out why he had behaved so uncharacteristically. The characters in movies also used to operate from a fixed position: if they were proper, they were supposed to look proper, and behave within certain patterns. What we call spontaneity now would have been called irrationality then. But since there are no set codes of behavior today, we accept the irrational. We like the diversion of surprising behavior in movies; we don't respond to those Charlton Heston heroes who lack irrational impulses. And we don't want over-elaborated motivation—we want just enough for us to get the sense of what a person is about.

In *Dog Day Afternoon*, we don't want any explanation of how it is that Sonny (Al Pacino) lives in both heterosexual and homosexual marriages. We accept the idea because we don't really believe in patterns of behavior anymore—only in behavior. Sonny, who is trapped in the middle of robbing a bank, with a crowd gathering in the street outside, is a working-class man who got into this mess by trying to raise money for Leon (Chris Sarandon) to have a sex-change operation, yet the audience doesn't laugh. The most touching element in the film is Sonny's inability to handle all the responsibilities he has assumed. Though he is half-crazed by his situation, he is trying to do the right thing by everybody—his wife and children, the suicidal Leon, the hostages in the bank. In the sequence in which Sonny dictates his will, we can see that inside this ludicrous bungling robber there's a complicatedly unhappy man, operating out of a sense of noblesse oblige.

The structure of *Dog Day Afternoon* loosens in the last three-quarters of an hour, but that was the part I particularly cared for. This picture is one of the most satisfying of all the movies starring New York City because the director, Sidney Lumet, and the screenwriter, Frank Pierson, having established that Sonny's grandstanding gets the street crowd on his side against the cops, and that even the tellers are on his side, let us move into the dark, confused areas of Sonny's frustrations and don't explain everything to us. They trust us to feel without our being told how to feel. They prepare us for a confrontation scene between Sonny and Leon, and it never comes, but even that is all right, because of the way that Pacino and Sarandon handle their contact by telephone; Sonny's anxiety and Leon's distress are so pure that there's no appeal for sympathy—no star kitsch to separate us from the nakedness of the feelings on the screen.

This kind of male acting is becoming much more common in movies. In the past, the corruption of stardom has often meant that the actor was afraid of carrying a role through and exposing the insides of a character; a star began to have so large a stake in his own image that he was afraid of what the audience might think of the revelation. But new stars such as Pacino and Nicholson and Gene Hackman and Robert De Niro go as far into their characters as they can psychologically allow themselves to go; that's how they work. Robert Redford *could* do that, but he has been holding back—he doesn't want you not to like the people he plays.

Yet if Redford is the closest thing we've got to the self-congratulatory American Protestant Eagle who flourished in the Second World War movies, that eagle has had his wings clipped. Redford, with his glamorous remoteness and passivity, combines the romantic appeal of the inverts and the matinée idols of those days with a new, uneasy consciousness that is supposed to account for his passivity. The new heroes don't soar; they can barely see straight. The myopically spacey Timothy Bottoms plays such characters as the gentlest and least harmful of the representative Americans in *The White Dawn*; he's frazzled, out of it, ineffective. One of the reasons that there are so few women's roles is that men have coöpted them. In earlier decades, if a hero wanted something he went out and got it. Uncertainty was the basis of many of the women stars' roles; the women asked, "Do I dare?" and sat at home, wheedling and plotting. Now that the men are so uncertain, what could a woman wheedle out of them?

In primitive societies, and in this country until quite recently, a man proved his courage by exposing himself to a dangerous test. If there's any equivalent to that now, it's exposing himself to the danger of going crazy—so crazy that he loses the capacity to feel. (And women do it too.)

Historically, people have recognized strong individuals as heroes or heroines by their willingness to accept the responsibility for their acts. And in the past if a movie hero broke the law because he felt he had to, we could respect him for it, because we knew—as he did—that there would be consequences, and not only legal and social consequences but moral ones, too. Now we're in a period when we know that most wrongdoing—the worst wrongdoing especially—isn't socially punished. And it's terribly apparent that the wrongdoers face no moral consequences. So it's not surprising that the standard action-movie heroes today aren't men who, after searching their consciences, violate the law; the heroes now are law-breakers at heart. What appears to separate them from the villains is that they're lawbreakers trying to confirm that they're courageous men. Whether they seek this confirmation of their masculinity on the police force or in crime or, like the rebel McMurphy, in an insane asylum, they're all lawless. On TV, when cops like Baretta (who's all heart) or the slimy-smart Starsky and Hutch club someone on the head, they explain that there was no other way. The law doesn't apply to them, and reading a prisoner his Miranda rights is just a joke, since they know their prisoners are guilty. And lawbreakers like the Burt Reynolds heroes know that if they're arrested the cops will kick the hell out of them, so the Miranda rights are a joke to them, too. The bond between the lawless cops and the law-breakers is contempt for the law.

When there doesn't appear to be any alternative to Clint Eastwood's relentless law-givers and Burt Reynolds' self-satisfied lawbreakers, it's easy to see why we get Ken Russell and *Tommy*, who isn't a man, but a numb child. It's as if the tough-guy movies said, "Either you feel our way or you feel nothing." Androgynous catatonia is the answer to repulsive macho. The alternative to *Macon County Line* and *Walking Tall* and *White Line Fever* sure as hell isn't Fred Astaire anymore; it's closer to David Bowie.

Nicolas Roeg's *The Man Who Fell to Earth*, which stars David Bowie, is *The Little Prince* for young adults; the hero, a stranger on earth, is purity made erotic. He doesn't have a human sex drive; he isn't even equipped for it—naked, he's as devoid of sex differentiation as a child in sleepers. (He seems to be the first movie hero to have had his crotch airbrushed.) Yet there's true insolence in Bowie's lesbian-Christ leering, and his forlorn, limp manner and chalky pallor are alluringly tainted. Lighted like the woman of mystery in thirties' movies, he's the most romantic figure in recent pictures—the modern version of the James Dean lost-boy myth. Nicolas Roeg has a talent for eerily easy, soft, ambiguous sex—for the sexiness of passivity. In his *Don't Look Now*, Donald Sutherland practically oozed passivity—which was the only interesting quality he had. And at the beginning of *The Man Who Fell to Earth* (which was shot in this country with an American cast except for Bowie), when the stranger splashes down in a lake in the Southwest and drinks water like a vampire gulping down his lifeblood, one is drawn in, fascinated by the obliqueness and by the promise of an erotic sci-fi story. It is and it isn't. The stranger, though non-human, has visions of the wife and kiddies he has left—an old-fashioned nuclear family on the planet Anthea. He has come to earth to obtain the water that will save his people, who are dying from drought, but he is corrupted, is distracted from his mission, and then is so damaged that he cannot return. Although Roeg and his screenwriter, Paul Mayersberg, pack layers of tragic political allegory into *The Man Who Fell to Earth*, none of the layers is very strong, or even very clear. The plot, about big-business machinations, is so uninvolving that one watches Bowie traipsing around—looking like Katharine Hepburn in her transvestite role in *Sylvia Scarlett*—and either tunes out or allows the film, with its perverse pathos, to become a sci-fi framework for a sex-role-confusion fantasy. The wilted solitary stranger who is better than we are and yet falls prey to our corrupt human estate can be said to represent everyone who feels misunderstood, everyone who feels sexually immature or "different," everyone who has lost his way, everyone who has failed his holy family, and so the film is a gigantic launching pad for anything that viewers want to drift to.

A former cinematographer, Roeg has more visual strategies than almost any director one can think of. He can charge a desolate landscape so that it seems ominously alive, familiar yet only half recognizable, and he photographs skyscrapers with such lyric glitter that the United States seems to be showing off for him (the better to be despoiled). The people pass through, floating, using the country without seeing its beauty. Roeg's cutting can create a magical feeling of waste and evil, but at other times his Marienbadish jumpiness is just trickery he can't resist. In *The Man Who Fell to Earth*, the unease and sense of disconnectedness between characters also disconnect us. Roeg teases us with a malaise that he then moralizes about. His effects stay on the surface; they become off-puttingly abstract, and his lyricism goes sentimental—as most other Christ movies do. In *Blow-Up* and *The Passenger*, Antonioni showed a talent (and a propensity) for mystification; it would be a present to audiences if just once he would use his talent frivolously—if, instead of his usual opaque metaphysical mystery, he'd make a simple trashy mystery, preferably in those *Réalités* travel spots he's drawn to. And it would be a blessing if Nicolas Roeg—perhaps the most visually seductive of directors, a man who can make impotence sexy—turned himself loose on the romance of waste.

...

Bowie's self-mocking androgyny is not a quality that one associates with the heroes of imperial nations. Imperial movie heroes are just about gone, and even much of what comes out on the American screen as sexism isn't necessarily the result of conviction; it may be the sexist result of simple convenience. In the movies or on television, the two cops in the police car don't have to think about each other. When a cop-hero's partner is shot, it's supposed to be worse than anything, but the reason it's worse than anything is always explained *after* he's been shot. Then the survivor—let's call him Frank—explains that Jim took the bullet for him, that Jim was the one Frank spent more time with than anyone else. And Frank's wife can say, "Frank and Jim were more married than we are"—and she says it sympathetically. She understands. The theme of mateship is such a clean, visible bond. It doesn't have the hidden traps of the relationship between men and women, or between lovers of the same sex. In a number of movies, the actors playing the two cops seem palpably embarrassed by the notion that women are those creatures who come into the story for a minute and you jump them. Some are embarrassed that that's all you do with them; others are relieved that that's all you have to do—because if there's anything more it may involve the problem of what men are supposed to be in relation to women.

Two human beings who are sexually and emotionally involved cause pain to each other, and it takes more skill than most writers and directors have to deal with that pain. Besides, with the Supreme Court decision leaving the determination of what is pornography to the communities, almost any treatment of the psychology of sex may get a film into serious legal problems. The porno filmmakers, whose investment may be thirty-five thousand dollars a picture, are closed in one city, hop to another, and come back with a few cuts or a different title. Porno films are all over the place, so it looks as if the screen is wide-open, but actually the studios aren't taking chances on sexual themes.

The changes in movies, responding to the changes in the national psychology, have come about mostly unconsciously. The comedies now are almost all made by Jewish directors—directors who are themselves anarchic comics. Comedies are no longer about how to win or how to be a success, but about trying to function in the general craziness. Some of the veteran directors may face insoluble problems—a director's craft isn't enough to see him through when that craft is itself an expression of the old, fixed patterns. In a country where the Protestant ethic doesn't seem to have worked out too well, it makes sense that directors of Catholic background—Francis Ford Coppola and Brian De Palma, of Italian-Catholic parents; Martin Scorsese, of Sicilian origins; Robert Altman, from a German-Catholic family in Kansas City, Missouri—speak to the way Americans feel now. These men have grown up with a sense of sin and a deep-seated feeling that things aren't going to get much better in this life. They're not uplifters or reformers, like some of the Protestant directors of an earlier era, or muckraking idealists, like some of the earlier Jewish directors. Pictures such as *Mean Streets* and *Taxi Driver, California Split* and *Nashville, The Godfather, Part II,* and the new *Carrie* combine elements of ritual and of poetry in their heightened realism. The Catholic directors examine American experience in emotional terms, without much illusion—in fact, with macabre humor. The Western heroes faced choices between right and wrong; these directors didn't grow up on right-and-wrong but on good-and-evil—and then they lost the good.

If *Jaws* represents a new affability about the tough American male, it also contains a token of a new ruthlessness. There's a lull in the action, a becalmed interlude, which is filled by a long monologue delivered by Robert Shaw. He tells the ultimate shark horror story—it's worse, even, than anything that we see in the movie. The story he tells concerns the men of the *Indianapolis,* a heavy cruiser that was torpedoed after delivering key elements of the atomic bombs to be dropped on Japan. As Shaw, in drunken, sepulchral tones, describes the events, the survivors were attacked by sharks, which returned day after day, using the ever-smaller group of survivors as a feeding ground. Actually, it is not known how many of the *Indianapolis* crew died because of sharks, or how many died from exposure, or from injuries sustained when the ship was hit. The monologue, conceived by Howard Sackler, embellished to a length of nine pages by John Milius, and then trimmed by Spielberg and Shaw to a feasible length, could easily have dealt with a fictitious ship, but using the correct name gave it an extra plausibility. In the rest of *Jaws,* we're worked over right in the open, but in this *Indianapolis* episode we're fooled by a hidden confusion of historical fact and sadistic fantasy. The writers probably didn't consider—or were simply indifferent to—the nightmarish pain that their gothic embroidery would give to the relatives of the men who died in those waters.

The only morality that many of the best young filmmakers appear to have is an aesthetic morality. They may show us geysers of blood that tear us apart, but they're true to what they think is good filmmaking. In their movies, the human logic is secondary to the aesthetic logic. A movie is like a musical composition to them: they'll put in a bloody climax because they need it at a certain point. They're not afraid of the manipulative possibilities of the medium; they revel in those possibilities and play with them. Catholic imagery has a kind of ruthlessness anyway—the bleeding Jesus, the pierced, suffering saints. But even without a Catholic background, Spielberg is as ruthlessly manipulative as Scorsese or De Palma (though he doesn't rely on instinct as much as they do—he plans, like Eisenstein). Film is their common religion. For some people in the audience, their films may be too shocking; they overwhelm us emotionally in a way that more crudely manipulative directors don't, and so people tend to become much more outraged by a *Taxi Driver* than by a *Towering Inferno*.

New action films often seem to be trying so hard to beat the tube that they reach right out to grab us—not with the technique of a Steven Spielberg but by crowding out any aesthetic distance. There has always been an element of dread in the pleasure of suspense movies, but it was tangled up with childish, fairy-tale excitement and the knowledge that the characters we cared about would come out safe; the dread was part of the fun. But in many current movies the suspense is nothing more than dread. The only thing that keeps us watching some films is the fear of what the moviemakers are going to throw at us next. We don't anticipate the climactic scenes pleasurably; we await them anxiously, and after the usual two hours of assault the punishment stops, and we go home relieved, yet helplessly angry.

On the basis that they can't say they were bored, large numbers of people seem willing to accept heavily advertised shock-and-dread pictures (such as *Marathon Man*) as entertainment. But in a neat cultural switch, a sizable number of educated people who used to complain of Hollywood's innocuous pampering, and who went to foreign films for adult entertainment, now escape to bland French romances, such as the Lelouch pictures or *Cousin, Cousine*, to find the same innocent reassurance that the mass audience used to obtain. They've become afraid of American movies, and not just of the junk but of *The Godfather, Part II*, *Nashville*, and the best this country has to offer. They're turning to Europe for cuddly sentiments —for make-out movies. The success of *Cousin, Cousine*, a rhythmless, mediocre piece of moviemaking, may be in part attributable to its winsome heroine (Marie-Christine Barrault), who is sexy in a fleshy smiling-nun way, and in part to its silliness. With its wholesome carnality, *Cousin, Cousine* is so pro-life that it treats sex like breakfast cereal. It features adultery without dirt—adultery as carefree nonconformity—and the way the chorus of understanding kids applauds the parents' displays of innocent happy sensuality this could be the first Disney True Life Adventure about people.

{*The New Yorker*, November 8, 1976}

:: Hot Air

In *Network*, Paddy Chayefsky blitzes you with one idea after another. The ideas don't go together, but who knows which of them he believes, anyway? He's like a Village crazy bellowing at you: blacks are taking over, revolutionaries are taking over, women are taking over. He's got the New York City hatreds, and ranting makes him feel alive. There *is* something funny in this kind of rant—it was funny in Fred Wiseman's *Welfare*, too; with the number of things that are going wrong in the city, it's a bottomless comedy to see people pinning their rage on some one object, person, or group, or a pet collection of them. Cabdrivers used to get it off on Mayor Lindsay, liberals on the moon landings, and now Chayefsky's getting it off on television. Television, he says, is turning us into morons and humanoids; people have lost the ability to love. Who— him? Oh, no, the blacks, the revolutionaries, and a power-hungry executive at the UBS network named Diana Christensen (Faye Dunaway). In Chayefsky's 1958 movie *The Goddess*, the Marilyn Monroe–type heroine (Kim Stanley) sought movie stardom, fame, and adulation in order to compensate for her inability to love. This empty girl was supposed to symbolize our dreams; moviegoers were his morons then. Chayefsky said in 1958 that his heroine "represents an entire generation that came through the Depression with nothing left but a hope for comfort and security. Their tragedy lies in that they never learned to love, either their fellow humans or whatever god they have." God and love came together in his 1959 play *The Tenth Man*, which ended with an old man saying of the hero, whose demon (of lovelessness) had been exorcised, "He still doesn't believe in God—he simply wants to love—and when you stop and think about it, gentlemen, is there any difference?" This mushy amalgam of God and love

545

is Chayefsky's faith, and if you don't share it you're tragic. The new goddess, the unprincipled career girl Diana Christensen, is explained in *Network* in these terms: "She's television generation. She learned life from Bugs Bunny. The only reality she knows comes to her over the TV set." What Chayefsky is really complaining about is what barroom philosophers have always complained about: the soulless worshippers at false shrines—the younger generation.

In Chayefsky's last film, *The Hospital* (1971), the fiftyish Jewish chief of medicine (George C. Scott) has lost his potency, fails at suicide, and is disappointed in his children; he blows off steam about what's wrong with the society but ridicules the Puerto Rican community-action groups who march on the hospital. After an affair with a young Wasp (Diana Rigg), who urges him to leave with her, he decides that *somebody* has to be decent and responsible, and so, with his potency restored, he stays to make his stand for sanity. Youth-baiting played a strong part in *The Hospital*, but Chayefsky's slapstick exaggeration of the chaos in a big-city institution had so much silly, likable crackpot verve that the diatribes against the disrespectful younger generation could be shrugged aside. *Network*, however, is all baiting—youth, TV, the culture, the universe. The UBS network has been taken over by a conglomerate, and Howard Beale (Peter Finch), a veteran anchorman whose ratings have slipped, is given two weeks' notice by executives who want to jazz up the news to make it more entertaining. Angry at being dumped, Beale goes out of control, and his blasts on the air about "this demented slaughterhouse of a world we live in"—blasts sprinkled with cusswords—accomplish what his restrained behavior didn't: his ratings go up. His best friend, the head of the news division—the fiftyish hero, Max Schumacher (William Holden), who is Paddy Chayefsky in the guise of the unimpeachable Ed Murrow—loses his fight to keep the news independent. The chief of operations (Robert Duvall) fires him and turns the news division over to Diana Christensen, the vice-president in charge of programming. So when Beale begins to have visions (either he's having a breakdown or he's in a state of religious exaltation) and is advertised as "the Mad Prophet of the airwaves," Schumacher is on the sidelines, and has nothing to do but hang around Diana Christensen, with whom he has an affair, and denounce her, television, and us soulless masses. The Mad Prophet and the sane prophet both deliver broadsides—enough to break a viewer's back. The screen seems to be plastered with bumper stickers.

The central gag in *Network*—Howard Beale becomes the first man killed because of lousy ratings—sounds like a good premise for a farce about TV, which has certainly earned farce status. (And, even if it hadn't, satire doesn't have to be fair to be funny.) But in the *Network* script Chayefsky isn't writing a farce: he's telling us a thing or two. And he writes directly to the audience—he soapboxes. He hardly bothers with the characters; the movie is a ventriloquial harangue. He thrashes around in messianic God-love booziness, driving each scene to an emotional peak. When Schumacher tells his wife (Beatrice Straight) that he's in love with Diana, his wife launches into a high-powered speech about "all the senseless pain that we've inflicted on each other," referring to his affair as "your last roar of passion before you settle into your menopausal years." It's a short, self-contained soap opera; she hits her peak—then she's invisible again. The director, Sidney Lumet, keeps the soliloquies going at a machine-gun pace. The movie might have been modelled on that earlier talk binge, Billy Wilder's *One, Two, Three*; Lumet is right—it's best not to let the words sink in. With Schumacher experiencing a "winter passion" and discussing his "primal doubts," you have to hurtle through to the next crisis. Lumet does Chayefsky straight, just as Chayefsky no doubt wanted. The film looks negligently made; the lighting bleaches the actors' faces, like color TV that needs tuning, and the New York views outside the office and apartment windows feel like blown-up photographs. The timing in most of the scenes is so careless that you may be aware of the laugh lines you're not responding to, and there's a confusing cut from Diana and Schumacher planning to go to bed together to Howard Beale in bed by himself. *Network* even fails to show the executives at meetings getting carried away by the infectiousness of Diana Christensen's ideas—getting high on power. But Lumet keeps it all moving.

Chayefsky is such a manic bard that I'm not sure if he ever decided whether Howard Beale's epiphanies were the result of a nervous breakdown or were actually inspired by God. Yet Beale's story has a fanciful, Frank Capra nuttiness that could be appealing. Peter Finch's sleepy-lion head suggests the bland, prosperous decay of an anchorman whose boredom is swathed in punditry. His gray aureole is perfect: the curly, thick hair, cropped short, is the only vigorous thing about him. (Does Finch, who is British-Australian, seem American? Not really, but then does Eric Sevareid, who comes from North Dakota?) If Chayefsky meant Beale to represent his idealized vision of the crusading mandarin journalists of an earlier day who are now being replaced by show-biz anchorpersons, Finch is miscast, but his fuzzy mildness is likable, and in a picture in which everybody seems to take turns at screaming (Robert Duvall screams the loudest) Finch's ability to seem reserved even when he's raving has its own satirical charm. Unfortunately, when Beale's wild-eyed ramblings are supposed to make his ratings zoom up, you can't believe it; he doesn't give off enough heat.

Beale the Prophet's big moment comes when he tells TV viewers to open their windows, stick out their heads, and yell, "I'm mad as hell and I'm not going to take this anymore!" But is the viewers' obedience proof of their sheeplike response to TV or is it evidence that the Prophet has struck a nerve — that the public is as fed up as he is? Considering that the entire picture is Chayefsky sticking his head out the window and yelling (in Chayefsky's world, that's how you prove that you're capable of love), it must be that Beale's message is supposed to be salutary. Yet there's no follow-through on this scene, and that's where the movie goes completely on the fritz. Chayefsky whirrs off in other directions — Max's winter passion for Diana, and the Saudi Arabians taking over the conglomerate.

Early on, Howard Beale is awakened at night by the voice of the Lord or some Heavenly Messenger, who affectionately calls him "Dummy" and tells him what he must do on the air. The voice may be simply Beale's delusion, but how are we to interpret the turn of events when Beale is summoned to a meeting with the piggy-eyed master salesman Arthur Jensen (Ned Beatty), the head of the conglomerate, and Jensen addresses him as "Dummy"? Jensen, a corn-pone Grand Inquisitor, tells Beale that the multinational corporate state is the natural order of things now, and that he should embrace this one-business world, in which all men will be taken care of as humanoids. Converted, Beale asks the TV audience, "Is dehumanization such a bad word?" He preaches his new corporate faith — "The world is a business . . . one vast, ecumenical holding company." But people don't want to hear that their individual lives are valueless; he loses his ratings and is killed for it. Chayefsky, it seems, can be indignant about people becoming humanoids, and then turn a somersault and say it's inevitable and only a fool wouldn't recognize that. And he's wrong on both counts. There are a lot of changes in the society which can be laid at television's door, but soullessness isn't one of them. TV may have altered family life and social intercourse; it may have turned children at school into entertainment seekers. But it hasn't taken our souls, any more than movies did, or the theatre and novels before them. I don't know what's worse— Beale's denunciations of the illiterate public (Chayefsky apparently thinks that not reading is proof of soullessness) or Schumacher's pitying tone. When Schumacher tells Diana Christensen that she can feel nothing, while he's O.K. because he can feel pleasure and pain and love, you want to kick him. Doesn't Chayefsky realize that everybody can feel—even a kittycat?

The screw-up inside Chayefsky's message of kindness shows in the delight he takes in snide reactionary thrusts. Diana Christensen has no difficulty coöpting an Angela Davis–like activist (Marlene Warfield), the Communist central committee, and an extremist group that's a parody of the Symbionese Liberation Army and the Black Panthers. (Chayefsky can't even resist a sideswipe at Patty Hearst.) Christensen propositions them to perform terrorist crimes—kidnappings, robberies, hijackings— on a weekly basis, in front of a camera crew, and their only quarrel is over money. Whatever one's disagreements with Angela Davis, she's hardly a sellout. Yet Chayefsky's venom is such an exuberant part of him that the best scene in the movie is the slapstick negotiating session in which the black revolutionaries, their agents, and the network attorneys haggle over residuals and syndication rights, and a revolutionary who wants to be heard fires his pistol to get some order. This is in the paranoid-comic-strip style of Norman Wexler, the scriptwriter for *Joe*, *Serpico*, and *Mandingo*. Chayefsky's speeches may be about humanism, but baiting gets the old adrenalin going.

And what of Diana Christensen, the hopped-up *Cosmopolitan* doll with power on the brain? Look at her name: the goddess of the hunt, and some sort of essence of Christianity? In bed, on top of Schumacher, she talks ratings until orgasm. Chayefsky, in interviews, actually claims that he has created one of the few movie roles in which a woman is treated as an equal; this can be interpreted to mean that he thinks women who want equality are ditsey little twitches—ruthless, no-souled monsters who take men's jobs away from them. Diana Christensen is, Schumacher says, "television incarnate"—that is, she is symptomatic of what's spoiling our society. And, in case we don't get Chayefsky's drift, he presents us with that contrasting image of a loving woman who has the capacity for suffering—Max's wife, to whom he returns after he leaves rotten Diana.

As Schumacher, Holden is in good form, and now that he has stopped trying to conceal the aging process his sunken-cheeked, lined, craggy face takes the camera marvellously—he has a real face, like Gabin or Montand. He does a lot for the movie—he's an actor with authority and the gift of never being boring—but he can't energize the phoniness of a man who claims to be superior to his society. This hero is trampling out the vintage where the sour grapes of wrath are stored. Dunaway chatters as Kim Stanley did in *The Goddess* (Chayefsky must believe that women talk because of their tinny empty-headedness), and even when she's supposed to be reduced to a pitiful shell by Holden's exposing her "shrieking nothingness" she's ticky and amusingly greedy. She snarls at underlings and walks with a bounce and a wiggle. In the past, Dunaway hasn't had much humor or variety; her performances have usually been proficient yet uneventful—there's a certain heaviness, almost of depression, about them. It's that heaviness, probably, that has made some people think her Garboesque. A beautiful woman who's as self-conscious as Faye Dunaway has a special neurotic magnetism. (The far less proficient Kim Novak had it also.) In this stunt role, her usual self-consciousness is turned into comic rapport with the audience; she's not the remote, neurotic beauty—she's more of a clown. And though her Diana isn't remotely convincing—she's not a woman with a drive to power, she's just a dirty Mary Tyler Moore—it's a relief to see Dunaway being light. She puts us on the side of the humanoids.

The watered-down Freudianism that Chayefsky goes in for—i.e., people want fame or power because they're sick—seems to get by almost everywhere these days. It became popular with those analysts who, taking Hitler's crimes as evidence, deduced that he was sexually crippled; they really seemed to think they were explaining something. And it spread in TV drama and in movies as a form of vindictive, moralizing condescension. The trick in *Network*, as in *The Goddess*, is to use a woman's drive toward fame or success as the embodiment of the sickness in the society. What's implicit is that if she could love she wouldn't need anything more. You couldn't get by with this bulling if a man were television incarnate.

Network starts in high gear and is so confidently brash that maybe people can really take it for muckraking. But it's no more than the kind of inside story that a lot of TV executives probably would secretly like to write. Chayefsky comes on like a patriarchal Jackie Susann, and he likes to frolic with the folksy occult. What happened to his once much-vaunted gift for the vernacular? Nothing exposes his claims to be defending the older values as much as the way he uses four-letter words for chortles. It's so cheap you may never want to say **** again. Chayefsky doesn't come right out and tell us why he thinks TV is *goyish*, but it must have something to do with his notion that all feeling is Jewish.

{*The New Yorker*, December 6, 1976}

:: Marguerite Duras

Most of the well-known writers who have tried to direct movies have gone at it briefly and given up in frustration. Cocteau was an exception; Marguerite Duras is another. She has been writing scripts since 1959 (*Hiroshima, Mon Amour*) and directing her own scripts since 1966, and the control in her new film, *Le Camion — The Truck —* suggests that she has become a master. But there's a joker in her mastery: though her moods and cadences, her rhythmic phrasing, with its emotional undertow, might seem ideally suited to the medium, they don't fulfill moviegoers' expectations. Conditioned from childhood, people go to the movies wanting the basic gratification of a story acted out. Many directors have tried to alter this conditioning, breaking away from the simplest narrative traditions, and they've failed to take the largest audience with them. Duras doesn't even get near the mass of moviegoers, though somehow — God knows how — she manages to make her own pictures, her own way. Hers is possibly the most sadomasochistic of all director relationships with the audience: she drives people out of the theatre, while, no doubt, scorning them for their childish obtuseness. At the same time, she must be suffering from her lack of popularity. Her battle with the audience reaches a new stage in *The Truck*, in which the split between her artistry and what the public wants is pointed up and turned against the audience. She brings it off, but she's doing herself in, too. And so it isn't a simple prank.

There are only two people in *The Truck*: Marguerite Duras and Gérard Depardieu. They sit at a round table in a room in her home, and never leave it. Small and bundled up, her throat covered, her unlined moon face serene, half-smiling, Duras reads aloud the script of a film in which Depardieu would act the role of a truck driver who picks up a woman hitchhiker.

He would drive and ask a question or two; the woman would talk. Depardieu doesn't actually play the truck driver: this actor, whose physical and emotional weight can fill up the screen, is used as a nonprofessional. He merely listens trustingly, a friend, a student, as Duras reads. Hers is the only performance, and there has never been anything like it: controlling the whole movie visibly, from her position on the screen as creator-star, she is so assured that there is no skittish need for makeup, no nerves, quick gestures, tics. The self-image she presents is that of a woman past deception; she has the grandly simple manner of a sage. Unhurriedly, with the trained patience of authority, she tells the story of her movie-to-be about the woman hitchhiker—a woman of shifting identities, who drops clues about her life which are fragments and echoes of Duras' earlier works. This woman, a composite Duras heroine, strews a trail of opaque references to Duras' youth in Indo-China (the daughter of two French teachers, Marguerite Duras spent her first seventeen years there), and when the hitchhiker talks to the truck driver about her disillusion with the politics of revolution, and says that she has lost faith in the proletariat, that she believes in nothing anymore—"Let the world go to rack and ruin"—she speaks, unmistakably, for Duras herself. *The Truck* is a spiritual autobiography, a life's-journey, end-of-the-world road movie; it's a summing up, an endgame. The hitchhiker travels in a winter desert; she's from anywhere and going nowhere, in motion to stay alive. Reading the script, Duras speaks in the perfect conditional tense, beginning "It would have been a film—therefore, it is a film." And this tense carries a note of regret: it suggests that the script is to be realized only by our listening and imagining.

Her seductive voice prepares us for the unfolding of the action, and when there is a cut from the two figures at the table to a big blue truck moving silently through cold and drizzle in the working-class flatlands west of Paris, we're eager to see the man and woman inside. But we don't get close enough to see anyone. The truck crawls along in the exurbanite slum, where housing developments and supermarkets loom up in the void, Pop ruins. Its movement is noiseless, ominously so; the only sound is that of Beethoven's "Diabelli" Variations, and the images and music never quite come together rhythmically. With nothing synchronized, the effect is of doomsday loneliness. Quiet is Duras' weapon. The Beethoven is played softly, so that we reach toward it. The stillness provides resonance for her lingering words—those drifting thoughts that sound elegant, fated—and for the music, and for the cinematographer Bruno Nuytten's love-hate vistas of bareness and waste, like the New Jersey Turnpike in pastels. The foreboding melancholy soaks so deep into our consciousness that when the director yanks us back to the room, you may hear yourself gasp at the effrontery of this stoic, contained little woman with her mild, Chairman Mao deadpan. When we were with the truck, even without seeing anyone in it we felt that "the movie"—our primitive sense of a movie—was about to begin. And it's an emotional wrench, a classic rude awakening, to be sent back to Square One, the room. The film alternates between sequences in the room and sequences of the rolling truck, always at a distance. Each time she cuts to the outdoors, you're drawn into the hypnotic flow of the road imagery, and though you know perfectly well there will be nothing but the truck in the landscape, you half dream your way into a "real" movie. And each time you find yourself back with Duras, you're aware of being treated like a chump, your childishness exposed.

Buñuel played a similar narrative game in parts of *The Discreet Charm of the Bourgeoisie*, parodying the audience's gullibility by involving us in scary ghost stories and then casually interrupting them. But that was only one of his games and he wasn't onscreen himself pulling the rug out from under us, the way Duras is, returning to her narration, all dulcet modulations, as if she thought we'd be delighted to listen. The audience reacts at first with highly vocal disbelief and then with outbursts of anger, and walkouts. Even those of us who are charmed by her harmonious, lulling use of the film medium and in awe of her composure as a performer are conscious that we have, buried under a few layers, the rebellious instincts that others are giving loud voice to. They're furious in a way they never are at a merely bad, boring movie, and this anger is perfectly understandable. But it's high comedy, too: their feelings have been violated by purely aesthetic means—an affront to their conditioning.

When *The Truck* opens at the New York Film Festival this week, there's likely to be a repetition of the scene in May at Cannes. After the showing, Marguerite Duras stood at the head of the stairs in the Palais des Festivals facing the crowd in evening clothes, which was yelling insults up at her. People who had walked out were milling around; they'd waited to bait her. It might have been a horrifying exhibition, except that the jeering was an inverted tribute—conceivably, a fulfillment. She was shaken: one could see it in the muscles of her face. But Robespierre himself couldn't have looked them straighter in the eye. There can't be much doubt that she enjoys antagonizing the audience, and there is a chicness in earning the public's hatred. *The Truck* is a class-act monkeyshine made with absolutely confident artistry. She knows how easy it would be to give people the simple pleasures that they want. Her pride in not making concessions is heroic; it shows in that gleam of placid perversity which makes her such a commanding camera presence.

She can take the insults without flinching because she's completely serious in the story of the despairing hitchhiker. In her method in *The Truck*, she's a minimalist, like Beckett, stripping her drama down to the bones of monodrama, and her subject is the same as his: going through the last meaningless rites. ("I can't go on. I'll go on.") What *The Truck* doesn't have is Beckett's bleak, funny commonness. Beckett sticks to low-lifers, and his plays are the smelly vaudeville of the living dead, the grindingly familiar slow music of moronic humanity. Duras is bleakly fancy, with a glaze of culture. She's all music, too, the music of diffuseness, absence, loss, but her spoken text is attitudinizing—desultory self-preoccupation, mystification. Not pinning anything down, she leaves everything floating allusively in midair. This is, God help us, a vice women artists have been particularly prone to. Who is this hitchhiker on the road of life? Ah, we are not to know. Indefiniteness is offered as superiority to the mundane, as a form of sensuousness. It's a very old feminine lure—presenting oneself as many women, as a creature of mystery, and, of course, as passive and empty, disillusioned and weary. Dietrich used to do it in sequins, feathers, and chiffon. Duras clothes it in Marxist ideology, and puts forth her disaffection as a terminal, apocalyptic vision: Nothingness ahead. Some of her remarks ("Karl Marx is dead," and so on) have a tinny, oracular ring. (You wouldn't catch out Beckett making personal announcements.) The hitchhiker's declaration that she no longer believes in the possibility of political salvation is meant to have shock value; the world—i.e., Paris—is being told what Marguerite Duras' latest stand is.

There are some people who are too French for their own good. True film artist though she is, Marguerite Duras has a sensibility that's infected with the literary culture of a *précieuse*, and partly because of the development of movies out of the common forms of entertainment, this sensibility exposes itself on the screen much more than it does on paper. Faced with the audience's impatience, Duras fights back by going further, defiant, single-minded. There's something of the punitive disciplinarian in her conception of film art; *The Truck* is a position paper made into a movie. It's accessible, but it's accessible to a piece of yourself that you never think to take to the movies. Let's put it this way: if you were studying for a college exam and knocked off to go see *The Truck*, you wouldn't feel you were playing hooky. Duras makes us aware of our own mechanisms of response, and it's tonic and funny to feel the tensions she provokes. Her picture has been thought out with such supple discrimination between the values of sound and image that one could almost say it's *perfectly* made: an ornery, glimmering achievement. At the opposite extreme from popcorn filmmaking, it's a demonstration of creative force—which doesn't always cut as clean as that laser sword in Alec Guinness's hand.

{*The New Yorker*, September 26, 1977}

:: A Woman for All Seasons?

To say that *Julia* is well lighted doesn't do Douglas Slocombe's cinematography exact justice. It's *perfectly* lighted, which is to say, the color is lustrous, the images so completely composed they're almost static—picture postcards of its heroine Lillian Hellman (Jane Fonda) as a national monument. This is conservative—classical humanist—moviemaking, where every detail of meaning is worked out, right down to each flicker of light in the bit players' eyes. The director, Fred Zinnemann, does all the work for you, the way George Stevens did in *A Place in the Sun.* He does it beautifully—and there are very few directors left who know how to do it at all; the younger directors who aspire to this style, such as Alan Pakula or Dick Richards, don't achieve anything like the smoothness of Zinnemann's control, the glide of one sequence to the next. The man who made *From Here to Eternity* and *The Nun's Story* and *The Sundowners* hasn't forgotten his trade. Yet there's a cautiousness and reserve in his control now. Though Zinnemann takes a very romantic view of his two heroines— Lillian and Julia (Vanessa Redgrave)—the film is impersonal, its manner objective. Zinnemann's imagery isn't as inflated as David Lean's; he doesn't hold the frames too long; *Julia* is never ponderous. But this is important-motion-picture land, where every shot is the most beautiful still of the month. *Julia* is romantic in such a studied way that it turns romanticism into a moral lesson.

"Julia," one of the stories in *Pentimento, A Book of Portraits* (1973), Lillian Hellman's second volume of memoirs, is an account of how her childhood friend Julia involved her in smuggling fifty thousand dollars into Nazi Germany ("to bribe out many in prison and many who soon will be"). Of the stories in the book, it comes closest to Hellman's plays and scenarios; it's the one most like a movie—specifically, the anti-Nazi adventure movies made in Hollywood in the forties. The author uses the smuggling operation as a suspense mechanism, and as a framework for her recollections about Julia. Zinnemann lets this suspense element slip between his fingers, indifferently, as if it would be vulgar to grip the audience's emotions. The Georges Delerue score is lovely, in Delerue's special, under-orchestrated way, and gives the imagery a reminiscent edge, but *it* doesn't provide suspense, either. Trying to be faithful to Lillian Hellman's recollections, Zinnemann and Alvin Sargent, the screenwriter, construct an ornate superstructure of narration, dissolves, flashbacks spanning decades, and telepathic visions. Yet without suspense this superstructure has no engine inside. The film is all mildly anticipatory; it never reaches a point where you feel "This is it." Sargent has demonstrated his craftsmanship in the past (the most gifted writers sometimes regress to the poetic follies of adolescence, and that probably explains his other Lillian, in *Bobby Deerfield*), and he's really trying this time. There's some shrewd, taut writing, but you can see that he's harnessed. The script fails to draw you in, and the invented scenes of the heroines as young girls are flaccid—a literary form of calendar art, and photographed like *September Morn*. The constraint and inertness must go back to the decision to treat the story as literary history, as a drama of conscience, a parallel to Zinnemann's *A Man for All Seasons*, with Lillian Hellman herself as a legendary figure, and the relationships she has written about—with Dashiell Hammett (Jason Robards), Dorothy Parker (Rosemary Murphy), Alan Campbell (Hal Holbrook), and others—assumed to be common knowledge. Pity the screenwriter impaled on the life of a living person. And Sargent is bound by that person's short account, to which a high degree of art has already been applied. He might have been liberated if he could have changed the names and fictionalized the story; that way, he could have plugged the holes in the material and supplied what's missing in the characters, and some skepticism. But then the film would have lost its air of importance, history, lesson. And, of course, its selling point. What other movie has had its trailer built into an Academy Awards presentation, the way *Julia* did last March, when Jane Fonda made a speech introducing Lillian Hellman, who, head erect, acknowledged a standing ovation?

The film opens with Jane Fonda's recitation of the epigraph to *Pentimento*, a passage about old paint on canvas aging and revealing what was underneath, what was obscured "because the painter 'repented,' changed his mind." Speaking as the elderly Lillian Hellman, she says, "I wanted to see what was there for me once, what is there for me now." The flashback structure, too, suggests that there will be shifting perspectives, and throughout the movie we wait for the revelation of something lost from sight, displaced, hidden. Yet the narrator also tells us, "I think I have always known about my memory: I know when it is to be trusted . . . I trust absolutely what I remember about Julia." And actually there are no shadings that change, nothing brought up that was painted over, no hint of "repentance." Except for some needed exposition and some filler scenes, the movie limits itself to what the author provides, and her terse style locks her view of the past in place; there's no space for us to enter into it—not even any junk rattling around for us to free-associate with. What, then, is the point of the first quotation? This sort of fidelity— presumably for the sake of a polished, literate tone—fuzzes up whatever chances the film has for clarity in its first, complicated half hour. Lillian's memories of the years shared with Hammett and her efforts to write are interspersed with her memories of Julia, the opening night of *The Children's Hour*, the play that made her famous, and scenes on the train when she's carrying the bribe money across Germany to Berlin. You need to stare at the wigs to locate yourself in time. After a while, it becomes apparent that the filmmakers are trafficking in quotations and too many flashbacks because they can't find the core of the material.

They trust the author's memory, but can *we*? Who can believe in the Julia she describes—the ideal friend of her early youth, the beautiful, unimaginably rich Julia who never fails to represent the highest moon-struck ideals? If ever there was a character preserved in the amber of a girlhood crush, she's it. The gallant, adventurous Julia opens the worlds of art and conscience to the worshipful Lillian. She recites poetry and is incensed at the ugliness of the social injustices perpetrated by her own family; she goes off to study at Oxford, then to medical school in Vienna, intending to work with Freud; she plunges into the dangerous opposition to Hitler, writes letters to Lillian explaining the holocaust to come, and in the middle of it all has a baby. This saintly Freudian Marxist queen, on easy terms with Darwin, Engels, Hegel, and Einstein, might have been a joke with almost anyone but Vanessa Redgrave in the role. Redgrave's height and full figure have an ethereal, storybook wonder, and she uses some of the physical spaciousness that she had on the stage in *The Lady from the Sea*; she can be majestic more fluidly than anyone else (and there's more of her to uncoil). She has a scene all bandaged up in a hospital bed; unable to speak, she points with maybe the most expressive huge hand the screen has ever known. She handles the American accent unnoticeably—it's not that awful flat twang she used for Isadora. In close-ups, Vanessa Redgrave has the look of glory, like the young Garbo in Arnold Genthe's portraits; her vibrancy justifies Lillian's saying that she had "the most beautiful face I'd ever seen." Redgrave is so well endowed by nature to play queens that she can act simply in the role (which doesn't occupy much screen time) and casually, yet lyrically, embody Lillian Hellman's dream friend. Zinnemann has very astutely cast as the teen-age Julia a young girl (Lisa Pelikan) who's like a distorted Vanessa Redgrave—a fascinating, dislikable, rather creepy look-alike, who suggests that the intellectual goddess didn't appear out of a white cloud.

It's the dark cloud—Jane Fonda's stubborn strength, in glimpses of her sitting at the typewriter, belting down straight whiskey and puffing out smoke while whacking away at the keys, hard-faced, dissatisfied—that saves the film from being completely pictorial. It's a cloud-of-smoke performance; Bette Davis in all her movies put together couldn't have smoked this much—and Fonda gets away with it. It's in character. She creates a driven, embattled woman—a woman overprepared to fight back. This woman doesn't have much flexibility. You can see that in the stiff-necked carriage, the unyielding waist, even in the tense, muscular wrists, and in her nervous starts when anything unexpected happens. Her clothes are part of her characterization: Anthea Sylbert, who designed them, must have taken her cue from photographs of the author. These are the clothes of a woman who didn't choose them to be flattering—she chose them with a sense of her position in the world. They're expensive, selected with an eye to drama and to fashion—also not to get in her way. Outfitted in a style that combines elegance and impatience, Jane Fonda catches the essence of the Irving Penn portrait of Lillian Hellman reproduced in her first book of memoirs, *An Unfinished Woman* (1969). When she's alone on the screen, Fonda gives the movie an atmosphere of dissension, and she sustains this discordant aloneness in her scenes with everyone except Julia, with whom she's soft, eager, pliant. Her deliberately humorless Lillian is a formidable, uningratiating woman—her hair sculpted out of the same stone as her face. If you like her, you have to like her on her own implacable terms. How does a viewer separate Jane Fonda's Lillian Hellman from the actual Lillian Hellman? It's impossible to make clear distinctions between the live woman that Jane Fonda draws from (the performance could be called an inspired impersonation), the self-portrait in the story, and the semi-fictionalized activities on the screen. Almost anything one thinks or feels about this character seems an intrusion on a life, yet an intrusion that has been contracted for by Lillian Hellman herself—perhaps somewhat unwittingly.

The story itself has a *submerged* core: all of Hellman's attitudes, everything that goes into her woman's variant of Hemingway-Hammett stripped-down, hardboiled writing. Her prose is strong and clear, and also guarded, reluctant, pried out of a clenched hand. In the kind of situation-centered play Hellman writes, she doesn't give much of herself away. Her memoirs are dramatized, too, yet they're more exciting as drama than her plays are, since you can feel the tension between what she's giving you and what she's withholding. One expects a writer to trust his unconscious, to let go sometimes—not always to be so selective. Lillian Hellman carries thrift and plain American speech to a form of self-denial. The clue to some of the tension in the story "Julia" comes elsewhere in *Pentimento*—in "Turtle," the most compact Hemingway-Hammett story in the book, yet the one that reveals the cost of being hardboiled. In "Turtle," there are only two important characters—Hellman and Hammett, with whom she lived off and on for almost thirty years—and it's evident that for him strong and clear and definite meant masculine, while doubts and unresolved feelings were weak nonsense: feminine. Lillian Hellman tried to write (and to live) in a way that Hammett would approve of; he rejected much of what she actually felt, and she accepted his standards. (The question of why a woman of such strength and, in many ways, of such ruthless honesty should have deferred to the judgment of a man of lesser gifts than her own—that's the sexual mystery that would make a drama.)

The movie is about Hellman's career and doesn't really exist independently of one's knowledge of that career. The friendship between Julia and Lillian is obviously the emotional basis—the original material—for *The Children's Hour*. In that play, scandalmongers spread a sexual rumor about the relationship of two young women teachers, destroying their friendship and their hopes. Here, in *Julia*, Lillian is out drinking in a restaurant with

Sammy (John Glover, who shows a nasty vitality, like an American Edward Fox), the brother of a former schoolmate. He says that "the whole world knows about you and Julia," and she slugs him, knocking him back in his chair and then slamming the table over on top of him as she leaves. (People in the theatre applauded.) In the melodramatic Victorian code that is integral to hardboiled writing, the suggestion of homosexuality is a slur—it sullies the purity of the two women's relationship. Only contemptible people—curs like Sammy—think like that. They don't know how to behave; they lack standards. (This was the theme that came out all too nakedly in Hellman's third book of memoirs, the 1976 *Scoundrel Time*.) The failure to look beyond "right" and "wrong" has limited Hellman as a dramatist, and in "Julia" (though not in other stories in *Pentimento*) she thinks in the same terms—judgmentally. "Julia" is an expression of outraged idealism—sexual, political, and in all areas of personal conduct. It is in this story that she shows the beginnings of her own political conscience, started and nurtured, according to her account, by Julia. And it is Julia's dedication to fighting Fascism and her subsequent mutilation and murder that serve as the concrete justification—the personal experience— behind Lillian Hellman's embittered attitude toward those she regards as cowardly or dishonorable. The motive force of the story is that those who have not lived up to her conception of honor stand morally condemned for eternity.

In the film, at the last meeting of Lillian and Julia, in a café near the railroad station in Berlin, Lillian turns over the money she has smuggled in, and Julia says to her, "Are you still as angry as you used to be? I like your anger. . . . Don't you let anyone talk you out of it." There's no way for viewers to understand what Julia is referring to: in their scenes together, Lillian has never demonstrated any anger. Julia has been the daring leader, railing at injustice, going off and doing something about it. Lillian has been the docile follower, the naïf. In the movie version of *A Man for All Seasons*, a respectable job of monument-making, Zinnemann enshrined the martyred Sir Thomas More as a man of conscience; audiences weren't forcibly reminded that what More got himself beheaded for was the belief that the Pope represented divine law. What people could take away from the film was that More stood by his principles and died for them. In *Julia*, it isn't nearly as clear why Lillian is a monumental figure. In the episode of carrying the money to Berlin, she's more of a hazard than anything else;

the operation is so efficiently organized and she is supported by such resourceful anti-Nazi underground aides that she hardly seems to be needed at all.

And so it has to be from Lillian's mentors that we get her measure. As Hammett, Robards, who is gruff and funny at the beginning, has nothing to do once the film gets under way—he's just the all-wise, all-knowing Dash standing by, with love. But Dash is there for a reason: he's a judge of writing of such supreme authority—a Sainte-Beuve at the very least—that when he tells Lillian that *The Children's Hour*, which she has just finished, is "the best play anyone's written in a long time," there can be no question about it. Julia is the saintly political activist who certifies Lillian's anger as instinctive morality, and Dash is the stamp of approval that certifies her greatness.

The most difficult thing for an actor to suggest is what goes into making a person an artist—the tensions, the richness. And this is particularly difficult in the case of Lillian Hellman, who doesn't have that richness, and who in her own account makes herself so innocent of intellectual drives that anger seems to be her creative fount. If Julia's last advice to Lillian actually was to hang on to her anger, it was bad advice. Anger blinds Lillian Hellman as a writer. But anger is what holds the story "Julia" together, and the movie doesn't have it. At moments, Jane Fonda supplies something better, because she understands how to embody the explosive Hellman resentment. She gets at what anger does to you. It won't let you relax. It boxes you in: you're on your own. When—as Lillian—she walks into Sardi's on the opening night of her hit, twitching slightly from drunken nervousness, revelling in the attention she's getting while stiffly living up to her own image of herself as the distinguished playwright, you want more of her. You feel that Fonda has the power and invention to go on in this character—that she could crack this smooth, contemplative surface and take us places we've never been to. The film's constraint—its not seizing the moments when she's ready to *go*—is frustrating. Perfectionism has become its own, self-defeating end.

{*The New Yorker*, October 10, 1977}

:: Shivers

There's an ecstatic element in Brian De Palma's new thriller *The Fury*: he seems to extend the effects he's playing with about as far as he can without losing control. This inferno comedy is perched right on the edge. It may be to De Palma what *The Wild Bunch* was to Peckinpah. You feel he never has to make another horror movie. To go on would mean trying to kill people in ever more photogenically horrific ways, and he's already got two killings in *The Fury* which go so far beyond anything in his last film, *Carrie*, that that now seems like child's play. There's a potency about the murders here—as if De Palma were competing with himself, saying "You thought *Carrie* was frightening? Look at this!" He's not a great storyteller; he's careless about giving the audience its bearings. But De Palma is one of the few directors in the sound era to make a horror film that is so visually compelling that a viewer seems to have entered a mythic night world. Inside that world, transfixed, we can hear the faint, distant sound of De Palma cackling with pleasure.

Most other directors save the lives of the kind, sympathetic characters; De Palma shatters any Pollyanna thoughts—any expectations that a person's goodness will protect him. He goes past Hitchcock's perversity into something gleefully kinky. In *Carrie*, he built a two-way tension between our hope that the friendless, withdrawn, telekinetic heroine would be able to sustain her Cinderella happiness at the school prom and our dread of what we feared was coming. De Palma builds up our identification with the very characters who will be destroyed, or become destroyers, and some people identified so strongly with Carrie that they couldn't laugh—they felt hurt and betrayed. *The Fury* doesn't have the beautiful simplicity of the Cinderella's-revenge plot of *Carrie*, and it doesn't involve us emotionally in such a basic way; it's a far more hallucinatory film.

The script, which John Farris adapted from his novel, is about two teen-agers, spiritual twins who have met only telepathically. They are superior beings; in a primitive tribe, we are told, they would have become the prophets, the magicians, the healers. In modern civilization, they become the prisoners of a corrupt government (ours), which seeks to use them for espionage, and treats them impersonally, as secret weapons. In the opening scenes, set on a beach in Israel, the psychic boy, Robin (Andrew Stevens), is captured by an agent, Childress (John Cassavetes). The picture deals with the efforts of Robin's father, Peter Sandza (Kirk Douglas), to find him. The search centers in Chicago, where Sandza enlists the help of the psychic girl, Gillian (Amy Irving). Douglas gives a creditable professional-powerhouse performance; his quest has a routine action-film quality, though, and doesn't affect us emotionally. Once again, the suffering center of a De Palma film is a young girl. Amy Irving (she was the chestnut-haired, troubled Sue Snell, the survivor of the prom, in *Carrie*) brings a tremulous quality to *The Fury*; she's lyrical in the most natural way. The script is cheap gothic espionage occultism; she humanizes it. Both Gillian and Robin have the power to zap people with their minds. Gillian is trying to cling to her sanity—she doesn't want to hurt anyone. And, knowing that her power is out of her conscious control, she's terrified of her own secret rages. There's a little of the young Sylvia Sidney in Amy Irving's apprehensive, caught-in-the-glare-of-headlights beauty. Her sense of alarm makes us feel that real lives are at stake. With her blue, heavy-lidded almond eyes, she can look like an Asiatic princess in a fairy tale or a mask of tragedy. Farris's complicated, rickety plot doesn't give Robin an opportunity to demonstrate his prodigious gifts before Childress corrupts them. And it doesn't develop the core relationship of Robin and Gillian, so that we'd feel her need to get to him (and to avenge him). This film's dark, symphonic terror might seem almost abstract if Amy Irving weren't there all the way through, to hold it together. De Palma's virtuosity and her unaffected performance play off against each other, to the great advantage of both.

There's a third major collaborator: Richard H. Kline, whose deep-toned, velvety cinematography keeps the whole movie vibrating. Kline, who shot *King Kong*, knows how to light to create hyperbolic imagery; scenes such as a telepathic vision on a staircase and gunfire on the streets at night have the luster of a binful of garnets, amethysts, cat's-eyes. The compositions have so much depth and heavy shadow that objects stand out as if they were in 3-D; one can touch the metallic sheen of the cars, respond to Robin as a sculptural presence. There's also a fourth major collaborator: John Williams, who has composed what may be as apt and delicately varied a score as any horror movie has ever had. He scares us without banshee melodramatics. He sets the mood under the opening titles: otherworldly, seductively frightening. The music cues us in. This isn't going to be a gross horror film; it's visionary, science-fiction horror. De Palma is the reverse side of the coin from Spielberg. *Close Encounters* gives us the comedy of hope, *The Fury* the comedy of cruelly dashed hope. With Spielberg, what happens is so much better than you dared hope that you have to laugh; with De Palma, it's so much worse than you feared that you have to laugh.

Obviously, De Palma was offered this project because Robin and Gillian have telekinetic powers, like Carrie's, and, just as obviously, although he uses some effects similar to those in *Carrie*, he's too original not to have embroidered them and turned them into something different. The violence is presented in such a stylized, aestheticized way that it transcends violence. When Peter Sandza is in a commandeered Cadillac at night in a pea-soup fog and the cars chasing him go up in balls of flame, the scene is so spectacularly beautiful that it hardly matters if one doesn't know why he sends his car flying into Lake Michigan; maybe he's just blowing off steam — having a destruction orgy because De Palma felt that this flourish was *visually* necessary to complete the sequence. There is a joke involving an amusement-park ride which is surely one of the great perverse visual gags of all time; one knows exactly what's going on, yet here, too, one is struck by the languorous richness of the scene. The joke itself has been aestheticized. Most directors are so afraid of losing our attention that if two people are sitting together talking we're not allowed to see what's happening around them. De Palma pans around the rooms and landscapes slowly — a Godardian ploy — to give us more and more to look at, and to key up our expectations. He doesn't quite make good on his promises: he doesn't provide the crucial actions — the payoffs — within the circling, enlarging movements. But the expansiveness is essential, because of the stodgy dialogue; he anticipates the boredom of the ear by providing excitement for the eye.

No other director shows such clear-cut development in technique from film to film. In camera terms, De Palma was learning fluid, romantic steps in *Obsession*; he started to move his own way in *Carrie*—swirling and figure skating, sensuously. You could still see the calculation. Now he has stopped worrying about the steps. He's caught up with his instructors—with Welles in *Touch of Evil*, with Scorsese in *Mean Streets*. What distinguishes De Palma's visual style is smoothness combined with a jazzy willingness to appear crazy or campy; it could be that he's developing one of the great film styles—a style in which he stretches out suspense while grinning his notorious alligator grin. He has such a grip on technique in *The Fury* that you get the sense of a director who cares about little else; there's a frightening total purity in his fixation on the humor of horror. It makes the film seem very peaceful, even as one's knees are shaking.

The Fury isn't tightly structured; there are rising and falling waves of suspense, and De Palma's visual rhythms outpace the story. (Sometimes the characters talk as if they hadn't noticed that the movie has gone past what they're saying.) Randall Jarrell once quoted some lines from Whitman and commented, "There are faults in this passage and they *do not matter*." The visual poetry of *The Fury* is so strong that its narrative and verbal inadequacies *do not matter*. No Hitchcock thriller was ever so intense, went so far, or had so many "classic" sequences.

Carrie Snodgress returns to the screen in the role of Hester, Peter Sandza's lover and confederate; she's so pale and thin-faced that she's unrecognizable until one registers her eyes and hears that purring, husky voice of hers which seems to come out of furrowed vocal cords. Her plaintive, low-pitched normality helps *The Fury* to touch the ground now and then; fortunately, she goes out of the picture in a tense, slow-motion death-knell sequence that does her full honor. Fiona Lewis, who plays the woman Childress assigns to watch over Robin and satisfy his sexual needs, is not so lucky; she goes out of the picture in perhaps the most gothic way that any beloved has ever been dispatched by her lover. Her exit is topped only by that of Childress, and this is where De Palma shows his evil grin, because we are implicated in this murderousness: we want it, just as we wanted to see the bitchy Chris get hers in *Carrie*. Cassavetes is an ideal villain (as he was in *Rosemary's Baby*)—sullenly indifferent to anything but his own interests. He's so right for Childress that one regrets that there wasn't a real writer around to provide dialogue that would match his gloomy, viscous nastiness. He's been endowed with a Dr. Strangelove dead arm in a black sling (and there's a nice touch: his dead arm hurts), but only his end is worthy of him. This finale — a parody of Antonioni's apocalyptic vision at the close of *Zabriskie Point* — is the greatest finish for any villain ever. One can imagine Welles, Peckinpah, Scorsese, and Spielberg still stunned, bowing to the ground, choking with laughter.

{*The New Yorker*, March 20, 1978}

:: Fear of Movies

Are people becoming *afraid* of American movies? When acquaintances ask me what they should see and I say *The Last Waltz* or *Convoy* or *Eyes of Laura Mars*, I can see the recoil. It's the same look of distrust I encountered when I suggested *Carrie* or *The Fury* or *Jaws* or *Taxi Driver* or the two *Godfather* pictures before that. They immediately start talking about how they "don't like" violence. But as they talk you can see that it's more than violence they fear. They indicate that they've been assaulted by too many schlocky films—some of them highly touted, like *The Missouri Breaks*. They're tired of movies that reduce people to nothingness, they say—movies that are all car crashes and killings and perversity. They don't see why they should subject themselves to experiences that will tie up their guts or give them nightmares. And if that means that they lose out on a *Taxi Driver* or a *Carrie*, well, that's not important to them. The solid core of young moviegoers may experience a sense of danger as part of the attraction of movies; they may hope for new sensations and want to be swept up, overpowered. But these other, "more discriminating" moviegoers don't want that sense of danger. They want to remain in control of their feelings, so they've been going to the movies that allow them a distance—European films such as *Cat and Mouse*, novelties like *Dona Flor and Her Two Husbands*, prefab American films, such as *Heaven Can Wait*, or American films with an overlay of European refinement, like the hollowly objective *Pretty Baby*, which was made acceptable by reviewers' assurances that the forbidden subject is handled with good taste, or the entombed *Interiors*.

If educated Americans are rocking on their heels—if they're so punchy that they feel the need to protect themselves—one can't exactly blame them for it. But one can try to scrape off the cultural patina that, with the aid of the press and TV, is forming over this timidity. Reviewers and commentators don't have to be crooked or duplicitous to praise dull, stumpy movies and disapprove of exciting ones. What's more natural than that they would share the fears of their readers and viewers, take it as a cultural duty to warn them off intense movies, and equate intense with dirty, cheap, adolescent? Discriminating moviegoers want the placidity of *nice* art—of movies tamed so that they are no more arousing than what used to be called polite theatre. So we've been getting a new cultural puritanism—people go to the innocuous hoping for the charming, or they settle for imported sobriety, and the press is full of snide references to Coppola's huge film in progress, and a new film by Peckinpah is greeted with derision, as if it went without saying that Bloody Sam couldn't do anything but blow up bodies in slow motion, and with the most squalid commercial intentions.

This is, of course, a rejection of the particular greatness of movies: their power to affect us on so many sensory levels that we become emotionally accessible, in spite of our thinking selves. Movies get around our cleverness and our wariness; that's what used to draw us to the picture show. Movies—and they don't even have to be first-rate, much less great—can invade our sensibilities in the way that Dickens did when we were children, and later, perhaps, George Eliot and Dostoevski, and later still, perhaps, Dickens again. They can go down even deeper—to the primitive levels on which we experience fairy tales. And if people resist this invasion by going only to movies that they've been assured have nothing upsetting in them, they're not showing higher, more refined taste; they're just acting out of fear, masked as taste. If you're afraid of movies that excite your senses, you're afraid of movies.

In his new book *The Films in My Life*, François Truffaut writes, "I demand that a film express either the *joy of making cinema* or the *agony of making cinema*. I am not at all interested in anything in between; I am not interested in all those films that do not pulse." Truffaut's dictum may exclude films that some of us enjoy. You couldn't claim that *National Lampoon's Animal House* expresses either the joy or the agony of making cinema. It's like the deliberately dumb college-football comedies of the thirties—the ones with Joan Davis or Martha Raye—only more so; it's a growly, rambunctious cartoon, and its id anarchy triumphs over the wet-fuse pacing, the blotchy lighting, and the many other ineptitudes. In its own half-flubbed way, it has a style. And you don't go to a film like *Animal House* for *cinema*, you go for roughhousing disreputability; it makes you laugh by restoring you to the slobby infant in yourself. (If it were more artistic, it couldn't do that.)

But that sort of movie is a special case. Essentially, I agree with Truffaut. I can enjoy movies that don't have that moviemaking fever in them, but it's enjoyment on a different level, without the special aphrodisia of movies—the kinetic responsiveness, the all-out submission to pleasure. That "pulse" leaves you with all your senses quickened. When you see a movie such as *Convoy*, which has this vibrancy and yet doesn't hold together, you still feel clearheaded. But when you've seen a series of movies without it, whether proficient soft-core porn like *The Deep* or klutzburgers like *Grease*, you feel poleaxed by apathy. If a movie doesn't "pulse"—if the director isn't talented, and if he doesn't become fervently obsessed with the possibilities that the subject offers him to explore moviemaking itself—it's dead and it deadens you. Your heart goes cold. The world is a dishrag. (Isn't the same thing true for a novel, a piece of music, a painting?)

This pressing against the bounds of the medium doesn't necessarily result in a good movie (John Boorman's debauch *Exorcist II: The Heretic* is proof of that), but it generally results in a live one—a movie there's some reason to see—and it's the only way great movies get made. Even the madness of *Exorcist II* is of a special sort: the picture has a visionary crazy grandeur (like that of Fritz Lang's loony *Metropolis*). Some of the telepathic sequences are golden-toned and lyrical, and the film has a swirling, hallucinogenic, apocalyptic quality; it might have been a horror classic if it had had a simpler, less ritzy story. But, along with flying demons and theology inspired by Teilhard de Chardin, it had Richard Burton, with his precise diction, helplessly and inevitably turning his lines into camp, just as the cultivated, stage-trained actors in early-thirties horror films did. Like them, Burton had no conviction in what he was doing, so he couldn't get beyond staginess and artificial phrasing. The film is too cadenced and exotic and too deliriously complicated to succeed with most audiences. But it's winged camp—a horror fairy tale gone wild, another in the long history of moviemakers' king-size follies. There's enough visual magic in it for a dozen good movies; what the picture lacks is judgment—the first casualty of the moviemaking obsession.

What Boorman has in surfeit is what's missing from *Heaven Can Wait*: there isn't a whisper of personal obsession in the moviemaking. The film has no desire but to please, and that's its only compulsiveness; it's so timed and pleated and smoothed that it's sliding right off the screen. This little smudge of a movie makes one laugh a few times, but it doesn't represent moviemaking—it's pifflemaking. Warren Beatty moves through it looking fleecy and dazed, murmuring his lines in a dissociated, muffled manner. The film has to be soft-focussed and elided—a series of light double takes—because if Beatty raised his voice or expressed anything more than a pacific nature, the genteel, wafer-thin whimsy would crumble.

There's no way I could make the case that *Animal House* is a better picture than *Heaven Can Wait*, yet on some sort of emotional-aesthetic level I prefer it. One returns you to the slobbiness of infancy, the other to the security of childhood, and I'd rather stand with the slobs. I didn't much mind *Heaven Can Wait* when I saw it. Some of the lines have Elaine May's timorous, unaccountable weirdness. (Those jokes of hers come at you like wobbly cannonballs; you're never sure which ones will hit.) And in their marginal roles Dyan Cannon (a frenzied, lascivious bunny) and Charles Grodin (a discreet lizard) play off each other like cartoon confederates. It wasn't bad. Why, then, does it offend me when I think about it? Because it's image-conscious celebrity moviemaking; Beatty the star (who is also the producer and the co-director and even takes a co-writing credit) wants to be a nice guy, the same way Burt Reynolds does in *Hooper*. They go soft on themselves and act on one cylinder. They become so *dear*—Beatty the elfin sweet Jesus, and Reynolds the macho prince who hides his saintly heart—that they're not functioning as artists; they've turned into baby-kissing politicians.

As Hooper, Reynolds risks his life and injures himself in order to protect a little mutt, and afterward, while in pain, he's bawled out by a huffy official from an animal-protection society who doesn't recognize his devotion to dogdom. But *we're* sure not kept in the dark. In this slapstick celebration of the "real people" in Hollywood—the stunt men—the director, Hal Needham, lays out the gags for us as if we were backwoodsmen, and when it's time for him to show his stuff by staging the breathtaking stunts that the movie keeps telling us about, he fumbles every damn one of them. The camera is always in the wrong place; it's as if Needham had a tic that made him turn his head at the crucial moment. And it's almost a sickness — the repetition mania, the falling back on exhausted conventions. The hero has a live-in girlfriend (Sally Field) who is an irrelevant drag on the action, just like the worrying wives of old. As Hooper goes off to perform the most dangerous stunt of his life, she delivers the line that emerged from the compressed lips of generations of movie wives: "I won't be here when you get back." Was there ever one of them who carried out the threat? (The alternative was the John Ford woman, who said, "Matt, be careful.")

Reynolds has a faithful audience for pictures in which he doesn't attempt anything he hasn't done before. A half-cocked piece of movie-making like *Hooper*, with its neo–John Wayneism (we red-blooded men who aren't afraid of risking our bodies are the true chivalrous knights of America, the only ones you can trust), is accepted as "a kick." The public has genuine affection for Reynolds' West Coast wise-guy swagger, and it doesn't seem to matter to people that in *Hooper* his merriment often seems a tired reflex. (That moon face crinkles on call.) Even if the press treated *Hooper* or a Clint Eastwood picture as contemptuously as it did *Convoy*, those pictures might not be hurt at box offices.

It's no accident that the directors who have an appetite for the pleasure and complexity of moviemaking are so often abused in the press. Their films are likely to grip people, and in impolite ways. These directors can't resist subverting the old forms that give comfort to audiences. And, given the hell of dealmaking and the infinite number of things that can go wrong during a production, a director who cares about the rhythm and texture of his imagery is likely to turn into a mixture of pompous bore, master strategist, used-car salesman, maniac, and messiah — in short, a major artist. And yes, he'll try for too big an effect, or he'll upset the balance of a neatly structured pipsqueak script. The pressures of dealmaking squeeze the juice out of him, but still, in his sheer burning desperation to make movies, he'll try to turn a dud into *something*. And maybe he'll sustain that drive for only a part of the picture and he'll let the rest of it go to hell. How can moviemakers sustain their energy? How can they believe they should give the public of their best when the kids want to get Greased over and over and the literate adults go off to their cozy French detective comedy? Whom can they make movies *for*? They have every reason to be bitter and confused. (And they are, they are.)

Audiences hiss the sight of blood now, as if they didn't have it in their own bodies. They hiss those bloody scenes that have the power to shock them, even when the blood isn't excessive. Bergman gets away with shocking effects; in *Cries and Whispers*, he even shows vaginal blood, and no one dares hiss. But in *Eyes of Laura Mars*, where the first flash of bloodletting comes right at the beginning, and in *The Fury*, where the bloodshed is stylized, hyperbolic, insane, audiences who seem hypnotized by the urgency in the moviemaking still hiss the blood. They seem to be saying, "I don't need this!" They hiss the blood as if to belittle it, to make it less menacing. And these movies are treated with condescension.

Movies have upset repressive people right from the start, but the old Hollywood studio heads learned to appease pressure groups by keeping a lid on sacrilege and eroticism, and by making sharp moral distinctions between the violent acts committed by good guys and those committed by bad guys. Probably the movie that did the most to overturn all this was *Bonnie and Clyde*, in 1967. Lingering sensuously on violent imagery, the director, Arthur Penn, brought our hidden, horrified fascination into the open. Eisenstein had plunged us into violence, and so had Buñuel and Kurosawa and many others, but this was an American movie made by an American director—in color—and it was saying, "Don't turn your head away, there's something horrible and rapturous going on." Louis B. Mayer and the old Hollywood simplicities were finally undermined. In 1969, Peckinpah's *The Wild Bunch* came out—a traumatic poem of violence with imagery as ambivalent as Goya's. And as the Vietnam War dragged on and Americans became more and more demoralized and guilt-ridden, our films splattered blood at us—so much blood that going to the movies was often a painful, masochistic experience. The lurid didacticism was generally hypocritical: every crummy action-adventure picture that didn't know how to keep the audience's attention except by piling on massacres pointed to the war as a justification. And people became particularly incensed over the balletic, slow-motion scenes; although there's a psychological rationale, as well as an aesthetic one, for this "eternity in an instant" treatment of falls and accidents and horrors, it began to seem a mere device to force us to stare at gruesomeness.

People had probably had it with movie violence long before the war was over, but they didn't feel free to admit that they really wanted relaxed, escapist entertainment. Now that the war has ended, they talk about violence in movies as if it would plunge us back into that guilty mess. There's a righteousness in their tone when they say they don't like violence; I get the feeling that I'm being told that my urging them to see *The Fury* means that I'll be responsible if there's another Vietnam. During a brutal fight in *Who'll Stop the Rain*, there were cries in the audience—on the order of "O.K., enough!"—and applause for the cries. These weren't the good-natured catcalls that are heard at stupid movies; it was an escape from the power of the fight. It's a way of closing off what you feel. I think I first became conscious of this audience mechanism back in the mid-forties, when I saw *Dead of Night* on its opening day in a crowded theatre and the audience laughed raucously during Michael Redgrave's greatest—most terrified—moments. The tension had got too much for them, and they turned philistine, rejecting their own emotional immersion in his performance. That's what people are doing now, on a larger scale. Maybe it's partly because they want to put the war behind them, but there's more to it: they're running away from flesh and blood on the screen. They have lost the background of security that used to make it easy for them to respond to suspense stories. Now, when they're always conscious of the violence in the society and are afraid that it's going to be coming at them when they leave the theatre, they don't want to see anything frightening on the screen. They've lost the hope that things are going to be better—that order will return. So they go to the movies to be lulled—to be gently rocked to sleep. (*Heaven Can Wait*—the acclaimed movie of the summer—is a lullaby.) What may be behind all this is the repression of the race issue. People feel that there's violence out there, and they want to shut it out. Movies, more than any other form of expression, are capable of bringing us to an acceptance of our terrors; that must be why people are afraid of movies.

Was *Convoy* punished because of the blood Peckinpah has made us look at in the past? It got the bum's rush, though it's a happy-go-lucky ode to the truckers on the roads, a sunny, enjoyable picture, with only ketchup being splattered (in a mock fight in a diner). The lighting suggests J.M.W. Turner in the American Southwest, his eyes popping with surprise. Seeing this picture, you recover the feelings you had as a child about the power and size and noise of trucks, and their bright, distinctive colors and alarming individuality. Peckinpah uses the big rigs anthropomorphically. Each brawny giant in the procession has its own stride; some are lumbering, others are smooth as adagio dancers, while one bounces along and its trailer shimmies. At night, when a frightened driver pulls out of the line to go off alone in the darkness, the truck itself seems to quaver, childishly. The trucks give the performances in this movie, and they go through changes: when the dust rises around them on rough backcountry roads, they're like sea beasts splashing spume; when two of them squeeze a little police car between their tanklike armored bodies, they're insect titans. The whole movie is a prankish road dance, and the convoy itself is a protest without a cause: the drivers are just griped in general and blowing off steam. They want the recreation of a protest.

Sam Peckinpah talks in code, and his movies have become a form of code, too. *Convoy* is full of Peckinpah touches, but you can't tell the put-on from the romantic myth; his cynicism and his sentimentality are so intertwined by now that he's putting himself on. He has a mocking theme here that's visual: the spaciousness of the land and the pettiness of men's quarrels. But the script doesn't play off this disparity, and so, when the spaciousness overwhelms the lawman's spite that set the convoy in motion, it's the plot (rather than mankind) that seems silly. The film barely introduces the characters, and one of the funniest, J.D. Kane's Big Nasty, who talks in a voice so deep it might be his mammoth truck talking, is lost sight of. And here, as in *Cross of Iron*, Peckinpah can't shoot dialogue; he doesn't seem to know anymore how people talk. (Also, the post-synchronization is so poor that the voices seem disembodied.) The visual music of the moving trucks is enough to carry the film for the first hour, but when the truckers stop for the night at an encampment, the movie stops; there's no narrative energy to keep it going.

The actor at the front of the convoy, Kris Kristofferson, isn't convincing as a horny trucker grabbing a sad-eyed waitress (Cassie Yates) and hopping into the truck for a quickie; Kristofferson lacks the common touch that might have given the movie some centrifugal force. But, with his steely blue eyes, and his hair and beard blowing in the wind, he's as majestic as the big trucks, and his reserve is appealingly heroic. Kristofferson doesn't overact, and his charm is so low-key and easy that even the disembodied sound doesn't damage him—it goes with his faintly detached personality. The sound is rough on the other performers, though; they seem not quite there. Kristofferson is partnered by Ali MacGraw, who has never seemed anywhere, and some of the resentment directed against the film may be because of her. She is a truly terrible actress, of the nostril school. (Did she study under Natalie Wood?) As the camera comes closer, the nostrils start flexing—not just for anger, for *any* emotion. Her role makes her seem soft and spoiled and rich, and she doesn't react to a situation, she comments on it, in a hideously superior way. When she's really working hard, she adds a trembling lip (reminiscent of Jackie Cooper as a child) to her tiny repertory of expressions. She isn't around a lot, though, and Kristofferson doesn't pay much attention to her (which saves him).

It isn't clear whether Peckinpah walked away from *Convoy* after presenting his first cut, or was barred from the final editing, or how much Graeme Clifford, who finally put it together (he was the editor on Nicolas Roeg's *Don't Look Now*), is responsible for. But there are lovely editing transitions and fast, hypnotic rhythms and graceful shifts of stationary compositions. Sequences with the trucks low in the frame and most of the image given over to skies with brilliant white clouds are poetic gestures, like passages in Dovzhenko. The film has a springiness of spirit, and a lust for drifting white desert sand; it's so beautiful (yet funny) that often you don't want the camera to move—you want to hold on to what you see. Probably Peckinpah intended to make a simple action movie, but something in him must have balked at that. He saw the trucks and the skies and he kept shooting, like Eisenstein when he saw the faces of the Indians in Mexico.

No American movie this year has been as full of the "joy of making cinema" as Martin Scorsese's *The Last Waltz*, his film of The Band's Thanksgiving, 1976, concert in San Francisco. He shot it while he was still involved in *New York, New York*—which was full of the "agony of making cinema." In *The Last Waltz*, Scorsese seems in complete control of his talent and of the material, and you can feel everything going right, just as in *New York, New York* you could feel everything going wrong. It's an even-tempered, intensely satisfying movie. Visually, it's dark-toned and rich and classically simple. The sound (if one has the good luck to catch it in a theatre equipped with a Dolby system) is so clear that the instruments have the distinctness that one hears on the most craftsmanlike recordings, and the casual interviews have a musical, rhythmic ease. Why was it so hard to persuade people to go see it? Were they leery of another rock-concert film? Were they tired of hearing about Scorsese? All of that, maybe, and possibly something more. They swooned and giggled over *A Star Is Born*, but *The Last Waltz* is a real movie, and it must have given off some vibration that made them nervous. They couldn't trust the man who'd made *Mean Streets* and *Taxi Driver* to give them a safe evening.

The fun of a movie thriller is in the way it plays on our paranoid fantasies; we know that we're being manipulated and yet—if the manipulation is clever enough—we give over to it. But can people respond to this as entertainment if they're on such edgy terms with themselves that they're afraid of being upset? In the press coverage of *Eyes of Laura Mars*, the reviewers seem to be complaining that it's a thriller—or, rather, an effective thriller. Their being frightened seems to make them resent the film as immoral. *Eyes of Laura Mars*, Irvin Kershner's seductive whodunit, is up against attitudes that a comparable fantasy, such as Polanski's *Rosemary's Baby*—also about justifiable female paranoia—didn't have to face. *Laura Mars* operates on mood and atmosphere, and moves so fast, with such delicate changes of rhythm, that its excitement has a subterranean sexiness. It's a really stylish thriller, and Faye Dunaway, with long, thick dark-red hair, brings it emotion and presence, as well as a new erotic warmth. (Her legs, especially the thighs, are far more important to her performance than her eyes; her flesh gives off heat.) More womanly and more neurotically vulnerable—even tragic—than before, she looks as if she'd lived a little and gone through plenty of stress. She's glamorously beat out—just right to be telepathic about killings. Caped and swathed in clothing, with her glossy pale face taut against the lustrous hair (so thick it's almost evil), she's both Death and the Maiden. No Hollywood sex goddess has ever presented so alluring an image of kinky Death herself.

The scabrous is part of the elegant in this film; Laura Mars is a celebrity fashion photographer who specializes in the chic and pungency of sadism. The pictures she shoots have a furtive charge; we can see why they sell.

Her photographic sessions, with burning cars and half-naked models strutting around their prey, are set up so that we get a sense of friction between the models, who are acting as killers and victims, and the buzzing, over-intense city, where everyone seems to be on a stage. Laura's pictures are, in fact, single-image versions of high-style blood thrillers, such as *Laura Mars*. The humor in the movie is in the mixture of people who drift through the celebrity-circus milieu. Models who in their poses look wickedly decadent may be just fun-loving dingalings; unself-conscious when they're nude, they put on their gaunt insouciance with their clothes. In this high-fashion world, decadence is a game. But the creepiness of the environment isn't. The frames are packed with abrasive movement, and we see the dreck right next to the glamour, the dirty fingers that handle the expensive photographs. In the rush and bickering confusion of Laura's work life, she's dependent on her scruffy, wild-eyed driver (Brad Dourif), who's into God knows what, and her agent-manager (René Auberjonois), who probably hates her, because he has to take care of all the technicalities of time and place and money while she's being "creative." She has no one to trust. And so the harassed, frightened Laura falls in love with a police lieutenant (Tommy Lee Jones), who comes from a different, working-class world and represents simple values, old-fashioned morality. In many ways, it's a subtle, funny movie. Laura's voice is heavy with emotion, the policeman's is light and high and boyish; they're as unlikely a pair of lovers as you would ever hope to see. With the help of Michael Kahn, who was the editor, Kershner glides over the gaps in the script and almost manages to trick viewers past the mediocre lighting. He gets us to experience the jangled, onstage atmosphere viscerally. Brad Dourif's excitable driver makes us laugh, because he epitomizes New York's crazed messengers and hostile flunkies; he's so wound up he seems to have the tensions of the whole city in his gut. The film has an acid-rock texture, while Tommy Lee Jones, with his cat burglar's grace, his sunken eyes, rough skin, and jagged lower teeth that suggest a serpent about to snap, takes us into the world of punk.

In *Laura Mars*, you barely see any violence; it comes across by suggestion and a few quick images. But it's violence of a particular kind (and this may explain the angry, moralistic reactions to the film): the danger is to the eyes. If the killer had gone for the throat, probably the movie wouldn't be so frightening and wouldn't be considered immoral. (Of course, it wouldn't have any point, either.) *Laura Mars* violates our guardedness about our eyes. The most dreaded thing that can happen to what many regard as their most sensitive organs happens in this picture; like *Un Chien Andalou*, it attacks what we're watching the movie with. *Eyes of Laura Mars* hasn't the depth of intention (or the art) to upset us profoundly, it doesn't go at the eyes like *King Lear* or *Oedipus Rex* or the *Odyssey*, it just touches lightly on our dread. But this movie has enough "pulse" to make us register how horribly vulnerable our bodies are. And people in the audience who are used to TV, with its car crashes and knifings and shootings that have no pain or terror in them, and no gore, feel violated: how dare a movie scare them, and how dare it attack their taboo about the eyes? Has their world become so close to a paranoid fantasy that they no longer experience any of the primal fun in being frightened?

One film has shocked me in a way that made me feel that it was a borderline case of immorality—Hitchcock's *Psycho*, which, because of the director's cheerful complicity with the killer, had a sadistic glee that I couldn't quite deal with. It was hard to laugh at the joke after having been put in the position of being stabbed to death in the motel shower. The shock stayed with me to the degree that I remember it whenever I'm in a motel shower. Doesn't everybody? It was a good dirty joke, though, even if we in the audience were its butt. I wouldn't have wanted to see *Psycho* that first time alone in a theatre (and I sometimes feel a slight queasiness if I'm by myself late at night somewhere watching a horror film on TV). But that's what a theatrical experience is about: sharing this terror, feeling the safety of others around you, being able to laugh and talk together about how frightened you were as you leave.

Those people who are trying to protect themselves from their own violence and their own distress by not going to see anything that could rock the boat are keeping a very tense cool. There's something crazily repressive in the atmosphere. They're rejecting the rare films that could stir them, frighten them, elate them. And they're accepting the movies in which everything happens affectlessly and even bloody violence can be shrugged off. Within a few years, everything has turned around. Violence that makes you feel afraid has replaced sex as what's offensive, exploitative, dirty; since the end of the war, particularly, this kind of violence has become pornographic—it's as if we thought we could shove muggers and urban guerrillas under the counter. Movie sex, meanwhile, has become trivialized—made casual. It's posh call-girl sex, *Playboy* sex; there's no hatred or possessiveness or even passion in it. (Imagine the sour rage and depth of desire a director like Peckinpah might show us if he made a movie about sex.) What does it mean when someone says to you in a prissy, accusing tone that he "doesn't like" violence? Obviously, he's implying that your ability to look at it means that you *like* it. And you're being told that you're made of coarser stuff than he is. He's found a cheap way to present his cultural credentials. There's something snobby in all this; sex is chic but violence is for the animals. The less worldly still ask, "Why can't they make movies about *nice* people?" It's the comfort of order that's wanted— everything in its place. It used to be that well-brought-up ladies were not expected to be able to stand the sight of blood; they were expected to be so protected from sex and blood and flesh and death that they would faint if exposed to what the common people had to learn to look at. It was considered an offense to them to bring up certain subjects in their presence. Now the same sort of delicacy is once again becoming a mark of culture and breeding. Squeamishness—surely with terror and prurient churnings under it?—is the basis of this good taste.

The people in Woody Allen's *Interiors* are destroyed by the repressiveness of good taste, and so is the picture. *Interiors* is a puzzle movie, constructed like a well-made play from the American past (such as *Craig's Wife*), and given the beautiful, solemn visual clarity of a Bergman film, without, however, the eroticism of Bergman. *Interiors* looks so much like a masterpiece and has such a super-banal metaphysical theme (death versus life) that it's easy to see why many regard it as a masterpiece: it's deep on the surface. *Interiors* has moviemaking fever, all right, but in a screwed-up form— which is possibly what the movie is all about. The problem for the family in the film is the towering figure of the disciplined, manipulative, inner-directed mother (Geraldine Page). She is such a perfectionist that she cannot enjoy anything, and the standards of taste and achievement that she imposes on her three daughters tie them in such knots that they all consider themselves failures. Alvy Singer, the role Woody Allen played in *Annie Hall*, was just such a compulsive, judgmental spoilsport, and Allen's original title for that film was *Anhedonia*—the lack of the capacity for experiencing pleasure.

Among the many puzzling aspects of *Interiors*: How can Woody Allen present in a measured, lugubriously straight manner the same sorts of tinny anxiety discourse that he generally parodies? And how intentional is most of what goes on under the friezes and poses? Are we expected to ask ourselves who in the movie is Jewish and who is Gentile? The characters are so sterilized of background germs that the question is inevitably raised, and one of the film's few overt jokes is an overheard bit from a television show in which an interviewer asks a boy, "What nationality were you at the time of your birth?" and the boy answers, "Hebrew." Surely at root the family problem is Jewish: it's not the culture in general that imposes these humanly impossible standards of achievement—they're a result of the Jewish fear of poverty and persecution and the Jewish reverence for learning. It's not the joy of making cinema that spurs Woody Allen on (as he made clear in *Annie Hall*, he can't have that kind of joy), it's the discipline of making cinema. The movie, with its spotless beaches, is as clean and bare as Geraldine Page's perfect house: you could eat off any image. The prints of *Interiors* were processed on a new film stock, and during the showings for the press and people in the industry in Los Angeles, Allen had the print returned to the lab after every screening to be washed. Which makes this the ultimate Jewish movie. Woody Allen does not show you any blood.

The father (E. G. Marshall) asks his wife for a divorce and then marries a plump, healthy, life-force woman (Maureen Stapleton), and so there are two mothers. The tall, regal first mother, an interior decorator (who places a few objects in a bare room), wears icy grays and lives among beiges and sand tones; the plebeian stepmother bursts into this hushed atmosphere wearing mink and reds and floral prints. This is the sort of carefully constructed movie in which as soon as you see the first woman caress a vase and hover over its perfection you know that the second woman will have to break a vase. The symbolism—the introduction of red into the color scheme, the broken vase, and so on—belongs to the kind of theatre where everything was spelled out. But under this obviousness there are the layers of puzzle. The two mothers appear to be the two sides of the mythic dominating Jewish matriarch—the one dedicated to spiritual perfection, the other to sensual appetites, security, getting along in the world, cracking a few jokes. It's part of the solemn unease of the film that no one would want either of them for a mother: they're both bigger than life, and the first is a nightmare of asexual austerity, the second an embarrassment of yielding flesh and middle-class worldliness. If the two are warring for control of

Woody Allen, the first (the *real* mother) clearly has him in the stronger grip. She represents the death of the instincts, but she also represents art, or at least cultivation and pseudo-art. (As a decorator, her specialty, like Woody Allen's here, seems to be the achievement of a suffocating emptiness.) Maureen Stapleton, the comic life force, lacks *class*. The film might be a representation of the traditional schizophrenia of Jewish comics, who have had the respect for serious achievement planted in them so early that even after they've made the world laugh they still feel they're failures, because they haven't played Hamlet. Groucho Marx talked morosely about not having had the education to be a writer, and said that his early pieces for the *New Yorker* were his proudest achievement. For Woody Allen, the equivalent is to be the American Ingmar Bergman.

The three daughters represent different aspects of the perfectionist neurosis. The oldest (Diane Keaton) is a well-known poet, determined, discontented, struggling with words while unconscious of her drives; the middle one (Kristin Griffith) is a TV actress, dissatisfied with her success, and snorting cocaine; the youngest (Mary Beth Hurt), who looks like a perennial student, rejects sham and flails around, unable to find herself. In plays, the youngest is generally the one who represents the author, and whenever you see a character who's stubbornly honest you know that you're seeing the author's idealized vision of some part of himself. With Mary Beth Hurt, if you have any doubts all you have to do is look at how she's dressed. (You'll also notice that she gets the worst—the most gnomic—lines, such as "At the center of a sick psyche there is a sick spirit." Huh?) She's unsmiling—almost expressionless—closed in, with specs, hair like shiny armor (it says hands off), and schoolgirl blouses and skirts. She's like a glumly serious postulant, and so honest she won't dress up; determined not to be false to her feelings, she actually dresses down for her father's wedding to the "vulgarian," as she calls her. (She's there under duress, and her clothes are an implicit protest.) She's the Cordelia, the father's favorite who refuses to lie, even to the mother, whom she alone in the family truly loves (she guiltily hates her, too).

The men's roles are relatively minor; Sam Waterston's part, though, is the only one that's unformed in the writing and doesn't quite fit into the formal plan. Geraldine Page is playing neurosis incarnate, and the camera is too close to her, especially when her muscles collapse; this failure of discretion makes her performance seem abhorrent. But Maureen Stapleton livens things up with her rather crudely written role. Hers is the only role that isn't strictly thematic, and you can feel the audience awake from its torpor when she arrives on the scene and talks like a conventional stage character. Diane Keaton does something very courageous for a rising star. She appears here with the dead-looking hair of someone who's too distracted to do anything with it but get a permanent, and her skin looks dry and pasty. There's discontent right in the flesh, while Kristin Griffith, the TV sexpot, appears with fluffy hair, blooming skin, and bright white teeth—the radiance that we normally see in Keaton. This physical transformation is the key to Keaton's thoughtful performance: she plays an unlikable woman—a woman who dodges issues whenever she can, who may become almost as remote as her mother.

For Allen, who is a very conscious craftsman, it is surely no accident that the mother's impoverished conception of good taste is sustained in the style of the film. But what this correlation means to him isn't apparent. *Interiors* is a handbook of art-film mannerisms; it's so austere and studied that it might have been directed by that icy mother herself—from the grave. The psychological hangups that come through are fascinating, but the actors' largo movements and stilted lines don't release this messy material, they repress it. After the life-affirming stepmother has come into the three daughters' lives and their mother is gone, they still, at the end, close ranks in a frieze-like formation. Their life-negating mother has got them forever. And her soul is in Woody Allen. He's still having his love affair with death, and his idea of artistic achievement (for himself, at least) may always be something death-ridden, spare, perfectly structured—something that talks of the higher things. (If this, his serious film, looks Gentile to people, that may be because for Woody Allen being Jewish, like being a comic, is fundamentally undignified. This film couldn't have had a Jewish-family atmosphere—his humor would have bubbled up.) The form of this movie is false, yet it's the form that he believes in, and the form of *Interiors* is what leads people to acclaim it as a masterpiece.

People like Woody Allen for a lot of good reasons, and for one that may be a bummer: he conforms to their idea of what a Jew should be. He's a younger version of the wise, philosophic candy-store-keeper in *West Side Story*. His good will is built partly on his being non-threatening. He's safe—the schlump who wins, without ever imposing himself. People feel comfortable with him; the comedy audience may even go to *Interiors*—to pay its respects to the serious Woody. Woody Allen's repressive kind of control—the source of their comfort—is just what may keep him from making great movies. *Interiors* isn't Gentile, but it *is* genteel. He's turned the fear of movies—which is the fear of being moved—into a form of intellectuality. If only it were all a put-on.

{*The New Yorker*, September 25, 1978}

:: Bertrand Blier

The French writer-director Bertrand Blier has an authentic, lyrical impudence in *Get Out Your Handkerchiefs*, which was shown at the New York Film Festival on September 29th and 30th. This is the third in his series of male erotic fantasies. Blier, who is a novelist and the son of the well-known plump character comedian Bernard Blier, started to direct movies in the sixties, and then in 1974 made *Going Places* (the original title is *Les Valseuses*, French slang for testicles), and in 1976 *Calmos* (it turned up, without publicity, in New York last year under the title *Femmes Fatales* and disappeared almost immediately). Perhaps *Handkerchiefs*, a more subdued, deeper variation on the themes of those two films, will make it easier for audiences to respond to what he's about and to look at his earlier work without becoming incensed. When *Going Places* was released here, in 1974, it was variously described as "sordid," "loathsome," and "disgusting," and just this past March it was taken off the Home Box Office schedule because of complaints from affiliate stations. What is the picture's crime? Probably that viewers find themselves laughing at things that shock them. At one point, the two young roughneck protagonists (Gérard Depardieu and Patrick Dewaere) board a train and observe a beautiful, pure-looking young mother (Brigitte Fossey) nursing her baby in an otherwise empty car. They offer this madonna money to give them a sip and, apparently terrified of refusing, she accedes. When she gets off the train, her husband, a scrawny, pasty-faced soldier on furlough, is waiting, and as she walks to join him she has a silly, happy grin on her flushed face. Audiences have come to accept the dirty joking in Buñuel's films; the years, the honors, the press have given it a pedigree. But Blier's joking is so unself-conscious that it makes Buñuel's seem preconceived, almost pedantically outrageous. Blier gives us the kind of joke that can't be done by implication or symbolically—that has to be absolutely literal. This kind of joke has found only verbal form before, yet Blier visualizes it—as if that were the most natural thing in the world to do. The two roughnecks act out their sex reveries—in which, no matter what a woman says, she's really begging for it, so they're doing her a favor if they force themselves on her. And people watching this may be so fussed about the disreputability of what excites them that they can't accept the humor of their own situation. *Going Places* is an explosively funny erotic farce—both a celebration and a satire of men's daydreams—and some people find its gusto revolting in much the same way that the bursting comic force of the sexual hyperbole in Henry Miller's *Tropic of Cancer* was thought revolting.

Going Places shakes you up and doesn't seem to leave you with anything to hang on to. It's easy to find it upsetting and degrading. But that's part of what makes it funny. The two men's crude energy is overwhelming, grungy, joyous. Life to them is like a big meal: they go at it like hungry workmen tearing at a carcass of beef, with greasy fingers. They aren't hippies rejecting middle-class materialism; they have none of the sanctimonious counterculture glamour of the pals in *Easy Rider*. They're closer to the joyriding lowlifers in *The Wild One*. These two pals talk in rough lower-class accents and don't fit into modern urban France, with its homogeneous middle-class culture. They're outsiders without jobs or money who want to live the life of the rich and satisfy their appetites. So they help themselves to things: they snatch purses, steal cars, pilfer shops, and make passes at almost every woman they get near. They're not professional criminals; they just rip people off. They harass shopkeepers and work them up into a rage, but, in terms of the film, this is the only excitement the smug, bored shopkeepers get, and it's way in excess of any damage that the boys actually do. The atmosphere is that of classic farce, as in Ben Jonson: these two are no worse than the respected members of the bourgeoisie, they're just less skillful in their methods. It takes a half hour or so before a viewer grasps that the two pals (one is twenty-five, the other twenty-three) are guileless raw innocents and that almost everything they do backfires on them.

The tone of *Going Places* is startling, both brutal and lyrical. The men are barnyard characters with the kind of natural magic that the kids have in Vigo's *Zero for Conduct* and that Jean Renoir's Boudu has; there's a poetic logic in what they do. They pick up a compliant scraggly-blond waif, a beautician (Miou-Miou), who is so used to being treated as something inanimate—as garbage—that she thinks she is garbage. The two guys beat her up and abuse her. Yet they also like her, and they take turns trying to bring her to orgasm—one of them even encouraging and coaching the other. But she remains sad and frigid, and they become furious with her. In between their heterosexual episodes, Depardieu jumps Dewaere (he yelps); he has also suffered the indignity of being shot in the groin, sustaining what the doctor calls "an abrasion of the left testicle." After the failure with Miou-Miou, the two go off to find an experienced older woman who will feel something; they wait outside a women's prison, confident that discharged prisoners will be sex-starved, and a middle-aged woman (Jeanne Moreau) who has spent ten years inside emerges. They treat her royally, with food and attention, and she gives them a great night of sexual maternal passion. But in the morning she kisses them both as they sleep and commits suicide by putting a gun to her vagina. Shocked by this first encounter with real madness and pain, they go back to their frigid little beautician; they weep and she comforts them, and then, out of a sense of responsibility to the dead woman, the three of them travel to another jail to await the release of her son. He turns out to be physically unappealing and not quite right in the head, but when the four of them are off in the country at a hideaway and the two pals are fishing they hear their frigid girlfriend, who is in bed with the crazy jailbird, making cries of sexual arousal, and in a minute she rushes out, radiant, to tell them the happy news of her first orgasm. (They pick her up and dunk her in the river.) Once aroused, she is always eager, and the two pals keep swapping places in the back seats of stolen cars.

The social comedy in Blier's work is essentially sexual comedy: sex screws us up, we get nicked in the groin or jumped from behind, idiots make out better than we do, and some people are so twisted that no matter what we try to do for them they wreck everything. And sex between men and women is insanely mixed up with men's infantile longings and women's maternal passions. Sexually, life is a Keystone comedy, and completely amoral—we have no control over who or what excites us.

Going Places was perhaps the first film from Europe since *Breathless* and *Weekend* and *Last Tango in Paris* to speak to us in a new, firsthand way about sex and sex fantasies; it did it in a terse, cool, assured style influenced by

Godard, yet with a dreamy sort of displacement. (Godard achieved something similar in the postcards sequence of *Les Carabiniers*—also a two-pals movie.) When Blier's two pals are not in movement, they're disconsolate; they can't think of what to do with themselves from day to day. The landscapes without other people, the deserted places they go to, suggest a sex-obsessed dream world. These are cavemen who give women what in their exuberant male fantasies women want. The dialogue is slangy, the mood buoyant—flagrantly funny in a special, unpredictable way. You have no idea what may be coming. The distinctive aspect of Blier's method of work is that although his scripts are completely written in advance of the shooting—and he doesn't improvise—he writes in an improvisational manner. Most scenarists, like dramatists, think out their structure in terms of the development of a situation—with conflict and resolution. They instinctively plan it out and know where they're going. Blier writes psychological picaresques: he begins with a group of characters and a certain tone, and then he may veer off and go wherever his subconscious takes him. Where he ends up probably surprises and partly mystifies him, as it does us. But generally he's right to trust his impulses, because they take him somewhere we might not have got to in any other way. Crazy connections get made—things unexpectedly tie together. And there is, finally, an underlying set of themes which emerges, and it's much richer than if he'd stuck to a conscious plan. The limitation—if one chooses to regard it as that—of Blier's go-with-your-subconscious method is that, naturally, his films all have the same themes. But he has the wit to treat his own subconscious as a slapstick fantasy land.

Blier's method worked in *Going Places*, and it works in *Handkerchiefs*, but something went wrong in his sexual extravaganza *Calmos* (and the picture failed, even in France). The first half hour or so of *Calmos* is a hilariously scandalous dirty-boy romp. Blier has such economy that he goes right into the comedy; there are no preliminaries, no waste—you're laughing before you've settled into your seat. There are two pals again, but now they're forty-year-old boulevardiers who look like wax grooms on a stale wedding cake. One is a gynecologist (Jean-Pierre Marielle), and the other a baby-blue-eyed pimp (Jean Rochefort). The doctor can't bear to look at women's genitals anymore; the pimp is exhausted by women's sexual demands—he feels women are chasing him even in his sleep. When the doctor's wife

(Brigitte Fossey), hoping to tantalize him, offers herself for bondage — tells him she's ready for *anything* — he asks for foie gras. It's a dumb joke, but her nudity and his uncontrollable disgust make it lewdly, visually funny. The comedy is derived partly from a banal premise, a reversal of women's saying they have a headache. But the men's satiation — their demonstration of revulsion against sex — has real comic conviction. The two men run away together into the countryside, to a village where they eat and drink and wear old clothes and begin to stink. Calm, that's what they want. Eating is the only thing they can get excited about. They sit at a Rabelaisian feast, along with the local curé (Bernard Blier) and his helper, in an old house, and the cinematographer, Claude Renoir, makes the house, the food, the landscape sinfully beautiful. This opening is an inspired exploitation porno fantasy, with Renoir's images (and the music, by Georges Delerue) providing a feeling of grandeur and folly. But then the story enlarges and takes a science-fiction turn. It shifts from the lunacy and regressions of these two men to the sexual revulsion of men en masse. Blier and his co-scriptwriter, Philippe Dumarcay (who also worked on *Going Places*), lose the flavor and the characters, and the picture falls back on the stored-up debris of mass culture. The two men are joined by other escaping men; women demanding gratification come after them with guns, and it's a full-scale tedious war of the sexes until, finally, the two pals, old men now and shrivelled in size, are dropped out of a cloud onto an island, where they walk through the pubic hair of a giant black woman and slip into her vagina just as her giant black lover arrives to deflower her, and crush them. *Calmos* is an overscaled back-to-the-womb satiric fantasy — a male daydream about the impossibility of escape from the sexual wars.

How much distance does Blier have from his characters' foolishness? Well, at least enough to make us laugh at them. In a sense, *Calmos* is about sex rather than about women. A couple of guys coming out of a bar late at night might talk like this — about wanting to go home just to sleep but knowing that there's a woman waiting up for them, and not being able to face it. It's about the demands of sex on men who spent their youth chasing women and now — jaded — want a break from it. There's no macho in the male bonding of the Marielle and Rochefort characters; they just want to be left alone for a while — they want to go off and live like pigs. It's a funny idea, and though *Calmos* abandons it, there are still things to look at all through the picture. It was a stroke of genius to use Renoir and

Panavision: the images have clarity, depth, richness, sweep, and the color is deeper even then Decae's. Early on, there's a streetcar full of avid women—a not too bright idea that is given a redemptive comic intensity by Renoir's lighting. Throughout, the women are made repellently beautiful—they have a neon voraciousness. Brigitte Fossey, a blond cat with a perfect tiny mouth, is like sensual porcelain. The light on her is so metallic and cold that her makeup seems to be dry ice. Any man would fear to come to her: who could live up to the glittering desire in her cat eyes? And even the idea of the giantess (shot on a beach in Guadeloupe) is almost redeemed by Renoir's use of Eastman color and Panavision. No one but Blier has matched such raunchiness and such visual beauty; you have to have a true respect for raunchiness to do that.

The title *Get Out Your Handkerchiefs* suggests a mockery of such movies as *Love Story*, but it also carries another suggestion—that we *should* be prepared to weep at the perplexities of love. It's a gentler, more refined comedy than either of the others; our laughter is never raucous. The wildness of *Going Places* hasn't disappeared, though—now it's underneath. The impression that the film gives is of freshness and originality, and of an unusual serenity. Feelings are expressed that haven't come out in movies before, and in a personal voice of a kind we think of as novelistic, yet nothing is wasted in the shots. Everything is to the point, and so we sit trustingly as things drift along and work themselves out. Here, as in the two other pictures, we never know where the story is going, and there's a considerable shift of direction midway, but this time it's all reassuringly quiet. The music is by Mozart, by Delerue (writing in the spirit of Mozart), and by Schubert, and this has an additional modulating, controlling effect. The style is almost chaste.

The two protagonists are played by the stars of *Going Places*, Depardieu and Dewaere (it was written with them in mind), but they're not the boors they were before—there's no violence in them. They're polite, harmless workingmen—Depardieu a driving-school instructor, Dewaere a playground supervisor. The picture opens at Sunday lunch in a Paris café. Jug-faced and serious, the powerfully built Depardieu is eating robustly while his lovely dark wife (Carole Laure) pecks at her food. Suddenly, he begins expostulating; he explains to her that she doesn't eat because she's sick of his face. He says that he loves her and wants to make her happy, so he'll bring her the man sitting opposite her whom she's been staring at and wants to go to bed with. There's something Neanderthal about his clumsiness; he's telling her of his consideration for her while making a public spectacle of her misery and their sexual failure. He goes over, introduces himself to the bearded stranger (Dewaere), propositions him, and says, "If you get her to smile, you'll be my pal." From this first scene—which is as deft and quick and funny as scenes in Sacha Guitry's comedies, such as *Lovers and Thieves*—Blier is playing with his characters and with us. The wife certainly looks bored and depressed, but we don't see her eying Dewaere—who wears glasses, and looks rather vague and self-absorbed. He accepts the invitation, though, and becomes the wife's lover, and the men then take turns trying to impregnate her—it being their theory that she is silent and morose because a woman needs a child. What we do see once the two men become pals (without Dewaere's getting her to smile) is that neither one makes any emotional contact with her. Dewaere has the complacency of a literate simpleton. He owns five thousand of the Livre de Poche paperback classics; reading them and listening to Mozart are his life. And he proselytizes, and converts Depardieu to his interests, while the wife scrubs and knits. When a neighbor (Michel Serrault, the star of *Lovers and Thieves*) bangs on their door at night to complain of the sound of a Mozart record, Depardieu sits him down and converts *him*.

So far, it's an enchantingly quirky sex comedy. The situation of the sterile wife and the rattled husband has its classic-farce overtones; the cuckolded husband is generally rich and decrepit, of course, but this is a classic farce in modern slang, with a barrel-chested, virile young husband who cuckolds himself with complete casualness, on the spur of the moment. Yet the film's texture is soft and sensual; there's a velvety underlayer to the scenes. Jean Penzer's cinematography suggests another world—like something shot from a diving bell. Because of Blier's method, nothing is ever explained. It's clear the two men are chumps. But if they don't have any idea what's going on in the wife's mind, neither do we. And the secret of the film—its essence—is that Blier doesn't, either. Carole Laure, with her neat little choirboy head and her slender, sinuous body, is treated as an object throughout. But never with contempt. And Carole Laure is a wonderful reactor. Her elusive, doleful shades of feeling delight us, even though we can't be sure what they mean; we can't tell if her knitting is a way of escaping the men's idiocy or if her mind is blank, or both, but we enjoy entertaining the possibilities. Are the men right to think she will be happy only if she has a child? Maybe so, but they go about trying to give her one without ever getting through to her. Their obtuseness—their clumsiness —may be the reason they can't reach her, but then perhaps it's her unreachability that makes them so clumsy. She has the natural, yielding grace of a sapling.

In the second half, the classical elements vanish, and the picture becomes more mysterious, leisurely, and meditative. In all three of these films, the movement is from the city to the country—to the primeval wilderness—and it's always the men's propulsion. This time, the two men decide that the wife they've been sharing needs country air, and the three of them go off to be counsellors at a summer camp for the underprivileged. The camp has one wealthy child, a thirteen-year-old boy (the child who plays the part is billed only by his nickname, Riton, to protect him from notoriety); he has been sent there by his parents to obtain experience of the underprivileged, whom he will be dealing with when he takes over the family's industrial enterprises. He's a smart brat, with a genius I.Q., though he looks unformed; there is no suggestion of horniness about him, and the first time we see him, when the other children are picking on him, we might easily take him for a girl. But he's far more clever than the two pals, and he hasn't had any reason to feel that he's clumsy; he has his child's guile and seductiveness. He says and does the shrewd things that thirteen-year-olds must want to say and do but don't have the courage for, or the knowledge, except in their dreams. He uses entreaties drawn from Cherubino in *The Marriage of Figaro*. And he gets through to the wife. The men were right: she wanted a child.

The woman takes this little boy to her bed, and can't live without him, even if that means he must be kidnapped. When he has been sent away from her to boarding school, and is in the dorm at night telling his awed fellow-students the story of his conquest, and the woman herself tiptoes in and, in full view of all those boys, kisses him, we're watching a mythological romance. There are all the obstacles, such as the boy's parents, to be taken care of, but the two men (who turn into her clown attendants) help her, though it lands them in jail. How can they not help? The boy prodigy is like their Mozart. The film goes off in this weird direction, yet it all seems uncannily logical and prepared for. At the end, the woman has her child lover and is pregnant as well.

It's bewildering yet mysteriously right, satisfying, down to the pensive sounds of Schubert at the end. There's a gravity to this film—to Blier's generous, amused giving in to a sense of defeat. At some level, he has the feeling that what women want men for is to perpetuate the species—that they really want a child. And he has compounded this fantasy by having a child father the child, thus eliminating the need for men altogether. *Handkerchiefs* is a farce that turns into a fable. Now we recognize why everything about the young wife is so ambiguous—that melting look in her eyes, her shimmering beauty. Now we can understand Dewaere's double take when he was spending a night with her and said he wondered what her husband was doing, and she said "Who?" This is a sleeping-beauty fable, but told from the point of view of a man's erotic fears. This woman is to be awakened not by a prince but by a princeling. At the moment that her child lover is seducing her, in the sleeping quarters at the summer camp, the two chumps come down the hallway, pause outside her door, and discuss whether to go in. They decide that there's no reason to worry—the boy is too young. It's a funny moment, yet there's poetic tension in it, and the hallway has a palpable sensual beauty. They're losing out forever.

All three of these films are about two pals who don't really understand women—and their not understanding women is part of their bond. The teamwork of the actors is the true marriage. Depardieu, with his beautiful long jaw and his loping walk, and Dewaere, with his nearsighted vagueness (he's like a more delicate Timothy Bottoms), move together rhythmically. Marielle and Rochefort twitch and grimace and drop their eyelids in perfect counterpoint; their show of revulsion at women is the flirtation dance of impotent roués. The pal teams in these movies have intuitive rapport. They hang loose when they're together.

In *Handkerchiefs*, Blier's fantasy themes seem to turn against the male fantasist. There's pain along with the humor. The thirteen-year-old who arouses the wife is a variation of the jailbird who aroused the beautician, but, once aroused, the lovely wife does not want the men—she wants only the child. The two men who were so happy with the mother figure played by Moreau, and who wanted to be suckled on the train, are now rejected by the mother. Marielle and Rochefort at least found their way back to the womb, but Depardieu and Dewaere seem to be locked out. All they've got is each other, and at the end they're going off together, maybe to live happily like pigs. But that's not how it looks. Discharged from jail and carrying their belongings, Depardieu and Dewaere peer through an iron gate into the window of the solid, rich home where the wife they have lost sits contentedly knitting baby clothes, and then disappear down the road.

Blier's poetic logic is so coolly, lyrically sustained in *Get Out Your Handkerchiefs* that nothing that happens seems shocking. You feel you understand everything that's going on. But only while it's happening—not afterward. Afterward, you're exhilarated by the wit, and by your own amusement at how little you understand. What does the woman respond to in the child? His need? His foxiness? His strength? His childishness? It's a mystery. Sex is emotional anarchy.

Blier doesn't attempt to present a woman's point of view; he stays with the man's view of women, and that gives his films a special ambience. For a woman viewer, seeing *Handkerchiefs* is like a vacation in a country you've always wanted to visit. Reading a book such as *From Here to Eternity*, a woman enters an area of experience from which she has been excluded; seeing a Blier film, a woman enters a man's fantasy universe stripped of hypocrisy. Blier's films have no meanness about women; the wife in *Handkerchiefs* isn't neurotic—just elusive. Women are simply seen as different. A man friend of mine used to say, "If the first Martian who lands on earth is a male, I'll have more in common with him than I do with all the women on earth." Blier's is an art of exaggeration: he takes emotions and blows them up so big that we can see the things people don't speak about—and laugh at them. *Get Out Your Handkerchiefs* makes you feel unreasonably happy.

{*The New Yorker*, October 16, 1978}

:: The God-Bless-
America Symphony

A "magnificent hermaphrodite born between the savage and the civilized": that's how Balzac described Hawkeye, the Deerslayer —the idealized frontier hero of James Fenimore Cooper's Leatherstocking Tales. The steelworker hero of Michael Cimino's *The Deer Hunter* is the newest version of this American "gentleman" of the wilderness, and the film—a three-hour epic that is scaled to the spaciousness of America itself—is the fullest screen treatment so far of the mystic bond of male comradeship. It is steeped in boys' adventure classics, with their emphasis on self-reliance and will power, and their exaltation of purity of thought— of a physical-spiritual love between men which is higher than the love between man and woman, because (presumably) it is never defiled by carnal desire. The American wilderness of our literature is (as D.H. Lawrence wickedly put it) the boys' Utopia. *The Deer Hunter* is a romantic adolescent boy's view of friendship, with the Vietnam War perceived in the Victorian terms of movies such as *Lives of a Bengal Lancer*—as a test of men's courage. Yet you can feel an awareness of sex just under the diffused sensuality of the surface. The whole movie, with its monumental romanticism and its striving for a symphonic shape, is sexually impacted. It takes the celibacy of football players before the big game and attaches it to Vietnam. The hero, Michael (Robert De Niro), and his friends—Nick (Christopher Walken) and Steven (John Savage)—are as chaste as Norman Rockwell Boy Scouts; they're the American cousins of hobbits.

Cimino, who is thirty-nine, has directed only one previous film— *Thunderbolt and Lightfoot*, with Clint Eastwood and Jeff Bridges, in 1974, which he also wrote. He's a New Yorker and a Yale M.F.A. in graphic design who went into the Army and was a medic attached to a Green Beret unit training in Texas. When his interest turned to movies, he worked in documentary film and in commercials before he was able to use writing as a way to break into directing. His first credit was on *Silent Running*, in 1971; then he (and also John Milius) worked on the script of *Magnum Force* for Clint Eastwood, who had already arranged to give Cimino his chance on *Thunderbolt and Lightfoot*. His new film is enraging, because, despite its ambitiousness and scale, it has no more moral intelligence than the Eastwood action pictures. Yet it's an astonishing piece of work, an uneasy mixture of violent pulp and grandiosity, with an enraptured view of common life — poetry of the commonplace.

When we first see the three men, it's 1968 and they are in a steel mill, on the floor of the blast furnace; at the end of the shift, they go from the blazing heat to the showers. It's their last day on the job before they report for active duty, and the other workers say goodbye to them. Then they move through the casual sprawl of their hilly mill town, Clairton, Pennsylvania, to their nearby hangout — Welsh's bar — to guzzle a few beers and loosen up. Each step of their day is perceived in ritual terms. The big ritual is to come that night: Steven's wedding at the Russian Orthodox Church and then the celebration at the Clairton chapter of the American Legion, which is also the farewell party for all three. We spend about three-quarters of an hour in the church and the hall; the moving camera seems to be recording what's going on in this microcosmic environment — to be giving us an opportunity to observe people as they live their lives. The long takes and sweeping, panning movements are like visual equivalents of Bruckner and Mahler: majestic, yet muffled. Because of the length of this introductory section, and because it isn't dramatically focussed, we feel an anticipatory ominousness. Derivative as this opening section is (it's easy to see the influence of Coppola and Visconti, and probably Minnelli, too), it conveys a very distinctive love of rootedness and of the values of people whose town is their world. (It's the sort of world we used to see in French films of the thirties, with Raimu.) Cimino brings an architectural sense into his collaboration with the cinematographer, Vilmos Zsigmond, whose style here recalls his smooth long takes in *Deliverance* but has a crisp vitality, like his more recent work in *Close Encounters*. There may be a touch of *National Geographic* in the first views of the beautiful, gaudy interior of the Byzantine-primitive church, yet Cimino and Zsigmond take the curse off the usual limitations of Panavision and the heightless wide screen by panning down, down, slowly. They provide such an illusion of height that it's hard to believe the screen is the same shape that George Stevens once said was good only for high-school-commencement pictures. In the church, we see the faces of people we have already met; our eye is caught by John Welsh (George Dzundza), the cherub-cheeked bar owner, singing in the chorus. Here and in the Legion hall, there are uninterrupted panning movements in which we see people singing and dancing, flirting and fighting, and moving from one group to another. And it has a detailed clarity: we feel that we're storing up memories. There's something nostalgic about this ceremonial view of ordinary American community life even as it's going on. This town of Clairton is actually a composite of a number of locations, most of them in Ohio, but it becomes a clear geographical entity for us, and even the double mobile home that Michael and Nick share feels so accurate that it, too, seems rooted. Nothing was shot in a studio.

Cimino's virtuoso staging has a limitation: the brilliance of his panoramic ensembles sometimes gives us the idea that in seeing so many things so quickly we have come to know these people. They don't actually reveal much more than the convivial crowds in a beer commercial do, yet we're made to feel that what we see is all they are. (A great director would plant doubts in us.) And even with the dozen or so principal characters, the casting and the actors' physiognomies and intuitive byplay do most of the work of characterization; the dialogue is usually just behavioral chatter. When Cimino wants to make a point, it's usually an outsize point—a portent or an omen that reeks of old-movie infantilism. Someone draws Michael's attention to a nimbus around the sun, and he explains what the Indians used to say this formation meant. (Is Cimino invoking the mythology of Hawkeye and the great chief Chingachgook?) Steven and his bride, who is pregnant but not by him, are served wine in a double-cupped goblet, by the priest, who tells them that if they drink it down without spilling a drop they will have luck all their lives, and we see the small stains forming on the bride's white lace bodice. (Here it's *Smilin' Through* that's invoked.) Nick, the best man, makes Michael promise that, whatever happens to him, he will be brought back to this place, these trees. A grim-faced Green Beret just returned from Nam comes into the Legion bar during the party; the men ask him "What's it like over there?" and he replies with an obscenity. And so on. Cimino's talent is for breadth and movement and detail, and the superlative mix of the Dolby sound gives a sense of scale to the crowd noises and the voices and the music; we feel we're hearing a whole world. But Cimino doesn't know how to reveal character, develop it, or indicate what's going on in a human relationship. When Linda (Meryl Streep), one of the bridesmaids, catches the tossed bridal bouquet, and Nick asks her to marry him and she says yes, we don't know if she's in love with him or with Michael, with whom she exchanged glances earlier, or what Michael feels. Probably, Cimino doesn't know; he may think it doesn't matter. Michael keeps his distance from people, and he seems too pure to have anything particular in mind when he looks at Linda; he's saving his vital juices for chivalry.

After the party is over and the bride and groom have left for their weekend honeymoon, Michael and Nick and their pals—John Welsh and skinny, dark Stan, played by John Cazale, and huge, bearded Axel, played by Chuck Aspegren—climb into Michael's white '59 Cadillac with tail fins and drive to the mountains, for a last, ritual hunt before Vietnam. A couple of the men are still wearing their rumpled tuxedos, but Michael, who is the leader of the group yet also a man apart, emotionally hidden, and with a compulsive orderliness that makes the others uncomfortable, has stripped down and dressed for his date with the deer. Unlike such makers of epics as Coppola and Bertolucci, Cimino doesn't seem to want his themes to rise to our full consciousness (or perhaps even to his own), but he can't resist eroticizing the hunt—it's a sexual surrogate, a man's-man wedding. Michael climbs to the top of a virgin mountain and, with a snowcapped peak behind him and a male choir in the sky singing a Russian Orthodox liturgical chant and rain clouds swirling about him, stalks a buck and fells it with one clean shot. That's his consummation.

The five hunters drive back down to Welsh's bar, and there follows a scene that is possibly too clever: fat, baby-faced Welsh plays a Chopin nocturne, and the others listen attentively. It's a moment of communion before the parting of the ways. The music is lovely, and if one of the men— the amiable nonentity Axel, perhaps—had only fallen asleep this scene might have been as great as it wants to be. But with all of them demonstrating their innate sensitivity, showing us that beer sloshers' savage breasts are soothed by music and that their inarticulate feelings go far beyond what they talk about, it's too much like those scenes in which roomfuls of Hitler's lieutenants all swooned to Wagner. And it's just a shade too effective, too theatrical, when Cimino cuts from this solemn grace to the noise and hell of Vietnam.

It's in the contrast, though, between the Clairton sequences, with all those people joined together in slowly rhythmed takes, and the war in Vietnam, where everything is spasmodic, fast, in short takes, with cuts from one anguished face to another, that Cimino shows his filmmaking instinct and craft. But also his xenophobic yellow-peril imagination. It's part of the narrowness of the film's vision that there is no suggestion that there ever was a sense of community among the Vietnamese which was disrupted. We are introduced to Asians by seeing a soldier (North Vietnamese, or, perhaps, Vietcong—we can't be sure) open the door of a shelter, find women and children cowering inside, and then thoughtfully lob in a grenade. Michael, a Green Beret Ranger in an advance reconnaissance unit, spots the soldier machine-gunning a fleeing woman and her child, yells "No!," and hits him with a flame thrower. The impression a viewer gets is that if we did some bad things over there we did them ruthlessly but impersonally; the Vietcong were cruel and sadistic. The film seems to be saying that the Americans had no choice, but the V.C. enjoyed it. Michael meets up with Nick and Steven again, and the three are taken prisoner and are tortured strictly for their captors' pleasure. The prisoners are forced to play Russian roulette in teams while the Vietcong gamble on which one will blow his head off.

The Vietnam War—and, more particularly, Russian roulette—serves Cimino metaphorically as the Heart of Darkness; Michael, the disciplined Deer Hunter, doesn't succumb. He has the will and courage to save the three of them. These prison-camp torture sequences are among the finest-edited action scenes that I know of; they are so fast and powerful—and so violent—that some people will no doubt be forced to walk out. They are the very center of the film—the test it was preparing for. Although Michael, the superman who forces his friends to develop the will to survive, belongs to the boys'-book world of grit and sacrifice, the sheer force of these pulp atrocity scenes takes over one's consciousness. I say "pulp" because the Vietcong are treated in the standard inscrutable-evil-Oriental style of the Japanese in Second World War movies and because Russian roulette takes over as the ruling metaphor for all the action scenes in the rest of the movie, even in the later episodes in Saigon and back home. Why is Russian roulette used this way? Possibly because it goes so completely against the American grain—it's like a metaphor for the General West-moreland theory that Asians don't value human life the way we do. But also because it has a boyish vainglory about it: does one have the guts to pull the trigger? It's a boy's kicky idea of courage.

If *The Deer Hunter* had been a serious consideration of boys'-book val-ues, it might have demonstrated that they did not apply in the mechanized destructiveness of modern warfare—that Michael was basically as vulner-able as everybody else. But the fact is that Cimino believes they do apply, and so Michael is put up against curs and sadists; he's in a Victorian test of manhood. And no doubt many people will go along with the film and accept Michael, the superior being, as a realistic hero, because of the gen-eral understanding that comradeship and depending on your buddies and helping them is finally all that you can believe in when you're in the midst of war. Cimino, who believes in those Hemingwayesque one-clean-shot values that Michael (whom he has obviously named for himself) repre-sents, has framed the whole war in terms of that kind of courage. Every-thing that happens appears to be the result of the atrocities of the Vietcong. Yet the film's point of view isn't clear. The American helicopters are like Walpurgisnacht locusts coming down on your head, and no one who believed that the Americans behaved honorably in Vietnam would have staged the evacuation of Saigon as Cimino has done, with thousands of Vietnamese abandoned and despairing. And, although Michael proves himself by performing extraordinary feats of valor, he is not ennobled by them, as movie heroes used to be. *The Deer Hunter* is Beau Geste-goes-to-Vietnam, all right, but with a difference: when Michael returns to his home and goes up to the mountain peaks again, and the male choir chants, he has the deer in front of him but he doesn't kill it. Cimino has made a film that vindicates the boys'-book values (without them, Michael and his friends would not have survived the prison camp) and then rejects them.

This movie may offend conventional liberal thinking more by its com-mitment to parochial, "local" values than by any defense of the Vietnam War—for it makes none. Neither does it take any political position against the war. But the film's very substance—the Clairton community in con-trast with the Asian chaos—is the traditional isolationist message: Asia should be left to the Asians, and we should stay where we belong, but if we have to go over there we'll show how tough we are. This parochialism may be the key to why some people will reject the film in toto—even find it despicable in toto. Although cosmopolitan values were actually the ones that got us into Vietnam (the government planners weren't small-town American Legionnaires; they were Harvard men), it has become the custom to pin the guilt on the military "hawks." Michael is not a liberal hero, like the Jon Voight character of *Coming Home*; we can feel (without being told) that he's grounded in the rigid values of people who are suspicious of science and world affairs and anything foreign. Cimino is as careful to leave controversy out of his idealized town as Louis B. Mayer used to be. Clairton is abstracted from even those issues that people in beer joints quarrel about; no one ever asks what the Americans are doing in Vietnam, there are no racial jokes, and there isn't as much as a passing reference to strikes or welfare, or anything else that might show dissension, anger, or narrowness. And, of course, there are no homosexuals in the town (or even in the war); if there were, the film's underpinnings would collapse, and its eerie romanticism would become funny. In this film, evil itself is totally unsexual; Russian roulette is the perfect solution—Nick, who has had his soul burned out by it, goes AWOL and disappears into the dives of Saigon, where civilians play that game. Without sharing the implicit God-and-country, flag-on-the-door political assumptions of *The Deer Hunter*, one can see, I think, that, even with its pulp components and the racism of its Saigon dens-of-vice scenes and its superman hero, it is not merely trying to move people by pandering to their prejudices—it is also caught in its own obsessions. And, because it plays them out on such a vast canvas, it has an inchoate, stirring quality. Audiences can project into *The Deer Hunter* in a way they couldn't with such male-comradeship films as *Butch Cassidy and the Sundance Kid*, because it gives us the feeling that it's got a grand design lurking somewhere in those sensual rhythms and inconsistent themes.

In traditional American literature—in Mark Twain, say—the boys with pluck run away from proprieties, restrictions, manners, chores. Women represent the civilization that must be escaped. But in *The Deer Hunter* women are not even that much: they exist only on the margins of the men's lives. Steven's mother (Shirley Stoler, in a poor, mostly one-note performance) is a virago, his bride is a sallow weakling, and the bridesmaids are overly made-up and have too many curls; they're plump—stuffed with giggles. The only woman we see in Clairton who could attract a man of substance for more than a quick fling is Meryl Streep's Linda, who works in the supermarket; Streep has the clear-eyed blond handsomeness of a Valkyrie—the slight extra length of her nose gives her face a distinction that takes her out of the pretty class into real beauty. She doesn't do anything standard; everything seems fresh. But her role is to be the supportive woman, who suffers and endures, and it's a testament to Meryl Streep's heroic resources as a mime that she makes herself felt—she has practically no lines. There were three writers on this project in addition to Cimino (Deric Washburn, Louis Garfinkle, and Quinn K. Redeker worked on the story with him, and Washburn did the screenplay), but Linda is a presence rather than a character. She's a possibility glimpsed, rather than a woman, or even a sex object—least of all, a sex object. Michael and Nick, the two central characters, both have some sort of commitment to her, without our knowing what either of them feels for her—it's a very limp triangle. She is the film's token of romance, and Cimino's unwillingness to go beyond Victorian tokenism muddies the film when Michael returns from Vietnam and his relations with Linda consist mostly of the exchange of unhappy, solicitous looks. Does he love her but feel that she's pledged to Nick, who he thinks is dead? (There's no clue to why he would think Nick was dead.) Michael shows no physical desire for Linda. They lie on a bed together, he fully clothed—should we know what they're thinking? We don't. And when, for one night, they're under the covers together, without their clothes, and he rolls over on top of her, the scene is deliberately vague, passionless. He never even kisses her—would that be too personal? He was hotter for the deer.

Finally (and improbably), Michael learns that Nick may still be alive, and goes back to Vietnam to find him and pull him out from the Heart of Darkness. The scenes in Vietnam, with all those people clamoring to survive, and with him going back in there to rescue a man who doesn't care to live, are so sweeping yet so slick that they're like Coppola without brains or sensibility. Exotic steaminess is pushed to the melodramatic limit, as Michael, looking for his friend, passes through the inferno of war and enters Saigon's sin city, operating in the midst of flames and human misery. The film's last hour, in which it loses its sure progression and its confident editing, would have been far less wobbly if Michael had not come home until after he had made this rescue attempt. As it is, he returns from

Vietnam twice, and during the period when he's home for the first time the story weaves back and forth, with fumbling scenes of Michael trying to make up his mind whether he should go see Steven, who's in a hospital. This period is unformed; it lacks resonance and gives us the impression that we're missing something—that pieces of the plot have been cut out.

It's possible that Cimino grew as an artist during the years of making this film (the production costs doubled, to thirteen million) but was locked into certain fantasy conceptions, and was never able to clarify the characters without violating the whole deer-hunting mystique he'd started with. And even after he'd shot the sequences that re-created the obscenity of the evacuation of Saigon, he was still committed to the gimmickry of the roulette game of life and death. *The Deer Hunter* is a small-minded film with greatness in it—Cimino's technique has pushed him further than he has been able to think out. His major characters don't articulate their feelings; they're floating in a wordless, almost plotless atmosphere, and their relations aren't sharp enough for us to feel the full range of the film's themes. Too many of the motifs are merely symbolic—are dropped in rather than dramatized. At times, we feel that we're there to be awed rather than to understand. We come out knowing the secondary characters—John Cazale's weak Stan (who hits women and kills deer sloppily) and George Dzundza's music-loving Welsh and John Savage's simplehearted, ingenuous Steven—far better than we know Michael or Nick.

This isn't because De Niro and Walken don't do their jobs. Walken seems completely authentic one minute and totally false the next, because he has so little that's definite to project that he's straining. Yet he has never been so forceful on the screen, and when he's feverish and wet in the Vietnamese jungle and his hair is plastered down on his head, his large eyes, sharp chin, and jutting cheekbones suggest Falconetti in *The Passion of Joan of Arc*; he has a feminine delicacy without effeminacy. He's right for his part, but his rightness for it is all that the part is. And this is true of De Niro. He's lean, wiry, strong. Physically, he's everything that one wants the hero to be. (The only thing that's unheroic about him is that he's still using the cretinous grin he developed for *Bang the Drum Slowly*.) He fails conspicuously in only one sequence—when he's required to grab Nick's bloody head and shake it. You don't shake someone who's bleeding, and De Niro can't rise above the stupidity of this conception; even his weeping doesn't move us. We have come to expect a lot from De Niro: miracles. And he delivers them—he brings a bronze statue almost to life. He takes the Pathfinder-Deerslayer role and gives it every flourish he can dream up. He does improvisations on nothing, and his sea-to-shining-sea muscularity is impressive. But Michael, the transcendent hero, is a hollow figure. There is never a moment when we feel, Oh my God, I know that man, I am that man.

{*The New Yorker*, December 18, 1978}

Invasion of the Body Snatchers is more sheer fun than any movie I've seen since *Carrie* and *Jaws* and maybe parts of *The Spy Who Loved Me*. The scriptwriter, W.D. (Rick) Richter, supplies some of the funniest lines ever heard from the screen, and the director, Phil Kaufman, provides such confident professionalism that you sit back in the assurance that every spooky nuance you're catching is just what was intended. It's a wonderful relief to see a movie made by people who know what they're doing. They're also working with a deliciously paranoid theme: trying to hang on to your human individuality while those around you are contentedly turning into vegetables and insisting that you join them. The film takes off from the 1956 *The Invasion of the Body Snatchers*, directed by Don Siegel—a low-budget Allied Artists movie (about $350,000) that has an honored place in film history, because of its realistic atmosphere (it's set in a drab, isolated small town that seems to close in on the characters) and the solid, frightening theme, which is essentially the idea that Ionesco developed in *Rhinoceros*. (Americans seem to have better luck when they treat surreal paranoid ideas in low-down science-fiction form.) Siegel's version was subjected to executive bowdlerizing: most of the humor was excised, and a prologue and an epilogue were tacked on to provide a hopeful resolution. Even so, it's a tight little economy-package classic. The new version is wilder and more fantastic, with perhaps the best use of Dolby stereo yet—the sound effects have you scared and laughing even before the titles come on. This Phil Kaufman version is so sumptuously made that it looks very expensive, even though it was done on what is now considered a small budget (under three and a half million, with a sizable chunk of that going into the post-production work on the sound.) The pre-title rumbling roar suggests how God might have started the Creation if only He'd had Dolby. The first images, which are of diaphanous gelatinous spores wafting upward, have a spectral comic beauty; it's like being in a planetarium while something awesomely, creepily sexy is taking place. This is a full-scale science-fiction horror fable, a realization of the potentialities of the material. For undiluted pleasure and excitement, it is, I think, the American movie of the year—a new classic.

The story is set in San Francisco, which is the ideally right setting, because of the city's traditional hospitality to artists and eccentrics. Probably nowhere else have people considered so many systems of thought and been through so many interpersonal wars; San Franciscans often look shell-shocked. The various outcroppings of the human-potential movement have had an unexpected result: instead of becoming more individual, people in therapeutic groups get so self-absorbed in their various quests that they appear dulled out. And so when the gooey seeds from space come down in the rain over San Francisco and cling to leaves and establish root systems and blossom, and each flower pod develops into a fetus that grows large enough to replace an individual as he sleeps, while the old body crumbles into a small pile of garbage, it is not surprising to hear the reborn flower people proselytizing for their soulless condition as a higher form of life. "Don't be trapped by old concepts," one of them says. The story simply wouldn't be as funny in New York City, where people are not so relaxed, or so receptive to new visions. There are no a-priori rejections in San Francisco.

The hip-idyllic city, with its gingerbread houses and its jagged geometric profile of hills covered with little triangles and rectangles, is such a pretty plaything that it's the central character. The movie itself is like a toy; it's all filigree, in the way that *The Manchurian Candidate* is. As the malignant growth sprouts brilliant-red blossoms, we hear the film's first words: in the bland, bored tone of someone who's trying to fill up the time, a teacher who's out with her class says, "There's some more flowers, kids. Go pick them." That has got to be a famous first line. For the opening third of the picture, almost every scene has a verbal or visual gag built into it, and throughout there's a laciness to the images—to the way the interiors include exterior views of the whimsical, Victorian-dollhouse architecture, and the bright-colored sanitation trucks gobbling up waste matter.

Elizabeth (Brooke Adams), who works at the Department of Health, picks one of the carnal red flowers on her way home. When she gets there, Geoffrey (Art Hindle), her laid-back lover, is sprawled out watching basketball on TV; he kisses Elizabeth without taking off his earphones and gets excited only when he hears a terrific play—he pushes her aside so he can see it. Geoffrey, who's a dentist, is so quintessentially laid back you don't know what keeps him vertical, or in such good shape. He just seems to have been manufactured with muscles: that's the model. The flower is left near his side of the bed, and in the morning he no longer goes with the flow; he gets up with a stolid sense of mission, dresses up as if he were a Rotarian huckster, and takes a bundle out under his arm and tosses it into a waiting garbage truck. And as he goes about the city he makes eye contact with other people, who all know what's on each other's minds—it's as if they were governed by Muzak. (Watching the clear-faced, neatly dressed, upstanding Geoffrey, you suspect that Werner Erhard was the original spore.) Scared by the change in him, Elizabeth tells her boss, Matthew (Donald Sutherland), that Geoffrey isn't Geoffrey, that "something is missing." But then she goes to a cocktail party celebrating the publication of a new how-to-be-happy book by Dr. Kibner (Leonard Nimoy), the city's leading chic psychiatrist, who suavely explains that she thinks Geoffrey has changed—has become less human—because she's looking for a chance to get out of their relationship. (Kibner is as smug as the psychoanalyst in *Cat People* explaining to Simone Simon that she only fantasizes turning into a leopard.) And Elizabeth, who knows she's beginning to have romantic urges toward her boss, half accepts Kibner's explanation.

In most science-fiction movies, the stalwart characters would have nothing to lose to the pod people; they have already been vegetablized by the lack of imagination of the filmmakers. But Kaufman and Richter have managed to give substance to the fear of losing one's individuality, by creating believable, likable characters. Brooke Adams doesn't have the sullen-washerwoman look she had in *Days of Heaven*; her turned-down mouth has an odd attractiveness, and her Elizabeth is smart and resilient, with a streak of loony humor. (She spins her eyeballs, like the great Harry Ritz.) Even her flat voice is funny here: she uses vocal affectlessness as a deadpan, and rings trick low notes on it. (The women in this movie are every bit as strong and sharp—and foolish—as the men, without any big point being made of it.) As heroes go, Sutherland may not be a world-beater, but at least he's plausible and stays in character. And the other leads play genuine

San Francisco weirdos. Jeff Goldblum, who knows enough to disregard his handsomeness, and to stick with a huffy, distracted timing that is purely his own, is Jack Bellicec, a furiously angry poet who is proud of taking six months to decide on a word, and Veronica Cartwright is his wife, Nancy, who works in their Turkish-bath establishment—Bellicec Baths—as desk clerk and masseuse. Veronica Cartwright has such an instinct for the camera that even when she isn't doing anything special, what she's feeling registers. She doesn't steal scenes—she gives them an extra comic intensity. When Nancy Bellicec greets someone by scrunching up her face, her whole goofy soul is in her expression. What the film catches with this devoted pair is their domestication of nuttiness—they wouldn't love each other so much if they weren't both a little cracked. San Francisco is a city full of people who are sure they could write better than the successful writers in their midst, and probably could, but they're too busy living and griping to try. Jack's contempt for the best-selling Dr. Kibner is the contempt of a writer who doesn't put anything on paper for the fraud who does. Phil Kaufman (who makes his home there) and Rick Richter (who was on the locations throughout the shooting) have got the conversational tone of the culture down pat. The Bellicecs must protect their eccentricity: it's the San Francisco brand of humanity. This film is almost like a surreal variant of Simone Weil's thesis that the people who resisted the Nazis weren't the good, upright citizens—they were the dreamers and outcasts and cranks. There's something at stake in this movie: the right of freaks to be freaks—which is much more appealing than the right of "normal" people to be normal.

There are some amazing special effects: the plant tendrils that sneak over sleeping people, and the fetal pods that bleed when they're crushed, and a dog joke that is perhaps a nod to *The Fly* and *The Mephisto Waltz* and the famous dog in *Yojimbo* but is also pure Dadaism. *Invasion of the Body Snatchers* gives the impression of a supernatural and fantastic visual style, though the cinematography, by Michael Chapman, is very straightforward. This may be because of the unusual delicacy of his work. The daylight scenes, with sharp primary colors that aren't posterish in the Godardian way, because of a softening use of secondary colors, emphasize the orderly movements of the pod people, which are so at odds with the iridescent bauble of a city. At night, of course, the city is theirs. Much of the photogenic power of the material (it's based on Jack Finney's early-fifties *Collier's* serial *The Body Snatchers*) comes from the fear of night and sleep: if a character closes his eyes, he may not be himself when he wakes up. When the first version was made, the filmmakers thought of calling it *Sleep No More*. Chapman has a special feel for night subjects, as he demonstrated in *Taxi Driver* and *The Last Waltz*, though his work on Kaufman's *The White Dawn* was also eerie and mysterious. He shows a gift here for bringing out the personality of the city locations; there's a finely drawn, cluttered grace in his San Francisco, and it intensifies the horror, in the same way that the characters' idiosyncratic styles of humor do. When the four principals run down Telegraph Hill, with a phalanx of pod people in pursuit, and dash to the Embarcadero, they cast long shadows, like figures in one of de Chirico's almost deserted piazzas. Parts of this film have a hellish beauty, like Cocteau's *Orpheus* and, more recently, *The Fury*.

There are small disappointments. Elizabeth tells Matthew of the conspiratorial meetings of the pod people before we actually see them meet. And Matthew has a sequence of racing from one telephone booth to another which is charged with meaningless tension and has no particular payoff. Perhaps the scenes in which pods are being dispatched to other cities are not as elegantly staged as they might be. And there may be a few times when the generally dazzling score, by Denny Zeitlin, the jazz pianist turned San Francisco psychiatrist, overpowers the action, but the music is a large contributor to the jokes and terrors. There is also a truly inspired electronic effect, devised by the sound expert Ben Burtt: the pod people make a shrieking, warning cry that suggests an inhuman variant of the rhythmic trilling-screaming sounds of the women in *The Battle of Algiers*. In that film, it was a cry for freedom; here it's a cry for conformity.

There's a great entertainment-movie tradition of combining high jinks and artistry, and this film belongs to it. Michael Chapman, the cinematographer, can be spotted in a corridor, leaning against a mop, and Robert Duvall, who played Jesse James in Kaufman's first major studio film, *The Great Northfield Minnesota Raid*, is visible as a priest on a playground swing. (As a benediction for the movie?) Don Siegel turns up, playing a cabdriver. And there's a reënactment of what is generally remembered as the end of the 1956 version (it's how the movie would have ended if the studio hadn't slapped on the "Get me the F.B.I." epilogue), with Kevin McCarthy, the star of that version, once more banging on car windshields. He yells,

"They're here! Help! They're here!" But this time he isn't saved—he's finished off. There are also fog-enshrouded shots of the Transamerica pyramid. (Transamerica is the parent company of United Artists, which financed this picture.) *Invasion of the Body Snatchers* doesn't take itself too seriously, yet it plunges into emotional scenes with a fast, offhand mastery. At night, Matthew stands on the terrace of his apartment, where he and his three friends have holed up, and looks down at the four adult-size fetuses that are almost ready to replace them. He wants to smash those bodies, but he can't destroy the ones of his friends, because they're so close to human that it would be like killing people he loves. He can smash only his own reproduction. This set of variations on the 1956 film has its own macabre originality; it may be the best movie of its kind ever made.

{*The New Yorker*, December 25, 1978}

from
TAKING IT ALL IN

:: Why Are Movies So Bad?
or, The Numbers

The movies have been so rank the last couple of years that when I see people lining up to buy tickets I sometimes think that the movies aren't drawing an audience—they're inheriting an audience. People just want to go to a movie. They're stung repeatedly, yet their desire for a good movie—for *any* movie—is so strong that all over the country they keep lining up. "There's one God for all creation, but there must be a separate God for the movies," a producer said. "How else can you explain their survival?" An atmosphere of hope develops before a big picture's release, and even after your friends tell you how bad it is, you can't quite believe it until you see for yourself. The lines (and the grosses) tell us only that people are going to the movies—not that they're having a good time. Financially, the industry is healthy, so among the people at the top there seems to be little recognition of what miserable shape movies are in. They think the grosses are proof that people are happy with what they're getting, just as TV executives think that the programs with the highest ratings are what TV viewers want, rather than what they settle for. (A number of the new movie executives come from TV.) These new executives don't necessarily see many movies themselves, and they rarely go to a theatre. If for the last couple of years Hollywood couldn't seem to do anything right, it isn't that it was just a stretch of bad luck—it's the result of recent developments within the industry. And in all probability it will get worse, not better. There have been few recent American movies worth lining up for—last year there was chiefly *The Black Stallion*, and this year there is *The Empire Strikes Back*. The first was made under the aegis of Francis Ford

Coppola; the second was financed by George Lucas, using his profits from *Star Wars* as a guarantee to obtain bank loans. One can say with fair confidence that neither *The Black Stallion* nor *The Empire Strikes Back* could have been made with such care for visual richness and imagination if it had been done under studio control. Even small films on traditional subjects are difficult to get financed at a studio if there are no parts for stars in them; Peter Yates, the director of *Breaking Away*—a graceful, unpredictable comedy that pleases and satisfies audiences—took the project to one studio after another for almost six years before he could get the backing for it.

There are direct results when conglomerates take over movie companies. At first, the heads of the conglomerates may be drawn into the movie business for the status implications—the opportunity to associate with world-famous celebrities. Some other conglomerate heads may be drawn in for the girls, but for them, too, a new social life beckons, and as they become socially involved, people with great names approach them as equals, and it gets them crazy. Famous stars and producers and writers and directors tell them about offers they've had from other studios and about ideas they have for pictures, and the conglomerate heads become indignant that the studios they control aren't in on these wonderful projects. The next day, they're on the phone raising hell with their studio bosses. Very soon, they're likely to be summoning directors and suggesting material to them, talking to actors, and telling the company executives what projects should be developed. How bad are the taste and judgment of the conglomerate heads? Very bad. They haven't grown up in a show-business milieu—they don't have the background, the instincts, the information of those who have lived and sweated movies for many years. (Neither do most of the current studio bosses.) The conglomerate heads may be business geniuses, but as far as movies are concerned they have virgin instincts; ideas that are new to them and take them by storm may have failed grotesquely dozens of times. But they feel that they are creative people—how else could they have made so much money and be in a position to advise artists what to do? Who is to tell them no? Within a very short time, they are in fact, though not in title, running the studio. They turn up compliant executives who will settle for the title and not fight for the authority or for their own tastes—if, in fact, they have any. The conglomerate heads find these compliant executives among lawyers and agents, among lawyer-agents, among television executives, and in the lower echelons of the companies they've taken over. Generally, these executives reserve all their enthusiasm for movies that have made money; those are the only movies they like. When a director or a writer talks to them and tries to suggest the kind of picture he has in mind by using a comparison, they may stare at him blankly. They are usually law-school or business-school graduates; they have no frame of reference. Worse, they have no shame about not knowing anything about movies. From their point of view, such knowledge is not essential to their work. Their talent is being able to anticipate their superiors' opinions; in meetings, they show a sixth sense for guessing what the most powerful person in the room wants to hear. And if they ever guess wrong, they know how to shift gears without a tremor. So the movie companies wind up with top production executives whose interest in movies rarely extends beyond the immediate selling possibilities; they could be selling neckties just as well as movies, except that they are drawn to glamour and power.

This does not prevent these executives from being universally treated as creative giants. If a studio considers eighty projects, and eventually twenty of them (the least risky) go into production, and two of them become runaway hits (or even one of them), the studio's top executive will be a hero to his company and the media, and will soon be quoted in the *Los Angeles Times* and *The New York Times* talking about his secret for picking winners—his intuitive understanding, developed from his childhood experiences, that people want a strong, upbeat narrative, that they want to cheer the hero and hiss the villain. When *Alien* opened "big," Alan Ladd, Jr., president of the pictures division of Twentieth Century-Fox, was regarded as a demigod; it's the same way that Fred Silverman was a demigod. It has nothing to do with quality, only with the numbers. (Ladd and his team weren't admired for the small pictures they took chances on and the artists they stuck by.) The media now echo the kind of thinking that goes on in Hollywood, and spread it wide. Movie critics on TV discuss the relative grosses of the new releases; the grosses at this point relative to previous hits; which pictures will pass the others in a few weeks. It's like the Olympics—which will be the winners?

There are a lot of reasons that movies have been so bad during the last couple of years and probably won't be any better for the next couple of years. One big reason is that rotten pictures are making money—not necessarily wild amounts (though a few are), but sizable amounts. So if studio heads want nothing more than to make money and grab power, there is no reason for them to make better ones. Turning out better pictures might actually jeopardize their position. Originally, the studios were controlled by theatre chains—the chains opened the studios in order to have a source of supply. But the studios and the theatre chains were separated by a Supreme Court order in 1948 and subsequent lower-court rulings; after that, the studios, operating without the protection of theatres committed in advance to play their product, resorted to "blind bidding" and other maneuvers in order to reduce the risk on their films. It's only in the last few years that the studios have found a new kind of protection. They have discovered that they can get much more from the sale of movies to television than they had been getting, and that they can negotiate presale agreements with the networks for guaranteed amounts before they commit themselves to a production. Licensing fees to the networks now run between $3,000,000 and $4,000,000 for an average picture, and the studios negotiate in advance not only for network showings and later TV syndication (about $1,500,000 for an average picture), and for pay television (between $1,000,000 and $1,500,000), but for cable TV, the airlines, cassettes, and overseas television. And, of course, they still sell to foreign distributors and to exhibitors here, and much of that money is also committed in advance—sometimes even paid in advance. So if a film is budgeted at $8,500,000, the studio may have $14,000,000 guaranteed and—theoretically, at least—show a profit before shooting starts, even if $4,000,000 is allowed for marketing and advertising. And the studio still has the possibility of a big box-office hit and *really* big money. If a picture is a large-scale adventure story or has superstars, the licensing fee to the networks alone may be between $15,000,000 and $25,000,000, and the total advance guarantees may come to almost double the budget. Financially, the only danger in an arrangement like this is that if the film goes seriously over budget the studio can still lose money. That's why directors who have the reputation of always coming in on schedule are in steady demand even if they've had a long line of box-office failures and their work is consistently mediocre, and why directors who are perfectionists are shunned as if they were lepers—unless, like Hal Ashby, they've had some recent hits.

The studios no longer make movies primarily to attract and please moviegoers; they make movies in such a way as to get as much as possible from the prearranged and anticipated deals. Every picture (allowing for a few exceptions) is cast and planned in terms of those deals. Though the studio is very happy when it has a box-office hit, it isn't terribly concerned about the people who buy tickets and come out grumbling. They don't grumble very loudly anyway, because even the lumpiest pictures are generally an improvement over television; at least, they're always bigger. TV accustoms people to not expecting much, and because of the new prearranged deals they're not getting very much. There is a quid pro quo for a big advance sale to television and theatres: the project must be from a fat, dumb best-seller about an international jewel heist or a skyjacking that involves a planeload of the rich and famous, or be a thinly disguised show-business biography of someone who came to an appallingly wretched end, or have an easily paraphrasable theme—preferably something that can be done justice to in a sentence and brings to mind the hits of the past. How else could you entice buyers? Certainly not with something unfamiliar, original. They feel safe with big-star packages, with chase thrillers, with known ingredients. For a big overseas sale, you must have "international" stars—performers who are known all over, such as Sophia Loren, Richard Burton, Candice Bergen, Roger Moore, Clint Eastwood, Burt Reynolds, Alain Delon, Charles Bronson, Steve McQueen. And you should probably avoid complexities: much of the new overseas audience is subliterate. For a big advance sale to worldwide television, a movie should also be innocuous: it shouldn't raise any hackles, either by strong language or by a controversial theme. And there must be stars, though not necessarily movie stars. It has recently been discovered that even many Americans are actually more interested in TV personalities than in movie ones, and may be roused from their TV-viewing to go see a film with John Denver or John Ritter. In countries where American TV series have become popular, our TV stars may be better known than our movie stars (especially the ones who appear infrequently). A 1979 Canadian film, *Running*, starring Michael Douglas, who has appeared in a TV series and was featured in *The China Syndrome*, cost $4,200,000; by the time it was completed, the various rights to it had been sold for over $6,000,000. The lawyer-financier who set up the production of *Foolin' Around*, which stars Gary Busey, said he would not have made the picture without the television insurance of a supporting cast that included Tony Randall, Cloris Leachman, and Eddie

Albert. Nobody needs to have heard of these independently packaged pictures for them to be profitable, and, in some cases, if it were not contractually necessary to open the film in theatres in order to give it legitimacy as a movie, it would be cheaper not to, because the marketing and advertising costs may outstrip the box-office revenue (unless that, too, was guaranteed). On productions like these, the backers don't suffer the gamblers' anxieties that were part of film business in the fifties and sixties, and even in the early seventies. Of course, these backers don't experience the gamblers' highs, either. Movie executives now study the television Q ratings, which measure the public's familiarity with performers, and a performer with a high rating (which he attains if he's been in a long-running series or on a daytime quiz show) is offered plum movie roles — even if this means that the script will have to be completely rewritten for his narrow range or bland personality.

There is an even grimmer side to all this: because the studios have discovered how to take the risk out of moviemaking, they don't want to make any movies that they can't protect themselves on. Production and advertising costs have gone so high that there is genuine nervous panic about risky projects. If an executive finances what looks like a perfectly safe, stale piece of material and packs it with stars, and the production costs skyrocket way beyond the guarantees, and the picture loses many millions, *he* won't be blamed for it — he was playing the game by the same rules as everybody else. If, however, he takes a gamble on a small project that can't be sold in advance — something that a gifted director really wants to do, with a subtle, not easily summarized theme and no big names in the cast — and it loses just a little money, his neck is on the block. So to the executives a good script is a script that attracts a star, and they will make their deals and set the full machinery of a big production in motion and schedule the picture's release dates, even though the script problems have never been worked out and everyone (even the director) secretly knows that the film will be a confused mess, an embarrassment.

Another new factor makes a risky project still riskier; if a movie doesn't have an easily paraphrasable theme or big stars, it's hard to sell via a thirty-second TV commercial. (The networks pay a lot for movies, but they get much of it back directly from the movie industry, which increasingly relies on TV commercials to sell a film.) It's even hard for the studio advertising departments to figure out a campaign for newspapers and magazines. And so, faced with something unusual or original, the studio head generally says, "I don't know how to market it, and if I don't know how to market it, it will lose money." The new breed of studio head is not likely to say, "It's something I feel we should take a chance on. Let's see if there's somebody who might be able to figure out how to market it." Just about the only picture the studios made last year that the executives took a financial risk on was *Breaking Away*. And despite the fact that it cost what is now a pittance ($2,400,000) and received an Academy Award Best Picture nomination, Twentieth Century-Fox didn't give it a big theatrical re-release (the standard procedure for a nominated film) but sold it to NBC for immediate showing, for $5,000,000. So a couple of weeks after the Awards ceremony, just when many people had finally heard of *Breaking Away* and might have gone to a theatre to see it, it appeared, trashed in the usual manner, on television. The studio couldn't be sure how much more money might come in from box offices, and grabbed a sure thing. In order to accept the NBC offer, the studio even bypassed pay TV, where the picture could have been seen uncut. It was almost as if *Breaking Away* were being punished for not having stars and not having got a big advance TV sale. And the price was almost insulting: last year, Fox licensed *The Sound of Music* to NBC for $21,500,000, and licensed *Alien* to ABC for $12,000,000, with escalator clauses that could take the figure up to $15,000,000; Columbia licensed *Kramer vs. Kramer* to ABC for nearly $20,000,000, and United Artists got $20,000,000 for *Rocky II* from CBS. But then how do you summarize in a sentence the appeal of a calm, evenhanded film about fathers and sons, town boys and college boys, and growing up—a modest classic that never states its themes, that stirs the emotions by indirection, by the smallest of actions and the smallest exchanges of dialogue?

If a writer-director conceives a script for a fiery young actor—K., a young man with star potential who has not yet had a role that brought him to the consciousness of the public—and shapes the central character to bring out K.'s volatility and ardor, he is likely to be told by the studio head, "K. doesn't do anything to me." That rules out K., even if the studio head has never seen K. act (and chances are he wouldn't remember him if he had). The studio head doesn't care if K. could become a star in this part; he wants R., because he can get a $4,000,000 network sale with the impassive, logy R., a Robert Wagner type who was featured in a mini-series. And if the point is pressed, the studio head may cut off discussion with some variation of "I must know what I'm doing, or I wouldn't be in this job." If he is feeling expansive, he may go on with "I won't say that you can't make a good film with K., and some people—some critics and your friends—will like it. But a good picture to me is a successful picture—one that will make money." If the writer-director still persists, it's taken as a sign of stupidity. A finer-grained executive—one of the rare ones who loves movies—may put it to him this way: "I like K., I like you, I like the script. But I can't recommend it. It's an expensive picture, and the subject matter makes it a long shot. And if I back too many long shots that don't come in, I'm out on my ass." That's the distillation of executive timidity, and maybe it's better to get it from the coarser man: you can have the pleasure of hating him—you aren't made to sympathize with his plight. Since all the major studios basically play by the same rules, the writer-director will wind up with a picture that is crucially miscast and has a vacuum at its center. By the time it is released and falls by the wayside, and he is publicly humiliated, K., disgusted at not having got the part, may have accepted a dumb role in a TV series and become a hot new TV personality, whom all the movie studios are propositioning.

Chances are that even if the writer-director had been allowed to use K., he would have been completely enraged and demoralized by the time he started shooting, because the negotiating process can stretch on for years, and anyone who wants to make a movie is treated as a hustler and an adversary. "Studios!" said Billy Wilder, paraphrasing an old complaint about women. "You can't make pictures with 'em, and you can't make pictures without 'em." Everybody in the movie business has the power to say no, and the least secure executives protect themselves by saying no to just about anything that comes their way. Only those at the very top can say yes, and they protect themselves, too. They postpone decisions because they're fearful, and also because they don't mind keeping someone dangling while his creative excitement dries up and all the motor drive goes out of his proposal. They don't mind keeping people waiting, because it makes them feel more powerful. I'm describing trends; of course, there are exceptions—those who are known (and sometimes revered) for quick decisions, like David Picker in his United Artists days, and Daniel Melnick in his brief stints at M-G-M and Columbia, and David Begelman at

Columbia and now at M-G-M. But most of the ones who could say yes don't; they consider it and string you along. (Hollywood is the only place where you can die of encouragement.) For the supplicant, it's a matter of weeks, months, years, waiting for meetings at which he can beg permission to do what he was, at the start, eager to do. And even when he's got a meeting, he has to catch the executive's attention and try to keep it; in general the higher the executive, the more cruelly short his attention span. (They're television babies. Thirty seconds is a long time to them.) In this atmosphere of bureaucratic indifference or contempt, things aren't really decided—they just happen, along bureaucratic lines. (Generally, it's only if a picture is a hit that executives talk about having given it the go-ahead. They all angle for credit in the media.) During the long wait, the director has lost the cinematographer he wanted and half the performers; in order to get the necessary approvals, he has agreed to actors he knows are wrong, and he has pared down the script to cut costs, chopping out the scenes that once meant the most to him but that he knows he can't get in the tight, ten-week shooting schedule he has been forced to accept. And then, at the last minute, a few days before shooting is to start, the studio is likely to slice the budget further—and he's down to a nine-week schedule, which means trimming the camera moves that were half the reason he'd been eager to work on the idea in the first place. Is it any wonder if the picture that comes out has a sour spirit?

It may just barely come out anyway. If there's an executive shakeup during production or after the film is completed (and shakeups take place every few months), the new studio head has nothing to gain if the film succeeds (he can't take credit for initiating it); he may find it to his strategic advantage for the film to fail. The executives—bed-hoppers, who go from one berth to another—have no particular loyalty to the studio, and there isn't the lower-echelon executive stability to launch a film initiated during the old regime with the same care as one initiated during the new regime. It all depends on the signals that come from the top.

If a big star and a big director show interest in a project, the executives will go along for a $14,000,000 or $15,000,000 budget even if, by the nature of the material, the picture should be small. And so what might have been a charming light entertainment that millions of people all over the world would enjoy is inflated, rewritten to enlarge the star's part, and overscaled. It makes money in advance and sends people out of theatres complaining and depressed. Often, when people leave theatres now they're bewildered by the anxious nervous construction of the film—by the feeling it gives them of having been pieced together out of parts that don't fit. Movies have gone to hell and amateurism. A third of the pictures being made by Hollywood this year are in the hands of first-time directors, who will receive almost no guidance or help. They're thrown right into a pressure-cooker situation, where any delay is costly. They may have come out of sitcoms, and their dialogue will sound forced, as if it were all recorded in a large, empty cave; they may have come out of nowhere and have never worked with actors before. Even if a director is highly experienced, he probably has certain characteristic weaknesses, such as a tendency to lose track of the story, or an ineptness with women characters; he's going to need watching. But who knows that, or cares enough to try to protect the picture? The executives may have hired the director after "looking at his work"—that is, running off every other reel of one of his films. They are busy people. Network executives who are offered a completed movie commonly save time by looking at a fifteen-minute selection from it—a précis of its highlights—which has been specially prepared for them. God forbid that they should have to sit through the whole thing.

What isn't generally understood is how much talent and hard work are wasted—enough, maybe, to supply the world with true entertainment. A writer who is commissioned to adapt a book and turns in a crackerjack script, acclaimed by the studio executives, who call him a genius, then stands helplessly by as the studio submits it to the ritual lists of the stars and the directors whom they can get the biggest guarantees on. And as, one by one, the stars and directors who aren't right for the project anyway take months to read it and turn it down, the executives' confidence in the script drains away. If a star expresses tentative interest, contingent on a complete rewrite, they will throw out the snappy script and authorize a new script by a sodden writer who has just had a fluke hit, and when the star decides to do something else anyway, they will have a new script written for a different star, and another and another, until no one can remember why there was ever any interest in the project. It may be shelved then, but so much money has already gone into it that in a couple of years some canny producer will think it should be brought back to life and reworked to fit a hot new teen-ager from television—who eventually will decide not to do it, and so on. To put it simply: A good script is a script to which Robert Redford will commit himself. A bad script is a script which Redford has turned down. A script that "needs work" is a script about which Redford has yet to make up his mind. It is possible to run a studio with this formula; it is even possible to run a studio *profitably* with this formula. But this world of realpolitik that has replaced moviemaking has nothing to do with moviemaking. It's not just that the decisions made by the executives might have been made by anyone off the street—it's that the pictures themselves seem to have been made by anyone off the street.

The executives are a managerial class with no real stake in the studio; they didn't build it, it's not part of them, and they're moving on—into a bigger job at another studio, or into independent production (where there's more money), or to form their own companies. The executives just try to hold things together for the short period that they're going to be around; there isn't even an elementary regard for the conservation of talent. And, as in any chaotic bureaucracy, the personalities and goals of those at the top set the tone for all the day-to-day decisions; the top executives' apathy about the quality of movies infects the studio right down the line. The younger executives who are pushing their way up don't want to waste their time considering scripts that may not attract a star. For them, too, a good picture is a picture that makes money, and so after *The China Syndrome* clicked at box offices, they could be heard talking about what a wonderful craftsman its director, James Bridges, was, and after *The Amityville Horror*, with its unbelievably clunky script, by Sandor Stern, showed big grosses, they wanted to sign up Stern as a writer-director. At the bottom as at the top, the executives want to score; they want a hit, not just for the money but for the personal pleasure of the kill.

Part of what has deranged American life in this past decade is the change in book publishing and in magazines and newspapers and in the movies as they have passed out of the control of those whose lives were bound up in them and into the control of conglomerates, financiers, and managers who treat them as ordinary commodities. This isn't a reversible process; even if there were Supreme Court rulings that split some of these holdings from the conglomerates, the traditions that developed inside many of those businesses have been ruptured. And the continuity is gone. In earlier eras, when a writer made a book agreement with a publisher, he expected to be working with the people he signed up with; now those people may be replaced the next day, or the whole firm may be bought up and turned into a subdivision of a textbook-publishing house or a leisure-activities company. The new people in the job aren't going to worry about guiding a writer slowly; they're not going to think about the book after this one. They want best-sellers. Their job is to find them or manufacture them. And just as the studios have been hiring writers to work on screenplays, they are now beginning to hire writers to work on novels, which the publishers, with the help of studio money, will then attempt to promote to best-sellerdom at the same time that they are being made into movies. The writer Avery Corman has suggested "the horrifying prospect of a novelist being fired from his own book." It won't horrify the people who are commissioning these new books—pre-novelizations.

There are certain kinds of business in which the public interest is more of a factor than it is in the manufacture of neckties. Book publishing, magazines and newspapers, movies and television and live theatre—these are businesses, of course, but traditionally the people who work in them have felt privileged (by birth or ability or talent or luck, or by a combination of those factors). That has been true not only of the actors and journalists but of the entrepreneurs and the managers. There have always been a few businessmen in these fields who had the sensibility of artists (without the talent or the drive); if they had a good critical sense and a generous nature, they were appreciators of artists and didn't resent them. And so they became great producers in the theatre and movies, or great book and magazine editors. Contemporary variants of these people insist on being celebrity-artists themselves, and right now they all seem to be writing and directing movies.

In movies, the balance between art and business has always been precarious, with business outweighing art, but the business was, at least, in the hands of businessmen who loved movies. As popular entertainment, movies need something of what the vulgarian moguls had—zest, a belief in their own instincts, a sentimental dedication to producing pictures that would make their country proud of their contribution, a respect for quality, and the biggest thing: a willingness to take chances. The cool managerial sharks don't have that; neither do the academics. But the vulgarians also did more than their share of damage, and they're gone forever anyway. They were part of a different America. They were, more often than not, men who paid only lip service to high ideals, while gouging everyone for profits. The big change in the country is reflected in the fact that people in the movie business no longer feel it necessary to talk about principles at all. They operate on the same assumptions as the newspapers that make heroes of the executives who have a hit and don't raise questions about its quality.

When the numbers game takes over a country, artists who work in a popular medium, such as the movies, lose their bearings fast. There's a pecking order in filmmaking, and the director is at the top—he's the authority figure. A man who was never particularly attractive to women now finds that he's the padrone: everyone is waiting on his word, and women are his for the nod. The constant, unlimited opportunities for sex can be insidious; so is the limitless flattery of college students who turn directors into gurus. Directors are easily seduced. They mainline admiration. Recently, a screenwriter now directing his first picture was talking about his inability to find a producer who would take some of the burden off him; he said he needed a clone—someone who would know what was in his mind and be able to handle a million details for him. But anyone observing this writer-director would know that he needs a real producer, and for a much more important reason: to provide the sense of judgment he has already lost. Nobody really controls a production now; the director is on his own, even if he's insecure, careless, or nuts. There has always been a megalomaniac potential in moviemaking, and in this period of stupor, when values have been so thoroughly undermined that even the finest directors and the ones with the most freedom aren't sure what they want to do, they often become obsessive and grandiloquent—like mad royalty. Perpetually dissatisfied with the footage they're compulsively piling up, they keep shooting—adding rooms to the palace. Megalomania and art become the same thing to them. But the disorder isn't just in their heads, and a lot of people around them are deeply impressed by megalomania. What our directors need most of all, probably, is a sense of purpose and a subject that they can think their way through. Filmmakers want big themes, and where are the kinds of themes that they would fight the studios to express? It's no accident that the two best recent American movies are both fantasy fairy tales—childish in the fullest, deepest sense. Working inside a magical structure, Carroll Ballard in *The Black Stallion* and Irvin Kershner in

The Empire Strikes Back didn't have to deal with the modern world; they were free to use the medium luxuriantly, without guilt. You can feel the love of moviemaking—almost a revelry in moviemaking—in their films, as you can also in Walter Hill's *The Long Riders*, despite its narrative weaknesses and a slight remoteness. But we don't go to the movies just for great fairy tales and myths of the old West; we also hope for something that connects directly with where we are. Part of the widespread anticipation of *Apocalypse Now* was, I think, our readiness for a visionary, climactic, summing-up movie. We felt that the terrible rehash of pop culture couldn't go on, mustn't go on—that something new was needed. Coppola must have felt that, too, but he couldn't supply it. His film was posited on great thoughts arriving at the end—a confrontation and a revelation. And when they weren't there, people slunk out of the theatres, or tried to comfort themselves with chatter about the psychedelic imagery. Trying to say something big, Coppola got tied up in a big knot of American self-hatred and guilt, and what the picture boiled down to was: White man—he devil. Since then, I think, people have expected less of movies and have been willing to settle for less. Some have even been willing to settle for *Kramer vs. Kramer* and other pictures that seem to be made for an audience of over-age flower children. These pictures express the belief that if a man cares about anything besides being at home with the kids, he's corrupt. Parenting ennobles Dustin Hoffman and makes him a better person in every way, while in *The Seduction of Joe Tynan* we can see that Alan Alda is a weak, corruptible fellow because he wants to be President of the United States more than he wants to stay at home communing with his daughter about her adolescent miseries. Pictures like these should all end with the fathers and the children sitting at home watching TV together.

The major studios have found the temporary final solution for movies: in technique and in destiny, their films *are* television. And there's no possibility of a big breakthrough in movies—a new release of energy, like the French New Wave, which moved from country to country and resulted in an international cross-fertilization—when movies are financed only if they fall into stale categories of past successes. But once the groups that are now subsidizing studio-made films begin to weary of getting TV shows when they thought they were buying movies, there should be a chance for some real moviemaking. And when the writers and directors have confidence in what they want to express, if they can't find backing from the studios they ought to be able to find backers outside the industry who will gamble on the money to be made from a good picture, once it is completed. It's easier to make money on movies now: there are more markets, and we know now that the films themselves have a much longer commercial life than early moviemakers could have guessed. The studios may find that they need great moviemakers more than the moviemakers need them. Billy Wilder may be right that you can't make pictures with 'em, but of course he's wrong that you can't make pictures without 'em. There are problems both ways, but there may be fewer problems without them, and less rage.

It would be very convincing to say that there's no hope for movies — that audiences have been so corrupted by television and have become so jaded that all they want are noisy thrills and dumb jokes and images that move along in an undemanding way, so they can sit and react at the simplest motor level. And there's plenty of evidence, such as the success of *Alien*. This was a haunted-house-with-gorilla picture set in outer space. It reached out, grabbed you, and squeezed your stomach; it was more griping than entertaining, but a lot of people didn't mind. They thought it was terrific, because at least they'd felt something: they'd been brutalized. It was like an entertainment contrived in Aldous Huxley's *Brave New World* by the Professor of Feelies in the College of Emotional Engineering. Yet there was also a backlash against *Alien* — many people were angry at how mechanically they'd been worked over. And when I saw *The Black Stallion* on a Saturday afternoon, there was proof that even children who have grown up with television and may never have been exposed to a good movie can respond to the real thing when they see it. It was a hushed, attentive audience, with no running up and down the aisles and no traffic to the popcorn counter, and even when the closing credits came on, the children sat quietly looking at the images behind the names. There may be a separate God for the movies, at that.

{*The New Yorker*, June 23, 1980}

:: *The Chant of Jimmie Blacksmith*

The great Australian film *The Chant of Jimmie Blacksmith*, which was made in 1978 and has finally opened here, has almost nothing in common with the other Australian films of recent years. All of them partake of some of the fascination of movies set in unfamiliar terrain, but this one is large-scale and serenely shocking, with the principal characters shot against vast, rolling landscapes that are like wide, wide versions of the flat, layered backgrounds in Chinese wash drawings. *The Chant of Jimmie Blacksmith* was adapted from Thomas Keneally's novel, which is based on the case of Jimmy Governor, a half aborigine who went on a rampage and killed seven whites in 1900, the very year of Federation. (His hanging was delayed until after the ceremonies, so as not to embarrass the proud young nation by reminding it of what had been done to the natives.) The movie is about the cultural chasm that divides the natives and the European-spawned whites, and it's horribly funny, because the whites are inadequate to their own cruelties. The emotional effects of what these displaced Irish and Scottish and English do are much larger than the people themselves. The director, Fred Schepisi (pronounced Skepsee), has a gift for individualizing every one of the people on the screen; it takes him only a few licks to let us perceive how they justify themselves to themselves. Men who were at the bottom in Europe now command thousands of acres. Scrabbling tightwads, these white landowners got where they are by self-denial. Penny-pinching is a moral tenet to them, and they don't regard cheating the helpless aborigines as cheating, because the aborigines don't know how to save their money anyway. The aborigines live in the remnants of a tribal society with an elaborate structure of claims: men are obliged to give a share of their earnings to their kin, even if their kin are drunken and diseased and want the money only to go on a binge. And men offer their wives to visiting kin as a form of hospitality. To the whites, giving money away is unfathomable laxity, and since the black women are so easily available the white men treat the aboriginal settlements as brothels. The black women don't even have to be paid for their services, except with a bottle of cheap sherry for their husbands. The settlements are conveniently situated on the outskirts of the towns, far from the eyes of white women and children.

Jimmie Blacksmith (Tommy Lewis) is a product of one of these visits to a tin shanty, and because he learns quickly and is half white, the Reverend Mr. Neville (Jack Thompson), who runs the Methodist mission school, and Mrs. Neville (Julie Dawson) take him into their home when he's of an age to be useful. They train him to be polite and docile and teach him how important it is to gain a good reputation for work. Jimmie goes through his tribal initiation rites, but he grows up determined to escape the debased existence of aborigines in their hovels by working hard, buying land, and, as Mrs. Neville has advised him, marrying a nice white girl off a farm, so his children will be only a quarter black and the next generation scarcely black at all.

Sent out into the world, with the blessing of the Nevilles, he's a half-caste Horatio Alger figure, determined to show that his word is his bond and that he will stick to a job until it's done. Proper and well-mannered, he looks for work among clerks and prospective employers who call him Jacko and refer to him as a boong, a darkie, and a nigger. He doesn't take offense: these whites don't understand yet that he's different from the uneducated blacks. He smiles, so that they will see how willing he is, and eventually he gets his first job—making a post-and-rail fence to mark the boundaries of a huge farm. As he digs holes in the hard, dry earth, the vistas are lonely and bare; far in the distance, delicately etched trees look pale blue. After months of back-breaking work, Jimmie finishes the job, is underpaid, and is ordered off the property; denied a letter of recommendation as well, he flares up and tells the man that he knows why—it's because the man can't write. Jimmie is knocked flat. He goes from one fence-building job to the next, and we see how his employers react to his eagerness to prove himself a good worker. No matter how long and hard he works or how servile his behavior is, he never wins the civility or praise he longs for. These isolated farmers are terse, close-mouthed, as if even a little companionable chat would be profligacy, a waste. They can't resist finding fault with Jimmie's work and shorting him on his pay; thrift and mistrust have become second nature to them. Besides, they need to see him fail: it confirms the necessity of keeping the savages in their place. Since the aborigines have no legal rights, the farmers can feel generous-hearted for paying any part of what was agreed to. When Jimmie complains, he looks slightly wall-eyed from terror. The farmers show their fears in their tight faces whenever there's more than one black on their land. Jimmie has a half brother, laughing Mort (Freddy Reynolds), a teen-age aborigine who giggles with contentment. He walks enormous distances to come be with Jimmie and give him a hand on his jobs, but this additional presence upsets the bosses, who accuse Jimmie of turning their land into "a blacks' camp."

When Jimmie visits his tribal shantytown with Mort, a claim is made on them for money; Mort gives his little bit happily, but Jimmie flings a roll of bills down on the ground in disgust, because his inability to save money eats away at his hopes. He gets a job as a tracker and general underling with the New South Wales Mounted Police; barefoot in a thick, outsize uniform, he's a caricature of a policeman. He thinks of the uniform very righteously, though, and when the police raid a settlement, trying to find out which of the aborigines stabbed a debauching white man, Jimmie does just what his boss, Constable Farrell (Roy Barrett), tells him to do: he rides in smashing his club down on the head and shoulders of anyone within range. Then he proves his diligence by turning in the culprit—an old friend. It isn't until the brutish Constable Farrell gets boozed up and tortures and kills the prisoner that Jimmie wakes from his illusion that he is part of the master race. Barrett is so strong an actor that when the constable's full sadism comes into play you want to cower in your seat; Jimmie is forced to understand that he is as powerless as the mutilated corpse.

He runs off and finds work as a sweeper and cook's helper at a shearing contractor's, where a dim-witted, rutting servant girl (Angela Punch), a blond waif who has been coupling with the goatish cook (played by Thomas Keneally), presents herself to him, half naked. She becomes pregnant, and so he gets himself a white wife. His next employer, Newby (Don Crosby), allows him to put up a one-room shack, where he and his bride can live while he builds a fence around the Newby domain. Beyond him, there are always the pastel hills—so remote they're almost part of the sky—and the faint blue trees. The immensity of the plains mocks Jimmie's hope of gaining a good reputation; trying to improve himself, he's like a hair-raisingly foolish cross between Jude the Obscure and Gunga Din. Jimmie's pathetic wife brings him his only chance of realizing his ambition to have a home, like a white man. Yet when he hears the first cries of his wife's baby, his bare feet grip the earth in dance steps that suggest an atavistic rite. Unconsciously, he seems to be expressing his continuity with nature and his tribe. Mort arrives in a spirit of celebration, accompanied by a cousin and by Jimmie's uncle Tabidgi (Steve Dodds), a tribal elder, who is worried about Jimmie's marriage to a white woman and has brought him a talisman to keep him safe. They stay on and on, with the uncle sousing while Mort helps with the work, until Newby raises the familiar cry that the place is being turned into "a blacks' camp." Mrs. Newby (Ruth Cracknell) and Miss Graf (Elizabeth Alexander), a young schoolteacher who lives with the Newbys, want to save Jimmie's wife from the fate of living among blacks anyway, and so Newby tries to get rid of Jimmie and his black kin by starving the whole group out. Jimmie is baffled by the whites' hatred, baffled that these people—the only ones on his travels who have ever shown him any kindness—are humiliating him by denying him money for groceries and are trying to persuade his wife to leave him and become a servant to Miss Graf, who is getting married. They represent what he wanted a white wife for—he wants to be them. And so, of course, they enrage him the most.

When Jimmie explodes, you may feel a sudden chill that is quite unlike what you have felt at other films, because his actions don't come out of conscious militancy or a demand for political justice. They come out of helplessness and frustration. The speed of Jimmie's first, irrevocable action makes the image seem like something happening in a delirium; his motion is so fast you replay it in your head and it stays with you—an insane ritual. It's as if he had let his unconscious take over. Jimmie acts on the level on which he has been experiencing the insults and the condescension. After the first explosion, he says he has declared war. But even then he doesn't wage war directly against the men: he attacks the men's most prized possessions—their robust, well-fed women, their pink-and-white children. His prime target—though only semi-consciously—is the supercilious schoolie, Miss Graf. She is everything plump and prissy that Jimmie has aspired to. Her immaculate, high-toned respectability represents sexuality to him, just as the "gins"—the unpaid black prostitutes lying on the dirt floors of their hovels—represent it to the ranchers. His war is race war, sex war—a freakish parody of textbook war which is probably an accurate reflection of the forces let loose in colonial uprisings. It's a conflict between two debased, threatened cultures—one individualistic, one tribal—and it's Jimmie, rather than a full-blooded aborigine, who explodes because he has tried the individualistic white way and has been rejected. He and Mort go back over the hundreds of miles he has covered; he retraces his steps to take revenge for each humiliation he has suffered.

If the film has a hero, it's Mort, who loses his happy laugh when he is drawn into Jimmie's war, and never fully regains it. We feel for Jimmie, but we don't love him as we love Mort, who is instinctively kind and selfless. Mort is something like the noble Indians and Negroes of American literature, but he's not a warrior or a mighty hunter. There's nothing overtly heroic about him; he's essentially passive and relaxed—a loyal, easy-going bum in ragged tweeds. This bum makes us see what the Europeans have destroyed; he's the simplest yet the most civilized person in the movie. The tribalism he accepts means that he doesn't have to prove himself, like the tormented Jimmie: he is part of everything. Jimmie suffers from the perils of Christian individualism; he wants respect, property, whiteness, and his failure rots him and twists him. Mort has nothing yet feels rich. We understand Jimmie and his divided soul only too well, but we don't *understand* Mort—he's both transparent to us and totally mysterious. People in ethnographic documentaries sometimes combine these qualities, but this is just about the only time I have ever seen primitive mystery made flesh in an acted movie. It couldn't have simply happened this way through a lucky accident of casting, because, of course, the past eighty years have taken their toll of tribalism. (Now it is having a *conscious* resurgence, and it's no more simple or instinctive than reawakened tribal consciousness among American Indians or the neo-African movements among American blacks.) Mort became a Methodist, but it rolled right off him. Jimmie was so flagrantly naïve that he believed what the white missionaries taught the blacks; he's their patsy. The Reverend Mr. Neville comes to understand this, in horror and confusion: he has been giving his life to destroying the blacks. Yet how could Jimmie have improved his lot except by being the good native grateful to work for the whites? The alternative was drunkenness, and death at an early age from consumption or pneumonia.

The Chant of Jimmie Blacksmith is a triumph of casting and of coaching. With a shooting schedule of only fifteen weeks, and locations requiring that the crew travel five thousand miles, Schepisi had the job of blending a large company of the finest (white) stage and screen performers with aborigines—most of them nonprofessionals who were trained while the film was being made. (The star, Tommy Lewis, was a nineteen-year-old half-caste college student.) The professionals had to be really skillful, so as not to dominate their scenes with the amateurs; there are fine shadings in the work of actors such as Brian Anderson, who plays the objective-minded butcher and hangman, and Peter Carroll, who plays the wheezing red-haired McCreadie, an intelligent, neurasthenic schoolteacher who is taken hostage by Jimmie and is then carried piggyback to safety by Mort. The aboriginal performers—the men, particularly—come through vividly. They have the advantage of their unusual (to us) physiognomies. At times, Freddy Reynolds (Mort) and some of the others—whose features are not African, yet whose skins are dark—look like the actors in blackface who played Negroes in *The Birth of a Nation* and other early American films; they seem so different from American blacks that it sometimes throws you off when they're referred to by the same epithets. Two professionals among them are wonderful as sots: Jack Charles as the murdered prisoner, and Steve Dodds as the dazed Tabidgi, who is tried for murder and simply says, "You'd think it would take a good while to make up your mind to kill someone and then to kill them, but take my word for it, it only takes a second." (Of all the turn-of-the-century locations, only one arouses suspicion: the graffiti in a deserted sacred place are disconcertingly bright and much too legible—the four-letter desecrations spell irony.)

Schepisi, who was born in Melbourne on December 26, 1939 (his grandfather was an immigrant from a small island north of Sicily), began working in advertising at fifteen and went on to TV commercials and government documentaries. In 1970, he made a half-hour short called *The Priest*, which was part of the omnibus film *Libido*, and five years later he completed an autobiographical feature, *The Devil's Playground*, about his early-teen years in a Catholic seminary. (Keneally, a friend of his, played a priest.) An epic is not easily made, especially one that deals with the queasy emotions that attend the creation of a society built on racial oppression, yet *Jimmie Blacksmith* is only Schepisi's second feature; it's a highly sophisticated production, made in Panavision (the cinematographer was Ian Baker), and one of the rare movies in which a wide screen is integral to the conception.

Schepisi has trimmed fourteen minutes since the film was shown at Cannes in 1978, and though wide-screen imagery is difficult to edit for speed, he has achieved a glancing, leaping emotional progression that's very calm, very even. The score, by Bruce Smeaton, never crowds the viewer's emotions but is right there when it's needed. Schepisi picked great material, and in mapping out the screenplay he took much of the dialogue right from the book. This is generally a mistake, but not with Keneally, who is a dramatist as well as a novelist. He writes dialogue that jumps up from the page, bites you on the nose, and makes you laugh.

Published here in 1972, Thomas Keneally's novel is no longer in print; the library copy that I read hadn't been checked out since January, 1973. How did this book slip into neglect? Was it because the literary-publicity machine was in its modernist phase, when the most highly honored novels were intricate literary puzzles? Or did the thought "arid," so closely associated with Patrick White, smudge the wrong Australian? I began the novel around one in the morning, intending to read only a few chapters before going to bed. Although it's a short book (just a hundred and seventy-eight pages), I stayed up until five, reading it slowly, because I didn't want to diminish the pleasure by going too fast. The book is like Nat Turner's story as a great lusty ironist—an Irish Nabokov, perhaps— might have written it. I didn't want to lose the full shape of the story by interrupting it until the next day; anyway, I had to read it in one sitting, because the rhythms propel you forward. They're oral rhythms—not just in the dialogue but in the prose cadences. The book itself is the chant, and it's inexorable. The novel and the movie add to each other. Keneally's passion comes out in barbaric, pixillated humor; Schepisi's vision is less comic, but his work is visually impassioned, and it, too, seems inexorable. The smooth, high-strung tone is set right at the start, and I don't think there's an inexpressive frame of film in the entire movie. Schepisi's chant has a different rhythm: Keneally writes spiccato, Schepisi's moviemaking is legato. Keneally writes with the comic virulence of an Irish-Australian observing the stingy Scots, who can't open their fists even when they're the lords of a great land; Schepisi sees the meanness set against the expanses, sees the patterns of dark to light, with the people at the dark bottom of the image and the birds flying from the pastels to the whiteness at the top. Each, in his way, makes you feel that he has captured a nation's rhythm.

In recent years, the movies with the clearest social vision appear to be those rooted in a particular time and place: in the Sardinia of the Taviani brothers' *Padre Padrone*, with its patriarchal system; in Francesco Rosi's *Christ Stopped at Eboli* (which gave you the feeling that the camera arrived in the remote, mountainous peasant village with Carlo Levi in the thirties and left with him, and that the land and the people returned to darkness). Maybe it's because movies spouted so much humanitarian ideology in the past, and Hollywood showed us so many faceless throngs, that these exact, personal visions bringing us up close to their subjects have special, ecstatic force. *The Chant of Jimmie Blacksmith* is a dreamlike Requiem Mass for a nation's lost honor; that Schepisi should have financed it partly by his work in TV commercials is a joke that all moviemakers can appreciate. Keneally's book is full of jokes. A sample: "Press cartoonists sketched the nascent motherland. . . . In one hand she held perhaps a tome with a title such as 'British Civilization,' in the other a blank parchment entitled 'The Fresh New Page of Democracy.' She rather resembed Miss Graf."

{*The New Yorker*, September 15, 1980}

:: The Man Who Made
Howard Hughes Sing

Jean Renoir instinctively understood what he had in common with characters very different from himself, and when his people are at their most ludicrous—when they are self-pitying or infuriatingly contentious—he puts us inside their skins, so we're laughing at ourselves. Asked to explain how it was that he didn't separate his characters into the good ones and the bad ones, Renoir's answer was always "Because everyone has his reasons," and in his best films we don't need those reasons explained—we intuit them. The young American director Jonathan Demme has some of this same gift, and his lyrical comedy *Melvin and Howard*, which opened the New York Film Festival on September 26th, is an almost flawless act of sympathetic imagination. Demme and the writer Bo Goldman have entered into the soul of American blue-collar suckerdom and brought us close enough to see that the people on the screen are us. Demme and Goldman have taken for their hero a chucklehead who is hooked on TV game shows and for their heroine his wife, who when she's off on her own and needs to work turns go-go dancer. And they have made us understand how it was that when something big—something legendary —touched these lives, nobody could believe it.

The lawyers and judges and jurors who were involved in the 1976–78 legal proceedings over the Howard Hughes will known as the Mormon will looked at Melvin Dummar, raked over his life, and couldn't believe that Hughes (who died in April, 1976) would have included Dummar among his beneficiaries. If you've seen Melvin Dummar on television, you may have observed that he's very touching—he looks like a more

fair-haired Andy Kaufman as Latka Gravas in the TV series "Taxi," and he
has that square, engaging naïveté that is so thoroughgoing it seems like a
put-on. Dummar does, in fact, have links to TV: he is the representative
debt-ridden American for whom game shows were created. He won a prize
on "Truth or Consequences" but was unsuccessful on "The Dating Game";
he once appeared on "Let's Make a Deal" wearing a string of oranges
around his neck and a hat shaped like an orange, and another time in the
same hat but with a duck on top with a sign that said "Quacking up for a
deal." Actually, Dummar was on "Let's Make a Deal" four times within a
period of five years (which is probably a record); in the hearings on the
will, an attorney said that this was a violation of federal law, and it was used
against him to indicate that since "theatrics and lying" were a way of life
for him, he could have faked the will and invented the story that he gave
to account for the bequest—the story of how one night around Christmas
of 1967 or early January of 1968 he had found Hughes in the desert and
given him a ride. Even Dummar's dreams were turned against him: an
attorney grilling his second wife in order to discredit him asked, "Mrs.
Dummar, didn't your husband once write a song which he entitled 'A
Dream Becomes Reality,' with this as one of the lines—'A beggar becomes
a king'?" And, of course, the attorney had a point: the Hughes bequest did
seem just like another one of Dummar's dreams, though it probably wasn't.
The new nonfiction detective story *High Stakes*, by Harold Rhoden, makes
a very spiky and convincing argument for the authenticity of the Mormon
will, which the whole country laughed at because of the inclusion of Melvin Dummar, who seemed like a pudgy hick. (Johnny Carson got a lot of
mileage out of Melvin Dummar jokes; for a while he was the national
chump.) Even the many eminent institutions that were also named as
beneficiaries didn't put up much of a fight for the will. Maybe their officers
couldn't believe Melvin Dummar belonged among the hallowed names.
More likely, these officers, knowing that the scary, powerful Summa Corporation, which controlled Hughes' wealth, would not relinquish this
fortune without a costly battle in the courts which Summa, with the
Hughes resources, could prolong into infinity, decided that it was wiser
simply to string along with the general attitude in the media that a will
in which Melvin Dummar was a beneficiary had to be a forgery. (The
will, dated March, 1968, which would have effectively dissolved the
Summa Corporation, left one-quarter of Hughes' estate to medical

research, one-eighth to four universities, and the remainder to be divided into sixteen parcels, among beneficiaries such as the Mormon Church, the Boy Scouts, orphans, Hughes' ex-wife, relatives, business associates, and Dummar, whose one-sixteenth would have amounted to over a hundred and fifty million dollars.)

But what if the meeting between Melvin Dummar and Howard Hughes took place just as Dummar said it did? What might have caused Hughes to remember Melvin a few months later and put him in his will? That's what *Melvin and Howard* tells us. By their own imaginative leap, Demme and Goldman make us understand what Howard Hughes might have seen in Melvin Dummar that the lawyers and reporters didn't see. Paul Le Mat (he was the disarming, spacy young hero in Demme's *Citizens Band*) is such an easygoing, non-egocentric actor that he disappears inside the role of big, beefy Melvin—a sometime milkman, sometime worker at a magnesium plant, sometime gas-station operator, and hopeful song-writer. Driving along the California-Nevada interstate at night in his pickup truck, Melvin has a bovine boyishness about him. He keeps himself in good cheer in the desert by singing "Santa's Souped-Up Sleigh"; the lyrics are his own, set to a tune he bought by mail order for seventy dollars, and when he sings—ostentatiously keeping time—you feel there's not a thing in that noggin but the words of the song. Jason Robards plays Howard Hughes, who hits a snag while racing his motorcycle in the desert and is flung into the air. He is lying in the freezing darkness when Melvin spots him—a bony old man in beat-out clothes, with a dirty beard and straggly long gray hair. When Melvin helps him into the front seat of the truck, next to him, he's doubled over in pain, and even as Melvin is wrapping him up to warm him there's a malevolent, paranoid gleam in his eyes. Melvin, who takes him for an old wino—a desert rat—is bothered by his mean expression, and in order to cheer him up (and give himself some company) he insists that the old geezer sing his song with him, or get out and walk.

Jason Robards certainly wasn't a beacon to his profession in last year's *Hurricane* or in the recent classic of nincompoopery *Raise the Titanic*, and it may be true that, as he says, he works in movies "to make it possible to work on the stage." But I doubt if he has ever been greater than he is here. This Hughes is so sure that people are only after his money that he distrusts everyone; he has bribed and corrupted so many high officers in business and government that he believes in nothing but the power of bribery. His thinking processes are gnarled, twisted; he begrudges the world the smallest civility and lives incommunicado from everyone. And here he is singing "Santa's Souped-Up Sleigh" while sneering at its cornball idiocy and looking over disgustedly, in disbelief, at the pleasure that this dumb bunny next to him takes in hearing his song. In recent years, Robards' Yankee suavity has occasionally been reminiscent of Walter Huston: his Ben Bradlee in *All the President's Men* recalled Huston in *Dodsworth*, and here, when his Howard Hughes responds to Melvin's amiable prodding and begins to enjoy himself on a simple level and sings "Bye, Bye, Blackbird," he's as memorable as the famous record of Huston singing "September Song." His eyes are an old man's eyes—faded into the past, shiny and glazed by recollections—yet intense. You feel that his grungy anger has melted away, that he has been healed. He and Melvin talk about how the desert, after rain, smells of greasewood and sage, and at dawn, just as they approach the lights of Las Vegas, where Hughes gets out, they smile at each other with a fraternal understanding that's a cockeyed, spooky miracle.

In an interview in the *Times* last year, Jason Robards pointed out that Robards was Hughes' middle name and that both of them had Loomises among their relatives. "They couldn't have cast anyone else as Howard Hughes," he said. "I figured I didn't have to do any preparation for the part. It's all built in genetically." What's built in genetically may be the way Jason Robards responds to an acting challenge: the son of an actor father and an actor all his life, he goes for broke in a way that never suggests recklessness. He just casually transports himself to new dimensions (that maybe nobody else has ever been in), as if he had been breathing that air all his life. Robards isn't on the screen for long, but Hughes suffuses the movie. You know he's there without your even thinking about him; he might almost be looking down on Melvin, watching what's happening to him. And this is what the picture is about. The moviemakers have understood the position that Howard Hughes has arrived at in American mythology, and they have used the encounter in the desert to confer a moment of glory on Melvin Dummar. Eight years later, when Melvin finds himself named in the will and realizes that the old coot who said he was Howard Hughes *was* Howard Hughes, he is awed—it's like being touched by God. When reporters, neighbors, and the curious and the crazy gather at his gas station, he hides in a tree and peers out at the crowd in terror.

Most of the movie is about Melvin's life during those eight years — the life that will look so makeshift and shoddy when it's examined in a court-room. Later in the morning after the encounter in the desert, Melvin's truck is repossessed, and his wife, Lynda (Mary Steenburgen), packs her things and takes their little daughter and goes off to live with another man, pausing only to murmur a regretful goodbye to the sleeping Melvin. They get a divorce, then remarry when she's hugely pregnant, but this marriage doesn't last long. Lynda can't stand Melvin's buying things that they never get to keep, and he can't stop kidding himself that his expensive, install-ment-plan purchases are somehow practical — that they're investments. So they never have anything — finally not even each other.

Mary Steenburgen was oddly tremulous in *Goin' South*, and though in *Time After Time* she was very sweet in an out-of-it way — a stoned cupcake — she didn't have the quickness or the pearly aura that she has here. Her Lynda Dummar has a soft mouth and a tantalizing slender wiggliness, and she talks directly to whomever she's talking to — she addresses them with her eyes and her mouth, and when they speak she listens, watching their faces. When she listens, she's the kind of woman a man wants to tell more to. Mary Steenburgen makes Lynda the go-go dancer so appealing that you realize she's the dream Melvin attained and then couldn't hang on to. Melvin is a hard worker, though, and he believes in family life. When Lynda leaves him, he's appalled by her exhibiting herself in strip joints; he keeps charging in and making scenes. Lynda is hurt by his attitude; she loves to dance, and she doesn't think there's anything lewd about what she's doing. In a way, she's right: Lynda could shimmy and shake forever and she still wouldn't be a hardened pro. Her movements are sexy but with a tipsy charm and purity. When her boss bawls her out because of a commotion that Melvin has just caused, she quits on the spot, whips off the flimsy costume that belongs to the boss, throws it in his face, and walks through the place naked, and she does it without making an event of it — it's her body. Melvin's second wife, Bonnie (Pamela Reed, who was Belle Starr in *The Long Riders*), isn't a romantic dream, like Lynda. She's a down-to-earth woman with a couple of kids who propositions him with a solid offer — marriage and her cousin's gas station in Utah, in a package deal. She makes the offer almost hungrily. Promising him a good marriage and a good busi-ness, she's like a sexual entrepreneur who feels she can use his untapped abilities and turn him into a success.

This is a comedy without a speck of sitcom aggression: the characters are slightly loony the way we all are sometimes (and it seldom involves coming up with cappers or with straight lines that somebody else can cap). When the people on the screen do unexpected things, they're not weirdos; their eccentricity is just an offshoot of the normal, and Demme suggests that maybe these people who grew up in motor homes and trailers in Nevada and California and Utah seem eccentric because they didn't learn the "normal," accepted ways of doing things. When Lynda is broke and takes her daughter, Darcy (the lovely, serious-faced Elizabeth Cheshire), to the bus station in Reno to send her to Melvin, she's frantic. Her misery about sending the child away is all mixed up with her anxiety about the child's having something to eat on the trip, and she's in a rush to put a sandwich together. She has bought French bread and bologna, and she takes over a table and borrows a knife from the man at the lunch counter so she can cut the bread; she salvages lettuce and tomatoes from the leftovers on someone's plate, and sends Darcy back to the counter to get some mustard and then back again to get some ketchup. The unperturbed counterman (played by the real Melvin Dummar) finds nothing unusual in this, and asks, "Is everything all right?" There's no sarcasm in his tone; he seems to understand what she's going through, and he wants to be helpful. She says, "Everything's just fine, thank you very much." She has dominated everyone's attention—she has practically taken over the station—yet the goofiness isn't forced; it's almost like found humor. It's a little like a throwaway moment in a Michael Ritchie film or a slapstick fracas out of Preston Sturges, but there are more unspoken crosscurrents—and richer ones—in Demme's scenes. While you're responding to the dithering confusion Lynda is causing in the bus depot, you're absorbing the emotions between mother and child. Darcy is often very grownup around her mother, as if she knew that Lynda is a bit of a moonbeam and needs looking after. But at the depot Darcy herself is so excited she becomes part of the confusion. Later, during Melvin and Lynda's remarriage ceremony in a Las Vegas "wedding chapel," Darcy is so impressed and elated that her whole face sparkles; she's like an imp Madonna. Throughout the movie, the children—Lynda's or Bonnie's, and sometimes all of them together— are part of an ongoing subtext: they're never commented on, and they never do anything cute or make a move that doesn't seem "true."

When Jonathan Demme does a thriller like *Last Embrace*, he seems an empty-headed director with a little hand-me-down craft, but in *Melvin and Howard* he shows perhaps a finer understanding of lower-middle-class life than any other American director. This picture suggests what it might have been like if Jean Renoir had directed a Preston Sturges comedy. Demme's style is so expressive that he draws you into the lives of the characters, and you're hardly aware of the technical means by which he accomplishes this—the prodigious crane and tracking shots that he has worked out with his cinematographer, Tak Fujimoto, and the fluid, mellow colors that probably owe a lot to Toby Rafelson's production design. The comedy doesn't stick out; it's part of the fluidity. And if you respond to this movie as I did, you'll hardly be aware (until you think it over afterward) that it has no plot, in the ordinary sense. (This could handicap it, though, in movie markets; the pitfall that a picture like this presents is that there's not a hard-sell scene in it. It's a soft shimmer of a movie, and the very people whom it's about and who might love it if they gave it a chance may not be tempted to see it.) There are a couple of flaws: the sequence of Melvin taking the will to the Mormon Church in Salt Lake City is so fast and cryptic it seems almost like shorthand, and if you've forgotten the stories that filled the papers a few years ago you may not understand what's going on; and the following sequence, of Melvin hiding from the crowd, doesn't have quite the clarity or the dramatic fullness that it needs. And there is a small lapse of taste: a shot too many of the blond Mrs. Worth (Charlene Holt), one of Melvin's milk-route customers—she lifts her head heavenward and mugs silly ecstasy at the prospect of his returning the next day, for another carnal visit. The dialogue is as near perfection as script dialogue gets—it's always funny, without any cackling. Bo Goldman, who is in his late forties, shared writing credits on *One Flew Over the Cuckoo's Nest* and *The Rose*, but this is his only unshared credit. (After spending a day with the real Melvin Dummar, Goldman decided he wanted to write the script; then he stayed with Dummar for a month and "got to love him," and came to know the two wives and Dummar's friends and relatives and neighbors.) The people in the movie—the large cast includes Charles Napier, John Glover, Gloria Grahame, Dabney Coleman, Michael J. Pollard, Martine Beswick, Susan Peretz, Naida Reynolds, Herbie Faye, and Robert Wentz—all seem scrubby and rumpled and believable; you feel that if you hung around Anaheim or L.A. or Reno you'd run into them. Maybe if you had been at the Sex Kat Klub at the right time, you'd have seen the dancer next to Lynda who was strutting her stuff with a broken arm in a big plaster cast.

Melvin and Howard has the same beautiful, dippy warmth as its characters. Paul Le Mat's Melvin, who barely opens his mouth when he talks, opens it wide when he sings. His proudest moment is probably the hit he makes at the dairy's Christmas party when he grins confidently as he sings a ballad about the gripes of a milkman. (The words, like the words of "Santa's Souped-Up Sleigh," are by the real Melvin Dummar.) Le Mat's Melvin often has a childlike look of bewilderment that he seems to be covering up by his beaming optimism. He's very gentle; he threatens physical violence only once—when he thinks that the assistant manager of the dairy (Jack Kehoe) is trying to rook him out of the big color TV set he has won as Milkman of the Month. Watching a game show, "Easy Street," on that set, he's like an armchair quarterback, telling the contestants which doors to choose to win the prizes. When Darcy is bored by it, he tries to justify his obsession by explaining how educational these shows are, but she isn't conned—she goes out to play.

Demme stages a segment of "Easy Street" (modelled on "Let's Make a Deal") which opens up the theme of the movie by giving us a view of game shows that transcends satire. Lynda, who has been selected as a contestant, appears in an aquamarine dress with tassels and an old-fashioned bellhop's hat, and when she does a tap dance that's as slow as a clog dance the audience starts to laugh. But she keeps going, and though she has more movement in her waving arms than in her tapping feet, she's irresistible. It's the triumph of adorable pluckiness (and the uninhibited use of her beautiful figure) over technique. The host of "Easy Street" (Robert Ridgely) combines malicious charity with provocative encouragement, and the enthusiastic applause confirms the notion that every TV audience loves someone who tries sincerely. In Ritchie's *Smile*, it was plain that the teen-age beauty contestants were not nearly as vacuous as they were made to appear (and made themselves appear), and here it's evident that Lynda the winner, jumping up and down like a darling frisky puppy, is putting on the excitement that is wanted of her. She's just like the pretty women you've seen on TV making fools of themselves, except that you know her; you know the desperation that went into choosing that tawdry dress and that's behind the eagerness to play the game—to squeal and act gaga and kiss everybody. The host personifies the game show, as if he were personally giving all the prizes. He's a pygmy metaphor for Howard Hughes. The game show is the illusion that sustains Melvin: that if you pick the right door, what's behind it is happiness.

Shortly after the probate trial on the Mormon will, the judge who had presided died of cancer; at his funeral service one of the speakers said that on his deathbed the judge told him that he hoped to meet Howard Hughes in the next world—that he had a question he wanted to ask him. The movie shows us a triumphant Melvin Dummar: he knows the answer. He also knows he'll never see the money. (Maybe Howard Hughes was the naïve one, if he thought that he could smash the monster corporation he had created.) Melvin Dummar was touched by a legend. Howard Hughes came to respect him, and so do we.

{*The New Yorker*, October 13, 1980}

:: *Used Cars*

Used Cars has a wonderful, energetic heartlessness. It's an American tall-tale movie in a Pop Art form, with a theme similar to that of *Volpone*. Remember the convict's advice that Nelson Algren quoted? "Never play cards with a man called Doc. Never eat at a place called Mom's. Never sleep with a woman whose troubles are worse than your own." This movie adds "Never buy a used car from a dealer whose slogan is 'Trust us.'" Its premise is that honesty doesn't exist. If you develop a liking for some of the characters, it's not because they're free of avarice but because of their style of avarice. Jack Warden plays twin brothers—the amiable codger Luke Fuchs and the vicious cutthroat Roy L. Fuchs—who run rival used-car lots across the street from each other in the booming Southwest. Luke has a bad heart, and every time he thinks of his skunky brother it gets worse; the only thing that keeps his business going is Rudy Russo. This fast-talking supersalesman, played by Kurt Russell, is so rambunctiously, ingeniously crooked that he's a standout—a star in the world of the mendacious. He's slick and sleazy—a vulgarian through and through. Kurt Russell was sensationally effective when he starred in the TV film *Elvis* early in 1979; here he goes further. His leap into satire blots away the ten Disney pictures he appeared in, between the ages of fourteen and twenty-four. His Rudy has an authentic loudmouth uncouthness; when he's momentarily stumped, his tongue seems to thicken helplessly. He's a son of a bitch, but not a bad guy. The film pits this crass, ferociously ambitious hero against the sneaky Roy L. They're feuding cartoon animals, both using dirty tricks. And when they land in court, the judge (Al Lewis) looks as if long, long ago he smelled something very rotten; it confirmed what he had suspected and he never let himself forget it.

The movie has a flow of visual-slapstick details and off-color verbal nuances that aren't ever punched up or commented on; they just keep flashing by. You see from the corner of an eye that the Mexican, Manuel (Alfonso Arau), who sells Rudy two hundred and fifty used cars (some of them taxis), conducts his illicit business out of his home in an old airplane that sits in the desert surrounded by cactus. The story line is built of small, wild frauds and jack-in-the-box jokes; they're all interconnected, and, amazingly, every one of them pays off. The film's super-hip use of corn is a home-grown surrealism that the director, Robert Zemeckis, and his co-writer and producer, Bob Gale (they were both born in 1951), have developed out of earlier American slapstick routines. The intricacy of the gag patterns is all theirs, and so is the way in which the clusters of gags come together—the momentum creates the illusion of being out of control. Zemeckis and Gale are compulsive jugglers, adding more and more balls. But this isn't simple gag comedy with kickers; the comedy is also in the characters, who keep kicking all the time. *Everybody* in the movie is funny—even Toby, Luke's dog. (Actually, you laugh more when the jokes involve Toby than you do the rest of the time, because whenever Toby is part of the chicanery on the lot, there's a cut to his trick and there isn't much else going on in the frame.) The whizzing plot mechanism may make some people feel that they've never been invited aboard—that the picture is speeding ahead without them. And it's vulgarly funny—which may repel some from boarding. Others have said they find it too cruel: there is a sequence in which Roy L. hires a demolition-derby driver to go across the street, pose as a customer, and take Luke for a ride so scary he'll have a heart attack, and Roy L.—he thinks—will inherit Luke's lot. When Luke staggers back into his office in his death throes, the scene might appear unconscionably prolonged if you weren't reacting to the jokes ricocheting off his stagger. Maybe it's just the timing in that sequence that throws some people off; the audience has no problem laughing when Rudy and his pals conceal Luke's death by burying him on the lot, sitting up in a 1959 Edsel.

The action is so fast that at times it's like an adolescent stunt, carried out convulsively—a fit. Everything is staged for motion; there isn't a static thought in this movie. The jokes aren't scattershot: *Used Cars* has the crazy consistency of a picture like *Bringing Up Baby* or *Shampoo*. The bluffs and the scams all play on the theme of trust (just as everything does in

Melville's *The Confidence-Man*). It's easy to see why Steven Spielberg, who sponsored Zemeckis and Gale, was drawn to their manic bravura: their moviemaking is a giant version of the toys he set in motion in *Close Encounters*. Spielberg was executive producer of their first feature, the 1978 *I Wanna Hold Your Hand*, and his picture *1941* was made from their screenplay, with John Milius as executive producer; both Spielberg and Milius were executive producers on *Used Cars*. All three of these Zemeckis-Gale projects have been commercial disappointments, and a friend of mine who couldn't stand *1941* said it was like having your head inside a pinball machine for two hours. I know what he meant: *1941* shows you talent without sensibility. And that's also why *Used Cars* seems adolescent, and maybe even pre-human. Like *1941*, it has a carnival atmosphere, and yes, there is something of a pinball machine about it. In both cases, the moviemakers start with a comic premise and take it as far as they can, expanding it with a soaring madness that seems to bring a metallic sheen to the images. What this way of working doesn't allow for is humanistic considerations; such considerations have rarely figured in farce, but Americans may have become touchy. When you see any version of *Volpone* on the stage or the screen, you're not likely to be offended by what it says about human greed, deception, mean-spiritedness. You think of the greed *Volpone* delights in as satiric distortion. But it can rub you wrong to see a used-car lot where everyone swindles everyone else; you may think you're seeing a metaphor of American life rather than a slapstick exaggeration.

Cold-bloodedness shouldn't need to be defended; you can't have pratfalls without it, and the sense of fun in Zemeckis and Gale's hyperbolic slapstick does more for us than pitting virtuous characters against the swindlers would. (It would be demeaning if every movie had to be "balanced," like a political discussion on TV, or like the Marx Brothers pictures made at M-G-M, which, at Irving Thalberg's insistence, were given a supposedly sane crooner and ingénue to balance the insane comedy.) In the context of *Used Cars*, anyone trying to be sane or virtuous would come across as a goosey dimwit, like poor Gloria Jean in *Never Give a Sucker an Even Break*. Zemeckis and Gale's movie is really a more restless and visually high-spirited version of the W. C. Fields comedies.

This picture is entirely made up of comic turns, and at its best there isn't a sincere emotion in it. Rudy's burly sidekick, Jeff, played by Gerrit Graham (he was Beef in *Phantom of the Paradise*), believes in omens, and not just in a small way—he believes totally in omens, and so he lives in spaced-out terror. Most of the time, he looks like a dodo bird in shock, and the gorgeous bimbos he generally has at his side are like feathered trophies. Luke's shell-shocked mechanic, Jim, whose standards of honesty are set by how things are done at Luke's lot, is played by Frank McRae. Given the workaday world in which Jim functions as an honest man, he can't help being funny. David L. Lander and Michael McKean (who's like an American Dudley Moore) play Freddie and Eddie, a pair of electronic wizards who help Rudy and Jeff cut into a Presidential address with their used-car commercials; Freddie and Eddie are like twin brothers, too, and they speak in a doubletalk jargon that suggests the language of robots. The film slides a bit when Rudy falls in love with Luke's long-estranged blond daughter, Barbara Fuchs, because Barbara seems too dainty and too easily duped. Though Deborah Harmon, who plays the part, has a good, eccentric voice and gives her lines little twists, her role doesn't have the hot-ziggety verve to match up with Kurt Russell's. The movie needed to go all the way; it shouldn't have pulled back into this pallid conventionality. (When Rudy says "Trust me" to Barbara, he actually means it.) The film recovers a bit, though. By the end, Barbara, who has appeared in time to take over her father's lot, is wising up, and she becomes a gyp artist, snookering a little old lady with a painted-over taxi. In the big finale, when, in order to keep Roy L. from grabbing the business away from Barbara, two hundred and fifty teen-age student drivers race Manuel's two hundred and fifty jalopies across the prairie, and Rudy jumps from car to car, like the hero of a Western jumping from horse to horse to stop the heroine's runaway coach, the picture adds up the way whoppers told by magnificent liars do.

Surprisingly, the cast works together more smoothly than the group that Spielberg assembled for *1941* did. And the gags interlock even more symmetrically. *1941* had a choppy beginning; it seemed to start with the story already under way, and Spielberg overdid some of the broad, cartoon aspects—several of the performers seemed to be carrying placards telling you what was wacko about them. But the U.S.O. jitterbug number is one of the greatest pieces of film choreography I've ever seen, and the film overall is an amazing, orgiastic comedy, with the pop culture of an era compacted into a day and a night. Its commercial failure in this country didn't make much sense to me. It was accused of gigantism, and it did seem huge, though part of what was so disarmingly fresh about it was the miniature re-creation of Hollywood Boulevard at night in 1941, with little floodlights illuminating the toy cars tootling around the corners and toy planes flying so low they were buzzing through the streets.

Spielberg and Zemeckis & Gale share a mania for comic invention, and there's the feeling of a playroom about their work. That has been true of the acknowledged masters of slapstick, though. Why hasn't *Used Cars* (which received some enthusiastic reviews) done better? The only big reason I can come up with is that maybe you have to be hooked on filmmaking to respond to it, because the jokes run all through and there aren't slowdowns or pauses for laughs. I loved the film, but I didn't laugh out loud a lot, because I was too busy looking at it. I've never seen another movie with the same kind of ravishing, bright Pop lighting, and the cinematographer, Donald M. Morgan, turns the used-car lot at night into a cityscape on the far side of the moon. The movie could be used for a film-school demonstration of dynamic composition and production design (even the clothes are photogenic and funny—Rudy and Jeff dress like natty astro-cowboys, in jeans and iridescent satin shirts). And the editing is by one of the modern masters, Michael Kahn. Maybe the failure is that of the moviemakers, who are so absorbed with their playthings that they fail to draw the audience in. But it could also be that *Used Cars* is so elegantly made and so continuously funny that audiences don't respond the way they would if the jokes were clumsily signalled. You have to bring something to this party. Rudy isn't just a creative sleazo. Why does he work for Luke, whose business is failing, rather than for the get-up-and-go Roy L.? For the challenge, of course. He's selling cars now, but he's still young: he's selling cars only until he can come up with the rest of the sixty thousand dollars it will take to buy the nomination for state senator. He's an American dreamer; he wants to go where the big bucks are. *Used Cars* is a classic screwball fantasy—a shaggy celebration of American ingenuity. Trust me.

{*The New Yorker*, November 10, 1980}

:: Religious Pulp, or
The Incredible Hulk

As Jake La Motta, the former middleweight boxing champ, in *Raging Bull*, Robert De Niro wears scar tissue and a big, bent nose that deform his face. It's a miracle that he didn't grow them—he grew everything else. He developed a thick-muscled neck and a fighter's body, and for the scenes of the broken, drunken La Motta he put on so much weight that he seems to have sunk in the fat with hardly a trace of himself left. What De Niro does in this picture isn't acting, exactly. I'm not sure what it is. Though it may at some level be awesome, it definitely isn't pleasurable. De Niro seems to have emptied himself out to become the part he's playing and then not got enough material to refill himself with: his La Motta is a swollen puppet with only bits and pieces of a character inside, and some semi-religious, semi-abstract concepts of guilt. He has so little expressive spark that what I found myself thinking about wasn't La Motta or the movie but the metamorphosis of De Niro. His appearance —with his head flattened out and widened by fat—is far more shocking than if he were artificially padded. De Niro went from his usual hundred and forty-five pounds to a hundred and sixty for the young fighter, and then up to two hundred and fifteen for La Motta's later days. (No man has ever made a more dramatic demonstration of the aesthetic reasons that people shouldn't get bloated.) And the director, Martin Scorsese, doesn't show us the trim, fast fighter and then let us adjust to his deterioration; he deliberately confronts us with the gross older La Motta right at the start, in a flash-forward.

At first, we may think that we're going to find out what makes Jake La

Motta's life special and why a movie is being made about him. But as the picture dives in and out of La Motta's life, with a few minutes of each of his big fights (he won the title in 1949), it becomes clear that Scorsese isn't concerned with how La Motta got where he did, or what, specifically, happened to him. Scorsese gives us exact details of the Bronx Italian neighborhoods of the forties—everything is sharp, realistic, lived-in. But he doesn't give us specific insights into La Motta. Scorsese and De Niro, who together reworked the script (by Paul Schrader and Mardik Martin, based on the book *Raging Bull*, by La Motta with Joseph Carter and Peter Savage), are trying to go deeper into the inarticulate types they have done before; this time they seem to go down to pre-human levels. Their brutish Jake is elemental: he has one thing he can do—fight.

Raging Bull isn't a biographical film about a fighter's rise and fall; it's a biography of the genre of prizefight films. Scorsese loves the visual effects and the powerful melodramatic moments of movies such as *Body and Soul*, *The Set-Up*, and *Golden Boy*. He makes this movie out of remembered high points, leaping from one to another. When Jake is courting the fifteen-year-old platinum-blond Vickie (Cathy Moriarty), he takes her to a miniature-golf course, and their little golf ball rolls into a little wooden church and never comes out. The scene is like one of a series in an old-movie montage showing the path to marriage. But Scorsese just puts in this one step; probably for him it stands for the series. And his neutral attitude toward La Motta is very different from that of forties movies. An idle remark by Vickie—that Jake's opponent in his next match is good-looking—makes Jake so jealous that he goes in and viciously, systematically destroys the kid's face. The movie doesn't throw up its hands in horror; it just looks on. Jake, who enforces long periods of sexual abstinence before his fights, becomes obsessed with the idea that Vickie is cheating on him; you feel that he *wants* to catch her at something. His suspicions lead him to smack her around and to beat up his brother Joey (Joe Pesci), who is his manager, sparring partner, and closest friend. The questions that come to mind (such as why Vickie stays with Jake, or why she leaves when she does, or even whether in fact she *is* unfaithful) clearly aren't germane to Scorsese's interest. Vickie doesn't react much; she accepts Jake's mounting jealousy passively.

Scorsese appears to be trying to purify the characters of forties movies to universalize them. Vickie is an icon—a big, lacquered virgin-doll of the forties. Tall and strong-looking, Cathy Moriarty has a beautiful glassy presence, like Kim Novak in her *Man with the Golden Arm* days, and the same mute sexuality. She recalls other iconographic presences—Jean Harlow, Lana Turner, and the knowing young Gloria Grahame—but she's tougher and more composed. Sitting at the edge of a swimming pool, her Vickie is a *Life* cover girl of the war years. She has sultry eyes and speaks in flat, nasal Bronx tones. It's lucky that Moriarty is big, because when Jake comes at her angrily, like a slob Othello, she looks as if she could take care of herself; there's no pathos. Joe Pesci's Joey is stylized in a different way: he may bring to mind the brother in a movie about a show-biz family. His speech sounds like patter, as if he were doing a routine with Abbott and Costello or the Three Stooges; he has the vocal rhythms of a baggypants comic from burlesque, and though his lines aren't especially funny, his manner is, and the audience responds to him gratefully, because he's so much saner and less monotonous than the Neanderthal Jake. It's Pesci's picture, if it's anybody's, because we can understand why Joey does what he does. Even when he goes out of control and smashes a taxi door repeatedly against a mobster who is caught half in, half out, we know that he's doing what Jake charged him to do. (As the big, gentle mobster, played by Frank Vincent, who's quietly effective, is having his bones broken, voluptuous, forlorn Mascagni music rises. Here, as in much of the movie, Scorsese's excesses verge on self-parody.)

Scorsese is also trying to purify forties style by using the conventions in new ways. If you look at forties movies now, the clichés (which bored people at the time) may seem like fun, and it's easy to see why Scorsese is drawn to them. But when he reproduces them, he reproduces the mechanical quality they once had, and the fun goes out of them. The cardinal rule of forties-studio style was that the scenes had to be shaped to pay off. Scorsese isn't interested in payoffs; it's something else—a modernist effect that's like a gray-out. Early on, when Jake's first wife is frying a steak for him and he complains that she's overcooking it, she hollers and picks up the steak as if she were going to throw it at him, but instead she puts it on his plate. The violence in the scene is right on the surface (she doesn't hold anything back), yet nothing comes of it, and shortly after that she disappears from the movie. We don't get the explosion we expect, but we feel the violence. Scorsese shows us Jake—snorting to himself, and with his belly hanging out—going to see Vickie to get his World Middleweight

Championship belt so he can hock the jewels from it, and the scene withers away. Yet we remember his banging on the belt to pry the jewels loose. Scorsese's continuity with forties movies is in the texture—the studio artificiality that he makes sensuous, thick, viscous; there are layers of rage and animosity in almost every sequence.

Raging Bull isn't just a biography of a genre; it's also about movies and about violence, it's about gritty visual rhythm, it's about Brando, it's about the two *Godfather* pictures—it's about Scorsese and De Niro's trying to top what they've done and what everybody else has done. When De Niro and Liza Minnelli began to argue in Scorsese's *New York, New York*, you knew they were going to go from yelling to hitting, because they had no other way to escalate the tension. Here we get more of these actors' battles; they're between Jake and Joey, and between Jake and Vickie. Listening to Jake and Joey go at each other, like the macho clowns in Cassavetes movies, I know I'm supposed to be responding to a powerful, ironic realism, but I just feel trapped. Jake says, "You dumb f—k," and Joey says, "You dumb f—k," and they repeat it and repeat it. And I think, What am I doing here watching these two dumb f—ks? When Scorsese did *Mean Streets*, *Alice Doesn't Live Here Anymore*, and *Taxi Driver*, the scenes built through language and incident, and other characters turned up. But when he works with two actors and pushes for raw intensity, the actors repeat their vapid profanities, goading each other to dredge up some hostility and some variations and twists. And we keep looking at the same faces—Jake and Joey, or Jake and Vickie. (They're the only people around for most of this movie.) You can feel the director sweating for greatness, but there's nothing *under* the scenes—no subtext, only this actor's version of tension. Basically, the movie is these dialogue bouts and Jake's fights in the ring.

The fights are fast and gory and are shot very close in. We're not put in the position of spectators; we're put in the ring, with our heads right up against the heads of the two fighters who are hammering away at each other, with slow-motion eruptions of blood and sweat splashing us. We're meant to see the fists coming as they see them, and feel the blows as they do; the action is speeded up and slowed down to give us these sensations, and the sound of the punches is amplified, while other noises are blotted out. These aren't fights, really; they're cropped, staccato ordeals. The punches are a steady series of explosions—a drummer doing death rolls. The pounding immediacy is grandiloquent—almost abstract.

The picture seems to be saying that in order to become champ, Jake La Motta had to be mean, obsessive, crazy. But you can't be sure, and the way the story is told Jake's life pattern doesn't make much sense. When he loses the title and gives up fighting, he opens a night club, where he's the m.c. and the comic, clowning around with the customers. I had no idea where this cheesy jokester came from: there was certainly no earlier suggestion that Jake had a gift of gab. And there is nothing to prepare us for the poster announcing that he's giving readings from Paddy Chayefsky, Shakespeare, Rod Serling, Budd Schulberg, and Tennessee Williams; we're in a different movie. At the end, before going onstage for his public reading, Jake recites Brando's back-of-the-taxi speech from *On the Waterfront* while looking in his dressing-room mirror. Scorsese is trying to outdo everything great, even the scene of De Niro talking to himself in the mirror in *Taxi Driver*. What does it mean to have La Motta deliver this lament that he could have been a contender instead of a bum when it's perfectly clear that La Motta is both a champ *and* a bum? (Is it a deliberate mockery of the simplicity of Schulberg's conception?) The whole picture has been made looking in a mirror, self-consciously. It takes a while to grasp that La Motta is being used as *the* fighter, a representative tormented man in a killer's body. He's a repulsive, threatening figure who seems intended to be all that and yet to have an element of greatness. He's a doomed strong man—doomed by his love for his wife and by his ability to fight. It's all metaphors: the animal man attempting to escape his destiny. When Jake, in jail on a morals charge, bangs his head and his fists against the stone walls of his cell and, sobbing in frustration, cries out, "Why? Why? Why? It's so f—king stupid! I'm not an animal," it's the ultimate metaphor for the whole film.

The tragedy in Scorsese's struggles with the material in both *New York, New York* and *Raging Bull* is that he *is* a great director when he doesn't press so hard at it, when he doesn't suffer so much. He's got moviemaking and the Church mixed up together; he's trying to be the saint of cinema. And he turns Jake's life into a ritual of suffering. In the middle of a fight, Jake is sponged by the men in his corner, and he has been injured so much that the water is dark: they're washing him in his own blood. Scorsese is out to demonstrate that he can have for his hero a brutish hardhead, a man with no redeeming social graces, and make you respect him. He must have been drawn to La Motta's story by its sheer plug-ugliness: here was a fighter who didn't even look graceful in the ring—he crouched and slugged. And

Scorsese goes to cartoon lengths to establish that Jake is a bad guy: Jake actually threatens to kill and eat a neighbor's dog. Scorsese doesn't want us to *like* Jake, because he wants us to respond on a higher level—to Jake's energy and his pain. He wants us to respect Jake despite everything we see him do. We're supposed to believe in his *integrity*. The Mafia bosses force Jake to throw a fight before they'll let him have a chance at the title. He throws the fight by just standing still and taking the blows; afterward, he weeps. It's a fall from grace: he has given up the only thing that counts. We're supposed to think, Jake may be a pig, but he *fights*. Scorsese appears to see Jake as having some kind of loony glory. But if you respond, possibly it's not to La Motta's integrity but to De Niro's; he buries the clichés that lesser actors might revel in, and is left with nothing to anchor his performance. He does some amazing things, though. In the ring taking punches, Jake seems to be crying, "Crucify me! Crucify me!" With anyone but De Niro in the role; the picture would probably be a joke. But De Niro gives you a sense of terrible pain that is *relieved* when he's in the ring. The film's brutality doesn't seem exploitative; it's mystical.

The magazine *Film Comment* has a feature, "Guilty Pleasures," which it runs intermittently: movie people list the works they wouldn't try to defend on aesthetic grounds but have enjoyed inordinately. When Scorsese offered some of his favorites in 1978, a thread ran through many of his selections. He says, "*Play Dirty* isn't a sadistic film, but it's mean. The characters have no redeeming social value, which I love." Of *Always Leave Them Laughing*, he says, "I admire the guts it took for Berle to make this autobiographical film about a completely dislikable guy." Of the hero of *I Walk Alone*, he says, "He has only one way to deal with his problems: brute force." Of *Dark of the Sun*, he says, "The sense of the film is overwhelmingly violent; there's no consideration for anything else. The answer to everything is 'kill.' " Scorsese likes movies that aren't covered in sentimental frosting—that put the surliness and killing and meanness right up front. But *Raging Bull* has the air of saying something important, which is just what he loved those cheapo pictures for not having. By making a movie that is *all* guilty pleasures, he has forged a new sentimentality. *Raging Bull* is about a character he loves too much; it's about everything he loves too much. It's the kind of movie that many men must fantasize about: their macho worst-dream movie.

Scorsese is saying that he accepts totally, that he makes no moral judgment. I think that by the last fight we're not supposed to care whether Jake wins or loses—we're supposed to want to be in there, slugging. Even the black-and-white is macho: it has something of the flashy, tabloid look of the original *Naked City* movie. But it's so hyper that you're aware of the art, which kills the tabloid effect. We don't get to see the different styles of La Motta's opponents: Scorsese doesn't care about the rhythm and balance of fighters' bodies. There's no dancing for these fighters, and very little boxing. What Scorsese concentrates on is punishment given and received. He turns the lowdown effects he likes into highbrow flash reeking of religious symbolism. You're aware of the camera positions and of the images held for admiration; you're conscious of the pop and hiss of the newsmen's cameras and the amplified sound of the blows—the sound of pain. Scorsese wants his B-movie seaminess and spiritual meaning, too. He wants a disreputable, lowlife protagonist; then he suggests that this man is close to God, because he is God's animal.

By removing the specifics or blurring them, Scorsese doesn't produce universals—he produces banality. What we get is full of capitals: A Man Fights, A Man Loses Everything, A Man Bangs His Head Against the Wall. Scorsese is putting his unmediated obsessions on the screen, trying to turn raw, pulp power into art by removing it from the particulars of observation and narrative. He loses the lowlife entertainment values of prizefight films; he aestheticizes pulp and kills it. *Raging Bull* is tabloid grand opera. Jake is the Brute Life Force, and the picture ends as he experiences A Surge of Energy. It's a Felliniesque ending: Life Goes On. The picture is overripe, ready for canonization. An end title supplies a handy Biblical quote.

{*The New Yorker*, December 8, 1980}

:: *Atlantic City*

Burt Lancaster started out, back in the 1946 *The Killers*, as a great specimen of hunkus Americanus. In Louis Malle's new comedy, *Atlantic City*, from a script by John Guare, Lancaster uses his big, strong body so expressively that if this were a stage performance the audience would probably give him a standing ovation. I don't see how he could be any better. He plays Lou, an old-timer who tries to keep up appearances; he irons his one good silk tie before going outside. Still dreaming of the good old days, when he was a flunky and bodyguard for big-time racketeers, Lou scrounges for a living as a numbers runner, making his rounds of Atlantic City's black slums and picking up bets of fifty cents or a dollar. He also takes handouts—and abuse—from Grace (Kate Reid), the widow of a mobster he used to work for. She has an apartment in the same building where he has a small, seedy room; she stays in bed, pampering herself, while he shops and cooks for her and walks her dog—a tiny poodle, which he hates. Grace is a hypochondriac and complainer, and she razzes him mercilessly; he accepts her reproaches, though he snarls to himself in weary resentment. You sense that he barely hears her anymore; Lou's thoughts are elsewhere. When he's in his room and looks out the window, across the airshaft, he can see into the apartment where Sally (Susan Sarandon) lives; hiding to the side, he watches her nightly ablutions when she comes home from her waitress work at the Oyster Bar in the Resorts International casino. She puts a tape of *Norma* on her cassette-player, cuts lemons in half, and rubs the juice onto her upper body. Excited, Lou hurries down to Grace's apartment, puts a record on, and crawls into bed with her.

Lancaster's acting in *The Killers* wasn't at all bad, but his physical

659

presence was so powerful in the busy years that followed that he became a caricature of an action star. Sometimes he was a satiric caricature (as in the 1952 *The Crimson Pirate*), and sometimes he was an impressive, highly sexual man of action (as in the 1953 *From Here to Eternity*), but in his many attempts to extend his range beyond action roles—in *Come Back, Little Sheba* (1952), *The Rose Tattoo* (1955), *The Rainmaker* (1956), *Separate Tables* (1958), *The Devil's Disciple* (1959), *The Young Savages* (1961), *Judgment at Nuremberg* (1961), *Birdman of Alcatraz* (1962), *A Child Is Waiting* (1963), and, most notably, in *Sweet Smell of Success* (1956)—you could often see him straining for seriousness, and it shrivelled him. (When Lancaster put on a pair of specs, he looked as if he'd been bled by leeches.) Probably no other major star took so many chances, and a couple of times—as the prince in Visconti's *The Leopard* (1963), and as the patriarch in Bertolucci's *1900* (1976)—he came through with a new weight of emotion. In those pictures, he seemed able to use his bull-like physicality with a new dignity and awareness. He was more physical than ever, but physical in the way that Anna Magnani (with whom he was teamed in *The Rose Tattoo*) was—battered, larger than life, vain, naked. In shallow action roles, he played bloody but unbowed; when he was working with Visconti or Bertolucci, he wasn't afraid to be bloody and bowed. And that's how he is here, but more so, because this time he isn't playing a strong man brought down by age and social changes: he's a man who was never anything much—he was always a little too soft inside—and Grace won't let him forget it.

Though I have a better time in the theatre at John Guare's plays than I do at the plays of any other contemporary American, I would not have guessed that his charmed, warped world and his dialogue, which is full of imagery, could be so successfully brought to the screen. In a Guare play, the structure isn't articulated. There's nothing to hold the bright pieces together but his nerve and his instincts; when they're in high gear, the play has the excitement of discovery—which you don't get in "well-crafted" plays. You're not stuck with the usual dramatic apparatus—the expository dialogue and the wire-pulling to get the characters into the planned situations. Instead, you get gags, which prove to be the explanations. *Anything* may turn up in a Guare play. In Joseph Papp's Public Theatre production of Guare's *Marco Polo Sings a Solo*, set on an Arctic island in 1999, Anne Jackson, who played Joel Grey's mother, revealed that her son was the first person in history to have only one parent: she was a transsexual, she explained, and had conceived him with semen saved from before her sex-change operation. In the same play, another character talked about Chekhov's *The Three Sisters*: "Those poor girls, all the time trying to get to Moscow. The town they lived in was only forty-eight miles from Moscow. In 1999 that town is probably part of greater downtown Moscow. They were in Moscow all the time." Guare's vaudeville jokes subvert traditional conceptions of drama. Anyone who has ever been embarrassed for the actors who had to fling a prop dead bird around the stage in *The Sea Gull* would have appreciated Anne Jackson's aside to the audience apropos of some similar props: "I don't know much about symbols, but I'd say that when frozen flamingos fall out of the sky, good times are not in store." In a foreword to the published version of his play *The House of Blue Leaves*, Guare wrote that what had got him out of a creative cul-de-sac was watching Olivier perform on successive nights in Strindberg's *The Dance of Death* and Feydeau's *A Flea in Her Ear*. In his imagination, they blended, he said, and became one play, and he asked himself why Strindberg and Feydeau shouldn't get married, or at least live together.

I have resorted to quoting from *Marco Polo* because I would like to suggest Guare's comic style without uncorking *Atlantic City*. Let me just indicate how the jokes function: Lou reminisces about the glories of this resort town in the days when there were real songs, like "Flat Foot Floogie with the Floy Floy," and he adds, "The Atlantic Ocean was something then." You laugh in recognition that for him life has lost its savor. Guare's one-liners are more deeply zany than we're accustomed to. His characters sound as if they had all invented themselves and their life histories right on the spot. And Guare has a way of shaping a funny line of dialogue so it goes loop-the-loop into pathos. Sometimes I think that his is the only kind of theatrical pathos that's really enjoyable; it erupts suddenly, when a character's invention can't go any further and he's left with truth. But it's still part of a gag. Kate Reid's Grace, lying amid boxes of chocolate and rose satin quilted covers, may remind the lucky few who saw Guare's most intense and macabre play, *Bosoms and Neglect*, of her performance as the bedridden, blind, and cancerous old Irish mother, Henny. (When Henny is in the hospital for surgery, her son visits a woman he picked up in Rizzoli's—a blond bibliophile who tries to seduce him with her first editions. He describes his mother's torments, and she cries, "I suddenly have this image of being blind. Oh God. Never to be able to browse.")

Guare was one of the three writers who worked with Miloš Forman on the 1971 *Taking Off*, but the film's sensibility was Forman's. *Atlantic City* is a collaboration much like that of Elia Kazan and Tennessee Williams on, say, *Baby Doll*. Louis Malle has entered into Guare's way of seeing—a mixture of observation, flights of invention, satire, perversity, anecdote, fable. And depth of feeling—what Lancaster, in the finest performance he has ever given (with the possible exception of his work in *1900*), brings to the film. And he brings it to the jokes.

Near the beginning of the film, one of the vast, curvy old Baghdad-by-the-sea buildings that date from Atlantic City's days as a resort community is dynamited; this rock-candy relic is making way for the new hotel-casinos, which have been shooting up since New Jersey legalized gambling there, in 1976. (It was chosen partly because it's on an island and can be closed off from the mainland.) Malle's Atlantic City is very different from the seedy, decrepit one in which Bob Rafelson shot *The King of Marvin Gardens*, in 1972. The destruction and construction that go on in all cities are accelerated in the new Atlantic City; it suggests a giant movie lot, where sets are built and struck. This spa that became a racketeers' paradise during Prohibition and is now on its chaotic way to becoming Vegas with a beach is an improbable place; it gives a hallucinatory texture to the characters' lives. And it's the ideal real place for a Guare comedy—everything arriving and departing in one fell swoop. Atlantic City is the film's controlling metaphor. Malle and Guare must have let the city itself set the motifs: demolition and construction; decay and renewal; water, baths, ablutions; luck. The city says so much on its own that the moviemakers don't have to press down for meanings; if anything, they need to hold back (and they do).

When the rambling pleasure palace crumbles, the film takes up the story of another relic—Lou. The movie is a lyric farce, in which Lou and Sally, and Grace also, realize their dreams, through a series of accidents and several varieties of chicanery. Sally has been training to become a croupier, under the tutelage of the Frenchman (Michel Piccoli) who gave her the Elizabeth Harwood tape of *Norma*. Her plans are disrupted when her wormy husband (Robert Joy) hitchhikes into town with her pale, sweetly zonked younger sister Chrissie (Hollis McLaren), who is hugely pregnant by him. They turn up, scuzzy from the road and with their packs on their backs, at the sleek casino where Sally works. Sally's husband expects her to let them crash at her place until he can dispose of a bundle of cocaine that he stole in Philadelphia. Once he arrives, nobody in the movie seems to have any principles or to have heard of honesty. (Chrissie doesn't even believe in gravity.) Lou—through a fluke—gets hold of the money from the cocaine, and starts behaving like the sport he has always wanted to be. He spreads the wealth around and squires Sally to an expensive restaurant; she's eager to learn more about the world, and, little as he knows, he's a fount of knowledge compared with her.

The role of the ignorant Sally, a back-country girl from Saskatchewan who hopes to work her way to Monte Carlo, is essentially that of Gabrielle in *The Petrified Forest*, and, for once, Susan Sarandon's googly-eyed, slightly stupefied look seems perfect. She doesn't rattle off her lines in her usual manner; she seems to respond to the freshness and lilt of the dialogue. In Malle's last film, *Pretty Baby*, she was mysteriously beautiful when she was posing nude for photographs, but she gave an inexplicably petulant and vapid performance; she did so much ruminating she was cowlike. Susan Sarandon has sometimes come through in strange circumstances, though; the permutations of her rattle provided the sprightliest moments of *The Other Side of Midnight*. Maybe she seems so skillful here because this is the best part she's ever had on the screen. Her double takes are very delicate; she keeps you tuned in to her feelings all the time. Sally's expression is frazzled yet affectionate when she looks at her Hare Krishna–ite little sister. Hollis McLaren (she was the half-mad girl in *Outrageous!*) brings a winsome dippiness to the role of gullible Chrissie, a flower child born into the wrong era. Simplicity like Chrissie's seems almost soothing, but not if you're her sister and don't know what to do with her. What can you do with a pregnant angel?

When I see a Guare play, I almost always feel astonished; I never know where he's going until he gets there. Then everything ties together. He seems to have an intuitive game plan. That's how this film works, too. It takes Malle a little while to set up the crisscrossing of the ten or twelve major characters, but once he does you can begin to respond to the interior, poetic logic that holds this movie together. By the second half, *Atlantic City* is operating by its own laws in its own world, and it has a lovely fizziness. Everything goes wrong and comes out right. It's no accident that Guare said Feydeau had helped him out of a cul-de-sac. We get the pleasure of seeing everything sorted out, as it is in a classic farce, except that the perfect pairings, the slippers that fit, the kindnesses rewarded have the dadaist quality of having been plucked out of the air.

The casting is superb, and each time a performer reappears you look forward to what he's going to do this time. There are just a few minor disappointments. Acting in English, Piccoli doesn't have his usual nuanced control (he overemphasizes his lines), but he certainly knows how to play a practiced European lecher; in one scene he circles around Sally, like a weary dancer. A murder sequence in a hydraulic parking structure is perhaps too tricky; it looks as if it was a bitch to shoot and edit. But there are almost constant small pleasures, such as Lou's meeting an old pal, Buddy (Sean Sullivan), who has become a washroom attendant, and swapping stories, and a hospital sequence, in which Robert Goulet, on behalf of Resorts International, presents the casino's check for a quarter of a million dollars to the Atlantic City Medical Center, the Frank Sinatra Wing, and sings to an audience of patients brought down to the lobby to make the presentation a media event. (It's like an epic-size Bill Murray routine.) One sequence appears to drift, but then has a great conclusion: Sally and Lou go to the house that she plans to share with nine other croupiers-in-training. (Each of the ten is studying to deal a different game—baccarat, blackjack, and so on.) Sally takes Lou to the room she needs to paint, and when they're alone he tells her that he watches her at night. She is moved and he can see that she is going to let him make love to her. He pushes her blouse down from her shoulders and looks at her ripe young flesh, and his watery eyes are full of reverence and regret.

This picture has just about everything that *Pretty Baby*, which was also made in this country, and in English, lacked. Every line of dialogue in *Pretty Baby* was stiff. It was clear that the person who made the film was a director, but it was hard to believe that he'd ever worked with actors before. In *Atlantic City*, Louis Malle is in full control and at his ease, and his collaboration with John Guare produces a rich, original comic tone. Sometimes the most pleasurable movies seem very slight, because they don't wham you on the noggin. Malle's skill shows in the way he keeps this picture in its frame of reference, and gives it its own look. Visually, it's extraordinary, though in a way that doesn't hit you on the noggin, either. The lighting is vivid but muted and indirect. A whole room may be in focus, yet with very little light—no more than the modulated light you see on cloudy days. The cinematographer, Richard Ciupka, is a young Québécois (the film was financed partly by Canadian funds); his work here suggests Storaro—it's like studio lighting but softer. The whole city seems to be in deep focus; you're sharply aware of old and new, age and youth. The ocean breezes are chilling to Lou; he's bundled up as he makes his rounds. But by the end he enjoys looking at the ocean again. The movie is a prankish wish-fulfillment fantasy about prosperity: what it does to cities, what it can do for people. There's a closing image of a massive building—the wrecking ball keeps pounding it, and it keeps refusing to yield. When you leave the theatre, you may feel light-headed, as if there were no problems in the world that couldn't be solved.

{*The New Yorker*, April 6, 1981}

:: Hey, Torquemada

As Nero in Mel Brooks's *History of the World—Part I*, Dom DeLuise is so greedy and sated that his eyelids droop from the weight of the food in his stomach; wreathed in fat, burping from indigestion, he goes on eating. DeLuise has always been funny in a distinctive, angelic, slightly hallucinated way. Even as the Polish assassin in *The End* (where he was so creatively crazy that he seemed to be inventing a new type of dementia right before your eyes), he was still well meaning. Not here: this Nero is rotten through and through, and DeLuise embraces rottenness with blissful abandon. It gives him a new dimension: he's funny in a great tradition of shameless low comedy. So is the movie. Structurally, *History*— a series of bawdy sketches—is a jamboree, a shambles. It's a floating burlesque show that travels from one era to the next, lampooning the specialties of each age—its particular infamies. Brooks is the writer, the director, and the star. His staging is often flaccid and disorderly, and he has never quite mastered the technique for building a film sequence, so even when he and the dozens of other comics in the cast are racing about, the movie often feels static. It's powered by its performers, though, and their way with a joke. It's an all-out assault on taste and taboo, and it made me laugh a lot.

Once the film gets past the Stone Age, Brooks is the star of each section: he's Moses, he's Comicus (a standup philosopher who performs for Nero), he's Torquemada, and he's Louis XVI, as well as a royal servant who doubles for Louis. We get more of the maniac side of Brooks than ever before, and it's enough to give this picture a charge of pure energy. I wish that he had selected less familiar periods of history. Rome has already been worked over (*A Funny Thing Happened on the Way to the Forum*, *Roman*

Scandals, The Boys from Syracuse, O.K. Nero!), and so has French court life (most recently in Richard Lester's *The Three Musketeers*, which had a chess game much like the one here). I'd rather see Brooks as an Etruscan, or maybe a Mayan, or he could have been an ancient Persian miniaturist, or a Shaker, or one of those anonymous artisans we're always hearing about who worked on the cathedral at Chartres. But he still finds plenty to do in Rome—which is full of tradesmen's signs that take you back to your first puzzlement over Roman numerals, and the use of V for U. All through the movie, there are graceful painted vistas, by the special-effects wizard Albert J. Whitlock.

History is about show business through the ages, and some of the routines are golden shtick: a vestal virgin says to a group of men, "Walk this way," whereupon each of the men imitates her sweet-young-thing saunter. (In *Young Frankenstein*, it was Igor's humpbacked slouch that was copied.) More specifically, the film is a parody of the Broadway-Hollywood approach to the squirmy "offensive" subjects: religion, the poor, and minorities—Jews, blacks, women, and homosexuals. The deluxe, tanned vestal virgins at Nero's court (courtesy of Hugh Hefner: they're actually *Playboy* playmates and models) are dressed in low-cut gowns, and every one of them has her bosoms squished together; they're riper versions of the Goldwyn Girls in *Roman Scandals*—what moviemakers used to call "pulchritude." Brooks may take a special delight in this kind of throwback; he may be saying that this aspect of show biz doesn't really change. He also revels in old theatrical effeminacy: Howard Morris is Nero's mincing court spokesman, Andreas Voutsinas is a fop hairdresser, and so on. They're exaggeratedly nelly, but they're not very funny, unless you find nelliness itself a howl—as burlesque patrons used to, and as Brooks probably still does.

Brooks doesn't modulate his material; he tends to keep everything at a manic pitch. Luckily, some of the comics he has rounded up preserve their own unruffled timing. When Beatrice Arthur, as a clerk at the unemployment office in Rome, questions the people in line, her unhurried, deep, ringing voice shrivels them. And there are quiet bits by Henny Youngman as a Roman chemist, by Jonathan Cecil as a bewildered popinjay at the court of Louis XVI, and many others. It's a great variety show: there are gags and routines by such people as Paul Mazursky, Ron Carey, Sid Caesar, Spike Milligan, Jackie Mason, Fritz Feld, Jack Riley, Ron Clark, John

Myhers, Jack Carter, Jan Murray, Pat McCormick, John Hillerman, Charlie Callas, John Gavin, Ronny Graham as Oedipus, Cloris Leachman as Madame de Farge, and Madeline Kahn as Nero's wife, the gum-chewing Empress Nympho, who has a voice that could shatter brass. Even Harvey Korman, who always seems to lose his bearings in Brooks's films, has a good bit when—as the prissy Count de Monet—he bashes his hand against a door, in anger at mispronouncing his own name. There are just two casting choices that stand out as mistakes: Shecky Greene as the lovelorn warrior Marcus Vindictus, the only man Nympho (a smart lady) rejects; Greene, who seems to have taken off the weight that Dom DeLuise gained, lets you see him trying to act funny. And Mary-Margaret Humes as the vestal-virgin ingénue, Miriam, has been handed too many toothy closeups, and she's a romper—when she's pleased about something, she jumps up and down. At first, you think somebody is going to do a number on her; Groucho certainly would have.

Sometimes the casting is on the nose: for example, John Hurt as Jesus presiding over the Last Supper. But Brooks must have laughed so hard at the idea that he didn't develop it; the people in the audience who aren't familiar with Hurt's previous roles (as a supreme sufferer) have no way to share the joke. The whole, brief Last Supper sequence is inspired, though. And so is the best-edited and best-sustained part of the picture—the Spanish Inquisition as a big musical number, with Brooks as a dancing, singing Torquemada in a red-devil cassock, and with lyrics such as "Hey, Torquemada, what d'ya say?" "I just got back from the auto-da-fé." This sequence has a pedigree: the Inquisition was done as a musical number in the Harold Prince production of Leonard Bernstein's *Candide*—remember Sondheim and Latouche's lyrics "What a day, what a day for an auto-da-fé"?

When I saw *History*, there were hisses and walkouts during this number, and the film has been attacked as a disgrace by reviewers in the press and on TV. I bet nobody hissed or walked out on *Candide*. When Prince and Bernstein do it, it's culture; when Brooks does it, there's a chorus of voices saying, "He has gone too far this time." Earlier in the film, the dancer Gregory Hines, who makes a breezy film début as Comicus' Ethiopian pal, Josephus, tries to convince the slavers who are sending him to the circus to be eaten by lions that he's not a Christian but a Jew. With his loose-limbed body—his legs seem to be on hinges—he does a mock-Jewish dance, and then a shim-sham, and the racial humor didn't appear to bother the audience. But during the Inquisition, when nuns toss off their habits, and a giant torture wheel to which pious Jews are attached is spun in a game of chance, there were mutterings of disapproval. Yet it's Brooks's audacity—his treating cruelty and pain as a crazy joke, and doing it in a low-comedy context—that gives *History* the kick that was missing from his last few films. The Inquisition is presented as a paranoid fantasy, with Jews as the only victims, and when Torquemada whacks the knees of gray-bearded old men imprisoned in stocks—using them as a xylophone—you may gasp. But either you get stuck thinking about the "bad taste" or you let yourself laugh at the obscenity in the humor, as you do at Buñuel's perverse dirty jokes. The offensive material is a springboard to a less sentimental kind of comedy.

If Mel Brooks doesn't go "too far," he's nowhere—he's mild and mushy. It's his maniacal, exuberant compulsion to flaunt show-biz Jewishness that makes him an uncontrollable original. At his best, he is to being Jewish what Richard Pryor is to being black: wildly in love with the joke of it, obsessed and inspired by the joke of it. What *History* needs is *more* musical numbers with the show-biz surreal satire of the Inquisition section; it's the kind of satire that makes the Marx Brothers' *Duck Soup* a classic farce. Brooks goes wrong when he pulls back to innocuous lovability—when he has Gregory Hines say to him, "You're the first white man I even *considered* liking." (Now, if that had been "the first Jew . . .") Hines' dancing—the movie could have used more of it—deserves better than a suck-up line.

When Brooks has a hot streak on a TV talk show, you can see his mental processes at work, and amazing things just pop out of his mouth. He can't get that rhythm going on the screen with prepared gags. Some movie directors can give their material that surprise. Altman has often done it, and in *Hi, Mom!* De Palma did it, with a highly inflammatory race-relations subject. But Brooks isn't a great director—far from it. He's a great personality, though, and he moves wonderfully; his dancing in his Torquemada robes is right up there with Groucho's lope. Wearing a little mustache and with his lips puckered, Brooks as Louis XVI bears a startling resemblance to Chaplin in his *Monsieur Verdoux* period. I kept waiting for him to do something with this resemblance, but he didn't. Was he unaware of it? Lecherous Louis did, however, make me understand why women at the French court wore those panniers that puffed out the sides of their skirts;

we see those ballooning bottoms through his eyes. (Brooks may be wasting his talent by not appearing in other directors' movies while he's preparing his own.) As a director-star, he has the chance to go on pushing out the boundaries of screen comedy, because, despite the disapproving voices in the press and on TV, he can probably get away with it. Like Pryor, he's a cutie.

{*The New Yorker*, June 29, 1981}

:: Portrait of the Artist
as a Young Gadgeteer

At forty, Brian De Palma has more than twenty years of moviemaking behind him, and he has been growing better and better. Each time a new film of his opens, everything he has done before seems to have been preparation for it. With *Blow Out*, starring John Travolta and Nancy Allen, which he wrote and directed, he has made his biggest leap yet. If you know De Palma's movies, you have seen earlier sketches of many of the characters and scenes here, but they served more limited—often satirical—purposes. *Blow Out* isn't a comedy or a film of the macabre; it involves the assassination of the most popular candidate for the Presidency, so it might be called a political thriller, but it isn't really a genre film. For the first time, De Palma goes inside his central character—Travolta as Jack, a sound-effects specialist. And he stays inside. He has become so proficient in the techniques of suspense that he can use what he knows more expressively. You don't see set pieces in *Blow Out*—it flows, and everything that happens seems to go right to your head. It's hallucinatory, and it has a dreamlike clarity and inevitability, but you'll never make the mistake of thinking that it's only a dream. Compared with *Blow Out*, even the good pictures that have opened this year look dowdy. I think De Palma has sprung to the place that Altman achieved with films such as *McCabe & Mrs. Miller* and *Nashville* and that Coppola reached with the two *Godfather* movies—that is, to the place where genre is transcended and what we're moved by is an artist's vision. And Travolta, who appeared to have lost his way after *Saturday Night Fever*, makes his own leap—right back to the top, where he belongs. Playing an adult (his first), and an intelligent one, he has a vibrating physical sensitivity like that of the very young Brando.

Jack, the sound-effects man, who works for an exploitation moviemaker in Philadelphia, is outside the city one night recording the natural rustling sounds. He picks up the talk of a pair of lovers and the hooting of an owl, and then the quiet is broken by the noise of a car speeding across a bridge, a shot, a blowout, and the crash of the car to the water below. He jumps into the river and swims to the car; the driver—a man—is clearly dead, but a girl (Nancy Allen) trapped inside is crying for help. Jack dives down for a rock, smashes a window, pulls her out, and takes her to a hospital. By the time she has been treated, and the body of the driver—the governor, who was planning to run for President—has been brought in, the hospital has filled with police and government officials. Jack's account of the shot before the blow-out is brushed aside, and he is given a high-pressure lecture by the dead man's aide (John McMartin). He's told to forget that the girl was in the car; it's better to have the governor die alone—it protects his family from embarrassment. Jack instinctively objects to this coverup but goes along with it. The girl, Sally, who is sedated and can barely stand, is determined to get away from the hospital; the aide smuggles both her and Jack out, and Jack takes her to a motel. Later, when he matches his tape to the pictures taken by Manny Karp (Dennis Franz), a photographer who also witnessed the crash, he has strong evidence that the governor's death wasn't an accident. The pictures, though, make it appear that the governor was alone in the car; there's no trace of Sally.

Blow Out is a variation on Antonioni's *Blow-Up* (1966), and the core idea probably comes from the compound joke in De Palma's 1968 film *Greetings*: A young man tries to show his girlfriend enlarged photographs that he claims reveal figures on the "grassy knoll," and he announces, "This will break the Kennedy case wide open." Bored, she says, "I saw *Blow-Up*—I know how this comes out. It's all blurry—you can't tell a thing." But there's nothing blurry in this new film. It's also a variation on Coppola's *The Conversation* (1974), and it connects almost subliminally with recent political events—with Chappaquiddick and with Nelson Rockefeller's death. And as the film proceeds, and the murderous zealot Burke (John Lithgow) appears, it also ties in with the "clandestine operations" and "dirty tricks" of the Nixon years. It's a Watergate movie and on paper it might seem to be just a political melodrama, but it has an intensity that makes it unlike any other political film. If you're in a vehicle that's skidding into a snowbank or a guardrail, your senses are awakened, and in the second before you hit you're acutely, almost languorously aware of everything going on around you—it's the trancelike effect sometimes achieved on the screen by slow motion. De Palma keeps our senses heightened that way all through *Blow Out*; the entire movie has the rapt intensity that he got in the slow-motion sequences in *The Fury* (1978). Only now De Palma can do it at normal speed.

This is where all that preparation comes in. There are rooms seen from above—an overhead shot of Jack surrounded by equipment, another of Manny Karp sprawled on his bed—that recall De Palma's use of overhead shots in *Get to Know Your Rabbit* (1972). He goes even further with the split-screen techniques he used in *Dressed to Kill* (1980); now he even uses dissolves into the split screen—it's like a twinkle in your thought processes. And the circling camera that he practiced with in *Obsession* (1976) is joined by circling sound, and Jack—who takes refuge in circuitry—is in the middle. De Palma has been learning how to make every move of the camera signify just what he wants it to, and now he has that knowledge at his fingertips. The pyrotechnics and the whirlybird camera are no longer saying "Look at me"; they give the film authority. When that hooting owl fills the side of the screen and his head spins around, you're already in such a keyed-up, exalted state that he might be in the seat next to you. The cinematographer, Vilmos Zsigmond, working with his own team of assistants, does night scenes that look like paintings on black velvet so lush you could walk into them, and surreally clear daylight vistas of the city—you see buildings a mile away as if they were in a crystal ball in your hand. The colors are deep, and not tropical, exactly, but fired up, torrid. *Blow Out* looks a lot like *The Fury*; it has that heat, but with greater depth and definition. It's sleek and it glows orange, like the coils of a heater or molten glass—as if the light were coming from behind the screen or as if the screen itself were plugged in. And because the story centers on sounds there is great care for silence. It's a movie made by perfectionists (the editor is De Palma's longtime associate Paul Hirsch, and the production design is by Paul Sylbert), yet it isn't at all fussy. De Palma's good, loose writing gives him just what he needs (it doesn't hobble him, like some of the writing in *The Fury*), and having Zsigmond at his side must have helped free him to get right in there with the characters.

De Palma has been accused of being a puppeteer, and doing the actors' work for them. (Sometimes he may have had to.) But that certainly isn't the case here. Travolta and Nancy Allen are radiant performers, and he lets their radiance have its full effect; he lets them do the work of acting, too. Travolta played opposite Nancy Allen in De Palma's *Carrie* (1976), and they seemed right as a team; when they act together, they give out the same amount of energy—they're equally vivid. In *Blow Out*, as soon as Jack and Sally speak to each other you feel a bond between them, even though he's bright and soft-spoken and she looks like a dumb-bunny piece of fluff. In the early scenes, in the hospital and the motel, when the blond, curly-headed Sally entreats Jack to help her, she's a stoned doll with a hoarse, sleepy-little-girl voice, like Bette Midler in *The Rose*—part helpless, part enjoying playing helpless. When Sally is fully conscious, we can see that she uses the cuddly-blonde act for the people she deals with, and we can sense the thinking behind it. But then her eyes cloud over with misery when she knows she has done wrong. Nancy Allen takes what used to be a good-bad-girl stereotype and gives it a flirty iridescence that makes Jack smile the same way we in the audience are smiling. She balances depth and shallowness, caution and heedlessness, so that Sally is always teetering—conning or being conned, and sometimes both. Nancy Allen gives the film its soul; Travolta gives it gravity and weight and passion.

Jack is a man whose talents backfire. He thinks he can do more with technology than he can; he doesn't allow for the human weirdnesses that snarl things up. A few years earlier, he had worked for the Police Department, but that ended after a horrible accident. He had wired an undercover police officer who was trying to break a crime ring, but the officer sweated, the battery burned him, and, when he tried to rip it off, the gangster he hoped to trap hanged him by the wire. Yet the only way Jack thinks that he can get the information about the governor's death to the public involves wiring Sally. (You can almost hear him saying, "Please, God, let it work this time.") Sally, who accepts corruption without a second thought, is charmed by Jack because he gives it a second thought. (She probably doesn't guess how much thought he does give it.) And he's drawn to Sally because she lives so easily in the corrupt world. He's encased in technology, and he thinks his machines can expose a murder. He thinks he can use them to get to the heart of the matter, but he uses them as a shield. And not only is his paranoia justified but things are much worse than he imagines—his paranoia is inadequate.

Travolta—twenty-seven now—finally has a role that allows him to discard his teen-age strutting and his slobby accents. Now it seems clear that he was so slack-jawed and weak in last year's *Urban Cowboy* because he couldn't draw upon his own emotional experience—the ignorant-kid role was conceived so callowly that it emasculated him as an actor. As Jack, he seems taller and lankier. He has a moment in the flashback about his police work when he sees the officer hanging by the wire. He cries out, takes a few steps away, and then turns and looks again. He barely does anything—yet it's the kind of screen acting that made generations of film-goers revere Brando in *On the Waterfront*: it's the willingness to go emotionally naked and the control to do it in character. (And, along with that, the understanding of desolation.) Travolta's body is always in character in this movie; when Jack is alone and intent on what he's doing, we feel his commitment to the orderly world of neatly labelled tapes—his hands are precise and graceful. Recording the wind in the trees just before the crash of the governor's car, Jack points his long, thin mike as if he were a conductor with a baton calling forth the sounds of the night; when he first listens to the tape, he waves a pencil in the direction from which each sound came. You can believe that Jack is dedicated to his craft, because Travolta is a listener. His face lights up when he hears Sally's little-girl cooing; his face closes when he hears the complaints of his boss, Sam (Peter Boyden), who makes sleazo "blood" films—he rejects the sound.

At the end, Jack's feelings of grief and loss suggest that he has learned the limits of technology; it's like coming out of the cocoon of adolescence. *Blow Out* is the first movie in which De Palma has stripped away the cackle and the glee; this time he's not inviting you to laugh along with him. He's playing it straight, and asking you—trusting you—to respond. In *The Fury*, he tried to draw you into the characters' emotions by a fantasy framework; in *Blow Out*, he locates the fantasy material inside the characters' heads. There was true vitality in the hyperbolic, teasing perversity of his previous movies, but this one is emotionally richer and more rounded. And his rhythms are more hypnotic than ever. It's easy to imagine De Palma standing very still and wielding a baton, because the images and sounds are orchestrated.

Seeing this film is like experiencing the body of De Palma's work and seeing it in a new way. Genre techniques are circuitry; in going beyond genre, De Palma is taking some terrifying first steps. He is investing his work with a different kind of meaning. His relation to the terror in *Carrie* or *Dressed to Kill* could be gleeful because it was Pop and he could ride it out; now he's in it. When we see Jack surrounded by all the machinery that he tries to control things with, De Palma seems to be giving it a last, long, wistful look. It's as if he'd finally understood what technique is for. This is the first film he has made about the things that really matter to him. *Blow Out* begins with a joke; by the end, the joke has been turned inside out. In a way, the movie is about accomplishing the one task set for the sound-effects man at the start: he has found a better scream. It's a great movie.

{*The New Yorker*, July 27, 1981}

:: *Pennies from Heaven*

Pennies from Heaven is the most emotional movie musical
I've ever seen. It's a stylized mythology of the Depression which uses the
popular songs of the period as expressions of people's deepest longings —
for sex, for romance, for money, for a high good time. When the characters
can't say how they feel, they evoke the songs: they open their mouths, and
the voices on hit records of the thirties come out of them. And as they
lip-sync the lyrics their obsessed eyes are burning bright. Their souls are
in those voices, and they see themselves dancing just like the stars in movie
musicals.

Visually, the film is a tarnished romance. The sets are stylized — not just
the sets for the dance numbers but also the Chicago streets and stores,
the movie houses, the diners and dives, which are designed in bold, formal
compositions, for a heightened melancholy. This is our communal vision
of the Depression, based on images handed down to us: motionless streets
and buildings, with lonely figures in clear, cold light. The film actually recreates paintings and photographs that are essences of America. There's
a breathtaking re-creation of Edward Hopper's *Nighthawks* coffee shop,
and its held for just the right length of time. There's Hopper's interior of
a movie house with a woman usher leaning against the wall, and there are
bleary faces and purplish red-light-district scenes by Reginald Marsh, and
thirties photographs of desolation, such as a dark flivver parked in front
of a plain white clapboard house. These images blend in and breathe with
the other shots. The whole movie seems a distillation of that forlorn, heavily shadowed period, while the songs express people's most fervent shallow
hopes. When the hero, Arthur, a sheet-music salesman, a big talker just
smart enough to get himself into trouble, goes on his selling trips, from

677

Chicago to Galena, in 1934, the land is flat and deserted, with almost nothing moving but his little car chugging along the road.

As Arthur, Steve Martin has light-brown hair cut short, and when he calls up a song he has an expression of eagerness and awe that transforms him. You forget Steve Martin the TV entertainer, with his zany catch phrases and his disconnected nonchalance. Steve Martin seems to have forgotten him, too. He has a wild-eyed intensity here that draws you right into Arthur's desperation and his lies. Arthur believes the words of the songs, and he tries to get to the dream world they describe. At home in Chicago, he pleads with his wife for a little sex: he mimes a love song—"I'll Never Have to Dream Again"—and Connee Boswell's voice comes out of him. It's our first exposure to the film's device, and though we're meant to laugh or grin, Connee Boswell is saying something for Arthur that his petite and pie-faced wife, Joan (Jessica Harper), refuses to hear, and the mixture of comedy and poignancy is affecting in a somewhat delirious way. Joan cringes at Arthur's touch; she thinks his attempts to make love to her are evidence of a horrible, sullying perversion. Then, in the little town of Galena, when he's in a music store trying to get an order, a shy schoolteacher, Eileen (Bernadette Peters), walks in; Arthur mimes Bing Crosby singing "Did You Ever See a Dream Walking?" and Eileen dances to the music, and the two of them form romantic, thirties-movie-star silhouettes in his mind. Eileen is pale and gentle, a brown-eyed blonde with soft curls—tendrils, really. She looks malleable, like the young Janet Gaynor. Eileen lives in a song world, too, and she's eager to believe Arthur's lie that he isn't married. She also has a spicy, wanton side; she turns into a Kewpie doll when she mimes Helen Kane's boop-boop-a-doops in "I Want to Be Bad." She has everything that Arthur wants, except money. As the story develops, it's so familiar it's archetypal; it's a manic-depressive libretto. Alfred Kazin has written about the passion of "a period—the thirties— that has had no rival since for widespread pain and sudden hope." That's what this black-humor musical, which Dennis Potter adapted from his six-segment BBC mini-series, is about.

The lip-syncing idea works wonderfully; it's in the dialogue interludes that the movie gets off on the wrong foot. Most of these scenes need to be played faster—to be snappier and more hyperbolic, with little curlicues of irony in the performances to point things up. For example, we see a gigantic billboard showing Carole Lombard with a huge black eye in Faith

Baldwin's *Love Before Breakfast*. (It's the same billboard poster that appears in a famous photograph by Walker Evans, taken in Atlanta in 1936.) A little while later, with the Lombard poster looking on, a love-starved man grabs a blind girl, and when we next see her, dead, she has a black eye. The director, Herbert Ross, plays it straight, and so instead of being bizarrely, horribly funny it's peculiar. Black humor played too slow *is* peculiar; it may seem that the misery level is rising awfully high. Ross's deliberate pace makes the film's tone uncertain. Sometimes he doesn't go all the way with a shocking joke, or he muffles it, so the audience doesn't get the release of laughter. There's so little movement during the dialogue that the characters seem numbed out, and the audience's confidence in the film is strained—the discomfort of some of the viewers is palpable. I think our emotions get jammed up. Yet the scenes in themselves—even those that are awkwardly paced and almost static—still have a rapt, gripping quality. And even when a scene cries out for a spin, a further twist of artifice, the actors carry the day. Bernadette Peters has ironic curlicues built in, and her exaggerated Queens diction (which is certainly eccentric for an Illinois girl) gives her her own cheeping-chicky sound.

Besides Arthur and Joan and that heavenly angel cake Eileen, there are two other major characters. Vernel Bagneris (the director and star of the long-running show *One Mo' Time*) plays a homeless, stuttering street musician and beggar, the Accordion Man, whom Arthur picks up on the road, and it's Bagneris who mimes the title song. The version he lip-syncs isn't the happy-go-lucky Crosby version from the totally unrelated 1936 film that was also called *Pennies from Heaven*; it's that of Arthur Tracy, which is much darker and much more potent. The sorrow of the Depression and the hoping beyond hope are concentrated in this song and in the Accordion Man himself. Arthur Tracy's wrenching voice—it has tears and anguish in it—comes pouring out of the stuttering simpleton, and, as if the song had freed him, the Accordion Man dances, sensually, easily. With a photo-collage of the Depression behind him and a shower of shimmering gold raining down on him, he stretches and struts. I never thought I'd go around with the song "Pennies from Heaven" pulsating in my skull, but the combination of Arthur Tracy and Vernel Bagneris is voluptuously masochistic. Popular singers in the thirties brought out the meaning of a lyric as fully as possible, and the original recordings, which are used here, have the true sound of the period. (The bridges between these old arrangements and the dances—and the dance sequences themselves—are said to have been orchestrated "using antique recording equipment" to preserve the thirties sound; however it was accomplished, the result is worth the effort.) Where the movie misses is in the timing of the contrapuntal gags: after the Accordion Man has had his shimmering-gold epiphany, Arthur, feeling like a real sport, hands him a quarter. Ross somehow buries the connection, the shock. Everything in the material is double-edged; it's conceived in terms of extremes—the melodrama and the pathos on one side and the dream world on the other. Normal life is excluded. But the director keeps trying to sneak it back in; he treats the piled-on sentimental gloom tenderly, as if it were meant to be real life. (Would he be this afraid of the cruel jokes in *The Threepenny Opera?*)

The other major character—almost as much transformed as Steve Martin—is Christopher Walken, with dark, slicked-down hair. As Tom the pimp, who puts Eileen on the street, he has the patent-leather lounge-lizard look of a silent-movie wolf, and his scenes play like greasy magic. In his first movie musical, Walken, who used to dance on Broadway, has more heat and athletic energy than he has shown in his straight acting roles. He has never been quite all there on the screen; he has looked drained or packed in ice. (That's what made him so effective as the chief mercenary in *The Dogs of War*—that, and the tense way he walked in New York, like an animal pacing a cage.) Here, there's sensuality in his cartooned apathy, and when he first spots Eileen his eyeballs seem to pop out on springs. In a mock striptease in a saloon, he shows how powerfully built he is, and he's a real hoofer. He takes the screen in a way he never has before—by force, and with lewd amusement, particularly when he bares a grotesque valentine tattoo on his chest.

There hasn't been this much tap dancing in a movie musical in many years. Arthur does a derby-and-plaid-suit vaudeville routine with two other salesmen, who are played by Tommy Rall (best known to moviegoers as Ann Miller's partner in the 1953 *Kiss Me, Kate*) and spaghetti-legged Robert Fitch (best known to theatregoers as the original Rooster in *Annie*). It's a fast, showy number—to the Dorsey Brothers Orchestra's playing and the Boswell Sisters' singing "It's the Girl"—and the three men have wonderful frilly gestures as they curve and sway to imitate femininity, and use their hands to model their dream girls' shapes in the air. Steve Martin doesn't slow his celebrated partners down; he's spectacular—he really is

Steve (Happy Feet) Martin. In the film's most startling sequence, set inside the Hopper movie theatre with the weary blond usher, Arthur and Eileen sit watching *Follow the Fleet*. Arthur is transfixed, and as Astaire sings "Let's Face the Music and Dance" Arthur begins singing, too. He goes up on the stage, and Eileen joins him—two tiny, sharply edged figures in deep, rich color against the huge black-and-white screen images of Astaire and Rogers dancing, and they really seem to be there. They dance along with the stars on the screen, and then the two minuscule figures shift into black-and-white, and take over. Arthur is in tails, Eileen in a copy of Ginger's glittering gown with its loose fur cowl. And a chorus line of men in tails appears, tapping, like the men in *Top Hat*. It makes you gasp. Do Steve Martin and Bernadette Peters really dare to put themselves in Astaire and Rogers' place? Yet they carry it off. You may still be gasping when Arthur and Eileen leave the theatre (the exterior is a Reginald Marsh) and hear newsboys shouting the headlines. The police are looking for Arthur.

Herbert Ross has never shown much audacity in his other screen work, and when a director has been as successful as Ross has been with bland muck (*The Sunshine Boys, The Turning Point, The Goodbye Girl*), and has even been honored for it, it certainly takes something special to make him plunge in. Ross didn't go in far enough, but this is still quite a plunge. Dennis Potter's idea—obvious, yet strange, and with a pungency—provided the chance of a lifetime; Ross's collaborators must have felt it, too, and possibly they came up with ideas he couldn't resist. He had a superlative team. The production designer was Ken Adam, who designed the eight most imaginative James Bond pictures and also *Dr. Strangelove, Barry Lyndon*, and *The Seven-Per-Cent Solution*. The film's greatest splendors are those re-created visions—particularly the coffee shop with Arthur and Eileen as nighthawks, and Jimmy's Diner, which has a sliding glass wall, so that the Accordion Man can slip out into the rain to dance. Among its more obvious splendors is an Art Deco Chicago bank in which Arthur, who has tried to get a loan to open his own music shop and been turned down, dreams that he's deluged with money: to the music of "Yes, Yes!," performed by Sam Browne and the Carlyle Cousins, he and the banker (the matchless Jay Garner) and a batch of chorines perform in a dance montage that suggests the harebrained variations of Busby Berkeley montages.

The choreographer, Danny Daniels, does each number in a different theatrical style, and he palpably loves the styles that he reworks, especially the lowdown, off-color ones, like Walken's "dirty" sandwich dance—he's wedged between two blowzy whores. With the exception of a few routines with chorus girls as Rockette-style automatons, Daniels' choreography isn't simply dance—it's gag comedy, in which each dancer has his own comic personality. The dances are funny, amazing, and beautiful all at once. There are no problems of pacing here (except that a few numbers are too short and feel truncated). Several of them are just about perfection. And with teasers—comedy bits that prick the imagination. Bernadette Peters has a big production number ("Love Is Good For Anything That Ails You") that's like a dance of deliverance. Her classroom is transformed into something palatial and white, with children tapping on the tops of miniature grand pianos, and with her in silver and white, shimmying down the center aisle. (All the costumes are by Bob Mackie.) And when Arthur dreams of himself as a happy man, settled down with both Joan and Eileen, the three of them mouth "Life Is Just a Bowl of Cherries," like a radio trio. It's an indication of the depth of Jessica Harper's performance as the little witch Joan, shrivelled by repression and hatred, that it takes a second to recognize her as the pretty brunette in the trio.

The cinematographer, Gordon Willis, provides the lighting to carry out Ken Adam's visual ideas, and it's different from anything that I can remember Willis's ever doing before. The movie is about ordinary experience in a blazing, heightened form, and Willis keeps the level of visual intensity phenomenally high. At times, the color recalls the vivid, saturated tones in the 1954 *A Star Is Born*: the images are lustrous, and are often focussed on the pinpoint of light in the dreamer-characters' eyes when they envisage the pleasures celebrated in the songs. Eileen's eyes switch on and off, and so do the Accordion Man's; Arthur is possessed by the dream—his eyes are always on. My eyes were always on, too: even when I wanted to close up the pauses between the actors' lines, there was never a second when I wasn't fascinated by what was happening on the screen.

Despite its use of Brechtian devices, *Pennies from Heaven* doesn't allow you to distance yourself. You're thrust into the characters' emotional extremes; you're right in front of the light that's shining from their eyes. And you see the hell they go through for sex and money. Arthur, the common man with an itch, will do just about anything. When he blurts out something about his wife to Eileen, he covers his traces blubbering about how horribly she died in an accident, and then uses the invented tragedy to soften up Eileen so he can hop on top of her. He's a bastard, but you're not alienated from him; the songs lead him by the nose. As it turns out, the one character whose dream comes true is the pinched and proper Joan, who has dreamed of taking revenge on Arthur for his sexual demands on her.

There are cruel, rude awakenings; maybe they should be more heartlessly tonic, more bracing. But they do give you a pang. When Eileen is happily dreaming away in her classroom, seeing it as a tap dancers' paradise, with the children tapping and playing musical instruments, the principal comes in, enraged by the noise that the kids are making, and he takes a ruler and smacks the hands of a fat boy—a boy who has been proudly blowing on a tuba in her dream. The injustice to the boy—the humiliation—is one of those wrongs that some people are singled out for. The boy is fat, Arthur is horny, Eileen is gullible, the Accordion Man is inarticulate. This double-edged movie supplies a simple, basic rationale for popular entertainment. It says that though dreamers may be punished for having been carried away, they've had some glorious dreams. But it also says that the emotions of the songs can't be realized in life.

There's something new going on—something thrilling—when the characters in a musical are archetypes yet are intensely alive. This is the first big musical that M-G-M has produced on its lot in over a decade. The star, Steve Martin, doesn't flatter the audience for being hip; he gives an almost incredibly controlled performance, and Bernadette Peters is mysteriously right in every nuance. Herbert Ross and Ken Adam and Danny Daniels and Gordon Willis and Bob Mackie and the whole cast worked at their highest capacities—perhaps were even inspired to exceed them. They all took chances. Do you remember what Wagner said to the audience after the première of *Götterdämmerung*? "Now you have seen what we can do. Now want it! And if you do, we will achieve an art." I am not comparing *Pennies from Heaven* with *Götterdämmerung*. But this picture shows that the talent to make great movie musicals is out there, waiting.

{*The New Yorker*, December 21, 1981}

:: *Shoot the Moon*

There wasn't a single scene in the English director Alan Parker's first three feature films (*Bugsy Malone*, *Midnight Express*, *Fame*) that I thought rang true; there isn't a scene in his new picture *Shoot the Moon*, that I think rings false. I'm a little afraid to say how good I think *Shoot the Moon* is — I don't want to set up the kind of bad magic that might cause people to say they were led to expect so much that they were disappointed. But I'm even more afraid that I can't come near doing this picture justice. The characters in *Shoot the Moon*, which was written by Bo Goldman, aren't taken from the movies, or from books, either. They're torn — bleeding — from inside Bo Goldman and Alan Parker and the two stars, Diane Keaton and Albert Finney, and others in the cast.

Diane Keaton is Faith Dunlap, and Finney is her husband, George. The Dunlaps have been married about fifteen years and have four school-age daughters. George is a nonfiction writer who's had a rough time, whipping up free-lance articles to meet the bills. But now he has become reputable, and they are doing better financially and are comfortable in their big old house in Marin County, across the bay from San Francisco. Their relationship has been poisoned, though. Faith knows all George's weaknesses and failures, and her knowledge eats away at his confidence. "You always remember the wrong things," he tells her. So he's having an affair, and feeling so rotten about it that he sobs when he's alone. And though he tries to keep the affair secret from Faith, she learns about it and is devastated. She can't look at him; her anxious eyes turn away. When he says, "You look really pretty," she can't stop herself from saying, "You seem surprised." Her angry misery is almost like a debauch; it makes her appear sodden. When she's with him, her face sinks—it's the dead weight of her sense of loss. At a book-awards ceremony in San Francisco, she overhears photographers who have taken pictures of the two of them decide on the caption "George Dunlap and friend." She blurts out, "I'm not his friend. I'm his wife." The movie begins on the eve of the day when she drives him out of the house, and it covers the next months of separation.

Their oldest daughter, the thirteen-year-old Sherry (Dana Hill), who has known about her father's adultery, feels that it's treachery to her and to the whole family. She can't forgive him, and after he has moved out she refuses to talk with him or to go along when he drives the younger girls to school or takes them away for the weekend. She shuts him out of her life, and the bond he feels with her is so strong that this is even more intolerable to him than being shut out of his own home. The other girls are sunshiny, but Sherry's face goes slack, and she looks burned out, like her mother. Faith, though, can look young and animated when she isn't with George; the years just fall away when she smiles her ravishing, clown's smile. Sherry's mood doesn't lift. She has had the most love and the most pain. She's the embodiment of what went wrong between her parents, and she's always there.

The movie isn't labored, like Ingmar Bergman's *Scenes from a Marriage*. It's essentially the story of the husband and father as supplicant for re-admission into the family, but it touches on things without seeming to address them directly. It's like a person with many sides. There are gags that pay off and keep on paying off—they turn into motifs. And sometimes the lines of dialogue that seem funny or ironic go through a variation or two and become lyrical. Parker has caught the essence of Bo Goldman's melancholic tone in the theme music—"Don't Blame Me," picked out on the piano with one finger. That, too, is turned into a joke and then has its original tone restored. There's an amazingly risky sequence, set in the restaurant of a Northern California inn, where George and Faith meet by chance and have a rowdy spat that's played off against screwball-comedy circumstances, with an elderly, quavering-voiced woman singer using the theme song in a hopeless attempt to drown out their shouting, and a man at the next table taking exception to their loud use of vulgar language. Many of the scenes have details that touch off very personal feelings: George pulling down the note pad that hangs on a string in his car to write excuses for his children's being late to school; one of the girls leaning toward *The Wizard of Oz* on the TV and chanting the Wicked Witch's threats slightly ahead of Margaret Hamilton. In this movie, the people have resources; they try things out. They take a step forward, and then maybe they move back. The tension that George feels with Faith is gone when he's with his perfectly shallow new lover (Karen Allen). She tells him, "You're my friend, George. I like you. I love you. And if you don't come through I'll find somebody else." She means it; she's adaptable.

The kids had a real presence in Bo Goldman's script for *Melvin and Howard* (his other screen credits include co-writing *One Flew Over the Cuckoo's Nest* and *The Rose*), and they have an even stronger one here. The family has been close in the loose, Northern California manner; the kids talk as freely as the parents do, and they're at ease, the way the house is. The girls have moments of imitating their high-and-mighty and short-tempered parents and then dissolving in giggles; they bitch each other heartlessly and then do something in perfect unison. When they squeal and carry on as they watch their parents on TV at the book awards, you know that this movie was written from observation and directed that way, too. The interaction of the four girls with each other and with their parents and the interaction of the girls with each parent's new lover are part of the substance of the movie. Alan Parker has four children, and Bo Goldman is the father of six; that may be the bond that made *Shoot the Moon* possible. This movie isn't just about marriage; it's about the family that is created, and how that whole family reacts to the knotted, disintegrating relationship of the parents. The children's world—a world of fragmented, displaced understanding—overlaps that of the adults and comments on it. And the texture of domestic scenes with bright, sensitive kids squabbling and testing keeps the film in balance. Bo Goldman has too much theatrical richness in his writing to make an audience suffer. He lets people be the entertainers that they are in life.

The four girls are inventive—they slip in and out of roles. Instinctive vaudevillians, they're always onstage. And whenever they're around, the movie is a variety show. Faith is sensitive to the comedy and drama of her family—she's constantly soothing and adjusting, and helping the seven-year-old get equal billing. When the morose, separated George takes the three younger kids out, he works so conscientiously to keep them happy that he sounds completely false; they feel his strain and try to humor him.

When they're with him and his new lady, they try to play their parts, to keep tension to a minimum. (The comedy here is in how transparently they assume these roles.) And the sign of Sherry's confusion is her insistence on bringing up just the things nobody wants to have brought up, on forcing her parents into bad scenes. Yet she is never a pain. She keeps the atmosphere raw, and rawness is what makes this movie get to you.

Albert Finney, who has been sleepwalking in his recent movie appearances, is awake and trying out his reflexes. There's a profound difference in Finney; this is not a performance one might have expected from him. He uses all the impacted sloth and rage that show in the sag and weight of his big, handsome face. Locked out, George looks stunned, as if he'd been hit over the head—you can see the emotions fermenting in him that he himself isn't conscious of. He doesn't know that he's going to explode when he does. In a sequence in which he goes to the house doggedly determined to give Sherry her birthday present, Faith tells him that Sherry won't see him, and bolts the door. All he knows is that he has to get to Sherry. He kicks at the door and then he suddenly smashes a glass panel, sticks his arm in and pushes the bolt, rushes upstairs, grabs the child and spanks her, brutally. Sherry reaches for a scissors and holds him off with it. And then they huddle together, sobbing, and he, unforgiven, caresses her, pleading for a chance. It's one of the saddest, greatest love scenes ever put on film; you feel you've lived it, or lived something so close to its emotional core that you know everything each of them is going through. When George leaves, in disgrace, he trudges out carrying the present; then, a few paces away from the lighted house, he suddenly breaks into a run. Both as a character and as an actor, Finney seems startled and appalled by what has been let loose in him. His scenes seem to be happening right in front of us—you watch him with the apprehensiveness that you might feel at a live telecast. Keaton is Faith, but Finney seems both George and Finney. He's an actor possessed by a great role—pulled into it kicking and screaming, by his own guts.

Diane Keaton may be a star without vanity: she's so completely challenged by the role of Faith that all she cares about is getting the character right. Faith's eyes are squinched and you can see the crow's-feet; at times her face is bloated from depression, and she has the crumbling-plaster look of an old woman. Keaton is tall but not big, yet she gives you a feeling of size—of being planted and rooted, while George is buffeted about. He doesn't know how he was cast loose or what he's doing at sea. He has done it to himself and he can't figure out why. Throughout the movie, he's looking for a dock—he's reaching out to his wife. But Faith is unyielding; she doesn't want more pain. Very few young American movie actresses have the strength and the instinct for the toughest dramatic roles—intelligent, sophisticated heroines. Jane Fonda did, around the time that she appeared in *Klute* and *They Shoot Horses, Don't They?*, but that was more than ten years ago. There hasn't been anybody else until now. Diane Keaton acts on a different plane from that of her previous film roles; she brings the character a full measure of dread and awareness, and does it in a special, intuitive way that's right for screen acting. Nothing looks rehearsed, yet it's all fully created. She has a scene alone in the house in the early days of the separation—soaking in a tub, smoking a joint and singing faintly (a Beatles song—"If I Fell"), getting out to answer the phone, and then just standing listlessly, wiping off her smudged eyeliner. It's worthy of a Jean Rhys heroine; her eyes are infinitely sad—she's cracking, and you can sense the cold, windy remnants of passion that are cracking her. But this scene is a lull between wars. Faith is rarely alone: she still has her life around her—she has the kids and the house. (And that house, with its serene view, is itself a presence; it's upsetting when George smashes the door.) Faith can ignore George and start having a good time with a rather simple new fellow (Peter Weller)—a workman-contractor who puts up a tennis court for her in the grove next to the house. But George can't ignore her, because she's still holding so much of his life—the kids, the house, all the instinctive adaptations they had made to each other. George can't take anything for granted anymore.

Alan Parker and Bo Goldman circle around the characters, observing their moves and gestures toward each other; the movie is about the processes of adaptation. That's why that sequence at the inn is so funny and satisfying. In *Melvin and Howard*, it was a great moment when Howard Hughes got past his contempt for Melvin and they spoke together about the smell of the desert after the rain, and finally were friends and so close that they didn't need to talk. In *Shoot the Moon*, the only time that George and Faith reconnect is in their drunken dinner at the inn when they start eating out of the same plate and yell at each other, and then they wind up in bed together. What a relief it is for George—for a few hours he can live on instinct again.

This film may recall Irvin Kershner's 1970 *Loving*—a story of separating that had a high level of manic pain. But the wife in that (played with great delicacy by Eva Marie Saint) wasn't the powerhouse that Faith is. Faith doesn't back down when she and George fight, and her angry silence is much stronger than George's desperate chatter—Faith has no guilt. *Shoot the Moon* may also call up memories of *Long Day's Journey Into Night*, in the theatre or on the screen. But in that, too, the husband held the power. George is powerless. He has an extraordinary reconciliation scene with Sherry: she runs away from her mother on the night of a party celebrating the completion of the tennis court, and comes to find him, and they talk together on a pier, sitting quietly, with George's brown cardigan pulled around them both to keep out the chill. But when he takes Sherry back home and sees Faith and her lover and their guests and the strings of festive lights on the tennis court, he's filled with a balky, despairing rage—you can almost see his blood vessels engorging. He has been stripped of too much of his life; throughout the film he has been losing emotional control, breaking down—he can't adapt.

Alan Parker doesn't try to rush things or to prove himself. His energy doesn't come all the way through to the surface, as an American director's might; it stays under, and it's evenly distributed. George becomes resentful of any sign of change in Faith's or the children's lives, but the film doesn't over-emote—it looks at him and at the others very steadily. It's a measure of the quality of Parker's direction that no one in the picture asks for the audience's sympathy. When George is self-pitying, as he is in a sequence of visiting the ruins of Jack London's house and telling his kids what a great author London was and how someone set fire to the house the night before the great author was supposed to move in, his maudlin tone is played off against the girls' questions and remarks about London's marriages and children; they all project their own feelings onto the Londons—it becomes a comedy routine. This is an unapologetically grown-up movie. Though Alan Parker doesn't do anything innovative in technique, it's a modern movie in terms of its consciousness, and in its assumption that the members of the movie audience, like the readers of modern fiction, share in that consciousness.

Probably Parker couldn't have brought it all off with such subtlety and discretion if he hadn't had the collaborators who were with him on his other features—the producer Alan Marshall, the cinematographer

Michael Seresin, the production designer Geoffrey Kirkland, and the editor Gerry Hambling. They must have helped free him to devote his full attention to the cast. He directs the actors superbly. Diane Keaton and Albert Finney give the kind of performances that in the theatre become legendary, and, in its smaller dimensions, Dana Hill's Sherry is perhaps equally fine. And the three child actresses—Viveka Davis as Jill, Tracey Gold as Marianne, and Tina Yothers as Molly—are a convincing group of sisters and the very best kind of running gag. Even George Murdock, who has a single appearance as Faith's dying father, is remarkable—the old man has a clear head. Parker has created a completely believable family and environment (the picture was all shot on location), and he has done it in the wet days and foggy light of a country and a culture that aren't his own. And he has given us a movie about separating that is perhaps the most revealing American movie of the era. *Shoot the Moon* assumes the intelligence of the audience, as *Bonnie and Clyde* did; it assumes that people don't need to have basic emotions labelled or explained to them. When you see *Shoot the Moon*, you recognize yourself in it. If there's a key to the movie, it's in one simple dialogue exchange. It comes at the inn when George and Faith are in bed, lying next to each other after making love. She talks about how much she used to love him and then:

FAITH: Just now for an instant there—I don't know—you made me laugh, George—you were kind.

GEORGE: You're right, I'm not kind anymore.

FAITH: Me neither.

GEORGE: You're kind to strangers.

FAITH: Strangers are easy.

:: *Richard Pryor Live on the Sunset Strip*

When Chaplin began to talk onscreen, he used a cultivated voice and high-flown words, and became a deeply unfunny man; if
he had found the street language to match his lowlife, tramp movements,
he might have been something like Richard Pryor, who's all of a piece—a
master of lyrical obscenity. Pryor is the only great poet satirist among our
comics. His lyricism seems to come out of his thin-skinned nature; he's
so empathic he's all wired up. His 1979 film *Richard Pryor Live in Concert*
was a consummation of his years as an entertainer, and then some. He had
a lifetime of material at his fingertips, and he seemed to go beyond himself.
He personified objects, animals, people, the warring parts of his own body,
even thoughts in the heads of men and women—black, white, Oriental—
and he seemed to be possessed by the spirits he pulled out of himself. To
those of us who thought it was one of the greatest performances we'd ever
seen or ever would see, his new one-man show *Richard Pryor Live on the
Sunset Strip* may be disappointing yet emotionally stirring. His new routines aren't as fully worked out; Pryor hasn't been doing the stage appearances that he used to do—hasn't, in fact, given any one-man shows since
the 1979 film was shot—so these routines haven't been polished and sharp-
ened, and they're not as varied. The material—specially prepared for this
film, which was shot at two performances at the Hollywood Palladium—
is rather skimpy, and a lot of it is patterned on routines from the first. Pryor
doesn't seem as prickly now—he doesn't have the hunted look, or the old
sneaky, guilty gleam in his eyes. He says he isn't angry anymore, and he
seems to have been strengthened—he's more open. This probably has

691

something to do with the vast public outpouring of affection for him after his near-fatal accident in June, 1980, when (as he acknowledges here) the dope he was freebasing exploded and set him on fire.

Pryor must have realized that millions and millions of people really wished him well, felt grateful for the pleasure he'd given them, and wanted him to live. How does an ornery, suspicious man who brought the language and grievances of the black underclass onto the stage deal with acceptance? (This is not a problem that Lenny Bruce, who brought the backstage language of the tawdriest levels of show business onto the stage, ever had to face.) Pryor doesn't appear sweetened, exactly. Even in the films in which he has played Mr. Nice Guy to children or whites, the stickiness hasn't clung to him; he's shed it. And he's always come clean with the audience. Pryor's best jokes aren't jokes in the usual sense—they're observations that are funny because of how he acts them out and because of his inflections. He constantly surprises us and makes us laugh in recognition. He tells us what we *almost* knew but shoved down, so when we laugh at him we feel a special, giddy freedom. That hasn't changed—he isn't soft in *Sunset Strip*. He tries on some benign racial attitudes and then drops them very fast—that's how you know he's still alive and kicking. He's different, though. You may sense that there has been a deepening of feeling, that there's something richer inside him, something more secure.

At the same time, he's adrift as a performer, because he isn't sure that he's got his act together. And he hasn't. The pressure of a one-man show before a huge crowd and on camera must be just about heart-stopping if you haven't been working in front of big live audiences. And that first film made him a legend; he has the pressure here of an audience expecting history to be made. This film doesn't build the performance rhythm that the 1979 film did; it's very smoothly put together, but in a meaningless way—you don't feel that you're experiencing *Pryor's* rhythms. Is the editing bad, or were the editors trying to stretch the material to this eighty-eight minute length? (Why are there so many cutaways—at just the wrong time—to laughing, dressed-up people in the front rows? You half expect to see a star or two among them. It makes the movie feel canned.) Haskell Wexler headed the camera crew, and the color looks true and clear, and Pryor, in his scarlet suit, black bow tie and shirt, gold shoes, and a snazzy designer belt with a piece hanging straight down, is vividly close to us. But he has trouble getting going. He has hunches—he touches on things and you wait to see what he'll do with them. And most of the time he doesn't do anything with them; they don't develop into routines—he just drops them. Midway, he starts getting into his swing, in a section about his experiences during the filming of parts of *Stir Crazy* in the Arizona State Prison. He goes on to talk about a trip he took to Africa, and it's a scene—he can live it. He turns himself into a rabbit, a bear, a lion, a couple of cheetahs, and a fearful gazelle. You feel his relief when he does the animals; a lot of the time he has been looking for his place on this stage, and now he has something physical to do. But then there's a sudden break. Voices, ostensibly from the audience, can be heard. One of them calls, "Do the Mudbone routine," and, rather wearily, saying that it will be for the last time, Pryor sits on a stool and does the ancient storyteller Mudbone, who in the seventies was considered one of his great creations. And the movie goes thud. This section feels like an interpolation—it doesn't have the crackle of a performer interacting with an audience. It's almost as dead as what happens when Johnny Carson asks an aging celebrity to tell the joke he used to tell that always broke Johnny up. Pryor looks defeated, shot down. The sudden dullness is compounded by his sitting: we're used to seeing him prowling—accompanied, when the spots hit the curtain behind him, by wriggling shadows.

When he picks up his act again, he talks about freebasing, and the feelings he had about his pipe—it talks to him, and he becomes the pipe. We feel as if we were actually listening to his habit talking to him. And he builds up a routine about his wife and his friend Jim Brown telling him what cocaine was doing to him. But "the pipe say, 'Don't listen.' " And then he tells about the hospital and about Jim Brown's visiting him every day. He's a great actor and a great combination of mimic and mime; he's perhaps never more inspired than when he assumes the personality of a rebellious organ of his body or of an inanimate object, such as that pipe—or Jim Brown. This is the high point of the film. When he becomes something or someone, it isn't an imitation; he incarnates the object's soul and guts. But he doesn't have enough material to work up the rhythmic charge he reached before Mudbone. What he has in *Sunset Strip* is the material for a forty-minute classic.

The picture is full of wonderful bits, such as his demonstration of how he loses his voice when he's angry at his wife, and to those unfamiliar with Pryor's infectiousness and truthfulness and his unfettered use of obscenity, and to all those who missed his 1979 film, it may be a revelation. But the greatness of *Richard Pryor Live in Concert* was in the impetus of his performance rhythm—the way he kept going, with all those characters and voices bursting out of him. When he told us about his heart attack, he was, in almost the same instant, the helpless body being double-crossed by its heart, the heart itself, a telephone operator, and Pryor the aloof, dissociated observer. We registered what a mysteriously original physical comedian he is, and we saw the performance sweat soaking his collarless red silk shirt. (There's no visible sweat this time.)

If he fulfilled his comic genius in *Live in Concert*, here he's sampling the good will the public feels toward him. Audiences want him, they love him, even in bum movies, and he appears to be experiencing a personal fulfillment. But he hasn't yet renewed himself as an artist: it may seem cruel to say so, but even the routine on his self-immolation is a pale copy of his heart attack. In the first film, there was a sense of danger; when he used the word "nigger," it was alive and raw. When he uses it here, it just seems strange. He's up against something very powerful: the audience may have come expecting to see history made, but history now is also just seeing Richard Pryor. He knows that he doesn't have to do anything. All he has to do is stand there and be adored. And he knows there's something the matter with this new situation, but he doesn't know how to deal with it.

{*The New Yorker*, April 5, 1982}

:: *E. T. The Extra-Terrestrial*

Steven Spielberg's *E.T. The Extra-Terrestrial* envelops you
in the way that his *Close Encounters of the Third Kind* did. It's a dream of a
movie—a bliss-out. This sci-fi fantasy has a healthy share of slapstick comedy, yet it's as pure as Carroll Ballard's *The Black Stallion*. Like Ballard,
Spielberg respects the conventions of children's stories, and because he
does he's able to create the atmosphere for a mythic experience. Essentially, *E.T.* is the story of a ten-year-old boy, Elliott, who feels fatherless
and lost because his parents have separated, and who finds a miraculous
friend—an alien, inadvertently left on Earth by a visiting spaceship.

If the film seems a continuation of *Close Encounters*, that's partly because
it has the sensibility we came to know in that picture, and partly
because E.T. himself is like a more corporeal version of the celestial visitors at the end of it. Like *Close Encounters*, *E.T.* is bathed in warmth, and it
seems to clear all the bad thoughts out of your head. It reminds you of the
goofiest dreams you had as a kid, and rehabilitates them. Spielberg is right
there in his films; you can feel his presence and his love of surprises. This
phenomenal master craftsman plays high-tech games, but his presence is
youthful—it has a just-emerged quality. The Spielberg of *Close Encounters*
was a singer with a supple, sweet voice. It couldn't be heard in his last film,
the impersonal *Raiders of the Lost Ark*, and we may have been afraid that
he'd lost it, but now he has it back, and he's singing more melodiously than
we could have hoped for. He's like a boy soprano lilting with joy all through
E.T., and we're borne along by his voice.

In Spielberg's movies, parents love their children, and children love their
siblings. And suburban living, with its comfortable, uniform houses, is
seen as a child's paradise—an environment in which children are protected

and their imaginations can flourish. There's a luminous, magical view of Elliott's hilly neighborhood in the early-evening light on Halloween, with the kids in their costumes fanning out over the neatly groomed winding streets as each little group moves from one house to another for trick-or-treat, and E.T., swathed in a sheet and wearing red slippers over his webbed feet, waddles along between Elliott and his teen-age brother, Michael— each of them keeping a firm, protective grip on a gray-green four-digit hand. E.T. isn't just Elliott's friend; he's also Elliott's pet—the film catches the essence of the bond between lonely children and their pets. The sequence may call up memories of the trick-or-treat night in Vincente Minnelli's *Meet Me in St. Louis*, but it's more central here. All the imagery in the film is linked to Halloween, with the spaceship itself as a jack-o'-lantern in the sky, and the child-size space visitors, who have come to gather specimens of Earth's flora, wrapped in cloaks with hoods and looking much like the trick-or-treaters. (The pumpkin spaceship is silent, though when you see it you may hear in your head the five-note theme of the mother ship in *Close Encounters*, and the music that John Williams has written for *E.T.* is dulcet and hushed—it allows for the full score that the movie gets going in your imagination.)

E.T. probably has the best-worked-out script that Spielberg has yet shot, and since it seems an emanation of his childlike, playful side and his love of toys, it would be natural to assume that he wrote it. But maybe it seems such a clear expression of his spirit because its actual writer, Melissa Mathison, could see what he needed more deeply than he could himself, and could devise a complete structure that would hold his feelings in balance. Mathison was one of the scenarists for *The Black Stallion* and is a co-writer of *The Escape Artist*; it probably isn't a coincidence that all three of these films have young-boy heroes who miss their fathers. Writers may be typecast, like actors; having written one movie about a boy, Mathison may have been thought of for another, and yet another. In *E.T.*, she has made Elliott dreamy and a little withdrawn but practical and intelligent. And very probably she intuited the necessity for Elliott, too, to be bereft—especially since Spielberg himself had experienced the separation of his parents. Mathison has a feeling for the emotional sources of fantasy, and although her dialogue isn't always inspired, sometimes it is, and she has an ear for how kids talk. Henry Thomas, who plays Elliott, and Kelly Reno in *The Black Stallion* and Griffin O'Neal as the boy magician in *The Escape*

Artist are not Hollywood-movie kids; they all have an unusual—a magical —reserve. They're all in thrall to their fantasies, and the movies take us inside those fantasies while showing us how they help the boys grow up. Elliott (his name begins with an "E" and ends with a "T") is a dutiful, too sober boy who never takes off his invisible thinking cap; the telepathic communication he develops with E.T. eases his cautious, locked-up worries, and he begins to act on his impulses. When E.T. has his first beer and loses his inhibitions, Elliott, at school, gets tipsy, and in biology class when each student is required to chloroform a frog and then dissect it he perceives his frog's resemblance to E.T. and sets it free. (His classmates follow suit.) The means by which Elliott manages to kiss a pretty girl who towers over him by at least a head is a perfectly executed piece of slapstick.

It's no small feat to fuse science fiction and mythology. *E.T.* holds together the way some of George MacDonald's fairy tales (*At the Back of the North Wind, The Princess and the Goblin, The Princess and Curdie*) do. It's emotionally rounded and complete. The neighborhood kids whose help Elliott needs all come through for him. Even his little sister, Gertie (Drew Barrymore), is determined to keep the secret that E.T. is hidden in Elliott's room. And when Elliott's harried mother (Dee Wallace) rushes around in her kitchen and fails to see E.T.—fails to see him even when she knocks him over—the slapstick helps to domesticate the feeling of enchantment and, at the same time, strengthens it. Adults—as we all know from the children's stories of our own childhoods, or from the books we've read to our children—are too busy and too preoccupied to see the magic that's right there in front of them. Spielberg's mellow, silly jokes reinforce the fantasy structure. One of them—Elliott on his bicycle dropping what look like M&M's to make a trail—seems to come right out of a child's mind. (Viewers with keen eyes may perceive that the candies are actually Reese's Pieces.) Among the costumed children radiating out on Halloween is a tiny Yoda, and the audience laughs in recognition that, yes, this film is part of the fantasy world to which Yoda (the wise gnome of *The Empire Strikes Back*) belongs. And when E.T.—a goblin costumed as a ghost—sees the child dressed as Yoda and turns as if to join him it's funny because it's so unaccountably right.

Henry Thomas (who was the older of Sissy Spacek's two small sons in *Raggedy Man*) has a beautiful brainy head with a thick crop of hair; his touching serio-comic solemnity draws us into the mood of the picture.

When one of the neighborhood kids makes a fanciful remark about E.T., Elliott reprimands him, rapping out, "This is reality." Dee Wallace as the mother, Peter Coyote as a scientist who from childhood has dreamed the dream that Elliott has realized, and the other adult actors are the supporting cast. Henry Thomas and E.T. (who was designed by one of the authentic wizards of Hollywood, Carlo Rambaldi) are the stars, and Drew Barrymore and Robert MacNaughton, as the teen-ager Michael, are the featured players. Elliott and his brother and sister are all low-key humorists. When Michael first sees E.T., he does a double take that's like a momentary paralysis. Elliott has an honestly puzzled tone when he asks Michael, "How do you explain school to a higher intelligence?" Little Gertie adapts to E.T. very quickly—he may have the skin of a dried fig and a potbelly that just misses the floor, but she talks to him as if he were one of her dolls.

Spielberg changed his usual way of working when he made *E.T.*, and you can feel the difference. The visual energy and graphic strength in his work have always been based on his storyboarding the material—that is, sketching the camera angles in advance, so that the graphic plan was laid out. That way, he knew basically what he was after in each shot and how the shots would fit together; his characteristic brilliantly jagged cutting was largely thought out from the start. On *E.T.*—perhaps because the story is more delicate and he'd be working with child actors for much of the time—he decided to trust his intuition, and the film has a few fuzzy spots but a gentler, more fluid texture. It's less emphatic than his other films; he doesn't use his usual wide-screen format—he isn't out to overpower you. The more reticent shape makes the story seem simpler—plausible. The light always has an apparent source, even when it gives the scenes an otherworldly glow. And from the opening in the dense, vernal woodland that adjoins Elliott's suburb (it's where we first hear E.T.'s frightened sounds), the film has the soft, mysterious inexorability of a classic tale of enchantment. The little shed in back of the house where Elliott tosses in a ball and E.T. sends it back is part of a dreamscape.

The only discordant note is the periodic switch to overdynamic camera angles to show the NASA men and other members of the search party whose arrival frightened off the space visitors and who keep looking for the extraterrestrial left behind. These men are lined up in military-looking groups, and the camera shows us only their stalking or marching bodies—

they're faceless, silent, and extremely threatening. Their flashlights in the dark woods could be lethal ray guns, and one of them has a bunch of keys hanging from his belt that keep jangling ominously. The rationale is probably that we're meant to view the men as little E.T. would, or as Elliott would, but most of the time neither E.T. nor Elliott is around when they are. Later in the movie, in the sequences in a room that is used as a hospital, it's clear that when adults are being benevolent in adult terms they may still be experienced by children as enemies. But the frequent intrusive cuts to the uniformed men—in some shots they wear moon-travel gear and head masks—are meant to give us terror vibes. They're abstract figures of evil; even the American-flag insignia on their uniforms is sinister—in modern movie iconology that flag means "bad guys." And this movie doesn't need faceless men; it has its own terror. Maybe Spielberg didn't have enough faith in the fear that is integral to any magical idyll: that it can't last.

When the children get to know E.T., his sounds are almost the best part of the picture. His voice is ancient and otherworldly but friendly, humorous. And this scaly, wrinkled little man with huge, wide-apart, soulful eyes and a jack-in-the-box neck has been so fully created that he's a friend to us, too; when he speaks of his longing to go home the audience becomes as mournful as Elliott. Spielberg has earned the tears that some people in the audience—and not just children—shed. The tears are tokens of gratitude for the spell the picture has put on the audience. Genuinely entrancing movies are almost as rare as extraterrestrial visitors.

{*The New Yorker*, June 14, 1982}

:: Up the River

For all the hell that Werner Herzog reportedly went through to make *Fitzcarraldo*, which showed on the closing night of the recent New York Film Festival, the film itself is a leaden variation on his *Aguirre, the Wrath of God*. It's *Aguirre* without the inspired images or great subject. *Aguirre* was about the civilized Europeans who, in their greed for gold, travelled to the Amazon and enslaved and slaughtered Indians. It was about madness. The sixteenth-century Spanish ladies in long gowns, sitting in their sedan chairs and being carried over the face of a cliff in the pale-green Andes, the peaks partly obscured by clouds — that may be historically accurate, and it's as magnificently bizarre as any image on film. When we see the Spanish expedition in that phantom landscape, Herzog seems great. When he takes us closer, he's in trouble, because he hasn't worked out a style of acting to go with his vision. The performers in their bulky, richly textured costumes don't appear to have any idea what's wanted of them; they flex their face muscles and stare at each other significantly. But Herzog was in luck: as Aguirre, Klaus Kinski, wearing a metal helmet that seemed to be soldered to his skull, had so little to do that he kept acting up a grotesque storm. Aguirre's glassy blue eyes didn't blink; they seemed to have popped open and stayed that way. He was like an angry, domineering Bette Davis; he held his mouth like a dowager, pursing his lips and scowling, and he took command of a group of soldiers by the demonic force of his glare. Kinski's Aguirre was a crazy conquistador who always walked at a tilt, and when he stood still he was slanted backward or, occasionally, sideways; he achieved the effect of the angled sets in *Caligari* just with his own body, which told us how off-balance his mind was.

Aguirre even managed to have Gothic political overtones—it could be seen as a parable of Hitler's taking power. The movie is trancelike: we experience the disorientation of the Europeans lost in this primeval lassitude. And the absurd humor is like a wink that you can't quite believe you saw; there's no preparation for it and no follow-up—Herzog never acknowledges it. Suddenly, a Spaniard says of the arrow that has just hit him, "This is not an arrow," or a man's severed head keeps on talking, finishing the sentence he was speaking when it was lopped off. And there are frames that are charged with something that goes beyond what we think of as dream, or even nightmare: abandoned in the jungle, a hooded horse stands immobilized in helpless terror; the camera passes over the remains of a boat, with a tiny lifeboat dangling from its stern, lodged high in the treetops.

Though made in 1972, *Aguirre* wasn't released here until 1977, which turned out to be perfect timing. Until the sixties, American anti-war movies had attempted to be realistic about war, but in the post-Vietnam period the horror of that war was all mixed together with the drug culture, and for many people psychedelic intensification began to seem the only true realism. The imagery of *Aguirre*—visionary, skewed, cuckoo—was a hallucinatory horror trip. The film took the edge off Coppola's still-to-come version of Conrad's dreamlike *Heart of Darkness*; Herzog had made the white-intruders-vs.-the-natives trip first. (Some moviegoers cheered each time an Indian's poisoned arrow hit its mark.) *Apocalypse Now* was clearly influenced by *Aguirre*, and Coppola may have acknowledged the debt in a visual gesture: his image of a wrecked plane nesting in a tree was possibly an homage to Herzog, though it couldn't match the shivery wit of that boat. Coppola's image could be accounted for; Herzog's had the purity of madness.

It may have been the surreal triumph of the boat in the trees that sent Herzog back to the shrouded mountains and mucky jungles of Peru and got him into the five-year mess of making *Fitzcarraldo*. In 1894, an Irishman known to the Peruvians as Fitzcarrald made a fortune in the rubber trade by figuring out how to ship the rubber from an inaccessible stretch of land: he dismantled a riverboat and used hundreds of Indians to carry the parts overland from one tributary of the Amazon to another, where it was reassembled. When Herzog was told this story, he must have visualized the riverboat on a mountain—his earlier image writ large. Of course, a film about that incident wouldn't have much visual excitement if the boat was in pieces. Herzog had been fascinated by the logistical mystery of how the prehistoric stone blocks were brought to Carnac—a feat that probably involved an army of slaves working for many years, like the building of the pyramids. Putting things together, he decided on something that would dwarf the actual Fitzcarrald's accomplishment: *his* Indians would haul a three-hundred-and-twenty-ton steamboat (roughly ten times the size and weight of Fitzcarrald's vessel) up a mountain *intact*, and on a grade twice as steep as the one in the historical account. *Fitzcarraldo* is a movie made for an image. And so perhaps it's not surprising that still pictures of the steamboat on the mountain are more resonant than the film. In a sense, *Fitzcarraldo* wrecks the image by explaining it. The mystery evaporates when we see the impossible made possible—when we see the hauling process.

Movies are based on illusion—movies *are* illusion. The sound of Fred Astaire's taps was added to the soundtrack after his dances were shot; Garbo's laugh is said to have been dubbed in *Ninotchka*; when the tiny Yoda stood in the forest advising Luke Skywalker, they were both actually on a platform built a few feet above a studio floor. The magic of movies is in the techniques by which writers and directors put us in imaginary situations and actors convince us that they are what they're not. Then along comes the G. Gordon Liddy of movies, Werner Herzog, who apparently sees the production of a film as a mystic ordeal.

In making *Fitzcarraldo*, Herzog was proving his uncompromising integrity by housing his actors deep in the jungle and having them go through the hardships of the characters they play—only more so. He christened the jungle camp "Film or Death." Herzog thought that this movie would be a cheat if he used miniatures and mattes. There's some goofball puritanism operating in this man: he treats the challenges he sets up as if they had been imposed on him—as if he had been cursed. He thinks he's producing art because he turns the making of a film into such a miserable, difficult struggle for all concerned. But the art of the motion picture is fakery—even its most ascetic practitioner, Carl Dreyer, knew that. Dreyer didn't burn up the elderly woman who was tied to the stake in *Day of Wrath*, and chances are that the actors who played in *Ordet* didn't even have to down all that poisonous-looking black coffee. Robert Bresson didn't actually drive the girl who played in *Mouchette* to suicide. (Only the audience.)

Nothing destroys the spell of dramatic movies so jarringly as the intrusion of violence and pain that clearly aren't faked, such as the slaughter of an animal or the wire-tripping of a horse. Those are the real snuff films.

Fitzcarraldo is embarrassingly—infuriatingly—real; the Indians tugging at Herzog's steamboat are workers trapped inside his misconception of a movie. We may be appalled by the labors that are evident in *Fitzcarraldo*; we may even be impressed by them. But we always see them as exactly what they are: labors undertaken to be photographed. The story he has devised never takes hold; there isn't enough illusion for that. The plot seems no more than a pretext for the central image. At times, the ship slowly climbing the mountain does seem rather magical, but two hours and thirty-seven minutes is a long sit, and the deliberateness of Herzog's pacing can put you in a stupor. A lot of other things happen, but that's all they do; they don't develop and they're not followed through. Herzog has got himself into some zone between documentary and drama where neither works. It may be that his passion for authenticity is more religious than aesthetic, because he can't seem to make the images vivid—it's as if all his energy had gone into meeting the behind-the-scenes tests that he created for himself, his cast, and his crew (and, probably, his backers).

The actual Fitzcarrald, who was content to have his boat transported in pieces, was already rich; he succeeded in his maneuver and got wildly richer from it. Herzog has written his Fitz as a lovable loser, though with Klaus Kinski in the role very little of that comes through. We don't know quite what Kinski's Fitz is, because he's not like anyone else in the world (except maybe Bette Davis playing Rutger Hauer). Herzog has grafted another element onto the story of the historical Fitzcarrald by giving his hero a reason for wanting to get rich in the rubber trade: an obsession with building an opera house in the jungle and bringing Caruso to sing in it. (An opera house was in fact built on the Amazon, in Brazil, in 1896.) This makes Fitz more like a movie director—like Herzog himself, who certainly didn't use the six million dollars that *Fitzcarraldo* finally cost on pleasures of the flesh. Herzog needed the money so he could punish himself and everyone around him—in the cause of art. A man who at fourteen or fifteen decided that filmmaking was his vocation, Herzog has got an army of heathens with painted faces hauling his three-hundred-and-twenty-ton Cross up a mountain—and in the misproportioned narrative this is meant to be merely the first step toward the goal of bringing opera to the jungle. By the time the ship is over the hump, we're prepared to accept any token of a finish, and that's about what Herzog delivers.

In Les Blank's feature-length documentary *Burden of Dreams*, which is about the making of *Fitzcarraldo*, there's a brief scene of Jason Robards in the title role (before amoebic dysentery caused him to leave the picture). Just from Robards' presence in that one bit, it's clear that his Fitzcarraldo might have been a likable, charismatic Irish bum with a dream. And we can tell that Kinski's Fitz is intended to be a generous, good-hearted fellow, because he talks to a pet pig and he likes the native children—he gives them chips of ice, and when they cluster around him in his shack he plays his Caruso records for them (and the pig). But Kinski is megalomania incarnate. Even in a dishevelled white suit and a floppy white straw hat that he looks lost in, he gives off emanations that are far too outré for this role. With his goggling eyes and his big dome and the spikes of yellow-orange hair sticking out of it, he's an icon of stark raving freakishness. Kinski keeps an expression on his face until it looks fixed and mad; he never lets you forget that he's different from other men. If he ever had an ordinary "normal" range, he doesn't anymore. And Kinski only does a single. He's usually a single who gives what's needed, but not this time. Kinski's Fitzcarraldo isn't a man with a dizzy dream—he's a bored, fed-up actor eyeballing the camera. This means that Claudia Cardinale, in the role of Molly, the madam of a fancy whorehouse who finances Fitz's scheme, can't quite come into focus. Cardinale, with her big bright smile, is a warm and jovial Molly, and if Robards were opposite her we could understand why she is so protective of Fitz. Cardinale is ripely alive even in this asexual movie, and she stays in character like a real trouper, even though Kinski pats her or takes her arm routinely, and so her Molly seems rather too conveniently acquiescent, and somewhat simple.

There is a sequence that might have been a comic heartbreaker and might also have told us what we needed to know about Fitz and his past: At an abandoned railway station where he has gone to pull up some tracks that could be useful for guiding his boat down the mountain, he is greeted by a family headed by a black man, who beams with pleasure at the sight of him. The man is still loyally guarding the rails that Fitz had hired him to guard six years earlier, when he was involved in an abortive bringing-in-a-railroad venture. Almost unbelievably, Herzog doesn't shape the meeting so that Fitz has some response—perhaps becomes shamefaced about past failures and forgotten pledges, maybe promises to pay the man some of his back wages. The scene is just dropped. And nowhere is there a suggestion of when or how this scrounging dreamer developed his passion for Caruso. Herzog has always been great at flooding huge landscapes with music, and when Fitz stands on the prow of his ship with his head flung back and with Caruso's voice coming out of the phonograph next to him, it's obvious that he feels he's the king of all he surveys. But Herzog has said that he himself doesn't like opera—that he went once and walked out. (A bummer of a first opera bored him and he never went to another. Suppose somebody's first movie is *Fitzcarraldo* . . .) The one opera-house scene (it was staged by Werner Schroeter) is insulting to Caruso and the aged, crippled Sarah Bernhardt, whom it purports to represent. For no apparent reason, Bernhardt is played by a female impersonator. Or perhaps there is a reason—to make Fitz's obsession ludicrous. He sees the plump singer and the tottering old tart in the same performance that we do, and he's ecstatic.

The tone that Herzog is after in this film must be romantic irony; he looks at Fitz's passion from the outside and sees Fitz's goal—opera in the jungle—as something of a joke. The film is a parody variation of *Aguirre*: this time the protagonist doesn't want to rule—he just wants to be an impresario. And he isn't meant to be a madman—just a little nutty. In the documentary, when Herzog rages against the beauty of the wilderness— when he says that he hates it, that it's all vileness and fornication, and that "the trees here are in misery, the birds are in misery, they don't sing, they just screech in pain, even the stars up here look like a mess"—surely he means us to laugh at his ranting intensity? He's playing the obsessed clown, and that's what he must have had in mind for Fitz, whose big accomplishment is worthless, and who finally relaxes and enjoys himself with a bit of bravura that is his way of making good on his vow to bring opera to the banks of the Amazon. Yet while we're watching the movie it just seems to be an inept attempt at a heroic spectacular, and when we get to the ramshackle finish it's as if *Lawrence of Arabia* had dissolved in giggles.

The biggest disappointment in *Fitzcarraldo* is Peru. After a visually promising beginning, Herzog seems to lose interest in the external world (and no one in this movie has much of an internal world, either). The shots are repetitive and are held too long, and though they're lovely, they don't have the ghostly, kinky expressiveness of the great images that sustain one through the dragginess of *Aguirre*. And probably because of Herzog's ironic intentions the steamboat being towed up the mountain loses any metaphorical meaning. In some shots, it looks so fake I guess it has to be the real thing. The sight that we wait for turns out to be a bust: when the ship is poised at the very top, it looks like a big toy.

The moviegoers who attend Herzog pictures probably perceive his Sisyphean labors as a metaphor for how every artist is tested, and think the labors crazy but grand. And sometimes they are: at the end of *Aguirre*, when the madman is on the raft and the camera circles him, it's as if he were strangling within the circumference of his own hysteria. (He's like the thrice-encircled poet of "Kubla Khan.") But the visual grandeur has gone flat in *Fitzcarraldo*. There may be limits to the results an imaginative moviemaker can get if he keeps rejecting imaginative techniques. A man who has to do everything the hard way raises the suspicion that he's simply a hardhead. Herzog says things like "If I show a plastic ship going over a plastic mountain, it will be just a Hollywood movie, a cheap movie, and everyone will know it." Does Herzog actually go to the movies? (He seems to want only the torment of making them.) No one could deny the persistence of tacky-looking pictures, but even fifty years ago craftsmen in Hollywood (and at UFA, in Germany) were creating effects more than equal to Herzog's needs in *Fitzcarraldo*. It can't be that he's afraid of a plastic look; he knows better than that. He could have controlled the quality of process shots much more easily than he controlled the maneuvers of that ship, and he wouldn't have risked other people's lives doing it or put his co-workers through misery. He would have been free to work as a film artist—instead of playing Pharaoh. Herzog puts his effort in the wrong place. Is it that he's afraid of *not* being tested, of *not* having his ordeals? He needn't worry; these days nobody makes big, ambitious movies without passing through fire.

The footage of Herzog himself in the Les Blank documentary, standing and addressing the camera (though with eyes averted), is stronger than anything in his own movie. (He does have an inner life—and it's frightening.) If you see *Burden of Dreams*, you may not be able to think of *Fitzcarraldo* without remembering Herzog's almost priggish dissociation from his own acts. *Burden of Dreams* isn't a major work on its own, but it has an unusual effect: it makes *Fitzcarraldo* crumble in the memory—it merges with it. In the documentary, Herzog acknowledges the injuries and fatalities that occurred during the making of his picture, but he regards them as the unavoidable results of his commitment to film; they're setbacks—obstacles to the profession of moviemaker. A sainted liberal, he's deeply concerned about the Indians' sufferings over the centuries, and he assures us of his care not to contaminate them with Western culture. His tone is mournful as he rambles on about the terrible exploitation that has been killing them off, and it's bad enough to watch hundreds of them in the mud pulling at his damn steamboat without listening to him lament their tragic history. At one glorious point in his monologues to the camera, this humble fellow tells us that his dreams are the same as ours—that "the only distinction between me and you is that I can articulate them." This puts him in a class with the movie queen in *Singin' in the Rain* who dimpled prettily as she said, "If we bring a little joy into your humdrum lives, it makes us feel as though our hard work ain't been in vain for nothin'." Herzog *is* an artist, but he's also a faker—the most dangerous kind, possibly, because he doesn't know how to use his fakery except to make himself seem more holy than other people.

{*The New Yorker*, October 18, 1982}

Tootsie began with Don McGuire, who wrote what is said to have been a wild screenplay. After it was sold and Dick Richards was set to be the director, Robert Kaufman was hired to do a new draft. When Dustin Hoffman read Kaufman's version, he agreed to play in the picture, and brought in his playwright pal Murray Schisgal (with whom he had once tried to concoct a movie about a man impersonating a woman) to rework the material. Then the director, Dick Richards, was replaced by Hal Ashby, and Larry Gelbart was hired for yet another version. After that, Hal Ashby was replaced by Sydney Pollack, and Elaine May (who chose to be anonymous) was signed to do a rewrite; after her came the team of Barry Levinson and Valerie Curtin, and after them, Robert Garland. And with some of these people doing more than one draft, when the screenplay had to be submitted to the Writers Guild for arbitration over the issue of who should get the screen credit, three large cardboard boxes were needed to transport the more than twenty scripts. Pollack must have saved whatever he could of the best in each of them—*Tootsie* sounds as if one superb comedy writer had done it all. There is talk in Hollywood now of forming the I Also Wrote/I Almost Directed *Tootsie* Club. (The writing credit went to Larry Gelbart and Murray Schisgal.)

One of the things that Hollywood used to be good at was producing enjoyable, seemingly effortless entertainments, such as the Hepburn-Tracy *Pat and Mike*, Jean Harlow in *Bombshell*, Claudette Colbert in *Midnight*, Jean Arthur and Ray Milland in *Easy Living*, the Hepburn and Grant *Bringing Up Baby*, and later on, *Some Like It Hot*—films that were factory products and commercial as all hell but took off into a sphere of their own. Those movies continue to give so much pleasure that they have a special glamour. *Tootsie*—a modern addition to this company—has what the best screwball comedies had: a Can-you-top-this? quality. (And they often got it from relays of top writers—who were on the payroll, anyway, in those days.) Paying off this project's earlier writers and directors added heavily to its cost, and it took a rather scandalous one hundred shooting days—some of them, according to press and TV accounts, given over to squabbles between Hoffman and Sydney Pollack. But when the result is a *Tootsie* the expenses seem justified. And when Hoffman delivers the kind of performance he gives here, the talk in the media about his being overpaid seems beside the point. This movie is inconceivable without him. Once Hoffman was committed to the project, the scriptwriters began to shape the central character to fit him, and then they went further. In its final form, *Tootsie* is based on Dustin Hoffman, the perfectionist; he's both the hero and the target of this satirical farce about actors.

The central character, Michael Dorsey, is a brilliant, "uncompromising" New York actor whom no one wants to hire, because he makes things hell for everybody. A stickler for the "truth" in an actor's performance, he over-complicates things. He's a nut—acting is his mania. So, despite his gifts and his reputation among the young actors whom he coaches, at thirty-nine he's still frustrated—scrounging for a living and finding jobs as a waiter. At the start of the movie, he hasn't had any acting work in two years, and when his girlfriend (Teri Garr) goes up for an audition for a role in a soap and is rejected as the wrong type, he decides to try for the part himself. Made up as a woman, he presents himself as Dorothy Michaels, and lands the job.

Michael is dressed in skirts for about half the movie. This isn't a simple female impersonation, on the order of *Charley's Aunt*. Michael finds himself when he's Dorothy—not because he has any secret desire to be a woman but because when he's Dorothy he's acting. He's such a dedicated, fanatical actor that he comes fully alive only when he's playing a role, and you can see it in his intense, glittering eyes. There are always several things going on in Hoffman's face. He lets us see that Michael's mind is working all the time, and that he's making an actor's choices. Michael is thinking out Dorothy while he's playing her—he's thinking out what a woman would do. When he's giving a performance as Dorothy, he feels a freedom that he doesn't have when he's just Michael. Dorothy, in her fussy, high-necked dresses, has a definite personality—we in the audience become fond of her. She's a flirt, a joker: *she* doesn't have to take herself as seriously as Michael, the artist (who's all nerves), takes himself. She has a much less knotted personality than he has—he allows her to have the charm he denies himself. She also has a Southern accent, and a rather troubling voice; it slips around in a hoarse, neuter sort of way. But Michael is a meticulous actor: Dorothy's vocal patterns and her phrasing are very different from his. And when she's at the TV studio, playing the role of Emily Kimberly, the hospital administrator in "Southwest General," she takes on a brisk huffiness. Hoffman's performance works at so many different levels in this movie that when Michael is in women's clothes you keep watching his crooked, lipsticky smile and his mascaraed eyes, to see what's going on in his head. And when Michael is only Michael, you miss Dorothy, and Emily, too. You can believe that Michael would be a hit playing Emily Kimberly, because this scrappy woman, with thick wrists and oddly sharp, crooked teeth and a bouffant red hairdo, is more eccentrically, believably alive than anyone you're likely to see on the soaps. The performers I've caught (in my limited exposure as I flick from one channel to the next) have been a glazed, strangely slowed-down race of people, plagued by uncertainty; they move as if they were under water and seem to spend their lives on the telephone. Emily, who's fast-talking, overexcited, and absolutely sure of everything she says, would be bound to stir things up.

It's the film's notion that when Michael plays Emily he is driven to depart from his scripts and improvise whenever he feels that the lines she has been given aren't true to her character, and that his improvisations—his peppery rejoinders when the male head doctor is being condescending to Emily—endear him to women viewers. It would be easy to say that the movie was itself being condescending to women—that it was suggesting that it took a man to be tough and forthright enough to speak up for women's rights. Dorothy does seem to be bringing enlightenment into her co-workers' lives, and there's an element of self-congratulation (and self-aggrandizement, too) in the way Michael delivers his spontaneous feminist speeches. But it's also perfectly in character for Michael, experiencing male condescension for the first time, to feel it as an insult to Emily, his creation, and have her erupt in anger. Michael loves his characters more than he loves himself—Emily has to be fearless, a standard-bearer. Michael compulsively embroiders on the role of Emily and enlarges it; even in a hospital soap he's on a quest for the truth of his character. Michael isn't adaptable; he's a total, egocentric idealist. That's what has made him too cantankerous to be a working actor.

When Dustin Hoffman smiles—as Dorothy—he may be more sheerly likable as a movie star than he has ever been before. He gives a master actor's performance: he's playing three characters, and they're shaped so that Dorothy fits inside Michael, and Emily fits inside Dorothy. Even Hoffman's self-consciousness as an actor works in this performance; so does his sometimes grating, rankling quality (which is probably his idea of sincerity). The climactic scene that ends Michael's imposture isn't as well thought out as the rest of the picture, and the cutaway is abrupt; the scene needs reverberations or an aftermath—it's just shucked off. And there's an undercurrent that I could do without: the suggestion that Michael, through playing a woman, becomes a better man—more in touch with himself and all that. This doesn't come through strongly enough to do the movie much harm. It's the kind of increment of virtue that actors and directors speak of proudly, though, when they're giving interviews to papers or on television; they can make it sound as if this were why they made the picture—to improve our characters and their own, too.

What's good about Michael's playing Dorothy is that it enables Hoffman to show a purely farcical side of himself, and he has some inspired moments. After Michael has fallen in love with Julie (Jessica Lange), the star of "Southwest General," who has become very much attached to Dorothy, he has a scene in which he eagerly agrees to babysit with her infant, without having the faintest idea of what he may be letting himself in for. We can see Michael's harried mind clicking along inside Dorothy even during the babysitting. He tries everything he can think of to amuse the child, and after he has been sitting on the floor trying to quiet the kid by stuffing food into her, he falls back in exhaustion. With his legs spread out under his skirt and his big, fluffy head of hair sunk on his small body, he looks like a broken doll. And there's a brief gag scene with Michael, whose career has just been shattered, walking by a mime in Central Park who's in a precarious pose and knocking him over with a malicious touch—no more than a finger. This is the only time Michael ever shows any doubt about his vocation, and it's a passing, aberrant impulse—as if his head didn't quite know what his hand was up to.

Sydney Pollack, who was an actor in his earlier years, originally went to Hollywood (in 1961) as a dialogue coach for John Frankenheimer; essentially he's still a dialogue coach, and this works better for him here than it ever has before. Having dealt with stars most of his life, he knows how impossible they can be, and he has been able to make *Tootsie*

something practically unheard of: a believable farce. The picture has more
energy than anything else he has done; it's almost alarmingly well cast, and
the lines of dialogue collide with a click and go spinning off. Pollack himself gives some jabbing, fast readings; he plays a major role—that of
Michael's agent—with zest. Teri Garr has developed a shorthand style of
comedy that's all her own, and the audience has such strong empathy with
her that she can get her flighty, pent-up character across to us in a few terse
movements and phrases. The actress she plays dramatizes her reaction to
everything; she's always shrieking or on the verge of shrieking—in disbelief at what is happening to her. Yet Teri Garr always takes us by surprise;
she has become the funniest neurotic dizzy dame on the screen. As
Michael's roommate, an avant-garde dramatist, Bill Murray keeps dropping into the movie and making an observation or a comment, and his
inflections break up the audience every time. (He is said to have ad-libbed
his role.) As a lecherous, foolish old ham who plays the head doctor in the
soap, the veteran performer George Gaynes has a small comic triumph:
once you've laughed at him, even the sight of him triggers more laughs.
Dabney Coleman, as the director of the soap, doesn't seem to have come
up with anything fresh, but Charles Durning, who plays Julie's farmer
father, does some shrewd underplaying, especially in a scene in which you
can feel how badly he wants to wallop Michael.

When Jessica Lange appears, the movie changes from the crackling,
rapid-fire presentation of the hopes versus the realities of out-of-work
actors' lives to something calmer, and perhaps richer. She has a facial structure that the camera yearns for, and she has talent, too. Her face is softer
here than in *Frances*; her Julie is a dream girl, and she's like a shock absorber
to Michael. When he, dressed as Dorothy, sees her, some of his irascibility
melts away. Julie has honey-colored hair, and a friendly smile; she looks
freshly created—just hatched, and pleasantly, warmly spacy (enough to be
deeply impressed by Dorothy's high-principled talk about the theatre).
Jessica Lange helps to keep the movie from being too frenetic. There is
none of the usual actress's phoniness in her work; as Julie, she says her lines
in such a mild, natural way that it makes perfect sense for Michael to stop
in his tracks and stare at her in wonder. The picture is marvellous fun.

{*The New Yorker*, December 27, 1982}

:: Memory

The Night of the Shooting Stars (the original Italian title is
La Notte di San Lorenzo) is so good it's thrilling. This new film by Vittorio
and Paolo Taviani (who made the 1977 *Padre Padrone*) encompasses a vision
of the world. Comedy, tragedy, vaudeville, melodrama—they're all here,
and inseparable. Except for the framing-device scenes that take place in
a blue-lighted, fairy-tale present, *Shooting Stars* is set in a Tuscan village
and its environs during a summer week in 1944, when the American troops
were rumored to be only days away, and the Germans who had held the
area under occupation were preparing to clear out. But this setting is
magical, like a Shakespearean forest; it exists in the memory of Cecilia,
who is telling the story of what happened that August, when she was a
sultry six-year-old hellion (played by Micol Guidelli), and her family was
part of a group of a few dozen villagers who had decided to disobey official
orders. Convinced that the Germans, who had mined their houses, meant
to destroy the whole town—San Martino—that night, they stole out after
dark and went to find the Americans. The directors (who also wrote the
script, with Giuliani G. De Negri) are great gagmen—they aren't afraid to
let Cecilia exaggerate. She remembers herself as a tiny six-year-old who is
independent of adults and smarter than life. It doesn't take much stretch
of our imaginations to grasp that accidents that befell the child—such as
tumbling onto a basket of eggs—have become enlarged. The basket itself
has assumed heroic proportions, and, having been blamed for what she
couldn't help, the little girl takes a demonic joy in smashing the two eggs
that are still intact. The Cecilia we see never complains and always finds
ways to amuse herself; when she has witnessed an on-the-run wedding (the
groom is AWOL, the bride's pregnancy is close to term) even the hops she

takes, out of sheer pixilated excitement, are a bit higher than life. At this rushed wedding, an old man drinks a ceremonial glass of wine and gives a recitation about what happened to Achilles and Hector as if the Trojan War had taken place in his own lifetime. I think you could say that *Shooting Stars* is about how an individual's memories go to form communal folklore, and vice versa, so that we "recall" what we've heard from others as readily as what we've actually seen or heard. And the myth becomes our memory—the story we tell.

The Tavianis' style here is intellectualized, but their effects are unaccountable and gutty. Right at the start, in the chaos of a war that's lost but not yet over, and with Army deserters making their way home and hiding out from the Germans and the local Black Shirts, and with families split between Resistance fighters and Fascists, and nobody sure what the Germans will do before they pull out, San Martino is victimized by a practical joker who plays "Glory, Glory Hallelujah" on his phonograph. It's a marching version, with drums and woodwinds, of the old camp-meeting hymn that became "John Brown's Body" and later the "Battle Hymn of the Republic," and it begins softly, as if John Brown's brigades were at a distance and coming closer, and the townspeople, who have been cowering in their cellars, think that the Americans, their liberators, have arrived, and rush out to greet them. One boy is so sure of it, he sees them.

Galvano (played by Omero Antonutti, the powerful father of *Padre Padrone*) is the leader of the group that sneaks away in the night; at times he's like a theatre director. He tells his people to wear dark clothes for camouflage, and the whole troupe scrambles into black coats and coverings at the same time—it's like backstage at the opera, with everyone getting ready for the masquerade scene. And then there's another, quicker routine: the dogs who must be left behind, because their barking would betray the group, bark because they're being left behind. At last, Galvano's villagers are out in the country. They have been told that the Germans will blow up the town at 3 A.M., and when it's close to three they stand still and listen. We hear their thoughts, and then, exactly at three, distant shelling can be heard, and we see closeups of ears, like enlarged details of paintings by Uccello. The villagers listen to the destruction of San Martino—the only world they know—and we see their hands clenching their house keys, and see their expressions. Galvano doffs his hat and weeps for San Martino; a man throws his key away. It's an unostentatiously beautiful passage. The people mourn, but they're too excited to feel crushed: they're out on the road looking for Americans. In the morning, they take off their black clothes. The August landscapes are golden, and Cecilia is proud of her pleated, red print pinafore. It's made of the same material as her mother's sundress; they're wearing matching mother-daughter outfits.

Shooting Stars keeps opening up and compressing as it cuts back and forth between what happens to the group in the hills and what happens to the others, back in San Martino, who believed the authorities when they told them that they'd be safe if they took refuge in the cathedral. The elderly bishop, who has collaborated—has done what he was told—offers bland assurances to everyone while praying to God that he will really be able to protect his flock. (His prayer has a note of apprehensiveness; life is making a skeptic of him.) So many townspeople gather inside that the bishop runs out of wafers, but the people have brought loaves of bread with them and they break these into bits. He consecrates the bread, and everyone is given the Host—the ritual has never seemed more full of meaning. When the crowded cathedral explodes, the door blasts open and smoke pours forth; two priests bring the bishop out, and, dazed, he slumps in the square. The pregnant bride had become too ill to go on with the trekkers in the country, and her mother had hauled her back on a litter and taken her into the cathedral; now the mother tries to carry the mortally wounded, unconscious girl out, and the bishop, pulling himself to his feet, helps her. For a minute, they're both slightly bent over, facing each other and tugging at the helpless girl; they're forehead to forehead, and their eyes lock. It's an insane, cartoon effect—"This is what trusting in God and the Fascists gets you!"—and it makes the pain of the situation more acute. *Shooting Stars* is so robust that even its most tragic moments can be dizzyingly comic. When Richard Lester attempted black humor on the horrors of war (in the 1967 *How I Won the War*), the scenes were jokey and flat, and the people were no more than puppets. In *Shooting Stars*, black humor is just one tonality among many, and the exhausted mother and the double-crossed bishop aren't diminished by being revealed as dupes; having shared their rock-bottom moment, we feel close to them. Many voices are joined in these memories, and though the people who have headed out for freedom may look more courageous, the film doesn't degrade the ones who stayed behind. They had their reasons—children, old age, fears. In one way or another, they're all like that woman with the pregnant daughter.

Out on the roads, a Sicilian girl who has been shot by German soldiers—who is already dead—flirts and makes small talk with some stray G.I.s, Sicilian-Americans from Brooklyn, before she accepts her death. The only other movie director I know of who could bring off an epiphany like this is the Ukrainian Dovzhenko, the lyrical fantasist of the silent era. The Tavianis present their wildest moments of fantasy in a heightened realistic form; you believe in what you're seeing—but you can't explain why you believe in it. I think that we're eager to swallow it, in the same way that, as children, we put faith in the stories we heard at bedtime, our minds rising to the occasion, because what happened in them was far more real to us than the blurred events of our day. And for the grown woman Cecilia the adventures that she took part in have acquired the brilliance and vitality of legend.

San Martino is probably much like the town of San Miniato, between Pisa and Florence, where the brothers were born (Vittorio in 1929, Paolo in 1931), and which was the site of a massacre carried out by the Germans. (Their first short film—*San Miniato, July 1944*, made in 1954—was about this massacre.) The full fresco treatment they give the events of that summer in *Shooting Stars* is based partly on wartime incidents that they themselves witnessed when they were adolescents; they have said that everything they show actually happened—that the events they didn't witness they picked up "one by one . . . from all kinds of sources, official and otherwise." It's this teeming, fecund mixture, fermenting in their heads for almost forty years, that produces this film's giddy, hallucinated realism.

The movie is not like anything else—the Taviani brothers' pleasure in the great collection of stories they're telling makes it euphoric. It's as if they had invented a new form. In its feeling and completeness, *Shooting Stars* may be close to the rank of Jean Renoir's bafflingly beautiful *Grand Illusion*, and maybe because it's about the Second World War and Renoir's film was about the First, at times it's like a more deracinated *Grand Illusion*. Trying to pick the name by which he'll be known in the Resistance, a man who sings in church decides that he wants to be called Requiem. A married couple who belong to Galvano's group are out in the middle of nowhere, listening to the sounds of a warplane overhead, and the man holds his wife's compact up so she can see to put on her lipstick. Galvano's hungry people come across a watermelon patch, and the film becomes a bucolic festival; one girl can't wait for a melon to be cut open—she smashes it with her bottom. At night, all of them sleep piled on top of each other in a crater—a shell hole—as if their bodies had been flung there in a game of pick-up-sticks. And the image is so vivid that somehow you don't question it. Was this crater with its groundlings conceived as a secular joke on the seraphic figures floating in the painted domes of churches? You don't boggle at anything in this movie. The Tavianis have the kind of intuition that passeth understanding. An era is ending, the society is disintegrating, but they take a few seconds to show us Galvano, who has gone to a stream to bathe, standing still in the water, completely at peace—his mind a blank. It's a transcendent image. He could be anywhere and the water would renew him; he has a sense of balance. Galvano gets to consummate his lifelong dream, but before he goes to bed with the woman he has loved for forty years—the woman who hasn't been accessible until now, because she became part of the landed gentry—they kiss, and he tells her apologetically that his kiss would be better if he hadn't lost three teeth. What he's saying is "Do you know what you've made us miss?"

The film's greatest sequence is hair-raisingly casual—a series of skirmishes in a wheat field. Still looking for the American troops and spotting nothing but Germans, the villagers come to a wheat field and meet up with a group of Resistance fighters who need help with the harvest (or the Fascists will get it), and the villagers lend a hand. And suddenly all the ideological factions that have been fighting in the country are crawling around in the tall wheat. There's a civil war taking place in the fields, with men who all know each other, who in some cases are brothers or cousins, going at each other with clubs and guns and pitchforks. These are not noble peasants. Two old friends wrestle murderously, each demanding that the other surrender; the gentle bridegroom kills a fifteen-year-old Fascist, who is grovelling in terror, and the kid's father falls to the earth and scoots in a circle like an animal in agony. Scenes from this battlefield could turn into Anselm Kiefer's huge straw landscapes, which are like windswept, overgrown memorials that have come up out of the past—out of war and mud and destruction. At one chaotic moment, a couple of people who are tending a wounded old woman reach out at arm's length for the flask of water that a couple of other people have just given to a wounded man, and then, realizing that they're enemies, both pairs start shooting at each other—from a distance of about three feet. It's a pure sick joke, like something Godard would have tried in *Les Carabiniers* if he'd thought of it. In *Shooting Stars*, you're never reminded of a filmmaker who isn't a master.

The Taviani brothers say that if there is a theme running through their movies it's "From silence to communication," but they try to spoof their own theme, too. When Cecilia and another little girl meet up with two G.I.s, Cecilia's friend picks the one she likes, and he gives her a chocolate bar, but Cecilia's G.I. indicates that he has nothing to offer her. Silently, she makes funny ugly faces at him, and he replies in kind, and then, wanting to give her some token, he improvises—he blows up a condom as if it were a balloon, and she dances off with her prize. This, like several other scenes in the movie, is reminiscent of Rossellini's 1946 film *Paisan*; the Tavianis, who saw that film when they were university students in Pisa, say that it was *Paisan* that made them decide to become moviemakers. And so maybe this G.I.-condom scene can be passed over—it's effective in the thin, overcooked manner of *Life* journalism in the forties. It's an amusing parody of a whole batch of romantic encounters in wartime movies, but it's also a dismayingly pat little number.

In a sense, everything in *Shooting Stars* is a theatrical routine (but not on that level). The Tavianis' style keeps you conscious of what they're doing, and, yes, the technique is Brechtian, but with a fever that Brecht never had. The Tavianis make stylized unreality work for them in a way that nobody else ever has; in *Shooting Stars* unreality doesn't seem divorced from experience (as it does with Fellini)—it's experience made more intense. They love style, but it hasn't cost them their bite—their willingness to be harsh and basic. During the brief period when a movie is actually being shot, a director often wishes that he had someone to help him—someone who knew what was inside his head. These two do, and that may account for the calm assurance of the film and its steady supply of energy. Every sequence is a flourish, but there's heft in the Tavianis' flourishes, and no two have the same texture or tone. The shaping of the material is much more conscious than we're used to. The movie builds, and it never lets up—it just keeps channelling its energy in different directions. Even when *Shooting Stars* is at its most emotionally expansive, you're aware of the control the directors have. What they're controlling is exaltation. That's the emotional medium they're working in.

They use sound in a deliberately primitive way: the sound here—whether it's from nature or Verdi or the score by Nicola Piovani—makes memories flood back just as odors sometimes bring things back. It's sound of great clarity, set against silence. (A superb fanfare is heard during the film's main title—a fanfare followed by cannon fire and then, for a moment, nothing.) The memories the sound brings back come up out of the muck and are heavily filtered; they're distorted, and polished until they gleam. And the directors' visual techniques—their use of dissolves, especially—keep you conscious of the processes of memory etching in and eroding. The film's impassioned style is steeped in nostalgia. Cecilia's mythicized memories are her legacy to her own child, to whom she is telling this story at bedtime. For the Tavianis, as for Cecilia, the search for the American liberators is the time of their lives. For an American audience, the film stirs warm but tormenting memories of a time when we were beloved and were a hopeful people.

{*The New Yorker*, February 7, 1983}

from
STATE OF THE ART

:: A Masterpiece

It's deeply satisfying to see, finally, Luchino Visconti's magnificent 1963 film *The Leopard* in Italian, with subtitles, and at its full length — three hours and five minutes. It had been cut to two hours and forty-one minutes when it opened in this country, in a dubbed-into-English version that didn't always seem in sync, and with the color brightened in highly variable and disorienting ways. Now the movie has its full shape, and it couldn't have arrived at a better time. The new movies — especially the new American movies — have reached a low, low point. And here is a work of a type we rarely see anymore — a sweeping popular epic, with obvious similarities to *Gone with the Wind*. Set in Sicily, beginning in 1860, it's *Gone with the Wind* with sensibility — an almost Chekhovian sensibility. It doesn't have the active central characters that the American epic has; there's no Scarlett or Rhett. But it has a hero on a grand scale — Don Fabrizio, Prince of Salina, played superlatively well by Burt Lancaster. And it's so much better at doing the kind of things that *Gone with the Wind* did — showing you how historical events affect the lives of the privileged classes — that it can make you feel a little embarrassed for Hollywood. *Gone with the Wind* is, of course, a terrific piece of entertainment; *The Leopard* is so beautifully felt that it calls up a whole culture. It casts an intelligent spell — intelligent and rapturous.

The Visconti epic is based on the posthumously published, best-selling novel by Giuseppe Tomasi di Lampedusa — an impoverished Sicilian prince, like his hero. (The Lampedusa coat of arms bore a leopard.) The movie isn't what we normally call "novelistic," though; everything comes to us physically. Visconti suggests Don Fabrizio's thoughts and feelings by the sweep and texture of his life. The fabrics, the medal-laden military uniforms, the dark, heavy furniture, the huge palaces, with their terraces and broad marble staircases, and the arid, harsh landscapes they're set in are all sensualized—made tactile. Burt Lancaster has always been a distinctively physical actor, and this is a supremely physical role. We know the Prince by his noble bearing and the assurance of his gestures—they're never wasteful. He's at ease with authority; you can believe that he's the result of centuries of aristocratic breeding. There's grandeur in the performance, which Lancaster has acknowledged he modelled on Visconti himself (who, though not a Sicilian, was a count whose family titles were among the oldest and most noble in Europe). It is not merely that the Prince is in tune with his surroundings. They have formed each other: he and the Salina country palazzo basking in the yellow light outside Palermo are one.

The Prince's estates have dwindled, money is running low, but he keeps up the family traditions. He's not a romantic—he's a realist. He'll protect aristocratic values for as long as he can, and he'll do his best to protect the future of the Salina family—his wife and seven children, his nephew—and the household priest and all the other attendants. He bends to the times only as much as he needs to. In 1860, Italy was in the middle of a revolution. Garibaldi and his followers—the Redshirts—were trying to unify Italy and free the south and Sicily from Bourbon rule. The Prince's favorite nephew, the spirited, gallant Tancredi (Alain Delon), goes off to join Garibaldi; he goes with the Prince's blessing and a small bag of his gold— the Prince understands that the Bourbons will fall. He's a man with few illusions, a man of sense who suffers fools all the time and tries to cushion his impatience. When Garibaldi lands on Sicily with an army of about a thousand men, and there are skirmishes in the streets of Palermo, the Prince's neurasthenic wife (Rina Morelli) becomes hysterically frightened —she's a whimperer—and he, recognizing that they may be in danger, takes her and their brood to safety at the family holdings across the island in Donnafugata. Along the way, the servants lay out a picnic—they spread a vast white linen cloth, and dish after dish, while the grooms take care of the horses. (Corot should have been invited.) At Donnafugata, the Prince leads the procession of his people, weary, and covered with dust from the road, into the cathedral. Seated in the Salina family pews, they're like corpses—petrified, dead-wood figures.

The movie is about the betrayal of Garibaldi's democratic revolution, and about the wiliness of opportunists like Tancredi. ("Black and slim as an adder" was how Lampedusa described him.) Tancredi makes his reputation as a heroic fighter while he's an officer with Garibaldi's Redshirts, but as soon as power shifts to the Mafia-dominated, middle-class landgrabbers, he changes into the uniform of the new king—*their* king, Victor Emmanuel II, from the House of Savoy. He doesn't so much as blink when he hears the gunshots that mark the execution of the last of Garibaldi's loyal troops. The young Delon is perhaps too airy for the role. With his even features, small teeth, and smooth cheeks, he's a very pretty art object, perfectly carved. He'd make a fine, spry figure in an operetta, but he doesn't have the excitement or force to give Tancredi's actions the weight they might have had. (This Tancredi is as shallow as that other opportunist—Scarlett.) But the film is essentially about the Prince himself—the aging Leopard—and how he reacts to the social changes.

Lancaster provides the film's center of consciousness. We see everything that happens through Visconti's eyes, of course, but we feel we're seeing it through the Prince's eyes. We couldn't be any closer to him if we were inside his skin—in a way, we are. We see what he sees, feel what he feels; we know what's in his mind. He's fond of—and a little envious of—Tancredi, with his youth and verve. The Prince—he's only forty-five, but forty-five was a ripe age in the mid-nineteenth century—has perceived what the result of the revolution will be: the most ruthless grabbers will come out on top. There's a despicable specimen of the breed close at hand—the rich and powerful mayor of Donnafugata, Don Calogero (Paolo Stoppa), who is eager to climb into society. The Prince has a daughter who is in love with Tancredi, but the Prince understands that this daughter—prim and repressed, like his wife—is too overprotected and overbred to be the wife Tancredi needs for the important public career he's going after. And Tancredi, who has nothing but his princely title and his rakish charm, requires a wife who will bring him a fortune. And so when Tancredi is smitten by Don Calogero's poised and strikingly sensual daughter, Angelica (the lush young Claudia Cardinale, doing a bit too much lip-licking), the Prince arranges the match. (All this is presented very convincingly, and it's probably silly to quibble with a masterpiece, yet I doubt if a warmhearted father—and especially one sensually deprived in his relationship with his wife—would be so free of illusions about his daughter. And it seemed to me that he was more cut off from his children—one of the striplings is played by the very young Pierre Clementi, who has the face of a passionflower—than a man of his temperament would be, whatever his rank.)

Lighted by the justly celebrated cinematographer Giuseppe Rotunno, the movie is full of marvellous, fluid set-piece sequences: the dashing Tancredi's goodbyes to the Salina family when he goes off to join Garibaldi; the picnic; the church sequence. The original Italian prints may have had deeper brown tones and more lustrous golds—some of the scenes have a drained-out look—but there's always detail to exult in. Each time the Salina family assembles for Mass or for dinner, it's a big gathering. Some of the smaller, less opulent sequences are ongoing political arguments, like the ironic dialogue between the Prince and the timid worrywart family priest (Romolo Valli), or between the Prince and a family retainer who is his hunting companion (Serge Reggiani, overacting). This poverty-stricken snob, who's loyal to the Bourbons, is shocked that the Prince would approve of his nephew's marrying a girl whose mother is "an illiterate animal." The political issues that the film deals with are, of course, simplified, but they're presented with considerable cogency, and they're very enjoyable. Of the smaller sequences, perhaps the most dazzling is the conversation between the Prince and a petite, intelligent professorial gentleman (Leslie French) who has come with the official request that he stand for election to the Senate. (Victor Emmanuel II is a constitutional monarch.) Here, the Leopard—refusing the offer—shows his full pride. It's the most literary passage in the movie; it's the rationale of the script: the Prince explains the Sicilian arrogance and torpor, and how he and the land are intertwined. I doubt if any other director has got by even halfway with a fancy dialogue of this kind, yet it's stunningly successful here. Lancaster has held his energy in check through most of the performance; now he comes out blazing, and he's completely controlled. He has a wild, tragicomic scene, too, when the weasel-eyed Don Calogero comes to discuss Tancredi's proposal to his daughter. The sickened Prince listens to him, and then, in a startling move, picks up the little weasel, plants a quick, ceremonial kiss on each cheek to welcome him into the family, and plunks him down. It happens so fast we barely have time to laugh. Don Calogero's greed shines forth then in the satisfaction with which he enumerates each item of the dowry he will bestow upon Tancredi; it's as if he expected the Prince to cry "Hosanna!" for each acre, each piece of gold.

Probably the movie seems as intense as it does because the action isn't dispersed among several groups of characters, the way it usually is in an epic. We stay with the Prince almost all the time. Except for the fighting in the streets, there's only one major sequence that he isn't in—an episode in which Tancredi and Angelica wander about in unused parts of the rambling Salina palace in Donnafugata. The Prince's absence may not be the reason, but this episode doesn't seem to have any purpose or focal point, and it's also the only time the film's tempo seems off. Whenever the Prince is onscreen—whether in his study, where the telescopes indicate his interest in astronomy, or in the town hall, controlling his distaste while drinking a glass of cheap wine that Don Calogero has handed him—we're held, because we're always learning new things about him. And in the concluding hour, at the Ponteleone Ball—certainly the finest hour of film that Visconti ever shot (and the most influential, as *The Godfather* and *The Deer Hunter* testify)—it all comes together. At this ball, the Salinas introduce Angelica to society—to all the many Sicilian princes and aristocrats. Visconti's triumph here is that the ball serves the same function as the Prince's interior monologue in the novel: throughout this sequence, in which the Prince relives his life, experiences regret, and accepts the dying of his class and his own death, we feel we're inside the mind of the Leopard saying farewell to life.

Everything we've seen earlier, we now realize, was leading to this splendid ball, which marks the aristocrats' acceptance of the parvenus who are taking over their wealth and power. (The poor will stay at the bottom, and—in the Prince's view, at least—will be worse off than before; the new ruling class will not be bound by the tradition of noblesse oblige.) The Prince, alone by choice, wanders from one mammoth ballroom to the next, observing all these people he knows. Tancredi and Angelica have their first dance, and the Nino Rota score gives way to a lilting waltz by Verdi, which had been discovered just before the film was shot; Visconti was giving it its first public performance, and a piece of music may never have been showcased more lavishly. Visconti (and perhaps his helpers) certainly knew how to stage dance sequences. (The movie was edited in a month, yet the rhythmic movement of the whole film is intoxicatingly smooth.) Soon the crowded rooms are stifling and, with the women fluttering their fans, look like cages of moths. The Prince, strolling away from these overheated rooms, sees a bevy of adolescent girls in their ruffles jumping up and down on a bed while chattering and screaming in delight—overbred, chalky-faced girls, like his daughters, all excited. In a room where people are seated at tables feasting, he glances in revulsion at a colonel covered with medals who is boasting of his actions against Garibaldi's men. He begins to feel fatigued—flushed and ill. He goes into the library, pours himself a glass of water, and stares at a big oil—a copy of a Greuze deathbed scene.

It's there, in front of the painting, that Tancredi and Angelica find him. She wants the Prince to dance with her, and as she pleads with him their bodies are very close, and for a few seconds the emotions he has been feeling change into something close to lust. He envies Tancredi for marrying for different reasons from his own; he envies Tancredi for Angelica's full-blown beauty, her heartiness, her coarseness. He escorts her to the big ballroom, and they waltz together. It's Angelica's moment of triumph: he is publicly welcoming her into his family. He is straight-backed and formal while they dance, but his thoughts are chaotic. He experiences acute regret for the sensual partnership he never had with his wife, and a nostalgia for the animal vitality of his youth. His intimations of his own mortality are fierce. After returning the shrewd, happy Angelica to Tancredi, he goes to a special small room to freshen up. Coming out, he sees into an anteroom—the floor is covered with chamber pots that need emptying. Eventually, the ball draws to a close, and people begin to leave, but a batch of young diehard dancers are still going strong: they're hopping and whirling about to livelier music now that the older people have left the floor. The Prince arranges for his family to be taken home, explaining that he will walk. When he passes down the narrow streets, he's an old man. The compromises he has had to make have more than sickened him—they've aged him. His vision of the jackals and sheep who are replacing the leopards and lions ages him even more. He is emotionally isolated from his wife and children; he no longer feels any affection for the sly-faced Tancredi. He's alone.

The Leopard is the only film I can think of that's about the aristocracy from the inside. Visconti, the Marxist count, is both pitiless and loving. His view from the inside is not very different from that of Max Ophuls in *The Earrings of Madame de . . .* —which was made from the outside (though it was based on the short novel by the aristocratic Louise de Vilmorin). Ophuls' imagination took him where Visconti's lineage (and imagination) had brought him, and he gave us a portrait of a French aristocrat by Charles Boyer which had similarities to Lancaster's performance. But we weren't taken inside that French aristocrat's value system with anything like the robust fullness of our involvement with Lancaster's Leopard. If it weren't for the Prince's wiry, strong, dark-red hair and his magisterial physique—his vigor—I doubt if we'd feel the same melancholy at the death of his class. The film makes us feel that his grace is part of his position. We're brought to respect values that are almost totally foreign to our society. That's not a small thing for a movie to accomplish.

{*The New Yorker*, September 19, 1983}

:: The Perfectionist

Barbra Streisand's *Yentl* is rhapsodic yet informal; it's like a gently surprising turn of phrase. Set in the thriving Polish-Jewish communities of an imaginary, glowing past, the movie has its own swift rhythms. Its simplicity and unity are somewhat reminiscent of Jacques Demy's *The Umbrellas of Cherbourg* (1964); perhaps that's because the composer Michel Legrand wrote the scores for both, and the songs carry both films' emotional currents (though in totally different ways). Adapted from the Isaac Bashevis Singer story "Yentl the Yeshiva Boy," the Streisand film tells of a young woman who grows up in a tradition-bound community in which bright boys—yeshiva boys—live to study Torah. Coddled and prized, they sit at their books all day long, memorizing and reciting, debating moral issues, and attempting to fathom the unfathomable. Women are excluded from scholarship, but Yentl has a passion for religious study—she thinks it's the only way of life that's worthwhile. And so when her widower father (who has secretly taught her) dies, she dresses as a boy, sneaks away at night and goes off to enroll in a yeshiva in a distant town.

The beginning of *Yentl* is shaky. Streisand wants to make sure we get the idea that women are kept in ignorance, and she's a trace insistent. And the end is, I think, a flat-out mistake. But most of *Yentl* is, of course, its middle, which is glorious; it's like that of the story, though with different shades of humor. Yentl, a woman crowding thirty, passes as an adolescent student and feels like one. She's carefree and goofy; she has found herself— as a boy. (Yentl in disguise is definitely a boy, not a man. That's how the masquerade was conceived by Singer, and it works for Streisand the way it did for Katharine Hepburn when she passed as a boy in *Sylvia*

Scarlett.) You can believe that the people in the Jewish quarter accept this smart, smooth-faced student, who has taken the name of Anshel, as male, because she isn't so very different from a lot of precocious, little-shrimp kids who seem to grow only in the head. Anshel is a sprite: as the yeshiva student, Streisand doesn't have an image of Barbra Streisand to play, and she lets herself be this slender and defenseless kid showing off his knowledge. When Streisand is playing a character, it releases something in her—a self-doubt, a tentativeness, a delicacy. She seems physically lighter; her scale is human, and you can share something with her that you can't when she's planted there as Streisand (and seems domineering). The basic concept of this movie lets her release herself, and as the yeshiva boy she's giddy and winsome.

Her singing voice takes you farther into the character; the songs express Yentl's feelings—what she wants to say but has to hold back. Her singing is more than an interior monologue. When she starts a song, her hushed intensity makes you want to hear her every breath, and there's high drama in her transitions from verse to chorus. Her phrasing and inflections are so completely her own that the songs make the movie seem very personal. Her singing has an ardent, beseeching quality—an intimacy. And her vocal fervor lifts the movie to the level of fantasy.

Streisand sings with such passionate conviction that she partly compensates for the sameness of Legrand's tunes. A few of them are exciting in context, but "This Is One of Those Moments" and "Tomorrow Night" are so dull they seem to be all recitative, and Legrand's music simply doesn't have the variety, the amplitude, to do justice to Yentl's full emotional range. The Alan and Marilyn Bergman lyrics don't rise to the poetic richness of the occasion, either; songs such as "No Matter What Happens" and "A Piece of Sky" are tainted with feminist psychobabble and Broadway uplift. Streisand's eerily way-out-there-by-itself voice soars, striving to achieve new emotional heights, and the music is on a treadmill. But as the director Streisand does graceful tricks with the songs. She uses them to take the audience through time and space. Yentl begins a song, and it continues in voice-over as the action races ahead. The songs are montages and comedy routines, too, with images of what Yentl is singing about edited to the rhythm of the music. During the song "No Wonder," a dialogue scene takes place while Yentl/Anshel sings a wry, funny commentary on it, and it's all brought off rather softly, without fuss. As a musical, *Yentl* conveys the illusion that the songs simply grow out of the situations — which isn't altogether an illusion.

The movie loses its sureness of touch now and then, but it's unassuming. It's a homey, brightly lighted fantasy. Yentl's teacher papa (Nehemiah Persoff) has the apple cheeks and jolly gray beard of a Yiddish Kris Kringle. And when he dies and she leaves home, a big bird who represents his spirit hovers overhead, accompanying her on her travels. The place Yentl grew up in, the inn where she breaks her journey, the town where she passes the examination and is accepted as a yeshiva student — they all have the familiarity and the pastness of places we know from folktales. Only the big, clanging gates of the Jewish quarter, which are closed at night, seem unusual, and it may take a second or two to register what they are, because the movie doesn't emphasize the specific nature of its folklore. It takes it for granted. (In a scene in which Yentl, dressed as a boy, pays for a ride on a farmer's wagon and then isn't allowed to climb on board, the point that the people on the wagon are gentiles who are pulling a trick on her isn't fully shaped for the audience, and some moviegoers may be mystified.) But *Yentl* isn't a sweet, tame musical. Coming out of that ornery, mischievous Singer story, it couldn't be. There's a running theme in Singer: human beings keep trying to flirt with God, hoping that someday a line of communication can be established, but sex always gets in the way. Their wonderful good intentions are thwarted by the tingle of the groin.

Dressed as a boy, Yentl is no longer resentful of male privileges, and for the first time she feels attracted to a man. At the inn, just after she has left home, she meets the virile, bearded Avigdor, played by Mandy Patinkin (who makes the impact here that he failed to make in *Ragtime* and *Daniel*). Avigdor is friendly and warm. He's also charged up sexually. After years of the repressed life of a yeshiva student, he can hardly wait to be married to the luscious ripe peach who is pledged to him. Yentl, who is aroused by his sensual fever, accepts his suggestion that she come to his yeshiva, and when, as Anshel, she is accepted there and is considered a prodigy, Avigdor's eyes sparkle with pride. He plays big brother to her, and she becomes his study partner.

Maybe the magic of this Singer story (and of many of his other tales) is that the folkloric characters have been imbued with a drop of D. H. Lawrence's blood, yet they live in a time when confusing sexual urges are explained as the work of demons. "Yentl the Yeshiva Boy" is a folktale told by a sly trickster: its elements don't stay within the conventions of folklore. (It's as if the story were a river, and fish were trying to jump out of it.) Things take a turn toward the disturbing in "Yentl the Yeshiva Boy"; they become quite turbulent. There's darkness on the one hand and ribald comedy—even sex farce and burlesque—on the other, but the storyteller remains imperturbable.

In the movie, when Avigdor's fiancée, Hadass (Amy Irving), a beauty out of the erotic pages of the Old Testament, enters the picture, it becomes a series of dilemmas and metaphors. The three principal characters look at each other with longing, and sometimes with fear and bewilderment. They can't sort their emotions out. Avigdor, not knowing that Anshel is a woman, feels a closer companionship with her than he has ever known with anybody else of either sex. When Hadass's father cancels the wedding and Avigdor is distraught, Anshel, his confidant, shares in his pain. And the brooding, pitiful Avigdor, having lost Hadass, and loving his friend Anshel, wants Anshel to marry her; that way, Avigdor won't feel he has totally lost her. He threatens to go away if Anshel doesn't agree to the plan. Meanwhile, Hadass, whose love for the burly, strong Avigdor is a mixture of attraction and terror, begins to love Anshel for his gentleness—Hadass has found a "man" she doesn't feel afraid of. The baffled Yentl, who sees in Hadass everything that she herself didn't want to be and couldn't have been—who sees that Hadass is like a slave girl when she's around men—is jealous of her and at the same time touched by her. Hadass's submissiveness is mysteriously sultry. And Yentl/Anshel—as if in a trance, thinking to hold on to Avigdor and also captivated by Hadass—asks for her hand in marriage.

One moment, Yentl is a yeshiva boy, taking pleasure in being the smartest kid in the class; the next moment, she's got herself in a fix. There's only one end to this story, and it's the one that Singer gave it: Yentl must go down the road in search of another yeshiva. She is condemned to the life of study that she has chosen (and a Chassidic scholar can never learn enough). It isn't difficult to figure out the thinking behind the film's ending, in which Yentl, restored to women's clothes, goes off to America, where, presumably, freed from the binding traditions of the Old World, she can live as a woman and still continue her studies. The thinking is that you have to give the movie audience hope. (And there's even an attempt to show that Hadass will be changed by her encounter with Yentl/Anshel—that, Lord help us, she has had her consciousness raised.) Streisand tries to turn a story about repressed, entangled characters into a sisterhood fable about learning to be a free woman. She tries to transform a quirky folktale into a fairy tale. And it feels almost like a marketing choice.

But this is by no means a playing-it-safe movie. It's a movie about restrictive social conventions and about internal conflicts—about emotions and how they snarl you up. There are no chases, no fistfights or fights of any other kind. The picture is closer to the sensibility of the Ernst Lubitsch musical comedies than it is to films such as *The Turning Point* and *Rich and Famous*. And even when the characters' sex roles are blurred—when they're lost in a multitude of roles—Streisand as director keeps them all clear. Her vision is sustained—until the end. The closing shipboard sequence seems a blatant lift from the "Don't Rain on My Parade" tugboat scene in *Funny Girl*; it feels like a production number, and it violates the whole musical scheme of the movie. It also has Streisand wearing immigrant chic and playing the Streisand image. This misstep must have come from an excess of virtue. Streisand wants to give the audience an educational and spiritual message. She wants Yentl to be—gulp—a role model. Where Streisand's instinct as an artist fails her is in her not recognizing that Yentl exists on a magical plane, and that the attempt to make her a relevant, contemporary heroine yanks her off it. The script, by the English playwright and television writer Jack Rosenthal and Streisand, prepares for this ending by placing the action in 1904, but the Chassidic life that the movie shows belongs to an earlier, make-believe past. At the start of the film, a book peddler calls out "Storybooks for women! Sacred books for men!" By 1904, the novels—*War and Peace*, perhaps, or *Anna Karenina* or *The Brothers Karamazov* or *Middlemarch* or volumes of Dickens or Balzac—might have had more to tell Yentl than she could get out of the sacred texts. (A girl who couldn't study Torah may not have known how lucky she was. When Yentl sings defiantly "Where is it written what it is I'm meant to be?" the answer is: In those sacred books that she's so high on.) This musical creates its own frame of reference; its spirit is violated by earnest intentions. Streisand wants to create a woman hero, but when you read Singer, Yentl isn't the hero—the story is. And at its best the movie is the hero, too.

Streisand's long obsession with the material is well known; she began thinking about the story as a possible film in the late sixties, and bought the screen rights in 1974. Whatever the box-office results, her instinct was sound. It *is* the right material for her. And now that she has made her formal début as a director, her work explains why she, notoriously, asks so many questions of writers and directors and everyone else: that's her method of learning. And it also explains why she has sometimes been unhappy with her directors: she really did know better. *Yentl* is never static or stagy; the images move lyrically. The same intuitions that have guided Streisand in producing her records and her TV specials have guided her here—and taken her into some of the same traps. But, even if you object (as I do) to the choice of songs on her records and the manner of those specials, they're highly professional. Within her own tastes, she aims for perfection. Shooting on Czech locations and in English studios, and with the cinematographer David Watkin, Streisand has made a technically admirable movie, with lovely diffuse, poetic lighting and silky-smooth editing. And she brings out the other performers' most appealing qualities. It's a movie full of likable people. Steven Hill, who plays Hadass's father, gives marvellous line readings, and he has something of the same gnomish charm as Nehemiah Persoff's Papa; they're the elders as a child sees them. And Amy Irving's Hadass has a comically human dimension. The half-closed eyes of this slave princess as she serves dinner make her look as if she were deep in an erotic dream, but they are actually the result of her having had to be up at dawn to buy the fish. Her sleepy, plaintive beauty is the perfect foil for Yentl's skinny, anxious face. When Amy Irving just stands there, with her mass of thick, curly dark-red hair and with ornaments dripping from her head and body, she seems to be overcome by her own heavy perfume. She's dopey and she's sumptuous—she's the image of what women have wanted to be freed from, yet can't help wanting to be.

Streisand and Amy Irving play off each other with a kind of rapport that you don't see in movies directed by men. They have a scene in which Hadass, now in love with Anshel, tries to help him conquer his physical timidity—tries to seduce him—and Yentl is in pain as she backs away. It's a deeply ambiguous scene; thought went into it, as well as care. And toward the end of the film Streisand and Patinkin play a bedroom scene in which Avigdor, who has been sexually attracted to Anshel in the vagrant moments when he wasn't sick with love for Hadass, shows the limits of his understanding of a woman's needs. The scene is simply different from scenes conceived and directed by men; it has a different flavor. Avigdor is revealed as essentially a big, sweet Jewish hunk who could never accept a woman as an equal, and when he and Yentl part, the tapering, feminine hand she holds up in farewell puts a seal on his blindness. The whole movie has a modulated emotionality that seems distinctively feminine. That's part of why the independent-woman-on-her-way-to-the-new-land ending is so silly. There is something genuinely heroic in the mixture of delicacy and strength that gives this movie its suppleness. Within the forty-one-year-old star-director are the perfectly preserved feelings of a shy, frightened girl of twelve. She's also shockingly potent. So was Colette—and there's a suggestion of her in the Yentl who runs her fingers over books as if they were magic objects.

{*The New Yorker*, November 28, 1983}

:: Golden Kimonos

A friend of mine says that when you go to a Kon Ichikawa film "you laugh at things, and you know that Ichikawa is sophisticated enough to make you laugh, but you don't know why you're laughing." I agree. I've just seen Ichikawa's 1983 *The Makioka Sisters*, which opened in New York for a week's run and will open nationally in April, and although I can't quite account for my response, I think it's the most pleasurable movie I've seen in several months—probably since *Stop Making Sense*, back in November. The last hour (the picture runs two hours and twenty minutes) is particularly elating—it gives you a vitalizing mix of emotions. It's like the work of a painter who has perfect control of what color he gives you. At almost seventy, Ichikawa—his more than seventy movies include *The Key (Odd Obsession)*, *Fires on the Plain*, *An Actor's Revenge*, *Tokyo Olympiad*—is a deadpan sophisticate, with a film technique so masterly that he pulls you into the worlds he creates. There doesn't seem to be a narrative in *The Makioka Sisters*, yet you don't feel as if anything is missing. At first, you're like an eavesdropper on a fascinating world that you're ignorant about. But then you find that you're not just watching this film—you're coasting on its rhythms, and gliding past the precipitous spots. Ichikawa celebrates the delicate beauty of the Makioka sisters, and at the same time makes you feel that there's something amusingly perverse in their poise and their politesse. And he plays near-subliminal tricks. You catch things out of the corner of your eye and you're not quite sure how to take them.

The Junichiro Tanizaki novel on which the film is based was written during the Second World War and published in 1948, under the title *A Light Snowfall* (and it has been filmed twice before under this title—in

1950, by Yutaka Abe, and in 1959, by Koji Shima), but it has become known here as *The Makioka Sisters*. The women are the four heiresses of an aristocratic Osaka family. Their mother died long ago, and their father, who was one of the big three of Japan's shipbuilders, followed. Tsuruko (Keiko Kishi), the eldest of the sisters, lives in the family's large, ancestral home in Osaka and controls the shrinking fortunes of the two unmarried younger girls. The film is set in 1938, and the traditions in which these women were raised are slipping away, along with their money. Tsuruko and the next oldest, Sachiko (Yoshiko Sakuma), have married men who took the Makioka name, but its prestige has been tarnished by the behavior of the youngest of the sisters, Taeko (Yuko Kotegawa), who caused a scandal five years earlier, when she ran off with a jeweller's son and tried to get married, though the Makioka family's strict code of behavior required that Yukiko (Sayuri Yoshinaga), the next to youngest, had to be married first. The scandal was augmented, because the newspaper got things wrong—wrote that Yukiko had eloped, and then, when Tsuruko's husband complained about the error, mucked things up more in correcting the mistake. Taeko still lives in Sachiko's home, along with Yukiko, but she's trying to achieve independence through a career. She wants to start a business, but Tsuruko won't give her her inheritance until she's married, and she isn't allowed to marry. It's Catch-22. She's flailing around, and waiting for the demure Yukiko to say yes to one of her suitors.

Each suitor is brought to a formal ceremony—a *miai*—where the prospective bride sits across a table from the prospective groom, with members of their families and go-betweens seated around them. At thirty, Yukiko is a veteran of these gatherings, but she has still not found a man to her liking. During the year that the movie spans, there are several of these *miai*—each a small slapstick comedy of manners. The last, when Yukiko finally meets what she has been waiting for (and the camera travels up the suitor's full height), has a special tickle for the audience, because you can see exactly why Yukiko said no to the others and why she says yes to this one.

These *miai* are just about the only formal, structured events; in between them, Taeko gets into highly unstructured emotional entanglements—falling in love with a photographer who becomes ill and dies, taking up next with a bartender, becoming pregnant, sampling a few lower depths, and planning to go to work, which means another scandal. While Taeko wears Western clothes and goes off on her own, the exquisite, subdued Yukiko stays in her sister's house. (The two married women's houses are like theatres-in-the-round, with the four sisters and the servants as each other's audience.) Is Yukiko the priss that her Southern-belle curls and her old-fashioned-girl manner suggest? Not by what you catch in glimpses. Yukiko, who clings to the hierarchic family values of the past, with all the bowing and the arch turning away of the head and the eyes cast down, is inscrutable, like Carole Laure in Blier's *Get Out Your Handkerchiefs*. But we see the come-on in her modesty. That's what's enchanting in the older sisters, too. Taeko, the animated modern girl, the one asserting her sexual freedom, is the least teasing, the least suggestive, but when she's with the others and in a kimono she's lovely. They're beauties, all four of them, with peerless skin tones, and they move as if always conscious that they must be visual poetry. (And they are, they are.)

Yukiko appears to be the most submissive, but she's strong-willed, and she has a sly streak. Living in Sachiko's house, she dresses with the door open to the hall Sachiko's husband passes through. And when she sees him looking at her bare thigh, she covers herself slowly, seductively. Sachiko, who observes what's going on, gets so fussed she starts tripping on her kimono and bumping into things. When she sees her husband kissing Yukiko, she crushes a piece of fruit in her fist and shoves it into her mouth to keep from crying out. And she renews her efforts to find Yukiko a suitable husband.

Ichikawa has said, in an interview, that he took his cue from the book's original title, *A Light Snowfall*. He said that light snow, which melts away instantly, "expresses something both fleeting and beautiful," and that he looked at the sisters in these terms. And that may help to explain why it's so difficult to pin down the pleasure the film gives. It's like a succession of evanescent revelations—the images are stylized and formal, yet the quick cutting melts them away. It's not as if he were trying to catch a moment— rather, he's trying to catch traces of its passing. When the four stroll among the cherry blossoms in Kyoto, the whole image becomes cherry-toned and they disappear.

Ichikawa's temperament brings something more furtive and glinting to the material than Tanizaki gave it in the novel. (In its spirit, the movie actually seems more closely related to other Tanizaki novels, such as *The Key*, than it does to this one.) The film builds to its last hour; what's distinctive about the buildup is that the darts of humor don't allow you a full release. Taeko's first bid for independence involves becoming an artist, and her sisters speak of her work in perfectly level, admiring tones. Sachiko even pays for a show at a gallery. Taeko's art is the creation of dolls—exact, life-like small reproductions of girls in heavy makeup and elaborate gowns, and with eyes that open and close. They could be little Makioka sisters. This is sneak-attack humor, played absolutely straight—Ichikawa is satirizing the material from within. And when this kind of suppressed joke plays right next to sequences such as a display of shimmering golden kimonos that the Makioka girls' father had bought for Yukiko's wedding presents, with one after another placed center screen—a glorious celebration of textures and color—an unusual kind of tension and excitement builds in the viewer.

I don't know enough about the Osaka culture to interpret the film as social criticism or as an elegy to a vanishing form of feminine grace. (Ichikawa himself comes from the Osaka area.) But the actresses are perfectly believable as the works of art that women like the Makioka sisters were trained to be. And it's easy to be entranced with the world that the film creates. (The industrialization of Japan is kept on the periphery.) When the banking company that Tsuruko's husband works for transfers him to Tokyo, and Tsuruko doesn't want to leave the Makioka home—a cool palace of polished wood that seems built on an intimate scale—you don't want to leave it, either. The rich colors, the darkness, the low-key lighting—they're intoxicating. When Tsuruko decides to make the move, and her husband falls to his knees to thank her, it has the emotional effect of a great love scene. But the film's finest moment comes at the very end. It's a variation of Joel McCrea's death scene in Peckinpah's *Ride the High Country*, when the old marshal falls out of the film frame. Yukiko is going off to be married; she boards the train in soft vanishing snow, and we realize that she meant far more to Sachiko's husband than a casual flirtation. We see him alone, getting drunk, and he looks terrible—he's all broken up. Then images of the four sisters among the cherry blossoms are held on the screen in slow motion that's like a succession of stills. At last there's only Yukiko's head in the center of the screen, and the head of her disconsolate brother-in-law passes across the screen behind her and out of her life.

The horrible thing about Peckinpah's recent death was that he was the most unfulfilled of great directors. Like Peckinpah, Ichikawa has had more than his share of trouble with production executives, but he has weathered it, and there's a triumphant simplicity about his work here. This venerable director is doing what so many younger directors have claimed to be doing: he's making visual music. The themes are worked out in shades of pearl and ivory for the interiors and bursts of color outside—cherry and maple and red-veined burgundy. He's making a movie that we understand musically, and he's doing it without turning the actors into zombies, and without losing his sense of how corruption and beauty and humor are all rolled up together.

{*The New Yorker*, March 11, 1985}

from
HOOKED

:: Out There and In Here

"Maybe I'm sick, but I want to see that again."
—Overheard after a showing of *Blue Velvet*.

When you come out of the theatre after seeing David Lynch's *Blue Velvet*, you certainly know that you've seen something. You wouldn't mistake frames from *Blue Velvet* for frames from any other movie. It's an anomaly—the work of a genius naïf. If you feel that there's very little art between you and the filmmaker's psyche, it may be because there's less than the usual amount of inhibition. Lynch doesn't censor his sexual fantasies, and the film's hypercharged erotic atmosphere makes it something of a trance-out, but his humor keeps breaking through, too. His fantasies may come from his unconscious, but he recognizes them for what they are, and he's tickled by them. The film is consciously purplish and consciously funny, and the two work together in an original, down-home way.

Shot in Wilmington, North Carolina, it's set in an archetypal small, sleepy city, Lumberton, where the radio station's call letters are WOOD, and the announcer says, "At the sound of the falling tree," and then, as the tree falls, "it's 9:30." Not more than three minutes into the film, you recognize that this peaceful, enchanted, white-picket-fence community, where the eighties look like the fifties, is the creepiest sleepy city you've ever seen. The subject of the movie is exactly that: the mystery and madness hidden in the "normal." At the beginning, the wide images (the film is shot in CinemaScope ratio: 2.35 to 1) are meticulously bright and sharp-edged; you feel that you're seeing every detail of the architecture, the layout of homes and apartments, the furnishings and potted plants, the

745

women's dresses. It's so hyperfamiliar it's scary. The vivid red of the roses by the white fence makes them look like hothouse blooms, and the budding yellow tulips are poised, eager to open. Later, the light is low, but all through this movie the colors are insistent, objects may suddenly be enlarged to fill the frame, and a tiny imagined sound may be amplified to a thunderstorm. The style might be described as hallucinatory clinical realism.

When Mr. Beaumont, of Beaumont's hardware store, is watering his lawn and has a seizure of some sort—probably a cerebral hemorrhage—the water keeps shooting out. It drenches his fallen body, and a neighbor's dog jumps on top of him, frisking and trying to drink from the spray. The green grass, enlarged so that the blades are as tall as redwood trees, is teeming with big black insects, and their quarrelsome buzz and hiss displaces all other sounds. When Jeffrey Beaumont (Kyle MacLachlan), home from college to be near his stricken father and take care of the store, walks back from a visit to the hospital, he dawdles in a vacant lot and spots something unexpected in the grass and weeds: a human ear with an attached hank of hair, and ants crawling all over it. The ear looks like a seashell; in closeup, with the camera moving into the dark canal, it becomes the cosmos, and the sound is what you hear when you put a shell to your ear—the roar of the ocean.

Jeffrey's curiosity about the severed ear—whose head it came from and why it was cut off—leads him to Lumberton's tainted underside, a netherworld of sleazy interconnections. A viewer knows intuitively that this is a coming-of-age picture—that Jeffrey's discovery of this criminal, sadomasochistic network has everything to do with his father's becoming an invalid and his own new status as an adult. It's as if David Lynch were saying, "It's a frightening world out there, and"—tapping his head—"in here."

Wholesome as Jeffrey looks, he's somewhat drawn to violence and kinkiness. But he doesn't quite know that yet, and it's certainly not how he explains himself to Sandy (Laura Dern), a fair-haired high-school senior and the daughter of the police detective investigating the matter of the ear. She has become Jeffrey's confederate, and when she questions the nature of his interest in the case he speaks of being involved with "something that was always hidden," of being "in the middle of a mystery." Sandy tantalizes him with what she's overheard the police saying, and he tantalizes her with the strange, "hidden" things he learns about. During their scenes together, an eerie faraway organ is playing melodies that float in the air, and the sound italicizes the two kids' blarney. It's like the organ music in an old soap opera; it turns their confabs into parody, and tells us that they're in a dream world. Sometimes when Jeffrey tells Sandy what he thinks is going on it's as if he had dreamed it and then woke up and found out it had happened. Jeffrey himself is the mystery that Sandy is drawn to (perhaps the tiny gold earring he wears is part of his attraction), and you can't help giggling a little when she turns to him with a worried, earnest face and says, "I don't know if you're a detective or a pervert." She's still a kid; she thinks it's either/or. Jeffrey is soon withholding some of his adventures from her, because they're not just mysteriously erotic—they're downright carnal, and, yes, he's smack in the middle of it all. He has been pulled—with no kicking or screaming—into the inferno of corrupt adult sexuality.

Dorothy Vallens (Isabella Rossellini) is soft and brunette and faintly, lusciously foreign; she has had a child, and she's enough older than Jeffrey to have the allure of an "experienced woman." A torch singer in a night club outside the city limits, she wears a moth-eaten mop of curls and lives at the Deep River Apartments in musty rooms that look as if they'd sprouted their own furniture. The gloomy walls—mauve gone brown—suggest the chic of an earlier era, when perhaps the building was considered fashionable (and the elevator worked). Sandy has told Jeffrey that the police think Dorothy Vallens is involved in the mutilation case, and have her under surveillance. Jeffrey puts her under closer surveillance. The moviemaker doesn't do any interpreting for you: you simply watch and listen, and what ensues rings so many bells in your head that you may get a little woozy.

Hiding in Dorothy's closet at night, Jeffrey peeks at her through the slatted door while she undresses. She hears him and, grabbing a kitchen knife, orders him out of his hiding place and forces him to strip. When he has nothing on but his shorts, she pulls them down and begins fondling him, but sends him back into the closet when she has a caller—Frank the crime boss, Mr. Macho Sleazeball himself, played by Dennis Hopper. Frank is an infantile tough-guy sadist who calls her "Mommy," wallops her if she forgets to call him "Daddy," and wallops her harder if she happens to look at him. All this seems to be part of their regular ritual; he demands his bourbon (as if he's sick of telling her), has her dim the lights, and he takes out an inhaler mask (for some unspecified gas) to heighten his sensations during sex. (The gas is probably a booster to whatever drugs he's on.) He also uses a fetish—the sash of Dorothy's blue velvet bathrobe. Jeffrey, in his closet, doesn't make a sound this time; he's transfixed by what he can just barely see. It's like a sick-joke version of the primal scene, and this curious child watches his parents do some very weird things. After Frank leaves, Jeffrey attempts to help the weary, bruised woman, but all she wants is sex. She's photographed in a clinch, with her face upside down and her ruby lips parted in a sly smile that exposes her gleaming front teeth—especially the one that has a teasing chip, as if someone had taken a small bite out of it.

When Jeffrey comes to see her again, he knocks on the door. She greets him eagerly—almost reproachfully—with "I looked for you in my closet tonight." (That line is a giddy classic.) The third night, they're on her bed after a round or two of intercourse. Trying to overcome his reluctance to hit her, she asks, "Are you a bad boy . . . do you want to do bad things?" We know the answer before he does. He's having trouble breathing.

Isabella Rossellini doesn't show anything like the acting technique that her mother, Ingrid Bergman, had, but she's willing to try things, and she doesn't hold back. Dorothy is a dream of a freak. Walking around her depressing apartment in her black bra and scanties, with blue eye-shadow and red high heels, she's a woman in distress right out of the pulps; she has the plushy, tempestuous look of heroines who are described as "bewitching." (She even has the kind of nostrils that cover artists can represent accurately with two dots.) Rossellini's accent is useful: it's part of Dorothy's strangeness. And Rossellini's echoes of her mother's low voice help to place this kitschy seductress in an unreal world. She has a special physical quality, too. There's nothing of the modern American woman about her. When she's naked, she's not protected, like the stars who are pummelled into shape and lighted to show their muscular perfection. She's defenselessly, tactilely naked, like the nudes the Expressionists painted.

Jeffrey, commuting between Dorothy, the blue lady of the night, and Sandy, the sunshine girl, suggests a character left over from *Our Town*. (He lives in an indefinite mythic present that feels like the past—he's split between the older woman he has sex with but doesn't love and the girl he loves but doesn't have sex with.) Kyle MacLachlan is in just about every scene, and he gives a phenomenal performance. As the hero of *Dune*, he may have been swallowed up in the sand, but here he's ideally cast. His proper look is perfect for a well-brought-up young fellow who's scared of his dirty thoughts (but wants to have them anyway). And when Jeffrey and Laura Dern's Sandy first meet and they make each other laugh, you relax with them and laugh, too, because you know that the two performers are going to work together like magic. Laura Dern brings a growing-up-fast passion to Sandy's love for Jeffrey, and she has an emotional fire that she didn't get to demonstrate in *Mask* or *Smooth Talk*. Lynch takes a plunge when he stages the high-schoolers' party that Sandy takes Jeffrey to: the two of them begin to dance and begin to kiss, and can't stop kissing. "Mysteries of Love," the song that they're dancing to, is scored using an organ, but now the organ isn't mocking them—the music swells to do justice to their feelings. The sequence may recall Sissy Spacek's romantic whirl at the prom in De Palma's *Carrie*, but the tone is different: we're being told that these two are not going to let go of each other, that they're moving into the unknown together. And the song, with lyrics by Lynch and music by Angelo Badalamenti (who wrote the score), carries the emotion over to the later scenes when Sandy's belief in Jeffrey is tested. (The movie may frighten some adolescents, as *Carrie* did, though the violent images aren't obtrusive; you don't quite take them in at first—it's only as the camera is pulling back from them that you see them clearly.)

As the uncontrollable Frank, in his slick leather outfits, Dennis Hopper gives the movie a jolt of horrific energy. Frank is lewd and dangerous; you feel he does what he does just for the hell of it. (He uses his inhaler to heighten the sensation of murder, too.) And as Ben, one of Frank's business associates, Dean Stockwell is a smiling wonder; you stare at his kissy makeup, the pearly jewel that he wears halfway up his ear, his druggy contentment. Frank refers to Ben as "suave," but that's not the half of it. Miming to Roy Orbison's song "In Dreams," about "the candy-colored clown they call the sandman," he's so magnetic that you momentarily forget everything else that's supposed to be going on.

Actually, it's easy to forget about the plot, because that's where Lynch's naïve approach has its disadvantages: Lumberton's subterranean criminal life needs to be as organic as the scrambling insects, and it isn't. Lynch doesn't show us how the criminals operate or how they're bound to each other. So the story isn't grounded in anything and has to be explained in little driblets of dialogue. But *Blue Velvet* has so much aural-visual humor and poetry that it's sustained despite the wobbly plot and the bland functional dialogue (that's sometimes a deliberate spoof of small-town conventionality and sometimes maybe not). It's sustained despite the fact that Lynch's imagistic talent, which is for the dark and unaccountable, flattens out in the sunlight scenes, as in the ordinary, daily moments between parents and children. One key character is never clarified: We can't tell if Sandy's father (played by George Dickerson) is implicated in the corruption, or if we're meant to accept him as a straight arrow out of a fifties F.B.I. picture. Lynch skimps on these commercial-movie basics and fouls up on them, too, but it's as if he were reinventing movies. His work goes back to the avant-garde filmmakers of the twenties and thirties, who were often painters—and he himself trained to be one. He takes off from the experimental traditions that Hollywood has usually ignored.

This is his first film from his own original material since *Eraserhead* (which was first shown in 1977), and in some ways it's linked to that film's stately spookiness. Lynch's longtime associate, the cinematographer Frederick Elmes, lighted both films, and he has given *Blue Velvet* a comparable tactility; real streets look like paintings you could touch—you feel as if you could moosh your fingers in the colors. There are also reminders of the musical numbers in *Eraserhead*, which were like a form of dementia. (Lynch used an organ there, too.) With Rossellini singing at the club, and vocalists like Bobby Vinton on the soundtrack and tunes layered in and out of the orchestral score, *Blue Velvet* suggests a musical on themes from our pop unconscious. There are noises in there, of course, and Alan Splet, who started working with Lynch when he was doing shorts and has been his sound man on all his features (*Eraserhead* was followed by *The Elephant Man*, in 1980, and *Dune*, in 1984), combines them so that, say, when Jeffrey walks up the seven flights to Dorothy's apartment the building has a pumping, groaning sound. It could be an ancient furnace or foghorns or a heavy old animal that's winded. The mix of natural sounds with mechanical-industrial noises gives the images an ambience that's hokey and gothic and yet totally unpretentious—maybe because Lynch's subject is normal American fantasy life. Even that fetishized blue velvet robe is tacky, like something you could pick up in the red brick department store on Main Street.

Blue Velvet is a comedy, yet it puts us—or, at least, some of us—in an erotic trance. The movie keeps ribbing the clean-cut Jeffrey, yet we're caught up in his imagination. It must be that Lynch's use of irrational material works the way it's supposed to: at some not fully conscious level we read his images. When Frank catches Jeffrey with "Mommy" and takes him for a ride—first to Ben's hangout and then to a deserted spot—the car is packed with Frank's thugs, Dorothy, in her robe, and a large-headed, big-bellied woman in a short, pink skirt who has been necking with one of the guys. When Frank parks and he and his thugs start punching out Jeffrey, the pink-skirted woman climbs up on the roof of the car and, to the sound of that sandman song, dances aimlessly, impassively, like a girl in a topless bar. (She's in her dream world, too.) In a later scene, a man who has been shot several times remains standing, but he's no longer looking at anything; he faces a one-eared dead man sitting up in a chair, with the blue velvet sash in his mouth, and the two are suspended in time, like figures posed together in a wax museum, or plaster figures by George Segal retouched by Francis Bacon. Almost every scene has something outlandishly off in it, something that jogs your memory or your thinking, like the collection of fat women at Ben's joint, who look as if they were objects in a still-life. Or there may be something that just tweaks your memory, like the worrywart old maid—Jeffrey's Aunt Barbara (Frances Bay). Or a bit of comedy that's underplayed, like the shot of Jeffrey's mother (Priscilla Pointer) and Sandy's mother (Hope Lange) getting to know each other and looking interchangeable. (The only scene that feels thin—that lacks surprise—is Dorothy's lushly romanticized reunion with her child; for a few seconds, the film goes splat.)

It's the slightly disjunctive quality of Lynch's scenes (and the fact that we don't question them, because they don't feel arbitrary to us) that makes the movie so hypnotic—that, and the slow, assured sensuousness of his editing rhythms. This is possibly the only coming-of-age movie in which sex has the danger and the heightened excitement of a horror picture. It's the fantasy (rather than the plot) that's organic, and there's no sticky-sweet lost innocence, because the darkness was always there, inside.

The film's kinkiness isn't alienating—its naïveté keeps it from that. And its vision isn't alienating: this is American darkness—darkness in color, darkness with a happy ending. Lynch might turn out to be the first populist surrealist—a Frank Capra of dream logic. *Blue Velvet* does have a homiletic side. It's about a young man's learning through flabbergasting and violent experience to appreciate a relatively safe and manageable sex life. And when Sandy's father, speaking of the whole nightmarish business of the ear, says to Jeffrey, "It's over now," the film cuts to daylight. But with Lynch as the writer and director the homily has a little zinger. Sandy, who may have watched too many daytime soaps, has dreamed that the morbid darkness will be dispelled when thousands of robins arrive bringing love— a dream that she tells Jeffrey (to the accompaniment of organ music twitting her vision). When a plump robin lands on the kitchen windowsill, it has an insect in its beak.

{*The New Yorker*, September 22, 1986}

:: Irish Voices

The announcement that John Huston was making a movie of James Joyce's "The Dead" raised the question "Why?" What could images do that Joyce's words hadn't? And wasn't Huston pitting himself against a master who, though he was only twenty-five when he wrote the story, had given it full form? (Or nearly full—Joyce's language gains from being read aloud.) It turns out that those who love the story needn't have worried. Huston directed the movie, at eighty, from a wheelchair, jumping up to look through the camera, with oxygen tubes trailing from his nose to a portable generator; most of the time, he had to watch the actors on a video monitor outside the set and use a microphone to speak to the crew. Yet he went into dramatic areas that he'd never gone into before—funny, warm family scenes that might be thought completely out of his range. He seems to have brought the understanding of Joyce's ribald humor which he gained from his knowledge of *Ulysses* into this earlier work; the minor characters who are shadowy on the page now have a Joycean vividness. Huston has knocked the academicism out of them and developed the undeveloped parts of the story. He's given it a marvellous filigree that enriches the social life. And he's done it all in a mood of tranquil exuberance, as if moviemaking had become natural to him, easier than breathing.

The movie is set on the sixth of January, 1904, the Feast of the Epiphany. The Morkan sisters and their fortyish niece—three spinster musicians and music teachers—are giving their annual dance and supper, in their Dublin town house, and as their relatives and friends arrive the foibles and obsessions of the hostesses and the guests mesh and turn festive. The actors—Irish or of Irish heritage—become the members of a family and

753

a social set who know who's going to get too loud, who's going to get upset about what. They know who's going to make a fool of himself: Freddy Malins (Donal Donnelly)—he drinks. Even before Freddy shows up, the two Misses Morkan—ancient, gray Julia (Cathleen Delany), whose fragile face seems to get skinnier as the night wears on, and hearty Kate (Helena Carroll)—are worried. They're relieved when their favorite nephew, Gabriel Conroy (Donal McCann), arrives, with his wife, Gretta (Anjelica Huston); they can count on Gabriel to keep an eye on Freddy for them. It's the reliable, slightly pompous Gabriel—a college professor and book reviewer—who has an epiphany this night, and we, too, experience it.

During the party, Gabriel tries to entertain Freddy's excruciating old bore of a mother (Marie Kean), a self-satisfied biddy who smiles a sweet social smile at Gabriel but treats her son with contempt. Mrs. Malins wears an evening hat perched on her white ringlets and sits with one hand on her fancy walking stick; she's so old she seems to have the bones of a little bird, yet Freddy looks to her for approval, like a child. When he sees her expression, he's left openmouthed, chagrined, and with a faint—almost imperceptible—stutter. He shrinks. She thinks she would like him to be like Gabriel, but she and Freddy match up beyond one's saddest dreams. She sneers at him for not being the manly son she can be proud of, and turns him into a silly ass. Ever hopeful, he's crushed over and over again, his mustachioed upper lip sinking toward his chin.

Gabriel looks more authoritative than he feels. A stabilizing presence, and the man whose task it is to represent all the guests in a speech thanking the hostesses, he's like an observer at the party, but he's also observing himself, and he's not too pleased with how he handles things—especially his response to a young woman who chides him for spending his summer vacations abroad and for not devoting himself to the study of the Irish language. He would like to be suave with her, but he's so full of doubts about himself that he gets hot under the collar. And Gabriel feels his middle-aged mediocrity when he's speechifying. He plays the man of literary eminence, toasting Aunt Julia and Aunt Kate and their niece, Mary Jane (Ingrid Craigie), after calling them the Three Graces of the Dublin musical world. But when the assembled guests drink to them he sees the ladies' gaiety go beyond gaiety. They can't contain their pleasure at being complimented; Julia's hectic, staring eyes fill with tears, and a high flush appears on her ancient girlish dimples. And he gets a whiff of mortality.

The movie itself is a toast to Irish hospitality and to the spinster sisterhood of music teachers, which has probably never before been saluted with such affection. Starting with the sound of an Irish harp under the opening titles, and with frequent reminders of the importance of the pianists who play for the dancing at the party, the picture is about the music that men and women make, and especially about the music of Irish voices. At supper, the characters go at their pet subjects: opera past and present, and famous tenors, dead and alive. They know each other's positions so well that they taunt each other.

One of the guests—a tenor, Mr. D'Arcy (Frank Patterson)—has declined to sing, but after most of the others have left he succumbs to the pleading of a young lady he has been flirting with, and sings "The Lass of Aughrim." Gretta Conroy, who has been making her farewells and is coming down the stairs to join Gabriel, stands hushed, leaning on the bannister listening. Mr. D'Arcy's voice, resonating in the stairwell, has the special trained purity of great Irish tenors; the whole world seems still while he sings, and for a few seconds after. And Gabriel, seeing his wife deeply affected, is fired with sexual longing for her. He hopes to awaken her passion. But in the carriage she's sad and silent, while he makes clumsy conversation. When they reach the hotel where they are to spend the night, she falls asleep in tears after telling him about her youth in Galway and about a consumptive young boy, Michael Furey, her first love, who sang that song, "The Lass of Aughrim." Michael Furey had left his sickbed to come see her on a rainy night in winter, and died a week later, when he was only seventeen.

In the course of the evening, Gabriel has been evaluating how he's doing, and feeling more and more like a solemn stuffed shirt. Now everything he thought he knew about Gretta and himself has been sent whirling. He feels that his own love for her is a dismal thing compared with the dead boy's, and he gets beyond his own ego—he's moved by the boy's action. He thinks about carnal desire and about "the vast hosts of the dead." He sees Aunt Julia as she had looked a few hours earlier when she danced with him, and imagines that she will be the next to go. And Huston, having intensified our vision of the family life that the final passages of the story come out of, implicitly acknowledges that he can't improve on their music. In the story, these passages are Gabriel's thoughts. Here Huston simply gives over to them, and we hear them spoken by Gabriel, as the snow outside blends the living and the dead. Joyce's language seems to melt into pure emotion, and something in Gabriel melts.

Huston moved to Galway in the early fifties, and it was his home base for roughly twenty years—it's where Anjelica Huston and his son Tony Huston, who wrote the script, grew up. But when he made this movie he shot the Dublin interiors in a warehouse in Valencia, California, and the snow was plastic. Huston wasn't strong enough to travel; he completed the film early in the summer, and died in August, after his eighty-first birthday. The picture he left us is a tribute to Joyce, whose words complete and transcend what we've been watching. But the humor is from the two of them, and from the actors.

The movie is a demonstration of what, in Huston's terms, movies can give you that print can't: primarily, the glory of performers—performers with faces that have been written on by time and skill, performers with voices. It's as if Huston were saying, "Making a movie of a classic isn't anything as simple as just depriving you of the work of your imagination. Your imagination couldn't create these people for you. Only these specific actors could do it." And, of course, they could do it only with Huston guiding their movements and Tony Huston providing their words. And, yes, your imagination is now tied to these actors, but they bring a spontaneity and joy into the movie which you don't experience from reading the story.

It isn't simply that they physically embody the characters; they embody what the movie is saying. When Aunt Julia, once a respected local soprano, is prevailed on to sing, and comes out with "Arrayed for the Bridal," the quaver in her thin voice is theme music. So is her vaguely rattled look. Poor, effusive Freddy tells her that he has never heard her sing so well, then goes even further and tells her he has never heard her sing half so well. That's right out of the story, but it's different when we can see and hear the woman he's praising so idiotically. Cathleen Delany is superb as Julia, whose memory is fading, and who sometimes forgets where she is. There's a moment at the beginning when she's in the receiving line and looks at someone blankly; asked if she doesn't remember the person from last year, she rallies with "Of course, of course." She's leaving this world, but she's still a firm social liar. Donal Donnelly isn't just a great drunk; he knows how to play a drunk sobering up. By the end of the party, Freddy is almost a man of the world. Marie Kean's Mrs. Malins is such a smiley little dragon she makes you laugh; the performance is high clowning. And Helena Carroll's Aunt Kate is wonderfully obstreperous when she berates the pope for turning women (like her sister) out of the choirs and putting in little boys. Ingrid Craigie's Mary Jane, the peacemaker, soothes Aunt Kate's sense of injury (you know it's an oft-indulged sense of injury) and steers people to safe ground; Mary Jane has a softness about her, a loving docility. Dan O'Herlihy is the Protestant Mr. Browne, a florid old gent who is delighted to hear Kate lashing out at the pope; he fancies himself a gallant and jovially drinks himself to sleep. Huston never before blended his actors so intuitively, so musically.

The change in his work is in our closeness to the people on the screen. Freddy is such a hopeful fellow, always trying to please, that we can see ourselves in his worst foolishness. We can see ourselves in Julia and Kate and in the stiff, self-tormenting Gabriel. And when Anjelica Huston's Gretta speaks of Michael Furey and says "O, the day I heard that, that he was dead," we hear the echoes of the pain that she felt all those years ago. We hear them very clearly, because of the fine, unimpassioned way that the actress plays Gretta, leaving the tragic notes to Gabriel. Gretta's is only one of the stories of the dead, but Joyce wrote the work right after his Nora told him of her early great love, and it's the most romanticized, the most piercing. The stillness in the air during Frank Patterson's singing of the melancholy "Lass" is part of the emotional perfection of the moment. But the film finds its full meaning in the stillness of Donal McCann's meticulous tones at the end—in Gabriel's helpless self-awareness. He mourns because he is revealed to himself as less than he thought he was. He mourns because he sees that the whole world is in mourning. And he accepts our common end: the snow falls on everyone.

{*The New Yorker*, December 14, 1987}

::   The Lady From the Sea

Every now and then, I hear from young women who say that they want to write or direct movies but have no interest in car chases, coke busts, or shoot-outs. They want to make movies about personal relations and emotional states. Generally, I encourage them, while acknowledging my dread of the mess of vague, inchoate feelings that could be the result. I caution them that it takes more talent and more tough-mindedness to put a sensibility on the screen than it does to film a gunfight, and, lest they think that their desire is a specifically feminine one, I point out movies such as Kershner's *Loving*, Alan Parker's *Shoot the Moon*, Ichikawa's *The Makioka Sisters*, and Satyajit Ray's *Days and Nights in the Forest* and *The Home and the World*. But young women directors may be drawn to get at emotional states with less plot apparatus—almost nakedly.

Gillian Armstrong reports that when she began work on her new picture, *High Tide*, she pinned a note above her desk: "Blood ties. Water. Running away." That note tells us what the movie is about more truthfully than a plot summary would. Shot from a script by Laura Jones, *High Tide* is a woman's picture in the way that *Stella Dallas* was—it's about the mother-daughter bond. But it's also a woman's picture in a new way: Gillian Armstrong, the Australian who directed *My Brilliant Career* at twenty-seven and then made *Starstruck* and *Mrs. Soffel*, has the technique and the assurance to put a woman's fluid, not fully articulated emotions right onto the screen. And she has an actress—Judy Davis, the Sybylla of *My Brilliant Career* and the Adela Quested of David Lean's *A Passage to India*—who's a genius at moods.

As Lilli, one of three backup singers for a touring Elvis imitator, Judy Davis is contemptuous of the cruddy act, contemptuous of herself. Too smart for what she's doing, Lilli is a derisive tease—a spoiler. Feeling put down, the dumb-lug Elvis fires her, and she's left alone at the beginning of winter in a ramshackle beach town on the magnificent, windswept coast of New South Wales. There, stuck in the Mermaid Caravan Park while she tries to scrounge up the money to pay for repairs on her car, she encounters her teen-age daughter, Ally (Claudia Karvan).

When Lilli's young surfer husband died, she felt lost; she gave up the baby to her mother-in-law, Bet (Jan Adele), and has been drifting ever since, and getting stinko and passing out. Bet, a singer in talent shows at the local restaurant–night spot, who works at a fish-packing coop and runs a soft-ice-cream stand, is a rowdy, belligerent woman, and she's devoted to Ally: Bet has taken care of her for thirteen years, but has no idea how unhappy the girl is—the rules Bet lays down to protect the kid cut her off from other kids and make her miserable. Lilli has an immediate rapport with the lonely Ally, even before she knows that Ally is her daughter, and after she knows, she can't take her eyes off the kid. When they're at the public baths at the same time, Lilli stares at Ally's legs under the stall door; Ally is shaving them, and Lilli stands there tranced out, sick with love and longing.

This remote, working-class, tourist-town Australia suggests a corrupted frontier settlement. The view of the cliffs and the sea includes the rusted debris of the caravan dwellers; the Mermaid is like the seedy trailer parks on the outskirts of American towns, but with a more pervasive sense of rootlessness and movement. The men and women, in their faded denims and cheap pastels, blend with the blue of the water. These people survive by changing their occupations with the seasons; they work hard in small businesses that look as if they had been thrown up out of packing crates. You see the crumminess of the town in the big, garish joint where the Elvis act is put on, and where Bet sings. (All the entertainers hit the same high decibel level.) An aging cowboy headliner called Country Joe (Bob Purtell) performs there against a backdrop of a huge bull's skull, and you get a taste of matey entertainment at a smoker, where Lilli earns the money she needs by doing a strip. You also see some less coarse men: Colin Friels as a fisher-man who responds to Lilli's wry half smiles and likes her too much to watch her at the smoker, and Mark Hembrow as a garage mechanic who takes a chance on her and lets her have her car. Gillian Armstrong's style is crisp, and the camera whizzes past the scenic wonders, often turning rocks and road lines into abstractions. The superb cinematographer Russell Boyd chose to be his own camera operator this time—so he could have the excitement of giving Armstrong the fast tracking movement she wanted, and she could concentrate on the performances.

Lilli and her young teen-age daughter match up; you feel that they're true kin—they belong with each other. But their scenes together are courtship dances that Lilli keeps pulling back from, terrified of taking on the responsibility of motherhood when she hasn't been able to make it alone. You may intuit that her having abandoned the child who was her only hold on life is the reason she has trashed herself. She doesn't look at her failures that kindly, though. And Bet—piggy-faced and broad in the beam—tells her she's riffraff. At first, Bet seems threatening. It isn't until she has spent a night with Country Joe, and her steady fellow (John Clayton) has used his truck to ram Country Joe's fancy car, that we fully appreciate what a frank, lusty bawd she is. She wins us over when she seeks assurance from Country Joe that he feels the night with her was worth the damage to his car. Bet isn't a monster; she's simply the wrong person to be raising the slender, pensive Ally, whose emotions are hidden away, like her mother's. Even Bet's sensitivities are crude.

Jan Adele makes her film début as the overprotective Bet, but she's a former vaudevillian who has been in show biz since she was three, and has done everything from ballet in tent shows, through singing with bands, to TV comedy. All her experience informs her presence here; it's a real turn, and the fact that she acts in a totally different style from that of Judy Davis (and the fourteen-year-old Claudia Karvan) strengthens the movie. Jan Adele projects to the rafters; she hands you every emotion neatly tagged. She's marvellous at it; she gives you the sense that in this rough country Bet hasn't been exposed to much in the way of amenities, or subtleties, either. The drama is in our feeling that Lilli must not leave her daughter in the embrace of this raucous old trouper. Bet isn't in the spirit of the film.

Lilli is so overcast—so unsure of herself—that we feel a mystery in her, despite her level gaze. Tall, skinny, red-haired Judy Davis was only twenty-three when she played her first leading role onscreen—in *My Brilliant Career*, in 1979. She may never have looked as beautiful as she does here in a motel-room scene with Colin Friels: he's lying on the bed, and she's standing by the window with her wavy hair wet from the shower. She's like a sea goddess. The first time we see her in this movie, she's on the stage in a tawdry mermaid dress of sequins and ruffles. The first time we see Ally, she's in the water, floating in a tidal pool; then she gets on her father's old surfboard—surfing is her refuge from the noisy junkiness of life with Bet. And the sight of the sea is mucked up by what people have done to the coast.

Gillian Armstrong and her scenarist don't connect the dotted lines, and you don't want them to. I expected more to go on between Lilli and the Colin Friels character, maybe because Davis has a special serenity with Friels (he's her husband), but the script doesn't build on this accord. That's a small matter; so is Lilli's unnecessary waffling at the end. The movie's emotional suggestiveness may be off-putting to some people; they may be so trained to expect action that they'll complain that not enough is going on. But a great many young women are likely to feel that this is the movie they've wanted to make. (Some of them have already made pieces of it; the humiliation of the striptease has been the subject of many women film students' shorts.) The acute, well-written script acknowledges the basic ineffableness of some experiences, especially in a self-conscious scene toward the end where Lilli tries to explain to Ally why she deserted her. And it all goes together. It goes with the way Lilli looks when she's about to leave town and abandon her daughter for the second time; paying off the garage mechanic and thanking him, she's white as death. Judy Davis has been compared with Jeanne Moreau, and that's apt, but she's Moreau without the cultural swank, the high-fashion gloss. And there's no movie-ish gloss here, either. Men don't mistreat Lilli, and she doesn't mistreat them. She just screws herself over, and the film's only question is, Will she stop?

{*The New Yorker*, February 22, 1988}

from
MOVIE
LOVE

:: Unreal

Pedro Almodóvar may be the only first-rank director who sets out to tickle himself and the audience. He doesn't violate his principles to do it; his principles begin with freedom and pleasure. Born in 1951, this Spaniard from hicksville went to Madrid at seventeen, got a job as a clerk at the National Telephone Company in 1970, and, during the more than ten years he worked there, wrote comic strips, articles, and stories for "underground" papers, acted in theatre groups, composed film scores, recorded with a rock band, performed as a singer, and shot films in Super 8 mm. and 16 mm. He absorbed the avant-garde slapstick of the late sixties and the seventies along with Hollywood's frivolous and romantic pop, and all this merged with the legacy of Buñuel and with his own intuitive acceptance of loco impulses. Generalissimo Franco kept the lid on for thirty-six years; he died in 1975, and Pedro Almodóvar is part of what jumped out of the box. The most original pop writer-director of the eighties, he's Godard with a human face—a happy face.

His new *Women on the Verge of a Nervous Breakdown*, his seventh feature (since 1980), is one of the jauntiest of all war-of-the-sexes comedies. Pepa (Carmen Maura), an actress who works in TV and commercials, and does dubbing, turns on her answering machine and learns that she has been jilted. Infuriated at the way her long-time live-in lover, Iván (Fernando Guillén), has evaded direct contact with her—he can lie to the machine without fear of being challenged—she dashes around, on spike heels, in a short, tight skirt, trying to confront him. Angry and impatient, and imagining she doesn't want to be in her apartment without him, she instantly puts it on the market.

Pepa is so wound up about Iván that although her girl friend the lightheaded Candela (María Barranco) keeps phoning and chasing her, asking for help, Pepa, hearing nothing, answers that she doesn't have time. What Candela is trying to tell her is that her own lover has turned out to be a Shiite terrorist who was using her place as a base of operations, and she thinks the police are after her. Without registering Candela's words, Pepa takes her in. Meanwhile, blankly handsome Carlos (Antonio Banderas), who turns out to be Iván's son, comes to see the apartment, and brings his soon to be discarded fiancée, Marisa (Rossy De Palma, who looks startlingly like the double face of Picasso's 1937 portrait of Dora Maar). Iván's earlier lover Lucia (Julieta Serrano)—she's Carlos's mother—arrives in search of Iván; she was over the edge for twenty years and has just recouped her sanity. And when Pepa, on Candela's behalf, consults a feminist lawyer (Kiti Manver), the woman turns out to be Iván's newest lover—and the next candidate for a breakdown. All these women are sleek-legged and chic and made up as if they were painted in acrylics.

The artificial is what sends Almodóvar sky high. The movie has nothing to do with what passes for nature or realism. It starts with titles set against divided-screen fashion and cosmetics layouts that parody the bright, crisp American-movie openings of the fifties. (All that plugging away to be Mondrian-new and striking.) *Women on the Verge* looks as if it had been made by a mad scientist playing with chemical rainbow colors—John Lithgow in his lab in *Buckaroo Banzai*. When you were a kid, you wondered if your crayons would kill you if you ate them. These toxic colors are toxins for the pleasure of it; Almodóvar makes the artificial sexy.

The film's controlling metaphor is right there at the start, in those sharp-edged layouts: Almodóvar is after the phosphorescent glow of cosmetics in women's magazines. (It's dream-candy color. You don't just see it; you consume it, lustfully.) Pepa and the others in their short short skirts have created themselves in the image of hot, desirable women. They function in the world; they do fine. But when it comes to men, that sassy image may be all that's holding them together. The lovely, wacky Candela is always speeding between panic and ardor; she talks about being entrapped by the Shiites, and her earrings—they're little silver espresso-makers—dangle alluringly. Except for Lucia (who suspects the truth about herself), they all know they look great; that's not a small thing. (Lucia can't keep up her morale; her makeup slips and blurs.)

The movie links Carmen Maura's Pepa to the Hollywood goddesses who blew a trumpet to announce that they were entering the house of passion. Their emotional display was morbidly fascinating; Almodóvar and Maura take off on that display and go further into it. Pepa looks great even though she shows some wear and tear. It's in her nature to charge into things bang, head on, and get scuffed up. She doesn't mind; she enjoys flaunting the ravages of love. It's also in her nature to let off steam; she distracts the police, who come looking for Candela, by giving them a stormy account of intimate experiences. Almodóvar revels in her overdramatizing, but it's never held an instant too long; it's quick and buoyant. It's taken for granted. Pepa is both overtly nuts—a coquettish, fluttering wreck—and profoundly sane and practical. After she gets the kiss-off from the answering machine, she's so zonked on pills and misery that she accidentally sets her bed on fire. She stares at it for a few seconds, then flips her cigarette into the flames and puts them out with the hose from the terrace.

Women on the Verge is serenely unbalanced—a hallucinogenic Feydeau play. Mad-again Lucia, in pale pink, rides to the airport on the back of a motorbike, her wig rising and blowing in the wind. She's determined to catch up with Iván, and he's about to board a plane. Inside the terminal, her head, seen gliding by above a moving walkway, is the head of a mythological creature—a wiggy Fate. When the people in the airport hear a shot fired and try to protect themselves by hitting the floor, they stay down until Iván comes over to Pepa, who has raced Lucia there. Then they all get up at once, like the dancer-spectators in a musical version of a gangster picture. The Madrid of the film is a pop utopia; it's also—as the closing song has it—"Puro Teatro."

Almodóvar celebrates women because they run the theatrical gamut. Carmen Maura is his star, his muse, his comedienne because she's all histrionics; she doesn't make a move that isn't stylized. Yet she's snappy. And it won't take her Pepa twenty years to see through Iván. Gray-haired, vain, and elegant, he's the film's MacGuffin—a shell of a man, and perhaps an archetypal Spanish roué. A dubber by profession, he's a voice pouring out inanities. It pleases him to flatter virtually every woman he sees; he's complimenting himself on his aplomb, his powers of seduction. When he has something to say that might provoke an emotional response, he'd rather talk into a machine. He's a sly fellow: while dodging Pepa, he keeps leaving messages accusing her of avoiding him. (He tells her to pack up his clothes and leave the suitcase with the concierge.) Iván is right to communicate by machine: as a disembodied voice, he gives the illusion of masculine strength. In person, he's just a pretty illusion, like his son, Carlos, and the police officers and the men from the phone company who invade Pepa's apartment.

The script began with Cocteau's *The Human Voice*—the famous telephone monologue in which a woman tries to win back the lover who is leaving her. Almodóvar had already done a turn on the play in his last film, the 1987 *Law of Desire*; this time, the monologue grew into a comic revenge on his old employer the phone company. Pepa grabs her phone and throws it out the window, and she throws out its offspring, the answering machine, too. She's paying them back for the long waits for men to call and the lies listened to.

This high comedy is the most visually assured of the five Almodóvar movies that have opened here. *Law of Desire* and the 1986 *Matador* were more sultry and erotic; this one is fizzier, sexier. Earlier, you could see him trusting his intuitions and taking leaps; now you don't see the risktaking—he's just up in the air flying. The movie is all coincidences, and each new one adds to the crazy brio. What seem to be incidental jokes turn out to be essential parts of one big joke. This is a movie where after a while you can't tell sexy from funny.

{*The New Yorker*, November 14, 1988}

:: A Wounded Apparition

Some movies—*Grand Illusion* and *Shoeshine* come to mind, and the two *Godfathers* and *The Chant of Jimmie Blacksmith* and *The Night of the Shooting Stars*—can affect us in more direct, emotional ways than simple entertainment movies. They have more imagination, more poetry, more intensity than the usual fare; they have large themes, and a vision. They can leave us feeling simultaneously elated and wiped out. Overwhelmed, we may experience a helpless anger if we hear people mock them or poke holes in them in order to dismiss them. The new *Casualties of War* has this kind of purity. If you meet people who are bored by movies you love such as *The Earrings of Madame de . . .* or *The Unbearable Lightness of Being*, chances are you can brush it off and think it's their loss. But this new film is the kind that makes you feel protective. When you leave the theatre, you'll probably find that you're not ready to talk about it. You may also find it hard to talk lightly about anything.

Casualties of War is based on a Vietnam incident of 1966 that was reported in *The New Yorker* by the late Daniel Lang, in the issue of October 18, 1969. (The article was reprinted as a book.) Lang gave a calm, emotionally devastating account of a squad of five American soldiers who were sent on a five-day reconnaissance mission; they kidnapped a Vietnamese village girl, raped her, and then covered up their crime by killing her. The account dealt with the kind of gangbang rape that the Vietnam War had in common with virtually all wars, except that the rapists here, unable in general to distinguish Vietcong sympathizers from other Vietnamese, didn't care that the girl wasn't Vietcong. This indifference to whether a candidate for rape is friend or foe may not really be that much of an exception; it may be frequent in wartime. What's unusual here may simply be that a witness forced the case into the open and it resulted in four court-martial convictions.

A number of movie people hoped to make a film of the Lang article, and, though it was commercially risky, Warners bought the rights and announced that Jack Clayton would make the picture—an arrangement that fell apart. Plans involving John Schlesinger and other directors also collapsed, but the article may have been the (unofficial) taking-off point for one film that did get made: Elia Kazan's low-budget, 16-mm. *The Visitors*, of 1972, which Kazan himself financed. He used a prosecution for rape and murder as background material to explain why a couple of ex-servicemen released from Leavenworth on a technicality were out to get the former buddy who had testified against them. Eventually, in 1987, after Brian De Palma had a success with *The Untouchables*, he was able to persuade Paramount to pick up the rights to the Lang story, which he'd had in the back of his mind since 1969. A script was commissioned from the playwright David Rabe, the quondam Catholic and Vietnam vet who had written *Streamers* and other plays about the war (and had wanted to work on this material for some years), but, when De Palma was all set to film it in Thailand, Paramount pulled out. The picture finally got under way at Columbia—the first picture to be approved by the company's new president, Dawn Steel. Whatever else she does, she should be honored for that decision, because twenty years later this is still risky material.

Lang's factual narrative is based on conversations with Eriksson, the witness who testified against the other men, and on the court-martial records. (The names were changed to protect everyone's privacy.) Rabe's script follows it closely, except that Rabe dramatizes the story by creating several incidents to explain what led to the rape and what followed.

When Eriksson (Michael J. Fox), who has just arrived in Vietnam, is out in a jungle skirmish at night, a mortar explosion shifts the earth under him; he drops down, caught, his feet dangling in an enemy tunnel. De Palma photographs the scene as if it were an ant farm—he shows us aboveground and underground in the same shot. Eriksson yells for help, and in the instant that a Vietcong, who has been crawling toward the dangling legs, slashes at them with his knife, Sergeant Meserve (Sean Penn) pulls Eriksson out. A minute later, Meserve saves him again from that Vietcong, who has come out of the hole to get him.

In the morning, the soldiers enter a peaceful-looking village; they stand near the mud-and-bamboo huts and see a stream and bridges and, a little way in the distance, paddy fields where women and elderly men are working, under the shadow of harsh, steep mountains. The tiered compositions are pale, like Chinese ink paintings. Throughout the movie, everything that's beyond the understanding of the Americans seems to be visualized in layered images; this subtle landscape reaching to Heaven is the site of the random violence that leads to the rape.

Smiling and eager, Eriksson walks behind two water buffalo, helping an ancient farmer with his plowing. Brownie (Erik King), a large-spirited, joshing black soldier, who is Meserve's pal—they're both due to go home in less than a month—cautions Eriksson about his exposed position on the field and walks him back to where the Sarge is taking time out, with the other men. They're all relaxed in a clearing near this friendly village, but we become ominously aware that the villagers in the paddies are evaporating. Brownie is standing with an arm around Meserve when the pastoral scene is ruptured: bullets tear into Brownie from a V.C. across the stream. An instant later, a guerrilla who's dressed as a farmer runs toward the group and flings a grenade at them. Meserve spots him and warns Eriksson, who turns and fires his grenade launcher; by luck, he explodes the V.C.'s grenade. Then the screen is divided by a couple of split-focus effects: in one, Eriksson, in closeup, rejoices at his freak shot and is so excited that he lets the grenade-thrower slip away; in another, Eriksson is staring the wrong way while behind him a couple of women open a tunnel for a V.C., who disappears into it. Meanwhile, Meserve fires his M-16 rifle, and then, his face showing his agony, he uses his hand like a poultice on Brownie's wound. A soldier radios for medical help, and Meserve, never letting go of his friend, keeps reassuring him until he's loaded on a chopper.

In these early scenes, Meserve is skillful and resourceful. He's only twenty years old, and as Sean Penn plays him he has the reckless bravery of youth. He's genuinely heroic. But Brownie dies (as Meserve knew he would), and back at the base camp the men, who have readied themselves for a visit to a brothel, are stopped and told that the village adjoining the base has been declared off limits. It's too much for Meserve, who has been put in charge of the five-day mission to check out a mountain area for signs of Vietcong activity, and later that night he finishes briefing his men by telling them to be ready to leave an hour early, so they can detour to a village to "requisition" a girl. Eriksson half thinks the Sarge is kidding. It takes a while for him (and for us) to understand that Meserve is not the man he was; only a day has passed since his friend was killed, but he has become bitter and vindictive—a conscious trickster and sinner.

Has something in Meserve snapped? Paul Fussell writes in his new book *Wartime* that in the Second World War the American military "learned that men will inevitably go mad in battle and that no appeal to patriotism, manliness, or loyalty to the group will ultimately matter." So "in later wars things were arranged differently," he explains. "In Vietnam, it was understood that a man fulfilled his combat obligation and purchased his reprieve if he served a fixed term, 365 days, and not days in combat either but days in the theatre of war. The infantry was now treated somewhat like the Air Corps in the Second War: performance of a stated number of missions guaranteed escape." Meserve, who has led dozens of combat patrols, has reached his limit with only a few weeks to go; he turns into an outlaw with a smooth justification for anything. (The kidnapping is a matter of cool planning: the girl can be explained as a "V.C. whore" taken for interrogation.) When Meserve's five-man patrol, having set out before dawn, arrives at the village he selected in advance, he and Corporal Clark (Don Harvey) peer into one hut after another, shining a flashlight on the sleeping women until they find one to their taste—Oanh (Thuy Thu Le), a girl of eighteen or twenty.

The terrified girl clings to her family. Clark carries her out, and her mother and sister come rushing after him, pleading in words that are just jabber to the soldiers, who want to get moving before it's light. They've taken only a few steps when the mother desperately hands them the girl's scarf. It's a pitiful, ambiguous gesture. She seems to want Oanh to have the comfort of this scarf—perhaps it's new, perhaps it's the only token of love the mother can offer her daughter. Eriksson says "Oh Jesus God" when he sees the men's actions, even before the mother holds out the scarf. Then he mutters helplessly, "I'm sorry." He's sick with grief, and we in the audience may experience a surge of horror; we know we're watching something irrevocable. Clark, a crude, tall kid who suggests a young Lee Marvin, is irritated by the girl's crying and whimpering, and he stuffs the scarf into her mouth, to gag her.

...

The men climb high above the valleys and set up a temporary command post in an abandoned hut in the mountains; it's here that the sobbing, sniffling girl is brutalized. (Thereafter, she's referred to as "the whore" or "the bitch.") Eriksson refuses his turn to rape her, but he can't keep the others from tying her up, beating her, and violating her. He himself is assaulted when he tries to stop them from killing her. Eriksson is brave, but he's also inexperienced and unsure of himself. In the few minutes in which he's alone with the girl and could help her escape, he delays because he's afraid of being charged as a deserter. The opportunity passes, and we can see the misery in his eyes. Meserve sees it, too—sees that Eriksson finds him disgusting, indecent. And he begins to play up to Eriksson's view of him: he deliberately turns himself into a jeering, macho clown, taunting Eriksson, questioning his masculinity, threatening him. Meserve starts to act out his madness; that's the rationale for Penn's theatrical, heated-up performance. He brings off the early, quiet scenes, too. When Meserve shaves after learning of Brownie's death, we see that the hopefulness has drained out of him. Suddenly he's older; the radiance is gone. Soon he's all calculation. Although he was coarse before, it was good-humored coarseness; now there's cynical, low cunning in it. Fox, in contrast, uses a minimum of showmanship. He gives such an interior performance that it may be undervalued. To play a young American in Vietnam who's instinctively thoughtful and idealistic—who's uncorrupted—is excruciatingly difficult, yet Fox never lets the character come across as a prig. The two men act in totally different styles, and the styles match up.

And, whatever the soldiers say or do, there's the spectre of the dazed, battered girl ranting in an accusatory singsong. The movie is haunted by Oanh long before she's dead. The rapists think they've killed her, but she rises; in our minds, she rises again and again. On the basis of the actual soldiers' descriptions of the girl's refusal to accept death, Daniel Lang called her "a wounded apparition," and De Palma and his cinematographer, Stephen H. Burum, give us images that live up to those words—perhaps even go beyond them. Trying to escape along a railway trestle high up against the wall of a canyon, Oanh might be a Kabuki ghost. She goes past suffering into the realm of myth, which in this movie has its own music—a recurring melody played on the panflute.

That lonely music keeps reminding us of the despoiled girl, of the incomprehensible language, the tunnels, the hidden meanings, the sorrow. Eriksson can't forgive himself for his failure to save Oanh. The picture shows us how daringly far he would have had to go to prevent what happened; he would have had to be lucky as well as brave. This is basically the theme that De Palma worked with in his finest movie up until now, the political fantasy *Blow Out*, in which the protagonist, played by John Travolta, also failed to save a young woman's life. We in the audience are put in the man's position: we're made to feel the awfulness of being ineffectual. This lifelike defeat is central to the movie. (One hot day on my first trip to New York City, I walked past a group of men on a tenement stoop. One of them, in a sweaty sleeveless T-shirt, stood shouting at a screaming, weeping little boy perhaps eighteen months old. The man must have caught a glimpse of my stricken face, because he called out, "You don't like it, lady? Then how do you like this?" And he picked up a bottle of pink soda pop from the sidewalk and poured it on the baby's head. Wailing sounds, much louder than before, followed me down the street.)

Eriksson feels he must at least reveal what happened to Oanh and where her body lies. He's a dogged innocent trying to find out what to do; he goes to the higher-ups in the Army and gets a load of doubletalk and some straight talk, too. The gist of it is that in normal (i.e., peacetime) circumstances Meserve would not have buckled like this, and they want Eriksson to keep quiet about it. But he can't deal with their reasoning; he has to stick with the rules he grew up with. He moves through one layer of realization to the next; there's always another, hidden level. The longer Eriksson is in Vietnam, the more the ground opens up beneath him. He can't even go to the latrine without seeing below the floor slats a grenade that Clark has just put there, to kill him.

De Palma has mapped out every shot, yet the picture is alive and mysterious. When Meserve rapes Oanh, the horizon seems to twist into a crooked position; everything is bent away from us. Afterward, he goes outside in the rain and confronts Eriksson, who's standing guard. Meserve's relationship to the universe has changed; the images of nature have a different texture, and when he lifts his face to the sky you may think he's swapped souls with a werewolf. Eriksson is numb and demoralized, and the rain courses down his cheeks in slow motion. De Palma has such seductive, virtuosic control of film craft that he can express convulsions in the unconscious.

In the first use of the split-focus effect, Eriksson was so happy about having hit the grenade that he lost track of the enemy. In a later use of the split effect, Eriksson tries to save Oanh from execution by creating a gigantic diversion: he shoots his gun and draws enemy fire. What he doesn't know is that Clark, who is behind him, is stabbing her. He didn't know what was going on behind him after he was rescued from the tunnel, either. This is Vietnam, where you get fooled. It's also De Palmaland. There are more dimensions than you can keep track of, as the ant-farm shot tells you. And the protagonist who maps things out to protect the girl from other men (as Travolta did) will always be surprised. The theme has such personal meaning for the director that his technique—his own mapping out of the scenes—is itself a dramatization of the theme. His art is in controlling everything, but he still can't account for everything. He plans everything and discovers something more.

De Palma keeps you aware of the whole movie as a composition. Like Godard, he bounces you in and out of the assumptions about movies that you have brought with you to the theatre. He stretches time and distance, using techniques that he developed in horror-fantasy and suspense pictures, but without the pop overtones. He shifts from realism to hallucinatory Expressionism. When the wounded Brownie is flown out by helicopter, the movement of the yellow-green river running beneath him suggests being so close up against a painting that it's pure pigment. When Eriksson is flown out, it's at an angle you've never seen before: he looks up at the rotor blades as they darken the sky. These helicopters are on drugs.

Great movies are rarely perfect movies. David Rabe wrestles with the ugly side of male bonding; he's on to American men's bluster and showoff, and his scenes certainly have drive. But his dialogue is sometimes explicit in the grungy-poetic mode of "important" American theatre. The actual Eriksson was in fact (as he is in the movie) married and a Lutheran. He was also, as Daniel Lang reported, articulate. This is Eriksson talking to Lang:

> We all figured we might be dead in the next minute, so what differ-
> ence did it make what we did? But the longer I was over there, the
> more I became convinced that it was the other way around that
> counted—that *because* we might not be around much longer, we had
> to take extra care how we behaved.

Rabe uses these remarks but places them maladroitly (as a response to something that has just happened), and he makes them sound like the stumbling thoughts of a folksy, subliterate fellow reaching for truth:

> I mean, just because each one of us might at any second be blown away, everybody's actin' like we can do anything, man, and it don't matter what we do—but I'm thinkin' maybe it's the other way around, maybe the main thing is just the opposite. Because we might be dead in the next split second, maybe we gotta be extra careful what we do—because maybe it matters more—Jesus, maybe it matters more than we even know.

This passage is the heaviest hammering in the movie (and the poorest piece of staging), but it's also a clear indication of Rabe's method. De Palma works directly on our emotions. Rabe's dialogue sometimes sounds like the work of a professional anti-war dramatist trying to make us think. Still, there's none of the ego satisfaction of moral indignation that is put into most Vietnam films and what De Palma does with the camera is so powerful that the few times you wince at the dialogue are almost breathers.

This movie about war and rape—De Palma's nineteenth film—is the culmination of his best work. In essence, it's feminist. I think that in his earlier movies De Palma was always involved in examining (and sometimes satirizing) victimization, but he was often accused of being a victimizer. Some moviegoers (women, especially) were offended by his thrillers; they thought there was something reprehensibly sadistic in his cleverness. He *was* clever. When people talk about their sex fantasies, their descriptions almost always sound like movies, and De Palma headed right for that linkage: he teased the audience about how susceptible it was to romantic manipulation. *Carrie* and *Dressed to Kill* are like lulling erotic reveries that keep getting broken into by scary jokes. He let you know that he was jerking you around and that it was for your amused, childish delight, but a lot of highly vocal people expressed shock. This time, De Palma touches on raw places in people's reactions to his earlier movies; he gets at the reality that may have made some moviegoers too fearful to enjoy themselves. He goes to the heart of sexual victimization, and he does it with a new authority. The way he makes movies now, it's as if he were saying, "What is getting older if it isn't learning more ways that you're vulnerable?"

Cruelty is not taken lightly in this movie. In the audience, we feel alone with the sounds that come out of Oanh's throat; we're alone with the sight of the blood clotting her nose. The director has isolated us from all distractions. There are no plot subterfuges; war is the only metaphor. The soldiers hate Vietnam and the Vietnamese for their frustrations, their grievances, their fear, and they take their revenge on the girl. When Brownie is shot, Eriksson, like Meserve and the others, feels that they've come to fight for the defense of the villagers who knew about the hidden guerrillas and could have warned them. They feel betrayed. Could the villagers have warned them without being killed themselves? It's doubtful, but the soldiers are sure of it, and for most of them that's justification enough for what they do to Oanh. The movie doesn't give us the aftermath: Oanh's mother searched for her and got South Vietnamese troops to help in the search; the mother was then taken away by the Vietcong, accused of having led the troops to a V.C. munitions cache. De Palma simply concentrates on what happened and why.

Meserve and Clark and one of the other men feel like conquerors when they take Oanh with them. They act out their own war fantasy; they feel it's a soldier's right to seize women for his pleasure. Comradeship is about the only spiritual value these jungle fighters still recognize; they're fighting for each other, and they feel that a gangbang relieves their tensions and brings them closer together. When Clark slings Oanh over his shoulder and carries her out of her family's hut, he's the hero of his own comic strip. These men don't suffer from guilt—not in the way that Eriksson suffers for the few minutes of indecisiveness in which he might have saved Oanh's life. He's turned from a cheerful, forthright kid into a desolate loner.

At the end, the swelling sound of musical absolution seems to be saying that Eriksson must put his experiences in Vietnam behind him—that he has to accept that he did all he could, and go on without always blaming himself. De Palma may underestimate the passion of his images: we don't believe that Eriksson can put Oanh's death into any kind of sane perspective, because we've just felt the sting of what he lived through. He may tell himself that he did all he could, but he feels he should have been able to protect her. The doubt is there in his eyes. (I hear that baby's cries after almost fifty years.) What makes the movie so eerily affecting? Possibly it's Oanh's last moments of life — the needle-sharp presentation of her frailty and strength, and how they intertwine. When she falls to her death, the image is otherworldly, lacerating. It's the supreme violation.

{*The New Yorker*, August 21, 1989}

In the middle of *My Left Foot*, the movie about the Dubliner Christy Brown, a victim of cerebral palsy who became a painter and a writer, Christy (Daniel Day-Lewis) is in a restaurant, at a dinner party celebrating the opening of an exhibition of the pictures he painted by holding a brush between his toes. For some time, he has been misinterpreting the friendly manner of the woman doctor who has been training him, and who arranged the show, and now, high on booze and success, he erupts. "I love you, Eileen," he says, and then, sharing his happiness with the others at the table, "I love you all." Eileen, not comprehending that his love for her is passionate and sexual, takes the occasion to announce that she's going to marry the gallery owner in six months. In his staccato, distorted speech, Christy spits out "Con-grat-u-la-tions" so that the syllables sound like slaps, and then he lashes her with "I'm glad you taught me to speak so I could say that, Eileen." The restaurant is suddenly quiet: everyone is watching his torment as he beats his head on the table and yanks the tablecloth off with his teeth.

It's all very fast, and it may be the most emotionally wrenching scene I've ever experienced at the movies. The greatness of Day-Lewis's performance is that he pulls you inside Christy Brown's frustration and rage (and his bottomless thirst). There's nothing soft or maudlin about this movie's view of Christy. Right from the first shot, it's clear that the Irish playwright-director Jim Sheridan, who wrote the superb screenplay, with another Irish playwright, Shane Connaughton, knows what he's doing. Christy's left foot is starting a record on his turntable; there's a scratchy stop, and the foot starts it up again—Mozart's *Così Fan Tutte*. A few toes wriggle to the music, and then in a sudden cut the bearded head of the man that the musical toes belong to jerks into the frame, and we see the tight pursed mouth, the tense face, and the twisted-upward, lolling head with slitted eyes peering down. He's anguished and locked in yet excitingly insolent. Day-Lewis seizes the viewer; he takes possession of you. His interpretation recalls Olivier's crookbacked, long-nosed Richard III; Day-Lewis's Christy Brown has the sexual seductiveness that was so startling in the Olivier Richard.

The defiance in Christy's glance carries over when the film flashes back from the acclaimed young author and artist in 1959 to the birth, in 1932, of the crippled, twitching child—the tenth of twenty-two children born to the Browns—who is thought to be a vegetable. The child actor (Hugh O'Conor) is a fine matchup with Day-Lewis and does wonderful work, but the small Christy might affect us as a Tiny Tim if we didn't have the image of the adult blending with him. Lying on the floor under the staircase like part of the furniture, Christy watches the crowded family life dominated by the violent, heavy-drinking bricklayer father (Ray McAnally), and bound together by the large, reassuring mother (Brenda Fricker). Despite what the doctors say and what the neighbors think, Christy's mother persists in believing that he has a mind. One day when he's alone in the house with her, he hears her fall; pregnant and near term, she's unconscious at the bottom of the stairs, lying near the front door. He squirms and writhes, flinging his body downstairs, and then banging his foot against the door until a neighbor hears the commotion, comes to the house, and sends her off in an ambulance. But when the neighbors gather they don't praise the boy: they don't realize that he summoned them. Seeing him there, they think his mother fell while carrying this moron downstairs. I don't know that any movie has ever given us so strong a feeling of an intelligence struggling to come out, to be recognized.

Finally one day, the boy, seeing a piece of chalk on the floor and desperate for some means of asserting himself, sticks out his left foot (he later described it as "the only key to the door of the prison I was in"), works the chalk between his toes, and makes a mark on his sister's slate with it. The family, awed, watches. After that, his mother teaches him the alphabet, and his brothers push him around outside in a broken-down old go-cart— it's like a wheelbarrow—so he can play with them. He speaks only in strangled grunts, but some members of the family understand him (his mother always does), and his father, who calls Christy's cart his "chariot," boasts of his accomplishments. It's a great day for all of them when this pale, gnarled kid takes chalk in his toes and, with a gruelling effort at control, writes "MOTHER" on the floor. (Astonishingly, even at that moment you don't feel manipulated; the directing is too plain, too fierce for sentimentality.)

Day-Lewis takes over when Christy is seventeen and, lying flat in the streets, is an accepted participant in his brothers' fast, roughneck games. As goalkeeper for a soccer match, he stops the ball with his head. The whack gives you a jolt. It gives him a savage satisfaction; it buoys him up. Out with his brothers, Christy's a hardheaded working-class cripple. At home, he paints watercolors. And though he can't feed himself or take care of his excretory functions or wash or dress himself, his life is one romantic infatuation after another—he courts the girls with pictures and poems. (In some ways, his story is a whirling satire of the Irishman as impetuous carnal dreamer.)

This is Jim Sheridan's first feature film, but he's an experienced man of the theatre, with a moviemaker's vision and a grownup's sense of integrity. There's no overacting and none of the wordiness that crept into Christy Brown's later books. His autobiography, *My Left Foot*, published when he was twenty-two, is a simple account (with perhaps a surfeit of creditable emotions). His best-known work, the semi-autobiographical novel *Down All the Days*, published when he was thirty-seven (and smitten with Thomas Wolfe), is the kind of prose-poetry that's generally described as roistering and irrepressible. It's a chore to get through. But what a life he lived! Sheridan and Connaughton know that their story is not the making of an artistic genius: it's the release of an imprisoned comic spirit. What makes Christy Brown such a zesty subject for a movie is that, with all his physical handicaps, he became a traveller, a pub crawler, a husband, a joker. He became a literary lion and made a pile of money; *Down All the Days*, a best-seller, was published in fifteen countries. The movie may tear you apart, but it's the story of a triumphantly tough guy who lived it up.

In a section of the film called "Hell," the father is laid off work, the family has nothing to eat but porridge, and Christy can't paint, because there's no money for coal—he has to go to bed. (The boys sleep four to a bed, sardine style.) It isn't until Christy is nineteen that his mother is able to buy him the wheelchair that she's been saving for. She's tough, too: she won't touch the money even during the porridge days. (She has her own hell: nine of her children didn't survive infancy.) There's nothing frail about these people; they're strong, and they're uncannily intuitive. The mother, who has always understood what is going on in Christy, is aware of the danger that the woman doctor (Fiona Shaw) represents; the mother worries that the doctor has brought too much hope to Christy's voice.

The cinematographer (Jack Conroy) brings the family close to you, and the images of flesh—the broad-faced Juno-like mother, the sculptural pink jowliness of the father, the girls in their first experiments with makeup, the raw-faced boys—come at you the way they do in a Dreyer film. In one scene, a bulging vein divides Christy's bony forehead right down the middle; sometimes when he tries to talk, he drools spittle. There isn't a wasted shot in the movie. A Halloween fresco is instantly stored as something not to be forgotten. And there is a moment that is simply peerless when Mr. Brown, the head of the house, is laid low; he falls to the floor—to Christy's province—and Christy is face to face with his dead father. It's a mythic image. But it doesn't go on a second too long. Neither does the wake—a real Irish wake that ends in a brawl. A man there offends Christy, who uses his talented left foot to kick the glass smack out of the guy's hand. (Christy loves to drink so he can misbehave.)

Everything goes right with the movie—which probably means that Sheridan and Connaughton hit the right subject for them and surrounded Day-Lewis with just the right players. But probably none of it would have worked without him and his demonic eyes. (At times, Day-Lewis's Christy uses his eyes to speak wicked thoughts for him, as Olivier's Richard III did. They're flirts, these characters. As for the actors, when they're deformed they're free to be more themselves than ever.) Something central in Day-Lewis connects with what's central in Christy. You could say that they share a bawdy vitality, and they do, but it's much more than that. It's in the passion that Day-Lewis has for acting: he goes in to find (i.e., create) the spirit of the character so that he can release it. That's how he asserts himself. So he responds to Christy's need for self-assertion and his refusal to see himself as a victim. Christy Brown died, at forty-nine, in 1981; he choked on food at Sunday dinner. This great, exhilarating movie— a comedy about suffering—gives him new life as a legendary Irish hero.

{*The New Yorker*, October 2, 1989}

:: *The Grifters*

Anjelica Huston has a mysterious presence. You can't tell what its sources are, but it seems related to the economy of her acting. In *Prizzi's Honor*, she used her Brooklyn accent to open up the character; in *Enemies, A Love Story*, the suggestion of pain gave force to each thing she did, especially when she made the pain comic. Huston is already past the age at which Garbo retired, and there's nothing youthful about her—but then there never was. (There wasn't much that was youthful about Garbo, either; being considered ageless often means looking older than you are.) Huston doesn't flaunt her androgyny or seem ashamed of it. Agelessness and androgyny are simply among her attributes. She's overpoweringly sexual; young men might find her frightening.

That makes casting her as Lilly Dillon in *The Grifters* an intuitive sneaky-right decision, because the core of the story is the refusal of Lilly's son, Roy (John Cusack), to have anything to do with her. He's paying her back. In his childhood, she was cold and miserly; she withheld any kindness. Now that he's twenty-five and has been on his own since he was seventeen, she shows up. Lilly is tough and she's seductive; she's the dominatrix as mother, and he's afraid of her getting her hooks in him.

The Grifters is based on one of the punchier pulp novels by Jim Thompson—a bitter, somewhat repellent book with a misanthropic integrity. Published in 1963, it's about three scam artists (Lilly, Roy, and Roy's bubbly bedmate Moira*, played by Annette Bening)—people who never got a break and don't give anybody else a break. Each of these chisellers has his or her own methods and agenda; there's no yielding by any

---

*In the movie, it's pronounced Myra.

of them (and no redemption). The film retains Thompson's hardboiled pitilessness, and a tension is created by placing these fifties or early sixties characters in nineties L.A. locations; we feel piqued, jazzed up. Toying with L.A. film noir, the director, Stephen Frears, and the scriptwriter, Donald E. Westlake, do twisted, anomalous things. The Elmer Bernstein score tries for a tart, sour Kurt Weill effect, and doesn't quite bring it off, but Westlake keeps some of Thompson's slangy, compact dialogue and adds his own, which has a madcap edge. The movie starts with comic capers, then uses Thompson's class resentment and grim hopelessness to smack us with discord. We're watching a form of cabaret.

This criminal subculture doesn't come equipped with a detective as moral explorer. It's a void, where Roy, who holds a salesman's job as a cover, lives alone by rules he has devised for himself. A cautious, hard-eyed practitioner of the "short con"—fleecing cashiers by getting change for a twenty and slipping them a ten, or playing craps with trick dice—he doesn't have to worry about doing time in prison. Roy has repressed any signs of an identifiable personality, and he does nothing to attract attention; he won't let himself have friends—that's being a sucker. He makes himself colorless, and socks his money away. It's a horrible, grubby life—a mole's life—and he's an intelligent, handsome kid, who could have gone to college, who could have lived among people. It's his angry touchiness about his young mother (she was only fourteen when she had him) that keeps him in his miserable isolation. He's getting even with her by throwing his life away.

Frears introduces the three characters (in the sections of a vertically divided triple screen) as they arrive at the places where they're about to do their grifts. Each of the three is putting on the face that he or she presents to the world. We're formally meeting three false fronts. It's Lilly's dream that her son will go straight and be a loving comfort to her, but she herself works for the Baltimore syndicate: she travels, placing bets at the tracks. Annette Bening's Moira is a sex fantasy come to luscious life. She's irrepressible—a real tootsie—and it takes a while for her adorable, kittenish perversity to make you apprehensive. Moira the smiler has been trained in big cons—scams that rake in bundles of money but can also land you in prison—and she's out to make Roy her partner. Roy likes Moira in his bed, but he was jerked around by his mother and he's not about to get jerked around again. He hates feeling that people might want to make something of him; he's not interested in becoming anything. Cusack suggests that Roy is cocky enough to think that he's something already, that he's living on his own terms.

Roy turns both women down, but he's an innocent compared with these two blondes—the killer mom and the tease—who are close to the same age. (It's perfect that Cusack gives his most memorable line reading to the word "Mom.") The two women battle over Roy's essence—the money that's hidden in the clown paintings in his apartment. In the structure of the film, it's Roy who's the clown.

There's nothing to fill out in a Jim Thompson novel; there's no room for characterization. It's socially conscious thin stuff. The three are stuck. You grasp the limits of what's available to them and how hard their dreams hit those limits, and you see them try to break through by using each other. Frears and Westlake are smart enough not to attempt to make a big thing of it. They keep it snappy, and heighten the sexual electricity.

Bening's two-faced little-girl quality is dazzling—just what film noir thrives on. When Moira blames Lilly for Roy's rejecting her proposition and turns treacherous, Bening makes the shift convincing; she's a stunning actress and a superb wiggler. And film noir is enriched by two competing femmes fatales. Huston's power as Lilly is astounding. This actress generally plays tightly controlled characters. (Her Gretta Conroy in *The Dead* was an exception.) Lilly is usually peremptory, displaying the authority of a woman who has worked for big-time mobsters for years; her whole existence is based on manipulation and control. She's a thief trying to outwit the thieves she works for. When she isn't sure she's succeeding, we can read the terror under the control. She's like a trapped animal when her boss (Pat Hingle), who thinks she has tricked him, shows up to punish her. Hingle, sucking on a big cigar, is chilling; as the power m.c. pulling the strings, he gives what's probably his best performance ever, and Huston matches him. The scene has a jangle; it's *Cabaret* moved from Berlin to L.A.

Actors are con artists, and our entertainment is in watching them get away with things. When Lilly, at the close, comes down in the elevator at Roy's apartment hotel, you may be reminded of Mary Astor in the elevator at the close of John Huston's *The Maltese Falcon*, and when, a little before that, Lilly pulls a maneuver on her son that's just about the ultimate con, you may recall John Huston in *Chinatown* saying, "Most people never have to face that at the right time and right place, they're capable of anything."

The leading characters' acceptance of brutality in Martin Scorsese's *GoodFellas* fails to scare us, and it doesn't haunt us afterward—perhaps it isn't meant to. But by the end of *The Grifters* (which Scorsese produced) Lilly's ruthless amorality is shocking—it has weight—and I think that's because Anjelica Huston is willing to be taken as monstrous; she contains this possibility as part of what she is. And when Lilly shows her willingness to do anything to survive she's a great character. At the end of John Huston's *The Treasure of the Sierra Madre*, the fortune is dispersed to the winds; here it's gathered up. Anjelica Huston's Lilly bites right through the film-noir pulp; the scene is paralyzing, and it won't go away.

{*The New Yorker*, November 19, 1990}

This volume contains essays and reviews from ten books by Pauline Kael: *I Lost it at the Movies* (Boston: Atlantic Monthly Press / Little, Brown, 1965); *Kiss Kiss Bang Bang* (Boston: Atlantic Monthly Press / Little, Brown, 1968); *Going Steady* (Boston: Atlantic Monthly Press / Little, Brown, 1970); *Deeper into Movies* (Boston: Atlantic Monthly Press / Little, Brown, 1973); *Reeling* (Boston: Atlantic Monthly Press / Little, Brown, 1976); *When the Lights Go Down* (New York: Holt, Rinehart, and Winston, 1980); *Taking It All In* (New York: Holt, Rinehart, and Winston, 1984); *State of the Art* (New York: E. P. Dutton, 1985); *Hooked* (New York: E. P. Dutton, 1989); and *Movie Love* (New York: E. P. Dutton, 1991). The text of "Movies, the Desperate Art," the first essay in this volume, is taken from *Film: An Anthology*, ed. Daniel Talbot (New York: Simon & Schuster, 1959).

The reviews in the present volume are all reprinted in their entirety. Each has been taken from its first book publication. Where and when the review first appeared is noted at the end of each one. At *The New Yorker*, Kael generally reviewed a number of movies, each separately, for a weekly column. The following eighteen reviews are taken from pieces that originally included reviews of other films: "The Poetry of Images"; "Pipe Dream"; "Louis Malle's Portrait of the Artist as a Young Dog"; "Collaboration and Resistance"; "Moments of Truth"; "Survivor"; "Coming: Nashville"; "All for Love"; "Walking into Your Childhood"; "Shivers"; "Hey, Torquemada"; "Portrait of the Artist as a Young Gadgeteer"; "The Perfectionist"; "Golden Kimonos"; "Irish Voices"; "The Lady from the Sea"; "Unreal"; and "Satyr." An additional fourteen reviews are taken from pieces that originally contained reviews of other films not included here, but whose titles in this collection are now those of the works Kael is reviewing: "*Faces*": from "The Corrupt and the Primitive"; "*High School*": from "High School and Other Forms of Madness"; "*The Fred Astaire and Ginger Rogers Book*": from "Foundering Fathers"; "*Days and Nights in the Forest*": from "Lost and Found"; "*Sparkle*": from "Creamed"; "*The Truck*": from "Contrasts"; "*The Chant of Jimmie Blacksmith*": from "Australians";

"*Used Cars*": from "Dizzy, Dizzy, Dizzy"; "*Atlantic City*": from "Chance/Fate"; "*Pennies from Heaven*": from "Dreamers"; "*Richard Pryor Live on the Sunset Strip*": from "Comedians"; "*E. T. The Extra-Terrestrial*": from "The Pure and the Impure"; "*Tootsie*": from "Tootsie, Gandhi, and Sophie"; and "*The Grifters*" from "Mother, Husband, Brother." In a few instances a piece's subtitle in its original book publication has been omitted if it simply names the film or films under review.

Abbott and Costello, 654
Abe, Yutaka, 738
À Bout de Souffle (Breathless), 46–50,
 69, 123, 129, 162, 186, 188, 588
Academy Awards, 56, 218, 486, 490,
 558, 621
Actor's Revenge, An, 737
Adam, Ken, 681–83
Adams, Brooke, 607–8
Addams, Charles, 97
Adele, Jan, 759–60
Adjani, Isabelle, 500, 502–3
Adrian, Iris, 224
Adventurers, The, 316
Adventures of a Young Man, 101
Agee, James, 44; *Let Us Now Praise
 Famous Men*, 357
Agnew, Spiro, 316, 449, 451
Aguirre, the Wrath of God, 700–1, 705–6
Aherne, Brian, 469
Airport, 266–67
Albee, Edward, 179
Albert, Eddie, 619–20
Albright, Lola, 233
Alda, Alan, 628
Alexander, Elizabeth, 633
Alex in Wonderland, 373, 521–22

Alger, Horatio, 131, 631
Algonquin Round Table, 477
Algren, Nelson, 647
Alice Adams, 10
Alice Doesn't Live Here Anymore, 526,
 655
Alice in Wonderland, 493
Alice's Restaurant, 247–48
Alien, 617, 621, 629
All About Eve, 111, 137
Allégret, Catherine, 337
Allen, Dede, 171
Allen, Karen, 686
Allen, Nancy, 671–72, 674
Allen, Woody, 409–13, 493, 533, 581–85
Allied Artists, 606
All the President's Men, 641
Allures, 119
Almendros, Nestor, 504
Almodóvar, Pedro, 765–68
Alpert, Hollis, 113–14
Alphaville, 121
Altman, Robert, 279–80, 282, 384–85,
 387–88, 390, 392, 456–62, 542, 669
Always Leave Them Laughing, 657
Amarcord, 524
American Federation of Labor, 32, 37

American Film Theatre, 393
American Graffiti, 380, 382
American in Paris, An, 338
American International Pictures, 203–4, 215, 228, 298
Amis, Kingsley, 84
Amityville Horror, The, 625
Anatomy of Love, The, 305
Anderson, Brian, 635
Anderson, Broncho Billy, 473
Anderson Tapes, The, 296
Andersson, Bibi, 510
Andrews, Julie, 470
Andy Hardy, 165
Angeli, Pier, 445
Anger, Kenneth, 382
Anka, Paul, 389
Anna Christie, 165, 361
Anna Karenina, 165
Annie, 680
Annie Hall, 581–82
Antonioni, Michelangelo, 127–34, 180–81, 183, 293, 430, 528, 540, 568, 672
Antonutti, Omero, 714
Any Wednesday, 225
Aparajito, 82, 84
Apocalypse Now, 628, 701
Apollinaire, Guillaume, 65
Appaloosa, The, 345
Apu Trilogy, The, 80–89
Aragon, Louis, 184
Arau, Alfonso, 648
Arbuckle, Fatty, 473
Arcalli, Franco, 332
Ardrey, Robert, 514
Aristotle, 4
Arletty, 223, 427
Arliss, George, 3

Armstrong, Gillian, 758–59, 761
Armstrong, Louis, 56
Arsenic and Old Lace, 495–96
Artaud, Antonin, 184
Arthur, Beatrice, 667
Arthur, Jean, 410, 465–66, 481, 708
Ashby, Hal, 449, 451, 453–54, 618, 708
Aspegren, Chuck, 599
Asta, 482
Astaire, Fred, 54, 93, 141, 275, 347–52, 457, 468, 498, 539, 681, 702
Asther, Nils, 19
Astor, Mary, 785
Atalante, L', 337, 504
Athena, 5
Atlantic City, 659, 661–65
À Tout Prendre, 380
Attentat, L' (The French Conspiracy), 400–2, 405, 407–8
Auberjonois, René, 579
Aubrey, James, 316
Auden, W. H., 168, 388
Augustine, Marty, 389
Au Hasard Balthazar, 185
Austen, Jane, 360
Autobiography of Miss Jane Pittman, The, 422–25
Avventura, L', 69, 293–94, 339
Awful Truth, The, 465, 469–71, 480–82, 484, 493
Axelrod, George, 126, 208

Baby Doll, 662
Bacall, Lauren, 36, 168, 295
Bacharach, Burt, 249
Bachelor and the Bobby-Soxer, The, 485, 487
Bacon, Francis, 336, 751
Badalamenti, Angelo, 749

Bad Company, 399

Bad Day at Black Rock, 12

Bagneris, Vernel, 679

Bailey, Charles W., II, 207

Baillie, Bruce, 119

Bainter, Fay, 295

Baker, Ian, 635

Baker, Josephine, 13

Baker, Lenny, 520–21

Baldwin, Faith, 678–79

Ballad of Cable Hogue, The, 282

Ballard, Carroll, 119, 627, 695

Ballard, Lucien, 120, 512

Ballet Review, 349

Balzac, Honoré de, 319, 596, 734

Bananas, 297, 323, 409–11

Bancroft, Anne, 411

Band, The, 577

Banderas, Antonio, 766

Band of Outsiders, 123, 162, 282

Bang the Drum Slowly, 380, 604

Bankhead, Tallulah, 400, 468

Bara, Theda, 16, 50

Barbarella, 338

Barbieri, Gato, 337

Bardot, Brigitte, 203, 293–94

Barefoot Contessa, The, 5

Barefoot in the Park, 225

Barranco, María, 766

Barrault, Marie-Christine, 544

Barrett, Roy, 632

Barrie, George, 493

Barrow, Clyde, 155, 160–61

Barry, Julian, 432, 438

Barry, Philip, 486

Barry Lyndon, 681

Barrymore, Drew, 697–98

Barrymore, Ethel, 489

Barrymore, John, 16, 110, 117, 146, 149

Barrymore, Lionel, 489

Barthelmess, Richard, 232

Barzini, Andrea, 149

Bass, Saul, 53

Bassani, Giorgio, 306–8

Bates, Florence, 145

Batista, Fulgencio, 444

Battle of Algiers, The, 208, 402–7, 610

Bauer, Harry, 20

Baxley, Barbara, 460

Baxter, Keith, 152

Bay, Frances, 751

Bazin, André, 82, 303, 305; *What Is Cinema?* 308

Beatles, The, 688

Beat the Devil, 219, 385–86, 482

Beatty, Ned, 459, 548

Beatty, Warren, 139, 165–67, 279–81, 448, 450–53, 572

Beau Geste, 601

Beau Serge, Le, 50

Becher, John C., 523

Beck, Stanley, 432

Beckett, Samuel, 555; *Waiting for Godot*, 395

Bedtime Story, 115

Beethoven (*Un Grand Amour de Beethoven*), 20

Beethoven, Ludwig van, 314, 344, 553

Before the Revolution, 180, 273, 276, 382

Begelman, David, 622

Beggar's Opera, The, 8

Belasco, David, 230

Bell, Julian, 142

Bellamy, Ralph, 466, 480, 493

Belle de Jour, 231, 235, 238

Bellini, Vincenzo: *Norma*, 659, 662

Bellocchio, Marco, 178–81, 208

Bellow, Saul, 363

Belmondo, Jean-Paul, 46–47, 50, 274, 294

Belson, Jordan, 119, 230

Ben Barka, Mehdi, 400, 407

Bening, Annette, 783–85

Bennett, Constance, 168, 481

Benton, Robert, 155, 160, 163, 168–69

Bergen, Candice, 619

Berger, Helmut, 306–7

Berger, Thomas: *Little Big Man*, 270

Berghof, Herbert, 522

Bergman, Alan and Marilyn, 731

Bergman, Ingmar, 80–81, 121, 141, 168, 180, 194–99, 283, 449–50, 453, 462, 506–10, 574, 581, 583, 685

Bergman, Ingrid, 214, 465, 495, 498, 748

Berkeley, Busby, 3, 56, 681

Berle, Milton, 438, 657

Bernhardt, Sarah, 705

Bernstein, Elmer, 784

Bernstein, Leonard, 28, 52–54, 56; *Candide*, 668

Bernstein, Walter, 360

Bertolucci, Bernardo, 180–81, 208, 273–78, 331–37, 382, 457, 599, 660

Best Years of Our Lives, The, 10, 93

Beswick, Martine, 644

Bête Humaine, La, 337

Beverly Hillbillies, The, 267

Beymer, Richard, 53

Beyond the Law, 191, 334

Bicycle Thief, The, 83, 303

Bidault, Georges, 325

Big Brother and the Holding Company, 226

Big Knife, The, 389

Big Sleep, The, 93, 168, 385, 390

Billy Budd, 70–74, 395

Billy Jack, 323, 390

Billy the Kid, 158, 169–70

Birdman of Alcatraz, 660

Birth of a Nation, The, 198, 635

Bishop's Wife, The, 486

Bitter Tea of General Yen, The, 19

Björnstrand, Gunnar, 199–200

Black, Karen, 458

Blackboard Jungle, 14, 26, 37–38, 522

Black Magic, 146

Black Orpheus, 51, 53

Black Panthers, 549

Black Rose, The, 146, 148

Black Stallion, The, 615–16, 627, 629, 695–96

Black Widow, 2

Blake, William, 62

Blakley, Ronee, 459–60

Blank, Les, 704, 706

Blessed Event, 137

Blier, Bernard, 586

Blier, Bertrand, 586–95, 739

Blondell, Joan, 224

Blood of a Poet, The, 20, 512

Blow Out, 671–76, 774

Blow-Up, 127–33, 228, 263, 453, 461, 540, 672

Blue, James, 120

Blue Velvet, 745–52

Blume in Love, 373, 388, 521, 523

Bob & Carol & Ted & Alice, 386, 521

Bobby Deerfield, 558

Bob Newhart Show, The, 389, 424

Body and Soul, 653

Bogarde, Dirk, 200

Bogart, Humphrey, 48, 111, 136, 138, 142, 170, 219, 222, 240, 274, 385, 387, 389, 391, 416, 420, 477

Bogdanovich, Peter, 369

Böhm, Karl, 509
Bois, Curt, 213
Boisset, Yves, 407–8
Boland, Mary, 206
Bombshell, 362, 708
Bonerz, Peter, 424
Bonnie and Clyde, 154–73, 185, 187, 215, 248, 362, 367, 419, 453–54, 574, 690
Bonnie Parker Story, The, 156
Booke, Sorrell, 399
Boom Boom, 476
Boorman, John, 373, 571–72
Borges, Jorge Luis, 236, 276
Bori, Lucrezia, 475
Born, Max, 259
Born to Win, 297, 323
Born Yesterday, 362
Boswell, Connee, 678
Boswell Sisters, The, 680
Bottoms, Timothy, 538, 594
Bouise, Jean, 408
Bouquet, Michel, 408
Bouton, Jim, 389
Bow, Clara, 232
Bowers, William, 446
Bowie, David, 539–41
Bowman, Lee, 485
Boxcar Bertha, 382
Boyd, Russell, 760
Boyden, Peter, 675
Boyer, Charles, 16, 144, 468, 471, 729
Boyle, Peter, 525, 528
Boys from Syracuse, The, 667
Boys in the Band, The, 192
Bozzuffi, Marcel, 407
Brackett, Charles, 476
Brackett, Leigh, 390
Bradlee, Ben, 641
Brahms, Johannes, 292

Brando, Marlon, 16–17, 25–26, 28, 31–32, 37, 39, 50, 91, 93, 110–17, 146, 149, 167, 318–20, 331, 333–38, 405–6, 410, 441, 443–45, 490, 528, 655–56, 672, 675
Brautigan, Richard, 263
Bread, Love, and Dreams, 305
Breakfast at Tiffany's, 227, 362
Breaking Away, 616, 621
Breaking Point, 454
Breathless (À Bout de Souffle), 46–50, 69, 123, 129, 162, 186, 188, 588
Brecht, Bertolt, 184, 188, 202, 682, 718
Breener, Dori, 523
Brennan, Walter, 388
Bresson, Robert, 185, 292–93, 428, 702
Brewster McCloud, 456, 458
Brice, Fanny, 344
Brickman, Marshall, 411
Bride Wore Black, The, 218
Bridges, Beau, 374
Bridges, James, 625
Bridges, Jeff, 372–75, 380, 397–99, 596
Bridges at Toko-Ri, The, 9
Bright, Richard, 446
Bringing Up Baby, 93, 453, 465, 471, 481–82, 496, 648, 708
Bring Me the Head of Alfredo Garcia, 513, 515–16
Bronson, Charles, 619
Brontë, Charlotte, 504
Brontë, Emily, 504
Brook, Claudio, 238
Brook, Clive, 222
Brook, Peter, 50
Brooks, Albert, 528
Brooks, Mel, 666–70
Brooks, Richard, 486

Brothers Karamazov, The, 361–62
Brown, Christy, 779–82; *Down All the Days*, 781; *My Left Foot*, 781
Brown, Jim, 693
Brown, John, 714
Browne, Sam, 681
Bruce, Lenny, 432–39, 692
Bruckner, Anton, 90, 597
Bubbles, John W., 213
Buchanan, Jack, 468
Buckaroo Banzai, 766
Bugs Bunny, 546
Bugsy Malone, 684
Bujold, Geneviève, 285
Bullitt, 298, 301, 367
Bunny, John, 473
Buñuel, Luis, 87, 170, 180, 235–41, 291, 313, 376, 554, 574, 586, 765
Burden of Dreams, 704, 706
Burgess, Anthony: *A Clockwork Orange*, 310–12
Burn! 402, 405–6
Burnett, Carol, 410
Burroughs, William: *Naked Lunch*, 72–73
Burton, Richard, 3, 571, 619
Burtt, Ben, 610
Burum, Stephen H., 773
Busey, Gary, 373, 619
Butch Cassidy and the Sundance Kid, 247–50, 368, 602

Caan, James, 318–19, 514, 516–18
Cabaret, 323, 327, 389, 410, 433, 785
Cabinet of Doctor Caligari, The, 700
Cabin in the Cotton, 19
Cabin in the Sky, 213
Cacoyannis, Michael, 284–89
Cactus Flower, 266

Caesar, Sid, 667
Cagney, James, 111, 158–59, 209, 311, 351, 389, 400, 468, 527
Caine Mutiny, The, 9
Calcutta, 294
Calhoun, Rory, 9, 25
California Split, 456, 496, 542
Callas, Charlie, 668
Calmos (Femmes Fatales), 586, 589–90
Camelot, 131, 351
Camion, Le (The Truck), 552–56
Campbell, Paul, 42
Camus, Albert: *L'Etranger (The Stranger)*, 48
Candidate, The, 367
Candy, 362
Cannes Film Festival, 290, 554, 636
Cannon, Dyan, 493, 572
Cantor, Eddie, 16, 161
Capolicchio, Lino, 306
Capone, Al, 158, 320
Capote, Truman, 113, 360
Capra, Frank, 247, 495–96, 547, 751
Captain Newman, M.D., 401
Cara, Irene, 530
Carabiniers, Les, 198, 216, 589, 718
Cardinale, Claudia, 704, 725
Carey, Ron, 667
Carlin, Lynn, 191
Carlyle Cousins, 681
Carnal Knowledge, 367
Carné, Marcel, 337
Carney, Art, 437
Caron, Leslie, 338
Carpetbaggers, The, 316
Carradine, Keith, 459, 461
Carrie, 542, 564–67, 569, 606, 674, 676, 749, 776
Carroll, Helena, 754, 757

Carroll, Nancy, 468

Carroll, Peter, 635

Carson, Johnny, 639, 693

Carter, Jack, 668

Carter, Joseph, 653

Cartwright, Veronica, 609

Caruso, Enrico, 703–5

Cary, Joyce, 356

Casablanca, 27, 92, 116, 495, 515

Casque d'Or, 337

Cassavetes, John, 101, 190–92, 429–30, 565, 567–68, 655

Castel, Lou, 179

Castellano, Richard, 320

Casualties of War, 769–78

Cat and Mouse, 569

Cat People, 608

Caught, 70

Cavett, Dick, 333–34

Cazale, John, 443, 599, 604

Cecil, Jonathan, 667

Central Intelligence Agency, 103, 401, 511–12

Cervantes, Miguel de: *Don Quixote*, 240

Chabrol, Claude, 50, 267, 292

Chafed Elbows, 126

Chaliapin, Feodor, 177

Chamberlain, Richard, 228

Champion, 101

Chandler, Jeff, 9, 25

Chandler, Raymond: *Farewell, My Lovely*, 384; *The Long Goodbye*, 384–92

Chang, Anna, 477

Chant of Jimmie Blacksmith, The, 630–37, 769

Chaplin, Charles, 110, 127, 214, 303–4, 335, 361, 410, 413, 473, 488, 669, 691

Chaplin, Geraldine, 459, 461–62

Chapman, Michael, 526, 609–10

Charade, 93, 465, 468, 491, 497–99

Charles, Jack, 635

Charles, Ray, 141

Charley's Aunt, 709

Chase, The, 169

Chatterji, Soumitra, 354

Chatterton, Ruth, 481

Chayefsky, Paddy, 545–51, 656; *The Tenth Man*, 545

Chekhov, Anton, 108, 723; *The Cherry Orchard*, 85; *The Sea Gull*, 661; *The Three Sisters*, 661; *Uncle Vanya*, 451

Chelsea Girls, The, 191

Cherrill, Virginia, 488

Cheshire, Elizabeth, 643

Chevalier, Maurice, 327, 476

Chiari, Walter, 152

Chien Andalou, Un, 237, 580

Chienne, La, 337

Child Is Waiting, A, 190, 660

Children Are Watching, The, 303

Children of Paradise, 223, 457

Chimes at Midnight (Falstaff), 147, 149–53

China Is Near, 178–81

China Syndrome, The, 619, 625

Chinatown, 454–55, 517, 530, 785–86

Chinoise, La, 182–89, 276, 291

Chirico, Giorgio de, 610

Chodorov, Edward, 477

Chopin, Frédéric, 54, 599

Christie, Julie, 228, 279–81, 448, 450–51

Christ Stopped at Eboli, 637

Ciannelli, Eduardo, 483

Cimino, Michael, 417, 596–604

Cincinnati Kid, The, 453
Cinderella, 564–65
CinemaScope, 2, 9, 206, 213, 745
Cinéma vérité, 190, 335, 429
Cinerama, 229
Circle in the Square, 394
Cisco Pike, 454
Citizen Kane, 129, 147, 149, 180
Citizens Band, 640
City Lights, 488
Ciupa, Richard, 664–65
Clair, René, 9–10, 449
Claire's Knee, 278, 283, 504
Clark, Dane, 380
Clark, Ron, 667
Clarke, Mae, 389
Clash by Night, 71, 363
Clayton, Jack, 770
Clayton, John, 760
Clemenceau Case, The, 305
Clémenti, Pierre, 275, 726
Cleopatra, 97
Cleopatra Jones, 420–21
Clifford, Graeme, 577
Clift, Montgomery, 26, 29
Clive, Colin, 19
Clock, The, 213
Clockwork Orange, A, 310–15, 323
Close Encounters of the Third Kind, 566,
    597, 649, 695–96
Closely Watched Trains, 210, 215
Cobweb, The, 5, 36
Cocteau, Jean, 10, 20–21, 50, 122, 281,
    364, 505, 552, 768; *Les Enfants
    Terribles*, 307–8; *Orpheus*, 60
Cohen, Leonard, 282
Cohn, Roy, 298
Colbert, Claudette, 155, 481, 708
Cold, Ulrik, 508

Cold Wind in August, A, 233
Coleman, Dabney, 644, 712
Coleridge, Samuel Taylor: "Kubla
    Khan," 706
Colette, Sidonie-Gabrielle, 736
Collier, Constance, 145
Collier's, 610
Colman, Ronald, 220, 498
Columbia Pictures, 621–23, 770
Come Back, Little Sheba, 660
Coming Home, 602
Commare Secca, La, 180, 273
Committee, The, 424
Condon, Richard, 208
Confession, The, 402, 405, 407–8
Conformist, The, 273–78, 323, 331, 337,
    382, 445
Congreve, William, 114
Connaughton, Shane, 779, 781–82
Conrad, Joseph: *Heart of Darkness*,
    600, 603, 701
Conroy, Jack, 782
Conte, Richard, 320, 380–81
Conversation, The, 672
Convoy, 569, 571, 573, 575–77
Cooper, Gary, 17, 76–77, 111, 142, 479
Cooper, Jackie, 577
Cooper, James Fenimore: *Leatherstock-
    ing Tales*, 596, 598, 605
Coppola, Francis Ford, 316–18, 320–21,
    440, 442–43, 445–47, 454, 542, 570,
    597, 599, 603, 615–16, 628, 671–72,
    701
Cops and Robbers, 368
Corman, Avery, 626
Corman, Roger, 446
Cornered, 420
Cornford, John, 142
Corot, Jean-Baptiste-Camille, 724

Cosmopolitan, 113, 549
Costa-Gavras (Konstantinos Gavras),
   369, 402, 404–7
Cotten, Joseph, 149, 228
Cotton Comes to Harlem, 297
Countess from Hong Kong, A, 335
Countess Maritza, 476
Cousin, Cousine, 543–44
Cousins, The, 50
Cousteau, Jacques, 292
Coutard, Raoul, 120, 184
Coward, Noël, 468, 486
Coyote, Peter, 698
Cracknell, Ruth, 633
Craigie, Ingrid, 754, 757
Craig's Wife, 581
Crawford, Joan, 16–17, 111, 231,
   493–94
Crazy Quilt, The, 120, 422
Cries and Whispers, 507, 574
Crimson Pirate, The, 94, 496, 660
Crisis, 486
Crist, Judith, 94–95
Croce, Arlene: *The Fred Astaire &
   Ginger Rogers Book*, 347–52
Cromwell, Richard, 232
Crosby, Bing, 468, 490, 493, 678–79
Crosby, Don, 632
Crossfire, 12, 70
Cross of Iron, 576
Crowther, Bosley, 52, 55, 60, 78, 81, 84,
   95–96, 99, 102, 233, 151
Cry Uncle, 297
Cukor, George, 469–70
Cummings, Robert, 495
Cummins, Peggy, 156
Curtin, Valerie, 708
Curtis, Tony, 3, 14, 213, 465, 496
Cusack, John, 783, 785

Dadaism, 609
Daddy Long Legs, 9
Dailey, Dan, 141
Dall, John, 156
Damned, The, 275, 277
Dandy in Aspic, A, 207
Dangerous, 340
Daniel, 732
Daniell, Henry, 145
Daniels, Danny, 681–83
Danny Kaye Show, The, 521
Danova, Cesare, 378
D'Antoni, Philip, 298
Dark of the Sun, 657
Dark Victory, 224, 340
Darling, 281
Darnell, Linda, 460
Darwin, Charles, 559
Dating Game, The, 639
David and Lisa, 80–81, 232
Davis, Angela, 549
Davis, Bette, 16, 19, 110–11, 117, 144,
   146, 224, 340, 494, 560, 700, 703
Davis, Joan, 570
Davis, Judy, 758, 760–61
Davis, Ossie, 203, 217, 421
Davis, Miles, 292
Davis, Viveka, 690
Dawson, Julie, 631
Day, Doris, 36, 212, 224, 498
Day in the Country, A, 504
Day-Lewis, Daniel, 779–82
Day of the Jackal, The, 407
Day of the Locust, The, 388
Day of Wrath, 6, 702
Days and Nights in the Forest, 353–57, 758
Days of Heaven, 608
Dead, The, 753–57, 785
Dead End, 170–71

Dead End Kids, 54, 112, 114

Dead of Night, 575

Dean, James, 26, 34, 142, 432, 503, 539

Death of a Salesman, 8

Decaë, Henri, 120, 591

Deep, The, 571

Deer Hunter, The, 596–605, 727

De Gaulle, Charles, 324

De Havilland, Olivia, 111

Delany, Cathleen, 754, 756

Delerue, Georges, 68, 558, 590–91

Deliverance, 373, 597

Delon, Alain, 619, 724–25

Del Rio, Dolores, 224

DeLuise, Dom, 666, 668

DeMille, Cecil B., 5, 168, 257–58, 260, 277, 400

Demme, Jonathan, 638, 640, 643–45

Demy, Jacques, 211, 730

De Negri, Giuliani G., 713

Deneuve, Catherine, 503

De Niro, Robert, 374, 378, 380, 441–44, 525, 527–28, 538, 596, 604–5, 652–53, 655–57

Denner, Charles, 407

Denver, John, 619

De Palma, Brian, 542–43, 564–67, 669, 671–76, 749, 770, 773–77

De Palma, Rossy, 766

Depardieu, Gérard, 552–53, 586, 588, 591–92, 594–95

Derby, 323

Dermithe, Édouard, 179, 307

Dern, Laura, 746, 749

De Sica, Vittorio, 45, 81–83, 89, 149, 303–9

Desirée, 14, 115

Destination Tokyo, 489

Destry Rides Again, 481

Detective, The, 202

Devi, 80, 85–89

Devil and Daniel Webster, The, 396

Devils, The, 298

Devil's Disciple, The, 660

Devil's Playground, The, 635

Dewaere, Patrick, 586, 588, 591–92, 594–95

De Wilde, Brandon, 91, 94

Diary of a Chambermaid, 238, 240

Diary of a Mad Housewife, 297

Dickens, Charles, 316, 570, 734

Dickerson, George, 750

Dickey, James, 373

Dietrich, Marlene, 168, 222, 359, 428, 468, 481, 555

Dillinger, 516, 535

Dillinger, John, 158

Dillman, Bradford, 398

DiMaggio, Joe, 363

Dirty Dozen, The, 164, 298

Dirty Harry, 416–19

Discreet Charm of the Bourgeoisie, The, 554

Disney studios, 224, 298, 344, 544, 647

Dobson, Tamara, 420

Doctor Zhivago, 207, 281

Dodds, Steve, 633, 635

Dodsworth, 641

Dog Day Afternoon, 537

Dogs of War, The, 680

Dolby sound, 578, 599, 606–7

Dolce Vita, La, 257–61, 293, 379

Dona Flor and Her Two Husbands, 569

Donahue, Jack, 476

Donahue, Troy, 445

Donati, Danilo, 259

Donen, Stanley, 491

Don Juan, 426, 452, 454, 485, 501–2

Donnelly, Donal, 754, 756

Don't Bother to Knock, 361

Don't Look Now, 539, 577

Doqui, Robert, 461

Dorléac, Françoise, 503

Dorsey Brothers Orchestra, 680

Dostoyevsky, Fyodor, 570; *The Brothers Karamazov*, 72, 166, 734; *Crime and Punishment*, 166, 428; *The Double*, 275; *The Idiot*, 73; *Notes from Underground*, 525; *The Possessed*, 185

Double Indemnity, 48, 50, 93, 137, 386, 388

Douglas, Kirk, 3, 16, 111, 486, 497, 565

Douglas, Melvyn, 91, 94, 96, 471

Douglas, Michael, 619

Dourif, Brad, 579

Dovzhenko, Aleksandr, 83, 170, 278, 402, 577, 716

Downey, Robert, 126

Downhill Racer, 374

Drake, Betsy, 477, 486

Dream Wife, 487, 489

Dressed to Kill, 673, 676, 776

Dreyer, Carl, 702, 782

Dreyfuss, Richard, 380, 533–34

Dr. Strangelove, 129, 172–73, 229, 312, 568, 681

Du Barry Was a Lady, 213

Duck Soup, 481, 669

Duel in the Sun, 4, 34

Dufy, Raoul, 499

Dumarcay, Philippe, 590

Dumbrille, Douglass, 401

Dummar, Melvin, 638–46

Dumont, Margaret, 410

Dunaway, Faye, 165, 167, 545, 550, 578

Dune, 749–50

Dunne, Irene, 228, 465–66, 470, 481–82, 484–86

Duprez, June, 489

Duras, Marguerite, 552–56

Dürer, Albrecht, 454

Durning, Charles, 712

Duvall, Robert, 319, 446, 514, 546, 548, 610

Duvall, Shelley, 461

Dwyer, John, 32, 37

Dyer, John, 97–100

Dynasts, The, 5

Dzundza, George, 598, 604

Earrings of Madame de . . . , The, 8, 282, 305, 453, 728, 769

Earth, 83

Eastman color, 591

East of Eden, 5, 26, 34–36, 142

East Side, West Side, 423

Eastwood, Clint, 215, 414–18, 535, 539, 573, 596–97, 619

Easy Living, 213, 708

Easy Rider, 245–46, 367, 382, 587

Easy to Wed, 2

Eburne, Maude, 145

Eddy, Nelson, 476

Eden, Anthony, 325–26

Edge of Darkness, 198

Edge of the City, 101

Edwards, Blake, 126

Egan, Michael, 522

Egyptian, The, 17, 33–34

8½, 123, 133, 212, 228, 259–61, 379, 457

Einstein, Albert, 559

Eisenstein, Sergei, 83, 88, 122, 153, 163, 170, 402–3, 533, 543, 574, 577

Elephant Man, The, 750

Elgar, Edward, 314

Eliot, George, 360, 570; *Middlemarch*, 734
Eliot, T. S., 239
Ellington, Duke, 344
Ellsberg, Daniel, 301
Elmes, Frederick, 750
Elvira Madigan, 185, 249, 308
Elvis, 647
Elvis on Tour, 382
Emerson, Ralph Waldo, 117
Empire Strikes Back, The, 615–16, 628, 697
End, The, 666
Enemies, A Love Story, 783
Enfants Terribles, Les, 50, 179, 307–8
Engels, Friedrich, 559
Enter Laughing, 213
Enter Madam, 468
Entertainer, The, 108
Eraserhead, 750
Erhard, Werner, 608
Ericson, Eric, 509
Escape Artist, The, 696–97
Esquire, 84, 166, 360, 370
E.T.: The Extra-Terrestrial, 695–99
Etting, Ruth, 16
Euripides: *Medea*, 164; *The Trojan Women*, 284–86, 288
Eustache, Jean, 427–30
Evans, Walker, 679; *Let Us Now Praise Famous Men*, 159
Every Girl Should Be Married, 486
Everything You Always Wanted to Know about Sex, 409–11
Executive Action, 401
Executive Suite, 52
Existentialism, 299, 302, 336
Exorcist II, 571
Expressionism, 381, 526, 748, 775

Exterminating Angel, The, 236
Eyes of Laura Mars, 569, 574, 578–80

Faces, 190–93
Fairbanks, Douglas, Jr., 307, 483, 498
Fairbanks, Douglas, Sr., 16, 77, 474–75
Falconetti, Maria, 604
Fallen Idol, The, 9
Falstaff (*Chimes at Midnight*), 147, 149–53
Fame, 684
Fanfan the Tulip, 448
Fanon, Frantz, 405
Fantasia, 262, 344
Fargas, Antonio, 523
Farrell, Charles, 232
Farrell, Glenda, 480
Farrell, James T.: *Studs Lonigan*, 381
Farris, John, 565
Farrow, Mia, 465
Fat City, 399
Faulkner, William, 100–1, 222, 271, 301, 483; *The Wild Palms*, 46
Faye, Herbie, 644
Fear and Desire, 522
Federal Bureau of Investigation, 301, 610, 750
Feld, Fritz, 667
Feldman, Phil, 446
Fellini, Federico, 121, 123, 141, 168, 180–81, 228, 257–62, 277, 283, 377, 379, 524, 658, 718
Fellini Satyricon, 257–62
Femmes Fatales (*Calmos*), 586, 589–90
Fermi, Enrico, 404
Ferrer, José, 108, 213, 486
Ferreux, Benoît, 290, 295
Ferro, Pablo, 223
Feuchtwanger, Lion, 90

Feu Follet, Le (The Fire Within), 293–94

Feuillère, Edwige, 233

Feydeau, Ernest-Aimé, 449, 663, 767;
 A Flea in His Ear, 661

Fiddler on the Roof, 323

Field, Sally, 573

Fields, W. C., 149, 152, 206, 412, 649

Film Comment, 657

Film Culture, 6

Films and Filming, 99

Finch, Flora, 473

Finch, Peter, 546–48

Fine Madness, A, 120

Finian's Rainbow, 208

Finlay, Frank, 107–8

Finney, Albert, 684, 687, 690

Finney, Jack: *The Body Snatchers*,
 609–10

Fires on the Plain, 737

Fire Within, The (Le Feu Follet), 293–94

Fischer-Dieskau, Dietrich, 509

Fisher, Carrie, 451

Fisher, Eddie, 389

Fistful of Dollars, A, 416

Fists in the Pocket (I Pugni in Tasca),
 179–80

Fitch, Robert, 680

Fitzcarraldo, 700–7

Fitzgerald, Barry, 489

Fitzgerald, F. Scott, 68, 187, 295;
 "Babylon Revisited," 293

Fitzgerald, Geraldine, 373

Fitzgerald, Zelda, 68, 358

FitzPatrick, James, 2

Five Easy Pieces, 264, 368

Flaherty, Robert, 83, 177

Fleischer, Richard, 401

Florey, Robert, 137

Fly, The, 609

Flynn, Errol, 421

Follow the Fleet, 348–49, 681

Fonda, Henry, 77, 156, 466, 468,
 470–71

Fonda, Jane, 323, 338, 532, 557–58,
 560–61, 563, 688

Foolin' Around, 619

Fool There Was, A, 50

Ford, John, 77–78, 153, 171, 573

Forman, Miloš, 662

For Me and My Gal, 351

Fort Apache, 77

Fosse, Bob, 432–33, 438

Fossey, Brigitte, 586, 590–91

Foster, Jodi, 526–27

400 Blows, The, 50, 291, 428, 502

Four Nights of a Dreamer, 428

Fowley, Douglas, 145

Fox, Edward, 562

Fox, Michael J., 770, 773

Frances, 712

Francis, Kay, 485

Franco, Francisco, 238, 765

Frank, Melvin, 487

Frankenheimer, John, 207, 393, 396, 711

Franklin, Aretha, 345, 530

Frantic (Elevator to the Gallows), 292

Franz, Dennis, 672

Frears, Stephen, 784–85

Frederick, Pauline, 232

Freed, Donald, 401

Free to Be . . . You and Me, 434

French, Leslie, 726

French Connection, The, 298–302, 323,
 367, 401, 467

French Conspiracy, The (L'Attentat),
 400–2, 405, 407–8

Freud, Sigmund, 36, 42, 87, 238, 240,
 361, 363, 394, 490, 520, 550, 559

Freund, Karl, 137
Fricker, Brenda, 780
Friedkin, William, 298, 300
Friels, Colin, 759–61
Friendly Persuasion, 116
Friends of Eddie Coyle, The, 381
Friml, Rudolf, 53
Froman, Jane, 16
From Here to Eternity, 14, 27–29, 33, 103, 317, 557, 595, 660
Front Page, The, 483
Fugitive Kind, The, 112, 228
Fujimoto, Tak, 644
Funny Face, 161
Funny Girl, 344, 734
Funnyman, 422, 424
Funny Thing Happened on the Way to the Forum, A, 666
Furie, Sidney, 207, 345–46
Furthman, Jules, 168, 222
Fury, The, 564–69, 574–75, 610, 673, 675
Fussell, Paul: *Wartime*, 772

Gabin, Jean, 550
Gable, Clark, 17, 114, 155, 342, 361, 400, 466–67, 493–94
Gaines, Ernest J., 424–25
Gale, Bob, 648–49, 651
Game of Love, The, 233
Gang That Couldn't Shoot Straight, The, 374
Ganguly, Sunil, 355
Garbo, Greta, 16, 113, 131, 165, 286, 307, 359, 494, 550, 560, 702, 783
Garden of Evil, 9, 34
Garden of the Finzi-Continis, The, 305–9, 323
Gardner, Ava, 207, 531

Gardner, Herb, 434
Garfield, Allen, 460
Garfield, John, 36, 111, 380
Garfinkle, Louis, 603
Garfunkel, Art, 254
Gargan, William, 163
Garibaldi, Giuseppe, 724–26, 728
Garland, Judy, 316, 351
Garland, Robert, 708
Garner, Jay, 681
Garr, Teri, 709, 712
Garson, Greer, 17
Gavin, John, 668
Gay Divorcee, The, 349
Gaynes, George, 712
Gaynor, Janet, 17, 215, 678
Gazzo, Michael V., 446
Geer, Will, 401
Gehrig, Lou, 16
Gelbart, Larry, 708
Gélin, Daniel, 291
General, The, 9
Genet, Jean, 40, 293
Genevieve, 19
Genovese, Kitty, 130
Genthe, Arnold, 560
Gentleman's Agreement, 11, 93
Gentlemen Prefer Blondes, 361
Georgy Girl, 127, 231
Géricault, Théodore, 504
Gershwin, George, 53–54
Getaway, The, 511
Get Out Your Handkerchiefs, 586, 589, 591, 594–95, 739
Get to Know Your Rabbit, 673
Getting Straight, 270
Gibbon, Edward, 258
Gibbs, Anthony, 227
Gibran, Khalil, 128

Gibson, Henry, 389, 456

Gibson, William, 169

Gielgud, John, 152

Gill, Brendan, 100–2, 293

Gilliatt, Penelope, 96, 100

Girotti, Massimo, 336–37

Gish, Lillian, 60, 113

Glover, John, 562, 644

Go Ask Alice, 422, 425

Go-Between, The, 306, 308

Godard, Jean-Luc, 47–50, 120–24, 162, 178, 181–89, 199, 211, 216, 276, 282, 291, 337, 374, 461, 566, 589, 609, 718

Goddess, The, 545, 550

Godfather, The, 316–23, 367, 377, 381–82, 419, 440, 442, 454, 569, 655, 727, 769

Godfather: Part II, The, 440–47, 527, 536, 542, 544, 569, 655, 769

God's Little Acre, 71

Going My Way, 490

Going Places (Les Valseuses), 586–95

Goin' South, 642

Gold, Tracey, 690

Goldblum, Jeff, 523, 609

Gold Diggers of 1933, 56

Gold Diggers of 1937, 480

Golden Boy, 53, 653

Golden Coach, The, 8, 40–43, 163

Golden Dawn, 476–77

Golding, Louis, 381

Goldman, Albert: *Ladies and Gentlemen, Lenny Bruce!!* 436–37

Goldman, Bo, 638, 640, 644, 684–86, 688

Goldman, William, 248–49

Gold of Naples, The, 305

Goldwater, Barry, 94

Goldwyn, Samuel, 10, 486

Goldwyn Girls, 667

Gone with the Wind, 424, 517, 723

Goodbye, Columbus, 246, 306

Goodbye Girl, The, 681

Good Earth, The, 96

GoodFellas, 786

Goodman, Benny, 344

Goodman, Ezra: *The Fifty-Year Decline and Fall of Hollywood*, 362–63

Gordon's War, 420–21

Gorman, Cliff, 432, 434

Gould, Elliott, 385–87, 391–92

Goulet, Robert, 664

Governor, Jimmy, 630

Goya, Francisco, 318, 574

Grable, Betty, 359

Graduate, The, 192, 231–33, 530

Graham, Billy, 196

Graham, Gerrit, 649–50

Graham, Ronny, 668

Grahame, Gloria, 36, 644, 654

Gramatica, Emma, 304

Granach, Alexander, 140

Grande Illusion, La, 20

Grand Guignol, 111

Grand Hotel, 3, 5, 457, 462

Grand Illusion, 9, 327, 716, 769

Grand Prix, 169

Granger, Farley, 156

Grant, Cary (Archibald Leach), 111, 388, 465–99, 708

Grant, Lee, 448, 451

Grateful Dead, The, 226

Grave, Louis, 327

Grease, 571, 573

Great Depression, 140, 159–61, 171, 480–82, 545, 677, 679

Great Gatsby, The, 465

Great Northfield Minnesota Raid, The, 610

Green, Martyn, 399
Green Berets, The, 298
Greene, Ellen, 520, 522
Greene, Graham, 381–82
Greene, Shecky, 668
Green Hat, The, 307–8
Greer, Germaine, 400
Greetings, 296, 672
Greuze, Jean-Baptiste, 728
Grey, Joel, 389, 660
Griffith, D. W., 6, 8, 69, 122, 150, 153, 177, 278, 304
Griffith, Kristin, 583–84
Grifters, The, 783–86
Grodin, Charles, 572
Guare, John, 659–63; *Bosoms and Neglect*, 661; *The House of Blue Leaves*, 661; *Marco Polo Sings a Solo*, 660–61
Guerre Est Finie, La, 404, 408
Guevara, Ernesto "Che," 182
Guide for the Married Man, A, 225
Guidelli, Micol, 713
Guiles, Fred Lawrence: *Norma Jean*, 360
Guillén, Fernando, 765
Guinness, Alec, 556
Guitry, Sacha, 9, 592
Gun Crazy, 156
Gunfighter, The, 77
Gunga Din, 77, 481–82, 484, 488, 496
Gunn, Moses, 399
Gunsmoke, 513
Guthrie, Arlo, 250

Hackman, Gene, 170, 299, 301, 538
Hagegård, Håkan, 509
Hail, Hero! 401–2
Hair, 260, 432
Half a Sixpence, 207

Hall, Conrad, 249
Hall, Porter, 145
Hambling, Gerry, 690
Hamilton, Edith, 289
Hamilton, Margaret, 686
Hamlet, 8, 109
Hammerstein, Arthur, 476, 479
Hammerstein, Oscar, II, 476, 479
Hammerstein, Reggie, 476, 479
Hammett, Dashiell, 388, 558, 561, 563; *The Maltese Falcon*, 390–91
Hampton, Paul, 342
Hans Christian Andersen, 10
Harbach, Otto, 476
Hard Day's Night, A, 225, 227
Harding, Ann, 481
Harewood, Dorian, 530
Harlow, Honey, 432, 438
Harlow, Jean, 16, 168, 359, 362, 479, 654, 708
Harmon, Deborah, 650
Harold and Maude, 454
Harper, Jessica, 678, 682
Harper's, 28, 33, 37
Harper's Bazaar, 81, 128
Harris, Barbara, 461
Harris, Leonard, 528
Harris, Richard, 536
Harron, Robert, 232
Harry & Tonto, 437, 521–22
Harry Kellerman (Who Is Harry Kellerman and Why Is He Saying Those Terrible Things About Me?), 297
Hart, Lorenz, 16
Hart, Moss, 477, 487
Harvey, Don, 772
Harwood, Elizabeth, 662
Hauer, Rutger, 703
Hawks, Howard, 168, 482–83

Hawn, Goldie, 448, 451

Hayden, Sterling, 389

Hayes, Helen, 481

Hayes, John Michael, 120

Hays office, 348

Hayward, Susan, 3, 341, 531

Hayworth, Rita, 465

Healy, Ted, 301

Hearst, Patty, 549

Hearst, William Randolph, 160

Heaven Can Wait, 569, 572, 575

Hecht, Ben, 129, 168, 482–83

Hee Haw, 267

Hefner, Hugh, 667

Hegel, G. W. F., 559

Hellman, Lillian, 93; *The Children's Hour*, 559, 561, 563; *Pentimento*, 557–63; *Scoundrel Time*, 562; *An Unfinished Woman*, 560

Help! 227

Hembrow, Mark, 759

Hemingway, Ernest, 101, 142, 358, 387–88, 561, 601

Hemmings, David, 131

Henreid, Paul, 515

Henry V, 108–9, 151

Hepburn, Audrey, 465, 468, 499

Hepburn, Katharine, 285–86, 465–66, 469, 481–82, 484–85, 494–96, 540, 708, 730

Herbert, Victor, 53

Herrmann, Bernard, 528

Herzog, Werner, 195, 700–7

Hesse, Hermann, 263

Heston, Charlton, 537

He Who Must Die, 51

Hi, Mom! 669

High and the Mighty, The, 34

High Noon, 77, 116, 138

High School, 252–56, 369–70

High Tide, 758–61

Hill, Arthur, 514, 517

Hill, Dana, 685, 690

Hill, George Roy, 248

Hill, Steven, 735

Hill, Walter, 628

Hillerman, John, 668

Hindle, Art, 608

Hines, Gregory, 668–69

Hingle, Pat, 785

Hiroshima Mon Amour, 552

Hirsch, Elroy "Crazylegs," 16

Hirsch, Paul, 673

His Girl Friday, 18, 137, 466, 480, 482–83, 488

History of the World—Part I, 666–70

Hitchcock, Alfred, 50, 156, 168, 201, 221, 300, 491, 564, 567, 580

Hitler, Adolf, 90, 313, 323, 326, 550, 559, 600, 701

Hoffman, Dustin, 231, 380, 432, 434–38, 628, 708–11

Holbrook, Hal, 204, 217, 418, 558

Holden, William, 516, 546, 550

Holder, Geoffrey, 371

Holiday, 465, 482

Holiday, Billie, 340–46

Holinshed, Raphael: *Chronicles*, 151

Holmes, Phillips, 139

Holt, Charlene, 644

Home and the World, The, 758

Home Box Office, 586

Homer: *Iliad*, 327; *Odyssey*, 580

Hoodlum Priest, The, 120

Hooper, 572–73

Hopper, Dennis, 747, 749

Hopper, Edward: "Nighthawks," 677

Hopper, Hedda, 358

Horse's Mouth, The, 10
Hospital, The, 323, 546
Hot Millions, 216
Houdini, Harry, 16
Hour of the Wolf, 194–96, 217
House of Strangers, 320, 381
Houseboat, 489
Houseman, John, 148, 156
Howard, Trevor, 114
Howards of Virginia, The, 466, 492
Howe, James Wong, 101
How I Won the War, 226, 715
Hud, 91–103
Hudson, Rock, 212, 498
Hughes, Howard, 316, 638–46, 688
Hugo, Adèle, 500, 502–3, 505
Hugo, Victor, 500, 502, 505
Human Voice, The, 768
Humes, Mary-Margaret, 668
Hunter, Ross, 218
Hunter, Tab, 3
Hurricane, 640
Hurst, Fannie, 86
Hurt, John, 668
Hurt, Mary Beth, 583
Husbands, 429
Hustler, The, 372, 374
Huston, Anjelica, 754, 756–57, 783, 785–86
Huston, John, 5, 753, 755–57, 785–86
Huston, Tony, 756
Huston, Walter, 641
Hutton, Barbara, 475, 488, 490
Huxley, Aldous: Brave New World, 629

I Am a Fugitive from a Chain Gang, 369, 400
Ibsen, Henrik, 7, 397; The Lady from the Sea, 560; The Wild Duck, 661

Iceman Cometh, The, 393–99
Ichikawa, Kon, 737, 739–41, 758
I Ching, 263
Ikiru, 79
I'll Cry Tomorrow, 341
I Love My Wife, 264
Imitation of Life, 262
I'm No Angel, 93, 469, 481
Impossible Camera, The, 294
In Cold Blood, 213
Inheritor, The, 407
In Name Only, 485
Interiors, 569, 581–85
Interlenghi, Franco, 45, 379
International Longshoremen's Association, 32, 37
International Settlement, 224
In the Heat of the Night, 218–20, 453
Intolerance, 69
Invasion of the Body Snatchers (1956), 606, 610
Invasion of the Body Snatchers (1978), 606–11
Investigation of a Citizen above Suspicion, 400, 408
Ionesco, Eugene: Rhinoceros, 606
Ipcress File, The, 345
I Remember Mama, 10
Irene, 476
Irving, Amy, 565, 733, 735
It Happened One Night, 155, 468, 481, 496
It's a Big Country, 11
It's Always Fair Weather, 141
I Walk Alone, 657
I Wanna Hold Your Hand, 649
I Want to Live! 52, 157
I Was a Male War Bride, 496
I Was a Teenage Werewolf, 204

Jackson, Anne, 660–61

Jacobi, Lou, 523

Jaffe, Sam, 483

James, Henry: "Daisy Miller," 49, 362

James, Jesse, 155, 158, 610

James Bond, 110, 140, 420, 681

Jarrell, Randall, 567

Jaubert, Maurice, 503

Jaws, 533–34, 542–43, 569, 606

Jesus Christ, 539–40, 543, 572

Jesus Christ Superstar, 432

Jewison, Norman, 219–20, 222–23, 453

Joanna, 190, 193

Joan of Arc, 49, 230

Joe, 367, 549

Johnson, Lamont, 371, 373

John XXIII, 437

Jolson, Al, 16

Jones, Christopher, 204

Jones, Jennifer, 502

Jones, Laura, 758

Jones, LeRoi (Amiri Baraka), 237

Jones, Tommy Lee, 579

Jonson, Ben, 587; *Volpone*, 647, 649

Jory, Victor, 228

Jour Se Leve, Le, 19, 427

Joy, Robert, 662

Joyce, Alice, 232

Joyce, James, 27; "The Dead," 753–57; *Finnegans Wake*, 389; *Ulysses*, 459, 461, 753

Judgment at Nuremberg, 660

Jules and Jim, 64–69, 129, 163, 171, 211, 501

Julia, 557–63

Juliet of the Spirits, 110, 123, 212, 259–60

Julius Caesar, 61, 148, 165

Jung, Carl, 258

Jupiter's Darling, 5

Jutra, Claude, 380

Kafka, Franz: "Metamorphosis," 183

Kahn, Herman, 229

Kahn, Madeline, 668

Kahn, Michael, 579, 651

Kane, Helen, 678

Kane, J. D., 576

Karvan, Claudia, 759–60

Kauffmann, Stanley, 54–55, 59, 65, 68, 99

Kaufman, Andy, 639

Kaufman, George S., 412

Kaufman, Phil, 606, 608–10

Kaufman, Robert, 708

Kaye, Danny, 521

Kazan, Elia, 5, 8, 28, 30–31, 34, 662, 770

Kazin, Alfred, 678

Kean, Marie, 754, 756

Keaton, Buster, 9, 410, 413

Keaton, Diane, 320, 410, 445, 583–84, 684, 687–88, 690

Keats, John, 142

Keel, Howard, 4

Kehoe, Jack, 645

Keitel, Harvey, 378, 380, 526–27

Keith, Brian, 209

Keller, Helen, 163

Keller, Hiram, 260

Kellin, Mike, 520

Kelly, Gene, 54, 141, 213, 351

Kelly, Grace, 465

Kelly, Orry, 475

Keneally, Thomas, 630, 632, 635–37

Kennedy, Jacqueline, 436

Kennedy, John, 103, 401, 461, 467, 672

Kennedy, Robert, 461

Kerby, William, 373

Kershner, Irvin, 120, 536, 578–79, 627, 689, 758

Key, The, 737–39

Keystone Cops, 46, 162, 473, 482, 588

Kiefer, Anselm, 717

Killer Elite, The, 511–19

Killers, The, 659

Killing, The, 62

King, Erik, 771

King, Morgana, 445

King, Tony, 530

King, Walter Woolf, 410

King Kong, 566

King Lear, 85

King of Marvin Gardens, The, 662

Kinsey Report, 100

Kinski, Klaus, 700, 703–4

Kipling, Rudyard, 483

Kirkland, Geoffrey, 690

Kishi, Keiko, 738

Kiss and Make Up, 493

Kiss Me, Kate, 680

Kiss Them for Me, 489

Kitt, Eartha, 420

Kline, Richard H., 565–66

Klute, 296, 323, 688

Knack, The, 227

Knebel, Fletcher, 207

Knight, Arthur, 54, 95

Knight, Shirley, 228

Kohner, Susan, 262

Kolb, Ken: *Getting Straight*, 270

Korman, Harvey, 668

Kortner, Fritz, 140

Korty, John, 120, 422, 424–25

Kosleck, Martin, 400

Köstlinger, Josef, 508

Kotegawa, Yuko, 738

Kramer, Stanley, 11, 51, 218

Kramer vs. Kramer, 621, 628

Krasker, Robert, 70

Kristofferson, Kris, 576–77

Kubrick, Stanley, 60, 62–63, 228–30, 261, 310–14, 344, 522

Kurosawa, Akira, 76–79, 81, 151, 153, 512, 574

Ladd, Alan, 3, 76, 367

Ladd, Alan, Jr., 617

Ladies' Home Journal, 472

Lady Eve, The, 93, 471

Lady in the Dark, 8

Lady Sings the Blues, 340–46

Lafont, Bernadette, 426–28

Lahr, Bert, 488

Lamarr, Hedy, 359

Lambrakis, Grigoris, 404

Lamont, Duncan, 42

La Motta, Jake, 652–58

Lampedusa, Giuseppe di: *The Leopard*, 723, 725

Lancaster, Burt, 29, 203, 217, 401, 496, 659–60, 662, 723–26, 729

Lander, David L., 650

Landlord, The, 296, 451, 453–54

Land Without Bread, 240

Lane, Mark, 401

Lane, Priscilla, 496

Lang, Daniel, 769–70, 773, 775

Lang, Fritz, 55, 156, 571

Langdon, Harry, 481

Lange, Dorothea, 159

Lange, Hope, 751

Lange, Jessica, 711–12

Lansbury, Angela, 213

Lansky, Meyer, 446

Last American Hero, The, 370–75, 380, 399

Last Detail, The, 454–55

Last Embrace, 643

Last of Sheila, The, 369

Last Outpost, The, 468

Last Picture Show, The, 328, 367, 399

Last Tango in Paris, 331–39, 457, 503, 528, 588

Last Waltz, The, 569, 577–78, 610

Last Year at Marienbad, 67, 110, 127, 132–33, 540

Lathrop, Phil, 512

Latin Lovers, 2

Latouche, John, 668

Laughing Policeman, The, 415

Laughton, Charles, 146, 149

Laure, Carole, 591–92, 739

Laurel, Stan, 483

Laurel and Hardy, 182, 481, 483

Laurents, Arthur, 52

Lauter, Ed, 372

Laval, Pierre, 325

Law and Order, 251–52, 255

Law of Desire, 768

Lawrence, D. H., 238, 596, 732

Lawrence of Arabia, 705

Lawyer, The, 345

Leach, Archibald. *See* Grant, Cary

Leach, Elias and Elsie, 472, 488, 499

Leachman, Cloris, 619, 668

Lean, David, 273, 557, 758

Lear, Edward, 83

Leather Boys, The, 345

Léaud, Jean-Pierre, 332, 337, 426–28, 502

Lebrun, Françoise, 427–29

Lederer, Charles, 483

Lee, Gypsy Rose, 400

Left Handed Gun, The, 163, 169–70

Legend of Lylah Clare, The, 202

Legion of Decency, 64–65

Legrand, Michel, 345, 730–31

Lehar, Franz: *The Merry Widow*, 449

Lehman, Ernest, 52

Leigh, Janet, 3, 14

Leigh, Vivien, 31, 93

Lelouch, Claude, 543

Le Mat, Paul, 640, 645

Lemmon, Jack, 496

Lenin, Vladimir, 186

Lenny, 432–39

Leonardo da Vinci, 361

Leopard, The, 660, 723–29

Lester, Richard, 167, 225–28, 230, 246, 293, 667, 715

Let's Make a Deal, 639, 645

Let's Make Love, 361–62

Letter to Three Wives, A, 18, 137

Lettieri, Al, 320

Levant, Oscar, 320

Levi, Carlo, 637

Levine, David, 179

Levinson, Barry, 708

Lewis, Al, 647

Lewis, Fiona, 567

Lewis, Sinclair, 142; *It Can't Happen Here*, 203

Lewis, Tommy, 631, 635

Liberty, 139

Libido, 635

Liddy, G. Gordon, 702

Life, 11, 45, 654, 718

Life and Times of Judge Roy Bean, The, 418

Lift to the Scaffold (Frantic), 292

Light Snowfall, A, 737–38

Lilith, 166

Limelight, 27

Lincoln, Abraham, 171, 364

Lindsay, John, 296, 545
Liszt, Franz, 54
Lithgow, John, 672, 766
Little Big Man, 368
Little Fauss and Big Halsy, 345
Little Murders, 296
Live and Let Die, 371
Lives of a Bengal Lancer, 483, 596
Lizzani, Carlo, 208
Llewellyn, Richard: *None but the Lonely Heart*, 488
Lloyd, Harold, 412
Lockwood, Gary, 229
Logan, Joshua, 113
Lolita, 58–63, 81, 521
Lollobrigida, Gina, 149, 305
Lombard, Carole, 228, 343, 468, 481, 678–79
London, Jack, 689
Loneliness of the Long Distance Runner, The, 227
Lonely Are the Brave, 402
Long Goodbye, The, 384–92, 410
Long Gray Line, The, 18, 25
Long Hot Summer, The, 101
Long Riders, The, 628, 642
Lonsdale, Frederick, 486
Lonsdale, Michel, 294
Lord Love a Duck, 126, 362
Loren, Sophia, 149, 213, 304, 619
Lorre, Peter, 35, 140
Los Angeles Times, 617
Losey, Joseph, 292
Louis, Joe, 16
Love Before Breakfast, 679
Loved One, The, 246
Love Happy, 401
Love Me or Leave Me, 341
Love Parade, The, 476

Lovers, The, 291–94, 429
Lovers and Thieves, 592
Loves of a Blonde, 210
Loves of Isadora, The, 286, 560
Love Story, 270, 591
Loving, 689, 758
Lowell, Robert, 365
Loy, Myrna, 481, 485, 494
Lubitsch, Ernst, 223, 324, 387, 449, 476, 493, 734
Lucas, George, 380, 616
Luciano, Lucky, 466
Luck of Ginger Coffey, The, 120, 213
Lumet, Sidney, 394, 537, 547
Lund, Art, 373
Luxemburg, Rosa, 184
Lynch, David, 745–46, 749–52
Lyon, Sue, 62

M, 35
Maar, Dora, 766
MacArthur, Charles, 129, 482–83
Macbeth, 148
MacBird, 173
Macdonald, Dwight, 65, 78–79, 81, 84, 102–3, 114
Macdonald, George: *At the Back of the North Wind*, 697; *The Princess and Curdie*, 697; *The Princess and the Goblin*, 697
MacDonald, Jeanette, 476–77
Macgill, Moyna, 213
MacGraw, Ali, 577
Machiavelli, Niccolò, 417
Mackie, Bob, 682–83
MacLachlan, Kyle, 746, 748–49
MacMurray, Fred, 386, 496
Macnaughton, Robert, 698
Macon County Line, 539

Mad at the World, 38
Made for Each Other, 323, 368
Magee, Patrick, 312
Magic Flute, The, 506–10
Magnani, Anna, 40–43, 163, 660
Magnificent Ambersons, The, 85, 138, 147, 149
Magnum Force, 414–19, 597
Magritte, René, 292
Mahler, Gustav, 90, 597
Mahrer, Marty, 16
Maidstone, 334
Mailer, Norman, 117, 191, 333–35, 380, 456; *An American Dream*, 358; *The Armies of the Night*, 358, 365; *Cannibals and Christians*, 358; *The Deer Park*, 364; *Marilyn*, 358–66; *Miami and the Siege of Chicago*, 358; "The White Negro," 529
Main, Marjorie, 170–71
Major Dundee, 120
Makioka Sisters, The, 737–41, 758
Malden, Karl, 30
Malle, Louis, 290–95, 659, 662–64
Malraux, André, 184
Maltese Falcon, The, 9, 785
Mambo, 5
Mame, 484
Mamoulian, Rouben, 429
Man Called Horse, A, 536
Man Called Peter, A, 9, 25
Manchurian Candidate, The, 79, 93, 154, 156, 172, 207, 607
Mandingo, 549
Man in the Gray Flannel Suit, The, 227
Man Escaped, A, 292
Man for All Seasons, A, 158, 218, 558, 562
Mankiewicz, Joseph L., 5, 137, 148
Manners, David, 228

Man of Aran, 83, 177
Manson, Charles, 312
Manver, Kiti, 766
Man Who Fell to Earth, The, 539–41
Man with the Golden Arm, The, 654
Many Rivers to Cross, 5
Mao Zedong, 179, 186, 554
Marathon Man, 543
Marceau, Marcel, 127
March, Fredric, 397–98, 481
Marcorelles, Louis, 46–47
Marielle, Jean-Pierre, 589–90, 594
Marker, Chris, 178
Marley, John, 191
Marr, Sally, 432, 437
Marriage Italian-Style, 305
Married Woman, The, 121, 123
Marsh, Reginald, 677, 681
Marshall, Alan, 689
Marshall, E. G., 582
Martin, Jean, 402, 406–7
Martin, Mardik, 381, 653
Martin, Steve, 678, 680–81, 683
Marty, 33, 381
Marvin, Lee, 37, 394–96, 772
Marx, Groucho, 412, 583, 668–69
Marx, Harpo, 127
Marx, Karl, 25, 88, 182, 186, 403, 555, 559, 728
Marx Brothers, 410, 481, 649, 669
Mascagni, Pietro, 654
Masculine Feminine, 178, 182, 186, 291, 374
M*A*S*H, 279–80, 386–87, 410, 456
Mask, 749
Mason, Jackie, 667
Mason, James, 60–61, 491
Massari, Lea, 290, 294
Mastroianni, Marcello, 379, 400, 466

Matador, 768
Mata Hari, 165
Mathison, Melissa, 696
Mattei Affair, The, 400, 402
Mature, Victor, 477, 523
Maura, Carmen, 765–67
Mauri, Glauco, 178
Mauriac, François, 185
May, Elaine, 572, 708
Mayer, Louis B., 165, 574, 602
Mayerling, 185
Mayersberg, Paul, 540
Mayfield, Curtis, 530
Mazursky, Paul, 373, 388, 410, 520–24, 667
McAnally, Ray, 780
McCabe & Mrs. Miller, 279–82, 323, 451, 671
McCann, Donal, 754, 757
McCarey, Leo, 481
McCarthy, Joseph, 207, 364
McCarthy, Kevin, 610
McCartney, Paul, 131
McCormick, Pat, 668
McCrea, Joel, 481, 516, 740
McDowell, Malcolm, 311, 313
McGuire, Don, 708
McKean, Michael, 650
McKee, Lonette, 530–31
McLaglen, Victor, 483
McLaren, Hollis, 662–63
McLiam, John, 399
McLuhan, Marshall, 256, 269
McMartin, John, 672
McMurty, Larry, 98
McNaughton, Robert, 698
McQ, 535
McQueen, Steve, 222–23, 400, 619
McRae, Frank, 650

Mean Streets, 374, 376–83, 419, 444, 525–26, 542, 567, 578, 655
Medicine Ball Caravan, 382
Meet Me in St. Louis, 696
Méliès, Georges, 177
Melnick, Daniel, 622
Melville, Herman: "Benito Cereno," 11; *Billy Budd*, 70–74; *The Confidence-Man*, 60, 649; *Pierre*, 72
Melville, Jean-Pierre, 50
Melvin and Howard, 638–46, 686, 688
Member of the Wedding, The, 6–7, 27
Men, The, 27
Mendès-France, Pierre, 325
Mephisto Waltz, The, 609
Mercury Theatre on the Air, 149
Mérimée, Prosper: *La Carrosse du Saint Sacrement*, 40–41
Merry Widow, The, 449
Metro-Goldwyn-Mayer (M-G-M), 17, 206, 212, 340, 479, 622–23, 649, 683
Metropolis, 55, 571
Michi, Maria, 337
Mickey One, 169
Midler, Bette, 674
Midnight, 708
Midnight Express, 684
Midnight Cowboy, 246, 296–97, 367, 380, 387
Mifune, Toshiro, 75, 77
Mildred Pierce, 232
Milius, John, 417–18, 516, 534, 542, 597, 649
Milland, Ray, 471, 497, 708
Miller, Ann, 680
Miller, Arthur: *After the Fall*, 360, 364–65; *Death of a Salesman*, 364; *The Misfits*, 360
Miller, David, 401–2

Miller, Glenn, 16
Miller, Henry: *Tropic of Cancer*, 587
Miller, Marilyn, 476
Miller's Beautiful Wife, The, 305
Milligan, Spike, 667
Million, Le, 9
Miner, Jan, 432
Minnelli, Liza, 532, 655
Minnelli, Vincente, 278, 597, 696
Miou-Miou, 588
Miracle in Milan, 8, 303–4
Miracle Worker, The, 163, 169
Misfits, The, 360–62
Miss Julie, 7
Missouri Breaks, The, 569
Mistons, Les, 428
Mitchell, Millard, 477
Mitrione, Dan, 406–7
Moby Dick, 148
Moment of Truth, The, 208
Mondo Cane, 173, 227
Mondo Trasho, 260
Mondrian, Piet, 766
Monogram Pictures, 50
Monroe, Marilyn, 113, 167, 358–66, 465, 545, 550
Monsieur Verdoux, 669
Montand, Yves, 366, 402, 404, 406–7, 550
Montgomery, George, 387
Montgomery, Robert, 387, 494
Moon Is Down, The, 198
Moore, Dudley, 650
Moore, Mary Tyler, 550
Moore, Robin, 298
Moore, Roger, 619
Moorehead, Agnes, 149
Moravia, Alberto: *The Conformist*, 273
More, Thomas, 562

Moreau, Jeanne, 64, 67–68, 153, 218, 292–94, 501, 588, 594, 761
Morelli, Rina, 724
More the Merrier, The, 10
Morgan! 127, 231
Morgan, Donald M., 651
Moriarty, Cathy, 653–54
Morituri, 116
Morley, Robert, 301
Morocco, 168, 221–22
Morricone, Ennio, 408
Morris, Howard, 667
Morris, Oswald, 62
Morrissey, Paul, 429–30
Morrow, Vic, 26
Morton, Gary, 438
Mother, 402
Mother and the Whore, The, 426–31
Motown, 340
Mouchette, 702
Moulin Rouge, 27
Mozart, Wolfgang Amadeus, 10, 45, 249, 450, 591–93; *Così Fan Tutte*, 507, 779; *Don Giovanni*, 507; *The Magic Flute*, 210, 506–10; *The Marriage of Figaro*, 593
Mr. Blandings Builds His Dream House, 487
Mrs. Miniver, 146
Mrs. Soffel, 758
Mumford, Lewis, 172–73
Mummy, The, 137
Munch, Edvard, 195
Muni, Paul, 96, 209, 400, 438
Murders in the Rue Morgue, 137
Murdock, George, 690
Murmur of the Heart, 290–91, 294–95, 323
Murphy, George, 477

Murphy, Michael, 424, 458
Murphy, Rosemary, 558
Murray, Bill, 664, 712
Murray, Jan, 668
Murray, William, 513–14
Murrow, Edward R., 546
Music Room, The, 85
Mussolini, Benito, 273, 276, 307–8
Mutiny on the Bounty (1935), 479
Mutiny on the Bounty (1963), 70, 114
My Brilliant Career, 758, 760
My Darling Clementine, 77
My Fair Lady, 218, 471–72
My Favorite Wife, 465, 482, 484
Myhers, John, 667–68
My Left Foot, 779–82

Nabokov, Vladimir, 636; *Lolita*, 59, 65, 81, 161
Nadelman, Elie, 412
Nader, Ralph, 400
Naked City, The, 658
Naked Runner, The, 207, 345
Nana, 361
Nanook of the North, 83
Napier, Charles, 644
Napoléon, Louis, 500
Napoléon Bonaparte, 115, 230
Nashville, 456–62, 542, 544, 671
Nathan, George Jean, 395
National Aeronautics and Space Administration, 698
National Geographic, 597
National Lampoon's Animal House, 570–72
Navigator, The, 9
Nazarin, 236, 238, 240
Neal, Patricia, 98
Needham, Hal, 572–73

Nehru, Jawaharlal, 86
Nero, 257, 666–68
Network, 545–51
Never Give a Sucker an Even Break, 649
Never on Sunday, 51
New Centurions, The, 454
Newhart, Bob, 389, 424
Newman, David, 155, 160, 163, 168–69
Newman, Paul, 91–92, 94, 99, 101, 169, 248, 250, 400, 418, 497
New Orleans Funeral and Ragtime Orchestra, 412
New Republic, 54, 59, 65
New Wave, 46, 50, 292, 428, 431, 628
New York, New York, 577, 655–56
New Yorker, 101, 113, 293, 476, 583, 769
New York Film Festival, 195, 251–52, 275, 331, 334, 338, 353, 500, 554, 586, 638, 700
New York Herald Tribune, 94
New York Philharmonic, 56
New York Times, 56, 58, 81, 95, 182, 354, 617, 641
Next Stop, Greenwich Village, 520–24
Niagara, 361
Nichols, Mike, 232
Nicholson, Jack, 455, 534–35, 538
Niebuhr, Reinhold, 59, 61
Night and Day, 487, 490, 492–93
Nightcomers, The, 318
Night of the Iguana, The, 140
Night of the Living Dead, 391
Night of the Shooting Stars, The (La Notte di San Lorenzo), 713–19, 769
Nikki, 477–78
Nimoy, Leonard, 608
1900, 660, 662
1941, 649–51
Ninotchka, 702

Niven, David, 485
Nixon, Richard, 449, 451–52, 672
Noiret, Philippe, 408
None but the Lonely Heart, 487–91
Noonan, John Ford, 523
Nordin, Birgit, 508
Norman, Marc, 512
North by Northwest, 465, 491, 497–98
North Star, The, 10
Northup, Harry, 528
No Time for Comedy, 492
Not as a Stranger, 25
Notorious, 221, 465, 491–92, 495, 497–98
Notte, La, 67
Notte di San Lorenzo, La (The Night of the Shooting Stars), 713–19, 769
Novak, Kim, 550, 654
No Way to Treat a Lady, 297
Nun's Story, The, 317, 557
Nuytten, Bruno, 554
Nykvist, Sven, 198, 504, 508

Oates, Warren, 515–16
O'Brien, Edna, 504
Observer, 59, 96
Obsession, 567, 673
O'Connor, Donald, 54
O'Conor, Hugh, 780
Odd Couple, The, 207, 266
Odd Man Out, 27, 61
Odets, Clifford, 129, 362, 478, 487–89, 491
O'Donnell, Cathy, 156
Of Mice and Men, 246
O'Herlihy, Daniel, 3, 757
O'Horgan, John, 432–34
O.K. Nero! 667
Oland, Warner, 222

Olive Trees of Justice, The, 120
Oliver, Edna May, 145
Oliver, Rochelle, 523
Olivier, Laurence, 8, 107–9, 144, 165, 311, 400, 492, 661, 780, 782
Olvidados, Los, 8, 313
On Approval, 9
Once upon a Honeymoon, 485
Once upon a Time, 487
One, Two, Three, 547
O'Neal, Griffin, 696
O'Neal, Ryan, 369
O'Neal, Tatum, 369
One Flew over the Cuckoo's Nest, 644, 686
O'Neill, Carlotta, 397
O'Neill, Eugene, 95; *The Iceman Cometh*, 393–99; *Long Day's Journey into Night*, 162, 393, 395–96, 398, 689
Only Angels Have Wings, 168, 465–66, 482, 497
On the Avenue, 496
On the Waterfront, 9, 14, 27–35, 38, 103, 112, 142, 317, 322, 656, 675
Open City, 337, 404
Operation Petticoat, 487, 492
Ophuls, Max, 70, 122, 138, 179, 282, 324–25, 327, 337, 728
Orbison, Roy, 749
Ordet, 702
Ornitz, Arthur, 524
Orwell, George: *1984*, 310
Ossessione, 337
O'Steen, Sam, 530
Oswald, Lee Harvey, 401
Othello, 107–9, 148
Other Side of Midnight, The, 663
Our Dancing Daughters, 16
Our Dancing Mothers, 232

Our Town, 145
Outcast of the Islands, 2, 27
Outrageous! 663
Owl and the Pussycat, The, 297, 368
Ox-Bow Incident, The, 76

Pabst, G. W., 177
Pacino, Al, 318, 320, 441, 444–45, 537–38
Padre Padrone, 637, 713–14
Page, Geraldine, 204, 581–83
Paisan, 404, 718
Pakula, Alan, 557
Pal Joey, 211
Pan, Hermes, 349–50
Panama, Norman, 487
Panavision, 591, 598, 635
Panic in Needle Park, The, 290, 297
Papas, Irene, 286–87, 289
Paper Moon, 369
Papp, Joseph, 660
Paramount Pictures, 30, 206, 316, 447, 456–57, 468–69, 476–79, 482, 485–86, 493, 770
Parents Terribles, Les, 6–7
Parker, Alan, 684–86, 688–90, 758
Parker, Bonnie, 155, 160–61
Parker, Charlie, 295
Parker, Dorothy, 558
Parrish, Maxfield, 2
Partner, 275–77
Pasolini, Pier Paolo, 180
Passage to India, A, 758
Passenger, The, 540
Passion of Joan of Arc, The, 604
Pat and Mike, 93, 708
Pather Panchali, 82–84
Paths of Glory, 62
Patinkin, Mandy, 732, 735

Patterson, Frank, 755, 757
Patton, 301
Peck, Gregory, 26, 111
Peckinpah, Sam, 120, 148, 282, 511–19, 564, 568, 570, 574–77, 581, 740–41
Pedi, Tom, 399
Peerce, Larry, 246
Peer Gynt, 5
Pelikan, Lisa, 560
Pender, Bob, 473–75
Penn, Arthur, 160–63, 168–71, 247, 574
Penn, Irving, 560
Penn, Sean, 770–71, 773
Pennies from Heaven, 677–83
Penny Serenade, 485–86
Penzer, Jean, 592
People Will Talk, 487
Pépé le Moko, 49
Peretz, Susan, 644
Périer, François, 408
Period of Adjustment, 362
Perles de la Couronne, Les, 9
Perrine, Valerie, 372, 432, 438
Persoff, Nehemiah, 732, 735
Persona, 194, 196
Pesci, Joe, 653–54
Pétain, Philippe, 323–24, 326
Peters, Bernadette, 678–79, 682–83
Petri, Elio, 208
Petrified Forest, The, 663
Petronius: *Satyricon*, 259
Petulia, 205, 225–27, 246, 461
Phantom India, 294
Phantom of the Paradise, 649
Philadelphia Story, The, 466, 482, 495
Picasso, Pablo, 64–65, 766
Piccoli, Michel, 408, 662, 664
Picker, David, 622
Pickford, Mary, 474–75

Picture of Dorian Gray, The, 213

Pierson, Frank, 537

Pinal, Silvia, 238

Piovani, Nicola, 719

Pirandello, Luigi, 40

Pitagora, Paola, 179

Place in the Sun, A, 10, 93, 557

Planet of the Apes, 205, 211

Plato, 178

Playboy, 513, 580, 667

Play Dirty, 657

Play It Again, Sam, 410, 412

Play It as It Lays, 514

Point Blank, 173

Pointer, Priscilla, 751

Poitier, Sidney, 101, 218–19

Polanski, Roman, 454, 578

Pollack, Sydney, 203, 534, 708–9, 711–12

Pollard, Michael J., 644

Pontecorvo, Bruno, 404

Pontecorvo, Gillo, 208, 402–7

Pop Art, 161, 185, 189, 203, 263–64, 270, 340, 344, 358, 647, 651, 676

Porter, Cole, 16, 487, 492–93

Portrait of Jason, 211

Post, Ted, 418

Postmaster, The, 85

Postman Always Rings Twice, The, 337

Potemkin, 9, 163–64, 402

Potter, Dennis, 678, 681

Potter, Martin, 260

Pound, Ezra, 238; *Pisan Cantos*, 519

Powell, Dick, 387, 420

Powell, Jane, 3

Powell, Michael, 216

Powell, William, 220, 471

Power, Tyrone, 111

Preminger, Otto, 49

Preservation Hall Jazz Band, 412

President's Analyst, The, 207

Presley, Elvis, 62, 758–59

Pressburger, Emeric, 216

Pretty Baby, 569, 663–64

Price, Leontyne, 210

Pride and the Passion, The, 491

Priest, The, 635

Prince, Harold, 668

Prince and the Showgirl, The, 362

Prince of Foxes, 146–47

Prizzi's Honor, 783

Prodigal, The, 9, 25, 38

Producers, The, 183, 207

Production Code, 36, 133, 530

Prokofiev, Sergei: *Peter and the Wolf*, 510

Prouse, Derek, 97

Proust, Marcel, 27, 307

Proval, David, 378

Provine, Dorothy, 156

Pryor, Richard, 345–46, 669–70, 691–94

Psycho, 201–2, 299, 580

Public Enemy, The, 158–60

Public Theater, 660

Pudovkin, Vsevolod, 10, 402

Pugni in Tasca, I (*Fists in the Pocket*), 179–80

Punch, Angela, 632

Punch-and-Judy shows, 177

Purcell, Henry, 314

Purtell, Bob, 759

Puzo, Mario: *The Godfather*, 316–17, 442

Quai des Brumes, 28

Queen, The, 211

Queen Kelly, 6

Queen of the Stardust Ballroom, 530

Queneau, Raymond, 292
Quinn, Anthony, 319, 497–98, 534
Quo Vadis, 4, 14

Rabe, David, 775–76; *Streamers*, 770
Rachel, Rachel, 191, 234
Rafelson, Bob, 662
Rafelson, Toby, 644
Raft, George, 496
Raggedy Man, 697
Raging Bull, 652–58
Ragtime, 732
Raiders of the Lost Ark, 695
Raimu, 597
Rain, 361–62
Raines, Cristina, 458
Rainmaker, The, 660
Raise the Titanic, 640
Raisin in the Sun, A, 213
Rall, Tommy, 680
Rambaldi, Carlo, 698
Rand, Ayn: *The Fountainhead*, 220
Randall, Tony, 213, 619
Rashomon, 9, 78–79
Rathbone, Basil, 219
Ravetch, Irving, 100
Ray, Charles, 232
Ray, Nicholas, 156
Ray, Satyajit, 80–89, 138, 353–57, 758
Raye, Martha, 570
Razzia, 299
Reader's Digest, 9
Rebel Without a Cause, 142
Red Desert, 110
Red Dust, 362
Redeker, Quinn K., 603
Redford, Robert, 248, 250, 263, 399, 465–66, 538, 625
Redgrave, Michael, 575

Redgrave, Vanessa, 131, 285–86, 557, 559–60
Red Shoes, The, 216
Reed, Carol, 2, 381–82
Reed, Pamela, 642
Reflections in a Golden Eye, 318
Reggiani, Serge, 726
Règle du Jeu, La, 6
Reid, Kate, 659, 661
Reinhardt, Max, 8
Remsen, Bert, 496
Reno, Kelly, 696
Renoir, Claude, 42, 590–91
Renoir, Jean, 8, 40–43, 68, 82–83, 89, 122, 148, 209, 272, 321, 337–38, 355, 452, 504, 514, 587, 638, 644, 716
Renoir, Pierre-Auguste, 49
Republic Pictures, 148, 453
Resnais, Alain, 141, 227
Return of a Man Called Horse, The, 536
Rey, Fernando, 299
Reynolds, Burt, 539, 572–73, 619
Reynolds, Freddy, 632, 635
Reynolds, Naida, 644
Rhapsody in Blue, 27
Rhoden, Harold: *High Stakes*, 639
Rhodes, Erik, 348
Rhys, Jean, 688
Rich and Famous, 734
Richard Pryor Live in Concert, 691, 694
Richard Pryor Live on the Sunset Strip, 691–94
Richards, Dick, 557, 708
Richardson, Ralph, 151, 165
Richardson, Tony, 246, 293
Richard III, 109, 780, 782
Richter, W. D. (Rick), 606, 608–9
Rickles, Don, 438
Ride the High Country, 120, 516, 740

Ridgely, Robert, 645

Riefenstahl, Leni, 403

Riesman, David, 14–15

Rifleman, The, 513

Rigg, Diana, 546

Riley, Jack, 389, 667

Rilke, Rainer Maria, 90

Rio Bravo, 168

Rioli, Riccardo, 42

Rio Rita, 476

Ritchie, Michael, 643, 645

Ritt, Martin, 100–1

Ritter, John, 619

Ritz, Harry, 127, 496, 608

Ritz Brothers, The, 127

River, The, 42, 82

RKO Pictures, 350, 469

Roach, Hal, 481

Road to Damascus, 5

Robards, Jason, 111, 394–95, 558, 563, 640–41, 704

Robbins, Harold: *The Adventurers*, 316; *The Carpetbaggers*, 316

Robbins, Jerome, 52, 54

Robe, The, 14, 17, 139

Roberta, 348–49

Roberts, Oral, 437

Roberts, William, 373

Robeson, Paul, 108

Robespierre, Maximilien-François de, 554

Robin Hood, 75, 420, 444–45

Robinson, Amy, 378

Robinson, Bruce, 500

Robinson, Casey, 477

Robinson, Edward G., 111, 320

Robinson, Jay, 453

Robinson, Jackie, 16

Robson, May, 496

Roché, Henri-Pierre: *Deux Anglaises et le Continent*, 64

Rochefort, Jean, 589–90, 594

Rockefeller, Nelson, 672

Rockettes, 682

Rockne, Knute, 16

Rockwell, Norman, 596

Rocky II, 621

Rodgers, Richard, 16, 53

Rodin, Auguste, 319

Rodway, Norman, 152

Roeg, Nicolas, 539–40, 577

Rogers, Ginger, 54, 93, 275, 349–52, 485, 498, 681

Rogers, Roy, 456

Rogue Cop, 17–18

Rohmer, Eric, 504

Roma, 379

Roman Scandals, 666–67

Roman Spring of Mrs. Stone, The, 166

Romanus, Richard, 378

Romberg, Sigmund, 16

Ronet, Maurice, 292–93

Roof, The, 304

Room for One More, 486–87, 489

Roosevelt, Franklin, 480

Rooster Cogburn, 535

Roots of Heaven, The, 148

Rope, 156

Rosalie, 476

Rose, Jack, 487

Rose, The, 644, 674, 686

Rosemary's Baby, 391, 530, 567, 578

Rosenthal, Jack, 734

Rose Tattoo, The, 660

Rosi, Francesco, 208, 402, 404, 637

Ross, Diana, 341, 343–46

Ross, Herbert, 412, 679–81, 683

Ross, Katharine, 249

Rossellini, Isabella, 747–48, 750
Rossellini, Roberto, 198, 303, 404, 718
Rossini, Gioacchino, 314
Rosten, Norman, 360
Rota, Nino, 318, 445, 727
Roth, Philip: *Goodbye, Columbus*, 306–7; *Portnoy's Complaint*, 520–21
Rotunno, Giuseppe, 726
Rouch, Jean, 178
Roxie Hart, 18, 137
Rubirosa, Porfirio, 316
Ruggles, Wesley, 481
Rules of the Game, 129, 452–53
Rumann, Sig, 410
Running, 619
Russell, Ken, 539
Russell, Kurt, 647, 650
Russell, Rosalind, 466
Russians Are Coming, The Russians Are Coming, The, 453
Rutherford, Margaret, 153
Ryan, Robert, 70–71, 394–95, 398, 401
Rydell, Mark, 389

Sabrina, 18
Sacco and Vanzetti, 400, 408
Sackler, Howard, 542
Sade, Donatien-Alphonse-François de, 236
Saint, Eva Marie, 465, 689
Sainte-Beuve, Charles-Augustin, 505, 563
Saint-Exupéry, Antoine de: *The Little Prince*, 539
Sakuma, Yoshiko, 738
Salinger, J. D.: *The Catcher in the Rye*, 390
Salou, Louis, 223
Salvatore Giuliano, 404

Samson and Delilah, 4
Sanda, Dominique, 274, 277, 306–7, 338
Sand Pebbles, The, 169
Sandpiper, The, 140
Sandrelli, Stefania, 274
San Francisco Chronicle, 47
San Francisco Examiner, 47
San Miniato, July 1944, 716
Sansom, Ken, 388
Sarandon, Chris, 537
Sarandon, Susan, 659, 663
Saratoga Trunk, 213–14
Sargent, Alvin, 558
Sartre, Jean-Paul, 184
Satie, Erik, 293
Saturday Night Fever, 671
Saturday Review, 54, 95, 314
Saunders, John Monk, 477–78
Savage, John, 596, 604
Savage, Peter, 653
Savage Seven, The, 204
Sayonara, 115
Sayre, Joel, 483
Scalphunters, The, 203, 205
Scarface, 400
Scenes from a Marriage, 510, 685
Schaefer, George, 148
Schaffner, Franklin, 207
Schary, Dore, 156
Scheider, Roy, 401, 534
Schepisi, Fred, 630, 635–36
Schiller, Lawrence, 358
Schine, G. David, 298
Schisgal, Murray, 708
Schlesinger, Arthur, Jr., 59
Schlesinger, John, 246, 321, 770
Schneider, Maria, 331, 337–38
Schrader, Paul, 525, 653
Schroeter, Werner, 705

Schubert, Franz, 591, 594

Schulberg, B. P., 478

Schulberg, Budd, 28, 656

Schumach, Murray, 56–57

Schumacher, Joel, 530

Schwarzkopf, Elisabeth, 141

Scopes trial, 211

Scorpio Rising, 126, 382

Scorsese, Martin, 376–83, 525–28, 542–43, 567–68, 577–78, 653–58, 786

Scott, George C., 228, 323, 372, 423, 534, 546

Scott, Randolph, 26, 484

Scott, Robert F., 144

Seberg, Jean, 47, 49–50, 408

Seduction of Joe Tynan, The, 628

Segal, George (actor), 203, 323

Segal, George (sculptor), 751

Sellers, Peter, 59–61

Selznick, David O., 6

Semprun, Jorge, 404–5, 408

Sennett, Mack, 481–82

Senso, 337

Separate Tables, 660

September Morn, 558

Seresin, Michael, 690

Serling, Rod, 207, 656

Serpico, 549

Serrano, Julieta, 766

Serrault, Michel, 592

Serre, Henri, 65

Set-Up, The, 70, 653

Sevareid, Eric, 548

Seven Brides for Seven Brothers, 3

Seven Days in May, 207

Seven Faces of Dr. Lao, The, 213

Seven-Per-Cent Solution, The, 681

Seven Samurai, The, 79, 512

Seventh Seal, The, 80, 196, 507

Shadows, 190–91

Shaft, 297–98, 392, 421

Shakespeare, William, 440, 656, 713; *Coriolanus*, 395; *Hamlet*, 8, 45, 109–10, 583; *Henry IV*, 151–53; *Henry V*, 108–9, 151; *Julius Caesar*, 148, 165; *King Lear*, 85, 108, 152, 580, 583; *Macbeth*, 79, 108, 148, 151, 164; *The Merry Wives of Windsor*, 151; *A Midsummer Night's Dream*, 509; *Othello*, 107–9, 148, 654; *Richard II*, 151; *Richard III*, 109, 158, 780, 782; *Romeo and Juliet*, 52–53, 55–56; *Taming of the Shrew*, 216

Shame, 194, 196, 198–200

Shampoo, 448–54, 648

Shane, 10, 76, 93–94

Shanghai Express, 168, 222

Shapiro, Stanley, 487

Shavelson, Melville, 487

Shaw, Artie, 342

Shaw, Fiona, 782

Shaw, Robert, 533–34, 542

Shearer, Norma, 17

She Done Him Wrong, 93, 465, 469

Sheldon, Sidney, 487

Shelley, Percy Bysshe, 142

Shepherd, Cybill, 525, 527

Sheridan, Jim, 779, 781–82

Sherlock Holmes, 219

She Wore a Yellow Ribbon, 77

Shima, Koji, 738

Shire, Talia, 445

Shoeshine, 44–45, 149, 303–4, 769

Shootist, The, 535–36

Shoot the Moon, 684–90, 758

Shoot the Piano Player, 69, 162, 187

Shop on Main Street, The, 210

Show, 59

Shubert organization, 476, 478–79

Sidney, Sylvia, 156, 468, 565

Siegel, Don, 416, 535–36, 606, 610

Sight and Sound, 97

Sign of the Cross, The, 261

Signoret, Simone, 337

Signs of Life, 195

Silence, The, 194

Silent Running, 597

Silent World, The, 292

Silliphant, Sterling, 512

Silverman, Fred, 617

Simms, Ginny, 493

Simon, Michel, 337

Simon, Paul, 254

Simon, Simone, 608

Simon of the Desert, 236, 238–41

Sinatra, Frank, 29, 36, 141, 274, 316, 486, 664

Singapore Sue, 477–78

Singer, Issac Bashevis: "Yentl the Yeshiva Boy," 730, 732–34

Singing Nun, The, 225

Singin' in the Rain, 52, 54, 93, 410, 707

Sinners in the Sun, 468

Sinyavsky, Andrei, 184

Sisters, 391

Sitwell, Osbert, 453

Sjöström, Victor, 60

Skin Game, 323

Skipworth, Alison, 206

Sleeper, 409–13

Sleuth, 492

Slezak, Walter, 485

Sloane, Everett, 149

Slocombe, Douglas, 557

Smeaton, Bruce, 636

Smile, 645

Smiles of a Summer Night, 196, 449–50, 453, 507

Smilin' Through, 598

Smith, Bessie, 345

Smith, Lois, 523

Smith, Maggie, 107

Smooth Talk, 749

Smordoni, Rinaldo, 45

Smouldering Fires, 232

Snodgress, Carrie, 567

So Big, 52

Soldier of Fortune, 2, 5

Solinas, Franco, 402, 404–7

Somebody Up There Likes Me, 52

Some Like It Hot, 60, 465, 496, 708

Sondheim, Stephen, 52

Song of Bernadette, The, 502

Song of Songs, 429

Song to Remember, A, 27

Sophocles: *Oedipus Rex*, 108, 164, 580

Sorrow and the Pity, The, 323–28

Sounder, 421–22

Sound of Music, The, 225, 621

Southern, Terry, 237; *Blue Movie*, 332

South Pacific, 54

Spacek, Sissy, 697, 749

Sparkle, 530–32

Speer, Albert, 325

Spiegel, Sam, 28

Spielberg, Steven, 533, 542–43, 566, 568, 649–51, 695–99

Spitz, Mark, 386

Splet, Alan, 750

Spradlin, G. D., 446

Spy Who Loved Me, The, 606

Stalag 17, 27, 116

Stamp, Terence, 70–71

Stanley, Kim, 545, 550

Stanwyck, Barbara, 50, 388

Stapleton, Maureen, 582–84

Star Is Born, A, 16, 61, 578, 682

Starr, Blaze, 438

Stars Look Down, The, 27

Starstruck, 758

Star Wars, 556, 615–16, 628, 697, 702

State of Siege, 369, 402, 405–8

Steagle, The, 297

Steegmuller, Francis, 307

Steel, Dawn, 770

Steenburgen, Mary, 642

Stefanelli, Simonetta, 321

Steiger, Rod, 30, 219, 389

Stein, Gertrude, 64

Stella Dallas, 758

Stendhal: *The Charterhouse of Parma*, 273

Stéphane, Nicole, 179, 307

Sterling, Ford, 473

Stern, Bert, 358

Stern, Sandor, 625

Stevens, Andrew, 565

Stevens, George, 10, 77, 481, 483, 557, 598

Stevens, Leslie, 169

Stevenson, Adlai, 94

Stewart, James, 17, 111, 210, 388, 466, 468

Stir Crazy, 693

Stockwell, Dean, 749

Stokowski, Leopold, 344

Stoler, Shirley, 602

Stop Making Sense, 737

Stoppa, Paolo, 725

Storaro, Vittorio, 337, 665

Story of Adèle H., The, 500–5

Story on Page One, The, 489

Straight, Beatrice, 547

Strangers on a Train, 93

Strasberg, Lee, 360, 363, 446

Strauss, Johann, 230; *Die Fledermaus*, 476

Stravinsky, Igor, 344; *Oedipus Rex*, 288; *Le Sacre du Printemps*, 331

Straw Dogs, 323

Streep, Meryl, 599, 603

Streetcar Named Desire, A, 6, 27, 31, 93, 100, 112

Streisand, Barbra, 344, 423–24, 465, 532, 730–31, 734–35

Strindberg, August, 7, 66, 333; *The Dance of Death*, 338, 661

Stroheim, Erich von, 6, 10, 122

Student Prince, The, 4

Sturges, John, 12, 207

Sturges, Preston, 18, 59, 137, 410, 477, 485, 643–44

Sudermann, Hermann, 429

Sugarland Express, The, 451

Sullivan, Anne, 163

Sullivan, Ed, 161

Sullivan, Sean, 664

Summer Interlude, 196

Summer Stock, 351

Sunday Bloody Sunday, 321, 323

Sundays and Cybèle, 81

Sundowners, The, 218, 557

Sunset Boulevard, 9

Sunshine Boys, The, 681

Supreme Court, U.S., 541, 618, 625

Supremes, 343, 345, 530

Surrealism, 199, 236–40, 413

Susann, Jacqueline, 551

Suspicion, 491

Susskind, David, 114, 213

Sutherland, Donald, 539, 608

Suzy, 479, 493

Swain, Mack, 473

Swan Lake, 268

Sweet Charity, 362, 433

Sweet Smell of Success, 129, 213, 301, 660

Swing Time, 349, 352

Sylbert, Anthea, 560

Sylbert, Paul, 673

Sylvia Scarlett, 469–70, 540, 730–31

Symbionese Liberation Army, 549

Tagore, Rabindranath, 83, 85–86, 88

Tagore, Sharmila, 88, 353–54, 356

Take the Money and Run, 413

Taking Off, 662

Talk of the Town, The, 487

Taming of the Shrew, The, 216

Tanguay, Eva, 16

Tanizaki, Junichiro: *The Key*, 739; *A Light Snowfall* (*The Makioka Sisters*), 737, 739

Taplin, Jonathan T., 382

Tati, Jacques, 293

Tattoli, Eva, 178

Taviani, Paolo, 637, 713–14, 716–19

Taviani, Vittorio, 637, 713–14, 716–19

Taxi Driver, 525–29, 542–43, 569, 578, 610, 655–56

Taylor, Dwight, 348

Taylor, Elizabeth, 144

Taylor, Laurette, 348

Taylor, Robert, 17, 27, 111, 400, 527

Tea and Sympathy, 8

Technicolor, 35

Teilhard de Chardin, Pierre, 571

Temple, Shirley, 485

Tender Trap, The, 213

Tennyson, Alfred: "Enoch Arden," 484

Tewkesbury, Joan, 457–58

Thalberg, Irving, 649

That's Entertainment, 493

That Touch of Mink, 487, 498

Theodora Goes Wild, 481

There's a Girl in My Soup, 264, 268

Thesiger, Ernest, 145

They Live by Night, 156

They Shoot Horses, Don't They? 367, 387, 688

Thief of Paris, The, 294

Thin Man, The, 93, 468, 482

Third Man, The, 149, 381–82, 389

This Is My Beloved anthology, 51

This Is the Night, 468

Thom, Robert, 204, 217

Thomas, Henry, 696–98

Thomas, Philip M., 530

Thomas Crown Affair, The, 205, 220–23, 225, 453

Thompson, Jack, 631

Thompson, Jim: *The Grifters*, 783–85

Three Cases of Murder, 148

Three Coins in the Fountain, 2

Three Days of the Condor, 512

Three Musketeers, The, 476, 483, 667

Three Stooges, The, 654

Throne of Blood, 79, 151

Through a Glass Darkly, 197

Thunderbolt and Lightfoot, 596–97

Thuy Thu Le, 772

Tidyman, Ernest, 298

Time, 7, 32, 58–59, 100–1, 130, 361, 363

Time After Time, 642

Time-Life, 344

Times (London), 97

Times Gone By, 305

Titicut Follies, 252, 369

To Catch a Thief, 465, 491, 497–98

Todd, Michael, 5

To Have and Have Not, 92, 116, 168, 268, 271

To Kill a Mockingbird, 218

Tokyo Olympiad, 737

Tolkien, J. R. R., 263

Tolstoy, Leo, 209, 391, 442; *Anna Karenina*, 734; *War and Peace*, 6, 734

Tom and Jerry, 219

Tomb of Ligeia, The, 454

Tom Jones, 227, 293

Tomlin, Lily, 459, 461–62

Tommy, 539

Tone, Franchot, 479, 494, 497

Too Late Blues, 190

Tootsie, 708–12

Top Hat, 348–49, 681

Topper, 470, 481, 497

Topper Takes a Trip, 482

Tora! Tora! Tora! 401

Torn, Rip, 398

Törst, 196

To Sir with Love, 219

Touch of Class, A, 493

Touch of Evil, 567

Touch of Larceny, A, 61

Toulouse-Lautrec, Henri de, 530

Towering Inferno, The, 543

Towne, Robert, 450, 453–55

Tracy, Arthur, 679

Tracy, Spencer, 468, 485, 495, 708

Travels with My Aunt, 484

Travolta, John, 671–72, 674–75, 774–75

Treasure of the Sierra Madre, The, 18, 786

Trent's Last Case, 146

Trial, The, 8, 150

Trilling, Diana, 360

Trintignant, Jean-Louis, 273–77, 408

Triumph of the Will, 403

Trojan Women, The, 284–89

Trouble in Paradise, 223

Truck, The (Le Camion), 552–56

Truckline Café, 335

Truffaut, François, 50, 64–65, 68–69, 82, 162, 187, 218, 291, 412, 428, 500–5; *The Films of My Life*, 570

Trumbo, Dalton, 401–2

Truth or Consequences, 639

Tucker, Larry, 523

Tupamaro guerillas, 405–6

Turner, J. M. W., 576

Turner, Lana, 17, 218, 654

Turner, Nat, 636

Turning Point, The, 681, 734

Twain, Mark (Samuel Clemens), 602

Twentieth Century, 468, 481

Twentieth-Century Fox, 206, 358, 361, 373–74, 617, 621

20,000 Leagues under the Sea, 3, 61

Two Daughters, 85

Two English Girls, 503–4

2001: A Space Odyssey, 205, 212, 225, 228–30, 262

Two-Way Stretch, 47

Tyson, Cicely, 422–24

Uccello, Paolo, 153

Ugly American, The, 115

Ullmann, Liv, 198–99

Umberto D., 81, 303–4

Umbrellas of Cherbourg, The, 730

Unbearable Lightness of Being, The, 769

Undset, Sigrid: *Kristin Lavransdatter*, 210

Unfaithfully Yours, 137

United Artists, 456, 512, 611, 621–22

Universal Pictures, 206

Untouchables, The, 770

Up the Down Staircase, 254

Urban Cowboy, 675
Used Cars, 647–51
Ustinov, Peter, 70–74

Valentino, Rudolph, 16, 99
Valley of the Kings, 34
Valli, Romolo, 726
Valseuses, Les (*Going Places*), 586–95
Van Pallandt, Nina, 389–90
Vanzetti, Bartolomeo, 400
Variety, 58, 81
Varsi, Diane, 204, 217
Vega, Isela, 516
Veidt, Conrad, 140
Venanzo, Gianni di, 120
Verdi, Giuseppe, 180, 376, 719, 727;
    La Forza del Destino, 210; *Rigoletto*,
    276
Victor Emmanuel II, 725–26
Vidal, Gore, 169, 333
Vie Privée, 293
Vietnam War, 196, 198, 226, 255,
    367, 369–70, 372, 420, 533, 574–75,
    596–605, 701, 769–78
Vigo, Jean, 337, 504, 587
Village of the Damned, 204
Villa Rides, 454
Vilmorin, Louise de, 728
Vincent, Frank, 654
Vinton, Bobby, 750
Violent Four, The, 208–9
Violent Saturday, 5
Viridiana, 236–38, 240
Visconti, Luchino, 275, 337, 597, 660,
    723–25, 727–29
Visitors, The, 770
VistaVision, 2
Vitelloni, I, 377, 379
Vivaldi, Antonio, 41

Viva Maria! 203, 293–94
Vlady, Marina, 153
Vogue, 128
Voight, Jon, 602
Volonté, Gian Maria, 209, 400, 408
Vonnegut, Kurt, 263
Von Sternberg, Josef, 83, 122, 138, 168,
    221–22, 337
Von Sydow, Max, 198–200
Voskovec, George, 399
Voutsinas, Andreas, 667

Wagner, Richard, 600;
    Götterdämmerung, 683
Wagner, Robert, 622
Wakeford, Kent, 382
Wald, Jerry, 363
Walken, Christopher, 523, 596, 604,
    680, 682
Walking Down Broadway, 6
Walking Tall, 539
Wallace, Dee, 697–98
Wallace, Irving, 316
War and Peace, 5–6
Warden, Jack, 448, 451, 455, 647
Warfield, Marlene, 549
Warhol, Andy, 128, 191, 358–59, 429
Warner Brothers, 11, 206, 340, 389,
    416–17, 770
Warshow, Robert, 322
Washburn, Deric, 603
Way We Were, The, 398, 465
Waterston, Sam, 583
Watkin, David, 735
Wayne, John, 26–27, 76, 415, 535, 573
Way We Were, The, 398, 465
Webb, Alan, 152
Webber, Robert, 516
Weekend, 199, 588

Weill, Kurt, 784; *The Threepenny Opera*, 680

Weil, Simone, 327, 609

Weingarten, Isabelle, 426, 428

Welfare, 545

Weller, Peter, 688

Welles, Beatrice, 153

Welles, Gwen, 462

Welles, Orson, 45, 109, 122, 138, 144, 146–53, 167, 489, 567–68

Wellman, William, 158

Wentz, Robert, 644

Werner, Oskar, 65

West, Mae, 296, 465, 468–69

West, Nathanael: *The Day of the Locust*, 388

Westerner, The, 512

We Still Kill the Old Way, 208

Westlake, Donald E., 784–85

Westmoreland, William, 601

West Side Story, 51–57, 218, 584

Wexler, Haskell, 223, 692

Wexler, Norman, 549

What Did You Do in the War, Daddy? 126

When You're in Love, 468

Where's Poppa? 296

White, Patrick, 636

White Christmas, 18

White Dawn, The, 538, 610

Whitehall, Richard, 99

White Line Fever, 539

Whitlock, Albert J., 667

Whitman, Walt, 278, 567

Who Is Harry Kellerman and Why Is He Saying Those Terrible Things About Me?, 297

Who'll Stop the Rain, 575

Who's That Knocking at My Door? 382

Wiazemsky, Anne, 185

Wild Angels, The, 126, 204

Wild Bunch, The, 368, 512, 516–17, 564, 574

Wild Child, The, 504

Wilder, Billy, 547, 622, 629

Wilder, Gene, 183

Wilder, Thornton: *The Bridge of San Luis Rey*, 40; *Our Town*, 145, 748

Wild in the Streets, 203–5, 215, 217

Wild 90, 191, 334

Wild One, The, 37, 111, 587

Wild Strawberries, 196, 507, 510

Williams, Billy Dee, 341–42, 346

Williams, Esther, 17

Williams, John, 385–86, 566, 696

Williams, Tennessee, 8, 167, 397, 513, 656, 662; *The Glass Menagerie*, 512; *Period of Adjustment*, 362; *A Streetcar Named Desire*, 100, 364

Willis, Gordon, 445, 682–83

Wilson, Edmund, 384, 388, 390

Wilson, Flip, 306

Wilson, Scott, 213

Winchell, Walter, 13

Wind, The, 60

Wind and the Lion, The, 535

Windsor, Duke of, 493

Winfield, Paul, 420

Wings in the Dark, 468

Winn, Kitty, 290

Winters, Jonathan, 412

Winters, Shelley, 62, 204, 520–21, 524

Wise, Robert, 52, 158

Wiseman, Frederick, 251–52, 256, 369, 545

Wizard of Oz, The, 55, 686

Wolfe, Thomas, 781

Wolfe, Tom, 370–72, 375; *The Kandy-*

Kolored Tangerine-Flake Streamline Baby, 370
Woman Accused, The, 468
Woman of Affairs, A, 307–8
Woman's World, 10
Women on the Verge of a Nervous Breakdown, 765–68
Wonderful Night, A, 476
Wood, Natalie, 55, 577
Wood, Robin, 354
Woodstock, 382
Woodward, Joanne, 101
World of Apu, The, 83–84, 354
World War I, 65, 138, 144, 216, 326
World War II, 139–40, 216, 226, 323–26, 352, 367, 377, 404, 420, 488, 518, 538, 600, 716, 737, 772
Wray, Fay, 476–78
Writers Guild, 708
Wunderlich, Fritz, 509
Wynn, Keenan, 213, 461
Wynn, Tracy Keenan, 424

Yakuza, The, 454, 534
Yamada, Isuzu, 79
Yates, Cassie, 576
Yates, Peter, 616
Yeats, William Butler, 150
Yentl, 730–36
Yesterday, Today, and Tomorrow, 305
Yojimbo, 75–79, 609

Yoshinaga, Sayuri, 738
Yothers, Tina, 690
Young, Burt, 515, 517–18
Young, Gig, 514, 516–17
Young, Robert, 471
Young at Heart, 36
Young Frankenstein, 667
Young Girls of Rochefort, The, 211
Youngman, Henny, 667
Young Mr. Lincoln, 171
Young Savages, The, 660
You Only Live Once, 156–59, 163
You Only Live Twice, 229

Z, 299–300, 302, 402, 404–5, 407–8
Zabriskie Point, 262, 568
Zanuck, Darryl F., 17, 363
Zavattini, Cesare, 45, 303–4
Zazie dans le Métro, 292–95
Zeffirelli, Franco, 216, 275
Zeitlin, Denny, 610
Zemeckis, Robert, 648–49, 651
Zero for Conduct, 69, 587
Ziegfeld, Florenz, 476, 479
Ziegfeld Follies, 141
Zinnemann, Fred, 5, 218, 557–58, 560, 562
Zolotow, Maurice: *Marilyn Monroe*, 360
Zsigmond, Vilmos, 389, 597–98, 673
Zweig, Stefan, 90–91